TOPIC TWO
chapter two
Test

Data Processing for Decision-Making

Richard W. Brightman
Chairman, Business Division
Waubonsee Community College
Aurora, Illinois

Bernard J. Luskin
Associate Dean, Admissions and Records
Orange Coast College
Costa Mesa, California

Theodore Tilton
Chairman, Division of Science and Mathematics
Waubonsee Community College
Aurora, Illinois

Data Processing For Decision-Making

An Introduction to Third-Generation Information Systems

The Macmillan Company, New York
Collier-Macmillan Limited, London

First Printing

Library of Congress catalog card number: 68-12713

THE MACMILLAN COMPANY, NEW YORK
COLLIER-MACMILLAN CANADA, LTD., TORONTO, ONTARIO

Printed in the United States of America

Preface

Jules Verne's visions of one hundred years ago are little in the light of today's realities. One of the most significant and overwhelming of modern-day developments has been the growth of automated data processing techniques. The third-generation data processing systems that were inaugurated in 1964 with the introduction by International Business Machines Corporation of their System/360 computer series are a manifestation of this technical growth—one that promises to bring great benefits to business and other social organizations, but not without intensive preparation on the part of its users. The world is becoming increasingly aware of the potential that automated data processing systems hold for the business community, not only in the light of this new equipment, but also in terms of the role that it should play in modern life.

As we point out in the text, the use of guess and intuition as decision-making techniques has seen its day. Modern information systems are able to provide decision-makers with information the quality of which was undreamed of a decade ago. But these information systems and the data processing techniques and devices that make them work have become increasingly difficult to understand, as far as the manager or decision-maker is concerned. Misapplication of these valuable tools is worse than no application at all, and every manager must move to meet the challenge presented by data processing techniques. This book is designed to help develop an understanding of the role that data processing takes within information systems and within the structure of the business organization.

In writing this book, we have kept three categories of readers in mind: college students looking forward to careers as professional data processors; college students taking a course for general information; and business managers and executives desirous of understanding the lingo of data processing and of a deeper appreciation of the role of data processing in their organization.

College students who intend to pursue data processing as a career will find in this book information they will need to continue advanced study in computer programming, information systems, systems analysis, and unit record data processing systems.

For the students in other fields, this text supplies a general understanding of the role and techniques of data processing within business and other organizations. Accounting, social science, and science majors will find valuable its description of the nature of the information systems used in social organizations and of the tools used in performing scientific and statistical calculations.

Business managers will find this book useful in dealing intelligently with members of the data processing staff. As we point out, all too frequently, decision-makers are left to the mercy of their data processing advisory personnel. Never before has the quality of decision-making been so much under the influence of those *not* responsible for making the decision—the data processing staff members. Data processing, as a new profession, has more than its share, we believe, of charlatans and incompetents. To an important extent, this book is an effort to protect decision-makers from the vagaries of their information system and to prepare them to make better use of its potential.

Our book assumes no prior knowledge of data processing on the part of the reader. For the college student who studies it, this book starts with some basic ideas of business organization and information requirements and proceeds to technical discussions of the most current techniques and hardware used in information systems. There is no question that this is a *college* text and one that includes chapters which must be studied rather than casually read.

The last division of the book, "System/360 Assembly Language Programming," is included particularly for those who wish to become professional data processors and computer programmers. After observing third-generation computer systems development, it is clear that professional computer programmers of the very near future will look to a detailed knowledge of System/360 Assembly Language as the first step in becoming a competent computer programmer. Despite the efforts of manufacturers and others to develop programming systems easier to use than an assembly language, it is clear that maximum efficiency of use of those systems (COBOL, PL/1, RPG, and so on) depends upon a knowledge of the assembly language into which the higher level languages are first translated. Moreover, some knowledge of the computer system used to execute his program is quite necessary to the commercial programmer preparing an elaborate production program. Since this is the case, because of the nature of his programming assignment, he may as well use a machine-oriented programming language in order to take full advantage of the flexibility of his computer system. For these reasons, we have not shied away from including technical materials dealing with programming the System/360. We believe that, for the career-minded college student who looks to computer programming as an occupation in the field of data processing, the most valuable programming language to study is System/360 Assembly Language.

However, we also recognize that the System/360 is not an easy computer to learn to program without some understanding of basic computer operations and programming techniques. For this reason, Part III concentrates in a general manner on how computers operate, what their various hardware components do and how they do it, and how one programs a simple computer. A teaching device with which we have been experimenting with remarkable success is included in Part III as Chapter 12. This is a hypothetical computer known as CYBERNAC. Although in general we look upon hypothetical computers with skeptical eyes for reasons expressed in Chapter 12, CYBERNAC has proven to be one of the most useful teaching devices we have found. In learning computer programming and operations, students have difficulty understanding what a stored program is, loading the program, and setting the computer to execute the instructions of the program. CYBERNAC has been used to teach these ideas to several hundred data processing students at Orange Coast College with gratifying results. Using a cardboard or plywood mock-up of CYBERNAC which shows the various parts of the computer as shown in Figure 12-1, the instructor can illustrate each cycle of a computer's operation and impress upon students the various implications and consequences of stored program execution.

But the mock-up is only half of the story. In addition, John Clark of Orange Coast College has prepared a simulator that will cause an electronic computer capable of processing FORTRAN to assume the operating characteristics of CYBERNAC. Using this simulator, students can write programs for CYBERNAC which can then be executed on a real computer. In this way, they not only have the experience of learning to program a very simple computing device, but also of testing their programming efforts on a real computer. This adds realism to their learning experience and also requires accuracy of programming and thorough program checkout procedures as well. Details regarding the use of this simulator, including program listings and documentation of the loading procedures for an IBM 1620 Model 1 with disk drive, will be available with the teachers' manual for this text.

The development of this text began with the Summer Institutes in Data Processing which were conducted at Orange Coast College during the summers of 1963 to 1966. With the exception of material concerning third-generation computer systems, these materials were gathered and tested during the Institutes and in preparation for them. For this reason, we owe recognition to all of the teachers who participated in the Institutes for the help, unwittingly, perhaps, that they afforded us in gathering the information that we present here. Space prohibits giving individual recognition to each participant, but among those who contributed most significantly are Richard Reynolds of Orange Coast College, whose philosophy and business insight helped to inspire the first five chapters; Donald Ketchum of Chaffey College, who showed us that the basic logic of computer operations can be effectively taught in a short period of time; and John Clark of Orange Coast College for his development of the CYBERNAC simulator and advice on Part III of the text. Others, whose casual conversations about the teaching of data processing helped us to organize the materials, include Ben Micallef of Meritt College, Nels Overgaard of Cerritos College, Ben Matley of Mount San Antonio College, Carl Grame of De Anza College, and Lawrence Harvey of Foothill College.

Most of the information on the System/360 and other matters regarding third-generation computing systems was gathered at the IBM Education Center in Los Angeles and from publications of that company. We owe thanks particularly to Andrew Burgoyne, Joe Mona, and George Weller of the International Business Machines Corporation for their help in providing us with materials used in this text.

We would be remiss, indeed, if we did not draw attention to our typist, grammarian, and pedagogical editor, Kay Brightman, without whose help this book would have remained a pile of clippings and lecture notes.

R. W. B.
B. J. L.
T. T.

Contents

Part I. Information Systems and Decision-Making

Part II. Unit Record Information Systems

Part III. Electronic Information Systems

Part IV. System/360 Assembly Language Programming

Part I

Information Systems and Decision-Making

1

Decision-Making Processes in Organizations

Let us begin with a straight-forward idea: Men go into business because engaging in business activity satisfies some of their desires, principally that of making money, although other goals of business activity are also important. Data processing, an area of business activity of fast-growing importance and complexity, enables businessmen to more effectively achieve these goals—money-making or otherwise.

Although straight-forward, this idea is really quite complex. Most businessmen, educators, and other knowledgeable people recognize that there is a good deal about business activity that is difficult to understand. If this were not the case, then there would be fewer business failures. Actually, over one thousand businesses fail each month in the United States. Almost always, these failures result from someone's thinking that he knows a great deal about business when in fact he knows very little. The purpose of this chapter is to explore the basic ideas underlying business activity—not to present a great deal of knowledge about business but to point out that there is a great deal to know—and to introduce data processing as an important tool in implementing the most important business activity: decision-making.

Goals of Business Activity

Ask a businessman why he is in business and his answer will be quick and certain: "To make money." Many would accept this answer as not only the truth but the only reason that businesses exist. Actually, however, thousands of businessmen who go into business for themselves leave a job earning, say, $10,000 a year, invest their life's savings of several thousand dollars, and consider themselves successful to earn substantially less than the $10,000 they enjoyed while working for someone else. There must be, therefore, important reasons for businesses to carry on their activities besides earning a profit. It is true that no business can survive for very long without a profit, although some railroads and ship-building concerns have gone on for several decades at a loss. However, given acceptable performance with respect to earnings, businesses typically try to satisfy a wide variety of nonprofit objectives for the people who are associated with the enterprise.

As data processors, we will be more concerned with fairly sizeable businesses rather than with small companies. Consider, for example, a large corporation. Associated with this business are a number of different kinds of people, all of whom influence the behavior of the company and all of whom will look to the company to satisfy certain goals. So far, so good. The rub comes here: As one of the people associated with this company, the goals you expect it to satisfy will depend upon your relationship with the company and will differ markedly from those expected by other types of people associated with the business. If you are a customer, you look for quality of product, efficiency of service, and more product for your money. As the owner, you expect the highest possible monetary return on your investment—a goal that clearly conflicts with that of the company's customers. As a professional manager, say, president or treasurer, you may not own very much of the business. Your main concern with the corporation is your job. The goals you look to are your financial income and the prestige that goes with being a boss in a large business enterprise. In causing the company to reach for these goals, you may influence it to do things quite contrary to the desires of both the owners and the customers. As a worker, your goals include more income, greater fringe benefits, better working conditions, more paid vacations, and the like. In short, you want things that either reduce profits or cause the price of the company's product to go up, displeasing its customers, making the professional managers nervous and the company's owners anxious about their investment returns. Finally, as a general citizen, you may look to this company, as many do today to American Telephone and Telegraph, United States Steel, General Motors, DuPont, and other industry leaders, for certain social goals, including the promotion of cultural events, support of education and research activities, charitable activities, and the like—goals that again conflict with those of the owners, managers, workers, and customers.

What we are getting at is this: To best appreciate the impact of data processing on business activities, one must understand the context in which these activities take place, the way in which the business is organized. To best understand why organizations of people behave as they do, one must be aware of the goals that organizations are trying to satisfy and of the wide variety of conflicting goals that different members of the business organization expect to be satisfied.

Fortunately, if a way can be found for the company to produce its product or service more efficiently, that is, at less cost, many otherwise conflicting goals can be partially satisfied at once. Lower-cost operations generally mean more profits, which can be distributed to the owners as dividends, to the workers as wages and fringe benefits, to the managers as funds for plant expansion and other pet projects, and still perhaps leave some to finance the local symphony orchestra. All that is needed is to recognize that businesses in the United States exist primarily to produce things—automobiles, diaper services, toothpaste, machine tools, dry cleaning, and so on. If a way can be found to produce these goods and services more efficiently, then the goals of the business, whatever they are, will be more satisfactorily fulfilled.

This brings us to the central point of this chapter. Efficient business operation depends upon efficient management. This is axiomatic. Just as axiomatic, although still not recognized by a few businessmen, is the notion that efficient management depends upon efficient decision-making. Finally, efficient decision-making depends upon the information available to the decision-makers or managers. *Data processing, by enabling the business organization to provide its decision-makers with higher-quality information, enables them to make higher-quality decisions, thus making operations more efficient and allowing fuller satisfaction of the business' goals.*

In this way, we see that the role of data processing in satisfying organizational goals lies in increasing productive efficiency. Usually, efficiency in productiveness is manifested in a variety of forms: higher-quality products; reduced man-hours per unit of product; reduced operating expenses; increased production per time period; improved service; increased flexibility of operation; greater product uniformity; lower inventory levels; and improved appearance and internal operation of plant. The introduction of a new data processing system or information processing system alone will not guarantee these benefits to a business. Only if the information provided by the system is used by the managers to make more intelligent decisions will these things come about.

Decision-Making

Essentially, a decision is a choice between controversial alternatives—a choice because one has to choose between two or more paths of action, and controversial because one is initially, at least, unsure which path holds more promise. One way to make a decision is to guess. Another is to flip a coin. Still another is to choose not to choose, which means that the decision-maker decides not to do his job. This phenomenon occurs much more frequently than one might suppose. Ask any saleslady how difficult it is for a prospect to decide which dress or pair of shoes to buy, or to decide not to buy something she does not want, for that matter. Or ask a waiter how many people implore each other to order from the menu rather than to make up their own minds. Decision-making is very difficult work. Historically, businessmen operated on the common sense approach. When a business decision was necessary they made one based on intuition (they doubtless deplored their wives doing the same thing) or, at best, an educated guess.

Times have changed. Technology has advanced and businessmen have the ability to collect volumes of data and to perform quantitative analysis on these data to an extent undreamed of twenty years ago. As a result, business decisions are becoming pretty high-quality merchandise against which the guess or the intuitive approach cannot hope to compete successfully. Gone are the days when Daddy could set Johnny up in business for himself because Johnny was too dull to be an engineer or a scientist or for that matter too dull to do anything but run a business. If Daddy were to do that today, Johnny would fail. He would fail because he would not be able to compete with businesses that are turning more and more to scientific, quantitative approaches to making business decisions. He would fail because business today is a highly technical and quasi-scientific field demanding intelligent and forceful decision-making.

Scientific approaches to business decision-making are in large part the result of developments in the electronic data processing, that is, the computer, industry. The power of this new tool is enabling businesses large and small to increase the quality of their decisions many-fold. In fact the last few years have seen the development of a new field of business management known as *scientific management*, or *operations research*. These relatively new decision-making approaches will be the subject of the next chapter. Our purpose here is to discuss the environment in which business decisions are made and its influence on the nature of the decision-making process. The environment in which business decisions are made is the business organization.

Organization

Look at a business—any business, anywhere—and you will always see the one thing common to all businesses: people. Sometimes there are not many people, as with a corner newsstand operated by one person, but people are always associated with business enterprises. As a matter of fact, there are a number of businessmen and scholars who feel that all problems associated with production, finance, and distribution are essentially solved, that the one remaining problem facing the business enterprise is its people. This view points out how important people are in a business enterprise. The people associated with any business are of two basic varieties: the customers and the owners. This initial categorization of a business' people opens up a Pandora's box of troubles and conflicts. The purpose of business, you recall, is to satisfy goals. The chief goal of the business owners is to make a profit (among other things, perhaps), and the chief goal of the customers is to get the most for their money. Clearly, these goals conflict and cannot both be satisfied completely. At best, we can hope that both the customers and the owners will be reasonably satisfied, that is, that the owners earn a fair profit on their investment and that the customers receive a fair exchange for their money.

Having thus categorized the business's peoples into two basic groups, it is time to decide which one we care about. As data processors, we are primarily interested in the inner operations of the business. Although we should expect to be called on to process information about the business's customers, our purpose is to examine the inner workings of the business enterprise; we will, therefore, consider the owners and their affiliates and leave the customers to the economists and marketing experts.

The second thing you will see when you look at any business anywhere is that the owners are organized into some sort of team. This is true even of the single-owner newsstand. In this case, the owner performs many functions himself, allocating his time to each as he feels their importance to the success of his enterprise warrants. Part of the time he is the purchasing department; another part, the sales department; another, the accounting department; and so on. Notice that when the business organization is discussed here, we discuss how the work of the business is achieved rather than the legal relationships between the owners. In this way, we distinguish the *social organization*, which concerns relationships between people, from the *legal organization*, which is an expression of the legal status of the organization as an entity in society.

This is not to imply that the social organization is more important than the legal. Indeed, the three basic types of legal business organization in the United States—proprietorships, partnerships, and corporations—as well as their countless varieties and mutations, all require different data processing activities. For example, the tax accounting for proprietorships, partnerships, and corporations call for significantly different accounting techniques and, consequently, different data processing techniques. However, if our purpose is to gain an insight into the workings of a business enterprise with respect to how the owners are organized to achieve their goals and how various data processing techniques serve the organization, then we would do best to concentrate on the social organization of the business.

All that is known about organizations of people and how they work together (or do not work together) cannot be adequately discussed in one chapter of an introductory book on data processing. Sociologists have defined a substantial area of study known as *organization theory*, which is primarily concerned with large groups of more or less formally organized people who strive, through implementation of the organization's operating procedures, to achieve its specific goals.

Those who study data processing today are most often motivated to do so by a desire to understand and work with modern automated data processing methods, including electronic computers and other high-speed data handling devices. This kind of data processing is most useful to large organizations, small businesses having neither the amount of data nor the amount of money to justify or afford very elaborate data processing techniques. Because of this, we will consider topics that involve the organization of fairly large businesses. However, elaborate data processing techniques are becoming available to smaller businesses through service bureaus who offer automated data processing equipment to them on an hourly or job basis. We should recognize that what is known about the organization of large businesses can be useful in analyzing the behavior of small and medium-sized enterprises as well.

Structure of Organizations

The owners of the business determine the structure of the business organization. They do this by assigning themselves tasks to perform in the conduct of the company's business and by hiring employees to look after still other tasks. In this way, employees, including managers, are part of the owner variety of people associated with the business. In larger organizations that make use of automated data processing techniques, those who accomplish the day-to-day tasks and make the basic operating decisions as well as many policy decisions are employees, hired by the owners to run the company at the highest possible long-term profit. Whether employee or owner, each of the workers in the organization occupies a position that is more or less well-defined with respect to that of the other workers. Each of these positions within the company has certain working relationships with other positions. The pattern of these working relationships is known as the *structure* of the organization.

Scholars of organization theory view the structure of an organization in two senses: the formal structure of the organization, and the informal structure of the organization. The pattern of relationships in the formal structure is usually depicted as an organization chart (Figure 1–1). The formal structure of an organization indicates how the owners or chief policy-makers think the business should be run. Persons working within the organization can look to the organization chart for their official relationships with others who work in the company.

If you have ever worked in an organization of any size, however, you will be quick to remember that the organization chart tells only part of the story. Whereas the formal organization chart indicates how the bosses think the business should operate, its actual operation more often than not is markedly different. The actual relationships within an organization comprise its informal organization. The formal organization and the informal organization may be identical, but this is rarely the case. The formal organization is based on a hierarchy of authority and emphasizes a chain-of-command structure according to the official position of each individual within the organization. The informal organization, in addition to recog-

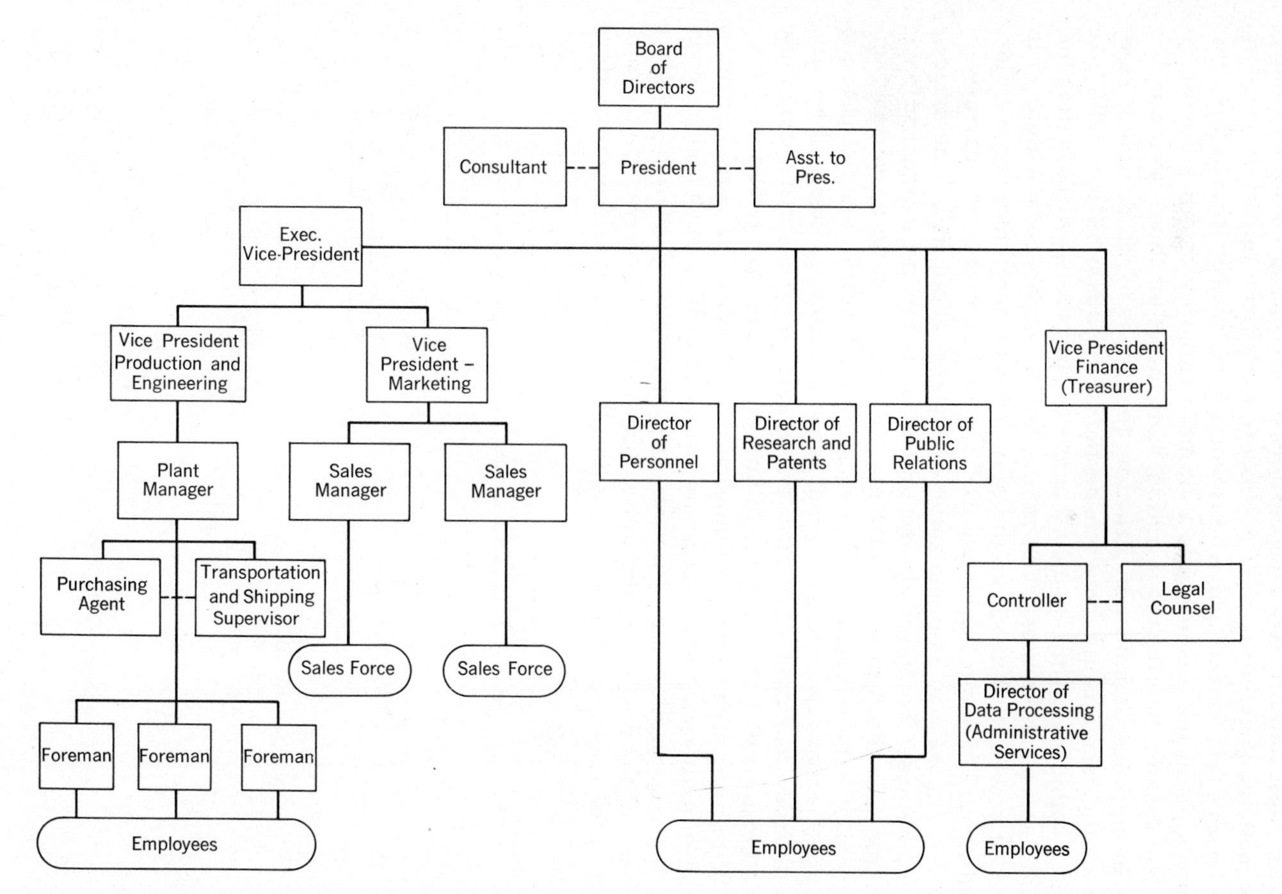

Figure 1–1. Typical business organization chart.

nizing these authoritative relationships, also recognizes that in actuality, the pattern of authority may not follow the official organization chart. The boss's son, for example, who is working his way up through the company to learn the business has a lot more authority as office boy or assistant cashier than the organization chart shows for those positions.

The informal organization structure, then, tries to tell the whole story about the relationships between people in the business. It tries to take into account friendships that exist across organizational levels in the company; special influences, such as the boss's son above; positions with special power attributes, like the duty sergeant in military organization; and so on. This story can be pictured, too, and often is by those who want to find out the way an organization really goes about its business. However, because the informal structure of each business organization is unique and the formal organization patterns are more universally employed, it is more useful here to examine the latter. In the discussion to follow, analysis of different formal organization structures will be used to illustrate relationships in business organizations. Understanding these relationships will also help one to understand informal relationships.

Within any organization the object is to establish working relationships, lines of authority, and a coordinated division of labor such that the goals of the organization are achieved. An organizational chart is simply a picture of the position of the individuals within the organization according to the type and levels of their skills. Within this concept we can draw

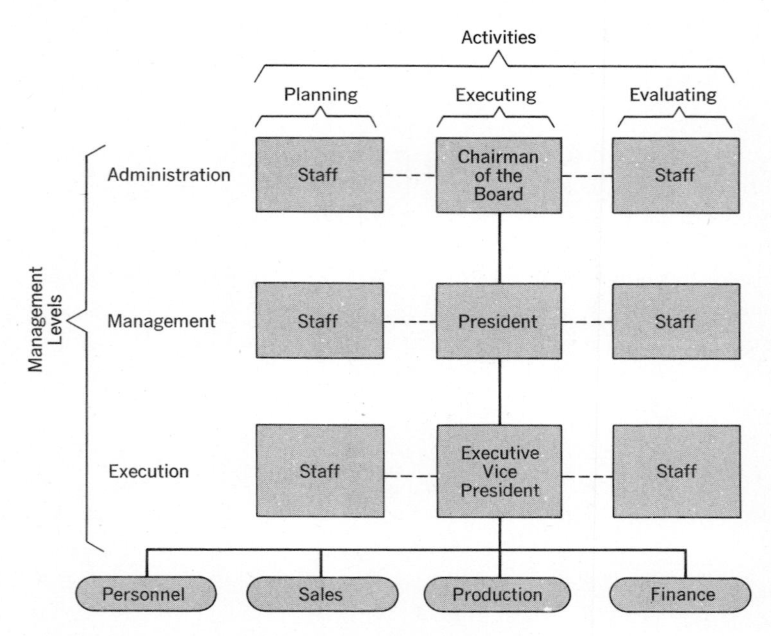

Figure 1–2. Basic activities of business organizations.

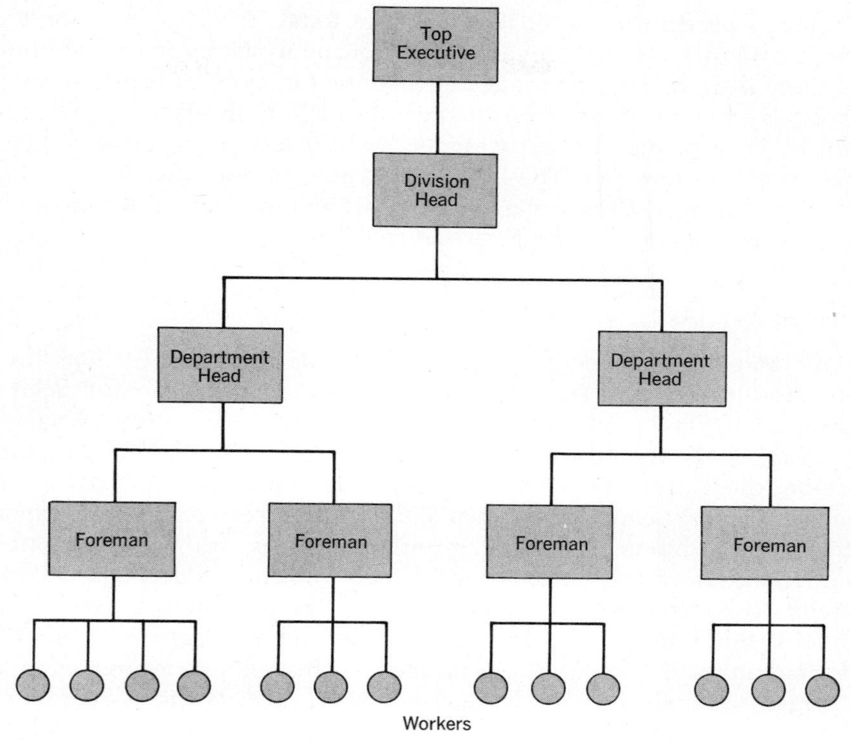

Figure 1–3. Typical line organization.

lines of delegated authority. We can further say that each level of authority has various responsibilities in terms of activities. The characteristic internal hierarchy of business organization has three levels: administration, management, and execution. The activities carried out by these levels are planning, evaluating, and executing. Figure 1–2 illustrates these activities as they relate to the basic business functions of sales, production, finance, and personnel.

Around this framework is built the formal or official structure of the organization. There are several generally accepted types of organization structure. They include *line organizations, line-staff organizations,* and a host of others that look to these two for their genealogy.

Line Organizations

Figure 1–3 shows a typical line organization. Basically, line authority is command authority and carries with it responsibility for accomplishment of objectives. Orders are issued and decisions are made in the line capacity. The line structure is the simplest and probably oldest type of organization and is used in many small businesses today. In the illustration the flow of authority is direct and unbroken from administration to execution, and there is no distinction made between the functions of people at various levels—that is, there is no distinction made with respect to what is done by each of the two departments, only that each department head supervises two foremen. The line organization is not often seen in this pure form. Usually, a line organization chart will indicate basic functional areas, such as marketing, finance, and so forth.

Line-Staff Organizations

An example of a line-staff organization appears in Figure 1–4. Staff functions are typically of a consultive nature—rendering advice and making recommendations, providing special and technical information, and serving in an advisory capacity to one or more line officers. This structure provides the line official with the opportunity to maintain both discipline and stability, while having the availability of staff services to bring expert information in terms of research, recommendations, record and statistical maintenance, and specialized skills to help him in his decision-making activity. The important distinction between line personnel and staff personnel is that line personnel make decisions and staff personnel provide information used to make those decisions. This puts data processing as an organizational activity clearly in a staff capacity. It is frequently

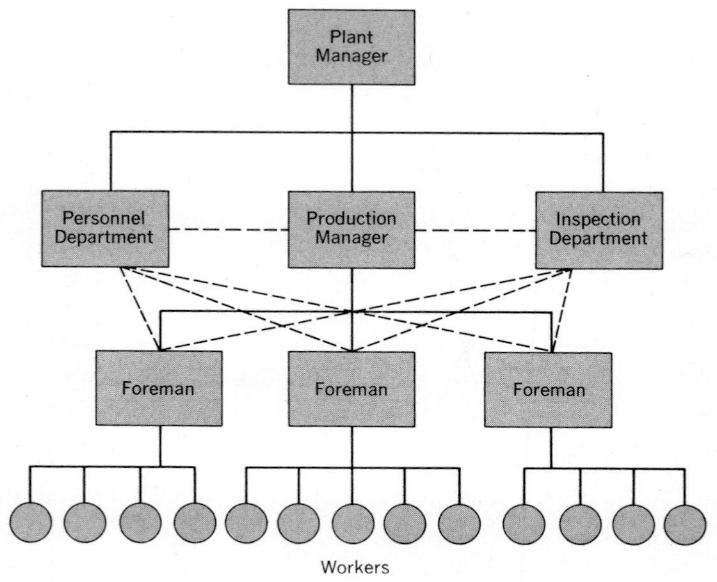

Figure 1–4. Line-staff organization.

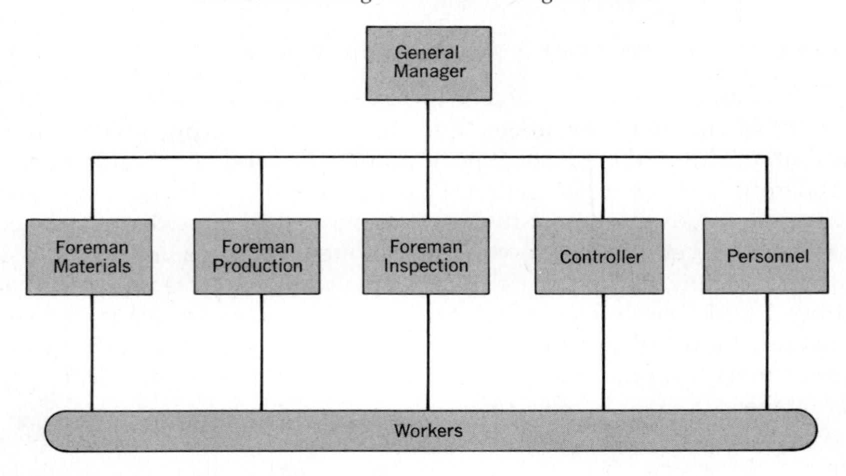

Figure 1–5. Functional organization chart.

charged, and rightly so, that staff personnel, because of their expertise in their subject fields, wield a great deal of power in the organization, an aspect of staff activities that frequently puts them into the position of making decisions rather than advising about them. Usually, this causes the organization great trouble in terms of affixing responsibility for the results of decision-making. A popular business adage has it that staff should be on tap, not on top.

Other Organizational Structures

There are several other types of organizational structures. These are basically offshoots of the line and line-staff concepts. The *functional organization* in which employees perform directly for two or more specialists is an example. This structure creates line relationships for those who in a line-staff organization would serve strictly a staff function. Overlapping responsibility is inherent in this type of structure and employees must maintain a multiple line relationship with those above them in the organizational structure. That is to say, employees are usually responsible to more than one boss, which is often confusing for worker and supervisor alike. Figure 1–5 illustrates part of a functional organizational chart.

Another offshoot of the line-staff organization structure is the *committee organization.* In this organizational form, decisions in functional areas are made by committees. The organization might have a production committee, a new product committee, a marketing committee, and so on. Although this method of organizing brings many skills and viewpoints to the decision-making activity, it suffers from the disadvantage of being exceptionally cumbersome and time-consuming. Quick decisions, often necessary in business dealings, are almost impossible to achieve.

Operating Aspects of Various Structures

Each of the formal structures a business might choose to adopt has a number of inherent advantages and disadvantages. The choice will depend on the kind of business it is, how large it is, and what kind of people are members of the organization. Figure 1–6 outlines the general advantages and disadvantages of the four common structures discussed here. It will not be very helpful to you to try to memorize this list. Use it to get a general feeling for how a group of people would operate under the conditions listed. Try to imagine why certain advantages are available to one structural form but not to others and which kinds of businesses would benefit most from the advantages or would be hindered least by the disadvantages.

As you might expect, business managers and executives do not always agree as to which structural form is best suited to their company. The success of any structure in terms of helping the organization meet its goals rests with the ability of its members to maintain and enforce the defined lines of authority and responsibility. Communications networks must be established, accurate and timely information must be available, and policies and procedures must be clearly defined and enforced.

Information Flow and Organization

It was pointed out earlier that successful business operation depends upon successful decision-making. Successful decision-making, you recall, is based upon information. A group of people organize themselves not only to allocate responsibilities and to share the work but to provide means of communication among the various activities taking place within the organization. A major purpose of any organizational structure is to cause information to flow to and from decision-makers so that they can make better decisions and so that their decisions can be implemented. Management, after all, is the process of converting information into action.

There is a good deal of action taking place in the day-to-day operations of a successful large business. The key operations are shown as Figure 1–7. Arrows depict the interrelationship of these operations in terms of the information that must flow from one to the others that need it to perform their functions. Thus, information about what and how much is bought is needed by disbursing in order to pay the vendor for the goods. It is also needed by receiving in planning on incoming shipments. Further examination shows that all operations are tied together in terms of information. The function of data processing in a company such as this one is to provide for the flow of information to the appropriate operation at the appropriate time.

Decision-makers use information from two sources. Some information comes from sources external to the company, such as government publica-

	Line Organization	Line/Staff Organization	Functional Organization	Committee
ADVANTAGES	1. Established lines of authority 2. No confusion of responsibility 3. Discipline easily maintained 4. Ease and speed of downward communication 5. Duties clearly defined	1. Established lines of authority 2. No confusion of responsibility 3. Discipline easily maintained 4. Staff increases depth of access of line personnel to knowledge 5. Cross relationships possible without breaking lines of authority 6. Assistance available in carrying out functions and responsibilities	1. Autocratic control eliminated 2. Less varied individual abilities required 3. Immediate services of specialist available	1. Advisory judgment and perspective available 2. Combined skills and abilities applied cooperatively to problems 3. Generally policy recommending groups 4. Supplemental ability to both line and staff
DISADVANTAGES	1. Lack of specialization of line officers 2. Variety of duties requires numerous skills 3. Spirit of teamwork and cooperation minimized by rigid lines of authority 4. Vertical communication difficult 5. Lack of expert advice 6. Loss of key personnel can cause immediate crippling effect	1. Communications slow due to larger working group 2. Possibility of misuse of staff or growth so that too many do too little 3. Organizational structure more complicated 4. More red tape 5. Higher expenditure in terms of personnel in hope of increased ability	1. Lines of responsibility not clear 2. Discipline may be sacrificed 3. Increased red tape 4. Overlapping authority	1. Slow 2. May be cumbersome 3. May be compromising and indecisive 4. Vague lines of authority 5. Requires extensive supervision 6. Increased red tape 7. Overlapping authority

Figure 1–6. Advantages and disadvantages of different organizational forms.

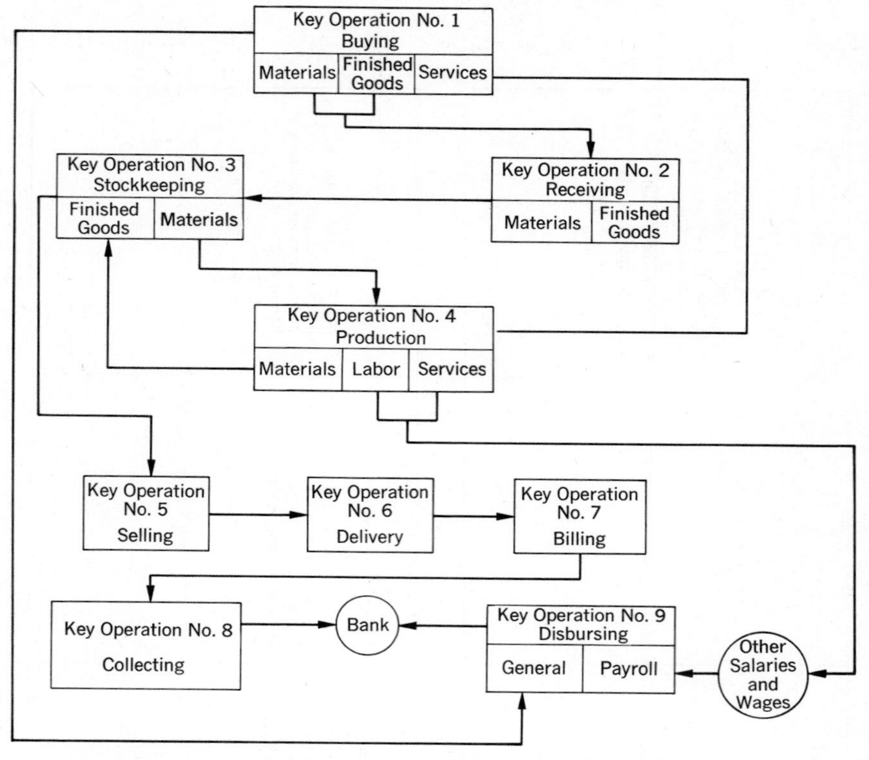

Figure 1–7. Interrelationship of key operations. (Courtesy, Moore Business Forms, Inc.)

tions, news articles, and the like. Other information comes from within the company, which frequently is information about the results of a decision made in the past either by the decision-maker receiving the information or by someone else. When a decision-maker receives information about the results of a decision he made in the past, we would say that he is getting feedback about his decision. It would certainly seem unreasonable to ask a business executive to make decisions and never let him know the outcomes of his efforts. Organization structures and the information systems that serve them always—if they are good ones—establish means by which a decision-maker is provided feedback about his decisions. These means are called *feedback loops.* A feedback loop works essentially like this: Given a chunk of information, a decision-maker makes a decision. Later, he receives feedback about what happened in response to his decisions. He uses this new information to modify his original chunk of information and then perhaps makes another decision, which is now based on better information. This appears graphically in Figure 1–8*a*. Notice that there are three basic components of the feedback loop. The information, the use of the information (in this case, the decision), and

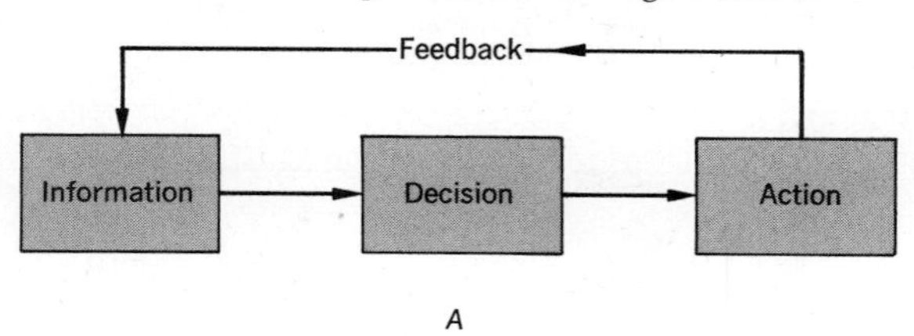

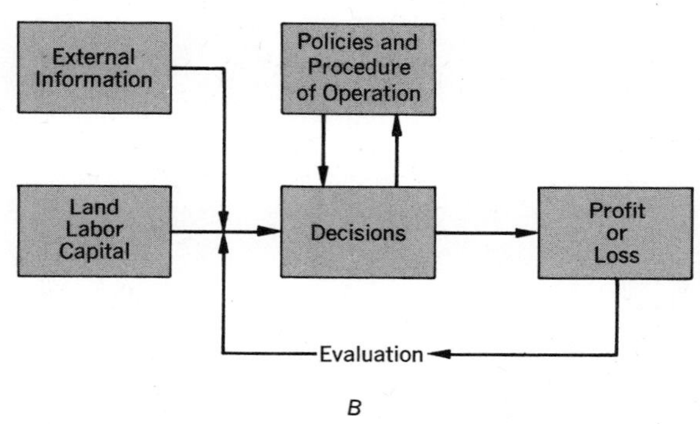

Figure 1–8. Feedback loop.

the action. Connecting these components are arrows representing the flow of information pertinent to that particular decision.

These three components can be applied to any production or decision-making operation. As a matter of fact, the total organization can be described by a feedback chart, as in Figure 1–8*b*. Notice that a decision is based on four types of information: the policies of the organization; external information; information about the availability of resources, land, labor and capital; and feedback about the results of past decisions which were implemented by productive activity. If the company's customers thought the productive activity was good, they bought the product, if not, they bought something else. This feedback information is used to modify productive operations accordingly. Figure 1–9 illustrates the same ideas put to use in a marketing system of a business and in an electronic computer system.

Analysis of the Organization and Its Information System

The manager of a modern business is in charge of a number of different systems each of which performs different functions. In a manufacturing organization, a complex system of machines and personnel is devoted to

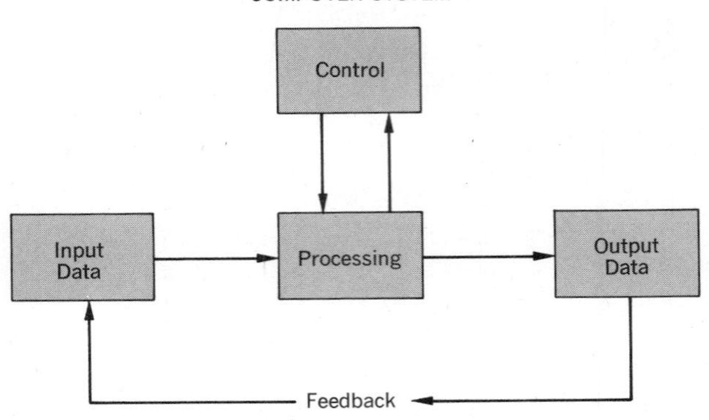

Figure 1–9. Feedback applications.

the production of the company's goods. Scheduling which machine to do what job and when and by whom is a difficult job, one that requires thorough knowledge of the entire production system. Similarly, every business has a communication system involving telephones, messengers, and perhaps teletype connections between facilities that are geographically separated. There is another system to fill customer orders, preparing some goods on a made-to-order basis, packaging goods, preparing invoices, shipping the goods, and perhaps following up of the order to help the customer make best use of what he has bought.

Still another system is concerned with billing the customer, determining what credit to extend to the customer, analyzing discount procedures, making adjustments, and the like. Probably the most difficult system to understand is the system of human relations that exists in every business organization. This system was the subject of much of the first portion of this chapter. The point of view we should take in the study of business information systems is one that shows an organization as a large system of activities designed to satisfy the goals of the business. Each of these activities—production, order-filling, customer billing, information flow, and so forth—is itself a system.

We are trying to visualize the business organization as a maze of interrelated manual, mechanical, electromechanical, electronic, and psychological systems that are entwined and strive together to achieve the goals of the entire organization. Ideally, the systems within the whole business system complement each other. The information system indicates to the production system what to produce and in what quantities to best satisfy the customers. The customer billing system aids the accounting and financial systems to determine the flow of funds and the marketing system by providing reports of customer activities. The marketing system complements the production system by determining not only what can be sold but what can be both sold and profitably produced.

In practice, however, the systems within the business organization do not always work together in the best possible fashion. The marketing system determines that it can sell thousands of private helicopters, say, for $5,000 apiece. The production system can find no way to produce these helicopters for less than $8,000. Rather than work together, the two systems point accusing fingers at each other using words such as "unrealistic," "uncooperative," "unimaginative." The customer billing system does not always provide the marketing system with customer reports. "It's hard enough," they say, "to do our own job of getting the bills out to the customers without trying to do the sales department's job, too!"

Most managers of large organizations will tell you that one of their most difficult jobs is to make all the systems within the business work together. Several decades ago, managers faced with this problem turned to specialists called, in those days, efficiency experts to help them make each system within the organization more effective in performing its specialized function. The effect was to make the whole business system more efficient by improving the efficiency of the subsystems, little was done to improve the effectiveness with which the subsystems worked together. More recently, managers have begun to recognize that to maximize the teamwork required of the subsystems for best performance of the whole system, increased reliance must be put by them on one of the subsystems, namely, the information system. This system provides the manager with the information he needs to best evaluate the operations of the entire system, in terms both of the individual efficiencies of the subsystems and of how well the subsystems complement rather than oppose each other. As with the analysis of any complex phenomenon, the analysis of a business's information system is best performed by persons who specialize in this sort of work. Persons who make a career of analyzing and developing information systems are known as *systems analysts*. In large part, they are an outgrowth of the defunct occupation of efficiency expert. However, instead of devoting their efforts to a subsystem or a part of a subsystem, they are concerned with the entire business system, particularly as to how the information system serves it.

A systems analyst, then, is concerned with the analysis of the organizational structure in terms of information flow, decision-making, and general improvement of business operations. Within the scope of the systems analysts duties, we find activities such as creating flow charts of documents, materials, work-in-process, information, and the like; preparing work distribution charts; preparing organizational charts; and designing physical layout charts of equipment and work stations. We also find the systems analyst involved in the design of business forms, developing new methods of records management and information storage, preparing operating manuals, conducting surveys of administrative methods, writing procedures for accomplishing routine tasks, and analyzing the equipment needed by the information system. Clearly, systems and procedures analysts, as they are sometimes known, perform activities that are part and parcel of every manager's job. Unlike a manager, however, the systems analyst is an adviser, a staff officer who makes no decisions but only provides information to those that do. Decision-makers turn to him to perform the analysis of internal business operations that require the knowledge of an expert in the field.

There are different types of systems analysts. Because electronic data processing is relatively new in the business information system, many systems analysts are not computer-oriented. Yet, because of the wide publicity that has been associated with electronic information systems, many persons believe that every systems analyst is a computer expert. Nothing could be further from the truth. Some persons who are known as systems analysts concern themselves only with the flow of documents within the offices and other work areas of the business facility. Still others limit themselves to the design of business forms and other documents to be used within the business and frequently in conjunction with the business's customers. It is true, however, that many systems analysts specialize in computerized information systems. In fact, many of these, because of their backgrounds as computer programmers or in other technical areas, are severely limited in vision to the hardware aspects of the information system in which they are operating. These machine-oriented individuals are called systems analysts only as a misnomer if they do not understand and appreciate the entire information system of the business organization.

Unfortunately, because many managers have been unfamiliar with the technical aspects of automated data processing, they have been at the mercy of just this kind of systems analyst. This has led to a good deal of "dog wagging" by persons limited in vision to their machines but who are placed in positions to influence the design of information systems. The result is an information system designed around a machine rather than around the information needs of the business. Professional business managers are becoming more aware of the technical aspects of automated information systems and recognize that the role of electronic data processing machinery can only be properly determined after a mastery of the information needs of the organization has been accomplished.

A system is essentially well-organized common sense, and a systems analyst must be able to work with common-sense ideas with ease. A systems analyst is a professional gamesman, too; he sees things that should be done to make the business more efficient and he plays the game of trying to get the people in the business to do things in the best way. His job is threefold: he determines what is being done now—a lot harder than one might expect; he determines what *should* be done and how; then he tries to implement the new method or the new system. The first two of these jobs are a lot easier than the last. Implementing a new system means asking the people in the business organization to change the way they have been doing things, perhaps for many years. Usually, the results of his efforts lie somewhere between what he perceives to be the ideal way of doing things and the way that people are accustomed to doing them. The closer the end result is to the ideal, the better the systems analyst. This points up the often neglected fact that in the analysis of a system and the subsequent design of a new system or changes in the old, the people operating in the system must also be considered. It is pointless to design an ideal system if the people in the business organization will not accept it. Thus, the systems analyst must also be a salesman, selling his ideas not only to those who will authorize the changes but also to those who must live with them.

Conclusion

In making an evaluation of the information needs of a business organization, the organization should be seen as a group of systems each performing certain specialized functions and each interrelated with the others into a total business system moving towards the satisfaction of the organization's goals. The prime function of management is to aid in the implementation of policies, procedures, and techniques that will result in operating savings, increased productivity, and general satisfaction of these goals. This is done by making better decisions based on the evaluation of continually better information in terms of accuracy and timeliness. The purpose of this text is to examine the ways in which such information is prepared and transmitted within the business system. We will return to the analysis of business systems and procedures in Chapters 4 and 5, where we will describe the basic tenets of business and information systems analysis and the basic automated data processing devices employed today by large businesses in the implementation of their information systems. Chapters 2 and 3 describe the family of quantitative business decision-making techniques that give rise to as well as result from the capabilities of modern data processing equipment.

The remainder of this book is devoted to automated techniques of data processing, including electronic data processing, electromechanical data processing, and other technical areas.

As a textbook in data processing, much has been left out. Strictly speaking, data processing includes much more than these things. Probably, however, most students will study these in courses which deal with data processing but which do not go by that name. Typewriting, accounting, bookkeeping, business machines and desk calculators, stenography, and a host of other college business courses are really courses in data processing but have not been considered as such because only recently have businessmen come to realize how important their information system is to them and have begun to think of data processing as something in itself worthy of their attention. While much of this recent attention to data processing is due to the remarkable developments in automated data processing methods, it should be remembered throughout the study of this book that today the vast majority of data processing does not use automated techniques at all but relies on manual techniques exclusively.

Study of the chapters to follow should not obscure the essential point that what is important to learn about data processing is not how machines are made to do magical things, because the machines and the techniques used to control them change very rapidly, but rather why the information should be processed, the form it should take, and to whom the information should flow to best serve those who must use it for high-quality decision-making so as to enable the business organization to meet its goals.

Questions

1. What are your goals in studying data processing? How many involve the enjoyment of material gain?
2. List specific goals that are likely to motivate business managers, factory workers, and corporation stockholders.
3. This chapter does not present a definition of the term *data processing.* Without looking up a definition, try to develop one yourself.
4. What is the most important distinction between a decision and a guess?
5. What is an organization? In what ways do business organizations differ from other organizations?
6. Draw an organization chart for an organization that employs the committee organizational structure.
7. What is the difference between line and staff relationships in an organization?
8. Develop an argument that supports the notion that a data processing department should be line rather than staff.
9. Why is it important for a systems analyst to understand the workings of the informal organization structure?

Scientific Decision-Making

How many warehouses should a manufacturer of food products desirous of minimizing both transportation and storage costs use in its distribution system? What is the best way to schedule jobs on a number of machines so as to make maximum use of each machine and at the same time meet production deadlines? How many cakes should a bakery shop bake to minimize the chance of being out of stock and incurring customer ill will and at the same time minimizing the chance of having to throw away many unsold cakes at the end of the day when it is uncertain exactly how many customers will ask to buy cakes? How many check-out stands should be installed in a supermarket so as to minimize the time that customers must wait in line and at the same time minimize the number of check-out stands standing idle during slow periods?

These questions and many others like them are the type that face business managers today and require answers—decisions, if you like—that frequently can be made with the use of scientific and mathematical techniques. In the previous chapter, we discussed the processes by which decisions were reached in a business organization. There, the relationships that exist between individual decision-makers in the business organization and the flow of information among them was analyzed. This chapter considers decision-making that utilizes quantitative techniques to analyze the information available to the decision-maker. These techniques are called *scientific decision-making* here because they involve decision-making processes that call upon scientific and quantitative methods of analysis.

The Nature of Scientific Decision-Making

Scientific decision-making is more often referred to by its practitioners as *operations research.* Defining scientific decision-making as the application of scientific techniques to decision-making, however, will not always satisfy the operations researcher when the terms *operations research* and *sci-*

entific decision-making are used interchangeably. The literature of operations research, which is quite abundant, shows considerable disagreement over what an adequate definition of this term should include. However, one definition that has been received with some unanimity of acceptance goes like this:

> "Operations research is applied *decision theory*. [It] uses any scientific, mathematical, or logical means to attempt to cope with the problems that confront the executive when he tries to achieve a thorough-going rationality in dealing with his decision problems."[1]

This definition describes a process of making decisions that is unlike that used by many businessmen in the past and in fact is not much like what many businessmen use today. Most businessmen today still employ the intuitive approach to decision-making, which relies on experience and subjective judgment almost entirely, with a minimum of quantitative analysis. Except for fairly large and progressive companies, scientific decision-making enjoys limited use.

There are two reasons for the lack of widespread use of operations research techniques by businessmen today. First, operations research is a relatively new field, and otherwise well-educated business decision-makers may not have had the opportunity to become acquainted with the potentials of this kind of work in terms of business success. Second, operations research requires considerable technical training, principally in the fields of mathematics and statistics, and most business executives have not had this training even to the extent of being able to appreciate what operations research can do for them, much less how it is done. Only within the last few years have professional schools of business begun to treat the subject in any depth. The Graduate School of Business at Stanford University, for example, as late as 1963 required no math other than high school algebra for those who aspired to enter their Master of Business Administration program. Now, that school has followed the example of other graduate business schools in the country like Harvard, Chicago, and Carnegie Institute of Technology and requires a year of college calculus for entry into the program. As we shall see, the picture is changing in the work-a-day world of business, too. The result of this increased interest in operations research is that both decision-makers and those who provide decision-makers with the information from which the decisions follow—that is, data processors—must be acquainted with the basic ideas of operations research and the basic kinds of problems and techniques to solve them that operations research deals with.

Although many businessmen look upon operations research as a new field, the ideas behind scientific decision-making have been around for

[1] D. W. Miller, and M. K. Starr, *Executive Decisions and Operations Research* (Englewood Cliffs, N. J.: Prentice-Hall, 1960), pp. 103–104.

some time. Systematic ways to think about business operations were first discussed as early as the beginning of the nineteenth century by such men as Charles Babbage, who is better known to data processors as one who made significant developments in the field of calculating machines, or, as we would call them, computers. Later, such men as Frederick W. Taylor, founder of "scientific management," or "Taylorism," as it is sometimes called by labor leaders; Frank Gilbreth, who developed therbligs, a measure of work effort expended by production workers; and Henry Gantt, who developed ways of charting the sequence of events and flow of work in industrial work situations all were applying scientific techniques to business problems.

However, few operation researchers would agree that the work these men did, however important, could be called operations research as it is known today. Today, operations research implies impersonal, rather rigid techniques of problem analysis and solution development, stressing scientific methods and employing a special tool called a *model*, about which more will be said later. Briefly, a model, as the term is used in operations research, is a mathematical expression of the operating system in which the problem exists and which represents, in mathematical terms, all the significant factors to be considered in arriving at a solution. It is the use of the model that distinguishes operations research or scientific decision-making from the earlier efforts of Taylor, Gilbreth, and others.

In summary, the basic notion of modern operations research can be set forth in two statements: (1) operations research employs quantitative instead of intuitive approaches to problem-solving; and (2) its method of approach employs mathematical and symbolic techniques of model-building. Or, as it has been put by one operations researcher: "Operations research is the art of giving bad answers to problems to which otherwise worse answers are given."[2]

There is abundant evidence that operations research is needed by modern businesses if they are to maximize their operational efficiency. A number of reasons for this have been suggested by managers and operations researchers. First, business operations today are far more complex than they were even a couple of decades ago. Companies that before World War II had to handle sales of $500,000 now face the problem of coping with sales of ten times as much. Giant companies such as General Motors Corporation, American Telephone and Telegraph, Ford, I. E. Du-Pont de Nemours, and International Business Machines cannot begin to cope with the highly complex operating problems and decisions that must be made without the use of some rational method of reaching solutions. Second, the business productive system can be looked upon as a system into which flow certain inputs and out of which flow certain outputs.

[2] T. L. Saaty, *Mathematical Methods of Operations Research* (New York: McGraw-Hill Book Co., 1959), p. 3.

Viewing a business as a whole system, as we did in Chapter 1, lends it to more rigid analysis, the kind of analysis generally associated with operations research techniques. Third, new production processes, including the use of more automated machinery, require more systematic scheduling of work through the productive facility. Rather than a foreman scheduling work through a network of interrelated machines, it is now necessary, because of the complexity of the equipment and the even more complex relationships between the machines, to use quantitative techniques, often performed by a computer, to provide for the most efficient use of equipment. Fourth, businessmen have come to recognize that many of their problems involve uncertainty. Uncertainty can be coped with by either hoping, guessing, or making some measure of the likelihood of an uncertain event occurring. Operations research, in its bag of tricks to help decision-makers, has statistical techniques which measure the probability of events happening and help determine the decision that will provide for the most desirable results whatever should happen. There is no way, of course, to completely predict the future, but there are techniques available that help both to minimize losses if things go badly and to maximize profits if things go well.

The use of operations research today is the result of several developments in the business world for several years. First of all, business managers had to recognize that "by guess and by golly" is no longer the most desirable way to arrive at a decision—if it ever was—and that more systematic and logical approaches to decision-making are required. Thus a change in attitude of business managers was necessary before operations research could be introduced into American business operations. Second, the development of computers and other automated data processing techniques has been necessary for some of the problems treated by operations research because the calculations involved can become so laborious and time-consuming that a decision could not be realized in the time necessary to implement it. Electronic computers, because of their ability to perform many calculations over a very short period of time now make problems solvable today which a few years ago were insolvable by virtue of the enormous number of calculations involved. Finally, the realization that business today is a highly technical field demanding increasingly sophisticated techniques has been brought home to many businessmen who earlier had depended on luck and intuition alone in making their decisions. This has come about through the loss of business to competitors who have been putting such techniques into practice and whose operating efficiencies have made them more formidable opponents in the marketplace. There is no quicker way to cause an American businessman to change his ways than to show how his operation can earn more profits, or how he can keep his competitors from taking business away from him.

These important developments came about gradually after World War II. The art of applying scientific techniques to solving operational problems got its start by its use in military operations during the war. In 1941, British scientists, having just developed radar, were asked by the military to determine the best way to use the new devices. The scientists approached this military problem with the same techniques they might use for strictly scientific problems. In short, they used what is known to scientific researchers as the *scientific method.* This method entailed carefully collecting data about the problem, analyzing the data by the use of mathematical and statistical techniques, developing a hypothesis to explain certain phenomena, and establishing theories that predicted behavior of certain elements in the problem. Then, using more data collected while the devices were under use, these scientists revised their theories and were able to develop the most effective means of employing this new military tool. It has been said that as a result of their efforts, the British defense capability was increased in efficiency by a multiple of ten. Having thus demonstrated the value of the scientific method to military operations problems in general, scientists and mathematicians were called upon during the war to analyze many other kinds of military problems, including determination of the best depth for depth charges to explode, increasing the accuracy of aerial bombing, and better deployment of ships in convoys.

After the war, however, businessmen seemed reluctant to introduce the scientific method into the analysis of their business operations, even in the face of its overwhelming success in military operations. This reluctance was based in part on ignorance and in part on fear of "ivory-tower idealism." Since the 1950's, however, operations research has grown in business applications, and more businessmen are turning to it, if for no other reason than to meet the competition of those businesses that have already introduced it. More often than not, operations research is introduced into a company when the company hires a consulting firm to solve a particular problem. Applying the scientific method to the problem, the consulting firm will often demonstrate to the company's management that impressive results can be achieved by dealing with operational problems in systematic ways. Later, the company assigns someone to the task of investigating operations research techniques as applied to other company problems, and perhaps in time an operations research department is formed. In 1963, it was estimated that one out of twenty of the country's businesses had operations research departments, or otherwise made use of operations research in the conduct of their affairs. Today, more than half of the largest one hundred companies in the United States have their own operations research departments.

The evidence is clear. Operations research, or scientific decision-making, has earned a place in the decision-making structure of American business. Because of this place, it is important for those who deal with the information needs of businesses to at least understand some of the basic ideas associated with this technique of business analysis. One should not expect to become an expert by reading these few pages. It is enough for him to understand the *kind* of problem being solved, not to be able to solve it.

The Basic Tool of Operations Research: The Model

A model, as the term is used in operations research, is a means of replicating real phenomena. The model airplane that a boy assembles replicates real aircraft and behaves in many important characteristics like real aircraft. This sort of physical model is useful to the boy in learning basic relationships about aircraft construction, control, and flight characteristics. In fact, model airplanes are used by adult aircraft designers in wind tunnels to determine the characteristics of real aircraft when moving through air at various speeds. At the same time, however, the model airplane cannot hope to replicate every characteristic of the real thing. There are important differences between the real world and models which are used to study real-world behavior. For this reason, no matter how thoroughly tested the model aircraft in the wind tunnel, the aircraft itself must be test flown to examine its flight characteristics under actual flight conditions. Like model aircraft, replicas can be developed to describe the significant behavior of many types of phenomena. Models can be constructed of oil refineries to determine the best mixtures of inputs and the best processing techniques to arrive at the desired outputs. Small models of factory floors and equipment to be housed in the factory are useful in laying out the best physical arrangement of the production facility. Models can be constructed of transportation networks to determine the most efficient number of warehouses, of production schedules to assure that a particular project will be completed on time, and of other less tangible operational phenomena, such as prediction of the number of hours a machine in a job-shop will stand idle when it is unknown exactly how many jobs during a given time period will require its use.

Some of these models are physical models, like the model aircraft and the plant layout model. Others, more abstract, are mathematical models in which the relationships are represented in terms of mathematical formulas. The oil refinery, the transportation network, and the production schedule are examples of models that are most often built on a mathematical rather than a physical basis. Whether more or less abstract, all models have certain characteristic features. They are used to analyze real-world behavior when the analysis of the actual phenomenon would be too cumbersome or too expensive. Models are simplifications of the real world. Again, as in the case of the model aircraft, all the characteristics and operating features of the real thing cannot be replicated in a model. Finally, as a result of their simplified representation of the real world, models often give somewhat inaccurate predictions of how the real world will behave.

There are three basic kinds of models. Physical models that look like the real thing are easy to construct and have certain useful purposes. Full-scale wooden mock-ups of modern aircraft, which are constructed before production on the real aircraft starts, are very useful in discovering errors of equipment placement made by a designer, in determining assembly sequences, and in the fabrication of large sheet metal parts.

One step removed from these physical models are models that are tangible and can be handled but do not look very much like the real thing. A globe, for example, does not really look much like the earth, but a great deal can be learned about the relationships between the continents, water masses and other geographic detail from studying it. Models such as this are frequently called *analog models.* An analog model is one that uses the characteristics of one physical structure to represent the characteristics of another; that is, the model is analogous to the real object being studied. Astronomers have used such models for several centuries in attempting to explain the behavior of bodies in the solar system and have constructed models which express the theories being tested. One such theory, for example, was a theory that the sun and the planets revolved around the earth. When this model failed to explain the observed behavior of the planets themselves, other models were developed, such as a heliocentric one in which the planets, including earth, revolved around the sun. Such models can be built of physical objects such as grapefruit, golf balls, and marbles; most of us have probably experimented at home with such models to see how eclipses of the sun and the moon might occur.

These models, which are analogous to the real-world phenomena being studied, can be further refined by expressing the relationships between the important factors as mathematical statements. Models that do this are the most abstract in nature and, by virtue of having no physical limitations with respect to manipulations, are the most versatile. Mathematical models are used by operations research to study business and economic phenomena. In mathematical analysis, the term *model* is used to mean a set of mathematical statements that describe the relationships between the several elements of the phenomenon being studied with enough accuracy to permit the model to be used to predict the outcome of the relationships during a particular event. For example, we might be interested in what might happen if we were to add sugar to a quantity of hydrochloric acid. One way to determine this would be to take a given quantity of hydrochloric acid and add a given quantity of sugar to it and watch to see what happens. This is perfectly feasible for problems that can be observed with ease and little cost. A way to predict what might happen without an actual experiment would involve building a mathematical model. One can express the characteristics of a given quantity of hydrochloric acid as a chemical formula and can also express the characteristics of a quantity of sugar in the same manner. These two equations form a model, and we can use the model to predict the reaction that occurs after the event of adding sugar to hydrochloric acid by adding the two chemical equations together. The sum of the two equations should be a chemical expression that describes the products that result when we actually add sugar to acid. If it does not, then our model does not work and a new one should be developed.

Mathematical models such as the one described above are particularly useful when the actual phenomena being studied cannot be experimented with to predict the outcome of different events. This is the case with almost all problems of business operations. One cannot experiment with customers or with employees or with a five million dollar factory to see "what would happen if . . ." What we can do is to express the significant relationships inherent in the problem in mathematical terms and, through mathematical manipulation, predict the outcome of different events. If the predictions based upon the model are often at odds with the real thing, then a new model must be developed to be used for predictive purposes. Such mathematical models use expressions such as equations and inequalities to describe the situation being studied.

One authority in the field outlines four basic equations that are used in operations research.[3] The first of these are *definitional equations*, which define relationships between certain variables. Retail price for example, might be expressed as

$$P = C + .4P$$

P is the retail price and C is the cost, or the amount the retailer had to pay for the unit of merchandise. In this case the retail price, in addition to consisting of the cost also includes a 40 per cent markup on retail.

Another type of equation is the *technological equation*, which expresses the results of physical processes. A factory's output, for example, might depend upon the number of machines it has and the number of employees available to operate the machines. Increasing the number of employees per machine might increase the output of the machine. Expressed as an equation, this might look like this:

$$O = ME$$

O is the factory output, M the number of machines, and E the number of employees. The output of the factory, given a certain number of employees

[3] Robert S. Weinberg, *An Analytical Approach to Advertising Expenditure Strategy*, Association of National Advertisers, 1960; cited in Abe Shuchman, *Scientific Decision Making in Business* (New York: Holt, Rinehart and Winston, 1963), pp. 95–101.

and machines, can be predicted by multiplying the number of employees by the number of machines available.

A third basic type of equation used in models which is particularly useful in studying the behavior of customers is the *behavioral equation.* Economists, for example, have long tried to describe consumption behavior of economic systems as an equation that relates consumer spending with national income. This equation usually looks like this:

$$C = a + bY$$

C represents the total spending in the economy for consumption purposes, that is, for consumer goods; a represents the minimum amount that will be spent regardless of the level of national income, representing the minimum level of living; b represents the portion of national income spent for consumption purposes above the minimum amount a; and Y represents national income, that is, the sum of all the earnings in the economic system during a given time period. This equation, in itself a simple model, describes a situation in which consumer spending rises and falls with national income. More generally, this consumption function, as it is usually called can be stated in more general terms:

$$C = f(Y)$$

This expression is read aloud as "C is a function of Y," or, in our previous example, "Consumption is a function of national income." A *function,* as used by mathematicians, is a device used to express the relationship between something that varies (in our case consumption) and the things that make it vary (national income). More technically, C is the *dependent variable,* Y is the *independent variable.* Functions are very important tools in mathematical analysis and for this reason, the data processor who works with those engaged in operations research activities should be familiar with them.

The fourth basic equation type expresses *constraints,* or limits of behavior, that are inherent in the situation being studied either through company policy, law, or other force. For example, General Motors might describe their maximum share of the automobile market as follows:

$$S = .5M$$

S is their dollar share of the automobile market and M is the total automobile sales for a given time period. In this case, the company is expressing its policy to capture exactly one-half of the automobile market. More often than not, constraints are expressed as *inequalities* rather than as equations. An inequality is an expression that sets a limit on a mathematical process. In our factory example above, it may be that no matter how many employees we hire, production per machine can never exceed ten units of product per hour. We would express this constraint of maximum production as:

$$O \leq 10M$$

As before, O represents output and M represents the number of machines in the factory. The symbol $\leq$ means "less than or equal to." It is one of several similar symbols used in expressing inequalities. These symbols are listed below:

Less than	$<$
Greater than	$>$
Less than or equal to	$\leq$
Greater than or equal to	$\geq$

Our example above tells us that output in our factory must always be less than or equal to ten units of output per machine per time period. In another situation, a businessman may decide that his plant must produce at least 1500 units per month in order to justify going into business. Letting P represent production, this constraint would be expressed as:

$$P \geq 1500$$

This would be read "production is greater than or equal to 1500 units."

Mathematical models—the kind used by operations research people—make heavy use of symbols, using letters of the alphabet to represent unknown quantities and in other ways expressing relationships in ways that puzzle the mathematically unsophisticated. While this can be very troublesome to nontechnical business managers, the symbolism used in operations research models is what gives them their great value. By representing symbolically the relevant characteristics of the problem, one is able to manipulate the characteristics and perform experiments on paper, whereas the relationships being represented symbolically may not permit manipulations or experimentation of any kind in the real world. For this reason, we should not expect mathematicians and operations researchers to abandon their symbols. Rather we should expect that as businessmen and in particular as data processors we prepare ourselves to understand mathematical symbolism and to be able to cope with mathematical analysis of business phenomena.

Businessmen who have a basic understanding of the use of models in scientific decision-making, at least to the extent of recognizing that particular problems lend themselves to the specific techniques, enjoy certain advantages. First, defining the problem in terms that can be expressed as a mathematical model forces the businessman to think through the problem with a great deal more care than might be used otherwise. Objectives are defined more realistically; the ways in which the objectives can be accomplished are considered more thoroughly; and the maximum effort that can be expended to make the objectives worth realizing is defined more critically, either as a dollar cost or as some other measure of effort.

Second, there is more accurate identification of the important factors to be considered in working for the solution to the problem. In the past, one of the chief reasons for poor decision-making has been the neglect of an important consideration only to find that, once the decision has been made, it is inappropriate in view of the neglected circumstance. The process of model building calls upon the businessman to discover all of the important factors of the problem and eliminate all the factors that do not matter.

Third, the use of models gives the business decision-maker a rational way to deal with uncertainty. Much of the decision-maker's work is done in an atmosphere of not knowing all the facts necessary to make the best decision. In particular, events to happen in the future may be uncertain. What will be the demand for our product? How many unacceptable parts are we likely to make? How many of our policy-holders will have a claim? In spite of this uncertainty, the businessman must make the best decision possible. This can be done by taking the uncertain events into account and treating them with a measure of their likelihood. Rather than guessing or hoping about the future, businessmen, through the use of models, can prepare decisions in terms of the most likely events and in such a way that minimizes the chance of loss if things do not go as predicted. In short, models, by permitting the use of probability analysis, give the businessman a tool that he can use to predict the future with greater accuracy than the guesswork he might have used without them.

But the use of models in decision-making has certain disadvantages, too. The model itself, being an abstraction of the real-world problem, requires oversimplification. Thus, a solution to a problem that fits the model perfectly may not fit the real world because simplification made the model too unrealistic. Even worse, a decision-maker, having once constructed a mathematical model, has an understandable reluctance to discard it even though it fails to predict the real-world situation as it should. It may even happen that the model builder begins to confuse the real world with the model he has constructed to help analyze it. For example, the simple model discussed above which dealt with consumption spending in an economic system may become, in the minds of beginning economics students, so synonymous with the real world that their judgments about consumer spending in the real world are based on that simple model. In fact, however, most of us would recognize that the amount that consumers spend for consumption purposes depends upon many things besides the level of national income and the minimum level of living. Cash balances in the bank, expectations of future income, and pressures from peer groups are just three of an uncountable number of reasons why consumers spend that are not necessarily included in this model.

The advantages of the use of models outweigh, in general, the disadvantages because when properly constructed and properly interpreted, models provide decision-makers with the means to predict real-world behavior without the necessity, usually prohibitive because of cost, of experimenting with the real world itself. The final test of a model, of course, is whether or not it really does represent the phenomena the model builder intended it to. If a model can be constructed that can accurately predict consumer demand, for example, then this is a useful model. A model that consistently causes the businessman to produce quantities in response to demands as predicted by the model, that never materialize, is a model that needs to be replaced. With care and systematic development and testing, models are the backbone of operations research. They are the means by which scientific decision-making is performed.

Questions

1. What is the difference between quantitative and intuitive approaches to problem-solving?
2. Develop a short, precise definition of *scientific method.* Do not consult a dictionary until after you have made your own definition.
3. Give examples, not used in the text, of each of the types of equations used in mathematical models.
4. Describe a function in your own terms. Give some examples of commonplace functional relationships.
5. Give examples not mentioned in the text of each of the three types of models used in operations research.

Scientific Decision-Making Techniques

In this chapter we examine in detail some specific techniques of scientific decision-making, or operations research. All of these techniques, of course, make use of models as described in the previous chapter.

Sampling

Probably the simplest kind of model used in business decision-making is the sample. Consider a manufacturer of firecrackers. Naturally, he is interested in the number of his firecrackers that will explode when properly lit. If none of them do so, people will stop buying his product. On the other hand, if all or almost all of the firecrackers explode, most customers will be satisfied enough to return for more. One way for the firecracker manufacturer to determine how many of a number of firecrackers will explode is to light them all; after this he knows exactly how many exploded. But we would not expect any businessman in his right mind to use this kind of quality control. What the manufacturer can do, however, is to pick a sample of the firecrackers and test them. Let's say he decides to take a sample of 100 firecrackers out of every 1,000 firecrackers produced. If, when lighting the 100 firecrackers in the sample he observes that all but six of them exploded, he might conclude that 94 per cent of the firecrackers he produces will do so. There are two comments which deserve to be made at this point. First, the manager must then decide what percentage of his firecrackers must explode in order to satisfy his customers. It may be that his customers will be satisfied if only three-quarters of the firecrackers explode, in which case the manufacturer can relax his production standards somewhat and perhaps reduce operating expenses accordingly. On the other hand, it may be that unless 99 per cent of the firecrackers explode his customers will become unhappy. In this case, he must maintain very high quality control standards in order to satisfy his customers.

The second comment concerns the reliability of the model. In this situation, the model is the sample and it is used to predict the real world, that is, the number of firecrackers out of each thousand which will explode when lit. The reliability of this model, that is, the accuracy with which it predicts the future, depends upon its size among other things. Clearly, a 100 per cent sample, that is, lighting every firecracker, is the most reliable method possible. Lighting none is the least reliable. Lighting 500 firecrackers is more likely to give an accurate prediction of the number out of 1,000 that will explode than lighting only one. The manufacturer must decide how accurate he wants his model to be. More specifically, he must decide upon the degree of accuracy that he will accept from his model as a predicter of the real world. He can design a model (100 per cent sample) that will produce an accurate prediction every time. Smaller samples will yield a higher probability of making an inaccurate prediction. Deciding upon the size of the sample that will provide the realiability desired is a problem of analyzing, among other things, the cost of sampling and the cost of inaccurate predictions. Solving this problem calls upon statistical theory which is beyond the scope of this book. Suffice it to say here that data processors may be called upon from time to time to deal with the calculations involving sampling and should be familiar with the basic ideas.

A sample, to be of use in predicting the real world, must be representative; that is, it must be so constructed so as to not have inherent inaccuracies. We would expect the firecracker manufacturer to pick his sample from all of the machines he has making firecrackers lest a faulty machine or one that is operating with exceptional efficiency produce a distorted prediction if only the firecrackers from that machine were sampled. There are several methods of picking a sample. One that is quite often discussed is the *random* sample. Many people believe that *random* means haphazard. This is not true. In sampling theory, the term *random* is used to indicate lack of bias and without plan. Care is taken in picking the sample, however, to insure that it is representative. Another frequently used sampling technique is known as systematic sampling, in which a sample is taken at regular intervals during a production run or is otherwise systematically selected from the entire population of items to be tested. Taking every tenth firecracker from every machine would constitute taking a 10 per cent sample in a systematic manner.

There are several other kinds of sampling methods which, while important, need not concern us here. Whatever the method used, sampling is a technique for dealing with uncertainty—for estimating how many customers will use a product without asking each of them, for checking the accuracy of manufactured products without inspecting each of them, and for other decision-making situations in which the real world must be predicted from a model.

Factor Analysis

Most business decisions involve the interaction of many different factors. Problems involving business operations can be analyzed in terms of these factors. A businessman might be interested in why production costs are rising and how to stop any further increases and even, perhaps, reduce them to former levels. An analysis can be made to determine the influence of the different factors that affect total production costs. Can costs be reduced, for example, by introducing a second production shift at wage rates slightly above the day shift rates and by eliminating overtime wages of one and one-half times the regular rates? This can be determined by calculating total costs of production when a second shift is used and comparing these costs with those incurred by overtime. The important observation to be made here is that all costs other than those being studied must be held constant. That is, all factors of the problem other than those factors—overtime wages versus second shift wages—must be held constant in order to determine the effect on production costs of the factors being studied. This is the basic nature of factor analysis. In real business situations, however, the problems are much more complex than this simple example and all the important factors cannot usually be isolated. As the term is used today by operations researchers, *factor analysis*, or *factor design and analysis*, refers to mathematical techniques for studying the complex interactions of many factors in a way that will indicate, with a minimum of experimentation, the most significant factors and the degree of their significance.

Factor analysis appears to have important applications in marketing and consumer research. A businessman, for example, who is interested in determining which has the greater effect upon sales—advertising in newspapers, over television, or on the radio—can perform factor analysis. Although he will not be able to determine with complete accuracy which is the most important and to what degree, he is better off than if he had just guessed. Most importantly, as with the case of sampling models, he is able to measure the likelihood that his model—in this case the mathematical construction of the factor analysis problem—will produce an inaccurate prediction of the real world and can then design the model to fit his requirements in terms of probable accuracy.

Replacement and Maintenance Models

An operator of a fleet of taxicabs faces a problem relating to the replacement of tires on his cabs. One way to solve this problem is to wait for a tire to wear out and then to replace that one tire. This solution has the advantage of getting the maximum use from each tire but suffers the disadvantage of high incidence of taxis being in a nonproductive situation while tires are being changed and further requires a crew to be on hand—whether working or not—at all times to change tires when needed. Another solution, at the other extreme, would involve changing every tire in every cab every month whether the tires are worn out or not. This has the advantages of never having a taxi "down" because of tire failure and of eliminating the need to have a tire crew always on hand, but it is very expensive in terms of tire costs. A replacement model is a mathematical technique to determine, in this example, how often to change tires so as to minimize the costs of buying tires, at the same time minimizing the costs of down-time because of tire failure. The same type of model can be used to determine how often to perform maintenance on operating machinery so to minimize both maintenance costs and down-time costs.

Another problem for which this kind of model can prove useful comes about when things being used do not wear out gradually but stop operating completely. The classic example of this is the light bulb. Imagine a business office with several thousand neon tubes installed in the ceiling to provide light for the workers. Replacing each tube after it burns out is a very expensive procedure requiring a permanent crew and many trips into the office for replacement purposes and requiring many "set-ups," when the crew must assemble its tools, set up ladders, and perform all the other tasks involved in changing a tube. These set-up expenses can be minimized by changing all tubes in a particular location at the same time, whether they are burned out or not. This costs a little more in terms of tube costs but the savings in terms of reduced set-up costs more than justifies it. The purpose of replacement models is to determine the optimum frequency for performing such replacements so as to minimize the total cost of replacements.

Linear Programming

Linear programming is one of a group of somewhat similar problem-solving techniques that are referred to as *mathematical programming*. Alone of the various operations research tools discussed in this chapter it is a recent development. The other tools used in operations research work have been around for some time and have been used by mathematicians and physical scientists before the techniques were introduced into business problems. Linear programming was developed during the 1950's and represents an important new way to solve quite a large number of business operational problems. Because of its wide applicability and because detailed examples of its basic concepts present excellent illustrations of how models are constructed and used in operations research, a more detailed treatment will be presented of linear programming than of other operations research techniques.

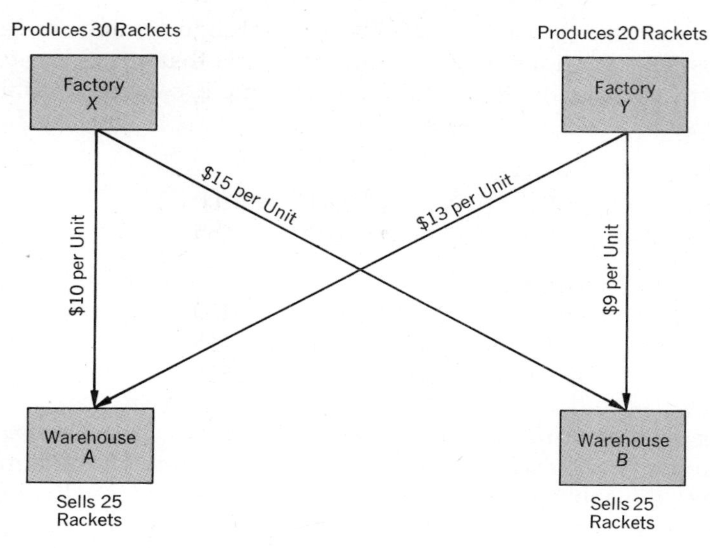

Figure 3–1. Transportation problem.

There are two basic kinds of problems that linear programming is capable of solving. Probably the classic problem is the so-called transportation problem. Imagine a manufacturer of tennis rackets who operates two production plants that are geographically separated and supply two warehouses that are also geographically separated. The two factories, Factory X and Factory Y, produce 30 rackets and 20 rackets per week respectively. The warehouses, A and B, each sell 25 rackets per week. It is possible for Factory X to supply both Warehouse A and Warehouse B with rackets. Similarly, Factory Y can supply both warehouses with rackets. The delivered total cost per racket, however, varies, depending upon which factory delivers to which warehouse. The total delivered cost for one racket from Factory X to Warehouse A is $10, from Factory X to Warehouse B is $15, from Factory Y to Warehouse A is $13, and from Factory Y to Warehouse B is $9. These relationships are shown in Figure 3–1.

The problem is to minimize the total delivered cost of tennis rackets to the warehouses for the entire business. Each warehouse must have exactly 25 rackets each week in order to meet orders from the retail stores it supplies. The optimum solution to this problem can be obtained by inspection, as follows:

Warehouse A receives:	
25 rackets from Factory X at $10 each	$250
Warehouse B receives:	
20 rackets from Factory Y at $9 each	$180
5 rackets from Factory X at $15 each	75
Total delivered cost	$505

The term *optimum* is used to describe this solution because none of the other possible solutions will result in total costs that are as low or lower than the total shown by this solution. For example, consider the following possible solution:

Warehouse A receives:	
20 rackets from Factory X at $10 each	$200
5 rackets from Factory Y at $13 each	65
Warehouse B receives:	
10 rackets from Factory X at $15 each	$150
15 rackets from Factory Y at $9 each	135
Total delivered cost	$550

It can be seen from these example solutions to this simple problem that there are many *possible* solutions. The purpose of linear programming is to discover the *optimum* solution without the necessity of evaluating every possible solution. In problems more complex than this one, the optimum solution cannot be found by simple inspection. If, for example, the tennis racket manufacturer had three factories and three warehouses each selling 25 rackets per week, the number of possible solutions would number in the tens of millions! Linear programming is a method that will solve this particular problem with less than ten mathematical operations.

The other basic type of problem to be solved using linear programming techniques occurs when a job must be done using limited resources. Resources can be limited in the sense that a machine has limited production capacity or there is a time limit placed on the degree to which some machines may be used to accomplish the job. Another limitation on resources lies in the need to employ several resources at once in order to perform the task when such simultaneous employment precludes the possibility of employing all of the resources in the optimum manner. Let's look at an example.

A manufacturer of small office tools has equipment available for short periods of time every week that can be used to produce ball-point pens and automatic pencils. These two products are produced only when the equipment needed to produce them is not being employed in other capacities since these products are not offered in the regular line of goods this company manufactures. Producing ball-point pens and automatic pencils is a fairly simple operation consisting of four basic steps. First, the body of the writing instrument is molded out of colored plastic kept in stock for this purpose. Then the bodies are sent to a printing machine that prints advertising messages, names, and other information on the bodies. The bodies then go to a machine which inserts the mechanism, either the ball and ink supply or the pencil lead mechanism, into the body. Following this, the instruments are sealed in small plastic packages suitable for hanging on display racks on counters of stationery stores, drug

Process	Production Capacity in Minutes Per 100 Units		Total Time Available Per Week in Minutes
	Ball Pt. Pens	Auto. Pencils	
Mold	10	7	120
Print	6	2	60
Assemble	2	1	30
Package	2	2	30

Figure 3–2. Production information for pen and pencil manufacture.

stores, and other retail outlets. The instruments are sold by the manufacturer in lots of 100 and each lot is sold at a gross margin of $3.40 for the pencils and $4.00 for the ball-point pens above direct manufacturing costs. That is to say, the pencils and the ball-point pens contribute $3.40 and $4.00 respectively to overhead and profits for each lot of one hundred.

The machinery used to produce the writing instruments has certain limitations with respect to production capacity per minute and to the total number of minutes each week that each machine is available for this work. Figure 3–2 shows the number of minutes required by each of the four processes to produce 100 of either ball-point pens or automatic pencils. It also shows the total amount of time each process can be used for the production of pens and pencils. The molding machine, for example, requires 10 minutes to produce 100 ball-point pens and 7 minutes to produce 100 automatic pencils and is available for this kind of work 120 minutes per week. Similarly, the packaging machine requires 2 minutes to package 100 pens, 2 minutes to package 100 pencils and is available 30 minutes per week. Viewed in terms of production capacity, the molding machine can produce each week 1,200 ball-point pens, or about 1,715 automatic pencils, or some mixture of the two products. Similarly, the assembly machine can product 1,500 ball-point pens per week, or 3,000 automatic pencils, or some mixture of both.

The problem faced by the manager of this operation is how many ball-point pens and how many automatic pencils should be produced in order to maximize the total contribution received from these products? Using the technique of linear programming to solve this problem involves expressing the relationships and the limitations of the situations in mathematical terms, that is, as building a mathematical model of the problem. To begin with, let's look at the profit contribution picture. It is desirable to sell some number of pens for a contribution of $4.00 per hundred plus some number of pencils for a contribution of $3.40 per hundred in such a way that no matter how many are produced of each of these items, the total contribution is maximized. An operations researcher would say that we are trying to maximize the following expression:

$$C = \$3.40P + \$4.00B$$

C represents total contribution; P represents the *number* of pencils (in units of 100) produced; and B represents the *number* of ball-point pens (in units of 100) produced. This equation has this to say: "Total contribution is equal to the sum of \$3.40 times the number of lots of 100 pencils that are sold plus \$4.00 times the number of lots of 100 ball-point pens that are sold." Clearly, it is a lot easier to write the simple equation above than it is to spell out the sentence that says the same thing.

The other relationships in this problem can be expressed using the same kind of mathematical shorthand. We know, for instance, that the maximum number of minutes per week that the molding machine can be used for manufacture of either ball-point pens or automatic pencils is 120. Letting B represent the number of ball-point pens produced and P the number of automatic pencils, we can express the constraints of the molding operation as follows:

$$10B + 7P \leq 120$$

In this expression, $10B$ represents the product of 10 minutes for each lot of 100 ball-point pens times the number of lots of ball-point pens manufactured. In this way, "$10B$" indicates the amount of time used by the molding operation to produce a given number of lots of ball-point pens, B. Similarly, $7P$ indicates the total amount of time needed by the molding machine to produce a given number of automatic pencils, P. The sum of these time factors must be less than or equal to the 120 minutes per week that the molding machine is available for this kind of production.

Writing all the limitations of the problem in mathematical terms, one would arrive at the following set of expressions:

$$\begin{aligned} C &= \$3.40P + \$4.00B && \text{(Contribution)} \\ 10B + 7P &\leq 120 && \text{(Molding)} \\ 4B + 6P &\leq 60 && \text{(Printing)} \\ 2B + 1P &\leq 30 && \text{(Assembly)} \\ 2B + 2P &\leq 30 && \text{(Packaging)} \end{aligned}$$

This set of expressions is a mathematical model of the production environment in which the pens and pencils are to be made. Linear programming is a mathematical technique for manipulating the expressions in such a way that values are found for P and B—the number of lots of pencils and ball-point pens to produce—that will maximize C, the total gross margin or contribution earned by the sale of the instruments. While it exceeds the purpose of this text to discuss the mathematical solution to this problem, it is simple enough to be solved using a graphical approach, that is, by replacing the mathematical model we have just constructed with an analog model, letting lines and areas be analogous to relationships in the real world we are studying.

Examine Figure 3–3*a*. This graph is constructed so that the horizontal axis represents the number of pencils that can be produced and the vertical axis the number of ball-point pens that can be produced. The dotted line labeled Assembly was drawn as follows. Look at the mathematical expression setting forth the constraints of the assembly process:

$$2B + 1P \leq 30$$

It tells us that the total amount of time available for assembly purposes is 30 minutes per week. Now, if we produce no ball-point pens at all, then all of the 30 minutes is available for automatic pencil production. In this 30 minutes per week, 30 lots of automatic pencils can be assembled, since it takes one minute to assemble one lot. The fact that the assembly process

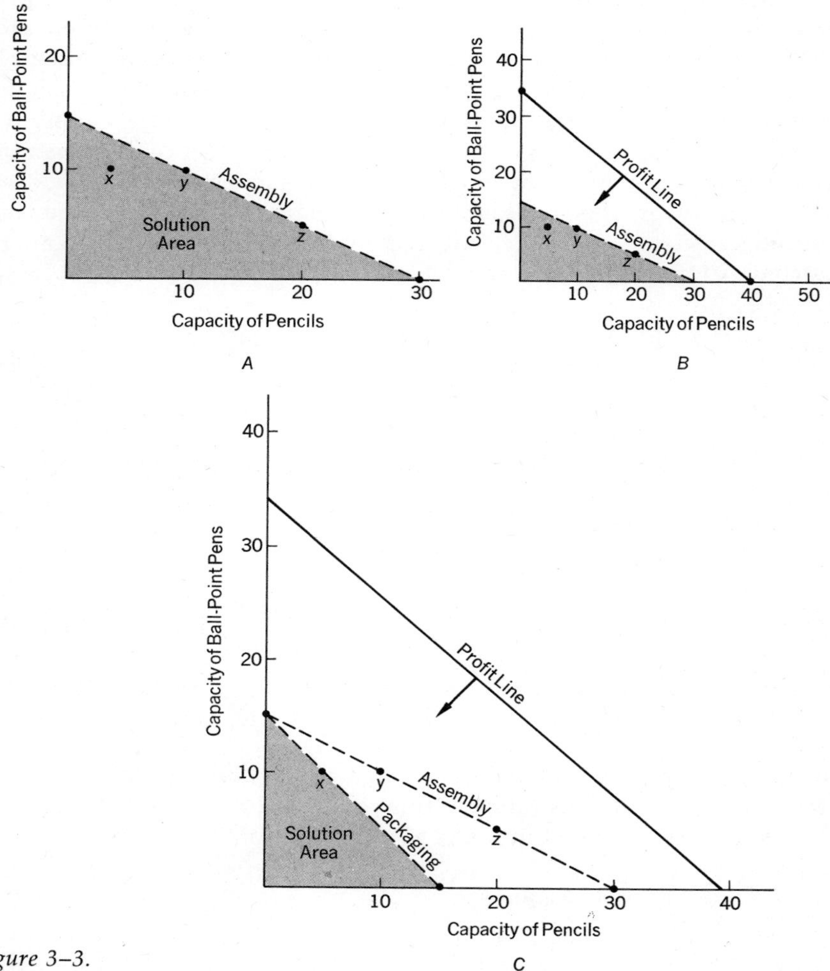

Figure 3–3.

can produce 30 lots of pencils is indicated by placing a dot at 30 on the horizontal axis of the graph in Figure 3–3*a*. On the other hand, if the assembly machine were used to assemble only ball-point pens during the 30 minutes available, then 15 lots of ball-point pens could be assembled since it takes 2 minutes to assemble each lot of pens. To represent this on the graph, a dot is placed at 15 on the vertical axis of the graph. The next step involves drawing a dotted line between these two points on the axes. This line represents the maximum output of the assembly process in terms of assembling all pencils (the point on the pencil axis), all pens (the point on the pen axis), or some combination of both pens and pencils.

The area between the Assembly line and the axes of the graph represents the possible production combinations or solutions. That is, any point in this area represents some combination of production of both pens and pencils that is possible in terms of what the assembly machine can produce in 30 minutes. Point *X*, for example, represents a combined production of 10 lots of ball-point pens, requiring 20 minutes of assembly time and 5 lots of automatic pencils requiring assembly time of 5 minutes. The total time required by the assembly process to assemble a combination of 10 lots of pens and 5 of pencils is 25 minutes. Since the assembly machine is available 30 minutes per week, this is a perfectly feasible combination. However, there might be a more *profitable* solution. The contribution associated with the solution represented by point *X* can be calculated as follows:

10 ball-point pens at $4.00	$40.00
5 automatic pencils at $3.40	17.00
Total contribution	$57.00

This figure can be calculated using the contribution formula developed in our model:

$$C = \$3.40P + \$4.00B$$

Substituting the number of lots of pens and pencils to produce, we arrive at:

$$C = \$3.40(5) + \$4.00(10) = \$57.00$$

Point *Y* represents a possible solution that yields more contribution and for this reason is more desirable. In this solution, 10 lots each of pens and pencils are assembled, yielding a profit equation of:

$$C = \$3.40(10) + \$4.00(10) = \$74.00$$

This solution utilizes the assembly machine for the full 30 minutes it is available, since 10 lots of pencils require 10 minutes and 10 lots of pens require 20. This explains why, in terms of the assembly machine, more contribution is earned by this solution. In general, it can be observed that any solution, or combination of products, that falls on the line is more profitable than one that does not because the line represents the maximum utilization of the machine.

Examine point Z. Point Z describes a solution in which 5 lots of pens are assembled requiring 10 minutes and 20 lots of pencils are assembled requiring 20 minutes. Again, all 30 minutes of assembly machine availability are utilized. The profit equation for this solution is as follows:

$$C = \$3.40(20) + \$4.00(5) = \$88.00$$

The most profitable solution of all those possible lies at the right-hand end of the Assembly line where all 30 minutes of available time are used to produce 30 lots of pencils:

$$C = \$3.40(30) + \$4.00(0) = \$108.00$$

This best solution with respect to the assembly machine can be solved without the necessity of working out the profit equation for each of the 30 possible solutions along the line. This can be done graphically as shown in Figure 3–3*b*. Figure 3–3*b* is the same as Figure 3–3*a*, except that the contribution equation was also drawn on the graph as a Profit line. The Profit line was drawn as follows: A level of production of 40 lots of automatic pencils was arbitrarily chosen and the amount of profits or contribution that would be earned if only 40 lots of pencils were calculated by multiplying 40 times $3.40 per lot to arrive at $136.00. A dot was put at the 40 mark on the Capacity of Pencils axis. (Since this level of production of pencils falls outside the area of possible solutions, it can never be attained —it would require 40 minutes of assembly time—but this does not matter for our purpose of drawing the Profit line.) Now, the $136.00 that could be earned if 40 lots of pencils were produced can be divided by $4.00 to determine how many lots of ball-point pens would have to be produced to yield the same profit:

$$\$136/\$4.00 = 34$$

Thus, to earn the same profits of $136.00 that would be earned if only pencils were produced, 34 lots of pens must be produced. A dot is placed on the Capacity of Ball-Point Pens axis representing 34 and a solid line, is drawn between the two dots. Any point on this line represents a combination of pens and pencils that will yield a profit of exactly $136.00. The best of the solutions can be found graphically by moving the Profit line directly toward the intersection of the axes of the graph, that is, in the direction of the arrow, until it touches a point on the Assembly line. The Profit line touches the point that indicates the solution of producing 30 lots of pencils and no ball-point pens. If the Profit line had a different slope, that is, if the relative profitability of pens and pencils were other than $3.40 to $4.00, the Profit line might intersect the other end of the Assembly line first, indicating that solution is best. Should the Profit line be parallel to the Assembly line, it would make no difference what the combination of products was; the profits would always be the same.

So far we have examined a graphical approach to find the best combination of pens and pencils to produce with respect to the limitations imposed upon us by the assembly machine. The other machines also impose limitations upon us, and these should be included in our analysis and by treating them in the same manner as the Assembly line. Figure 3–3*c* is exactly like Figure 3–3*b*, except that the line representing the limitations of the packaging machine have been included. It was drawn in exactly the same way as the Assembly line. If no ball-point pens were to be produced, the 30 minutes would be available to package pencils and, at 2 minutes per lot, 15 lots of pencils would be packaged. This quantity of packaging is indicated by a dot placed at 15 on the Capacity of Pencils axis. Similarly, if no pencils are packaged, then it would be possible to package 15 lots of pens and a dot is placed at the 15 point on the Capacity of Ball-Point Pens axis. A dotted line is drawn connecting these two dots and the area of possible solutions with respect to the packaging machine is shaded in. The limitations imposed upon us by the packaging machine are considerably more strict than those of the assembly machine. Points Y and Z representing possible solutions as far as the assembly machine is concerned are now unfeasible since the packaging machine cannot package the instruments fast enough to keep up. The most profitable solution as far as the assembly machine goes, that is, producing 30 lots of automatic pencils only, is also out of the picture since it is pointless to assemble these if they cannot be packaged. The range of possible solutions now is in the shaded area defined by the Packaging line. Moving the Profit line down again, we see that it now intersects the area of possible solutions at a point which indicates that 15 pens should be produced (requiring all of the 30 minutes available for packaging) and no pencils. The profits at this point are:

$$C = \$3.40(0) + \$4.00(15) = \$60.00$$

Point X is still a possible solution and although it now lies on the line, is still less than optimal in terms of the new conditions imposed by the packaging machine:

$$C = \$3.40(5) + \$4.00(10) = \$57.00$$

The limitations of the other two machines, the molding machine and the printing machine can be added to the graph shown in Figure 3–3*c* and the result will be Figure 3–4. In this figure, the Profit line has been redrawn so that it fits within the expanded size of the graph. The limitations of the molding and printing operations are indicated by the lines identified as Molding and Printing. It can be seen that these machines further restrict the size of the area (that is, the number) of possible solutions. The outer boundary of the area of solutions, drawn in a heavy line, is approached by the Profit line as before. The Profit line intersects the solution area first at a point indicating production of about 9.75 lots of automatic pencils and about 5.25 lots of ball-point pens. Since the production of these instruments must be in even lots of 100, the best combination of products includes 9 lots of automatic pencils and 5 lots of ball-point pens for a total contribution of:

$$C = \$3.40(9) + \$4.00(5) = \$50.60$$

There is no other combination of products which will yield a greater contribution than this one.

Linear programming using the analog model we have been using is fairly easily understood. However, the number of real-life situations in which this graphical method of solving the problem arises is severely limited. What if, for instance, the manufacturer above had three products to manufacture instead of just two? Here, a three-dimensional graph would be called for. Such an analog model can be built and possibly

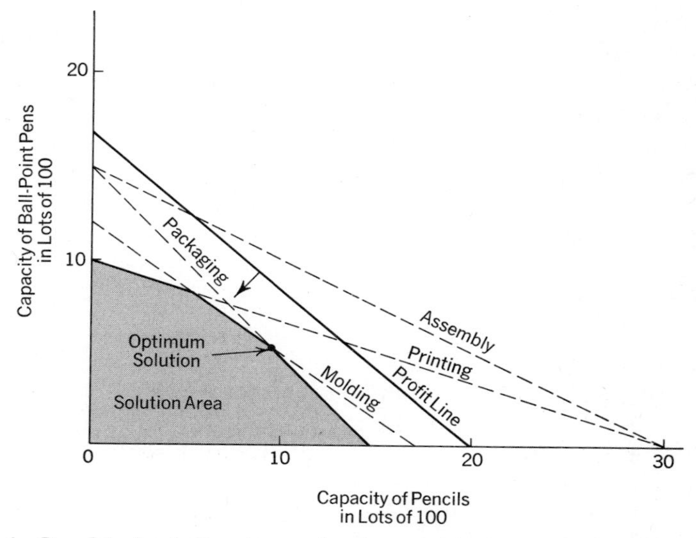

Figure 3–4. Graphical solution to production problem using linear programming.

drawn, but it is difficult to use. Planes are used instead of lines and the optimal solution can be found when the profit *plane* intersects the first peak in the *volume* of possible combinations. If there were 20 products to produce, it would require a 20-dimensional graph, which is clearly out of the question. Mathematical models, however, can be used to analyze these many-dimensional figures. Where analog models break down because of physical limitations, mathematical techniques for solving linear programming problems are the most widely used. Fairly complex problems involving several dimensions require considerable calculations to arrive at the optimum solution. Fortunately, most manufacturers of electronic computing equipment offer as a service to those who use their equipment programs written to solve certain kinds of problems in a general manner. Linear programming is one such problem. The data processor need only determine the various limitations and other conditions of the problem and submit these, together with the program to the computer system and the solution is found in a relatively short time. Because of the wide applicability of linear programming to many kinds of important business problems, data processors can expect to be called upon to process such problems more and more frequently as businesses begin to make more use of operations research techniques in decision-making.

Dynamic Programming

Dynamic programming and linear programming are close relatives in the same family of operations techniques known as *mathematical programming*. Linear programming, as we have seen, is a technique for finding the optimum solution to a given set of relationships. It is a method for helping the businessman make *one* decision. In the example above this decision was how many lots of each of ball-point pens and automatic pencils to make each week. Dynamic programming is a method to help the businessman make several interrelated decisions that must be made sequentially.

Frequently, situations arise in business operations in which the present decision depends on a past one. For example, a purchasing agent may decide to buy a certain raw material for the first time to meet the needs of a new production process in his plant. He develops a model that takes into account the expected usage rate of the material and its storage and ordering costs, and he uses the model to determine how much to order. When he orders the second time he must make another decision as to how much to order. Clearly, how much he will order the second time depends upon how much he ordered the first time and upon the accuracy of his estimates about material usage. His second decision is made in the light of what he decided in the past. Dynamic programming is a technique of operations research that allows for optimum decisions to be made regarding the time period to come regardless of any poor or, more euphemistically, "suboptimal" decisions that were made in the past. As in the case of linear programming, dynamic programming is a mathematical technique of solving operating problems that will find many more applications in the future.

Queuing Theory

A queue is a waiting line. Queuing theory is a method of studying the behavior of waiting lines in order to predict the length of the line and the various costs associated with its length and with trying to shorten it. Consider a businessman who has located his store in a large shopping center. Through experience he knows that one out of 36 passers-by will come in. However, he does not know how many are going to come in at one time, so he is unable to determine how many salesclerks should be available in the shop to serve customers. If there are not enough clerks, customers will form waiting lines—queues—and such waiting lines are costly in terms of dissatisfied customers and unsold merchandise. Queuing theory is a technique that lets the businessman solve his problem of minimizing total cost of selling by finding the number of salesclerks to hire that will minimize the cost salaries and at the same time minimize the costs of the waiting lines.

Frequently, queuing theory makes use of a simulation technique known as the *Monte Carlo technique*. Our businessman does not know how many customers at a time are likely to come in at once. He is able to simulate behavior of passers-by by developing a device (a pair of dice would do in this case) that would help him study the behavior of something else that occurs once out of 36 times on the average but is nevertheless irregular. By throwing a pair of dice and observing how many times two occurs and how often two occurs sequentially, he is able to simulate the behavior of passers-by who behave, as he has observed, in much the same way. This simulation coupled with the mathematical techniques of queuing theory will lead to the optimum number of salesclerks to have in the store.

Queuing theory has found several applications, ranging from treating the number of telephone calls a switchboard might receive at once—in which application, incidentally, the technique was developed; the number of ships to arrive at once at a docking facility; the number of supermarket checkout stands to install; and the optimum number of aircraft loading and unloading facilities to install at airports.

Decision Theory

Most businessmen face the unpleasant job of having to make a decision about something knowing that certain events may occur to make him regret the decision. He is uncertain as to whether or not these unfortunate events will happen. For example, an airline, wishing to schedule enough flights between two locations over a weekend knows that if it schedules too few, it will lose possible revenue and may incur the wrath of prospective customers. On the other hand, scheduling too many flights may result in unsold seats and high operating expenses per paying passenger. The decision must be made as to how many flights to schedule, and it must be made in the face of uncertainty as to how many passengers there will be. Decision theory is a method of applying certain techniques of statistical analysis to problems involving uncertainty in such a way as to minimize the degree to which the businessman is likely to regret the decision he made. It involves assigning measures of probability to the events the occurrences of which are uncertain. The various possible payoffs or losses that would occur for each of the possible events is calculated and statistical manipulations are performed that point the way to the most desirable decision. Decision theory does not provide a way to predict whether or not some event will happen, but it does provide a way to make an optimal decision when taking into consideration the likelihood of the events coming about.

Game Theory

Game theory is a close relative of decision theory in that their objectives are the same: to provide an optimal decision in the face of events the occurrence of which is uncertain. However, game theory takes into account one additional factor not found in decision theory: an opponent whose decisions, if correctly made, may be damaging to us and who will be adversely affected when we make good decisions. The simplest example of this sort of situation is a gin rummy game in which one player makes a good set of decisions at the expense of the other player since one player can win only what the other loses. This operates much like decision theory except that the behavior of one's competitors must also be taken into account. Knowing that you are evaluating his possible actions, a competitor may modify his behavior from what it would have been had he not known. As a consequence, situations in which game theory is appropriate are very dynamic in nature. Game theory handles rather well situations in which there are only two or three opponents, but in most business situations in which the competitors are somewhat numerous, its applications are severely limited. For this reason few, if any, applications have been made of game theory to practical problems.

PERT

PERT is a method of planning and control. The initials PERT stand for Program Evaluation and Review Technique. The technique was developed through the combined efforts of the U.S. Navy Special Projects Office, Lockheed Aircraft Corporation, and the management consulting firm of Booz-Allen and Hamilton for the purpose of controlling the interrelated activities involved in developing the Polaris guided missile. It is said to have saved years in the amount of time needed to complete the Polaris project.

The type of problem that PERT is used to help solve arises when the project involves many smaller tasks to be done within a time schedule that allows for the most effective sequence of events in completing the project. The basic question that a manager of such a project faces is this: "When shall I start task A in order that it be completed before task B must begin since the completion of task A is necessary for the commencement of task B. Moreover, task B must be completed before work can start on tasks C and D, which should be completed at the same time since both of them are necessary to begin task E. If there are many such tasks, the problem of expressing their interrelationships with respect to times needed for completion becomes very difficult.

PERT expresses the interrelationships of the activities within a project with the use of a device known as a *network.* A network is a pictorial representation of all the activities and events, with their estimated time needed to complete the project. Let us consider a few basic things that must be done to construct a house. The foundation must be laid, the plumbing and electrical circuitry installed, the framework assembled, the roof installed and covered, the walls plastered and painted, the floors finished, and the exterior painted. Clearly, some of these things must be completed before work can start on others. Figure 3–5 shows a PERT network expressing these basic activities. The ovals in PERT networks are usually called *events.* They are identified in this example by the type of activity they represent. The letter *S* in the leftmost oval indicates that that particular event is the start of the house-building project. The *C*'s in the other ovals tells us that these events are the completion of the activities being described. The numbers above the ovals are used for identification purposes as in discussing paths through the network, such as path 10-20-30-60-80-100-120. The lines or arrows in PERT networks represent the activities themselves as opposed to the events of their start or completion. Thus, once the event Completion of Framework takes place, the activities of installing plumbing, electrical wiring, and building the roof can begin. The numbers beside each activity or line represent the time it takes to complete that activity. In this example, the time is expressed in weeks. Once the project is started, it takes a week to complete the foundation. Two weeks later the frame is completed and work can commence on the roof and the electrical plumbing installation. Both of these latter jobs, which take two weeks each, must be completed before the interior is plastered, and so on until the completion of the entire house.

Even this simple example gives some insight into how such a picture

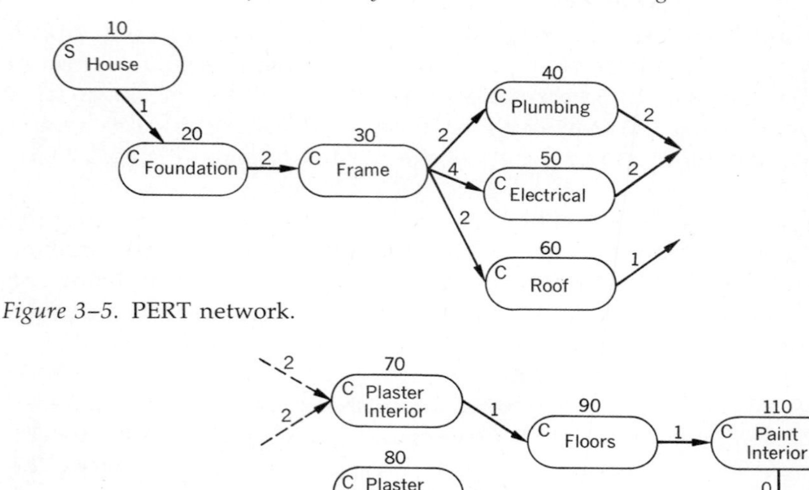

Figure 3–5. PERT network.

can be useful to the person who is in charge of completing the house in the most efficient manner. He knows, for example, that it is pointless to hire the electricians and plumber when the project is started since they will have to wait three weeks for the completion of the frame until they can start work. The manager also can see that the installation of the electrical system is a bottleneck requiring twice as much time for completion as the other activities that must be completed before work on the interior plastering can begin. In real-life applications, of course, the analysis is much more involved. Projects that have hundreds and perhaps thousands of interrelated activities require more than the casual analysis we have performed here in order to perfect the way in which activities must be started and coordinated to insure maximum efficiency. These techniques are quantitative in nature and fairly heavily draw upon statistical analysis in arriving at optimum solutions.

A close relative of PERT that deserves mention here is the Critical Path Method, or CPM as it is sometimes called. This is a mathematical technique for comparing the normal times and costs required to complete the project with those times and costs that would obtain if a crash program were inaugurated. In general, the *critical path* refers to the path through the network which defines the shortest possible time in which the entire project can be completed. In the house-building project above, this critical path is the 10-20-30-50-70-90-110-120 path. Another basic type of path through the network is the *slack path*, which is a sequence of events that requires less time than the critical path, that is, in which there is time left over in terms of the minimum time needed for the project.

Simulation

The operations research techniques discussed above all attempted to express certain relationships and factors in a given business problem to arrive at a solution for that particular operational problem. These larger models try to simulate an entire business system, rather than to treat one specific problem. For this reason, simulation is a much more elaborate model-making technique of analysis than other operations research methods. An oil refinery, for example, has many different types of inputs —crude oils, chemicals, heat, and processing times—and many different kinds and grades of outputs, including aviation gasoline, automobile gasolines, kerosene, and petrochemical products. The management of such a refinery well might wonder what the possible outputs of such an operation could be, given a set of inputs. By mathematical simulation of the entire refining process, management can predict with fair accuracy what inputs are needed in order to produce a desired set of outputs without the necessity of experimenting with the refinery itself.

Such techniques are generally called *systems simulation* and can be applied to a wide variety of business systems. The technique depends upon the operation researcher's ability to express the various relationships of the system in quantitative terms and then to construct the model in such a way that these expressions duplicate as accurately as possible the real-world system being simulated. This model is then subjected to the same kinds of events that might occur in normal and not-so-normal operating conditions and its performance "under fire" is observed and these observations are used to form predictions about the way the real-life system will perform under the same conditions. If the model behaves unrealistically to the extent that it is not a good predictor, then, as with the other types of models used in operations research, it is either modified or discarded.

Interesting applications of simulation techniques have been made in the aerospace industry and in the military, which has developed several so-called war games in which the tactical and strategic factors of real battle situations are simulated. Such games have proved to be valuable training aids to the armed forces, much the same as the famous Link trainers have become in simulating in-flight situations that pilots must face. Business management games have been developed for the same purpose. Such games simulate business environments and relationships in ways that are designed to train business managers in effective thinking about business problems and competitive techniques. Today there are dozens of such business games covering a range of business activities such as marketing, finance, production control, and general operating management. Many of these are now being used in business management curricula in colleges and universities.

Role of the Data Processor

The development of operations research techniques is the result of heavy demands upon businessmen to make consistently good business decisions. It would seem that if all businessmen tried to analyze all or even most of their operational problems with the use of these tools, there would be little need for active decision-making as most of us know it today, that is, as made by a businessman faced with controversial alternatives of action. Operations research, however, is not a panacea for business problems. It is helpful in picking the best alternative among several to solve a particular problem. It is not, however, a substitute for business judgment. Decisions still have to be made by men. Although operations research may be helpful to the men who are making the decisions, the results of the quantitative analysis afforded by operations research must still be tempered by the judgment of the one responsible for the decision. Judgments must be made as to the validity of the model being used, of the quality of the data being analyzed, of what problems are to be treated using these techniques. However grand the techniques of business analysis may become, there will always be a need for men to make the final decision and to stand ready to accept the responsibility for its quality. The basic activities of management—organization, planning, integrating, and measuring—must still be done under the supervision of the manager. Operations research may help him do a better job and probably will, but it will not do the entire job for him.

For the data processor, operations research represents business operating techniques that will call more and more heavily upon the equipment that he works with. Businesses and business managers are becoming increasingly aware of the value of scientific decision-making and of the ability of the electronic computer to perform the calculations involved. Computer manufacturers are developing an increasing number of generalized computer programs that allow business to make use of these techniques with a minimum of effort with high speed computers performing the calculations. The data processor must familiarize himself with the basic ideas underlying operations research and become acquainted with what techniques are best for what particular problems. Frequently, data processors are faced with this type of question by business managers who recognize that computers are valuable tools but are not familiar with how they work: "Can the computer tell me how many lots of ball-point pens and automatic pencils I should manufacture every week?" The answer to this sort of question is both yes and no. It is yes in the sense that an answer can be forthcoming from the computer. It is no in the sense that the computer provides no answers of itself. There is a program, or set of instructions, which will cause a computer to perform the calculations necessary for the analysis of the problem. This program was written by a man; the computer only does what it is told to do. The decision based upon the calculations must still be made by the manager. It is up to the data processor to answer the question, in this case, as yes. He cannot be expected to explain the intricate details of computer programming of a linear programming problem to the manager. He is expected, however, to recognize that the problem can be solved by linear programming techniques and that computer programs are available or can be written that will cause a computer to perform the calculations.

Many times in his day-to-day work, the data processor will be faced with such questions from those who have come to understand that the electronic computer is capable of performing seemingly miraculous feats of analysis. Truly, these are "electronic brains" which will run the business by themselves. The data processor knows this is not true, and, in time, so will his bosses, as will all business managers. In answering such questions, it is the responsibility of the data processor to recognize that a way to solve the problem exists and to advise the manager as to what will be necessary in order to use that particular technique. Sometimes, it may require hiring a consulting firm. Other times, it may involve executing a prewritten program after supplying the computer system with the appropriate information. The electronic computer, which makes many of the techniques of operations research feasible for modern businesses, will be called upon more and more in the future to perform such jobs. In the past, many computers have been used to perform rather traditional accounting and bookkeeping tasks for businesses. The computer provides business decision-makers new ways to perform their function which were not dreamed of ten years ago. The future holds even greater promise. In order for the data processor to keep up with his profession, he must keep himself up to date with these new uses of electronic data processing equipment. This chapter is meant to be a first small step in this direction.

Questions

1. If you rolled a die five times and the number four came up each time, could you then conclude, on the basis of this sample, that every time the die was rolled four would come up? Why not?
2. What are the two basic kinds of linear programming? What is the basic difference between them?
3. Explain the difference between linear programming and dynamic programming. Give examples where each might be used in business situations.
4. What applications involving business uncertainty can you think of that can be handled by businessmen using decision theory techniques?
5. What is the difference between game theory and decision theory?
6. Draw a PERT network showing what must be done to bake a cake, or

build a boat, or some other project in which activities needed for completion of the project can take place simultaneously.

7. In the network you prepared in question six, determine the critical path. What is the time difference between it and the path with the greatest slack?

4

Information Systems: Basic Considerations

Definition of Systems

So far, we have observed that the significant activity of successful managers was successful decision-making. Furthermore, it seems reasonable to expect that successful decision-making depends upon the information available to the decision-maker. In this chapter, we are to investigate the basic nature of business information systems and the role they play in providing the information needed by managers.

The term *system* is used to mean the method by which an individual or an organization accomplishes the tasks necessary to achieve its goals. Almost everything we do as individuals is done in some systematic manner, even though the system may be entirely subconscious. Brushing one's teeth in the morning, for example, is hardly something that demands great mental effort in terms of designing a system to get the job done. But the system is there, nevertheless, established unconsciously through numerous repititions. If you don't think this is so, tomorrow morning try changing your procedure. Pick up the toothpaste first instead of your toothbrush, or vice versa depending on your present system. You will soon discover that doing things slightly differently requires the development of a new system and consequently considerably more mental concentration on what it is you are doing than before. Now suppose you decide that this new procedure for brushing your teeth is far better than the old method, or will be when you grow accustomed to it. How much effort will it demand on your part to implement the system so that it becomes as automatic for you as the former method? Now, what if the new system requires that the toothpaste be relocated in the medicine cabinet and you must persuade the other members of your household to expect to find it in the new location when they brush their teeth, and more important to *return* it to the new location? These thoughts point up some of the difficulties facing those whose business it is to design and implement systems within business organizations involving hundreds and even thousands of individuals, all of whom may have to accustom themselves to the new way of getting things done. These are the types of difficulties systems analysts try to cope with.

Before pursuing these ideas further, it will be useful to define rather specifically certain terms that are frequently used in conjunction with business systems and systems analysis. The first of these is the term *objectives*, which, for most people, is synonymous with *goals*. These are the ends towards which the organization and its various parts work.

The term *decision* is used to mean a selection between controversial alternatives. The controversial nature of the alternatives is an important element of the decision-making process. Clearly, if one alternative solution to a problem is so far superior to all other possibilities, then no decision need be made; the problem is self-solving. However, most important business decisions involve problems for which there is no obvious solution. In these cases, the decision-maker, if he is to do the best job possible, must equip himself with as much information as possible. This is where the data processor comes in. In the past, as we have observed, many decisions made by businessmen were made on an intuitive basis, which is to say that the decisions were essentially guesses, albeit tempered by the experience and general knowledge of the decision-maker. Now, because of the advent of mass information handling techniques, decision-makers are able to better evaluate the alternatives that they face.

Policies are essentially decisions that have already been made. They represent standard organization reactions to predictable events and in a larger sense they become the basic precepts that guide administrative action and define authority, responsibilities, and criteria of evaluation. All of that is quite a mouthful and it means that the business organization has found a number of events that call for standardized decisions. Whenever such an event occurs, the standard organizational response will be implemented. A bank, for example, may refuse as a matter of policy to accept deposits to checking accounts unless the depositor gives his account number. Those who are wise in the ways of business organizations recognize that simply because it is the stated policy of an organization to do something in a particular manner is no reason to believe that things cannot be done differently. It is only a matter of finding the individual in the organization who has the authority to break the policy. In our example above, a depositor might ask to talk to the head teller. Failing there, he might request an audience with the operations officer, from him to the general manager, and so on. Sooner or later, someone will be found who can make a decision for an event that is an exception to the general policy of the organization.

In systems work, a good deal of use is made of the term *procedure*. A procedure is a series of logical steps for accomplishing a job. For example, the procedure for starting the engine of an automobile equipped with an automatic transmission might go like this: place transmission in neutral, insert key into lock, press accelerator pedal to the floor once and release, turn ignition key clockwise until starter motor starts, hold key in this position until engine starts, release key, put transmission in the position desired. Procedures that are formally specified are very important for most manufacturing operations. The steps that a worker on a production line must take, for example, to accomplish his task may be set forth in a manner designed to help train future workers to do the same work and to provide the basis for an analysis of what actions and movement the job entails. Such studies, often called time and motion studies, for manual tasks, whether on a production line or in an office, are used to find better ways to go about the job. A commonplace way to prepare such studies is to make a procedural flow chart. Its purpose, as we shall see in the next chapter, is to set forth in a graphic form those activities that must take place in the accomplishment of the task.

System has been defined already as the means by which an organization or an individual goes about accomplishing the tasks necessary to achieve its goals. Clearly, there is a close relationship between this term and the term *procedure. A system is a network of related procedures, the sum of which result in the accomplishment of the organization's goals.* Within the system that acts as the *modus operandi* for every organization are a number of *subsystems.* In fact, many systems analysts prefer to look upon the total business system as a nesting of subsystems the smallest unit of which is the procedure. Figure 4–1 shows in broad perspective how this might work for a company that is functionally organized into four areas: marketing, production, accounting, and personnel. The aggregate business system in this case is composed of the four subsystems that cope with these four areas of activity. Similarly, each one of these subsystems is broken down into subsystems, too. The accounting subsystem in this case has such subsystems as asset accounting, liability accounting, equity or ownership accounting, expense accounting, tax accounting and many others. Going a few steps further, the asset accounting system might appear as in Figure 4–2, which shows that it consists of subsystems involving the control of long-term and short-term assets. These subsystems, too, are composed of yet other subsystems. So it goes, with the systems breakdown becoming finer and finer until the finest element is reached. This final component is a procedure. Under accounts receivable, for example, subsystems are designed to assure that a customer's account is kept up to date. Such a subsystem would describe the flow of information from the sales operation, where the credit sales are made, and from the billing operation, which bills the customers and receives their payment. The manner in which the customers' bills are prepared may be the final procedure in this aspect of the overall system. Also, the receipt of payment and the initial recording of the receipt may be an activity best described as a procedure. (It should be pointed out here that our use of the term *procedure* as the smallest component of the network or nesting of subsystems within the overall business system does not square entirely with the generally accepted definition of the term. More generally, any set of logical steps designed to accomplish some task is a procedure. What we

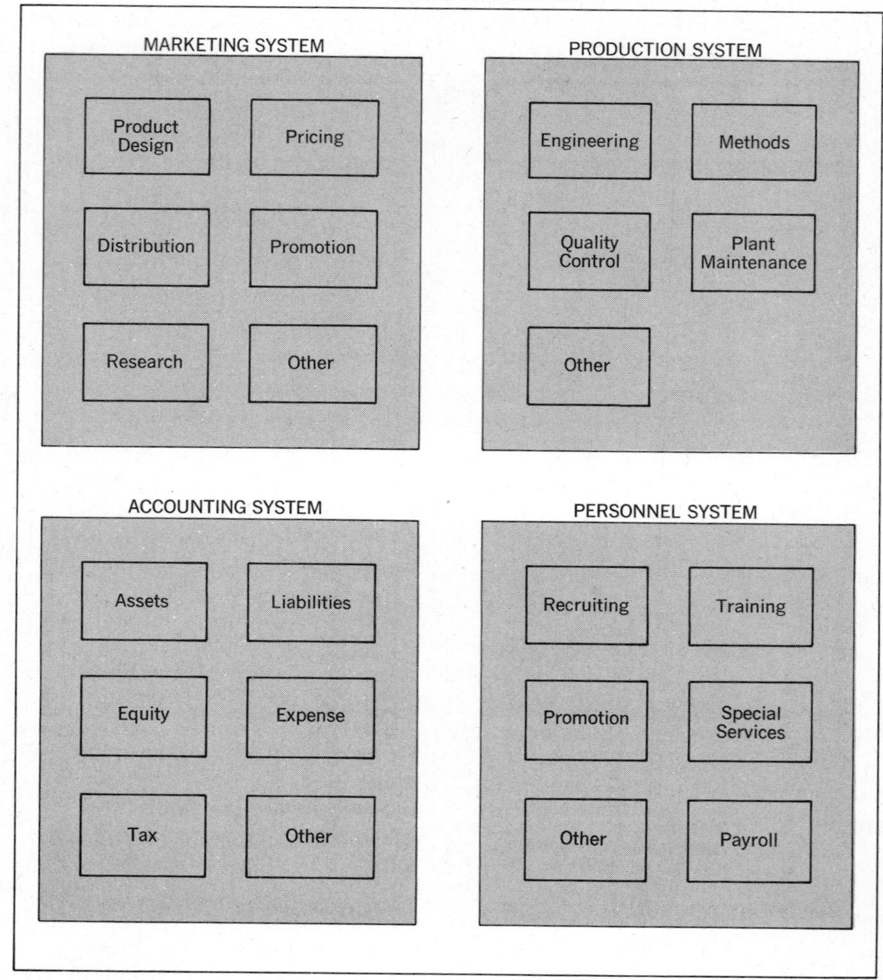

Figure 4–1. Nesting of subsystems within the overall business system.

might call a subsystem here might be looked upon as a procedure by someone else.)

Referring back to Chapter 1, consider how organizations are organized along functional lines, with authority flowing downward through the organization's structure (whether straight-line, committee, or what have you) in terms of the functional areas concerned with the basic activities of the business. From the president to a vice president in charge of marketing to managers of sales, advertising, and so forth to the final component in the organizational structure, the chain of command follows to an important extent the nesting of subsystems within the total business system.

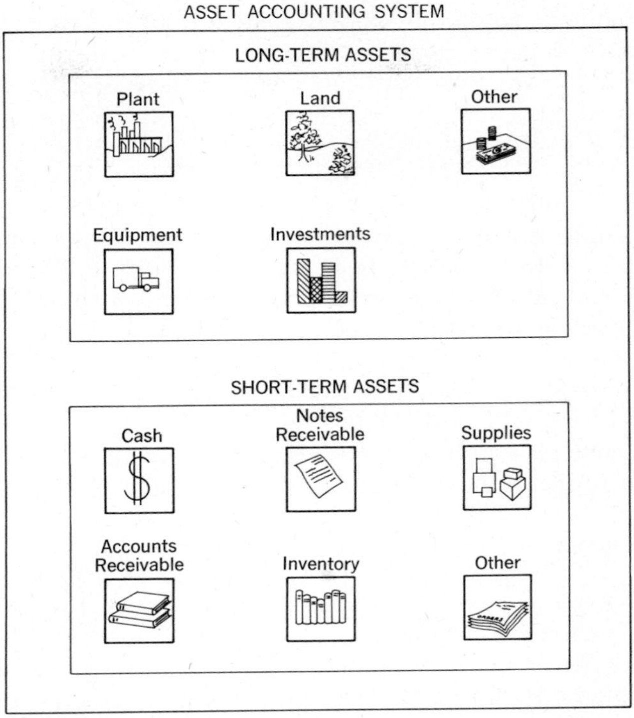

ASSET ACCOUNTING SYSTEM

LONG-TERM ASSETS

Plant Land Other

Equipment Investments

SHORT-TERM ASSETS

Cash Notes Receivable Supplies

Accounts Receivable Inventory Other

Figure 4–2. Nesting of subsystems within a subsystem.

An understanding of this sort of relationship between the form of the organization and the way in which systems are nested within the company is a prime requisite to the successful data processor. The reason for this lies in the nature of the system of most concern to the data processor: the information system. This system, unlike the others, cannot be thought of as being nested within larger networks of systems. This is because the information system serves all of the other subsystems within the organization. Although from the *formal* organizational standpoint, the information system, or data processing function, as it is more commonly called, often appears as a subsystem of the accounting system, many are beginning to recognize that it cannot be treated in the same manner as the other systems.

The Systems Department

Because many organizations have found that the relationships that exist between the various systems within the business and in particular those of the information system are complex and difficult to control, specialized organizations within the business have been developed especially for the purpose of analyzing and developing systems and procedures. The functions of such a department reflect the role that those involved in systems development and analysis play within the business organization.[1]

Organization Planning and Analysis

The systems department has become responsible for examining the formal organization of the enterprise and recommending changes that would improve its efficiency. Such a responsibility points up emphatically the broad nature of systems work within the organization and why it cannot be adequately considered as subsystems activity.

Systems Analysis and Design

Systems analysis will be discussed in the next chapter. It is the definitive responsibility of the systems department in that it concerns the functioning of the entire organization in terms of its activities as it strives to achieve its goals.

Management Audits

A management audit is a survey of the ways in which certain activities of the business are performed or the manner in which certain departments or even the entire organization goes about its work. Essentially, this is an efficiency study, to measure how well the organization, or parts of it, are being managed.

Preparation of Written Procedures

Describing the detailed manner in which things are to be done, the policies that are to be enforced and how, and other matters of day-to-day operations fall within the responsibilities of the systems department. These descriptions often employ flow charts. These, too, will be discussed in the next chapter.

Forms Design and Control

Transmission of information within the organization is usually effected through the use of business forms. The design of these forms and the procedures by which they are to be transmitted is a field of endeavor that can pay off handsomely in terms of increased efficiency of the information system and consequently of the entire business system.

[1] N. L. Senensieb, "Systems, Functions, Concepts and Programs," in Systems and Procedures Association, *Business Systems*, I (1963), pp. 3–4 to 3–29.

Report Analysis

Business reports, which are used by the business to transmit information internally to decision-makers and externally to stockholders, government agencies, and the like, are analyzed by the systems department for ways to increase their usefulness to those who receive them. Removing unnecessary and redundant information from a report and adding to it relevant information is a major step in improving the quality of decisions made by the users of the reports because it saves them time and provides them with pertinent information.

Records Management

The form that records take and the manner in which they are stored so as to make them available when needed and at the same time to minimize the cost of their maintenance is another activity that can produce great efficiencies in the organization's operations. In fact, this has become so important in the last few years that a specialized area within systems work has developed to meet its needs. This area is called *information retrieval* and will be discussed in Chapter 5.

Work Simplification

Work measurement and simplification as a field of business activity has been around a long time, getting its start with Frederick W. Taylor, who was mentioned in Chapter 2. In terms of the systems department, this activity tends to be confined to evaluating and improving the performance of office and clerical tasks, leaving production work measurement to the production control department and its industrial engineers. The same techniques are employed, however, for both groups to achieve the same ends—more efficient work methods through simpler and more effective procedures.

Work simplification as performed by the systems department involves the use of scientific methods to analyze business work procedures and enveloping more effective ways to get work done. There are several basic tools used in work simplification. These include work distribution charts, process flow charts, procedure flow charts, work measurement, and time and motion study. The first three of these, which are integral parts of systems analysis and design, will be discussed in the next chapter.

Work measurement is a technique of determing the time required to complete a unit of work in comparison with time standards that serve as a basis of control. Work measurement usually involves breaking down the job being studied into the most fundamental elements and analyzing these with a view towards increasing the efficiency with which the job is accomplished. Such analysis is familiar to industrial engineers who perform time and motion studies in analyzing the repetitive types of work done in manufacturing processes. This type of work analysis has found its way into the office where clerical procedures are analyzed using the same techniques. Time and motion studies analyze work activities in terms of *therbligs,* a term coined by Frank Gilbreth (therblig is Gilbreth spelled backwards). A therblig is a basic motion performed by one who is doing some manual task. There are over a dozen basic therbligs in common use, including such motions as find, assemble, use, search, grasp, and inspect.

Equipment and Facility Layout and Selection

The selection of office and data processing equipment and the physical arrangement of this equipment as well as the layout of office space in general has been delegated to the systems department. Once again, the assumption of this responsibility illustrates the close relationship between systems work and the preparation and flow of information and work within the organization.

Systems Implementation

One of the most difficult responsibilities of the systems department is implementing a new system. It is one thing to design a better way to do things; quite another to persuade others to adopt these ways. Most systems analysts will claim that the hardest part of their jobs is dealing with people within the organization and enticing them to change the way they have been doing things to a more effective way—the same kind of difficulty you would have in persuading your family to store toothpaste in a different location. There is no question in the minds of competent systems men that no matter how well the system is designed, no matter how much more effectively the job will be accomplished with the new system, unless it is properly implemented, all of the effort put into its design is wasted. At least half of the skill of being a good systems analyst lies in being able to persuade people of the desirability of turning to a new way of doing things. Remember, the people in the organization are there primarily to satisfy their own personal goals. Probably some or perhaps all of these personal goals conflict with those of the organization. For this reason, it may be futile to approach people with the argument of increased organizational efficiency alone to persuade them to change their methods. The systems man must be a true salesman in the sense of selling his product (a new system or procedure) by appealing to the personal needs and goals of those who must adopt his new system.

The position of the systems department within the organization, because of its characteristic crossing of functional areas within the organization's systems network is of a staff nature. Systems men are typically not line decision-makers, although they have the ability, because of the services they perform for decision-makers, to wield a powerful influence over the decisions that are made. Since the advent of automated data processing and its highly technical aspects, decision-makers frequently are at the mercy of their data processing and systems advisors. An indolent systems man, or an ignorant one, might advise a decision-maker that certain types of information are impossible to obtain with the information system available when, in fact, it is perfectly feasible to gather and present the information as required by the decision-maker. The decision-maker, because of his lack of technical knowledge of the field has no way of knowing this and will make do with what he has, perhaps making decisions of much lower caliber than would be possible if he was provided the additional information. In no other specialty field within the business has the success of the business depended so heavily upon the expertise and conscientiousness of personnel as in the case of data processing and data processing systems.

Tasks of the Information System

There are many different types of systems—or, as we have defined them, subsystems—operating within a business organization: a production system, marketing system, system of personnel administration, and so forth. From the data processor's standpoint, the system of most concern is the information system. This system, as was mentioned earlier, is conceptually unlike the other systems in that it cannot be viewed as nesting within any one broad system as was the case, for example, with the asset accounting system, which was entirely nested within the broader accounting system. Instead, it crosses organizational and system boundaries as a matter of necessity in performing its tasks within the organization. In this sense, the information system is a subsystem only of the *total system,* a position which has brought many systems analysts to the study and definition of the "total systems concept" by which is usually meant the entire business system and the manner in which it operates in the striving for organizational goal satisfaction. The basic task of any information system, of course, is to supply the organization's decision-makers with the information they need in order to make decisions. Because the organization must also provide information to outsiders, the information system must prepare and provide this as well. In the execution of these tasks, the information system calls upon a field of business specialization—data processing.

Data Processing

Data Processing is a term used in businesses to mean *the gathering, storing, processing, and transmitting of information* within the organization. From this definition, it can be seen that data processing is the heart of the organization's information system. Its importance is so great, in fact, that many businessmen and students of business organization behavior have come to attach to it an importance that is unjustified in terms of its functions within the organization. The basic role of the information system is to provide information to decision-makers in a form most suitable for developing high-quality decisions. Data processing, as the functional part of the information system, provides the tools and techniques used to achieve this task. Data processing relates to the rest of the business organization in a staff fashion. Data processing is part of the information system but, contrary to the belief of many professional data processors, is not the entire system and has no proper decision-making or policy-making function outside of the information system. In the performance of its duties as part of the information system, data processing makes use of seven definitive techniques, each of which should be familiar to everyone involved in any way with the field. Each of these techniques is discussed below.

Data Collection

Data collection means the gathering of original data to be entered into the information system. For example, sales information is considered to be original data taken from sales slips or cash register tapes at the time that the transactions were made. These data are recorded on *source documents,* in this example, the sales slips or cash register slips. Source documents are the media, then, used to enter the original data into the information system. Areas of activity within the data collection function of data processing involve the design of source documents, preparation of procedures for handling source documents, and initiating other data processing techniques on the source data and selection of mechanical and electronic devices to be used, if any, in the gathering of original data.

Classification

Data that are unorganized are still data, but *organized* data becomes information. Data not organized into some meaningful pattern can serve almost no useful purpose to those who must use it to make decisions. A formal definition of *classification* might go something like this: classification is the process of identifying each item of data and systematically placing it within a scheme that categorizes data according to common characteristics and features. The sciences, for example, have long paid heed to the necessity of classifying the phenomena they study. First, things are broadly divided into those that are living or have lived (organic) and those things that do not live and never have (inorganic). Living things are then classified as plants and animals; each of these is then classified into different phyla, then into classes, genus, species, and so on. Similarly, in business information, it is useful to classify information according to the logical characteristics of the data. Inventory records are classified according to type of inventory, use, source, and so forth. Customer records are often classified according to amount of average purchase and frequency of purchase, employees according to department, and sales records by salesman or geographic location. It is always difficult to draw clear lines that distinguish one classification from another. There are creatures which are part plant and part animal; there are things, such as viruses, which seem to be both alive and dead. Similarly, there are customers of businesses that defy classification. In spite of the numerous exceptions that are found to any classification scheme, it is useful to classify information.

SORTING

The term *sorting* is generally used by data processors as a verb meaning to arrange data into some kind of order. Many become confused about the distinction that should be made between data that have been sorted and data that have been classified. Classification means to assign an item of data to a category of data according to some logical characteristic that is common to all the data in the category. Sorting means to arrange items of data in some *arbitrary* order, alphabetically, numerically, or otherwise. The best example of this difference is the telephone directory. The entries in the white pages of the book are sorted alphabetically. This arrangement is arbitrary and your name appears in this portion of the directory entirely on the basis of how it happens to be spelled and upon the conventional way that we arrange our alphabet. Imagine how difficult it would be to make a listing of all the medical doctors in the telephone directory using only the white pages. This difficulty arises from the fact that the data in the white pages are not *classified* in any logical fashion whatsoever; they have simply been *sorted* alphabetically. On the other hand, examining the yellow pages, or the classified telephone directory, will yield all of the doctors in one place. This is so because the entries in this portion of the directory are arranged on the logical basis of occupation or service offered.

CALCULATING

Calculating is a process of performing mathematical operations upon data, which results in new data. Calculating is the only technique of data processing that produces new data. All the other techniques are limited to manipulating the original source data. Many dramatic developments have been made in the last few decades in the development of devices that perform calculation functions. Almost daily one can read newspaper announcements about the features of an electronic computer or of the applications now being performed by these devices. A large portion of this book is devoted to discussions of how these devices work and how they are used. It is important to recognize that the calculation is only one of several processes performed by the data processing function. While the computational ability of some devices has increased, their usefulness is still limited by such other functions as recording and communicating. An electronic computer that can perform several million multiplication operations every second is of no use if the results cannot be just as quickly presented as information to be used. One of the major problems of modern data processing equipment design has centered on developing recording and communicating devices (called input/output devices) that can handle data as fast as computers can produce it or use it.

Summarizing

Summarizing is a process of condensing data into more useful form. Consider the sales report shown in Figure 4–3. The sales figures shown for each salesman in the Sales column is known as a *detailed listing*. This detailed information is useful to a branch manager in terms of evaluating the performance of each salesman, but not very useful to, say, the president of the company who is more interested in the overall picture of the company's operations. For his purposes, the detailed information is summarized into branch totals, territory totals, and finally, the total sales for the company. Each of these three *levels* of totals is usually identified by data processors with specific terms that are in universal use. The detailed listing is one of these terms. The branch totals in this example are known as *minor totals*, the territory totals as *intermediate totals*, and the company total as a *major total*. Each of these levels of totals is known as a *summary total* indicating that information has been condensed in order to produce the total. Further, it can be seen that each level of total is a summary total of the next lower level, that is, the intermediate total is a summary of the minor totals, and the major total is a summary of the intermediate totals.

Recording

Recording is the process of expressing data in some form that is recognizable by either man or machine. The sales clerk, for example, when writing the details of a sales transaction on a sales slip is recording original data, or *source data* as it is frequently called, on a source document. Similarly, an accounting machine, when producing the sales analysis report shown in Figure 4–3, is recording detail and summary information. A device that writes information on magnetic tape is recording information to be read later by a machine, and a card punch that records data on a card in the form of holes punched into it is recording information to be read later by a machine. Recording of source data is often called *originat-*

Territory	Branch	Salesman	Sales	Branch Totals	Territory Totals
Eastern	New York	T. Dickson	$13,462.81		
		T. Tilton	8,391.69		
		S. Hiraoka	18,925.84		
				$40,780.34	
	Boston	D. Jeffries	7,321.92		
		S. Peterson	10,391.46		
		D. Pierce	14,382.61		
				32,095.99	
	Norfolk	S. Robinson	9,461.50		
		S. Long	7,392.85		
				16,854.35	
					$ 89,730.68
Western	Los Angeles	W. Scholtz	12,931.28		
		G. Saunders	6,921.75		
		R. Reynolds	5,320.92		
				25,173.95	
	San Francisco	B. Luskin	12,391.82		
		J. Clark	9,397.63		
		R. Bise	4,921.82		
				26,711.27	
					51,885.22
Central	Denver	L. Rutherford	7,822.50		
		A. Scofield	9,391.73		
				17,214.23	
	New Orleans	M. Ruth	13,862.50		
		D. Crowe	7,931.81		
		W. Johnston	4,621.20		
				26,415.51	
					43,629.74
			Company Total		$185,244.64

Figure 4–3. Sales analysis report.

ing and means, as the term implies, writing the original data for use later by the information system.

Communication

Communication is the process of transferring information or data from one point to another either within the organization or to users of information outside the organization. All of the other techniques of data processing are useless unless this one is performed adequately. For this reason, most data processors consider communications to be their most challenging problem. Whether the communications within the organization are performed via flow of paper forms, telephone lines, face-to-face contact, or some combination of these (which is almost always the case), developing an effective communication system as part of the information system is a goal towards which the major portion of the work of the systems department strives.

These seven processes are practiced by data processors using a wide variety of equipment ranging in simplicity from paper and pencil, as in recording operations, to very elaborate and expensive electronic computers used in some kinds of calculating operations. Many people, when using the term *data processing* intend for it to mean data processing as performed by automatic devices like computers, high-speed accounting machines, and the like. Acutally, the correct definition of data processing includes all methods and means of gathering, storing, processing, and transmitting of information. Furthermore, many people look upon data processing as a new field of automated techniques. Usually, this mistaken view is based upon a limited definition of data processing which includes only automated techniques. Actually, data processing has been with us for centuries, ever since early farmers decided to keep records of their crops, lands and cattle. The mark of one who understands data processing today is his recognition of the role data processing plays within the information system of organizations, whether the organizations be business, government, social, or whatever. Most likely, however, you were attracted to this field of study because of the dramatic advances that have been made in the technology of the field. In recognition of this, the major portion of this book is devoted to explaining the ideas behind these advances and how they are used within the information system.

Basic Information Needs of Large Organizations

The requirements for information in any organization depend on what the organization's purposes are and how these purposes are achieved. A large business organization is generally engaged in earning a profit and satisfying some of the other goals of smaller organizations and individuals within it, as well as satisfying demands made upon it by external groups. Figure 4–4 depicts some of the internal and external demands put upon modern large business organizations for information. Users of information above the double line in the center of Figure 4–4 are external users of information provided by the organization's information system. Customers require information about the status of their accounts; insurance companies require information about the status of assets and personnel insured; stockholders require information about dividends, earnings, and the financial position of the company; unions require information about union members, dues paid, and new employees; banks require information about bank account balances and check reconciliation; vendors require information about purchases and payment of accounts. One of the largest and most insistent external organizations that require information

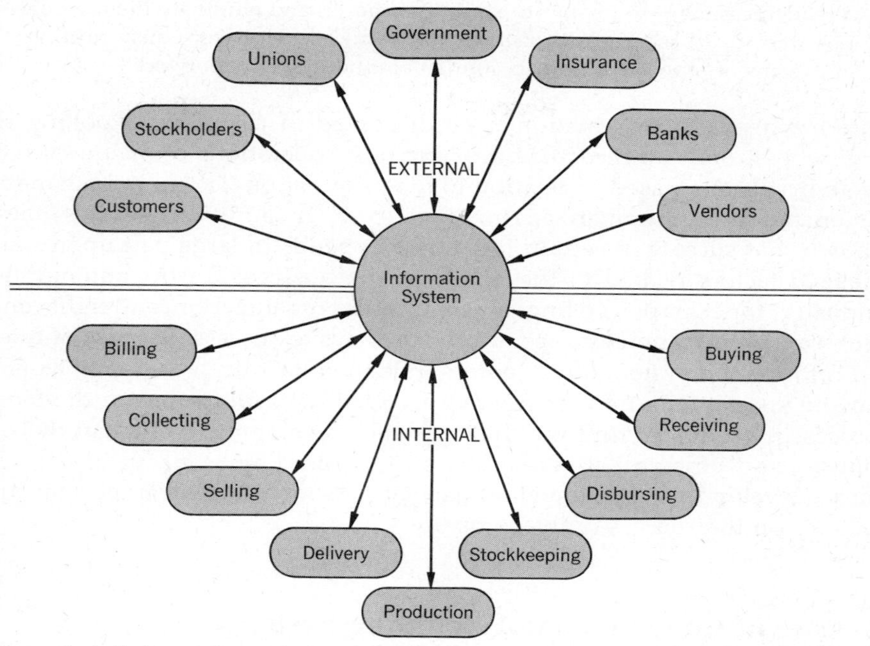

Figure 4–4. Information requirements for large business organizations.

from business organizations is the government, particularly, the federal government. An article appearing in a national newsmagazine a couple of years ago dramatically demonstrates the nature of some of the federal government's requirements for information imposed on all business and on large businesses, in particular.

> The U.S. Government requires the business community to file no fewer than 5,455 different reports during the year on a variety of subjects, ranging from employment to industrial inventories. Small businessmen complain that they sometimes have to pay the accountants who handle their forms more than they make themselves, and some big businessmen spend as much as $300,000 a year just answering Defense Department questionnaires. In a single year, one Midwestern farm-products company handled 173 different federal forms, ranging in frequency of filing from daily to annually, and finally turned in a total of 37,683 reports that involved 48,285 man-hours of work.
>
> When they looked out from under this mountain of paperwork and saw the President of the U.S. turning off unnecessary lights in the White House, a lot of businessmen decided that he was the kind of man who would understand their problem. So they began deluging him with letters asking that the Government also try to economize on the forms and questionnaries that they must deal with (sometimes under pain of stiff penalties). They read their man right. President Johnson has declared war on excessive paperwork

> for businessmen, promising to simplify reports, and eliminate them when possible. . . . Last week, in fact, Government agencies were busy turning out reams of reports on how to eliminate unnecessary paperwork.[2]

Internal needs of information were discussed in Chapter 1. Looking at Figure 4–4, one can recognize the nine basic operations of business that were briefly discussed in relation to the information flow in the business organization as summarized in Figure 1–7. In addition, studies have shown that success in certain industries depends in large part upon specialized factors related to the nature of the business. In the automobile industry, for example, styling, efficient dealer organization, and tight control over production costs seem to be the keys to success. Because of this, an information system for an automobile manufacturing company would devote special attention to these areas. Similarly, companies in the food processing industry find that new product development, efficient distribution, and powerful advertising are especially important. In life insurance, development of competent agency personnel has an important influence on the success of the company.

Failure of Conventional Accounting Systems

Conventional accounting systems with their emphasis upon historical, financial, and production data have in general failed to meet the information needs of modern large enterprises in today's competitive business environment. There can be no doubt that conventional accounting systems that have been in use since the first development of the double-entry bookkeeping system will have a place in the information system of business organizations for many generations to come. It is also clear, however, that these methods have become only a part of the total information system for the organization. This is difficult for many to accept, particularly those who have devoted most of their lives to mastering the intricacies of modern accounting practice. As a result, many otherwise progressive organizations, in relegating their data processing departments and their information systems to the control of the accounting department are put at a serious competitive disadvantage. The chief failing of conventional accounting systems as information systems lies in their failure to highlight the information most important to the decision-maker. These systems, by their nature, omit such important areas as information about the future; information that can only be expressed in nonfinancial terms, like the adequacy of customer service, quality of merchandise, and market share; and information about environmental conditions as they have a bearing upon the organization's operations. What is more, decision-

[2] *Time*, April 24, 1964, p. 94.

makers who are not trained in accounting theory and practice can make little use of many reports and documents prepared under the conventional accounting systems because of the arbitrariness of terminology and tradition in presenting accounting information.

From these considerations, it should be clear that each business organization will develop its own unique information system geared to meeting its own unique requirements as well as the standard information requirements found in all business organizations. The following chapter will consider the nature of systems analysis and design and how these techniques are used to develop these unique information systems.

Questions

1. Explain the difference between procedures and policies.
2. What is the relationship between systems and procedures?
3. Distinguish between classification and sorting.
4. What are the seven basic data processing processes?
5. Is there a relationship between "systems" and the total organization, the department, and the data processing hardware?
6. Explain the basic purpose of an information system.
7. Relate systems and data processing to the line/staff organization.
8. Can you see a need in large organizations for specialization in areas of systems analysis? If so, what type?
9. How does the information system of an organization differ from other subsystems within the organization?
10. What is the difference between a management audit and systems analysis and design?
11. In what way are decision-makers in an organization at the mercy of systems analysts and data processors?
12. Explain the difference between a source document and a report.
13. What is the distinction between *recording* data and *gathering* it?

5

Systems Analysis and Design

Definition and Objectives of Systems Analysis

In the last chapter, we examined the nature of business systems, with particular attention to information systems. The purpose of this chapter is to review the basic aspects of systems analysis and design.

Systems analysis is the process of evaluating all the aspects of a particular system and the situation in which the system operates. In its broadest sense, this involves the examination of the inputs into the system and the output requirements. The objective of this analysis is the design of a system to achieve the desired outputs in the most effective manner.

The design and development of a working system usually consists of three easily identifiable stages. The first of these is the study and design stage. At this point in the genesis of a system, the input and output are scrutinized and the means to use the input to achieve the desired output is developed. All too often, there is no formal effort on the part of the organization to make full use of this stage of development. Systems seem to *happen* in organizations without much thought being devoted to how the system should go about doing the job. This is because the *job* must be done, and the most expedient way is found in the press of the moment with little regard to future requirements to do the same work. Continued utilization of the emergency techniques bring a system of sorts into being. Systems analysis is a formalized attempt to avoid this haphazard manner of systems development.

The second stage of formalized systems development consists of the implementation of the system that was designed in the first stage. In the second stage, men, materials, and devices are joined together into a system that works. Still, however, the system is likely to be far from optimal. It is almost certain to be better than the haphazard system born of necessity, but experience has shown that regardless of the care that goes into the first stage of systems development, the operation of the system thus designed will bring many "bugs" to light that must be corrected.

The third stage of systems development, then, involves the day-to-day operation of the system and the continued analysis of the way in which the work is being done. Because of the nature of things, often the order of these stages is disturbed in actual practice. The third stage may come first, followed by the other two in sequence. Such a phenomenon comes about because of the haphazard method of systems development described above, which results in a working system the analysis of which begins after the work starts rather than before.

Even when a system is well-designed and well-implemented, there is still good cause to continued its analysis and evaluation. Changes in organizational policy, markets, government regulations, competition, new equipment, and a host of other developments make any system short-lived. For example, so-called third-generation computers, introduced in 1964, offered data processors a major advance in computer technology applications. This caused users of computing equipment to devote hundreds of man-hours to redesigning their information systems in such a way as to benefit most from the advantages offered by the new equipment. In general, a healthy, growing business organization will find continuous need for systems analysis, design, and redesign in order to maintain an efficient, competitive business organization.

Design of Information Systems

The basic truism of any systems analysis effort is first to understand the system now being used. This is much more difficult than the uninitiated might expect. Understanding the present system requires that a good deal of information be gathered, sample forms used in the system collected, costs calculated, effectiveness measured, interviews held with individuals who work within the system conducted, and direct observations made concerning the way things are now being done. Organizational relationships are an important subject of study in any systems analysis. Individuals working within the system do not always cooperate to the extent that the systems analyst might wish. This, of course, makes things considerably more difficult. People, once used to a particular way of doing things, are typically suspicious of different ways and of those who wish to develop new methods. They may not understand what the systems analyst is doing and may not feel motivated to help supply the information he needs. They may fear that the new system will eliminate the job they do and perhaps jeopardize their security. For any one of a host of reasons, the systems analyst finds that this stage of the design of an information system is difficult indeed.

When the basic information about the current system has been gathered, the systems analyst turns to the task of analyzing it for the purpose of discovering its weak points. Almost always, this analysis involves the use of flow charts and other documents that break the system down into basic procedures and present an aggregate picture of the flow of information and forms through the system and of the operations, often called *events,* that are performed by the individuals or stations in the system. Documentation such as this is the subject of a later section of this chapter. It serves not only the purpose of systems analysis but also provides official records of the systems being employed within the organization.

Once the documentation of the present system is complete, the analyst is now able to examine in detail the current system. Typically, this is done by locating the origin of a sample source document within the system, measuring the effort needed to produce it, the data needed for its correct preparation, the number of stations in the system that need copies of it, and the event that causes it to be prepared. Then the path of the source document is traced from station to station through the system and an analysis is made of the activities of each station with respect to this document and the subsequent preparation of other documents and reports resulting from these activities. Finally, the outputs of the system are examined and compared with the output desired. Once this analysis is completed, it is then possible to consider modifications of the system which will improve its efficiency or will result in more desirable output or both. Often, modifications leading to a better system involve the redesign of forms and reports and rerouting of existing forms in the system. Too, stations in the system might be eliminated because of redundant activities or merged with other stations for more coordinated overall effort. There are occasions when the desired modifications call for changes in the information-handling equipment—data processing equipment—used by the system. This is of most interest to those of us who are interested in data processing as a part of the information system.

When modifications of a system indicate that different data processing equipment is called for to produce the desired results, a specialized study of data processing equipment is initiated to determine what equipment and in what configurations would be best suited for the job. This specialized study is known as a *feasibility study.* More generally, a feasibility study is conducted whenever an organization wants to know whether or not automated electronic equipment, together with the related information system characteristics needed to maximize the effectiveness of the automated devices, would be an advisable change from the system in current use. A feasibility study also used to mean a study which examines the desirability of replacing one system of automated data processing devices with another, usually more elaborate, system. The factors to be considered, with respect to specific equipment configurations, include the following: a description of the equipment, with detailed information about its capabilities and how these will meet the requirements of the new system; the cost of the equipment, including a comparative cost analysis of leasing the equipment versus purchasing it; the availability of maintenance and machine service; the availability of physical facilities to house and operate the equipment; the extent to which computer programs written to control the equipment currently in use must be rewritten; when the equipment can be delivered; and what assistance the manufacturer can provide in programming the equipment and in other ways making it function within the system.

Systems design can be approached from the standpoint of modifying the existing system in such a way as to minimize the equipment costs of systems change or from that of increasing the efficiency of the system by speeding up the processes already taking place within it, usually through the introduction of automated data processing equipment. The latter approach, which promises greater efficiency within the old system, is often embraced by those who are taken with the more romantic aspects of electronic computer technology. Now that the initial glory of electronic computers has dulled, systems analysts are taking a more realistic view of the computer as a tool within the information system. Where before an organization might introduce a computer into its system for the sake of having a computer (indeed, we still see computer installations on the ground floors of office buildings behind plate glass windows so that passers-by will see them and be impressed with the forwardness of the company) and design its information system around it, manufacturers of computing equipment are called upon with increasing frequency to demonstrate how their equipment will best serve the particular information system under consideration.

A new or modified system, when designed and implemented into a working system then becomes subject to continued scrutiny to determine whether or not it is a good system—that is, whether or not it will present a substantial increase in the organization's effectiveness. One writer in the systems field suggests ten tests of whether or not the system is good. These tests provide an insight into the way in which new systems, particularly automated systems, affect business organizations.[1]

1. The system will be vigorously opposed by those whose empires within the organization will suffer because of its implementation. A system which disrupts no one's operating habits in the organization is probably irrelevant.

2. The system will be expensive. It is a mistake to justify an automated system by the savings it will incur because there probably will be no great reduction in the costs of the information produced by the system. The information will become more timely and otherwise more useful, however, and the study that went behind the system might well discover other cost-saving but non-hardware-oriented modifications.

3. A good electronic computer system can do work that cannot be done any other way. If a way can be found to do the job another way, say with a punched card system, even though it may involve more time, then the computer is not being utilized to its highest potential.

[1] Claggett, Jones, "Ten Tests," *Systems*, January 1965, p. 14.

4. The reports produced by the systems are real reports, not just listings of data. Recall that the difference between data and information is that information is data presented in the most useful form. A report is a device which transmits information, not data.

5. Information produced by the system and delivered to a station in the organization is *used.* If individuals receive reports from the system that are not used, then they should not get the reports—the system needs further modification.

6. The same report will not go to different levels of decision-makers in the organization. The president of a sales organization is more interested in branch sales totals than in detailed listings of all transactions. The information system should take into account the different needs for information at the different organizational levels and produce and deliver reports accordingly.

7. The automated system is not part of the conventional accounting system and control of the data processing department does not lie with the accounting department. As discussed in the last chapter, conventional accounting systems have failed to provide modern large businesses with the information they need. Putting a resource as potentially valuable as data processing as a bookkeeping tool of the conventional system is a serious mistake.

8. Top executives are familiar with data processing and appreciate what a good information system can do for the organization.

9. The system is viewed by the organization's decision-makers as a decision-making tool rather than as a means to reduce accounting costs.

10. Experts were called in *before* the system was designed and implemented, and they were called in for advice in designing the new system, not reassurance that the new system already designed is good.

Characteristics of Information Systems

It is always difficult to classify things and, as you might expect, things as complex and as unique as information systems are difficult to fit into neat classifications. While it may be difficult to determine for a particular information system the category to which it belongs, several different types of information systems can be identified in business organizations.[2] Each of these is briefly discussed below.

Centralized and Decentralized Systems

A centralized information system is one in which all of the functions of the information system—data gathering, processing, storage, and transmission—are performed by an organization clearing house of information. All of the reports and most of the forms and other documents that carry

[2] W. F. Williams, *Principles of Automated Information Retrieval* (Elmhurst, Ill.: The Business Press, 1965), pp. 37 ff.

information to decision-makers within the organization originate from this clearing house. Similarly, all of the data collected by the organization is done by the centralized system, where it is then stored and used to prepare the reports required.

A decentralized information system, on the other hand, is one that involves several rather autonomous information systems serving functional departments or suborganizations within the enterprise. Each of these gathers its own data, produces reports as needed by the department it is serving and stores data accordingly.

A good example of the contrast between centralized and decentralized information systems is provided by libraries of colleges and universities. A library is an information system, even though it typically does not serve decision-makers. Some libraries are completely centralized. The entire collection is housed under one roof and all users of the information system must go to the centralized library. Many colleges and universities, however, maintain departmental libraries which contain collections of books dealing specifically with the discipline of that particular department. Political science, philosophy, physics, mathematics, and other departments of the institution will maintain their own libraries. Often, such library systems are oriented around a main library, which contains a basic collection and also maintains records of the volumes kept by the departmental libraries. So, too, business information systems that are decentralized will have some form of centralized coordination (if the total information system is well-designed), which works for optimum effectiveness of the system.

Distribution-Oriented and Storage-Oriented Systems

A distribution-oriented system is one whose operations emphasize the transmission of information to decision-making stations throughout the organization. Its antithesis is the storage-oriented system, which is more concerned with the efficient storage of data than with its transmission to information users in the system. A library is a storage-oriented information system. Retrieving information from such a system requires a good deal of effort on the part of the individual who needs the information. American Airlines' SABRE information system, on the other hand, which is devoted to disseminating information about aircraft seat availability, is distribution-oriented. This system provides reservation desks with information on seating availability on airline flights within a few minutes after an inquiry is made.

Information System Size Classifications

An information system is considered small by authorities in the field if it has access to 50,000 or less records of information, where a record is an amount of information pertinent to something or somebody about which the organization needs information. An employee record, for example, might contain information concerning the employee's name, the date he came to work for the organization, his social security number, his birthdate, and so on. A record about an item of inventory might include information about its physical characteristics, the vendor from whom it is normally purchased, the amount of the item currently on hand, and other important bits of information. Information systems that store and have available up to one million records are usually considered medium-sized and large information systems are those which contain over one million records at any one time.

Data Retrieval and Document Retrieval Systems

Data retrieving information systems have the ability to take many different types of data stored in rather expensive storage devices and manipulate them in such a way that a desired report can be produced, often involving mathematical calculations. Document-retrieving systems, on the other hand, are able to produce a given document upon request, but with little or no manipulation of data possible. Such a system frequently makes use of microfilm and other recording techniques utilizing miniaturized reproduction in order to store documents and records. Upon inquiry, such a document can be reproduced on a screen-like device, or a "hard" copy of the original document can be produced. Once again, a library is a typical document-retrieving system, one that makes the actual documents available to users.

Historically, electronic data processing, as well as other forms of automated data processing, has concentrated on processing records rather than entire documents. In the last few years, increasing attention has been paid to a specialized area within the field of data processing known as *information retrieval*, which is the process of recovering documents or records from a collection of documents or other forms of complete records.

The basic task of information retrieval is to store the documents or records in a form that is best suited to serve the retrieval needs of the particular application. The key to success in accomplishing this task is *indexing*, a specific technique of classifying that builds a list of records and documents stored in the system, states where each item on the list is stored, and states how the information can be taken from storage for use and replaced. Because of the increased interest in information retrieval, dramatic advances have been made in the means by which documents are processed for storing. Some of these techniques involve the use of microfilm, aperture cards, and other means of reducing the document to minute proportions for economy in storage space. Recent advances in electronic computer technology and the development of mass data storage devices, to be discussed in a later chapter, have led to means of storing a drawing or other document in a form that essentially consists of data, which, interpreted by a computer program, will cause the computer to trace the drawing on a cathode ray tube display unit, much like a television screen, so that a user of the drawing may have immediate access to it and to thousands of others by simply indicating to the computer system which document he would like displayed. Moreover, techniques have been developed that permit the user to modify the drawing at the display tube device so that the data stored in the computer system will henceforth cause the new drawing to be traced when the document is called for.

Information retrieval is yet in its infancy. Because of economies that can be enjoyed by an information system using automated information retrieval as compared to the conventional file and library approach to document storage, increased emphasis can be expected to be placed on it in the future. This will require professional data processors to become more aware of the various techniques of the art.

Manual Versus Automatic Systems

Almost every information system combines both manual and automated techniques in getting its work done. Even systems that employ the most sophisticated computing equipment will find it necessary to buy pencils, too. It is conceivable to develop an information system that is entirely manual, in which all of the gathering, storage, processing, and transmission of data is accomplished without the use of automated devices of any kind. Such systems, except for rather small business organizations, are seldom found, and even very small businesses may employ cash registers, adding machines, and even postage machines for their mail. The degree to which an information system should be automated depends upon the speed with which information must be processed, the amount of information to be processed and stored, and the value of the information to the decision-maker as compared to the costs of automating the system.

Batch and Real-Time Systems

The most commonplace data processing systems are those that make extensive use of batch, or sequential, processing techniques. A batch technique is one that gathers and saves all transactions affecting a file of information and, after a specific time period has elapsed or after a given number of transactions have been accumulated, the file is updated all at once making use of the transactions that have been collected. For example, banks typically accumulate all the transactions affecting checking and savings accounts for a day and, the next day, record each transaction to the appropriate account. In this way, the file of customer checking accounts is always a day behind the actual transactions (deposits and withdrawals) that have taken place. This system, however, is economical for a bank to use because it permits considerable labor specialization and concentration of effort to do the updating job all at once. Updating each individual customer record as the transaction takes place is a much more costly practice.

Real-time systems do not gather transactions for processing at some later time but process each transaction as it occurs. Real-time systems promise to be one of the most exciting and important developments in the area of electronic data processing. For this reason, an entire chapter has been devoted to them.

Documentation

Documentation is the process of recording every step in a procedure or a system in such a way that it can be completely replicated in the future if it becomes necessary to do so. Such documentation takes the form of job descriptions, procedure descriptions, and flow charts. Descriptions, because they are made up of words, cannot always be easily digested or analyzed by the reader, particularly if the procedure is complex to any extent. For this reason, it is the usual process to document procedures and systems activities in the form of flow charts. Among the many different types of flow charts used by business information systems in their documentation efforts, there are a few widely accepted forms that deserve individual recognition. In addition to their usefulness in providing a record of the way a system or procedure works, these documents are essential for analysis of business operations. They are one of the basic tools of systems analysis.

Work Distribution Charts

Work distribution charts are used to analyze what jobs are being done within a given system or subsystem and which of the individuals working in the system is responsible for the performance of the work. There are many different formats used by different companies in the preparation of work distribution charts. An example of the information usually found on such a form is shown in Figure 5–1. The left column of the chart shows the basic activity of the organization unit (department, section, or whatever) being analyzed. In this case, this is a work distribution chart of a data processing department and the left column shows two of the reports regularly produced by this department, the weekly payroll and the weekly inventory status report. Across the top of the report is indicated the various positions or jobs that spend some time at each of the various tasks needed to achieve the basic activity. The supervisor, for example, spends three hours per week in scheduling production, equipment, and reviewing programs and reports with respect to the production of the

Activity	Position		Position		Position		Position		Position		Position	
	Supervisor	Hrs	Tab Operator	Hrs	Computer Operator	Hrs	Key Punch Operator	Hrs	Programmer	Hrs	Librarian	Hrs
Weekly Payroll	Schedules production, equipment. Reviews programs, reports	3	Operates sorters, collator	12	Mounts payroll tapes, attends computer during production.	16	Prepares time cards	10	Maintains program, implements new services	3	Files and locates tapes	5
Inventory Report	Schedules production, equipment. Reviews programs, reports	5	Operates sorter, reproducing punch	16	Mounts inventory tapes, attends computer during production.	10	Prepares usage and receipt cards	8	Prepares wiring panels, maintains programs	5		

Figure 5–1. Work distribution chart.

weekly payroll. Similarly, he spends five hours each week performing the same tasks relative to the inventory status report. Other employees, by job title, are listed across the top of the chart and one can determine for each what his specific tasks are and how much time is spent. A work distribution chart is usually supported by other, more detailed forms prepared by the employees themselves indicating how much time is spent in what tasks and for what basic activities.

Process Flow Charts

A procedure is a series of logical steps designed to accomplish some task. Analysis of procedures is necessary in order to improve them and to make them more efficient. One of the most useful tools in the analysis of procedures is the *process flow chart*, or *procedure flow chart*, a form on which the details of procedures are recorded in pictorial form so that, if it is a new procedure, it can be more effectively evaluated and if already in use, can be effectively reevaluated. The symbols used in process flow charts are shown in Figure 5–2.

Figure 5–3 shows a procedure analysis work sheet, which depicts the various steps taken when a collector of trading stamps presents these stamps for merchandise redemption at a redemption center. Each of the actions that takes place in this procedure is listed down the left portion of this form and is identified with a letter indicating which employee is performing that particular action, for example, *A* for order clerk, *B* for stock clerk, and *C* for manager. Symbols are darkened, showing the nature

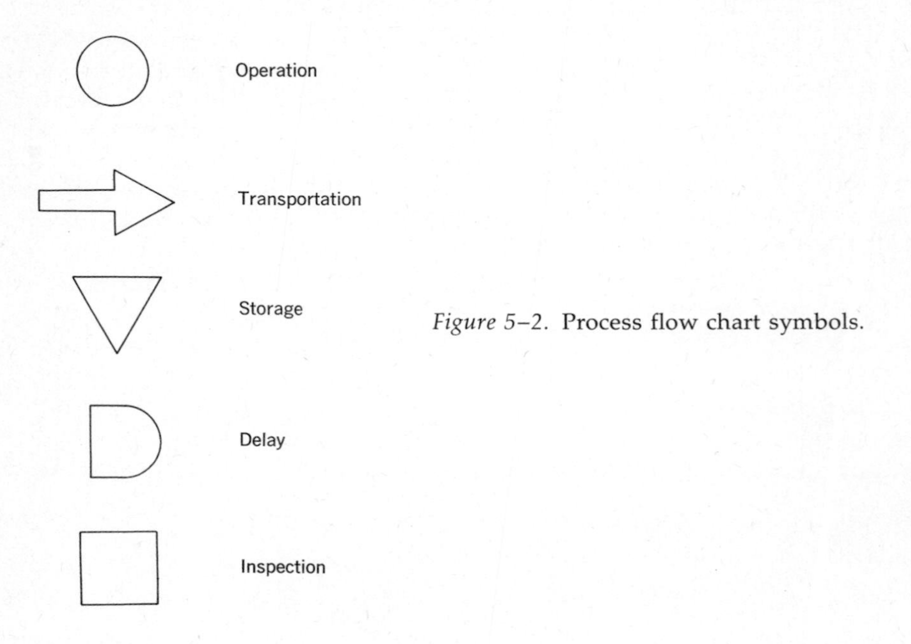

Figure 5–2. Process flow chart symbols.

PROCEDURE ANALYSIS WORK SHEET

SUMMARY	PRESENT NO.	PRESENT HRS.	PROPOSED NO.	PROPOSED HRS.	SAVINGS NO.	SAVINGS HRS.
○ OPERATIONS	10	1.08				
⇨ TRANSPORTATIONS	7	.07				
□ INSPECTIONS	1	.01				
D DELAYS	0					
▽ STORAGES	1	.01				
DISTANCE TRAVELED	90.2					

PROCEDURE CHARTED: Stamp Redemption

CHART BEGINS: Order Counter | CHART ENDS: Order Counter

CHARTED BY: Brightman | DATE: 4/30/67

☒ PRESENT ☐ PROPOSED

LINE NO.	STEPS IN PROCEDURE	OPER.	TRANSP.	INSPECT.	DELAY	STORE	DISTANCE IN FEET	TIME	ELIMINATE	COMBINE	SEQUENCE	PLACE	PERSON	IMPROVE
1	A. Prepares merchandise order from customer request	●					--	.05						
2	A. Carries order to stock room		●				15.0	.01						
3	A. Returns to order desk		●				15.0	.01						
4	B. Draws merchandise from stock	●					--	.12						
5	B. Enters withdrawal on bin record	●					--	.01						
6	B. Carries merchandise to order desk		●				15.0	.01						
7	B. Returns to stock room		●				15.0	.01						
8	B. Prepares requisition form to replace merchandise	●					--	.02						
9	B. Delivers requisition to manager		●				25.2	.02						
10	B. Returns to stock room		●				15.0	.01						
11	C. Checks requisition against master merchandise list			●			--	.01						
12	C. Prepares daily merchandise replacement order	●					--	.25						
13	A. Counts trading stamps offered by customer	●					--	.10						
14	A. Enters customer information in redemption book	●					--	.03						
15	A. Enters stamps received in redemption book	●					--	.01						
16	A. Stores stamps in safe					●	--	.01						
17	A. Collects sales tax from customer	●					--	.05						
18	A. Prepares tax receipt	●					--	.03						
19	A. Delivers merchandise and receipt to customer		●				--	.01						
20														
21	A. Order Clerk													
22	B. Stock Clerk													
23	C. Manager													
24														
	TOTALS	10	7	1	-	1	90.2	1.17						

APPROVED BY — DATE — PAGE 1 OF 1 PAGES

Figure 5–3. Procedure analysis worksheet.

of the activity, the distances traveled, and the amount of time required for each activity are recorded at the right of the form. At the top and bottom of the form is space for totals of time and distances and at the right edge are places to indicate what improvements might be made in the procedure. This work sheet has several details that could be profitably modified. Line 12, for example, indicates that the manager prepares a merchandise replacement order each time an item of merchandise is taken from stock. Surely, it would be more effective to prepare this order at the end of the day using all of the merchandise requisition forms at once. But if this is true, then why not have the stock clerk keep the requisition forms instead of delivering each one as it is written to the manager? This type of analysis is greatly facilitated by forms such as these.

Systems Flow Chart: Forms-Oriented

A systems flow chart is one that documents the activities within a system or subsystem involved in the accomplishment of some task. Symbols used in systems flow-charting are shown in Figure 5–4. Two basic versions of the systems flow chart concentrate upon either the flow of forms through the system or the chronological steps to be taken in accomplishing tasks. The forms flow chart, illustrated in Figure 5–5, shows the various activities that take place when a medium-sized department store orders and receives merchandise. This, then is a picture of the procedure or subsystem used by this organization to order and receive merchandise. Across the top of the figure are shown the various stations in the organization which take part in this particular procedure—the department buyer; the store manager; the accounting, purchasing, and receiving departments; and finally, although it is not part of the organization, the vendor of the merchandise is shown in order to give a more complete picture. (As with most of the examples in this text, this is not presented as the best way, necessarily, to do this particular job. The reader may enjoy analyzing this particular procedure from the standpoint of finding inefficient activities and developing better ways of doing the work.) The following description refers to the letters in the flow chart and explains the various activities taking place.

a. A purchase order is prepared by the department buyer in three copies. The purchase order is a source document.

b. Each purchase order must be approved by the store manager.

c. Copy three of the purchase order is retained by the department buyer; copies one and two go the accounting office.

d. The accounting office determines whether or not the department was open to buy with respect to this merchandise and, if so, records the purchase order and reduces the open to buy for the department.

e. Copy one of the purchase order is mailed by the accounting department to the vendor.

Processing — A major processing function.	**Input/ Output** — Any type of medium or data.
Punched Card — All varieties of punched cards including stubs.	**Perforated Tape** — Paper or plastic, chad or chadless.
Document — Paper documents and reports of all varieties.	**Transmittal Tape** — A proof or adding machine tape or similar batch-control information.
Magnetic Tape	**Disk, Drum, Random Access**
Offline Storage — Offline storage of either paper, cards, magnetic or perforated tape.	**Display** — Information displayed by plotters or video devices.
Online Keyboard — Information supplied to or by a computer utilizing an online device	**Sorting, Collating** — An operation on sorting or collating equipment.
Clerical Operation — A manual offline operation not requiring mechanical aid.	**Auxiliary Operation** — A machine operation supplementing the main processing function.
Keying Operation — An operation utilizing a key-driven device.	**Communication Link** — The automatic transmission of information from one location to another via communication lines.
Flow	The direction of processing or data flow.

Figure 5–4. Symbols used in systems flowcharting.

f. Copy two is sent to the receiving department to await the receipt of the merchandise.

g. Upon receipt of the merchandise, the receiving department prepares a receiving report.

h. Copy three of the purchase order is filed by the department buyer.

i. Receiving report is compared with purchase order by purchase department to determine that the merchandise received was the same as that ordered.

j. Copy two of the purchase order and the receiving report are filed by the purchase department.

k. The receiving report is compared to the purchase order by the department buyer. If correct, both are filed together.

l. The invoice prepared by the vendor is received by the purchasing department and compared with the purchase order.

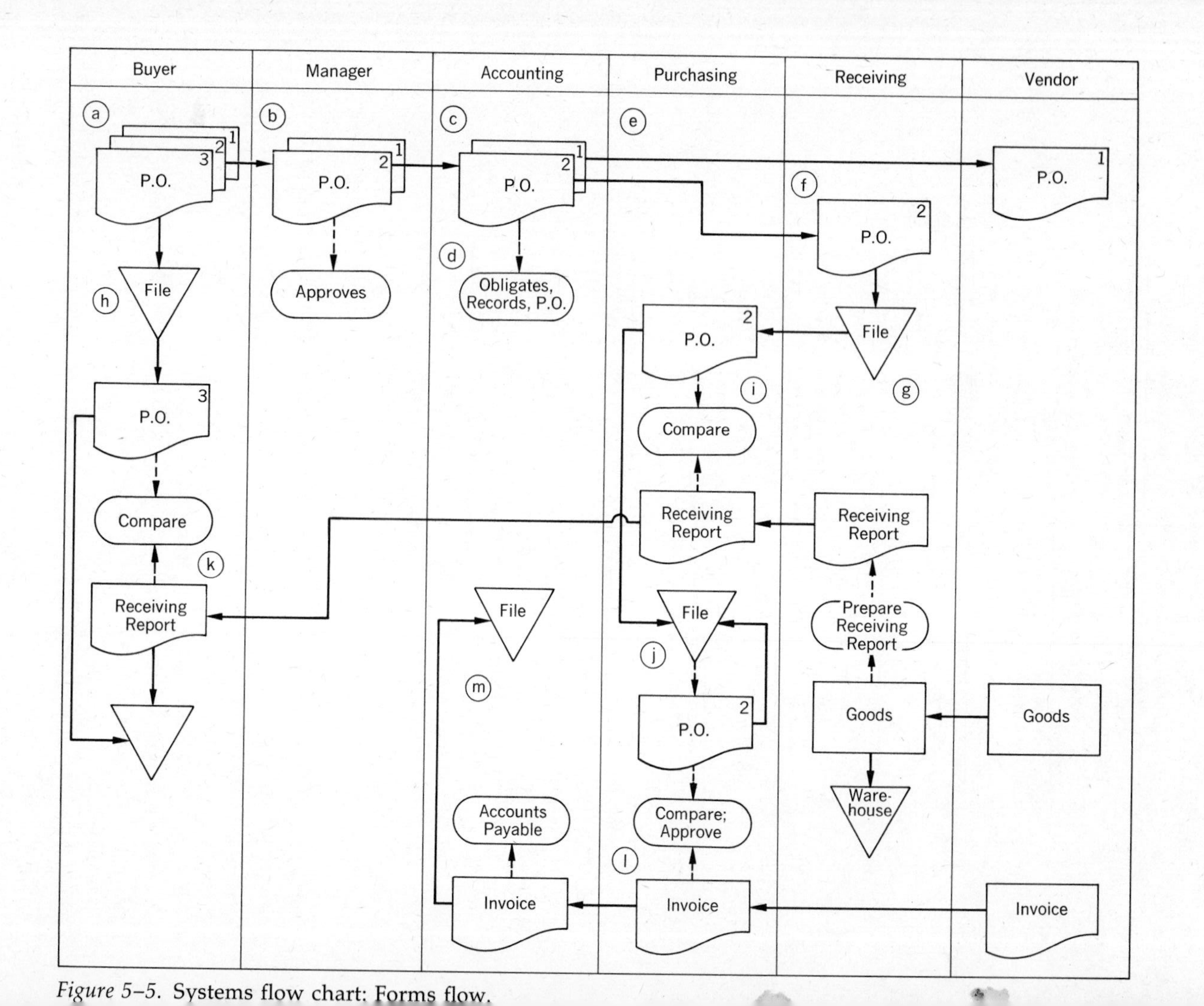

Figure 5–5. Systems flow chart: Forms flow.

m. The invoice, having been approved by purchasing for payment, is sent to the accounting department, where the amount to be paid is entered into the accounts receivable ledger. The invoice is filed by the accounting department.

Systems Flow Chart: Task-Oriented

A task-oriented systems flow chart is one that concentrates on the logical and chronological sequence of events in accomplishing some task. Figure 5–6 illustrates a systems flow chart that describes the steps to be

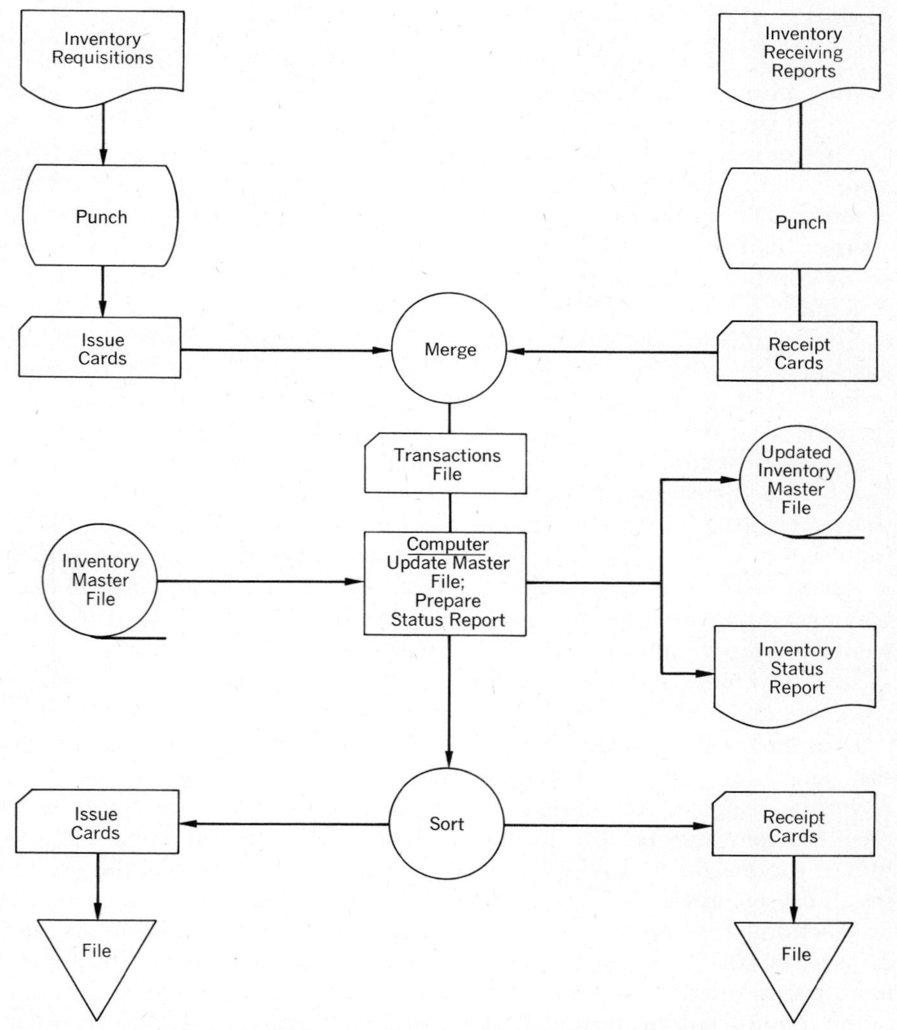

Figure 5–6. Systems flow chart: Inventory file updating and status report.

taken in updating a file of inventory records and producing a periodic inventory status report. Inventory issues and receipts cards are punched from requisition and receiving forms. These two sets of cards are then merged into a complete transactions file for the period that is made available to a computer, along with the inventory master file, which is maintained on magnetic tape. The computer uses the current transactions data to bring the inventory records on the tape up to date and also produces a report that specifies the status of the inventory. The transactions cards are separated into issues and receipts files and stored.

Program Flow Chart, or Block Diagram

Electronic computers do work in response to a set of instructions stored in the computer's memory. This set of instructions is known as a *program* and the persons who write the instructions are known as *programmers.* The systems flow chart in Figure 5–6 indicates, among other things, that a computer is used to update the inventory master file and to produce the inventory status report. The computer does these things in response to a set of instructions written by a programmer and stored in the memory of the computer, using techniques that will be described in detail later in this book. In the writing of the program, the programmer will make use of a fundamental tool of programming, the *program flow chart*, or *block diagram.* This document shows the logical sequence of steps that the computer system must perform in order to accomplish the task desired. Figure 5–7 shows a block diagram that depicts these steps. First, the heading of the inventory status report is written out on a printing device attached to the computer. The computer then reads the cards for the first transaction (the receipts and issues cards for one inventory item). Following this, an inventory record is read from the master inventory file, which is stored sequentially according to inventory item number on a reel of magnetic tape mounted on a device somewhat like a tape recorder attached to the computer. Since the inventory master file is arranged in ascending order, the computer will compare the number of the master record read with the item number of the transactions card just read. If the number of the transactions card is higher, then the appropriate inventory master record is further along the magnetic tape and another tape record is read and the comparison done again. This process continues until the item number on the transactions card is sensed to be equal to that of the master file. When this takes place, the updating of the master inventory record is initiated. If it should happen that the number on the transactions card was less than that just read from the master file, the transaction file was not properly in sequence and an error routing to handle this situation—to stop while an operator adjusts the files, or some other action—will be initiated. When the transactions item number and the master file item number are the same, then the inventory receipts for

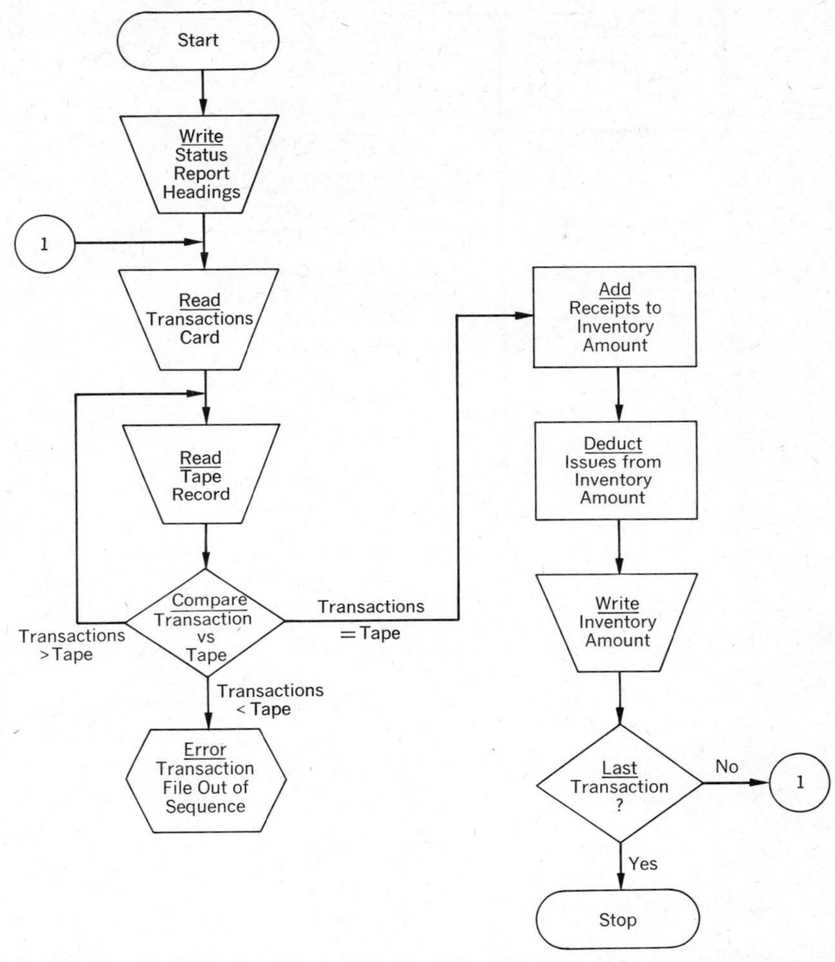

Figure 5–7. Program flow chart or block diagram for inventory file updating and status report.

the period of that item are added to the total inventory on hand figure, which is part of the inventory record, and the issues of that inventory item are deducted. The new inventory amount is written out on the report together with the inventory item number, and the card reader device is tested by the computer to determine if there are more transactions to process. If there are, then the program branches back to an instruction, which causes another set of transactions cards to be read. The *connector* numbered 1 indicates where control of the program is to transfer if the last transaction card has not been read and processed. If the last transaction card has been processed, the computer halts, and the updated

Symbol	
	Processing A group of program instructions which perform a processing function of the program.
	Input/Output Any function of an input/output device (making information available for processing, recording processing information, tape positioning, etc.).
	Decision The decision function used to document points in the program where a branch to alternate paths is possible based upon variable conditions.
	Program Modification An instruction or group of instructions which changes the program.
	Predefined Process A group of operations not detailed in the particular set of flowcharts.
	Terminal The beginning, end, or a point of interruption in a program.
	Connector An entry from, or an exit to, another part of the program flowchart.
	Offpage Connector A connector used instead of the connector symbol to designate entry to or exit from a page.
	Flow Direction The direction of processing or data flow.
Supplementary Symbol for System and Program Flowcharts	
	Annotation The addition of descriptive comments or explanatory notes as clarification.

Figure 5–8. Program flow chart or block diagram symbols.

master tape and inventory status report may be removed from the computer system.

Figure 5–8 shows the symbols typically used in program flow charting. Documentation in the form of flow charts serves two major purposes in systems analysis and design. First, as in the case, particularly, of procedural and forms flow charts, they serve as an important tool of analysis. Second, all such flow charts serve as records to be used to determine how things have been done in the past. In the case of block-diagramming, for example, it is extremely important that the programs written for computer execution be documented in such a manner that another programmer or a systems analyst who may not be an expert programmer can examine them and determine exactly what is taking place. The reason for this requirement stems from the frequent necessity to modify programs to satisfy different information requirements of the information system. Programmers, being in great demand, tend to have a high turnover rate in data processing installations; that is, they tend to change jobs rapidly as promotions and other opportunities are offered. For this reason, a program written today and needing modification in a few months must be understandable to programmers who were not involved in its original writing. The block diagram together with the coding of the program in the programming language used make up this essential documentation. Many computer installations have been plagued with inadequate program documentation resulting in substantial duplicated effort in rewriting programs that cannot be understood even by the programmer who wrote it and in considerable effort expended to analyze programs. Documentation of programs becomes even more vital when new computer equipment is installed. This almost always involves some reprogramming effort. Rewriting programs from one language to another or modifying the original programs in the original language in order that they may be executed on new computing equipment is impossible without proper documentation.

The Economics of Information

Information, as used by a business organization, is a resource, one which is used in a way that hopefully maximizes the organization's use of other resources—raw materials, labor, and physical facilities—in such a way that the goals of the organization are achieved in the most efficient manner. Like the other resources available to the organization, information is not a free commodity. In determining whether or not to employ a particular type of resource—a new raw material, or a new machine, for example—the business organization asks if the additional benefits it expects to reap from the use of this resource will exceed the additional costs of making the new resource available for use. Economists like to consider the marginal costs and the marginal utility of goods and services used by businesses and consumers. They define the marginal costs of a good or service as the additional cost to the consumer of one more unit of the good or service. Marginal utility is defined as the additional utility or usefulness as measured in some quantitative manner of the goods or services being consumed. Viewing economic goods and services from this marginal analysis viewpoint allows economists to develop certain rules of economic behavior. The most significant of these for our discussion here is the rule that states that consumption of a good or service will increase in units per time period until the marginal cost of the last economic good or service used is just equal to the marginal utility of that good or service.

What this means to those who are interested in the economic aspects of information systems is this. Information, as an economic good used by business organizations, can be made available to the organization at some cost. A little information is of great use to an organization. As more and more information becomes available, the organization finds it increasingly difficult to make as much use of it as was possible with the first few items of data. Thus, as the amount of information available to an organization increases, the usefulness of each additional unit of information decreases —that is, the utility of additional information decreases as more and more information becomes available. It is possible for a business organization to have more information than it can use. As consumers, we experience the same sort of thing. When consuming a good or service, the more we have of something, the less value additional units of that good or service have for us. One automobile may be very valuable to us and we may be willing to spend a great deal for it. Another automobile is of less value as a second car to us than the first was, the third even less valuable and it may happen that we would rather pay *not* to own a fourth automobile just to avoid the maintenance and insurance expense in supporting it.

On the other hand, while the usefulness of information decreases for an organization as more and more information becomes available, the cost of making more and more information available increases with each additional unit of information provided. The marginal costs of information increase as more information is produced. Determining the amount of information to be generated by an information system, then, becomes a balancing act. As information is provided in increasing quantities to the organization, its marginal costs rise while its marginal utility decreases. The optimal amount of information for an information system to provide will be that amount where the additional costs of one more unit of information are just equal to the additional monetary value of the utility of that information. Any amount of information greater than this will cost more than the utility gained will be worth. Any less than this will cost less than its usefulness will justify, and the organization will be induced to increase its demands for information. Economists are fond of preparing graphs of phenomena like this; such a graph is shown in Figure 5–9. This graph indicates that as the amount of information provided by the information system increases, the marginal cost of information increases and the marginal utility of the information decreases. The marginal cost and marginal utility lines intersect at the amount of information at which the marginal costs and marginal utilities are equal. Providing more or less than this amount of information will either provide more or less information than can be economically justified.

One of the most important tasks for the systems analyst as he relates to the information system is determining the optimal amount of information to provide the organization. While theoretically this is simply a matter of equalizing the marginal utilities and costs of information as discussed above, it is almost impossible to do this in any practical sense. Evaluating the cost of information can be done today with some accuracy, although it is a rare business organization that has taken the trouble to do so. Evaluating the utility of the information in dollars and cents terms is very diffi-

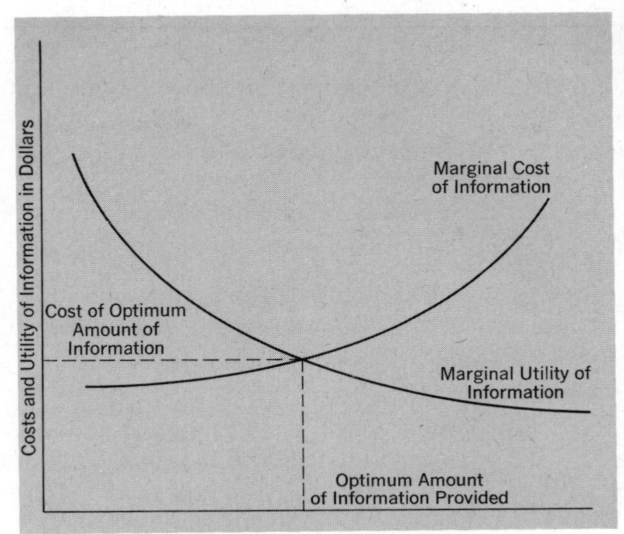

Figure 5–9. Marginal analysis of information costs and utilities.

cult, if not impossible. Despite the difficulties of applying marginal analysis to the determination of information availability to organizations, the theoretical framework upon which the technique depends still can serve as a guideline to those who must wrestle with this problem. Donald V. Etz of the National Cash Register Company, writing in *Datamation*, a professional journal of data processing, has this to say:

> At one time it may have been enough to announce, "I have a computer for sale," to have immediately a backlog of orders. But the phase soon passed, as real competition entered the picture. NCR was among the first to recognize the need to offer data processing systems, not mere computing hardware. But even this phase has nearly run its course. It is no longer enough to promise, "My system will provide you with hourly reports on your business, broken down by every permutation and combination of information category—and do it at less cost than my competitor's system." The manager, facing a growing mountain of paperwork, may well reply, as did the woman with 10 children to the readership surveyor: "Who reads?" Specifically, his questions may be: "Will I be able to assimilate and use all the information your system offers me? Will the decisions I am able to base on your EDP [Electronic Data Processing] system's information be sufficiently more profitable than those I am now making, without the benefit of this information, to justify the cost of your system?"[3]

[3] Donald V. Etz, "The Marginal Utility of Information," *Datamation*, August, 1965.

Questions

1. Explain the three stages incumbent on development of effective systems.
2. Discuss the way new systems might affect the business organization.
3. What is *information retrieval?*
4. How is indexing significantly related to information retrieval?
5. How are work distribution charts useful?
6. Explain and compare three different charting techniques.
7. What is the difference between a systems flow chart and a block diagram?
8. Why is documentation of computer programs valuable to an organization?
9. Discuss the concept: Information is an economic good.
10. What is the relationship between the marginal cost and marginal utility of information?

6

Information Science: A New Profession

The Beginnings of Automated Data Processing

Why must men count? How have men counted in the past and how do they count now? How did we get where we are, and for that matter, where are we? The Neanderthal Man's survival simply depended upon whether he was stronger or more clever than others living in the predatory fashion of society in those days. He simply fought the elements. He did not trade and he did not bother to keep records. However, as families or tribes began to form, men were driven by necessity to keep some sort of records. Perhaps, men started counting by stacking rocks or making tally marks on bark or hides. Eventually, they developed a system for counting. Probably because we have ten fingers, we now use a base ten system. Suppose we look at the admissible marks in our number system—0, 1, 2, 3, 4, 5, 6, 7, 8, and 9. Let's call them digits. We can count by this system, keeping a record of our tally marks. When we reach the highest admissible mark, we simply move over one column and indicate by a mark at what level we are in our system. For example, a 1 and a 0 (or "ten") indicate we have cycled through our total set of admissible marks one time and no more. Or, a 1 and 1 ("eleven") indicate we have cycled through our set of marks once with one left over. A 2 and a 2 indicate we have cycled through our set of marks twice with two left over, and so on. Simple? Of course. You could develop other systems of counting using different numbers of admissible marks and various number bases, and, probably, we would use such a system if we had other than ten fingers. Our point here is that anything once clearly explained becomes obvious. However, when something is unknown, we have to wait for its discovery to understand its simplicity. Keeping this in mind, let us look at the development of data processing into what we can now call information science.

Historically, as families and tribes grew, man was forced to calculate and keep records. He might have tied knots in a rope, or perhaps placed beads on a grooved board, which he called a *counter*. In any case, calculating and the keeping of records existed ages before history was formally recorded. For example, the abacus, a device using beads to represent decimal numbers, has been in use for some 2,000 years. Even today, it is more widely used than any other type of calculator. Babylonian records exist as far back as 4500 B.C. indicating that scribes recorded sales contracts on clay tablets in the commercial activities of that era. This method was improved significantly with the Egyptian development of papyrus and the calmus. Papyrus is a "paper" made by taking thin sheets of the bark of a reed plant and glueing them together. The calmus was a pointed pen also made from a reed. Actually, it is not known when these writing materials were developed. They could possibly antedate the Babylonian clay tablets. Later developments included improvements in writing media, such as parchment and, eventually, paper. Interestingly enough, paper did not replace the use of parchment in England until about 1495.

We attribute the development of the first actual bookkeeping system and the establishment of a fixed monetary system to the Babylonian Empire. The Greeks contributed to the development of business with inventory control systems, "day books," and "ledgers," while the Athenians were the first to employ a system of auditing records to obtain accurate facts and discover pilferage. In the tenth century A.D., Henry I established the Office of the Exchequer, the earliest known accounting system in England. Its operation initially revolved around the Domesday Book, used to record the value of all taxable estates in England.

The use of "debits" and "credits" was a contribution of the Italians in the fourteenth century, and to them we attribute the double-entry bookkeeping system used today and studied in all accounting and bookkeeping courses.

Manual methods of data processing were developed and refined very early in history, as we have seen, but not much was done to increase processing speed and efficiency until the 1800's, at which time the modern era of mechanical, electromechanical and electronic techniques of data processing began.

In the early 1600's, the table approach to arithmetic functions was used by John Napier, a Scot. One could multiply on a device known as "Napier's Bones" in which the use of the carry was employed. During the same century, Blaise Pascal in Paris developed a numerical calculator using the ten-tooth wheel in what was the first mechanical adding machine. The calculator rotated in steps from 1 to 9 and had a carry lever. In the 1800's, Dor Eugene Felt developed Felt's "Macaroni Box" which was the forerunner of the comptometer of today. At about the same period of time, Joseph Marie Jacquard developed the first punched card machine, which was a loom used to weave intricate designs into cloth, and a few years later Burroughs developed a more sophisticated adding and listing machine. Some of these devices are shown in Figure 6–1. They were all mechanical and hand-operated but were significant stepping stones to modern technology.

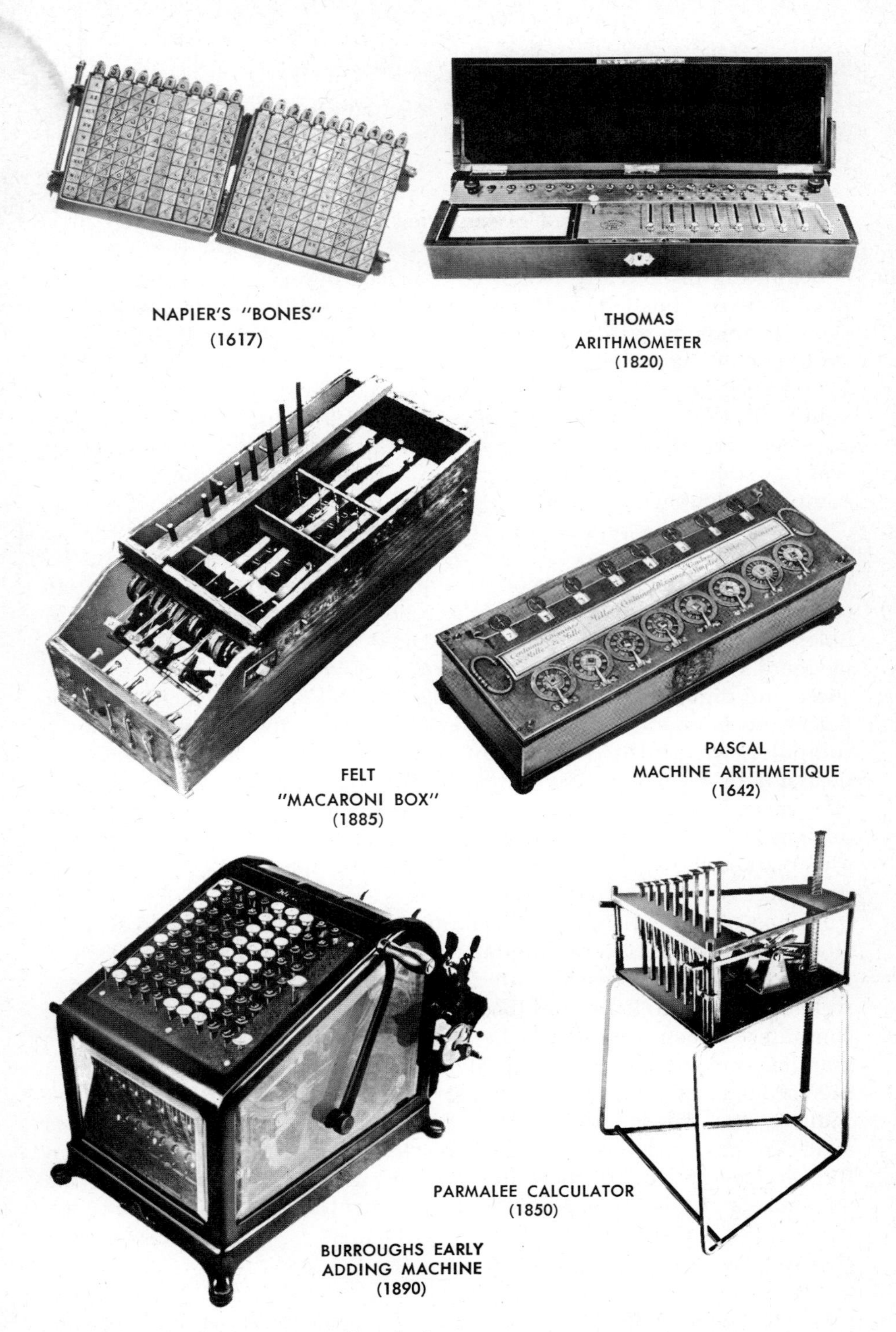

Figure 6–1. Early data processing devices.

The transition from man-operated mechanical accounting machines to electromechanical, punched card data processing occurred when Dr. Herman Hollerith, a Census Bureau employee, adopted Jacquard's principle—the system of a meaningful punched hole—and developed the first statistical machine actuated by punched cards. Between 1900 and 1915, punched card processing was adopted for use by over 300 companies.

Beginning in the early 1800's, but particularly while electromechanical processing of punched cards was becoming a reality, the embryo of computer technology was also beginning to develop. Charles P. Babbage, a professor of mathematics at Trinity College in England, developed the "Difference Engine," a digital machine designed to compute numerical values. The Difference Engine never really materialized practically, and Babbage turned his attention to the "Analytical Engine." This machine was intended to be the first completely automatic, general-purpose digital computer. Babbage died in 1871 without having perfected the machine.

Howard Aiken, a professor at Harvard, working with IBM from 1937 to 1944, was the first to successfully develop an electronic computer. Actually, this first computer, made up of 78 adding machines and desk calculators combined into one machine, was controlled with a roll of paper tape with holes similar to the player piano perforated roll. It combined the ideas of Jacquard's loom and Babbage's Difference Engine, resulting in the first successful digital computer. It was called the Mark 1. In 1946, ENIAC (for Electronic Numerical Integrator and Calculator), the second electronic computer, was finished at the University of Pennsylvania. ENIAC was designed by J. Presper Eckert and John W. Mauchly. Its primary purpose was special problem solution at the Aberdeen Proving Ground. These designers later developed UNIVAC (Universal Automatic Computer). This marked the birth of computer usage for business; UNIVAC I was the first successful commercial computer.

In the early 1950's, numerous computer manufacturers began to develop stored program, electronic digital computers, and in the late 1950's and 1960's, computer processing came fully into its own. Burroughs, Honeywell, Sperry Rand, RCA, and IBM have become well-known names in the computer industry, with IBM being the giant in the field. These firms manufacture computers ranging in size from small ones costing less than $100,000 to large computers valued at more than $5,000,000. The computer industry and data processing have pervaded large and small businesses alike. Today, if a company cannot afford its own computer, it can obtain the services of a data processing service bureau and reap many of the advantages of this important new management tool.

Computer Generations

Computer technology has grown in terms of "generations" of hardware characteristics and we speak of three generations of computers developed to the present time. The vacuum tube, limited memory computers produced by various manufacturers, were characteristic of the first generation and were primarily used in scientific applications. The second generation (1959–1964) encompassed the advent of large-scale, solid state components, microsecond random access, and large-scale memories. Both business and scientific applications were characteristic of this generation. Business applications generally were characterized by high volume input/output capabilities and minimal computations. Scientific applications included maximum computation, minimum input/output capability. There was much growth in terms of business applications during this period. Examples of second-generation computers include the IBM 1400 and 7000 series, the RCA 205 and Burroughs 5000.

During the development of the second-generation operating systems, programming languages were not standard. This made the job of training personnel harder and caused some problem in that a person gaining skill in a little-used hardware system had serious problems in terms of employment in an installation using the hardware of another manufacturer.

Third-generation computers such as IBM's System/360 are characterized by multiprogramming capability; time-sharing terminals; and increased main memory size. The 360, for example, is supposed to cover the "full circle" of needs of all users. It is appropriate for both business and scientific processing. Real-time processing is characteristic of third-generation computers. The necessity for batch processing has been significantly reduced.

Multiprogramming, that is, the execution of several programs in parallel rather than serial fashion as in the past, and multiprocessing by several interconnected processors using an array of peripheral equipment to handle a number of simultaneous jobs are examples of benefits to be gained in the third generation. Arithmetic units are now faster and microelectronics has provided substantially smaller circuits. Mass production of this type of circuit will reduce its previously prohibitive manufacturing costs. This, coupled with greater reliability, extensive use of communications terminals, and mass storage devices, serves as a giant step forward in computer technology.

The general trend, then, is toward a single family line of hardware and away from the multitypes of similar systems of the second generation. Industry will probably continue to evolve and develop toward the total information system and information science will come to play an increasingly important role at all levels within the business organization.

Modern technology has changed the pace and state of the world. The visions of Jules Verne in his science fiction of 100 years ago have turned out to be less wondrous than the technological realities of today. The world has gone through what has been called the second industrial revolution.

The Current State of the Art

In the last couple of decades, we have become accustomed to hearing such terms as automation, computers, data processing, systems, information science, and other, even more exotic nomenclature. The technology that is developing to cope with the successes of the contemporary industrial revolution and the burgeoning population is presenting industry with a gigantic problem. We are involved in what might be called a state of creative destruction. New methods, products, and equipment have been developing so rapidly that, in some cases, devices are practically obsolete before they hit the marketplace. Small companies have exploded in terms of size, and large companies have had to attempt to compete efficiently in an era of an educated, cost-conscious consumer. Adapting business organization and personnel to new methods of keeping records up to date, of billing, producing goods, selling and buying raw materials has become a serious problem. Over the past couple of years, we have witnessed the concept of creative destruction in action in the simple swing of the pendulum away from extensive use of unit record or punched card data processing equipment as primary hardware to a computer technology with unit record hardware being used only as support. The IBM 360 Model 20, for example, which rents for slightly more than the standard unit record installation, gives full unit record installation capability plus the capability of a computer thrown in.

There has been, as a result of a burgeoning technology, a scramble toward the development of more effective processing techniques and

Figure 6–2. Second and third generation computer components. A second generation component is shown to the right, consisting of one transistor and contacts. The thimble (left) shows fifty thousand transistors and contacts of the third generation components.

efficient systems. The advent of computerized hardware has placed us in a technological revolution equivalent to the nineteenth-century industrial revolution. In 1966, the United States had 63 per cent of the 44,000 electronic computers installed throughout the world—some 28,500 computers. This is a phenomenal number considering that in 1956 there were less than 800 computers in this country. Also in 1966, $5.4 billion worth of equipment in terms of analog and digital computers was shipped around the world. The comparison is even more vivid when we consider that in 1955 the value of all of the computers manufactured in the world was less than $200 million.

The need for computer programmers will increase 250 per cent within the next six years. By 1970, it is predicted that the total market for computers will be over $10 billion. Figures for the last ten years show a steady $1 billion-a-year increase in annual investment in electronic computers. The year 1965, for example, showed an increase of $2.5 billion. At this rate, by 1980, the investment in computers will be $20 billion a year and by 1990, over $30 billion. By the end of the 1970's, the number of computer installations will, at the present growth rate, at least double.

This development has led to statements such as these made by Richard Brandon at a data processing conference in 1966:

1. An almost unbelievable shortage of competent data processing personnel exists in the areas of qualified managers, analysts, and programmers.

2. More than 40 per cent of all data processing installations in the United States are failures. Of these, more than 90 per cent survive by crisis.

3. No industry has taken a tool of such unparalleled power and used it so badly.

4. Data processing management personnel themselves are incompetent—as managers, not as technicians.

Strong statements? Yes. A condemnation? Not really. Recent technological growth has given industry the capability of having at its fingertips information for decision-making purposes that has been heretofore prohibitively costly to obtain. Also, the volume of input/output activities on a day-to-day basis has compounded the problem. Many organizations suffer the necessity of solving today's problem today. Thus, appropriate planning, systems analysis and methodology have been unskilled and haphazard though adequate in meeting the existing crisis.

Many problems exist. Poor long-term planning, abominable documentation because of lack of time or trained staff, and pressures of day-to-day business activity are building monstrous problems with which industry must cope and for which it must find a solution. Differentiation in types of personnel, specialization, and more adequate training are helping to solve these problems. A vivid example of the problem is provided by the personnel hired by an uneducated management to aid in solving its problems. For example, there is a significant difference between a hardware-oriented systems analyst and a general systems analyst. This has been recognized, much to the dismay of many organizations and is a distinction that has become crucial in the past few years. The procedures analyst we knew during the 1940's and 1950's is not the hardware analyst needed today. The problems generated in many installations today were caused by the "theoretical" analyst who, instead of staying in his own field, attempted to bridge the hardware gap without proper training. This condition, in the past, was aggravated by management ignorance regarding the necessary qualifications of hardware data processing personnel. Stuffing in of this type of personnel was simply an attempt to fill the void. Management is now beginning to recognize the need for specialization and has become aware that an analyst competent to work with planning systems such as PERT or CPM is not necessarily the same type of analyst necessary for planning and scheduling hardware operations, and that the hardware analyst is not necessarily the best physical procedures man.

The above illustrates only one problem. We face shortages of competent programmers, operators, technicians, and a multitude of support personnel. All of this has brought about a new profession which we choose to call, for lack of a better term, *information science.*

Information Science as a New Profession

Because of the technological and organizational changes discussed earlier, a new group of occupational or professional areas has developed. Persons working in these areas deal with data information, and the systems and hardware that process and transmit information throughout the organization. Usually, these persons are known as data processors.

The selection and assignment of these data processing personnel is one of management's most difficult problems. Figure 6–3 depicts a basic hierarchy of data processing personnel, and Figure 6–4 shows the paths that might be followed in terms of one's progression in the field. The following sections analyze some of the personnel areas we have been discussing: hardware systems analysts, programmers, and technicians, especially operators. We will not here go into a discussion of support personnel such as customer engineers, sales representatives, and other equipment manufacturers' personnel. Neither will we go into management's point of view, except to say that it is incumbent on management to understand all types of personnel qualifications in depth if it is to properly perform its function. Also, management must have enough understanding of hardware and its capabilities to know what to expect of it and whom to hire in terms of qualifications to operate the equipment.

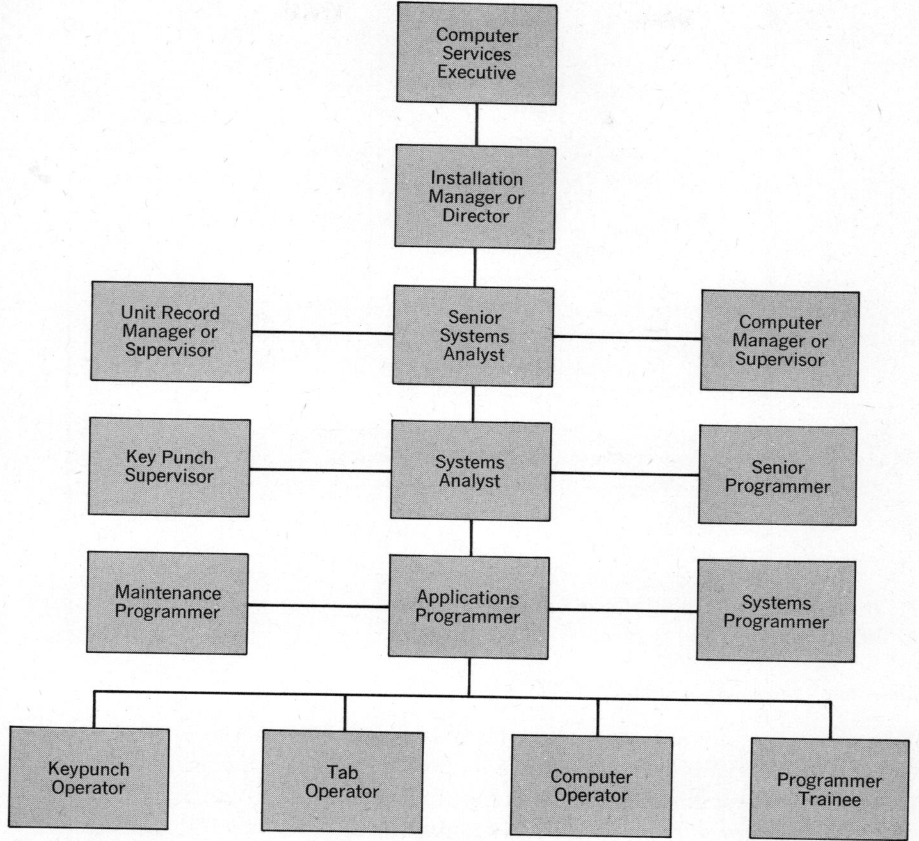

Figure 6–3. Hierarchy of data processing personnel.

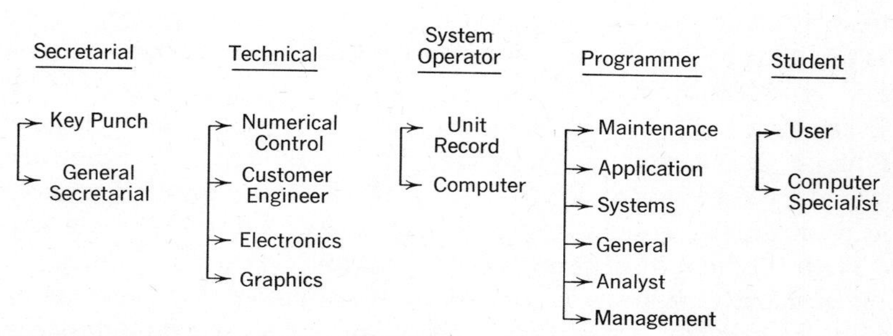

Figure 6–4. Path of achievement in data processing.

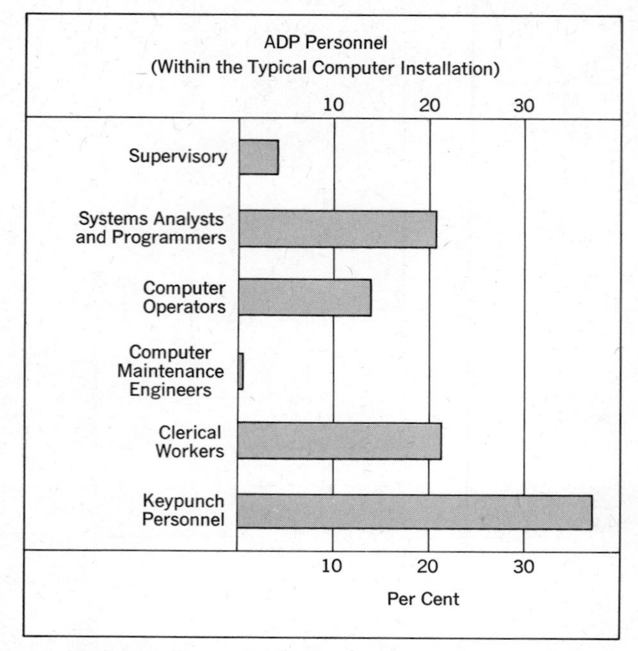

Figure 6–5. Distribution of personnel in a typical organization. (Courtesy, Bureau of Labor Statistics.)

THE SYSTEMS ANALYST

In many organizations, a supervisor is plagued by paperwork; he must direct and train his people, handle much routine work himself, have conferences and meetings, and make numerous emergency decisions. An effective supervisor can promote teamwork and improved performance at individual work stations. His aims are to make the work go more smoothly, decrease costs, educate people to do their jobs better, and implement more effective control over operations. In these cases, the supervisor is performing a systems function within his department. However, where a company is large and its activities varied, systems efficiency is today being studied and improved by what has come to be called *systems analysts.*

It is the job of the systems analyst to tie together the work of the various departments and to aid in accomplishing the above-mentioned economies for the total organization through a coordinated effort with the supervisors. With the advent of computer technology, those analysts who have specialized hardware skills work with the supervisors in systems areas where the supervisor is in the position of a user of data processing services. It is the job of the analyst to help the supervisor understand the problem, to define that problem so that it is more effectively applicable to data processing hardware solutions, and to assure that greater information service is provided.

In his role, the analyst must gather facts, analyze existing procedures, define problems, and make recommendations for improved systems or revised operations. As part of this he must help the functional departments of the business by determining the feasibility of new computer applications. The job of the hardware analyst is not conceptually different from the general analyst in definition, but he must bring to it distinct expertise in hardware operation.

The hardware-oriented analyst must have insight into sophisticated use of equipment, a management sense in terms of understanding organizational goals, imagination, and a good ability to communicate. All of these attributes must be pulled together and implemented with proposals and explanations documented in great detail. Of course, this is a general profile, and recognizing the existence of human frailties, management must use its own expertise in placing personnel into these positions. Improper assignment can breed much harm and dissension in the company. This is especially true since many departments may previously have had little service in terms of electronic or automated information systems. In some companies, one can find supervisors who are openly hostile to automated data processing of any kind.

PROGRAMMERS

There are more than 100,000 personnel engaged in computer programming in the United States today, and within the next ten years, that number will probably double. Again, since there are many types of programmers, we will pursue a general definition of computer programmer.

The programmer works with the systems analyst in reviewing the problem in terms of its solution by the hardware system. The programmer prepares systems flow charts and block diagrams, then codes and "debugs" programs to make them operational. Senior programmers generally analyze problems outlined by the systems analyst in terms of detailed equipment requirements and capabilities. They may also prepare instruction sheets to guide operators during production runs, and work on and evaluate existing programs with an eye to changes in equipment configurations or increased efficiency and maintenance.

Long hours and great attention to detail are required of programmers. The logic of the problem must be understood with all of its possible contingencies, and programmers are constantly challenged to develop programs that use the hardware with the optimum efficiency during actual production runs.

Many companies have *maintenance programmers* who spend most of their time modifying and maintaining existing programs. These companies will also have *application programmers* who are continually working on new and often specialized applications.

There is no specific number of programmers who might work in a company of a given size or on a given piece of computer hardware. A company may have from one to one hundred programmers on its staff. However, one thing common to medium-sized companies with 500 or fewer employees and using a medium-sized computer costing from $50,000 to $100,000 per year is this: the systems analysts must double in brass in terms of breadth of skill. They must, along with being able to define the problems effectively, get down to the nuts and bolts of making sure the programs are efficiently operational. In fact, there is a growing demand for *programmer analysts* who have the technical knowledge to analyze and write computer programs and who also have the responsiblity of overseeing the operation of the entire information system.

Systems Programmers

A *systems programmer* is one whose responsibility lies with maintaining the computer system's generalized operating programs and operating systems or "software" as these programs are called. An operating system is a complex of computer programs that serve the purpose of increasing the effectiveness of the computer system's operation. Operating systems, which will have a remarkably important role to play in third-generation computers, will be discussed in a later chapter of this book.

Operators

Machine operators generally fall into two basic categories: the career operator who has no aspirations to become an analyst or programmer and the operator who uses his operator's job as an entry level job for advancement. Operators manipulate control switches, control panels, storage devices, printers, readers, and punches as required by particular applications. They may work with auxiliary equipment, loading tape or magnetic disk packs according to specific instructions, and in card installations are proficient in card handling and processing techniques. They may have skill in observation of control panel lights with the ability to report deviations from standard operations and provide elementary program error diagnostics. In many cases, operators also assist in updating and maintaining operating records.

Becoming an accomplished person in any of the occupations we have discussed here is no small task in an era which, since the first space capsule was launched, has apparently operated on the premise that if it works, it is obsolete. New hardware, new problem-solving approaches, rapidly increasing software availability, increased sophistication of applications, and pressures from more sophisticated users for more and more service make it necessary for data processing personnel to work continually to maintain skills current with the existing technology.

Questions

1. Discuss the sequence of events that were most significant in the development of modern data processing technology.
2. What are the differences between the various computer generations?
3. What is the function of the systems analyst?
4. Explain various types of programming employment opportunities.
5. Discuss the relationship of technology, technicians, and management personnel in terms of today's industrialization.
6. What is meant by the concept of creative destruction?
7. What is meant by the term *total information system?*
8. What do you consider as the three major events contributing to the advent of modern computer systems?
9. Develop a definition of the term *information science.*
10. What is different about the third-generation of computer systems?
11. What considerations are implicit in determining whether upgrading of a company's hardware is warranted?

Part II

Unit Record Information Systems

7

Unit Record Data Processing

The Unit Record

As we have seen, data processing departments operating within the organizational structure apply specialized techniques of gathering, recording, classifying, sorting, summarizing, calculating, and communicating to the clerical routine entailed in the manipulation of data. In this perspective, data processing becomes the heart of the information system. There are several ways in which the techniques of data processing are applied: manually, mechanically, electromechanically, and electronically. Among the aims of the information system, in general, and of data processing, in particular, are speed of operation, elimination of duplication, multifunction usage of data, and efficient storage of data—all within a cost framework that the organization can afford. Our conceptual analysis of what data processing is and what it does can be meaningful only in terms of the tools employed. One such tool is the unit record, the punched card.

Punched cards are the basic element in a type of data processing system known as *unit record*, or *electromechanical*, data processing. A *record* is a body of data concerning some logical entity relating to the organization. An employee record, for example, is a body of data concerning such an entity—an employee. So are inventory records and customer records. A large business organization will maintain records for many different entities and purposes. A *unit* record is data concerning an entity contained in one physical unit of a particular medium—say, a piece of paper, a ledger card, or, of particular interest here, a punched card. This one card, into which data has been recorded as punched holes, can then be used to produce a variety of different reports and calculations involving information about this logical entity. In the chapters dealing with electronic data processing, you will encounter the term *logical record.* A logical record is a complete record of a logical entity. A unit record, on the other hand, may or may not be a complete record, but will contain data recorded on one unit of the medium, i.e., one punched card.

The use of punched cards goes back as far as 1801 when Jacquard used them in his automatic loom to control the colors of thread in the weaving process. In the 1880's a statistician named Herman Hollerith, an employee of the U.S. Census Bureau, developed a machine that used cards into which data were recorded in the form of punched holes. These cards were used to tabulate information needed for the annual census. This early punched card machine offered such an improvement over the former tabulating techniques used by the Census Bureau that the amount of time necessary to complete the job was reduced from twelve to eight years — an important reduction in view of the Constitutional requirement to take a census every *ten* years! In 1907, James Powers developed another type of punched card system, which was used in the 1910 census. In 1930, an Englishman named Perkins patented the idea of coding information around the edges of a card, a system you may have heard of as the "key-sort" system. Figure 7–1 shows the three basic types of punched cards used in the systems mentioned here. Today IBM uses the Hollerith-type punched card, Remington Rand Division of Sperry Rand uses the Powers system, and Royal-McBee is the major user of the Perkins edge-notched system.

A card into which data have been punched can cause many functions to be performed. Figure 7–2 indicates the usefulness of this basic data processing tool. If the punched hole will do all these things for us, we can deduce that its singular advantage is in providing us with the ability to perform a multitude of tasks from a hole that has only been punched once. Thus, the distinct advantage of punched card or unit record processing is the ability to "write it once," sometimes called the "integrated data processing" approach. In fact, if we look more closely, we can see only three fundamental activities that can be performed on data. We can record (punch or write); re-record; and reconstruct (calculate). These activities are all that are performed in what we have called the basic principles of data processing — gathering, recording, classifying, sorting, summarizing, calculating, and communicating.

Recognizing this, specific equipment has been developed which together will perform all of the above operations, each performing its specific function(s) and when brought together forming a bank of unit record equipment that will perform all of the clerical activities required for paperwork processing in the typical data processing installation. This equipment is known as tabulating (Tab), or electronic accounting machine (EAM), equipment, or unit record equipment. This installation is different from a computer installation, even though the computer may use punched cards for processing. The difference lies in the ways in which the pieces of equipment perform their tasks. Computers are *primarily electronic* devices although they do employ some mechanical and electrical parts. Unit record equipment is *primarily mechanical and electrical,* although here, too, some overlap exists into electronic functions. Whereas a unit

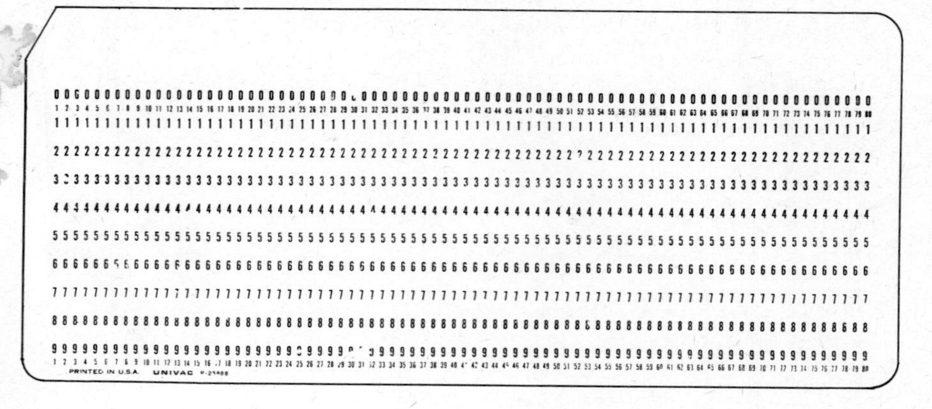

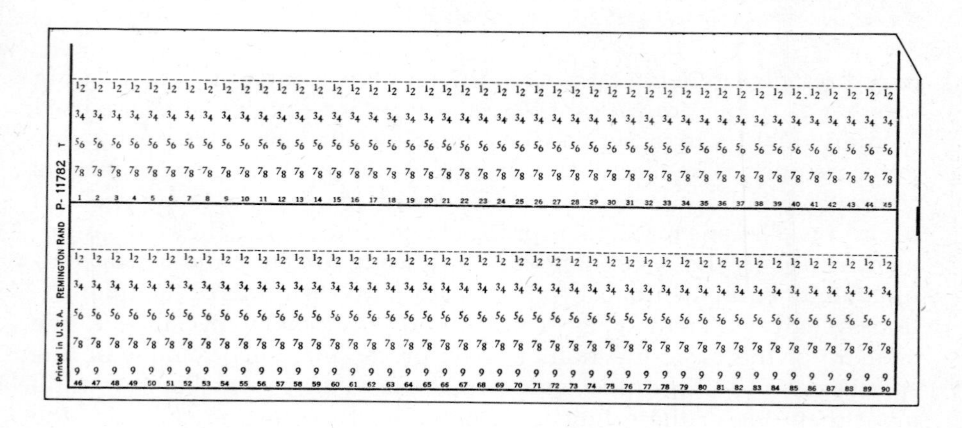

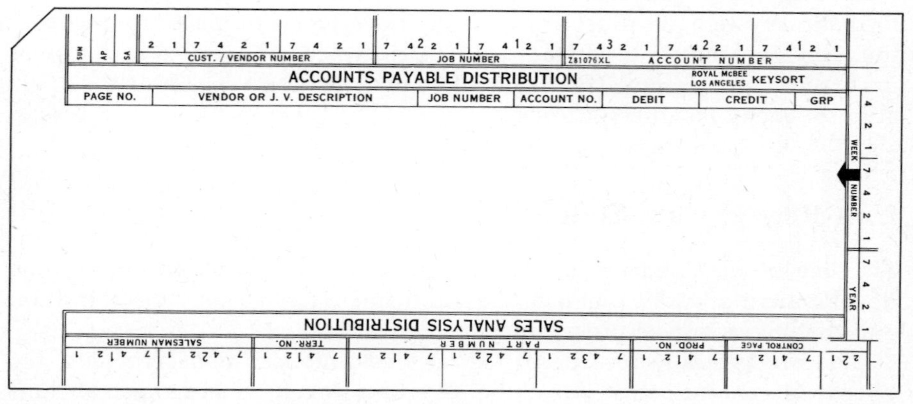

Figure 7–1. Three types of punched cards.

What the
Punched Hole Will Do

1 It will add itself to something else.
2 It will subtract itself from something else.
3 It will multiply itself by something else.
4 It will divide itself into something else.
5 It will list itself.
6 It will reproduce itself.
7 It will classify itself.
8 It will select itself.
9 It will print itself on the IBM card.
10 It will produce an automatic balance forward.
11 It will file itself.
12 It will post itself.
13 It will reproduce and print itself on the end of a card.
14 It will be punched from a pencil mark on the card.
15 It will cause a total to be printed.
16 It will compare itself to something else.
17 It will cause a form to feed to a predetermined position, or to be ejected automatically, or to space from one position to another.

Figure 7–2. Functions of the IBM punched cards. *(Courtesy, IBM)*

record *installation* involves several different types of equipment working together as a data processing system, unit record equipment is also used in individual units to support computer installations. A company may purchase only those machines that it feels will act as support in using its computer in an optimum fashion. However, many firms today use unit record installations for all their processing activities. The choice of equipment is usually the result of a feasibility study to determine which combination of equipment most appropriately suits the needs of the information system. Different types of unit record equipment specialize in one or more of the basic functions of data processing. One example of this specialization is shown in Figure 7–3. Some of the equipment may fulfill more than one of these functions; however, the function shown is the basic application of each machine.

To understand how the unit record equipment is integrated into an information system, we must first consider how data is prepared for processing. Also, we must understand some principles common to all types of unit record equipment. Then we will be in a position to examine the operation of each machine specifically.

Unit Record Data Codes

The use of punched cards and the write-it-once principle require the development of codes that facilitate recording data in a condensed fashion and that allow logical processing.

Data are typically recorded in three basic modes: *alphabetic data*, the twenty-six characters of our alphabet and a dozen or more special characters such as dollar signs, commas, ampersands, and the like; *numeric*

Figure 7–3. IBM 188 collator. One of the specialized pieces of unit record equipment. *(Courtesy, IBM)*

data, the characters of the decimal number system; and *alphameric data*, which is a combination of alphabetic and numeric characters. Of particular significance is the character-oriented nature of these recording modes. Commercial data processing is primarily concerned with processing records of information. Each record is a group of characters arranged and grouped in meaningful ways. Characters are grouped together into *data fields.* A data field is a complete unit of information about the entity of which a record is being kept. An employee record, for example, may contain several fields of data: a field for the employee's name, another for his number, another for his pay rate, and so on. A record, then, is a group of data fields about some logical entity; a field is a group of characters which provide numeric values or alphabetic information; and a character is a number, a letter, or some special symbol.

Any data coding system used with punched cards must allow for use of the three data modes. In unit record processing, incidentally, numeric codes predominate.

The IBM Punched Card

Figure 7–4 shows an IBM punched card. The IBM card is divided into 80 vertical *columns* numbered 1–80 from left to right. Each column is divided into twelve *punching positions* or *rows*, which are designated as follows: the topmost row is the 12 row, followed by the 11 row, the 0 row, then the 1, 2, 3, 4, 5, 6, 7, 8, and 9 rows successively. The punching positions for the digits 0–9 can be seen on the card in the illustration and correspond to the numbers printed on the card. Because the top row of the card is called the 12 row, the top edge of the card is called the 12 edge. Because the row closest to the bottom of the card is the 9 row, the bottom edge of the card is called the 9 edge. Knowledge of terminology is important here because cards feed in the various machines in different ways. In one machine cards might feed 12 edge first, face up, while in another they might feed 9 edge first, face down. Occasionally, you will encounter cards with colored stripes on them, or with the corners cut. These markings are used for visual identification and facilitating effective handling, but they have no importance with respect to machine processing.

Each of the 80 columns on the card may accommodate a digit, an alphabetic character, or some special character. The coding scheme used in IBM punched cards, by far the most widely used in data processing today, is known as the Hollerith code. This code divides the alphabet into three parts, or *zones*, A–I, J–R and S–Z, as shown in Figure 7–4. An alphabetic

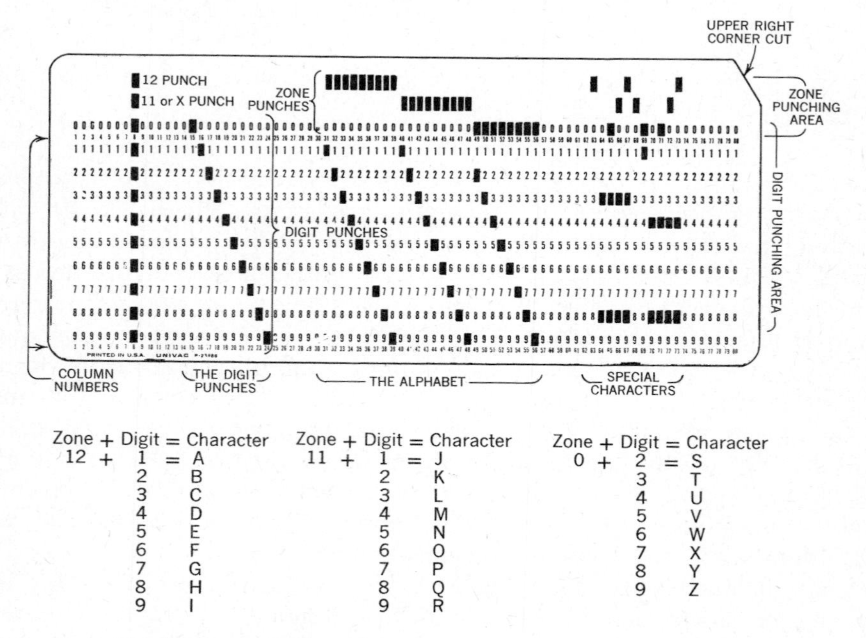

Figure 7–4. The IBM punched card.

character punched into a column of a card requires two punches, a zone punch (12, 11, or 0) indicating in which of the three zones the character is to be found and a digit punch determining the specific character within that zone. Thus, the letter M, for example, would require an 11 zone punch (indicating the second zone) and a 4 digit punch (the fourth character in that zone) in the same column; the letter A requires a 12 and a 1 (first zone, first character), an S, a 0, and a 2, and so forth. Probably, you will not want to memorize this code. However, because it is so widely used in data processing today and serves as the basis for other coding schemes, you should be able to quickly determine the Hollerith code for any alphabetic character. This can be done by visualizing the three zones of the alphabet and remembering the starting letters (and codes) of each zone: A (12–1), J (11–1), and S (0–2). Now, any character can be coded or encoded by counting up from one of these three starting points. A number in a column of a card may be represented by a single digit punch in a particular column. Figure 7–4 also shows the Hollerith combinations for alphabetical character representation. As you can see, it is possible to represent 80 characters of information on a single card. Generally, you will be working with groups, or *decks,* or cards and it becomes necessary in machine processing to mechanically distinguish between what we will call *master cards* and *detail cards.* For example, we might have a master card into which is punched a customer's name and address. This card may be followed in the deck by detail cards for that same customer each containing an order for merchandise placed by that customer. Unit record machines can distinguish certain cards or groups of cards because of identifying punches called *control punches*—in many cases, X punches that have been punched in the card. An X punch is an 11 punch in a particular column of a card which, in this case, would serve to distinguish a master card from a detail card.

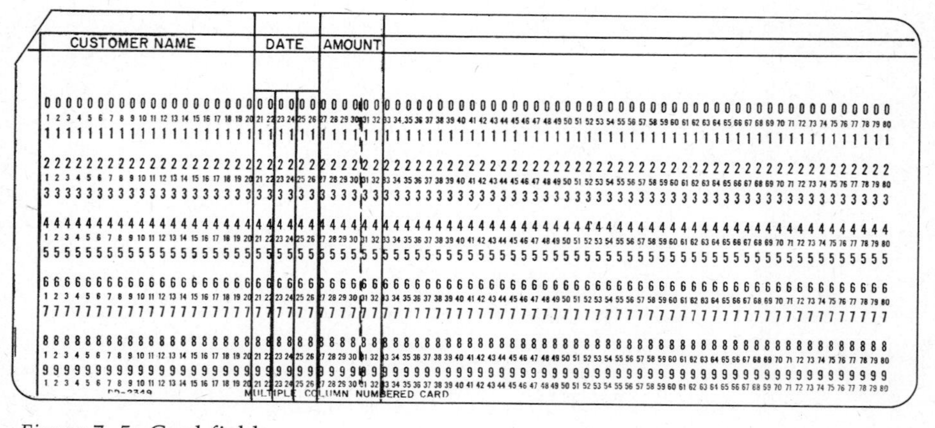

Figure 7–5. Card fields.

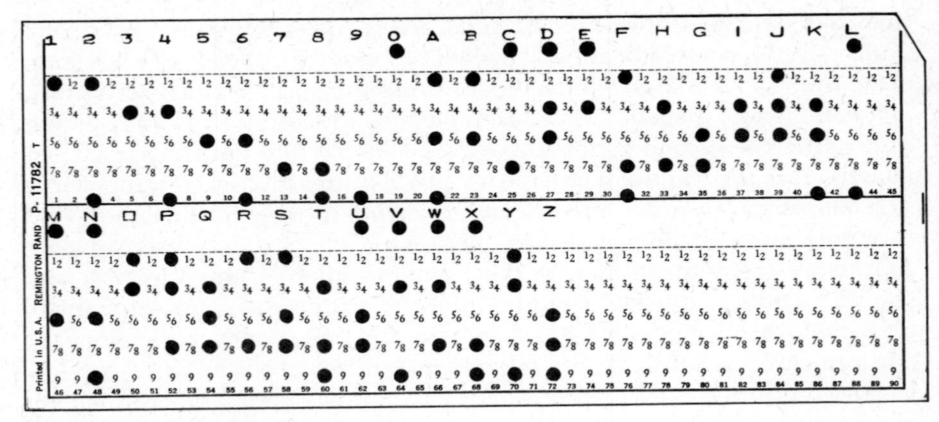

Figure 7–6. Remington Rand card.

Data may be punched in a card in one or more consecutive columns. These columns are called *fields.* A field may consist of one column to a maximum of 80 columns and is a group of columns set aside to be used for a specific purpose. The length of fields may be variable and depend on the length of the particular information to be included within them. Figure 7–5 clearly identifies a name field, date field, and amount field. A given field must be long enough to accommodate the largest number of characters which will be entered into it; when data requiring fewer characters than this are entered, blanks are left in the *high-order* or left-most positions of the field.

THE REMINGTON RAND CARD

The Remington Rand card, shown in Figure 7–6, is the same size and is made of the same paper as IBM cards. It uses round rather than rectangular holes and has 90 columns of information. Forty-five columns are arranged along the upper half of the card and 45 on the lower half. Each division has six rows, with odd numbers represented by a single hole in the proper row and the even numbers represented by two holes. Remington Rand cards are seldom found in data processing installations today and for this reason little time will be devoted to this system here.

ROYAL-MCBEE KEYSORT CARD

Another unit record system that has some specialized usefulness is the keysort system. This system makes use of cards into which data are recorded in the form of notches around the card edge and as small holes in the body of the card. One of these cards was shown in Figure 7–1. More consideration will be given this system at the end of this chapter with the discussion of manual methods of unit record data processing.

Advantages and Disadvantages of Unit Records

The punched card is based on the write-it-once principle. The use of the punched hole provides us with a means of increasing the utilization of data, gives us greater accuracy, and provides us with a permanent record of the activities performed.

Many distinct advantages other than these are gained from the use of punched cards: ease of assembly or reassembly for various tasks; easy recognition of data by machine or by an individual, particularly if the cards have been *interpreted*—that is, if the information punched in the card has also been *written* on the card; ease of storage; relatively low cost per unit of information; and applicability to use in many machines for many purposes. Punched cards are a very effective medium for data manipulation if recognition is taken of the limited amount of information that can be represented on a single unit record and if codes and fields are judiciously designed and used. However, care must be taken to insure that decks of cards remain intact. Cards are small and easy to lose and professional handling is a key factor in effective manipulation. Card stock is sensitive to moisture and extreme temperatures, or to dust. Therefore, control must be maintained in any installation to insure the proper physical condition of the cards for processing. In fact, effective card handling is a distinct sign of an effective data processor. Joggling decks appropriately and fanning cards before processing to eliminate sticking due to static electricity are important steps in preventing jams in the hardware.

IBM and Remington Rand cards are not compatible. However, the basic principles of data preparation, punching, and processing in terms of handling and machine control are fundamentally the same. We will examine some IBM equipment that fulfills the basic principles of unit record data processing. It must be kept in mind that understanding the principles and techniques of processing manipulation and handling is the important idea, not rote memorization of the abilities of the machines themselves. The remainder of this chapter discusses the means by which source data is punched into punched cards, how the resulting decks of data cards are placed in order, and some basic considerations of unit record processing equipment operation. The chapter to follow examines the methods by which unit record equipment is controlled or programmed.

Transcribing Written Records to Punched Cards

Before any manipulations in terms of adding, subtracting, dividing, multiplying, listing, reading, printing, summarizing, classifying, sorting, and so on, can take place, data must be properly and thoughtfully transcribed into punched holes. Basic to the transcription of these data is an

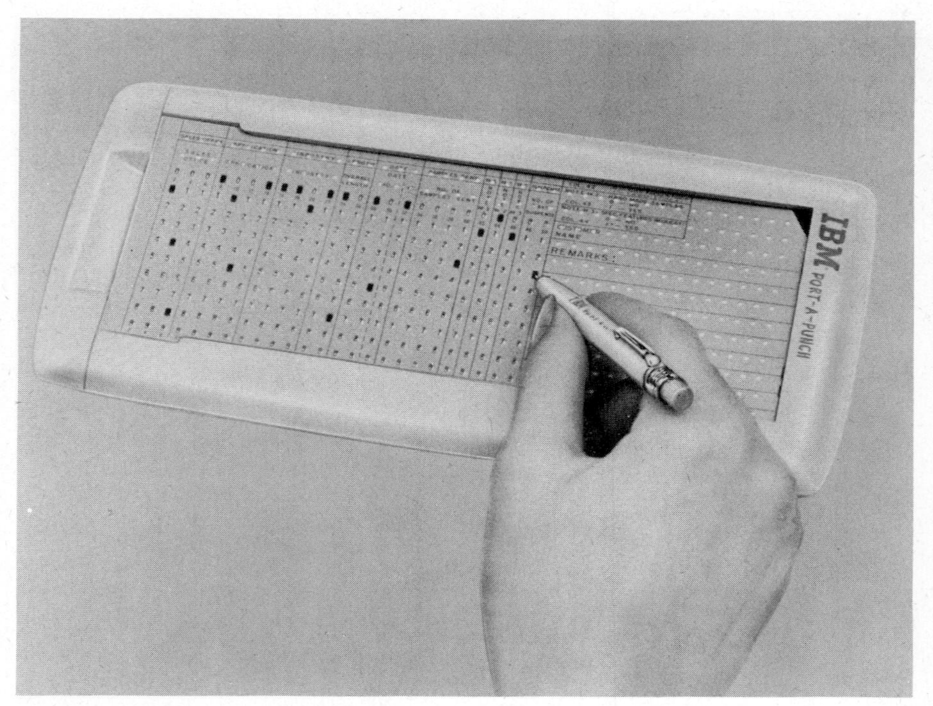

Figure 7–7. IBM Port-A-Punch device. *(Courtesy, IBM)*

understanding of your specific problem in terms of *constant data*, which is repetitive in nature, and *variable data*, which will be constantly changing in a particular application. We must know which data is to be manually punched into each card, which may be duplicated from one card to another, and which can be punched by machine into many cards.

Before a system can operate, it must have input. The input we are discussing here is the punched card. One way of transcribing data into punched cards might be with the IBM Port-A-Punch, a device used to manually poke out perforated holes in IBM cards one hole at a time. One of these is shown in Figure 7–7. Obviously, jobs requiring large volumes of cards preclude this method.

Two of the most commonly used card punch machines are the 024 and 026 card punches. The 026 is shown in Figure 7–8. The operation of both of these machines is basically the same, except that the 026 has a printing device that allows information punched into the card to be printed on the top edge of the card, whereas the 024 does not. There are two basic keyboards used on these card punches. The combination numeric and alphabetic keyboard in Figure 7–9 operates similarly to the keyboard of a typewriter for the alphabetic punching and a ten-key adding machine for numeric punching. The *numeric* keyboard is similar in set-up to the ten-key adding machine.

The basic punching mechanism of the card punch is the punch die. Associated with the keyboard is a set of twelve punch dies which provide for column-by-column punching of the zone and digit punches into the card.

As you can see in Figure 7–8, the keyboard is connected to the card punch by a cable that permits the operator to adjust it on the table for maximum comfort. In the upper righthand corner of the card punch is the *card hopper*, which may have a capacity of up to 500 cards. Cards are placed in this hopper face forward, 9 edge down, and are fed front card 9 edge first onto the punch bed. There are three card beds and two stations on the card punch. From right to left are the punch bed, then the punch station, the read bed, the read station, and the stacker bed, just below the stacker. In unit record equipment, cards are always fed from a hopper and after the appropriate operations have been performed, they wind up in a stacker. In the case of the card punch, cards are stacked 12 edge down, face up. A pressure plate holds them in position, and the last card punched

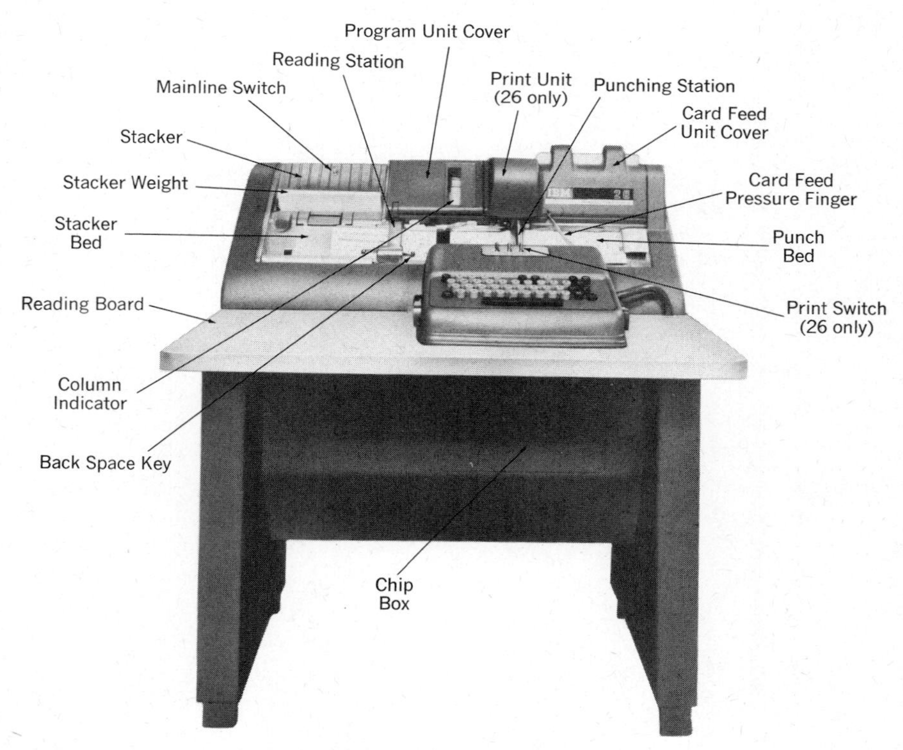

Figure 7–8. IBM 026 card punch. *(Courtesy, IBM)*

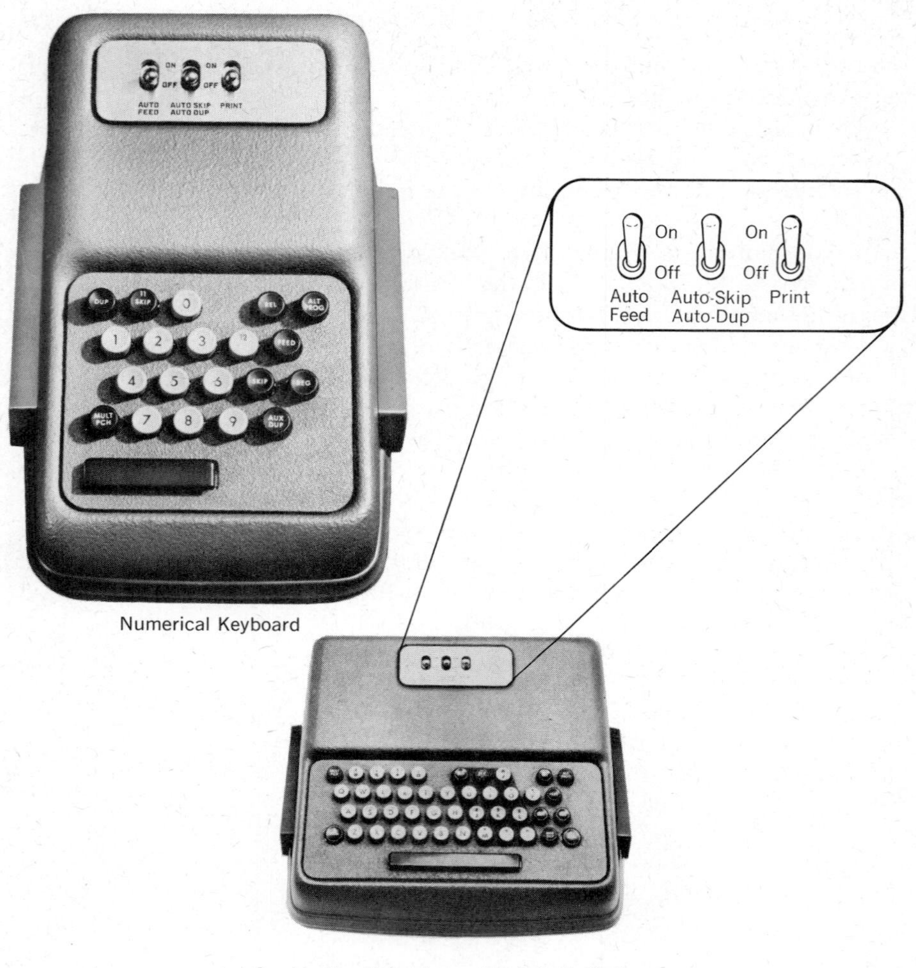

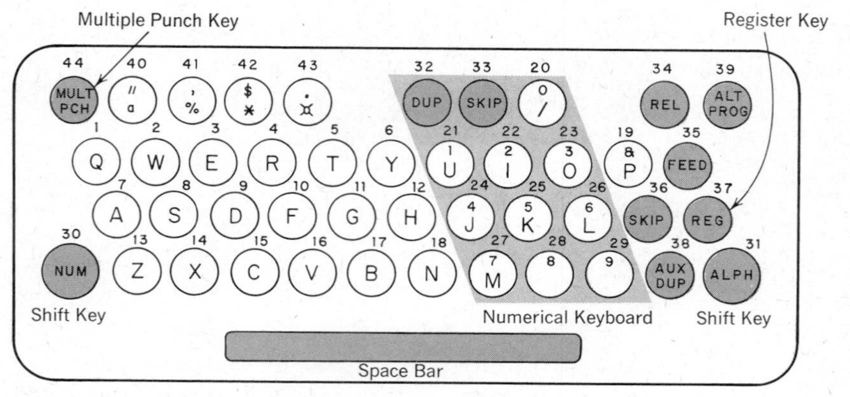

Figure 7–9. Card punch keyboards. *(Courtesy, IBM)*

winds up at the bottom of the stack. This way, the cards are stacked in the original sequence in which they were punched.

You will note the reading board onto which information can be conveniently placed for punching; the backspace key, which, as long as it is held down, backspaces cards at both stations in a column-for-column fashion; the chip box, which must be emptied periodically, and behind which are located the fuses. Also note the column indicator, which shows the next column to be punched. In the manual mode, the keyboard is in alphabetic shift. Therefore, if one wishes to punch a numeric character, he must hold down the numeric shift key.

The latest model of key punch manufactured by IBM is the Model 029. This key punch is quieter, faster on some automatic operations and has available an expanded character set to make it compatible with the character set used in the System/360 family of computer systems. Operation of the Model 029 Card Punch is essentially identical with the 024 and 026.

Manual Operation of the IBM Card Punch

In using the card punch, the first two cards must be fed by depression of the card feed key; others will then feed automatically, provided a card is properly registered at the punching station and the automatic feed switch is on. Punching takes place column for column from left to right in a serial fashion. When column 80 of a card passes the punching station, it moves across the read bed to the read station. That card registers at the read station simultaneously with a card at the punching station and another card is fed into the punch bed. The read and punch stations can operate in synchronization and there is an internal connection between them; thus, realizing that some information is repetitive from card to card, we can duplicate information from a card at the reading station to a card at the punching station by punching only the variable information and by duplicating information that we determine to be constant.

IBM Card Punch Operation Under Program Control

Under manual control, each punch requires depression of a key, or, in the case of duplication of information from one card at the read station to another at the punch station, the duplicate key must be held down until the appropriate number of columns have been duplicated. Under program control, operator efficiency is increased by devices for punching data automatically. The program unit in Figure 7–10 provides automatically for desired repetitive operations such as duplicating, skipping over columns, shifting from alphabetic to numeric and vice versa. Under program control star wheels are lowered so they make contact with the card. If a wheel falls through a punched hole, a circuit is created and specific action takes place.

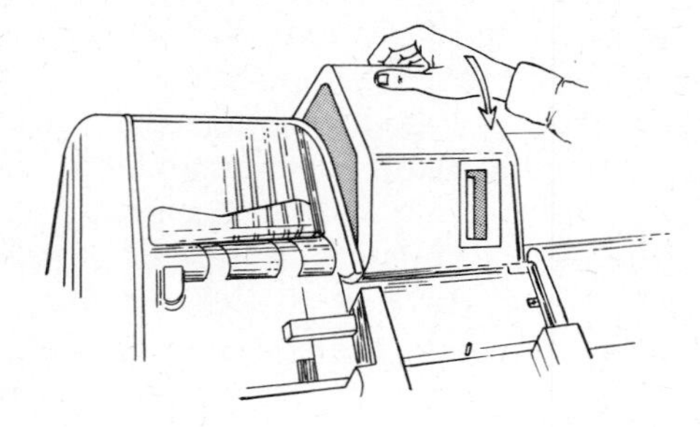

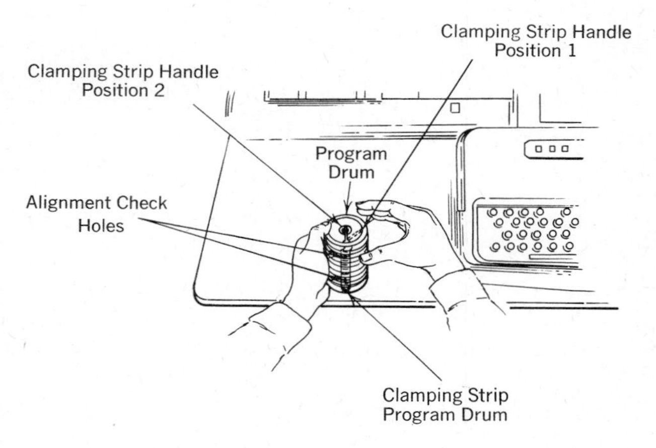

Figure 7–10. IBM card program unit and program drum (photo). *(Courtesy, IBM)*

Program Card

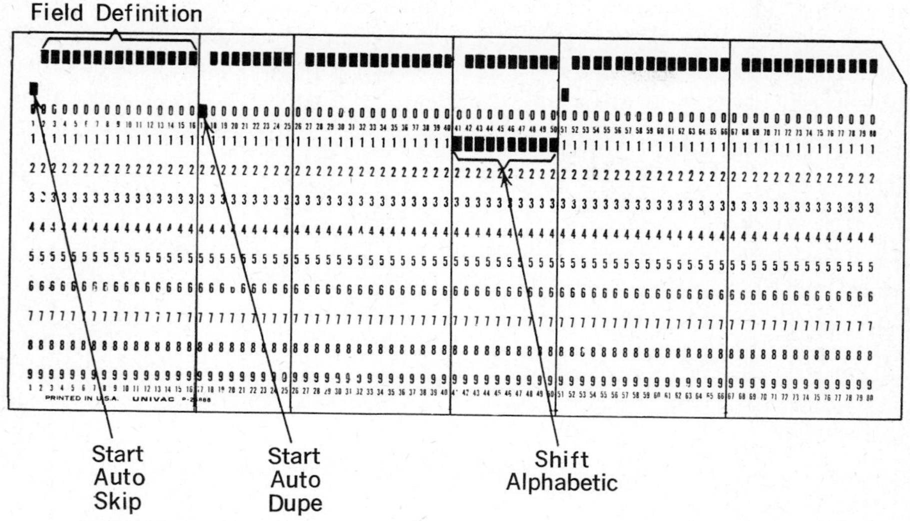

Figure 7–11. IBM card punch program card.

The rules for operating a card punch under program control and developing an appropriate program card are simple. The program card controls operation of the card punch column for column (Figure 7–11). Each of the columns in the program card contains a punch that causes certain functions to take place automatically. These punches, or codes, are shown:

Code or Punching Position	Function
12	Field definition
11	Start automatic skip
0	Start automatic duplication
1	Alphabetic shift

Under program control the card punch is in numeric shift unless the alpha shift code is placed in each column in which alphabetic information is to be punched.

Here are some rules for developing program cards:

1. A 12 punch is placed in each column except the first column of each field that has been defined.
2. The 11 or 0 punches are placed in the first column of any field in which skipping or duplication is desired. The remainder of the fields to be duplicated or skipped are defined by 12 punches as in field definition.
3. The 1 alpha shift code is placed in each column in which an alphabetic character is to be punched.

The program card is inserted around the program drum, making certain that the 9 edge of the card is positioned against the rim of the drum. If the clamping strip handle is turned so that the card is locked in place, and the card is flush against the 9 edge and is properly visible through the alignment holes, you are ready to insert the drum and begin operation.

Punched Card Verification

Verification, as the term is used in data processing, means to ascertain that data have been correctly recorded. To verify cards punched on an IBM card punch, an IBM verifier is used. The appearance of the verifier is almost identical with that of the card punch. To verify card punching operations, the verifier operator parrots the operations of the card punch operator. If an error is encountered, an error light on the verifier comes on. The operator may try to rekey the column three times by turning off the error indicator. On the third try, if the card is incorrectly punched, a notch is placed on the 12 edge of the card. If the card is correct, a notch is placed on the 80 edge. In this way, erroneous cards can be easily separated and corrected.

Arrangement and Rearrangement of Data: Sorting

One of the seven basic operations of data processing is sorting, that is, putting data into some kind of order. *Sorters* are machines designed to arrange decks of punched data cards in either alphabetic or numerical order. Understanding the way these machines operate requires a basic understanding of card reading and timing. In almost all unit record equipment, a data card, when being read, is transported over a brass roller and under a set of brushes, one for each of the eighty columns of the card. Figure 7–12 depicts a card passing between the metal read brush and contact roller. Although the sorter only has one brush, the same principle applies to all unit record equipment. The card is an insulator which prevents contact between the read brush and contact roller. The punched hole allows a circuit to be created between the brush and the roller and thus causes an electrical impulse to be generated. Every time a card is processed through a unit record processing machine, a card cycle occurs. The impulses generated when a card is read are in this manner timed. In the case of the 082 sorter, they are timed 9 through 12 since the card feeds 9 edge face down—that is, the impulses occur at 9, 8, 7, 6, 5, 4, 3, 2, 1, 0, 11, and 12 times during the card cycle. In general, a card cycle is that period of time necessary to complete a given set of operations in sequence and represents the total movement of the card through the machine. However, multimachine cycles, such as total cycles (which cause totals to be printed),

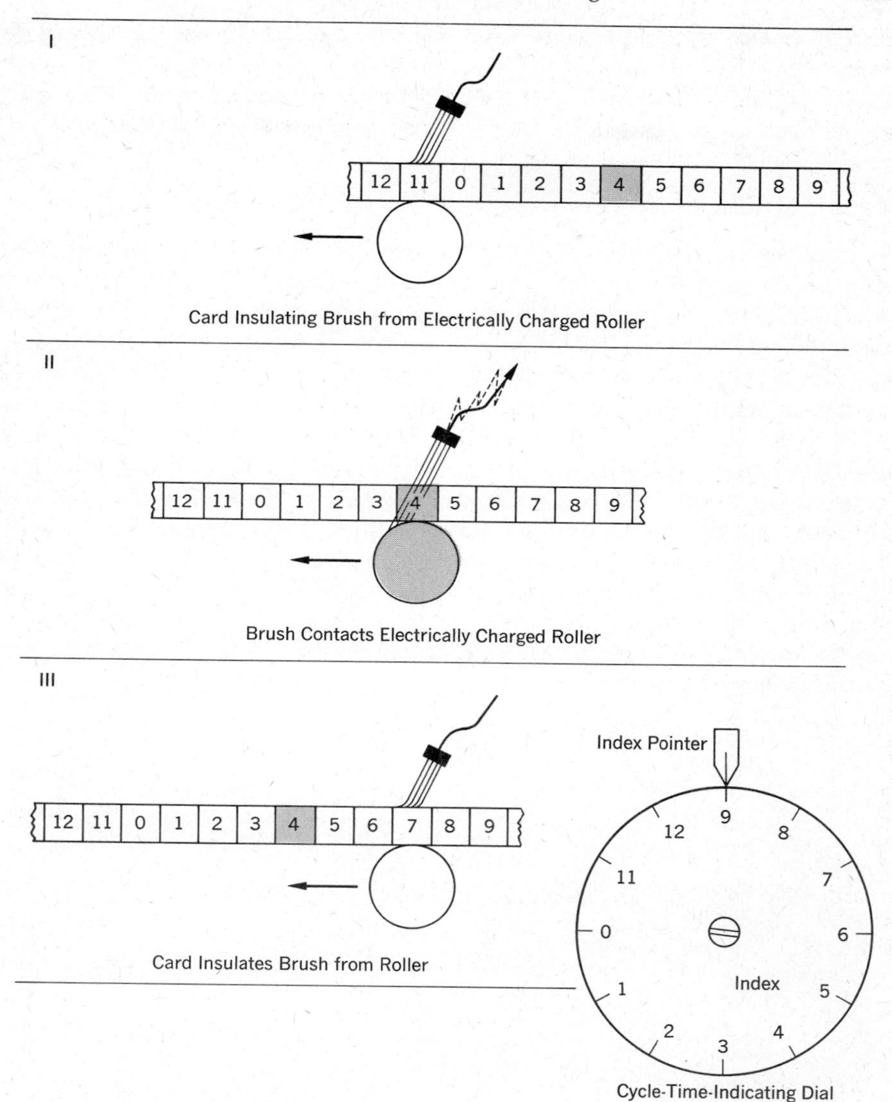

Figure 7–12. Card reading. *(Courtesy, IBM)*

punch cycles (which cause summary cards to be punched in conjunction with a reproducing punch attached to the accounting machine), and print cycles (which cause detail or summary lines to be printed), can occur during a given card cycle. Actually, all cycles performed by a machine are machine cycles—that period of time necessary to complete a machine operation. Some unit record equipment makes use of machine cycles that do not involve transporting a card and, therefore, has no machine times. Here, however, we are primarily interested in investigating the way in which electrical impulses are identified as ones or threes or elevens or whatever. This identification is accomplished with the use of an index dial, also shown in Figure 7–12, which rotates in conjunction with a card cycle, thus keeping track of the card read times as the card is being read.

Basic Operation of the IBM 082 Sorter

A picture of the IBM 082 Sorter is shown in Figure 7–13. Both the 082 and 083 sorters utilize the same operating features. The 083 is a faster machine, sorting cards at 1000 per minute, rather than at 650 per minute as is the case with the 082, and has a few convenient features not available on the 082. However, an understanding of the 082 will include all of the concepts needed to understand the 083, although the reverse is not the case. The main line switch, as shown, is located on the inside right leg of the 082. After turning it on, a 60-second warm-up period is required. A running light will come on when the machine is ready. Cards are placed into the card hopper 9 edge face down. Although the hopper has capacity for about 1200 cards, additional cards may be added without stopping the machine once the start key has been depressed to start feeding. The machine will automatically stop when a pocket becomes full; thus an operation can be started and an operator may move to another machine without fear of a problem.

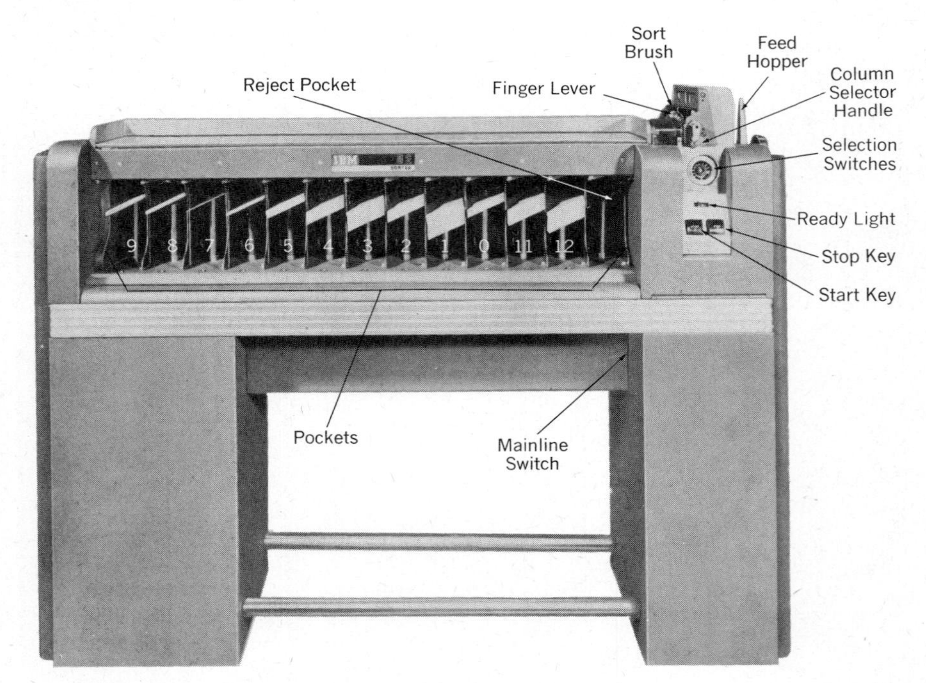

Figure 7–13. IBM 082 card sorter. *(Courtesy, IBM)*

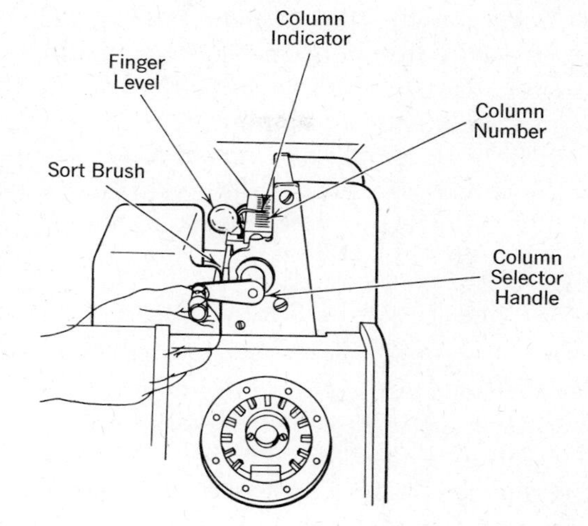

Figure 7–14. Column selection.

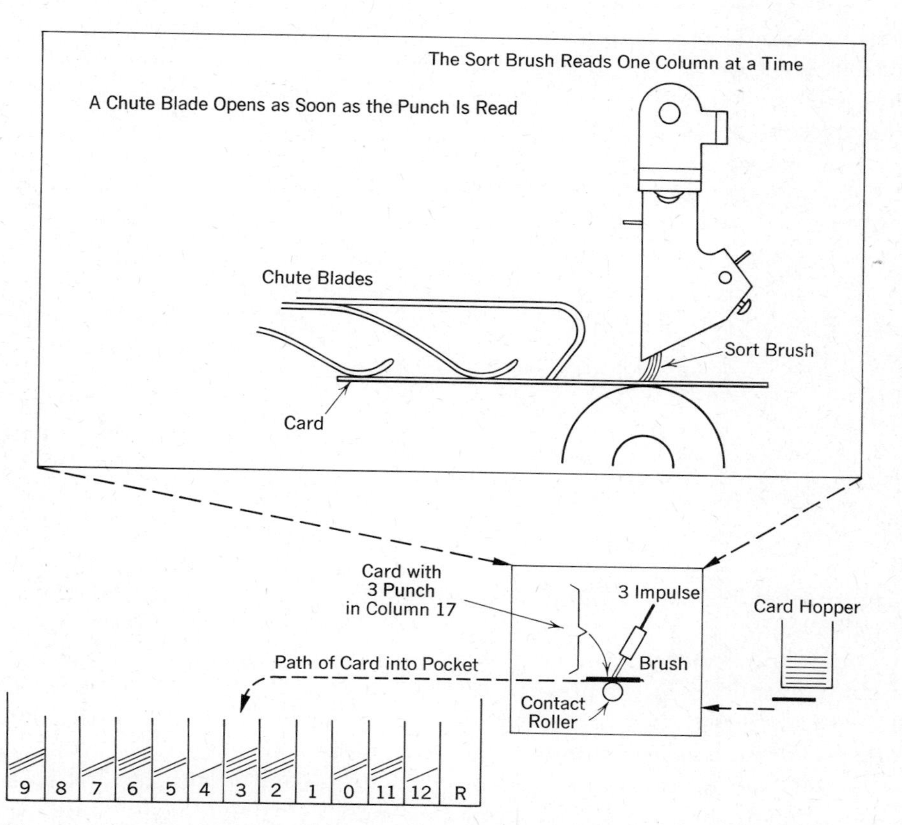

Figure 7–15. Path of cards through IBM 082 and 083 sorter. *(Courtesy, IBM)*

We noted earlier that the 082 through the use of the sort brush reads one column at a time. Note the column selector handle in Figure 7–14, which can be used to move the column indicator, the position of which corresponds to the column being read by the reading brush. Figure 7–15 indicates the path of a card into a given pocket on the sorter. Notice that the card passes under the read brush on a given column and then continues down the chute blades to the appropriate pocket.

Types of Sorting

A card field, we have observed, is a group of columns set aside which contains specific types of information. We will refer to the rightmost position, sometimes called the units position of the field, as the low order position and to the opposite end as the high order position of the field. Consider a card with three fields: state number in columns 19–21, county number in columns 40–41, and city number in columns 60–62. City is a three-column field, and cities, let us say, are numbered from 001 to 999. To sort cities in order, we would use the *reverse digit* method—that is, sorting column for column from the low order to the high order position, or to say it another way, units, within tens, within hundreds. It is difficult to visualize at first how this works. Let us imagine that we wish to sort the deck of cards according to city number so that it is organized in ascending sequential order. Assume, for the sake of simplicity, that we have only nine cards in the deck which are randomly arranged in this order:

537
022
246
555
335
421
965
883
081

The first card of this deck has 537 punched into it; the last has 081. Since this field has three columns or characters, we must make three passes through the sorter starting with the units or low-order position of the field. Figure 7–16 shows how the cards are arranged after each of the three passes. Note that the entire deck is in sequential order with 022 in front and 965 at the rear at the end of the third pass.

Suppose, now, we wanted to sort city within county within state. This would be known as a major-intermediate-minor sort, with state being the major field and city the minor. We would perform a reverse digit sort,

Pass One Units Position	Pass Two Tens Position	Pass Three Tens Position (Sort Complete)
081	421	022
421	022	081
022	335	246
883	537	335
965	246	424
335	555	537
555	965	555
246	081	883
537	883	965

Figure 7–16. Three passes of data deck through sorter.

beginning with the low order position of the minor field and proceed, in reverse digit fashion, backwards through the minor, intermediate, and major fields. Suppose we have a great volume of cards, say, 300,000, to sort on six columns. We know handling is going to be difficult. A way to simplify the handling difficulty of the sort, even though the machine operates at a constant speed, would be to block sort. Block sorting is a technique of dividing a large deck of cards into several smaller decks, by sorting first on the high order field or the high order position of the one field to be sorted. This operation results in several "blocks" that can be treated as separate sorting operations in which the normal reverse digit method is used. With our problem above, we would sort the high order column first. Stack the cards by group—that is, 700,000's, 600,000's, 500,000's, and so on—and then reverse digit sort each group and put them back together, 600,000's behind 700,000's and so on. This would not speed the operation, but it would make handling simpler. Also, if more than one sorter is available, other blocks may be sorted at the same time.

Let us now look at alphabetic sorting. Since cards pass through the 082 machine 9 edge first, and the card is sent down the chute blade of the first impulse generated during a given card cycle, and alphabetic characters are represented in Hollerith code by two punches in a given column, we have a problem. We must make two passes on each column for an alphabetic sort. A zone pass might be made first to block cards A–I, J–R and S–Z—that is, the 12, 11, and 0 zones. Note the sort selection switches in Figure 7–17. There are twelve switches plus the alpha sort switch, corresponding each to an 082 pocket and punching position on the card. When a sort switch is engaged, it deactivates the brush at that particular time in the cycle and causes the card to go into the reject pocket, or if a subsequent zone punch is picked up in that column, the card would fall in the appropriate zone pocket—12, 11, or 0. Therefore, a zone pass could be made by simply activating switches 1 through 9 and causing cards to fall in the zone pockets. There is an easier way. Activating the alphabetic sort switch deactivates the brush on punching positions 1 through 9 and causes the cards to fall into the appropriate zone pocket. By making both a

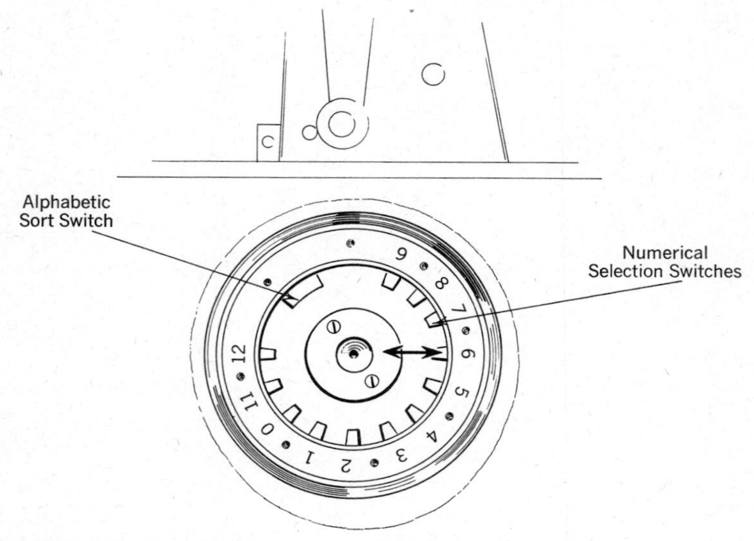

Figure 7–17. IBM 082 sort selection switches. *(Courtesy, IBM)*

zone and a digit pass on each column, we can use the reverse digit method for alpha sorting also. Usually, alphabetic sorting involves first sorting a column on the digit punches, then depressing the alpha sort switch and making a second pass on the same column. At the end of the second pass, the deck will be in the three zone pockets, and by placing the three parts, 12 zone first, then 11 zone, and 0 zone, the deck is in alphabetic order in that column.

In using any equipment, it is important to know how long a given job will take us. On the 082 sorter, we can use two simple formulae:

$$\frac{\text{cards} \times \text{columns}}{\text{read speed}} = \text{machine time}$$

and

$$\text{machine time} + \text{handling time} = \text{operating time}$$

Suppose we were going to sort 1300 cards on 5 columns at the 082 read speed of 650 cards per minute:

$$\frac{1300 \times 5}{650} = 10 \text{ minutes}$$

plus 25 per cent handling time, or 12.5 minutes total operating time.

The basic ideas of unit record processing have been briefly introduced in this chapter, along with information on how punched cards are prepared and how decks of such cards are assembled in desired order through sorting. The chapter to follow describes equipment that uses decks of cards such as these to produce information in the form of reports that businessmen then would use for decision-making and control purposes.

Questions

1. Explain the advantages to be gained by using the card punch under program control.
2. What benefits are derived for a company in attempting to automate portions of its information system?
3. How does the "write it once" principle apply to unit record data processing?
4. Under what circumstances is block sorting useful and what benefits are derived from its use?
5. If one had to sort 230,000 cards on four columns using an 083 sorter, what considerations must be used to determine the time necessary to complete the job and how long would it take?
6. What is the purpose of the sort selection switches on the 082 sorter?
7. Explain the principle of card reading in unit record equipment.
8. What is the difference between constant and variable data? Give examples.
9. Discuss three techniques involved in aiding an operator to perform card handling effectively.

Unit Record Equipment: Its Control and Function

The purpose of this chapter is to introduce the manner in which unit record equipment, other than card punches, verifiers, and sorters, which were discussed in the previous chapter, are controlled. Control of a unit record processing device is almost always accomplished through the use of a control panel, or wiring panel, as they are frequently called. These panels are prepared and mounted on the equipment, causing it to perform various functions. Changing the functions to be performed by the equipment is a matter of removing one panel and mounting another. Unit record equipment is in this manner *externally* controlled through the use of these control panels, a feature that helps to distinguish it from electronic digital computing equipment, which is controlled by programs stored internally in the memory device of the computer. Novices to unit record equipment are at first bewildered at the seeming complexity of a control panel, which may contain several hundred different wires. Actually, there is a fairly small number of ideas employed in the control of this type of equipment, none of which is difficult to understand.

Keep in mind as we work our way through the following examples of basic unit record equipment that the primary aim here is understanding of unit record *principles* and not of specific machine operation. Unfortunately, sophisticated hardware is often misused because the users have the ability to apply only the simplest methods of operation. It is up to the user to be dynamic and creative in applying these principles in operating the hardware with which he works for maximum effectiveness in terms of the aims of the information system. One chapter, such as this one, cannot hope to equip you with the technical information you need to be an expert unit record operator. Only the principles involved, together with basic technical features of unit record equipment operation, will be discussed. As a matter of fact, an understanding of the principles discussed in these chapters will enable you, with the help of IBM manuals, to prepare control panels which will perform the operations discussed in the sections to follow. This might seem difficult, but after one or two attempts you will find it not impossible.

Unit Record Equipment Control: Wiring

In Chapter 7, we examined reading brushes and how they generate electrical impulses. The impulse generated by a reading brush we will call a *directed impulse.* That impulse is generated in the machine by the circuit created when a hole in the insulating card is found and contact with the roller is completed. In unit record equipment, a directed impulse from a brush emanates at a control panel, and must be *redirected* through wiring to cause the machine to perform certain functions. (See Figure 8–1.) Sometimes, *manual* control panels, wired for temporary jobs, are used. Sometimes, control panels are *fixed* and covered for permanence. Fixed wires are barbed so that once inserted they are not easily removed or require the use of a special tool for removal, whereas manual wires are easily removable.

Wires are plugged into *hubs*, or holes, in the control panel. Two basic types of hubs are *exit hubs* and *entry hubs*. Directed impulses emanate from exit hubs. These impulses are generated from reading brushes or might be internally generated by a device known as an *emitter*, which

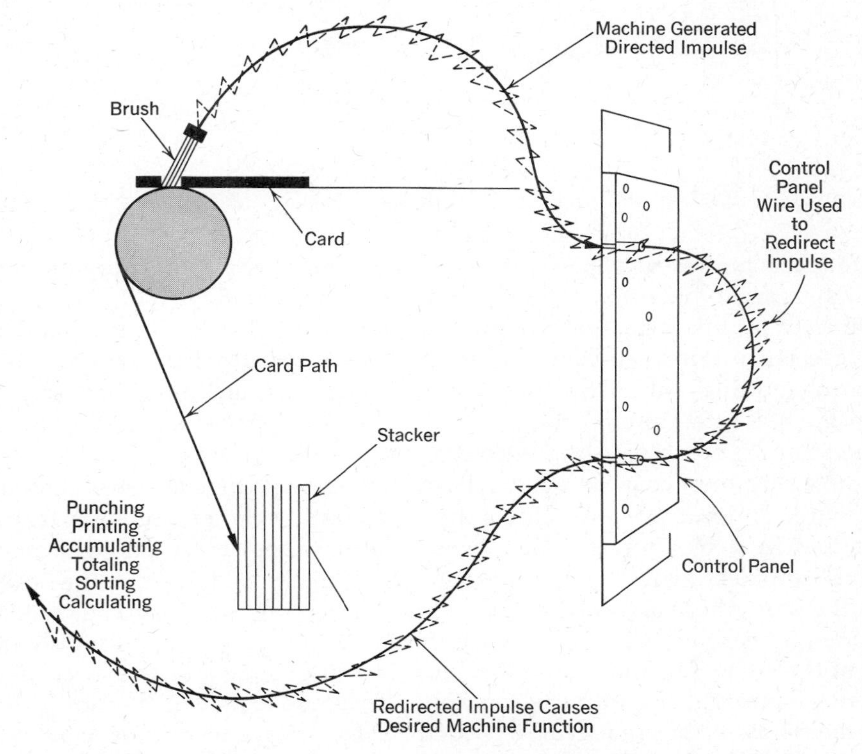

Figure 8–1. Directed electrical impulses emanating from control panel and being directed to perform some machine function. *(Courtesy, IBM)*

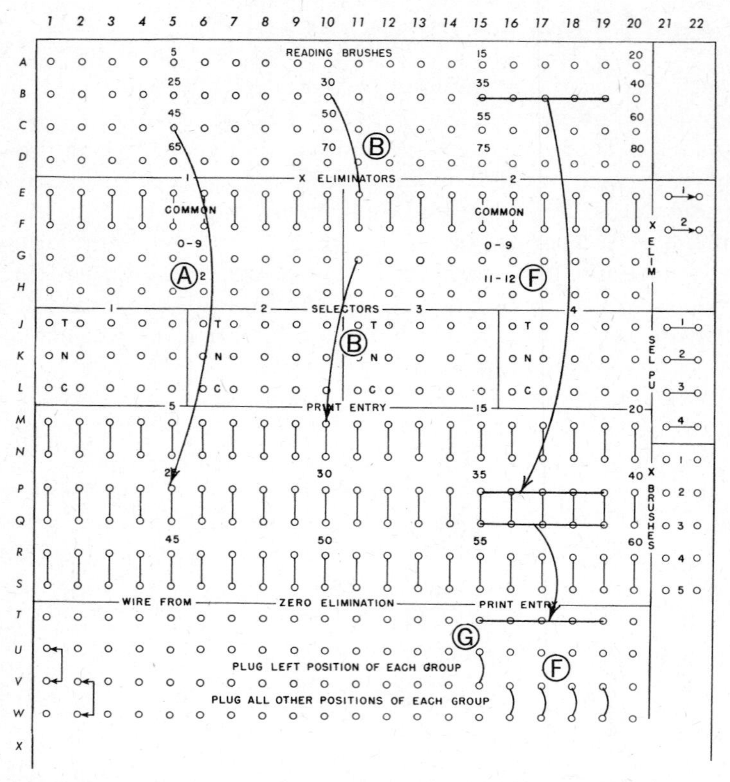

Figure 8–2. IBM 548 interpreter control panel. *(Courtesy, IBM)*

produces impulses at particular machine times which the programmer might want to plug into an entry hub to cause a specific function to occur. Directed impulses generating from exit hubs are redirected to entry hubs. These entry hubs can cause such activities as printing, punching, comparing, adding, subtracting, or totalling on various machines. Note wire A on the 548 interpreter panel in Figure 8–2. An impulse emanating from the reading brush exit hub enters print position 25, causing a character from a card to be printed. As the illustration shows, there are several types of wires and hubs. Many times a directed impulse can be used effectively more than once. Therefore, many entry hubs are set up as pairs of *common hubs.* Impulses sent through one common hub emanate through the other of the pair. These are indicated by a line connecting the hubs on a control panel. Sometimes, then, an entry hub can become an exit if an impulse is sent through its common hub. Multicommon hubs are known as *bus hubs.* As in Figure 8–3, an impulse sent into one would exit at each of the other three. These hubs are useful in reducing *split wiring,* a technique of attaching wires to other wires so that directed impulses can be plugged into several entry hubs. An impulse entering a split wire can be redirected

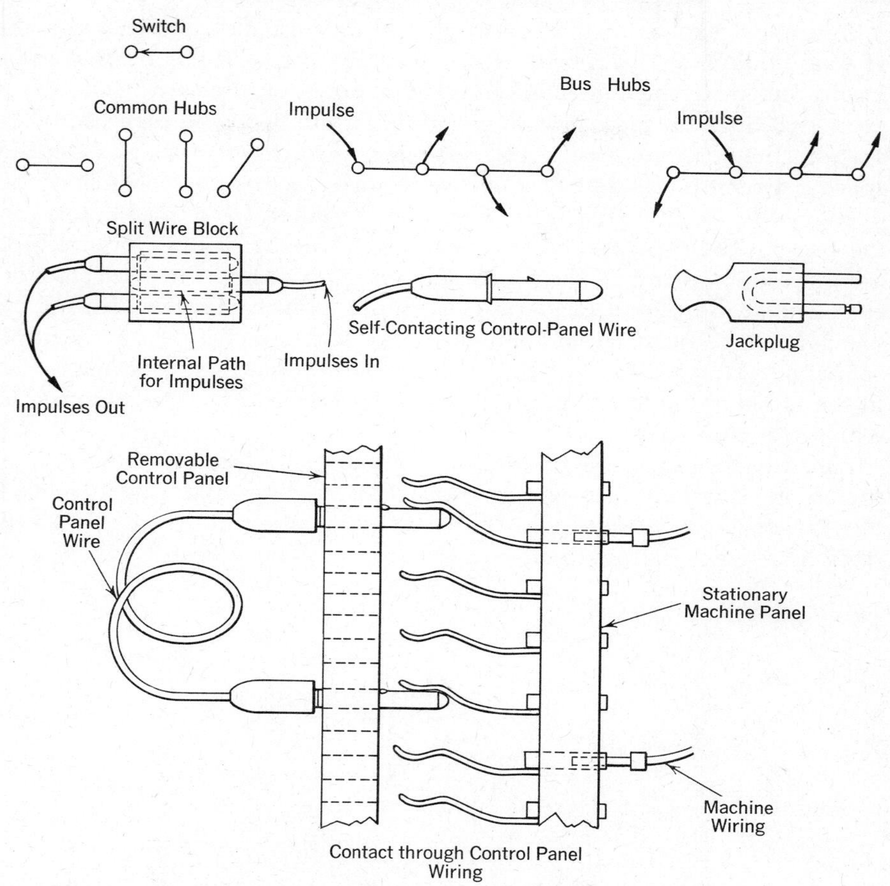

Figure 8–3. Types of control panel hubs. *(Courtesy, IBM)*

numerous times if need be. Keep in mind that what is accomplished through the hub depends on the timed impulse generated through it. *Switching hubs* or *neutral hubs,* which may be built internally onto control panels, allow certain sections of the panel to be turned on or off. Observe also the jackplug, a very short wire that may be used for connecting two adjacent hubs. This jackplug aids in reducing the number of wires running over the control panel.

Interpreting

Interpreting is the process of printing on a punched card the same information that is punched into it. Because the 548 interpreter, alluded to in Chapter 7, embodies some of the concepts common to all EAM equipment, let's discuss some of its operating principles more thoroughly.

Figure 8–4 shows a 548 interpreter, its control panel, and that portion of a card on which it can print. The interpreter can read holes punched in a card and print the characters thus represented on the card itself. It can print two lines on a card, as depicted in Figure 8–4. The printing takes place in the space above the 12 row (upper printing position) and in the space between the 11 and 12 rows (lower printing position). Which of the two printing positions will be used is determined by setting a knob in the back of the machine. One pass through the machine is required for each line to be printed. The 548 can print a maximum of 60 characters on each line at the rate of 60 cards per minute. Notice that the printing on the 548 is one-third larger than that of a card punch that can print 80 characters. This makes it easier to read; also, a significant advantage lies in the fact that the information need not be printed over the column into which it is punched.

Cards are placed in the card hopper 12 edge first face up and are interpreted and passed to the card stacker. Cards may be continuously added; the stacker has a *stop lever* which stops the machine if it becomes full. The main line switch is used to turn the machine on. The start key, which must

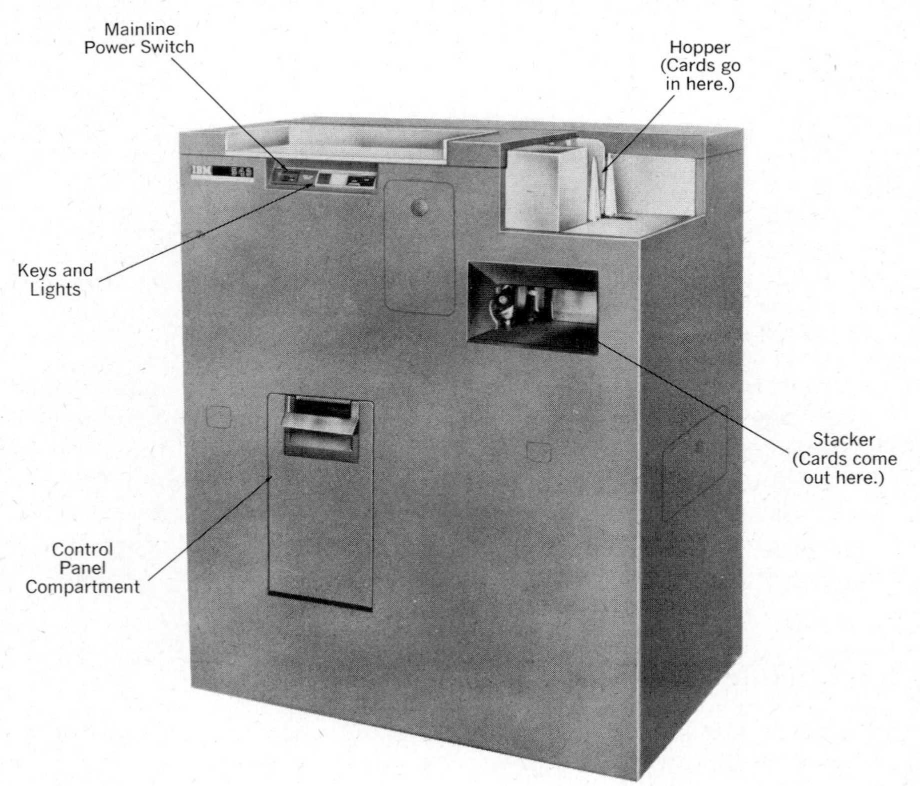

Figure 8–4. IBM 548 interpreter control panel (above) and printing area (opposite). *(Courtesy, IBM)*

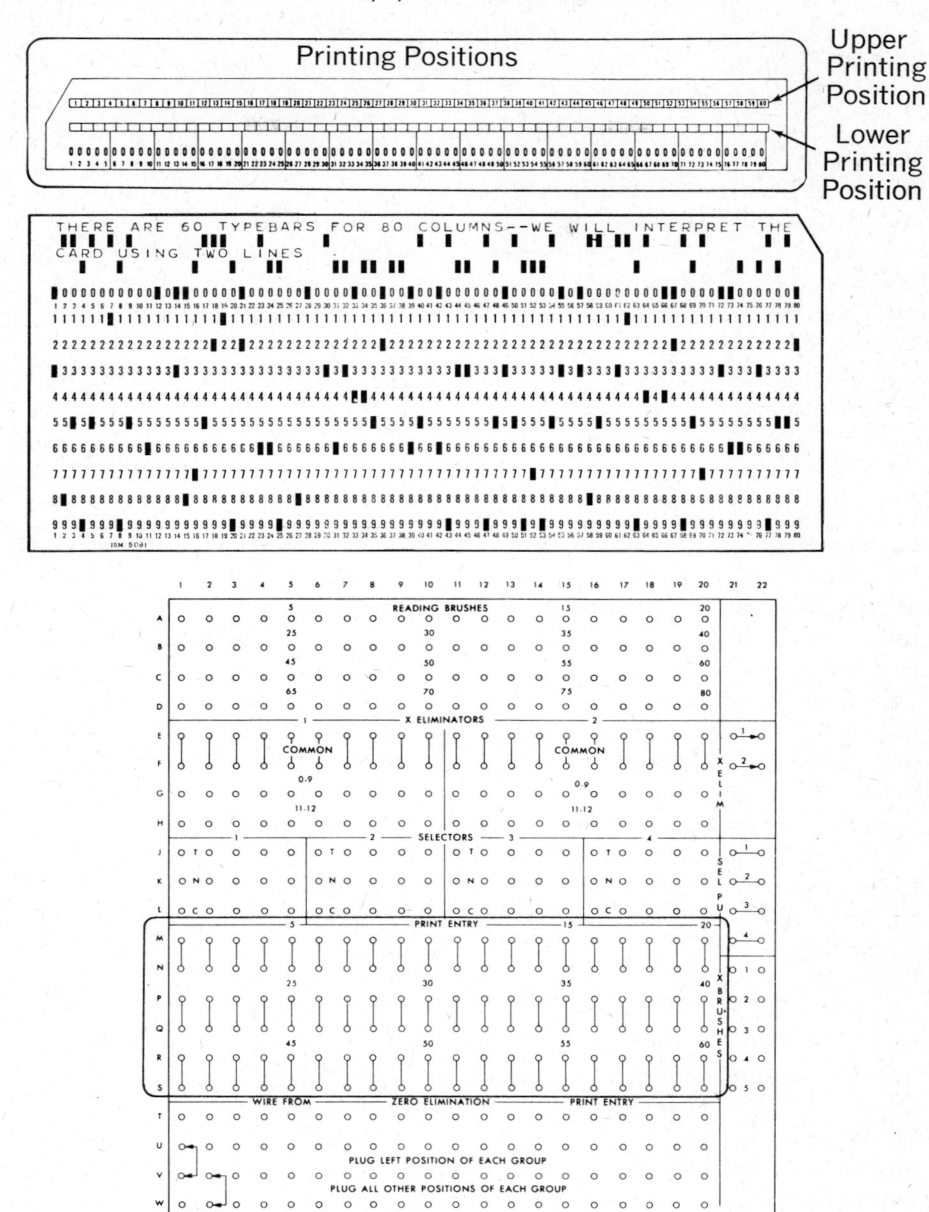

be held down for three cycles, starts cards processing. As in all IBM unit record equipment, there is a ready light that indicates that the machine is on. The stop key can be used to stop processing at any time. Pressing the start key resumes interpreting at the point at which the machine left off. This characteristic is common to all unit record equipment. It might be interesting to note at this point that, since cards feed through the interpreter 12 edge face up, care must be taken in restacking the cards. The card furthest from the front of the deck—that is, the last card of a given group—will be interpreted first.

On the control panel in Figure 8–4 are shown the 80 reading brush exit hubs, one for each of 80 reading brushes set over the card columns. This is characteristic of all unit record equipment (except sorters) and computers in which cards are read. Each reading brush exit hub may be wired to a print entry hub to cause printing to take place on a specific print position. For example, wire A in Figure 8–2 will cause the character punched in card column 25 to print in print position 50. Let us now look at those devices on the 548 that represent common EAM and data processing principles—namely, switches, selectors, X eliminators, and zero eliminators.

Switches and X Elimination

The switches on the control panel of the 548 are jackplugged to turn on the X eliminators. (Jackplugging a switch on a control panel is the same as flipping a toggle switch.) We noted earlier that X punches (or eleven punches) are frequently used to distinguish master from detail cards. Suppose column 25 (wire A) in our card contains a valid bit of numeric data that we want printed on the card and also contains an X punch to be used for some control purpose. If we wire as in A, an alphabetic character will print, since both the 11 and digit punch will be read and thus be printed. Our object is to print only the numeric character. The X eliminator permits the separation of zone and digit impulses and has three sets of hubs—common, 0–9, and 11–12. Each common hub will accept any impulse, and it will be available at the other common if we want to use it for some additional purpose. Also, there is an internal connection between common, 0–9, and 11–12. However, 0–9 will only accept or emit impulses 0 through 9, and the 11–12 hubs only 11–12 impulses. Keeping in mind that a 1 punch in a card, for example, generates an impulse at *one time* and an 11 generates an 11-timed impulse in the card cycle, if we wire as in B from reading brush 30 into common and from 0–9 to the print position, recognizing that only 0–9 timed impulses can escape from that hub, the 11 (X) will be lost and only the digit will be printed. Thus, we have allowed only the numeric portion of the column to print on our card. The X eliminator is sometimes referred to as a *column split* because of its ability to split a given column into numeric and zone portions.

Zero Elimination

If we want to suppress insignificant high order zeros in a given field, we wire as in F in Figure 8–2. The zero eliminator is wired from the other common hubs of the field where suppression is desired just as it would be printed, that is, from high to low order positions of the field, and jack-plugs would be placed as in the diagram. The leftmost position indicates the beginning of the field as in G.

SELECTION

Selection, as the term is used in unit record data processing, means selecting one of two fields to be used for some purpose. There are two basic types of selection: *field selection* – reading from two fields and making a decision to print or punch the information from only one of these fields; and *class selection* – reading one field and printing or punching into one of two different fields.

To understand either type of selection, we must examine another feature of unit record equipment: X brushes. X brushes are special brushes timed so that they read only X punches. They are located in front of the read brushes on the 548 and are shown in Figure 8–5. The 548 has five X brushes any or all of which may be used to determine whether or not there are X punches in particular columns. If there is an X punch in a particular column, the equipment is to perform one function; if there is not, another.

In Figure 8–6 are shown examples of field and class selection. Let us analyze the simple class selection problem shown there. We need to determine whether there is an X punched in column 80 of the card. If there is, we would like the information in the data field punched in card columns 21–25 to print in Field B; if there is no X punched in column 80, we would

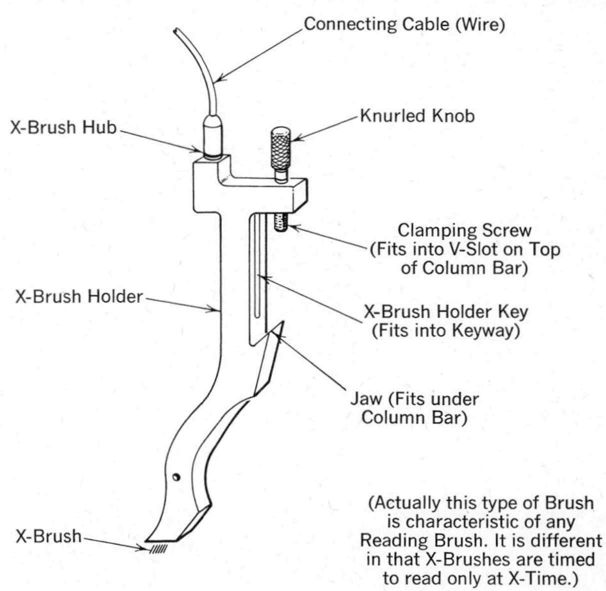

Figure 8–5. A diagram of one of the five X brushes in the IBM 548 interpreter. *(Courtesy, IBM)*

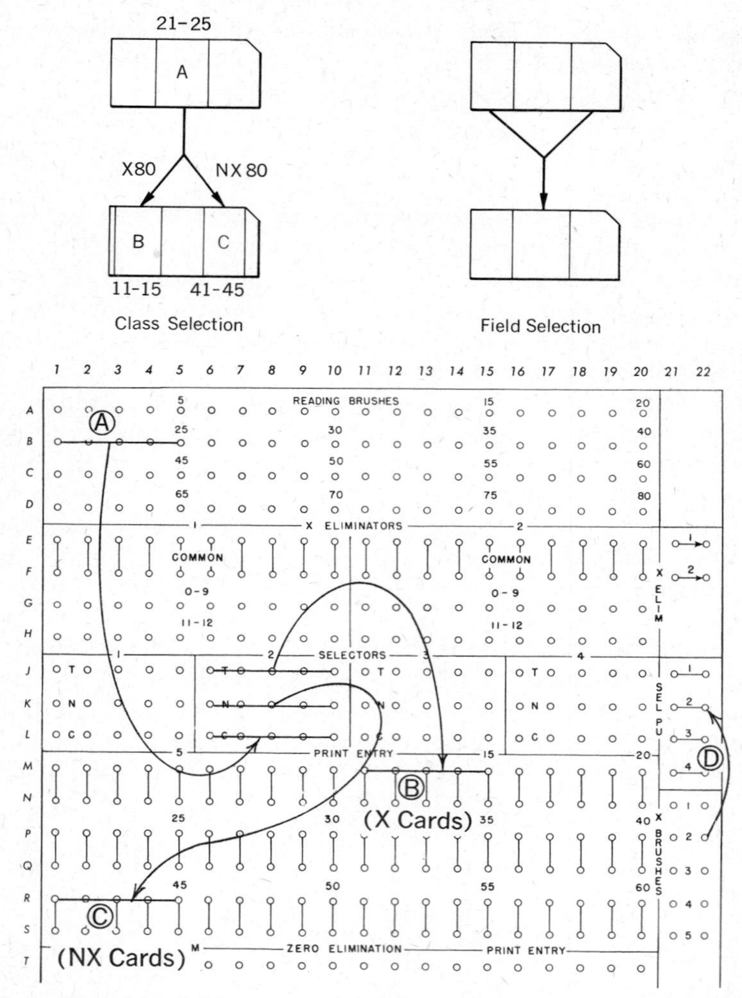

Figure 8–6. Class and field selection and control panel wired for field selection. *(Courtesy, IBM)*

like it printed in Field C. This process requires use of a selector which picks a field on the basis of an X or no-X condition. Figure 8–7 shows a selector. Selectors are each composed of three hubs and a pick-up hub. There is normally an internal connection between the common hub and the normal hub; any impulse put into common comes out of normal, which may then be wired to print. However, you will note that the armature on the selector is connected to a pick-up hub. If the pick-up hub receives an X impulse (read by an X brush), it swings the armature to the transfer position, thus causing an internal connection between common and transfer instead of common and normal. Therefore, we would wire as in Figure 8–6: if there is no X, from read exit hubs 21–25 into common

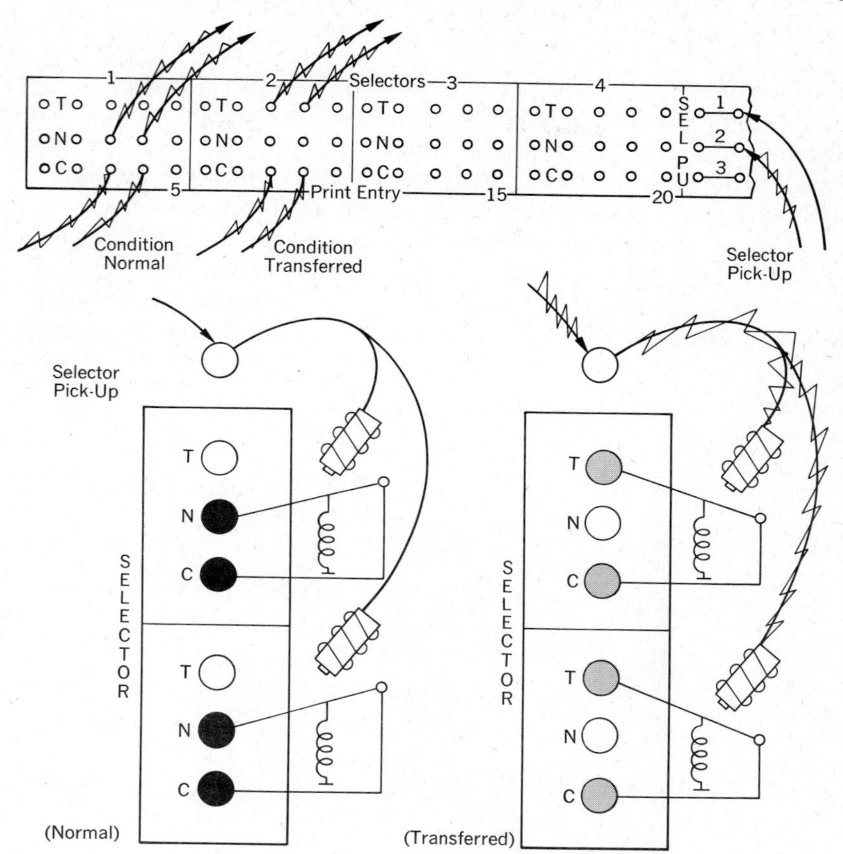

Figure 8–7. Selector operation.

and out of normal to print entry hubs 41–45 for printing; and if there is an X, from transfer to print entry hubs 11–15. Thus, in the case of an X punch in the column, the selection will be transferred internally and data columns 21–25 would print in Field B. We make the selector operative by connecting the X brush, which is set to read that column, to the proper selector pick-up, as in D in Figure 8–6.

We have briefly examined the 548 interpreter. There are other models of interpreters, such as the 557, which interprets at a speed of 100 cards per minute rather than 60 as with the 548, can print on any one of 25 different lines, and uses print wheels instead of typebars. Most importantly, we have surveyed the tools used in unit record programming or wiring, as it is called. We are aware now of the function of control panels, hubs, jackplugs, and wires. We have explored, though briefly, features common to all unit record equipment: X eliminators, X brushes, and selectors, and we have seen the conceptual principles of both class and field selection. These principles apply generally to all unit record equipment. They also apply to computer processing.

Reproducing

The 514 reproducing punch depicted in Figure 8–8 has as its main function various forms of automatic preparation of cards. In transcribing information, the reproducer has the ability to reproduce from one card to another in either the same or different columns. Observe the main line switch, which is turned on to supply operating current and also the common features of equipment we have discussed before, such as the start and stop buttons. The comparing indicator signals incorrect reproducing operations. If an error in punching occurs, it can be traced by using the comparing indicator on which a magnet will drop visually, indicating the

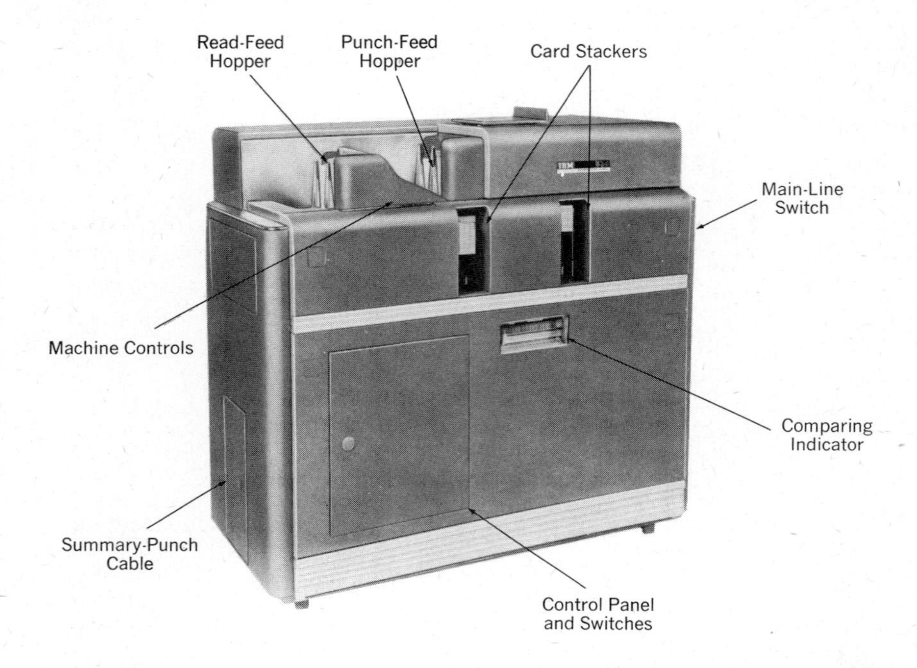

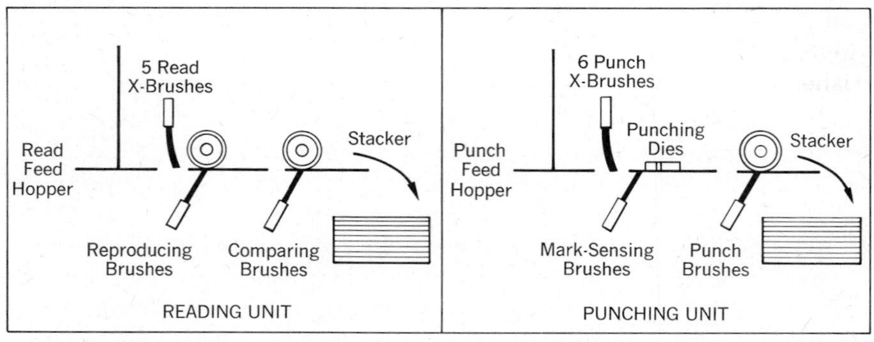

Figure 8–8. IBM reproducing punch and internal schematic. *(Courtesy, IBM)*

column in which the error occurred. This is similar to the verifying operation on the card punch.

The schematic in Figure 8–8 shows the internal structure of the reproducer. The machine is divided into two units—a reading unit and a punching unit—which may be used independently or in conjunction, depending on the operation to be performed. Each unit has a feed hopper that holds approximately 800 cards, which are fed 12 edge face down. Cards feed from the hoppers, pass under the brushes and punch dies, and proceed to one of the two stackers, each of which holds about 1000 cards and has an automatic lever that stops the machine if the stacker becomes full.

The two basic categories of operation of a reproducer are *gangpunching* and *straight reproducing*. Gangpunching is a technique of reading a master card of a deck of cards and using the information read to punch data into subsequent detail cards in the same deck. Subcategories of gangpunching include interspersed master gangpunching and offset gangpunching.

Straight reproducing involves reading one deck of cards and using the information read to punch another deck of cards, which may or may not be identical to the original deck but which nevertheless contains the same data. Subcategories of reproducing include class-selected reproducing (which is similar to class selection on the interpreter), field-selected reproducing, combined reproducing and gangpunching, summary punching, and mark sensing.

Again let us emphasize that although these operations are specific functions of the reproducer as a link in the unit record system, they are critical concepts where computers, with unit record equipment as support, are used.

GANGPUNCHING

Gangpunching involves automatically copying punched information from a master card into one or more following detail cards. (See Diagram A of Figure 8–9.) The punch die shown in the schematic represents a set of 80 punch dies, one for each column on the card. Punching takes place using impulses generated from the holes in a card being read at the punch brushes and through control panel wiring being channeled back to the punch dies, causing those columns read at the punch brushes to be punched at the punch dies. It follows, then, that as each card moves from the punch brushes to the stacker, and the card following moves to the punch brushes, that card becomes a set-up card or master card for the following card which has then moved under the punch dies.

Interspersed Master Gangpunching. Diagram B of Figure 8–9 shows an interspersed gangpunching operation using multiple masters. In this case, each master card has an X punch in column 80, which is read by one

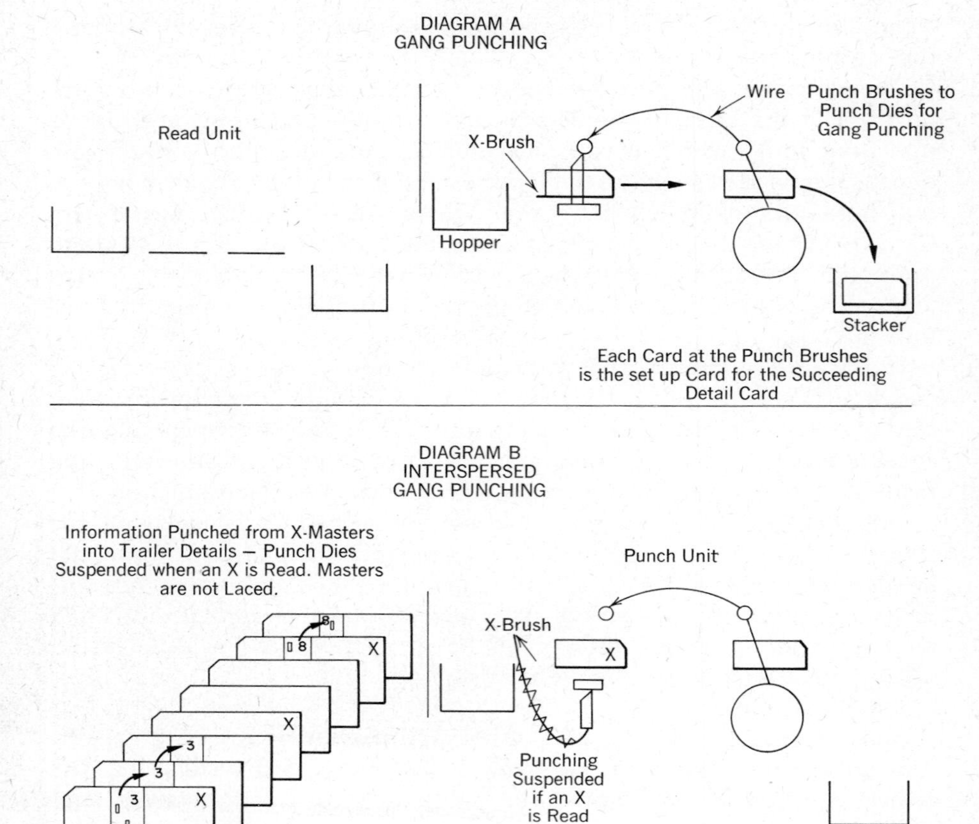

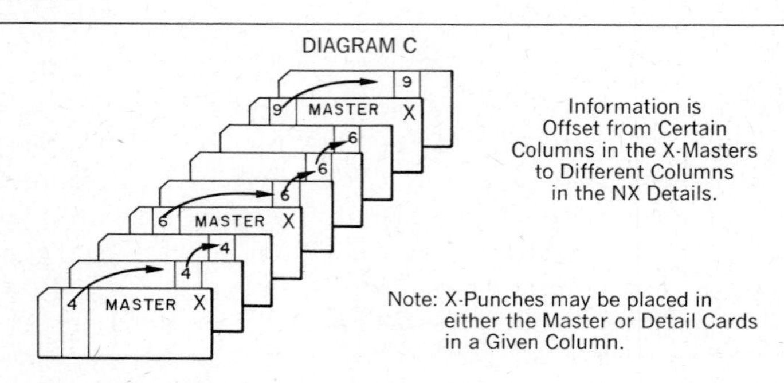

Figure 8–9. Gangpunching.

of the machine's X brushes. If the machine reads such an X, it can be wired not to punch into that card. Therefore, as the cards proceed through the punching unit, each master card becomes a new set-up card for its succeeding detail cards. Master cards that have a control punch (an X punch) in column 80 will not be punched with information from the preceding card, which is a detail of an earlier master card. The control punch in the master card thus prevents erroneous information from being punched into it through the use of the selector principle discussed earlier in this chapter.

Offset Gangpunching. Diagram C of Figure 8–9 illustrates offset gangpunching. In this case, we are punching from certain columns in master cards to different columns in the succeeding detail cards. Data from columns read by the reading brushes are directed to the punch dies representing the fields into which the data are to be punched.

Verification. After cards are gangpunched, they can be compared for accuracy. This is done in the reading unit, where there are two sets of brushes—reproducing brushes and comparing brushes. There is also within the machine a comparing unit that controls the status of the comparing indicator on the front of the machine. The comparing unit is made up of 80 comparing magnets for the 80 reproducing brushes and 80 more magnets, one for each of the comparing brushes. Wiring for comparing of various punching operations is accomplished by wiring from the reproducing brushes into one set of comparing magnets and from the comparing brushes into the other corresponding magnets. Data read from a card at the comparing brushes is compared with that of a card at the reproducing brushes, and if there is a difference in punches for the columns wired, the error column is indicated on the comparing indicator. The comparing indicator shows the condition of the comparing magnets, which, when differing information is sensed, stop the operation of the machine and prevent further processing until they are reset by lifting a lever to the left of the comparing indicator. The reading unit, like the punching unit, also has X brushes so that the last card of one group need not be compared with the first of another. Diagram A of Figure 8–10 shows a comparing unit schematic.

Straight Reproducing

We observed earlier that the punching and reading units can be used in conjunction. This is done in straight reproducing operations. As in Figure 8–10, Diagram B, data read from the card at the reproducing brushes is punched into a card at the punch dies. The card just punched moves to the punch brushes where it is compared with the card from which the data were punched, which is now at the comparing brushes.

Selected Punching. Two other operations performed by the reproducing punch— class- and field-selected reproducing—are depicted in Figure 8–11. This operation is performed using selectors as discussed in our study of the interpreter.

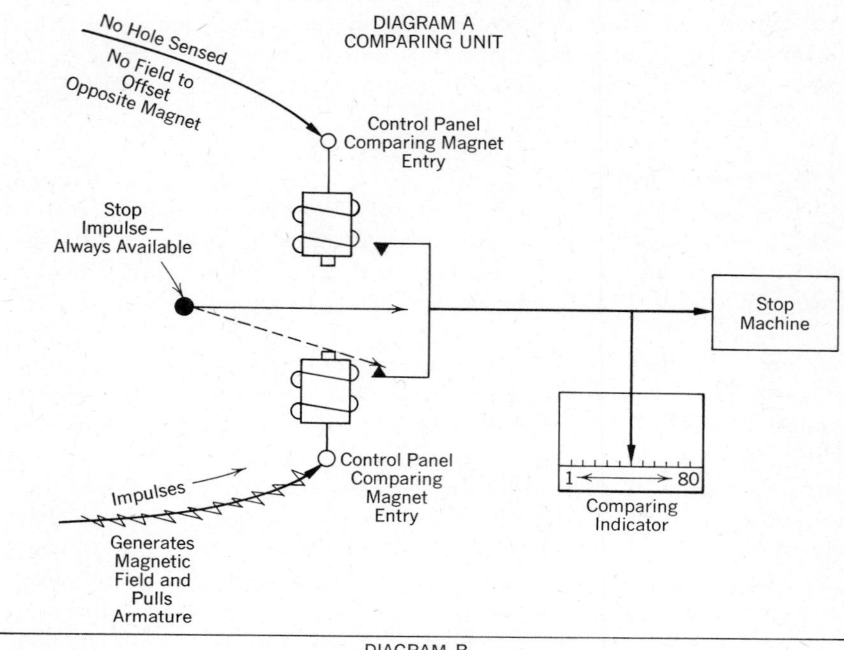

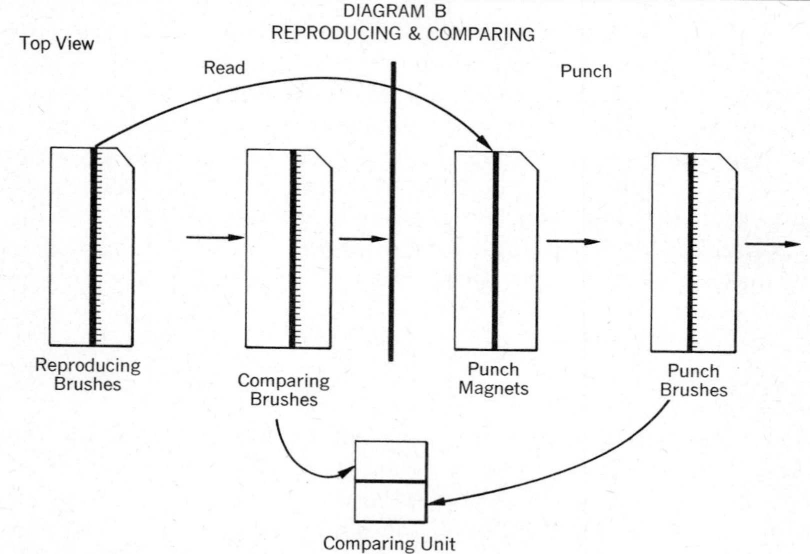

Figure 8–10. Comparing unit schematic diagram.

Summary Punching. Summary punching is a unique operation in that data read into or computed within an accounting machine are transmitted through a cable from the reproducer which is inserted into the accounting machine. These data are punched into summary cards. Thus, the combin-

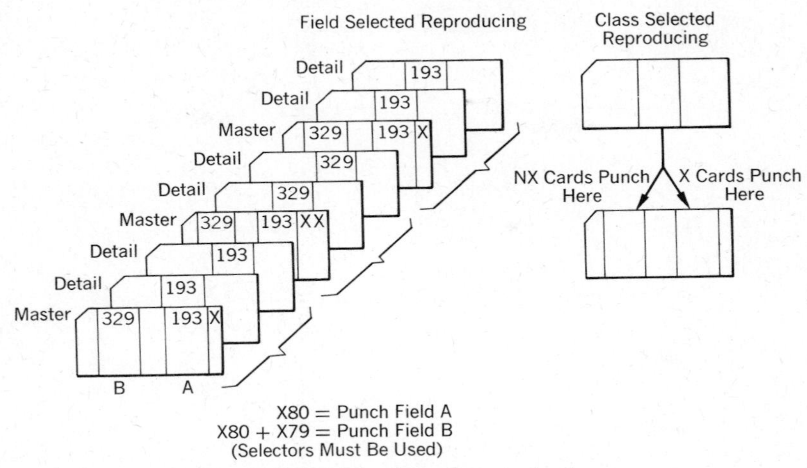

Figure 8–11. Class selected and field selected reproducing.

ing of these two machines to perform this operation facilitates summarizing totals of large amounts of data into small numbers of cards, thus reducing card handling and effecting ease of storage.

Mark Sense Punching. Mark sense punching is a process of converting electrically conductive pencil marks on a card into punched holes in that same card. In the preceding chapter, we analyzed the IBM card in detail. Look at the cards in Figure 8–12. Each card can have 27 mark sense positions, each of which can be read by a mark sense brush in the punch side of the reproducer. It takes three card columns to accommodate one mark sense position. Three columns for one mark sensed punch times 27 positions equals 81 card columns, but the 80 edge of the card leaves enough room for the 81st column.

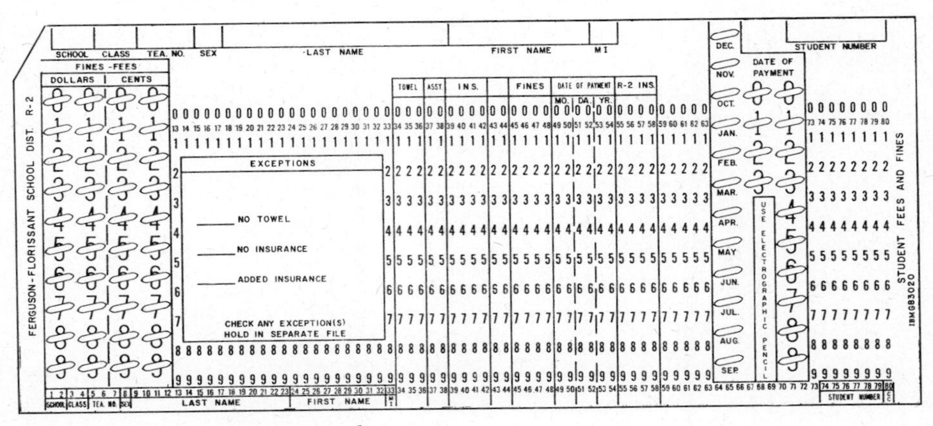

Figure 8–12. A mark sense card.

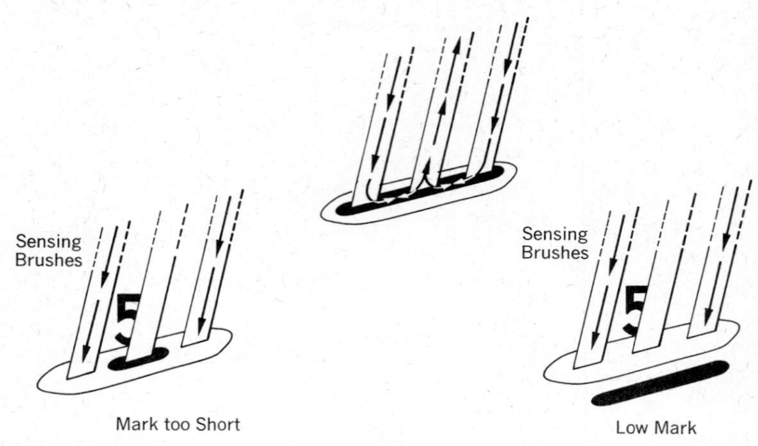

Figure 8–13. Mark sense reading. *(Courtesy, IBM)*

Ordinary pencil leads do not usually contain enough graphite to create an electrical circuit adequate for energizing the punch dies. Therefore, special mark sense pencils must be used.

As a marked card passes through a reproducer with the mark sensing special feature, each pencil mark is read by three electrical contacts (brushes). Electrical impulses flow down through the outer brushes and through the mark and up the middle brush if the card has been properly marked. Thus, an electrical circuit is completed and a punch die operates (see Figure 8–13). Marks can be erased by passing an eraser over the entire mark to remove the graphite deposit sufficiently enough to eliminate conductivity. It is important when mark sensing to use a hard, smooth surface. When a soft surface is used many times, the pencil creates an indentation and the mark sense brushes pass over the marked area without the proper circuit being created. It is often difficult in looking at a mark to tell if it will cause punching to take place. If great blocks of cards are to be marked, constant surveillance of the brushes is necessary because graphite may tend to collect and inappropriate punches may occur owing to short circuits. A verification device installed in reproducers with the mark sensing feature is called the double punch blank column detection device. It does just that: checks for double punches and blank columns on a card, which, incidentally, are commonplace error conditions. However, if a case occurs where a double punch in a column is a necessary part of the job, this feature cannot be used.

End-Printing

Another reproducer in common use is the 519 document-originating machine, which performs all those functions applicable to the 514 we have been discussing, but in addition performs the function of end-printing.

The end-printing unit in the 519 is a small interpreting device housed on the punch side of the machine which can print figures on the 1 edge of the card. The functioning of the 519 is otherwise essentially the same as the 514.

We have now looked at transcription of data in two ways: column-by-column punching, or serial punching, as in the card punch, and row-by-row, or parallel punching, as accomplished by the reproducing punch. On some types of more sophisticated punches, such as the 1403 reader-punch that may be attached to a 1401 computer system, the use of 80 punch brushes and punch dies and the functions performed are the same as those performed by reproducing punches, with the exception of the introduction of the computational ability of the associated computer.

Collating

Classifying data—that is, filing cards in proper logical order for processing in subsequent operations—is a time-consuming task, particularly if the number of data cards is great. The collator is a machine specifically designed for various types of filing. We will analyze the filing operations performed on the 085 collator, shown in Figure 8–14.

Again note that the main line switch (right side) must be turned on to provide power to the machine. This is different from the start key that initiates processing. The start key must be depressed for three cycles before automatic feeding becomes operative. Although there is a stop key that will stop the operation at any time and allow it to be restarted again, the machine automatically stops as the last card leaves its hopper. The run-out key must then be depressed to process the remaining cards. This is an important point because many jobs have been spoiled by an operator removing the cards when the machine stops and departing for subsequent operations, leaving cards in the machine where they may also spoil the next application and certainly will be missed from their proper place in the deck just collated.

Actually, there are two 800-card hoppers, the upper one being called the secondary feed hopper, and the lower, the primary feed hopper. Both hoppers feed through to 1,000-card stackers, which, as in all unit record machines, stop processing if full. There is also an error light that comes on when an error condition in processing occurs.

Functions of the Collator

Card Selection. X cards, or cards containing an X punch in a given column, first cards of a group, last cards of a group, single card groups, zero balance cards, and no-X cards can be selected from a deck of cards.

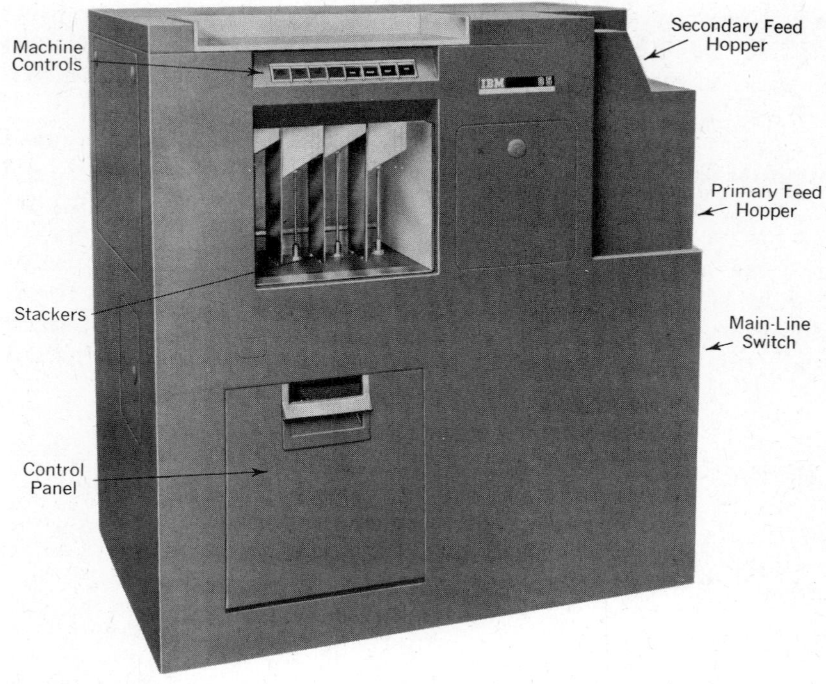

Figure 8–14. IBM 085 collator. *(Courtesy, IBM)*

Sequence Checking. Card files can be checked for ascending or descending order and the machine can be controlled to stop and turn on an error light if a sequence error occurs.

Merging. Two files of cards already in sequence can be joined or merged into a single deck, which would then be in ascending numerical order.

Merging with Selection. Sometimes a merging operation similar to that described above involves assembling a deck of cards by combining a deck of master cards with a deck of transaction, or detail, cards in such a way that each master card in the merged deck is immediately followed by the transaction cards with the same control number—product number, customer number, or the like. When there is no transaction card to be thus associated with a master card, it is useful sometimes to select out of the merged deck this unmatched master. Merging with selection is a technique of accomplishing this.

Matching. In an operation similar to merging with selection, two decks are read simultaneously by the collator and each pair of cards is compared.

Cards that do not have a counterpart in the other deck are stacked separately. The result is two decks of cards that have matching control fields and a third deck that contains cards which were unmatched in the comparing process. This operation differs from merging with selection in that the matched pairs are not filed together into one deck but rather are put into separate decks.

Blank Column Detection. Along with each of the above operations, the machine can perform blank column detection, in which it determines that all card columns have been punched. Detection of a blank column will be registered by the blank column detection lights and the collator will stop.

Principles of Operation

Let us now look at the interesting schematic of the 085 collator as shown in Figure 8–15. Cards are fed 9 edge first face down into the primary and secondary card hoppers at an operating speed of 240 cards per minute from each feed. Actually, since either one or both of the feeds may be used, the speed of the machine will vary from 240 to 480 cards per minute machine processing time.

In the primary feed, there is a set of 80 sequence read brushes and 80 primary read brushes and a sequence unit into which 16 columns of data on a card can be wired. The cards then pass through the primary feed from the primary brushes to the sequence brushes, and the same field can be compared for ascending or descending sequence by the primary and sequence read brushes. Suppose we were comparing cards on only one column and the cards were punched 1, 2, 4, 5, 6, 9, 8. Obviously the 9 is

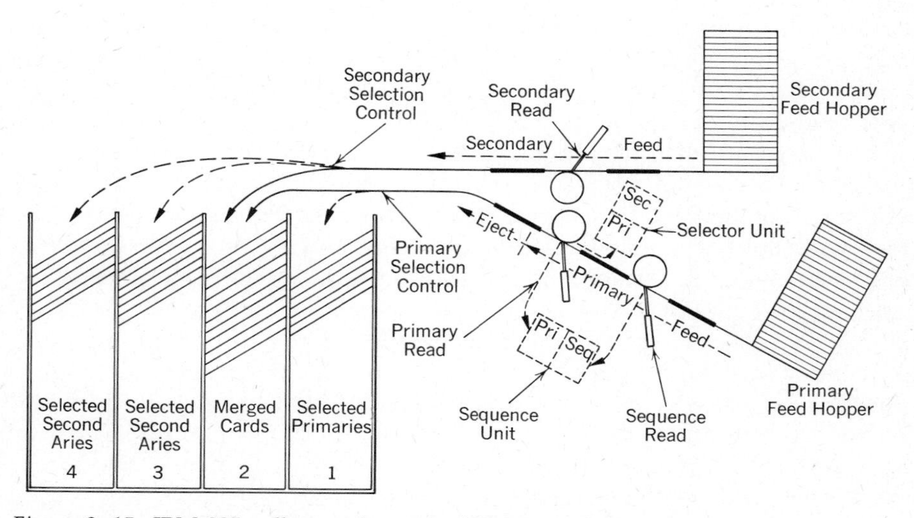

Figure 8–15. IBM 085 collator schematic. *(Courtesy, IBM)*

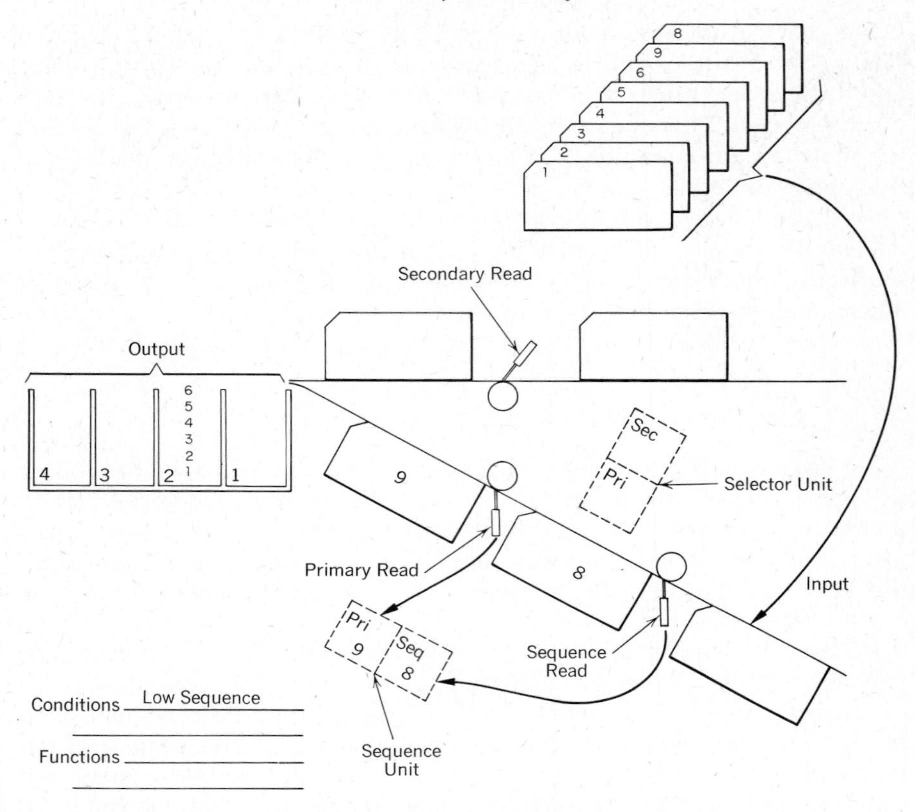

Figure 8–16. Low sequence condition in collator. *(Courtesy, IBM)*

out of order. This would be called a low sequence error because 9 is read into the primary side of the sequence unit and the 8 into the sequence side as shown in Figure 8–16. The condition of the sequence comparing unit would be low sequence. Suppose the cards were punched 9, 7, 6, 4, 5, 3 in descending order. In this case, we would have a high sequence condition that would also cause an error as shown in Figure 8–17.

The schematic in Figure 8–15 shows that the chute blades of the primary feed will allow cards to go only into pockets 1 and 2. Cards from this feed will normally go to pocket 2 unless selected through wiring control to go into pocket 1. Let us look now at the secondary feed with its single set of 80 read brushes. Note that the chute blades in the secondary feed will only allow cards to drop into pockets 2, 3, and 4, and all cards will go into pocket 2 unless selected. Normally, the secondary feed is wired into the secondary side of the selector comparing unit and compared with cards read at the primary read brushes of the primary feed, which is wired into the primary side of the sequence unit.

There are various other models of the collator in use today, one of which

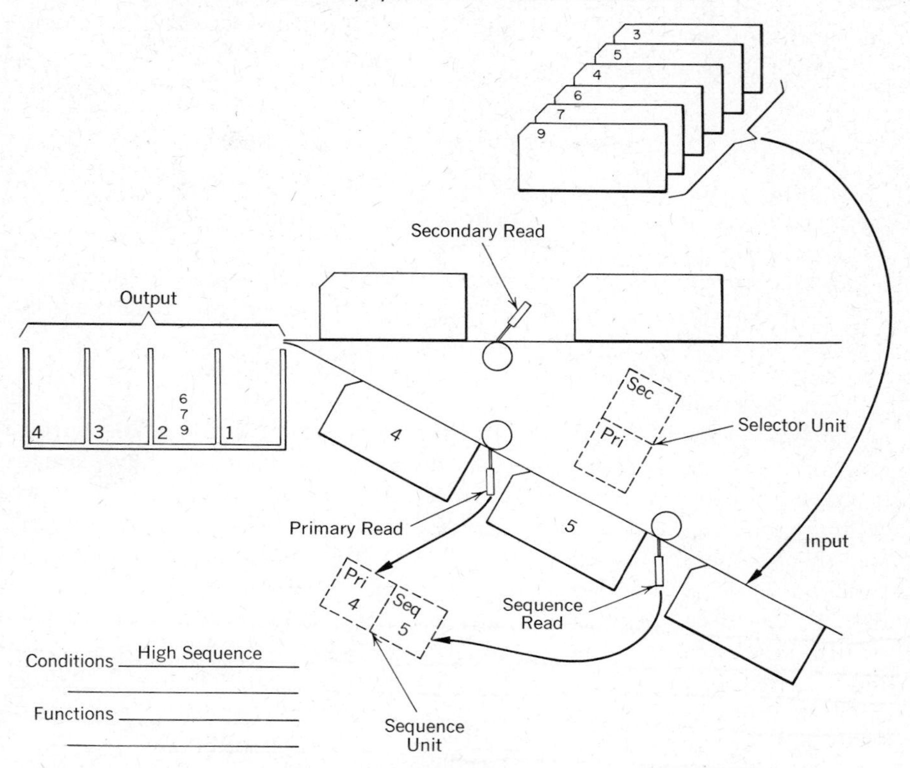

Figure 8–17. High sequence condition in collator. *(Courtesy, IBM)*

is the 188 collator. Its particular difference from the 085 is not conceptual but in speed and technology; it operates at 650 cards per minute per feed and has solid state components—transistors, diodes, and so on—compared to the completely electromechanical 085.

Tabulating and Accounting

So far, we have observed the punching, sorting, reproducing, and collating of data. We have considered manipulation of the sequence of data cards and observed some of the basic techniques of unit record equipment wiring. The ultimate purpose of all this activity is printing, tabulating, and preparation of printed reports. The primary tabulating devices used for report generation in unit record installations are the IBM 402 and 407 accounting machines.

The accounting machine has both arithmetic and printing capabilities. It can print reports on continuous form paper or, as we discussed earlier, can be hooked to the reproducer and data read from cards processed by it can be punched on summary cards. There are other models of accounting machines, such as the 403, 408, and 419, but 402's and 407's predominate and all perform basically the same functions.

ACCOUNTING MACHINE FUNCTIONS

Accounting machines can read figures punched in cards and then print them out or use them to accumulate totals by addition or subtraction. The basic operations of the accounting machine are detail printing or listing, which occurs when data from each card passing through the machine is read and listed; group printing, which occurs when the machine accumulates amounts and prints minor, intermediate or major group totals; and summary punching, which we have already discussed.

Figure 8–18 shows the 402 accounting machine. We will look primarily at the 402, pointing out significant differences from the 407. The buttons and switches are, for all practical purposes, like those we have already discussed concerning other machines. Accounting machines make use of tape-controlled carriages, which aid in manipulation of report formats and in page handling. The carriage or paper transport mechanism is controlled by holes punched in a tape, which is affixed to a tape-reading device. The tape has numbers down the side, each of which denotes the position of a printing line on the form being printed. The tape is divided into 12 channels into which holes are punched to cause various functions, such as skipping and total control, to take place. An analysis of Figure 8–19 will show how the control tapes aid in formatting reports.

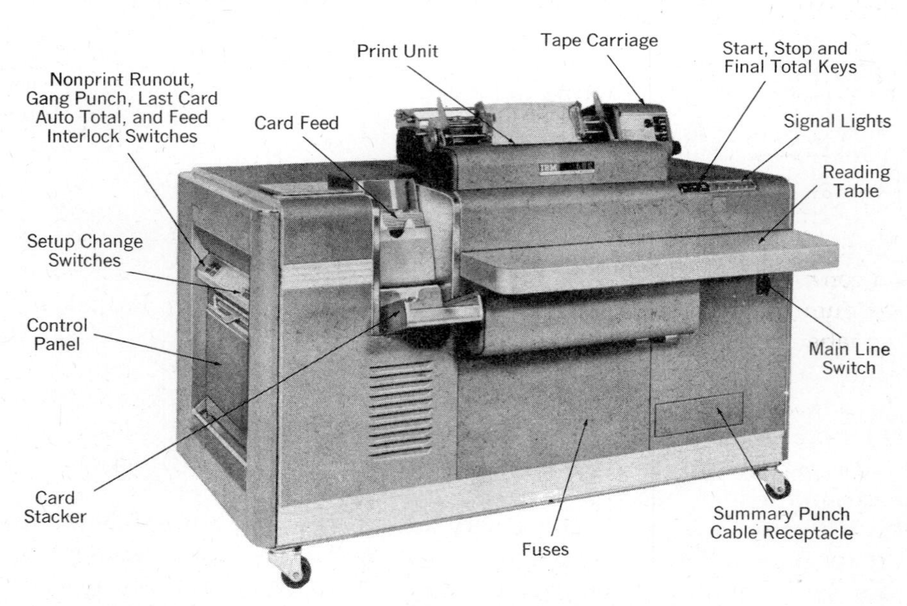

Figure 8–18. IBM 402 accounting machine. *(Courtesy, IBM)*

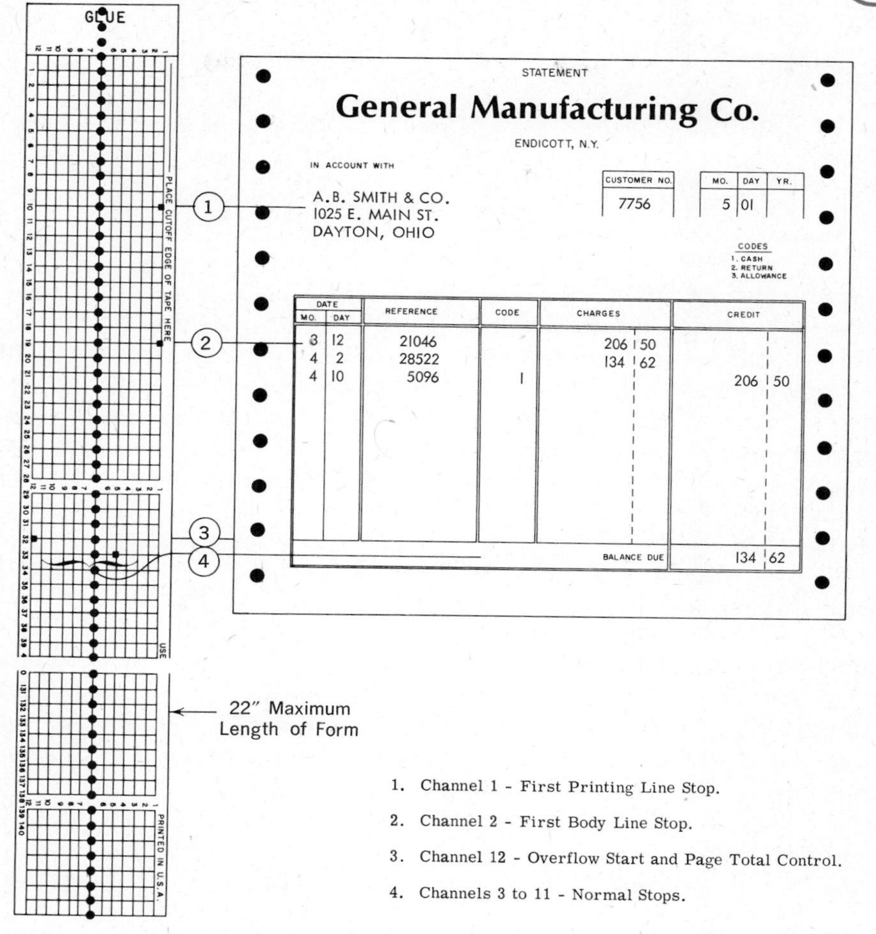

Figure 8–19. Carriage control tape and functions. *(Courtesy, IBM)*

Printing on the 407 occurs using alphameric wheels and may be done on continuous form paper, whereas the 402 uses type bars, some of which are numerical only, and some of which are alphanumeric, containing both alphabetic and numeric information.

Summarizing

The accounting machine embodies an accumulating feature. The 402 has 80 and the 407 has 112 separate accumulators, or counters, as they are usually called. These counters are of various sizes, but each operates on the same principle as the automobile odometer. They are mechanical and operate with rotating wheels, each numbered 0–9, with the ability to carry, as in addition operations. Information read from a card is wired to

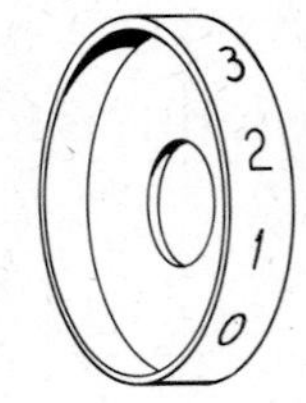

Figure 8–20. Accounting machine counters. *(courtesy, IBM)*

a counter entry, which causes it to be added into the counter. Contents of counters can be printed or transferred to another counter by totalling the particular counter. Examples of 402 counters are seen in Figure 8–20.

The accounting machine can find subtotals of numerical data by causing minor, intermediate, major, and final totals to take place on given conditions through control panel wiring. Examples of typical accounting machine output reports with various types of totals identified can be seen in Figure 8–21.

Manual Unit Record Systems

In the last chapter, we mentioned the Royal-McBee or Keysort system of edge-notched cards. In this type of unit record, data are represented by notches made in appropriate positions along the edge of the cards. (See Figure 8–22.) The coding scheme used for notching data into the edge of the cards is called modified binary coded decimal and is composed of the digits 7–4–2–1. Symbols of the decimal numbering system are recorded into each character position by notching one or two positions in the character. A 4 is represented by a 4 notch, a 6 by both a 4 and a 2 notch. This coding scheme is similar to that known as the Binary Coded Decimal, or BCD, system which represents decimal data in binary form. BCD is a coding scheme that records decimal characters using only ones and zeros —the two characters used in the binary number system. The positions in BCD are 8–4–2–1 as compared with 7–4–2–1 in the edge-notch system. The method of coding characters is the same, however, and for this reason, the 7–4–2–1 system is called modified BCD. In Figure 8–23 a comparison is made between modified binary coded decimal and binary coded decimal. As you can see, the modified system, while still allowing the representation of all decimal characters in four positions, saves one notching position. This is a valuable saving when you think of notching values into many hundreds or thousands of cards for use in various applications in organizational processing.

Figure 8–24 shows the keysort batch groover, which is designed to notch large groups of cards with identical information. As many as 50 cards can be grooved at once. The machine has an alignment pin to center

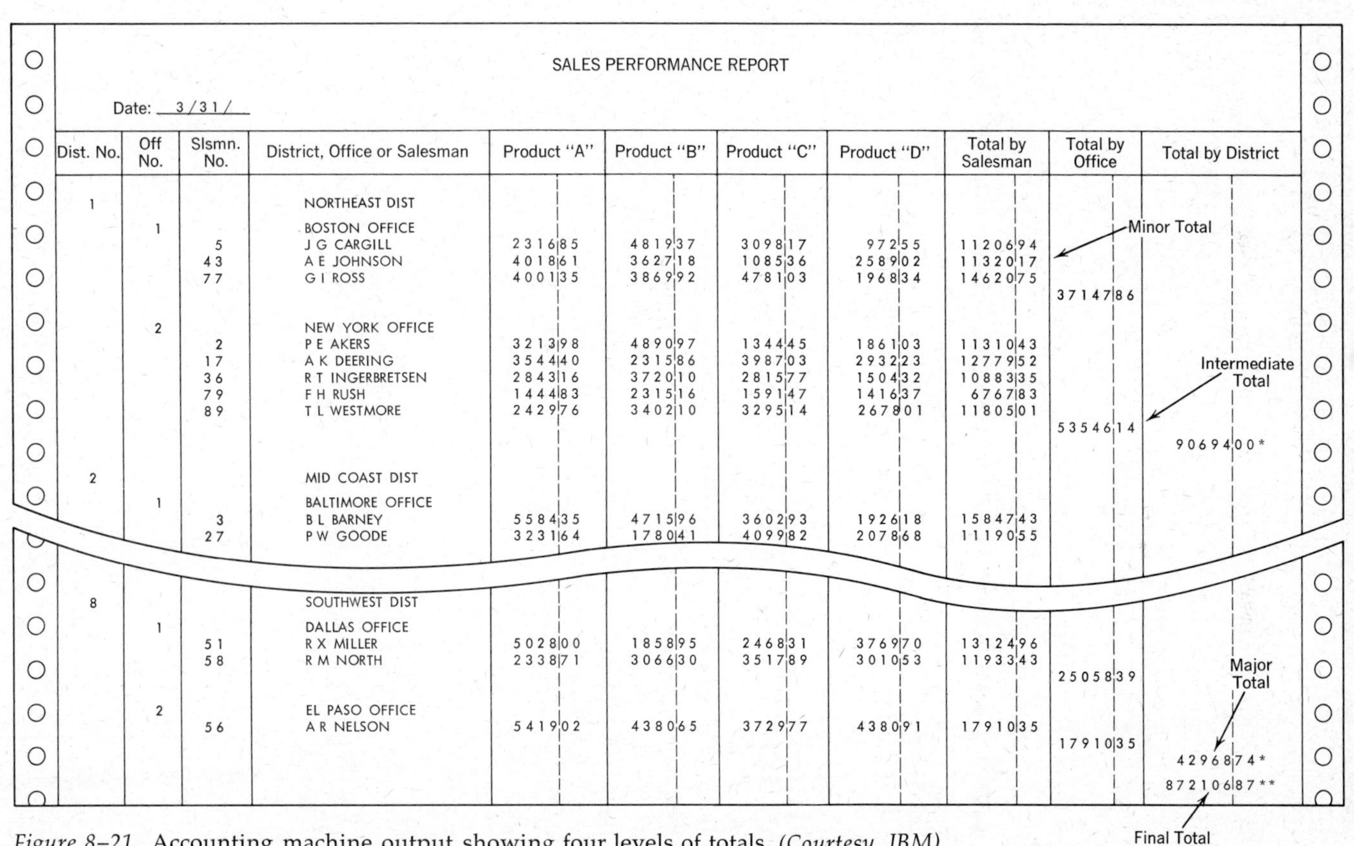

SALES PERFORMANCE REPORT

Date: 3/31/

Dist. No.	Off No.	Slsmn. No.	District, Office or Salesman	Product "A"	Product "B"	Product "C"	Product "D"	Total by Salesman	Total by Office	Total by District
1			NORTHEAST DIST							
	1		BOSTON OFFICE							
		5	J G CARGILL	2316 85	4819 37	3098 17	972 55	11206 94		
		43	A E JOHNSON	4018 61	3627 18	1085 36	2589 02	11320 17		
		77	G I ROSS	4001 35	3869 92	4781 03	1968 34	14620 75		
									37147 86	
	2		NEW YORK OFFICE							
		2	P E AKERS	3213 98	4890 97	1344 45	1861 03	11310 43		
		17	A K DEERING	3544 40	2315 86	3987 03	2932 23	12779 52		
		36	R T INGERBRETSEN	2843 16	3720 10	2815 77	1504 32	10883 35		
		79	F H RUSH	1444 83	2315 16	1591 47	1416 37	6767 83		
		89	T L WESTMORE	2429 76	3402 10	3295 14	2678 01	11805 01		
									53546 14	
										90694 00*
2			MID COAST DIST							
	1		BALTIMORE OFFICE							
		3	B L BARNEY	5584 35	4715 96	3602 93	1926 18	15847 43		
		27	P W GOODE	3231 64	1780 41	4099 82	2078 68	11190 55		
8			SOUTHWEST DIST							
	1		DALLAS OFFICE							
		51	R X MILLER	5028 00	1858 95	2468 31	3769 70	13124 96		
		58	R M NORTH	2338 71	3066 30	3517 89	3010 53	11933 43		
									25058 39	
	2		EL PASO OFFICE							
		56	A R NELSON	5419 02	4380 65	3729 77	4380 91	17910 35		
									17910 35	
										42968 74*
										872106 87**

Figure 8–21. Accounting machine output showing four levels of totals. *(Courtesy, IBM)*

SUMMARY 7 4 2 1 7 4 2 1 7 4 2 1 7 4 2 1 7 4 2 1 7 4 2 1 7 4 2 1 7 4 2 1
THOUSANDS HUNDREDS TENS UNITS
PRODUCTION ORDER NUMBER
PRINTED IN U.S.A.

PRODUCTION ORDER NUMBER		DESCRIPTION		DATE - START	DATE - FINISH
6027		Animal Cage		Aug.30	Sep.4
QUANTITY - ORDERED	QUANTITY - PRODUCED	PRODUCT CLASS - MODEL NO.	PART NO.	MATERIAL	
35	35	01 138		OUTSIDE PURCHASES	25 00

WESTERN METAL PRODUCTS CO.
LOS ANGELES, CALIFORNIA

JOB COST SUMMARY

OPERATION	Shear	Punch	Assemb.	Ship		
DEPARTMENT	6	7	8	9		
HOURS						
LABOR $						
OVERHEAD $						
TOTAL $						

LABOR	
OVERHEAD	
TOTAL COST	
SCRAP COST	4 20
NET COST	
COST PER PIECE	

© 1965 MCBEE SYSTEMS
DATA PROCESSING PRACTICE SET - FORM PS-13-2
© W15853E MODEL NUMBER PRODUCT CLASS FINISH DATE MONTH

Figure 8–22. Royal-McBee edge-notch card and coding scheme. (Copyright © 1965 by McBee Systems, Royal Typewriter Company, Inc., a division of Litton Industries.)

cards under the knife. The knife is operated manually by pulling the handle forward. Figure 8–24 depicts the keysort keypunch which is used to notch large quantities of information. One side of the card is notched at a time. The keypunch looks and operates much like an adding machine. It can both punch and read as well as list and total arithmetically on a tape.

Cards can be manually punched by using the Keysort Hand Punch (Figure 8–24). The hand punch is used to notch a single position at a time. Errors in notching can be corrected by using gummed stickers called card savers. This saves making a new card when an error occurs. (See Figure 8–25.)

Binary Coded Decimal				(Decimal Equivalent)	Modified Binary Coded Decimal			
8	4	2	1		7	4	2	1
			1	1				1
		1		2			1	
		1	1	3			1	1
	1			4		1		
	1		1	5		1		1
	1	1		6		1	1	
	1	1	1	7	1			
1				8	1		1	
1			1	9	1		1	
No Groove				0	No Groove			

Figure 8–23. Comparison of BCD and modified BCD. (Zeros omitted for clarity.)

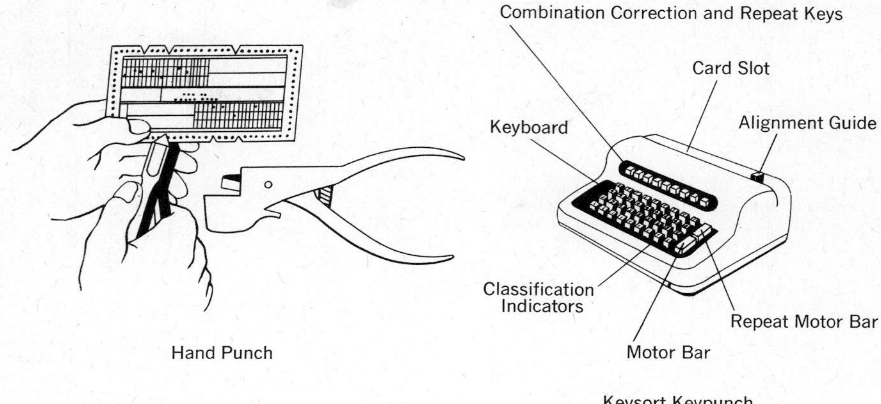

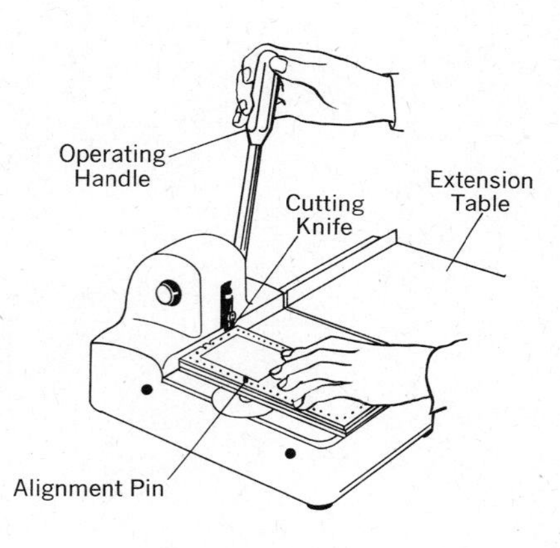

Figure 8–24. Keysort batch groover, keypunch, and hand punch. (Courtesy, McBee Systems, Royal Typewriter Company, Inc., a division of Litton Industries.)

Card Savers Are Gummed Stickers Used to Correct a Notching Error or to Save Creating a New Card If a Classification Is Changed. Sheets of Card Savers Are Perforated Into Sections of Three Holes and Bound in Book Form. To Apply:

1. Tear along Long Perforation.
2. Fold Slightly along Short Perforation.
3. Moisten the Gummed Side.
4. Align Holes of Card Saver with Holes of Keysort Card in from the Back.
5. Fold other Half Forward over the Edge of the Card and Press Down to Secure all Edges.
6. The Card Is now Ready for Renotching.

Figure 8–25. Keysort card savers. (Courtesy, McBee Systems, Royal Typewriter Company, Inc., a division of Litton Industries.)

BASIC TECHNIQUE

A new operator can quickly attain a high degree of sorting efficiency without previous experience or mechanical aptitude. It is merely necessary to follow certain basic principles and techniques.

Sorting the Long Side

1. Place a convenient handful of cards (approximately 1" or slightly larger) on the Alignment Block with the front of the cards facing the operator and the side to be sorted at the top.
2. Holding the cards loosely with the left hand, jog them against the guide of the Alignment Block.

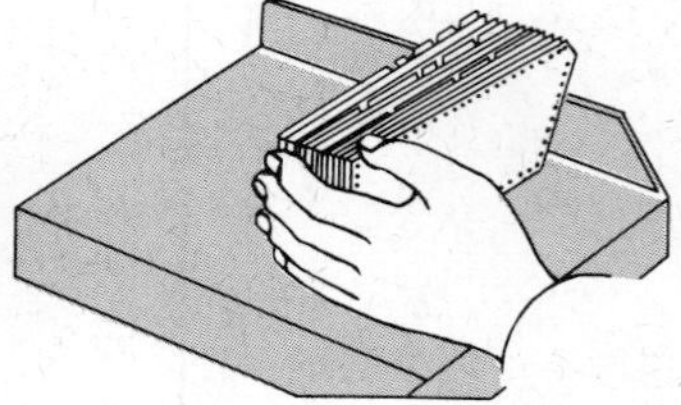

3. Grasp the cards close to the position to be sorted.
4. Hold the handle of the Keysorter firmly with the right hand. Keep the fingers away from the needle at all times.
5. Insert the needle in the position to be sorted until the front card is approximately one inch from the handle.

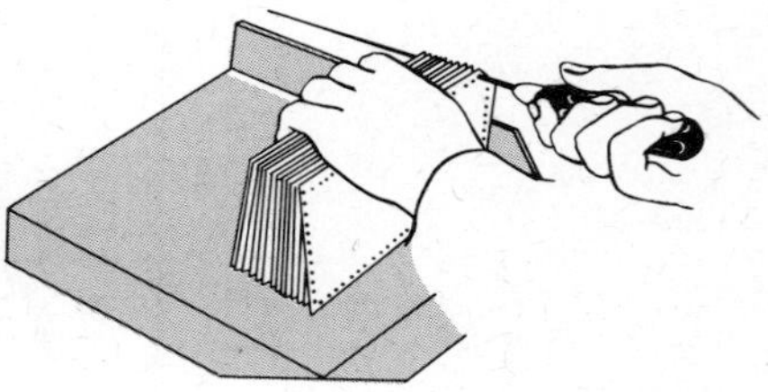

6. Slide the left hand to the left side of the cards. Hold them lightly with only slight pressure of the thumb and fingers against the cards.

7. Move the handle of the Keysorter to the left and at the same time move the cards to the center of the Alignment Block. Hold the cards with the left hand. Exert pressure with thumb in the lower left corner.

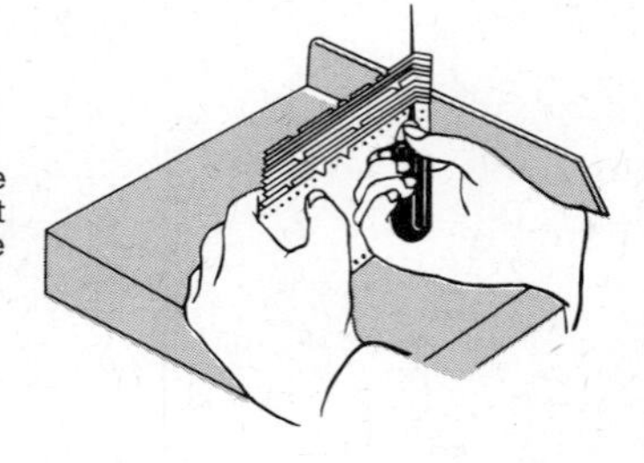

Notched cards can be sorted by using a simple keysorter or sorting needle and an alignment block. An operator can actually attain a high degree of efficiency in sorting using this method. Figure 8–26 goes through sorting using the keysorter in a step-by-step fashion. The same sorting methods as used with the IBM 082 and 083 sorters—direct sorting, block sorting, and reverse digit sorting—can be accomplished manually using the sorting needle. A direct sort on a single position field can be accomplished by simply inserting the needle and lifting the cards. Sup-

The inside of the fingers should be flush against the beveled edge of the cards.

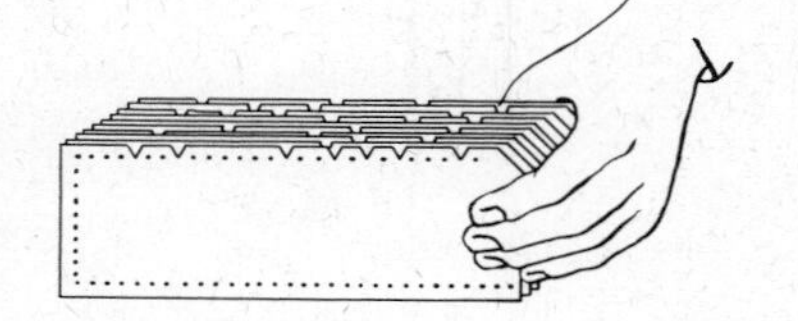

8. Swing the Keysorter to the right until resistance is felt. This will cause the cards to spread out on the needle. For Sequence Sorting (see following section), release the pressure of the left hand. Spread the fingers to balance the cards that will fall.

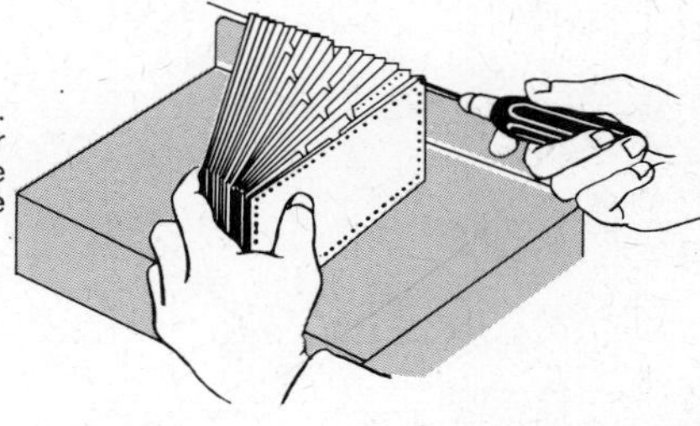

9. Lift Keysorter slightly—approximately one-half inch from surface of the Alignment Block. Strike the cards several times against the guide of the Alignment Block, at the same time gently raising the Keysorter away from the cards that are falling.

10. If some cards stick and do not fall, grasp all the cards, placing the thumb and fingers in the upper left hand corner of the cards that are still on the needle. Move the cards towards the center of the Alignment Block. Lower right hand slightly; release the pressure of the left hand and strike the cards again to break loose those that do not fall in the first operation.

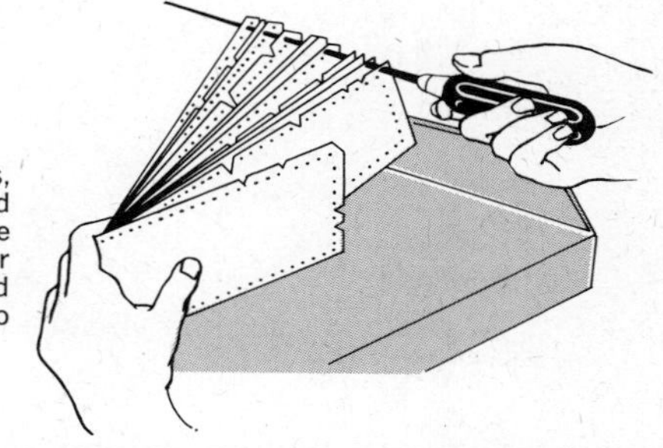

Figure 8–26. Step-by-step method of using the Keysorter. (Courtesy, McBee Systems, Royal Typewriter Company, Inc., a division of Litton Industries.)

pose we represented six in a one-position field for day shift and no notches for night shift. We can see how easily these could be separated.

Edge-notched cards can also be processed electromechanically through the use of the tape punch/reader depicted in Figure 8–27. This machine can also punch information into the body of the card and can read and tabulate information from the body of a card onto a tape similar to a standard adding machine tape.

It should be apparent from the manual system we have investigated

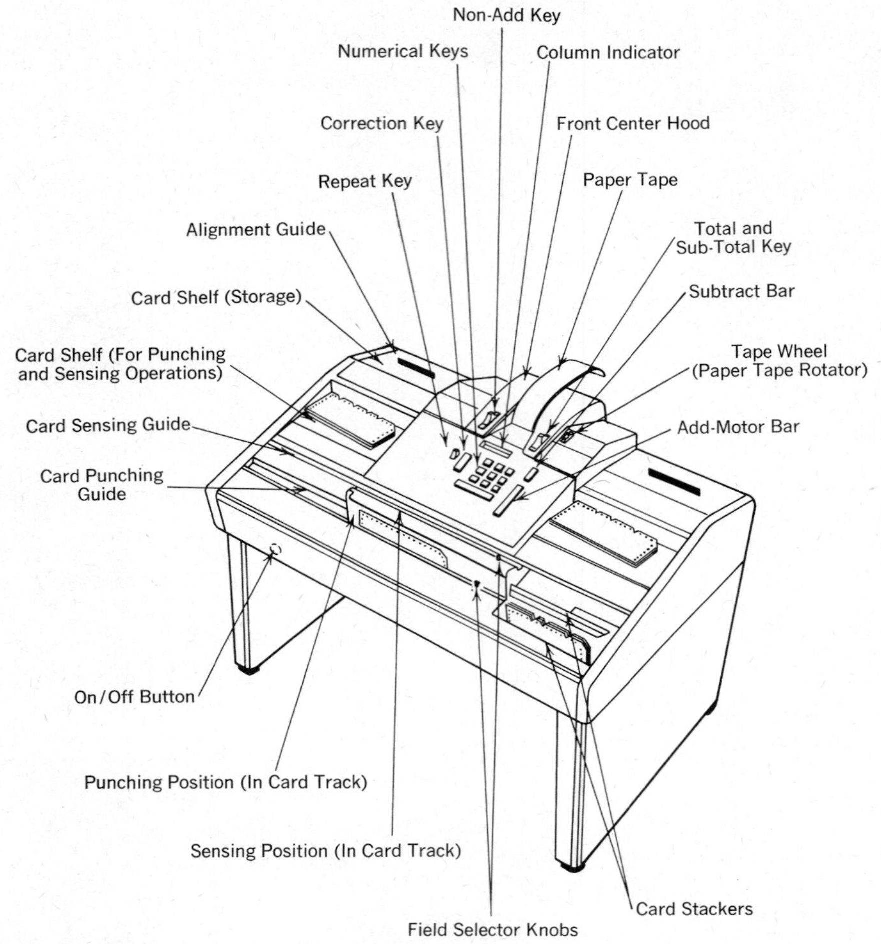

Figure 8–27. Keysort tape punch/reader.

here that the principles we applied during our discussion of tabulating equipment are directly applicable to manual systems as well and that basic methods of data processing remain constant. It is technology and our skill in its implementation that changes.

Third-Generation Unit Record Processing

The term *third generation,* as used by data processors, refers to the latest stage in the development of electronic data processing techniques. Unit record processing has, in the past, typically been performed by the type of electromechanical equipment described in this and the previous chapter. Unit record data processing—the processing of records contained on a unit of a recording medium (like a punched card)—can and has been performed using electronic equipment. As has been pointed out here, the ideas of unit record processing and the functions of unit record equipment carry over into computerized data processing, and in the past a number of hybrid devices have been used that are both electromechanical and electronic in nature. These devices usually performed calculating functions involving multiplication, division, and other operations beyond the powers of the equipment described in these chapters.

The advent of third-generation computer systems brought with it a computer the purpose of which is primarily unit record data processing. This computer system is one of the IBM System/360 family of computer systems and is known as the Model 20. The heart of the System/360 Model 20 is the *Multi-Function Card Machine* or MFCM illustrated in Figure 8–28. This machine is a versatile card-handling input/output device for the system to which can be attached a number of other devices, such as high-speed printers, magnetic tape drives, and a processing unit or computer. A typical Model 20 installation would include a 2020 Processing Unit, a 2560 MFCM, and a high-speed printer that, depending upon the model, can print up to 750 lines per minute.

The Model 20 is a stored-program computer system and in this respect differs from other unit record processing equipment that is programmed externally with the use of wired control panels. Electronic computers are controlled by programs—written instructions that are to be sequentially executed. Programs are stored for execution in the computer system's

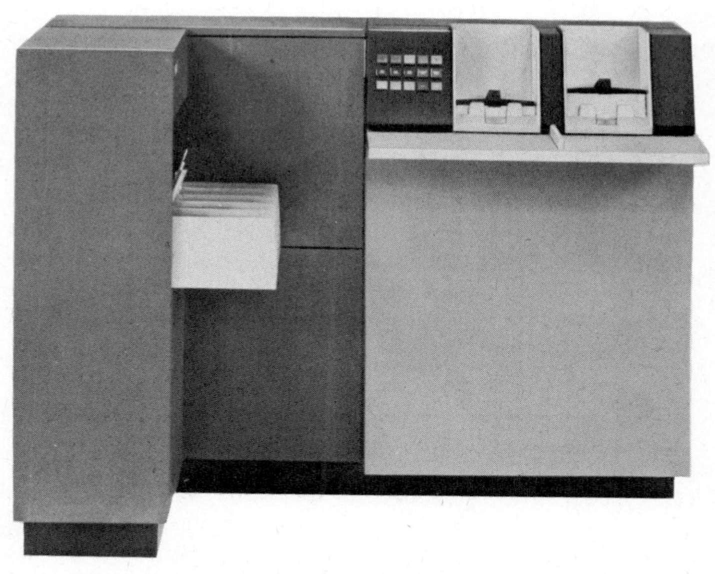

Figure 8–28. IBM 2560 multi-function card machine. *(Courtesy, IBM)*

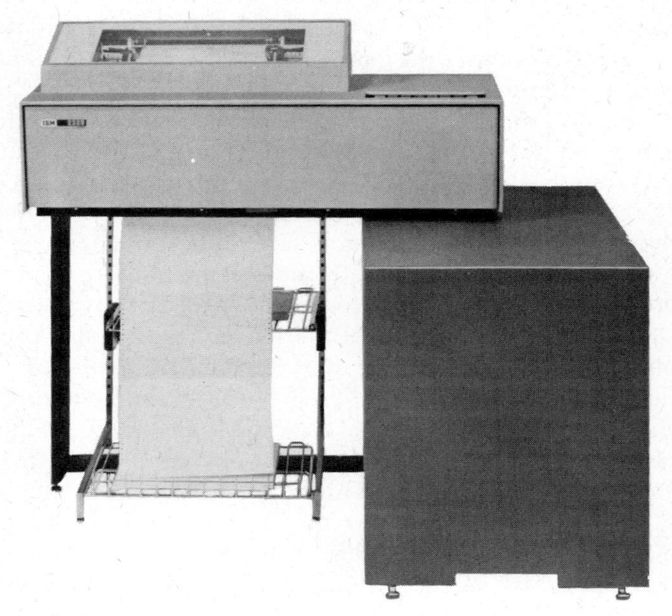

Figure 8–29. IBM 2203 printer. *(Courtesy, IBM)*

memory—a device that stores data to be processed by a computer system. Writing programs for computers is the subject of later chapters. The Model 20 is programmed using a programming language known as RPG, for Report Program Generator, a method of writing computer instructions which is particularly useful for the type of business reports produced by unit record installations. It can also be programmed using techniques discussed in a later chapter on computer programming.

The main advantages of Model 20 utilization in unit record installations over more conventional electromechanical equipment include higher throughput, or faster completion of jobs; greater calculating and data manipulating power; reduced card handling (since one machine now does what many were required to do before); and *upward compatibility*, by which is meant the ability to upgrade the computer system to a more sophisticated model of the System/360 without substantial reprogramming.

Unit Record Equipment and the Future

Unit record equipment has a distinct place in professional data processing and will be used for a long time to come. In view of the tremendous growth in the number of computer installations, the skyrocketing investment in computer equipment, and other dramatic technological developments, some believe that unit record equipment has seen its day and is

Figure 8–30. IBM 2020 central processing unit. *(Courtesy, IBM)*

now obsolete. However, many small firms that heretofore could not afford automated data processing equipment can now enjoy its use. Moreover, one of the greatest benefits unit record equipment can offer business information systems is support to computer installations.

Important also is the realization that the handling concepts we have applied to unit record equipment in this chapter also apply directly to computer processing. Merging, matching, merging with selection, gang-punching, selective reproducing, interpreting, sorting, and all of the other functions discussed here are implicit in effective data processing, whether accomplished through electromechanical means or electronically. These are concepts which will remain constant. Only the mechanics of their implementation will change with the technology.

Questions

1. Explain the difference between directed and redirected impulses.
2. Reading brushes are associated with which type of hub—entry or exit?

3. What is the purpose of a common hub? How does this purpose differ from bus hubs?
4. Explain the advantages of the 548 over the 026 in terms of printing information.
5. What is the purpose of a column split and how does it operate?
6. Explain the use and purpose of X brushes.
7. Discuss the principles and applications related to the use of selectors. How does a selector work?
8. How does offset gangpunching differ from interspersed gangpunching?
9. What are comparing magnets used for and how do they work?
10. Explain mark sensing.
11. What are the main functions of a collator?
12. What conditions would occur if you were sequence checking cards in an 085 and the cards were in this order: 9, 7, 6, 8, 9, 3, 2?
13. Describe the typebars on a 402.
14. How is format control obtained on the 402?
15. Discuss the report generating advantages of the 402.
16. Compare the bank of unit record equipment you have studied with IBM System/360 Model 20.

Part III

Electronic Information Systems

Operation and Programming of Electronic Digital Computers

In the last twenty years, we have witnessed the introduction of three generations of computer systems. These machines have offered man a means of increasing his productivity by expanding his capability of performing tasks that he would not have dreamed of attempting prior to the computer. Practically every industry owes its present state, in part, to the digital computer. There are four factors that make the digital computer such a valuable tool: (1) speed of operation, (2) permanent memory, (3) accuracy, and (4) automatic operation.

The speed with which computers can perform operations is beyond the comprehension of even those who have been associated with them for some time, much less the novice. The computer carries out its orders (instructions) one step at a time, but these steps, in many instances, are executed at speeds approaching one ten-millionth of a second. In one minute of operation, many computers can carry out more calculations than a man could perform in a lifetime. It is not uncommon for modern-day computers to add 250,000 sixteen-digit numbers in less than one second.

Permanent memory for data storage purposes is another factor that makes the computer highly valuable. Computers can store large volumes of data and at the whim of the operator recall any or all of that data for inspection or processing. A company may want to know how many of its employees have a particular skill. The computer under appropriate program control could recall from its permanent memory files all of those employees with the desired skill and give management the desired report in a matter of minutes.

The accuracy with which data may be handled and operated upon is another of the computer's valuable traits. Multiplication or division problems performed by the computer can be calculated to twenty decimal places as accurately as to four decimal places.

Automatic operation plays a very significant role in the computer's value. Since it has the ability to store and recall data, it follows that it can store and recall a set of instructions. In fact, it can store and execute these instructions in sequence without any human intervention. This has many advantages, chief of which is the ability to execute a series of sequential instructions that are stored in the memory of the computer and that can be executed over and over again without the necessity of presenting the instructions to the computer more than once. Thus, calculations to prepare a weekly paycheck for an employee can be performed as many times as there are employees for whom a paycheck must be prepared without the necessity of providing separate instructions for each employee pay record to be processed. This set of instructions, which must obviously be written to handle all possible contingencies in a particular application, is known as a *stored program* when stored in the computer system's memory. The importance of the stored program to electronic data processing will become clearer later in these chapters. Suffice it to say here that it has been heralded as the most significant advance to date in computer technology. Its development was accomplished by a man named Von Neumann and frequently the stored program concept is called the Von Neumann principle.

Using these desirable characteristics, computers can balance bank accounts, figure payrolls, check income tax returns, update insurance records, control a firm's inventories, send bills to customers, simulate the design and effect of the design of aircraft or missiles, perform heart research, and a myriad of related jobs. Computers play a role of some sort in every industry and profession. In light of this, challenging new careers are opening for the able high school or college graduate. The future progress of many businesses and, in fact, the country will rely heavily upon people who can understand and solve scientific, social, and industrial problems on the computer. The design of the Supersonic Transports (SST's) was impossible without the use of the computer. Some of the decisions made by the computer during this design would have taken man a lifetime to make. The computer has the ability, not only to aid in the design, but also to simulate the flight of the finished product under varying environmental conditions. Many large cities are discussing the possibility of 200- and 300-mile-per-hour public transportation systems for moving millions of people from place to place within cities and surrounding areas. Scheduling and operating trains running minutes apart at these speeds will require many split-second decisions that cannot be accomplished by man alone. The computer has made its mark in society as a highly valuable tool and in coming years society will lean even more heavily on the computer for support.

Computer Types

Computers are powerful tools to be sure, but they are not "electronic brains," "electronic giants," "thinking machines," or, in fact, any kind of a giant electronic monster possessing mysterious powers and wisdom.

Probably, the best way to classify a computer in this sense would be to say that it is an exceptionally fast and accurate moron capable of manipulating data and making a few very elementary decisions based upon the nature of the data being processed. One of the primary functions of these chapters is to dispel some of the mystery surrounding black boxes which sit in air-conditioned rooms pumping out reams and reams of reports. Computers are completely useless without man, for he must not only tell the computer what to do, but how to do it as well. Moreover, computers' vocabularies are very limited. This forces man to express highly complex problems in relatively simple terms if he wishes to use computers as problem-solving devices.

Analog Computers

When solving problems, computers are dealing primarily with values expressed as numbers using either a counting or a measuring scheme. A computer using a measuring scheme is usually making an analogy between two conditions. For instance, a speedometer is used to make an analogy between the rotation of a shaft and the speed with which an automobile is travelling. A thermostat makes an analogy between the warping of a bimetal strip and the temperature of an object. A gasoline gauge is making an analogy between the position of a float and the amount of gasoline in a tank. A calculating machine or computer that makes analogies between numbers and directly measurable quantities such as voltage, rotations, resistance, and so on, is known as an *analog computer.* These computers are in wide use in controlling manufacturing processes, oil refining, and in the missile and space industry. For example, if one is given the diameter of a pipe and the rate of flow of the fluid in the pipe, it is a simple task to determine the amount of fluid that has passed a specified point in a given amount of time. The amount of fluid passing a point can be controlled either by using pipe of a different diameter or controlling the rate of flow of the fluid through the pipe. If the pipe is of constant diameter, then the amount of fluid passing a point may be controlled by changing the rate of travel of the fluid. An analog computer works very efficiently in cases such as this. The analogy is made between the speed of the fluid in the pipe and the volume of fluid passing a certain point. Thus, the computer can be made to control the speed required to produce a given volume of the fluid. The computer can be used continuously to monitor the velocity of the fluid and adjust this velocity almost immediately to meet the volume requirements of a specified mixture.

Digital Computers

A *digital computer* deals with numbers by counting. It accepts numbers in the form of coded digits and operates on them by a counting process.

Adding machines and cash registers are good examples of digital computers.

Each type of computer (digital or analog) has its place in industry and one was not designed to replace the other by any stretch of the imagination. They were meant to supplement each other. In fact, many of the computers used in missiles and spacecraft programs represent a combination of digital and analog computers and are known as *hybrid* computers. The strong or appropriate features of each are used to perform its specialty. One of the big advantages of the digital computer over the analog variety lies in its accuracy. It is a very rare analog computer that can come up with answers accurate in the third decimal place. In a digital computer, this presents no problem whatsoever. Although more accurate than the analog computer, the digital computer is somewhat slower in its total operation. Once the job to be done is defined properly, then decision for the type of computer (analog or digital) to be used is made almost automatically. For the remainder of this and the chapters to follow, our discussion will be restricted to digital computers because for commercial applications digital computers are used virtually exclusively.

Computers Defined

The word *computer* is very general and strictly speaking could be applied to a variety of devices. Throughout the industry, the word computer usually refers to a stored program digital computer. Another type of computer will usually be referred to by name as analog, special purpose, hybrid, synchronous, and so on. In general, a computer is any device capable of accepting data, applying prescribed processes to this data, and yielding results of these processes. A digital computer is one capable of accepting and operating on only the representation of digits or other characters that have been coded in a digital fashion. A stored program digital computer is a computer that has the ability to perform sequences of internally stored instructions with the added ability of operating upon the instructions themselves. Also, it has the ability to alter the sequence of instructions based on previously calculated results or the desires of the computer operator. Thus, the word *computer* will be taken here to mean a stored program digital computer.

Prior to the introduction of third-generation data processing systems, computers were classified as either scientific or commercial. The particular characteristics of the system which made it fall into one or the other of these classes was its input, processing, and output requirements. Most commercial applications are concerned with high volume input and output and relatively little computation, whereas the scientific applications require little input and output and complex calculations. However, problems being solved by businesses are becoming as complex and are requiring as much calculation as some scientific applications, and scientific applications are requiring much more input and output. Third generation computer manufacturers attempt to provide one system that can handle scientific, commercial, and communications applications and provide for better information retrieval capabilities. Thus, a large or small business need not worry about a commercially oriented computer for one application and a scientifically oriented computer for another. One system should be able to handle all of its data processing needs.

How Do Computers Do Work?

We implied previously that a computer is essentially a robot and as such it must be instructed to perform tasks desired by the user. Each computer is designed to perform only a specified number of operations. To make the computer perform these operations, we must supply it with instructions that it "understands." *Instructions* define basic operations to be performed and tell the computer where the required data needed to carry out this operation are located. Any problem, simple or complex, must be broken down into a set of these instructions before the computer can go to work solving the problem. For example, a computer may be wired internally to automatically execute a multiplication operation. Of course, it would be wired to carry out other operations as well, but let's concentrate for the moment on the multiplication section. If we wish to use this feature of the computer, we must somehow indicate that multiplcation is desired by using an instruction with an appropriate operation code that calls for multiplication. Then we will need to tell the machine where it is to look in its memory for the multiplier and multiplicand and, in some cases, tell it where in its memory to place the product. When we give the computer the correct commands (instructions), it will proceed to follow these commands (like the robot it is) and produce the desired result.

A program is a series of instructions expressed in a form that the machine can use and in a sequence that causes a desired result to be achieved. When we speak of methods of processing data, we must realize that these include a method of getting the information into the system, the equipment to be used for processing, a method of storing the information (internally or externally), some way to get the results out of the system, and a set of instructions for processing the information.

Actually, a computer solves problems in much the same way as you do. Suppose you have been hired by a company to perform payroll calculations but that you do not understand the procedure to be followed under varying conditions (i.e., overtime calculations, statuatory deductions, and so on). You do, however, possess the ability to read, perform basic calculations, write checks (once the amount has been determined), and follow directions. The supervisor for whom you are working has devised a foolproof plan whereby a man with your limited abilities can calculate weekly pay and write checks without really understanding what he is doing. He has decided to set up boxes similar to post office boxes. Each box is numbered in sequence (1, 2, 3, . . .) and inside each box is an instruction. He informs you that you are to start at box 1 and carry out the instructions in that box, proceed to box 2, 3, and so on in sequence, carrying out all of the instructions until you have processed the last man's time card and written the last check for the last man. The appearance of your work station is shown in Figure 9–1.

The day begins and you take your place at your work station. According to the supervisor, you are to look at the instructions in box 1, execute them, and go on to sequentially higher numbered boxes unless instructed by one of the instructions to do otherwise. Reaching into box 1 you find that the instructions tell you to clear the calculator to zero and to empty boxes 14 through 19. This you do, after which you replace these initial instructions back into box 1. In box 2 you find instructions telling you to

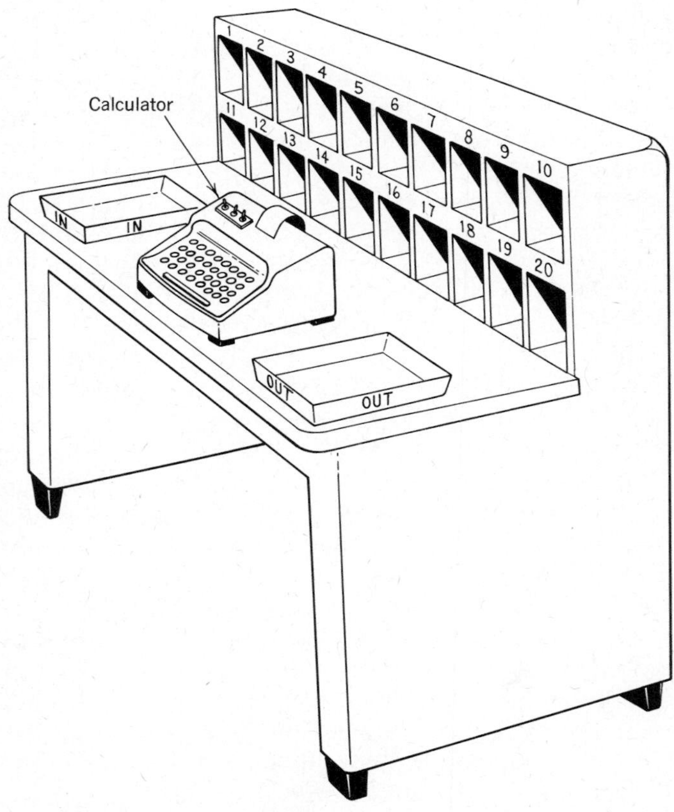

Figure 9–1. Payroll clerk work station.

reach in the box labelled IN, take the card on top of the deck and place it beside the calculator. Box 3 tells you to examine the time on the card and determine whether or not this man has worked over 40 hours this week. If he has not you are to proceed to box 4. If he has worked over 40 hours, proceed to box 11. In box 4, the instructions are to multiply his hourly rate indicated on the card by the number of hours indicated on the card and save this result in box 14. Box 5 gives you the procedure for calculating withholding tax and instructions to save this information. Box 6 details the calculations for FICA and instructs you to save these results. Box 7 asks you to determine from the card whether or not this employee is on the pension plan. If he is, proceed to box 8. If not proceed to box 9. In box 8, the procedure for calculating pension plan deductions is outlined. You are instructed to save this result as well. Box 9 instructs you to add up all of his deductions and subtract this amount from his gross pay. This yields his net pay. Box 10 instructs you to write his check, place it in the out box and proceed to box 11. Box 11 instructs you to subtract 40 from his total hours worked and save this result. Box 12 tells you to take the result just saved and multiply it by the overtime hourly rate indicated on the card and save this result. Box 13 tells you to multiply 40 by his normal rate, add this result to the figure just saved.

When the supply of cards in the IN box has been exhausted, you are to sit and wait for more cards and continue in the same routine.

The procedure outlined above in words may be expressed diagrammatically as in Figure 9–2. This is referred to as a *block diagram* of the procedure you are to follow. If a computer were solving this payroll problem, it would proceed in a similar fashion except at much greater speed. Instructions would have to be provided to the machine and stored in its memory. The act of writing these instructions is called programming. The set of instructions is called the program, and the person writing these instructions is called the programmer. Once the instructions have been written (in a format usable by the computer) and loaded into the machine, they will be executed in sequence in much the same fashion as you did in calculating the payroll for the company.

Prior to writing the program for any computer, the problem to be solved must be thoroughly analyzed and a detailed method of attack for the computer must be outlined. All logical procedures and algorithms must be dictated in advance so the computer can follow these procedures without further intervention by the operator of the machine. The step-by-step process of outlining these procedures is best accomplished by means of a block diagram for which rules and details for writing will be presented later. Figure 9–2 represents a rough block diagram for the sequence of operations to be performed in our payroll example. Closer analysis of the problem just solved reveals that basically we are concerned with five components: the *IN box*, the *OUT box*, the *pigeon holes (memory)*, the *calculator*, and the *person controlling* the sequence of operations. In a com-

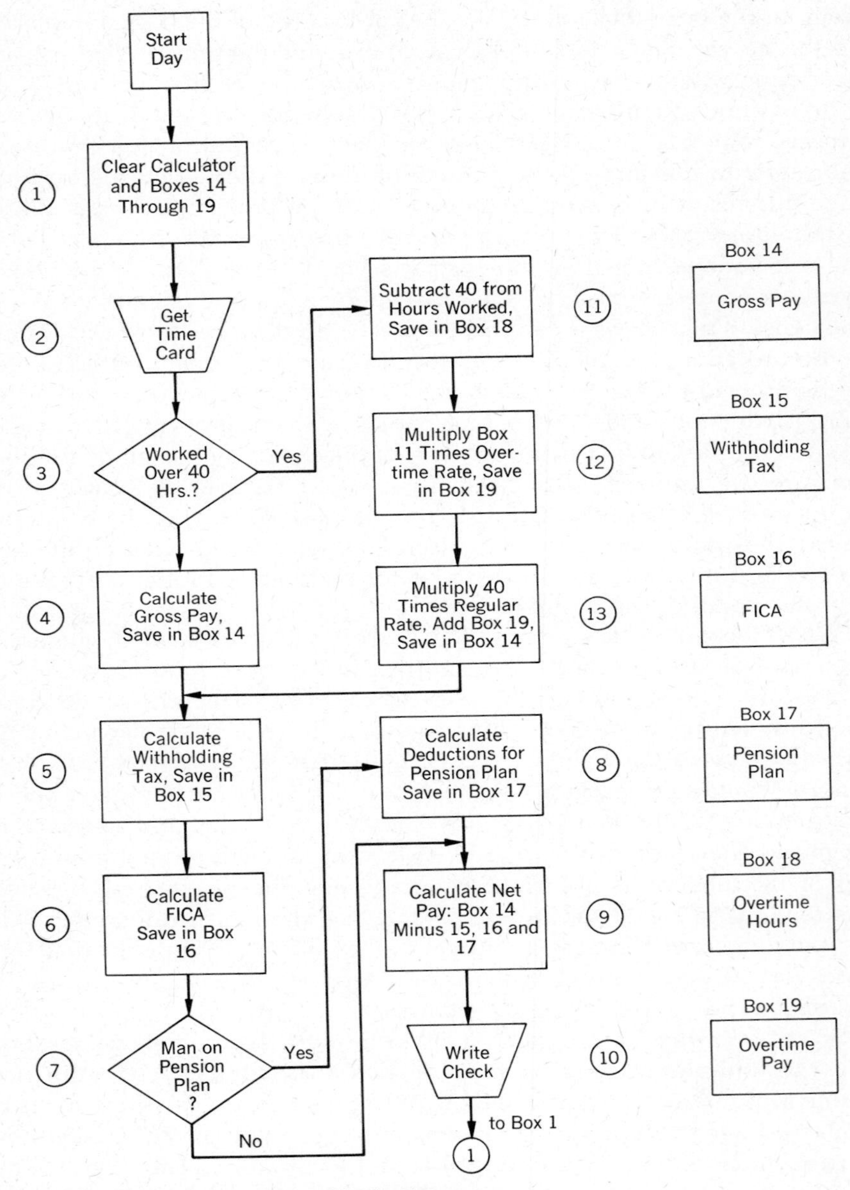

Figure 9–2. Payroll calculation block diagram.

puter, we are also concerned with these five elements. Although we give them different names, they basically perform the same function. The *input device* in the computer is analogous to the IN box in our problem, the *output device* to the OUT box, the *arithmetic unit* to the calculator, the computer's *memory* to the pigeon holes, and the *control unit* in the computer to the person controlling the operations. Each of these devices will be discussed in more detail later in this chapter.

Computer Data Representation

You will recall that in our definition of a digital computer we mentioned that it must be capable of accepting the representation of digits or other characters that have been coded in a digital fashion. At this time, we would like to examine some of these coding schemes. In the chapter on numbering systems, one of the primary objectives was to make the reader aware that data need not be represented in the familiar decimal form to be understood or usable. This idea applies to the internal representation of data in the computer as well. Although foreign to us, this form of representing numbers in the machine is very meaningful to that particular computer.

Binary Techniques of Representing Numbers and Characters

Initial designers of digital computers attempted to represent information inside the machine in much the same fashion as it was written externally. For example, to store the number 24 inside the computer, they attempted to use two vacuum tubes, each conducting currents at different levels. The tens vacuum tube was to conduct current at a level proportional to the digit 2 and the units vacuum tube was to conduct at a level proportional to the digit 4. Initial adjustment of the tubes was satisfactory, but as the tubes started to wear, the level of conduction that was required to represent the digit 2 was reduced to representing a level proportional to the digit 1—obviously an undesirable situation. Further study of coding schemes and circuit analysis revealed that it was possible to represent data by merely turning a tube on or off and not having to worry about ten different voltage levels. This technique required more tubes, but accuracy of representation was much more important than the number of tubes used. Thus, to store the number 24, five instead of two tubes were necessary, if the number were to be coded in pure binary. The configuration would have appeared as shown in Figure 9–3.

Now, if the tube were on (conducting), the corresponding power of 2 represented by that tube was significant. If the tube were off (not firing), the corresponding power of 2 was to be used as merely a place holder.

Computer design has come a long way in the past twenty years, but the same principles for data representation are still used. Vacuum tubes have been replaced by transistors and these, in turn, replaced by microminia-

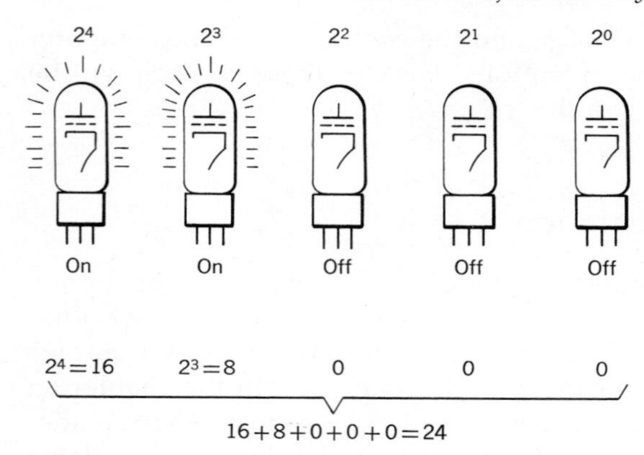

Figure 9–3. Tubes representing binary data.

turized circuits, which consist not only of transistors but also of other components and which occupy less space than formerly needed for a transistor alone. Wired circuits have been superseded by solid logic technology, but internal data representation remains basically the same.

The reader will become familiar with representation of numeric data in the binary system from the chapter on number systems, so we will proceed directly into methods of representing alphabetic and decimal data.

One of the prime considerations of the computer designer is establishing the number of different characters to be represented in his computer's memory. One designer may decide to store nothing but numbers in his machine, whereas another may wish to store both numbers and alphabetic characters in his. Once this decision has been made, a technique for storing this data must be devised.

Let us suppose that we, as designers, have decided that our machine is to have the capability of storing in any one memory location any one of the ten numeric digits of the decimal number system, the 26 letters of the alphabet, and 12 special characters—48 characters in all. We would like to use the "on-off" principle in storing this data, so as to maintain maximum reliability. The question is, how many of these "on-off" switches do we need for each memory location? Suppose we tried four of these switches (bits). We would find that in four bits, only 16 different configurations are possible ($2^4 = 16$) (Figure 9–4). We have 48 characters to represent and each representation is to be unique. Examining a five-bit counter, we find that $2^5 = 32$ different configurations are possible—still not enough! Going to six bits gives us $2^6 = 64$ different configurations—too many—but we must use this many to assure that we can store our 48 desired characters. Thus, for this particular computer, each memory location will consist of at least six bits.

Now, we must name these positions so that we may recognize data

How many different positions must be provided to make 16 possible number configurations available? A 1 or 0 is possible in each position.

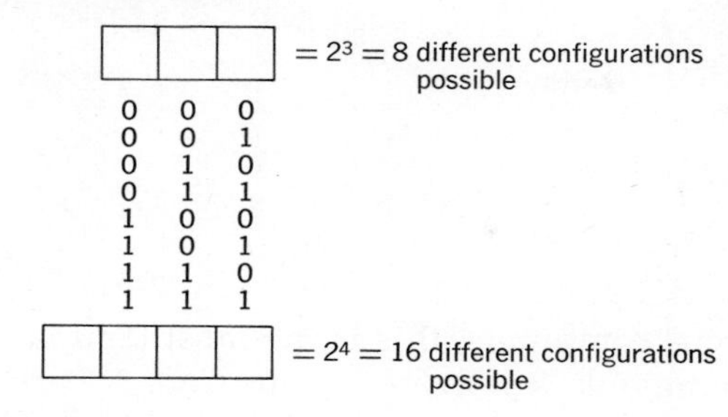

Therefore, the number of different combinations possible in n binary boxes $= 2^n$

Figure 9–4. Binary values.

when it is stored. Let's visualize our six bits as shown in Figure 9–5, where the letters and numbers have been selected to correspond with data in the punched card as follows:

Card	*Core*	
No zone	A and B bits off	Zone Bits
Zero zone	A bit on, B bit off	
11 zone	A bit off, B bit on	
12 zone	A bit on, B bit on	
0 numeric	8 and 2 bits only	Numeric Bits
1 numeric	1 bit on only	
2 numeric	2 bit on only	
3 numeric	2 bit and 1 bit on only	
4 numeric	4 bit on only	
5 numeric	4 bit and 1 bit on only	
6 numeric	4 bit and 2 bit on only	
7 numeric	4 bit, 2 bit and 1 bit on only	
8 numeric	8 bit on only	
9 numeric	8 bit and 1 bit on only	

Thus, if the letter E enters the machine via a punched card (Hollerith Code 12–5), it will be stored in a memory location as:

B ●
A ●
8 0
4 ●
2 0
1 ●

The number 6 is stored in a memory location as:

B 0
A 0
8 0
4 ●
2 ●
1 0

For commercial computers, this is the most familiar form of representing data. It is commonly known as Binary Coded Decimal (BCD). Note that each memory location has the capability of storing 64 different characters, but if only 48 are to be used, the machine will have to provide for recognizing the remaining 16 characters as invalid and for notifying the operator of this condition. Thus, if a memory location received a character from the input device which does not produce one of the 48 desired configurations, it is the machine's responsibility to signal a validity error so that steps are taken to correct the situation.

Parity

Transferring data from one location in memory to another involves some fairly complex electronic operations. There is always the possibility of the circuitry dropping a bit of information during the transmission. This is remote, but may occur. In BCD machines, another bit is attached to the

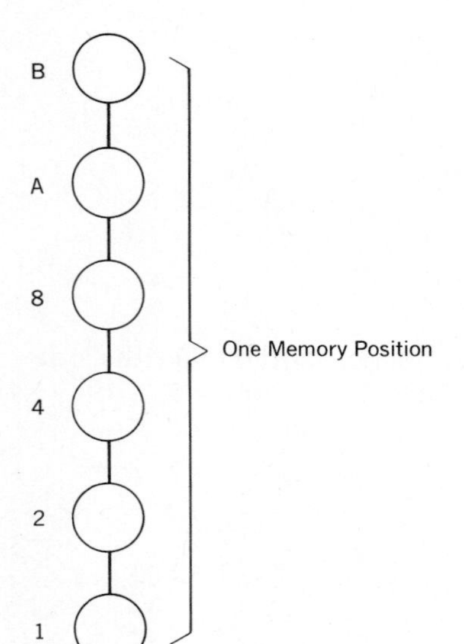

Figure 9–5. Alphabetic coding scheme for internal data storage.

six bits that are used for character representation. This bit is called a *check,* or *parity, bit* and is usually depicted as a C in the same manner as A and B zone bits. Its sole function is to guarantee that an odd number of bits are always on in any one core location (for odd parity machines). Thus, the letter E would be stored in one memory location as:

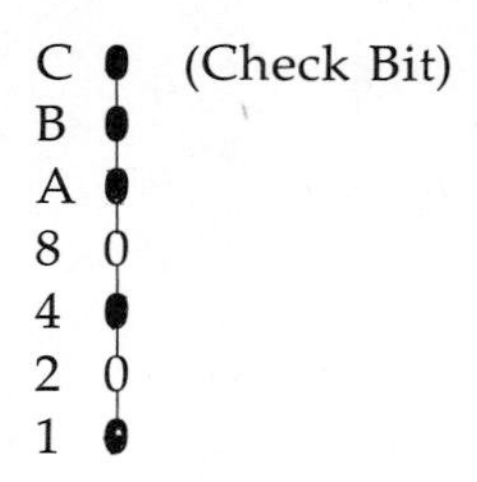

The letter T would be stored in one memory location as:

C (Check Bit)
B
A
8
4
2
1

Note that the check bit is used to establish "oddness" in any one memory location. Should a character be transferred from one memory location to another and a bit inadvertently lost or gained in the transmission, an error would be detected immediately, for an even number, instead of odd number, of bits would be on. This condition would cause the computer to stop or to perform some special function.

Field Definition and Computer Words

The internal memory of BCD machines may be thought of as composed of many of these seven-bit switches capable of holding up to 64 different configurations. This concept presents one very significant problem: how does the machine detect where data fields, consisting of a number of adjacent memory positions, start and end? To provide a means of defining different lengths of fields in computer memory devices, computer designers added one more bit to the seven. This bit is used to detect the most significant character in a field of data. Some refer to this as a *flag bit,* others as a *word mark bit.* An eight-bit representation for each character is used in the IBM 1401. In the IBM 1620, which can store numbers only, a six-bit representation is used for one memory location. Figure 9–6 illustrates the number 7146 stored in BCD in the IBM 1401 and IBM 1620 computers in

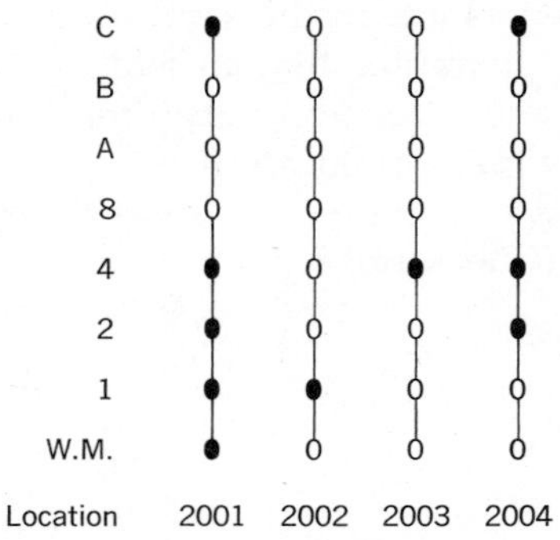

IBM 1401 representation of the number 7146 as a field

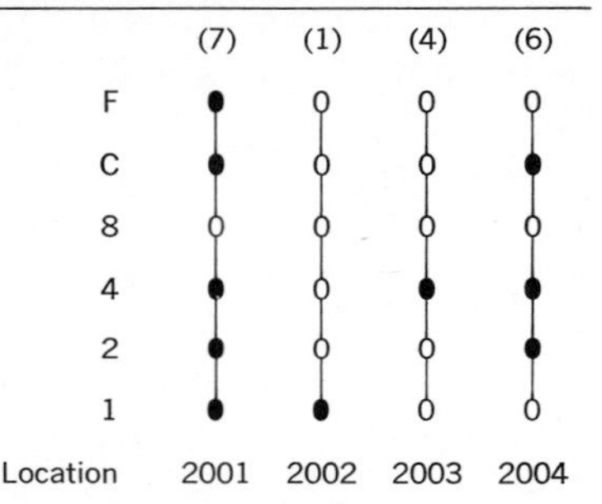

IBM 1620 representation of the number 7146 as a field

Figure 9–6. Character representation in 1620 and 1401 computers.

locations 2001 through 2004. Note that the memory position associated with the 7 in both cases has the added bit turned on. This bit is used for field identification. If the programmer wished to reference the number 7146, he would instruct the machine to get the field located at memory location 2004 in either case. According to the type of instruction used, the machine would pick up all of the information from 2004 and consecutive lower numbered memory positions until a flag or word mark was sensed, indicating that access had been given to a complete field of data. Thus, records in the IBM 1620 and 1401 may consist of many different fields of varying length, the length of the field being detected by the presence of a flag or word mark. Machines possessing this feature are classified as *variable word length* computers. This is the most common type used by commercial data processors.

At the other end of the computer spectrum are scientific computers. Data representation in these machines is best accomplished by using "words" of binary data. In these machines, a word consists of a fixed number (say 32) of binary bits, which implies that in these computers all data are classified as *fixed word length* fields of binary data. If the word length were 32 bits, then, the largest number that could be stored in any one location would be $2^{32} - 1$. The high order bit is usually reserved for the sign of the data. Instructions for these machines are designed primarily to operate on these "words" of information, whereas in variable word length computers, the instructions are designed to operate on fields of varying length.

In the IBM System/360 computer system, several data formats can be used. This is in keeping with the "one system for all applications" idea. When processing scientific data, it can be instructed to operate on words, and when processing commercial data, it can be instructed to operate on characters. In most applications, a combination of the two modes of operation is desirable. The System/360 uses eight rather than six bits to represent characters and a set of eight binary digits in System/360 memory is known as a *byte*. This indicates that in one memory location, 2^8 equals 256 different representations that may be realized. Of course, with 256 different configurations available, the largest number possible is 255. The range of values in an eight-bit, or one-byte, memory position goes from 00000000 to 11111111, that is, from 0 to 255 (11111111 base 2 is equivalent to 255 base ten). Thus, there are 256 different values, including zero.

Data represented in the System/360 uses a code generally referred to as the Extended Binary Coded Decimal Interchange Code (EBCDIC). In a chapter to follow, the EBCDIC representation of data in the 360 will be discussed in more detail.

Binary Number Representation

The reader has observed that representing data in a form that can be used by a computer presents no particular challenge. Once it has been established that groups of two-way, or binary, switches will be used to represent the data, then all that remains is to devise a scheme whereby different switch configurations represent different characters. This same idea applies to the representation of numbers in binary machines, that is, machines that have the capability of handling binary data. To represent numeric quantities in these systems does not present as difficult a problem as that of trying to represent characters, for the ground rules used in the development of number systems in general may be employed. Chapter 16 of this book deals with number systems in general. This section will be devoted exclusively to the binary numbering system. (Should the reader wish more detail and examples, he should refer to Chapter 16. However, no greater understanding of number systems than that developed here will be required for the rest of the book save Part IV.)

When representing characters in a computer (as opposed to the representation of numbers) any number of different schemes may be utilized, for within any given system only a finite number of characters need be represented uniquely. In representing numbers, however, we need a technique which will be consistent for the representation of an infinity of quantities. In the base ten numbering system, the position of each digit (0–9) is significant. The same concept is found in the base two system. For example, in the base ten system, the number 514 represents:

$$(5 \times 10^2) + (1 \times 10^1) + (4 \times 10^0)$$

In the base two system, the number 1011 represents:

$$(1 \times 2^3) + (0 \times 2^2) + (1 \times 2^1) + (1 \times 2^0).$$ [1]

Were we presented with the binary number 110111 and asked to determine its value as represented in the familiar base ten system, we would proceed with the conversion as follows:

$$\begin{aligned} 110111_2 &= (1 \times 2^5) + (1 \times 2^4) + (0 \times 2^3) + (1 \times 2^2) + (1 \times 2^1) + (1 \times 2^0) \\ &= (1 \times 32) + (1 \times 16) + (0 \times 8) + (1 \times 4) + (1 \times 2) + (1 \times 1) \\ &= 32 + 16 + 0 + 4 + 2 + 1 \\ &= 55_{10} \end{aligned}$$

This technique may be applied to the conversion of all whole numbers from the binary system to the decimal system. (More sophisticated techniques for conversions of this type are outlined in Chapter 16.)

Suppose now that we were presented with the inverse problem—that is, given a number in the base ten system to convert it to one in the base two system. A little reflection on this problem by the observant student should reveal that this process involves determining the highest power of two present in the base ten number and its remainders after this power of two has been removed. For example, consider trying to convert the number 55_{10} to base two. The first question we would ask is what is the highest power of two present in the number 55? Since $2^4 = 16$, $2^5 = 32$, and $2^6 = 64$, we note that the answer to our question above is 5. This would indicate that we must have a 1 present in the position signifying 2^5. Now, after removing $2^5 = 32$ from 55, we are left with 23. We now ask the same question of this number 23. Since $2^3 = 8$, $2^4 = 16$, and $2^5 = 32$, we note that the answer is 4, indicating we need a 1 in the position representing 2^4. After removing 16 from 23, we are left with 7. The highest power of 2 in 7 is 2, indicating that a zero is to be present in the position representing 2^3 (since $2^3 = 8$) and a 1 present in the position representing 2^2. Removing 2^2 from 7, we are left with 3, which has one 2 and 1 left over. This gives us the bits (binary digits) necessary to fill all of the positions from 2^5 down to 2^0. We get, as expected, 110111_2 for the representation of 55.

[1] Any number except zero raised to the zero power; for example, 10^0 is always equal to 1. Thus, $10^0 = 1$ and $2^0 = 1$.

This procedure may be shortened somewhat by observing that nothing more than division by 2 repetitively is involved; for example:

		Remainder
2	55	
2	27	1
2	13	1
2	6	1
2	3	0
2	1	1
	0	1

Note that reading the remainders from bottom to top (110111) gives us our result in base two.

At this time we would like to present some of the fundamentals of addition in base two. The addition table for base two appears as:

+	0	1
0	0	1
1	1	0c

For example:

$$0 + 0 = 0$$
$$0 + 1 = 1$$
$$1 + 0 = 1$$
$$1 + 1 = 0 \text{ with a carry}$$

To add two numbers in base two, we may use the table above and note that any carries are to be moved to the adjacent column on the left. Adding 11_2 to 01_2, we proceed in much the same fashion as we do when adding numbers in base 10.

```
c c
  1 1
  0 1
-----
1 0 0
```

Note that $11_2 = 3_{10}$, and $01_2 = 1_{10}$, and $3_{10} + 1_{10} = 4_{10} = 100_2$. In adding the bits in the righthand column, we see from the table that $1 + 1 = 0$ with a carry. This carry is represented by the c in the left column. Adding this carry (1) to the 1 below it, we get 0 with a carry. This carry is represented by the c to the left of the bits. Now the 0 of this result is added to the 0 in that column to give us 0 as our middle bit. Finally, since there are no more bits, we bring the carry down and get our result 100_2. As a final example, let us examine the addition of 101101_2 to 011100_2.

$$\begin{array}{r} c\ c\ c\ c \\ 1\ 0\ 1\ 1\ 0\ 1 \\ 0\ 1\ 1\ 1\ 0\ 0 \\ \hline 1\ 0\ 0\ 1\ 0\ 0\ 1 \end{array}$$

To check our result, we can convert the numbers above to decimal, add them together and convert this answer to binary. Hopefully, we shall arrive at the same result.

$$\begin{aligned} 101101 &= (1 \times 2^5) + (0 \times 2^4) + (1 \times 2^3) + (1 \times 2^2) + (0 \times 2^1) + (1 \times 2^0) \\ &= (32 + 0 + 8 + 4 + 0 + 1) \\ &= 45 \\ 011100 &= (0 \times 2^5) + (1 \times 2^4) + (1 \times 2^3) + (1 \times 2^2) + (0 \times 2^1) + (0 \times 2^0) \\ &= (0 + 16 + 8 + 4 + 0 + 0) \\ &= 28 \\ 28 + 45 &= 73 \end{aligned}$$

		Remainder
2	73	
2	36	1
2	18	0
2	9	0
2	4	1
2	2	0
2	1	0
	0	1

Reading backward we get:

$$1001001_2$$

This is the same result we obtained when we added the two given binary numbers together.

Computer Memory Addressing

Once the reader realizes that each machine has its own (not necessarily unique) coding scheme for representing data, addressing schemes for computers may be more easily understood. In our post office box example, we decided to label each box from 1 to 20 and in each box we stored instructions or results of calculations. We made no restriction as to the number of instructions that could be held by one box nor to the size of the result that one box could accept. When working with digital computers, it is very important that the programmer be aware of the limitations placed on one storage location. In the IBM 1401, one storage location can hold a digit no larger than 9. This applies to the IBM 1620 as well. One position of storage in the System/360 can hold a number as large as 255 expressed in binary, and in the IBM 7090, one storage location could contain a number as large as $2^{36} - 1$.

The basic addressable unit in the 1401 and 1620 is a six-bit (BCD) position; in the 7090, it is a 36-bit word, and in the System/360, it is an 8-bit byte. To say that a machine has 8,000 memory positions is to say that 8,000 positions may be addressed, that is, accessed, and may be used to hold a portion of a field of data or a portion of an instruction, but this does not tell the whole story. One must know exactly what kind of information can be held in one addressable position of storage. Then, he can determine whether or not this is the best machine for his applications. Consider a 12,000-position 1401 and a 20,000-position 1620. Which has more storage available to the programmer? For operations on numeric data only the 1620 has 8,000 more positions of storage, but for operations using alphabetic data, the 1401 has more storage (by 2,000 positions) since the 1620 must use two memory locations to store one alphabetic character. A computer programmer usually addresses storage areas by number and these range from 0 up to the storage capacity of the machine minus 1. Thus, a 64,000, or "64K," computer would contain addresses numbered from 0 through 63,999.

Referring once again to our check-writing example, we notice that in the memory are stored instructions as well as data. In a computer, this is also the case, except that in the case of some computers every instruction does not require the same amount of storage. Some instructions may use only one storage position and others as many as twelve, depending on the type of computer.

Computers can be classified by referring to the type of instructions and data they have the ability to handle. We may refer to a machine as variable word length, fixed instruction length; fixed word length, fixed instruction length; variable word length, variable instruction length.

Computer Program Execution

Since the storage device or memory device in the computer must be capable of storing both data and instructions, the computer must have some kind of technique for distinguishing between the two. This is accomplished through use of a very precise timing device used to tell the computer when to examine an instruction and when to execute an instruction. In this chapter, we will use the terminology *access the instruction* and *execute the instruction.*

Let us imagine that stored in memory cell 100 is a command to add the contents of cell 200 to cell 300 and store the result in cell 300. Be sure to distinguish between the addresses of the data (200 and 300) and the actual data present in these locations. Various computers will execute this instruction in different ways. Some computers have the ability to add one memory location directly to another (add to memory logic) where others must use intermediate storage areas known as registers in the execution of the instruction. For our purpose, let us assume that our computer is of the latter type. For the sake of discussion, we will also assume that we are working on a fixed word length machine which possesses the following:

1. A location counter, which is used to tell the machine where in memory the next instruction is to be found.
2. Registers to be used to hold the intermediate results. These registers will be assumed to be 32 bits (one word) in length. We will refer to these as general purpose registers.
3. An instruction register, which is used to store the instruction being executed.
4. Appropriate circuitry to carry out the addition operation.

A schematic of our computer appears in Figure 9–7*a*.

Now, we will examine the details of executing the add command situated in memory cell 100. At the beginning of the *access instruction cycle*, our location counter should be positioned at 100. Now, the machine will go to the location indicated by the location counter, read an instruction there and place this instruction in the instruction register. Once the instruction has been placed in the instruction register, the timer will indicate that the access cycle has been completed. At the completion of the access cycle, our schematic would appear as shown in Figure 9–7*b*. Now the timer indicates that we should begin execution of the instruction in the instruction register. The type of add circuitry in our machine will determine the internal mechanics to be followed during the addition process. We will assume that our machine follows the process outlined below.

During the initial phases of the execute cycle, the instruction in the instruction register will be analyzed for type. Once it has been determined that an add instruction is to be executed, the necessary electronic switching inside the machine will take place to effect an addition operation. Since the command indicates that we are to add the contents of memory location 200 to the contents of memory location 300, the machine will automatically place the contents of cell 300 into the general purpose register, add the contents of cell 200 to the general purpose register, and store the contents of the general purpose register back into cell 300. After execution of this instruction, our schematic appears as shown in Figure 9–7*c*. The location counter has been increased so as to indicate the next memory cell (this was done at the end of the previous access cycle), so the machine is automatically ready to access and execute the next instruction in sequence.

This example has been simplified for the sake of discussion, but the

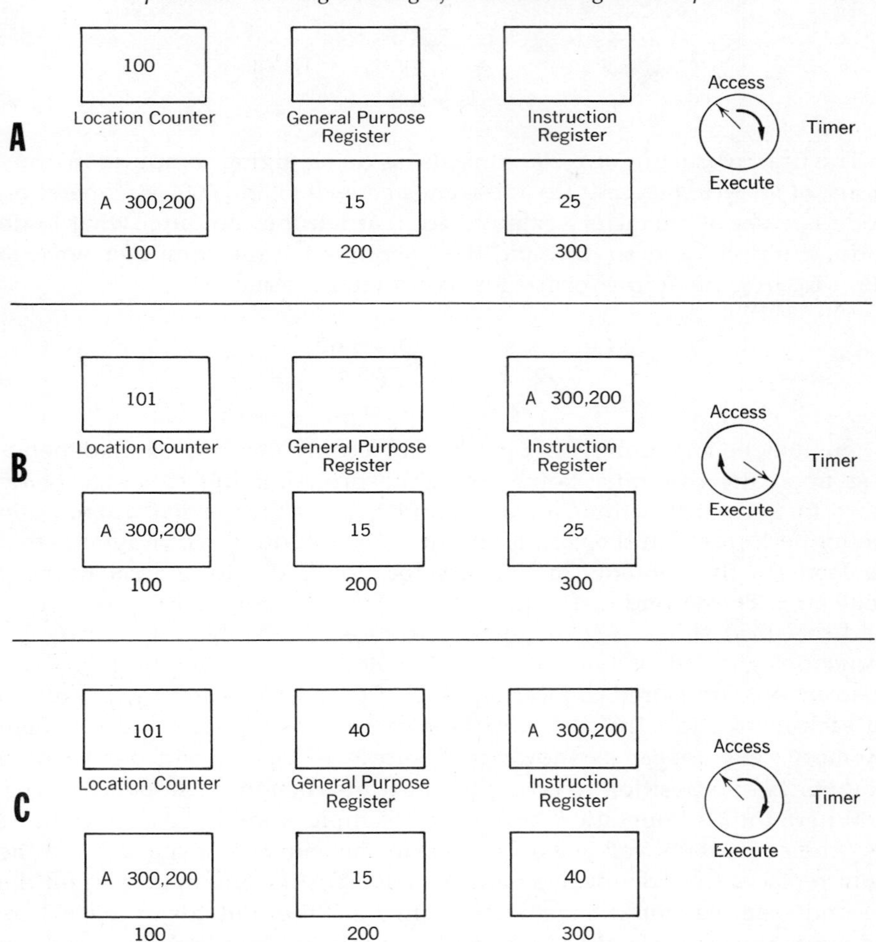

Figure 9–7. Access and execution of computer instruction.

idea is sound. The hypothetical computer under discussion had the ability to automatically place the data in the general purpose register, add the appropriate data to this register and store the sum. In the System/360, this operation must be suggested to the computer in a little more detail. Roughly speaking, the add command in the System/360 is not as versatile as the one described above. To perform this operation in the System/360, we would be required to instruct the machine to place the information from one of the memory cells into a general purpose register, to add the contents of the associated memory cell to this register, and finally to store the contents of this register in a specified memory location. For the sake of discussion, let us suppose that the general purpose register is numbered 5. Then our sequence of instructions to carry out the addition described above would be:

L 5,200
A 5,300
ST 5,300

The first instruction, L 5,200 consists, as do all digital computer instructions, of an *operation code* (L) and some *operands* (5 and 200). An operation code is a set of characters or numbers that tell the computer what to do (add, multiply, and so on), and the operands tell the computer what to do it to. In general, the format for a computer instruction is:

Op Code	Operands
XXX	XXXX XXXX

There may be any number of operands in a computer instruction depending upon the computer being used, the programming language being used to write instructions for the computer, and the particular operation being performed. In the case of the first instruction, the computer is told to load (L) the contents of memory location 200 into general purpose register 5. The second instruction adds (A) the contents of 300 to register 5, and the third stores (ST) the answer in location 300. Note that three instructions instead of one must be executed. Let us imagine that these instructions are stored in locations 100, 101, and 102. After the execution of each instruction, the contents of the computer's registers and pertinent memory cells appear as shown in Figure 9–8. Once again our location counter is in a position to access the next instruction in sequence for us.

Where the add operation in the first example could have been defined as "the contents of cell 200 are added to the contents of cell 300 and the sum replaces the previous contents of cell 300," the add operation for the second example would have been defined as "the contents of cell 300 are added to the contents of general purpose register 5 and the sum is held in register 5." Thus, the results of the additions are identical, but the method of obtaining the result is different. This points out the need for carefully reading and understanding the function of each instruction in the computer you propose to program, for without this understanding effective programming is impossible.

Program Development

In the development of a computer program, the first factor to consider is the type of data available as input. Another factor is the number and type of instructions available for use. Another is the procedure to be used in solving the problem. Finally, a careful analysis must be made of the output requirements of the program. Once decisions have been made for each of the above factors, the programmer represents the solution of his problem

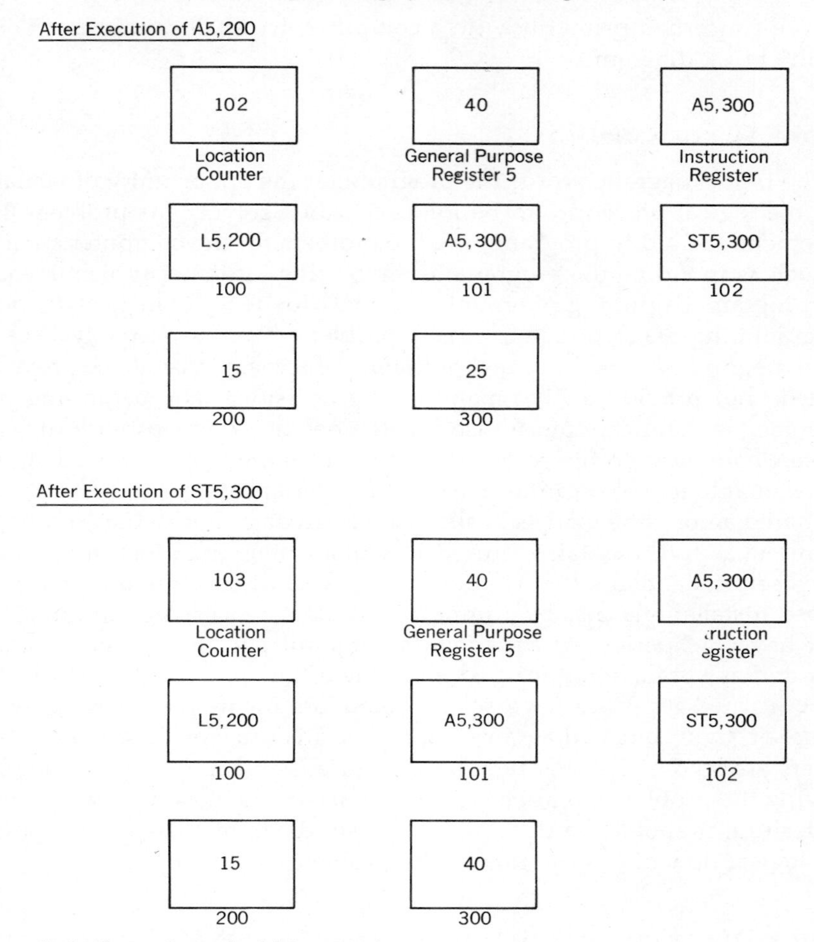

Figure 9–8. Execution of add instruction.

graphically. This will be accomplished by means of block diagrams and flow charts. Some persons use the words block diagram and flow chart interchangeably. We would prefer to make a definite distinction between them. A block diagram is a graphic representation of the procedures by which data is processed within a given computer system. A flow chart is a graphic representation of the data processing system in which information from source documents is converted to final documents. A block diagram spells out the procedure to be followed for the handling of data in a specific machine, whereas a flow chart indicates how data will flow through the entire system. A programmer graphically representing the solution to his problem in a specific computer would construct a block diagram, whereas a systems analyst trying to chart the path of a document through his data processing installation would use a flow diagram. Since we are concerned primarily with a computer, we shall concentrate solely on the block diagram.

Block Diagramming

The block diagram affords the programmer the opportunity of visualizing the logical procedure to be followed when solving his problem. It is a tremendous aid in programming the problem for the computer solution as well as in aiding the programmer in locating difficult problem areas in his program. Beginning programmers have a tendency to neglect the block diagramming stage of solving their problem. This is probably because most beginning programming problems are easily visualized mentally and do not provide for too many logical decisions. The beginning programmer is handicapping himself if he does not learn to block diagram these elementary problems, for the time will come when he needs to use this valuable tool and cannot for lack of experience.

Shared among the many so-called experts in data processing are varying opinions as to the detail required in a block diagram. Most installations use a set of standards that should be followed when block diagramming. Those installations just beginning to use data processing equipment or that have inexperienced supervision are similar to the novice programmer and as yet have not learned the value of this powerful tool, or if they have learned its value have set no standards for its use. Consequently, some of their block diagrams represent insufficient information and others are so detailed that they become impossible to follow. The logic of solving the problem should be clearly depicted in a block diagram. If more is desired, it should be done in a separate diagram so as not to confuse the logical flow of the solution to the problem.

Block Diagramming Symbols

To date there has been no universal standardization of block diagramming symbols. Within each company, certain symbols are reserved for specific operations, but these vary from company to company. For the purpose of the ensuing discussion, we shall adopt the symbols shown in Figure 9–9.

Block Diagram Example

Consider a general block diagram of the calculation of payroll for a company as shown in Figure 9–10. We recommend that the procedure illustrated by the following diagrams be adhered to when the reader attempts to block diagram his problems for a computer. Figure 9–10 provides a general picture of the procedure to be used in the solution of this problem to the programmer and anyone interested in the method of solu-

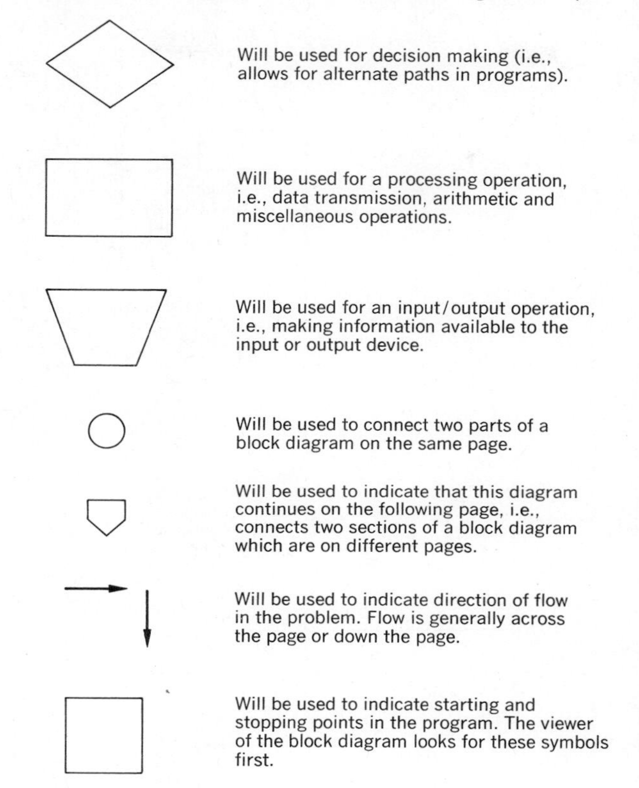

Figure 9–9. Block diagram symbols.

tion. If more detail on any one of the blocks were desired, detailed block diagrams of those blocks could be prepared. Consider the more detailed block diagram of block 100 shown in Figure 9–11. If one desires more detail on, say, block 110, he could similarly prepare a detailed block diagram of this block. It might appear as shown in Figure 9–12.

Using block diagrams in this fashion allows the programmer to examine the detail of any section without losing sight of the overall picture. Also, if an error in results is observed, the detailed diagram for each section may be analyzed without distraction from the rest of the procedure. The block diagram should not contain detailed machine instructions. This detail is handled when the problem is programmed for the computer. A block diagram was not meant to be a series of boxes around computer instructions, but rather presents to the viewer a series of logical steps to be used when solving a specific problem.

In the case of block diagrams, the statement that a picture is worth a thousand words is particularly appropriate. This picture presents the solution to a problem in a clear, easy-to-follow fashion. As you become more sophisticated in data processing, you will find that the block diagram is

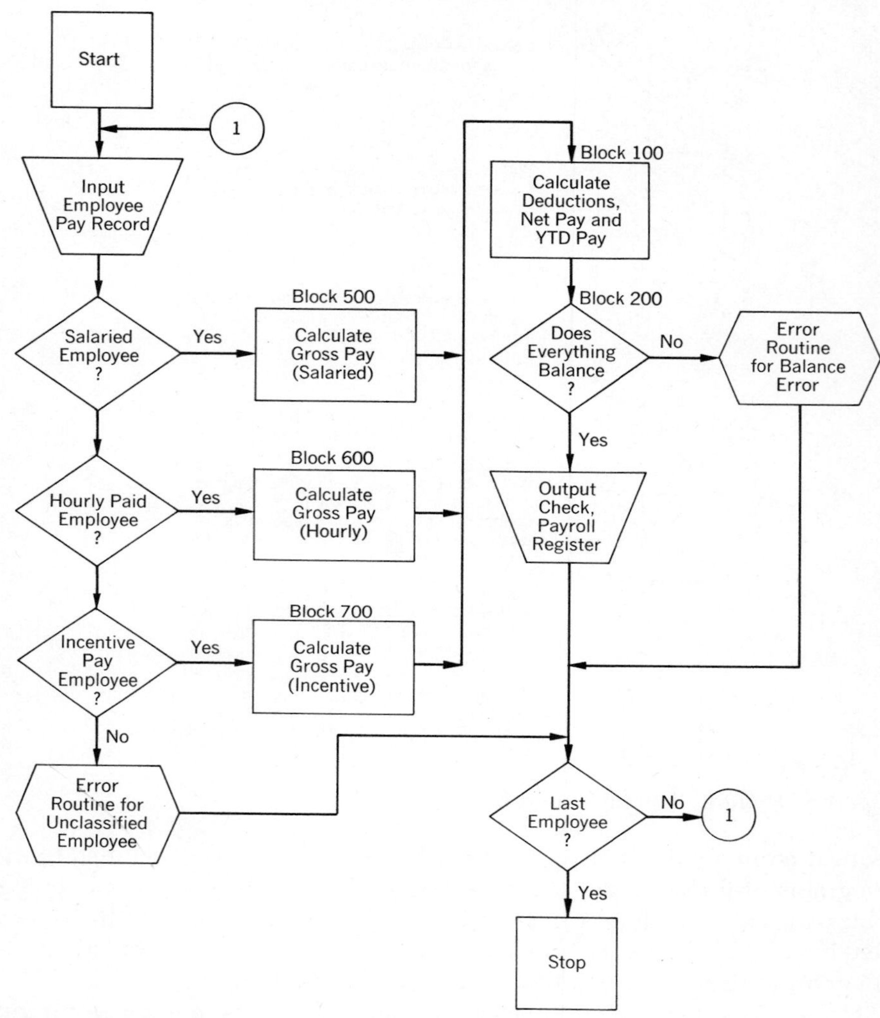

Figure 9–10. Block diagram example.

probably the most valuable communicative link between man and machine. Some believe it is the key to understanding the methods and techniques of computer programming and data processing in general.

Steps in Program Development, Check-Out, and Execution

Problem Definition

Prior to investigating the five components of a digital computer in more detail in the next chapter, we will summarize briefly the steps required

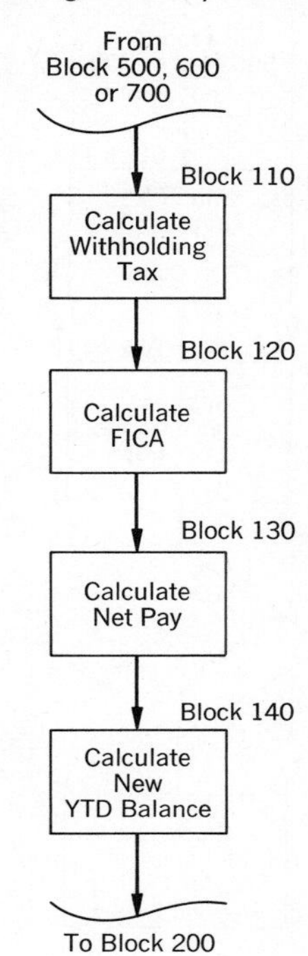

Figure 9–11. Detail block diagram of Block 100.

for proper program preparation and execution. The first, and probably the most important, is problem definition. There are probably more programs that do not work as they were intended because of poor problem definition than because of any other factor. This phase of program preparation should take into account the limits of the problem, the nature of the input and output requirements, handling of exceptional cases by the program, and probably most important, future requirements for this program.

Block Diagramming

Once the problem has been defined and carefully analyzed, we can proceed to the second step—preparing the block diagram. This tool has been discussed previously. It, along with a brief written explanation, provides the company and the programmer with program documentation. The explanation should be written in such a fashion that a person two years from now could read it and understand the purpose of the program, its requirements, and how it works.

Coding

Once the block diagram and its associated detailed block diagram have been completed, we are ready to code the problem. In this phase of pro-

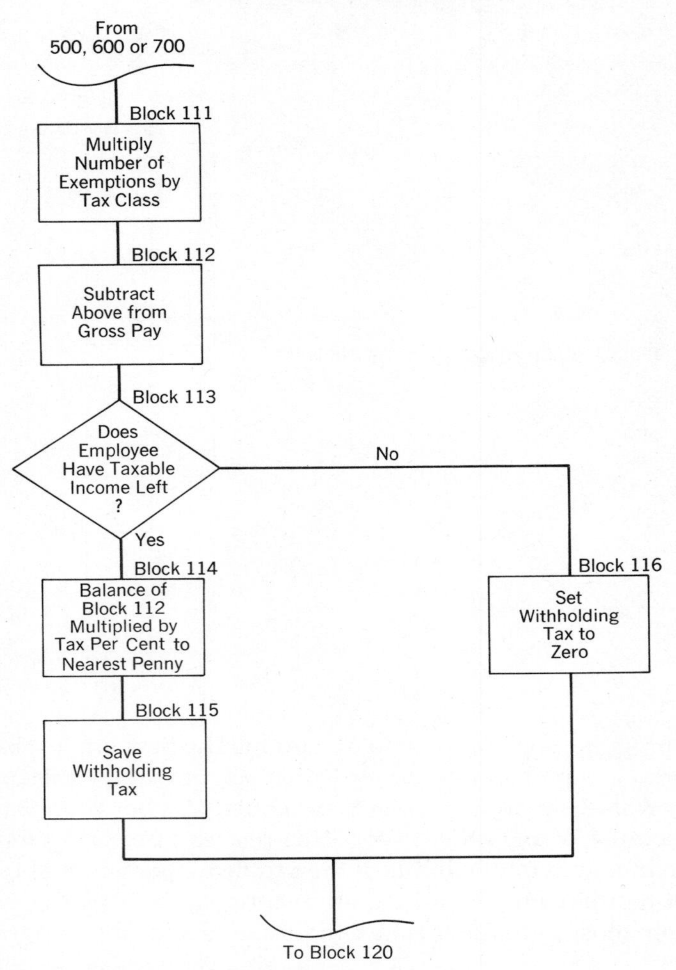

Figure 9–12. Detail block diagram of box 110.

gram preparation, we are translating the logic and the operations to be performed, as indicated by the block diagram, into a language that can be understood by the computer. Each computer manufacturer has recommended forms to be used when coding problems for his machine. Also provided by most manufacturers is a package of "software" which includes programs that help to write application programs. Writing programs in machine language is no easy task and very few programmers actually use this type of coding. To relieve the programmer's burden of machine language coding, manufacturers provide programmers with a language that is much easier to use when coding problems. The machine being what it is, can work with only its own language (machine language). This forces the manufacturer to supply, along with this easier-to-code language, a program to translate the language that the programmer uses to code his problem into machine language with which the computer can work. This program may be thought of as a translator, translating instructions from the form written by the programmer into a form suitable for the computer. One of the more common types of these languages is the System/360 Assembly Language, which is discussed in later chapters.

Punching

After the program has been coded, the next task to be performed is punching the program into cards. This must be done with extreme care, for one character punched in the wrong column can be disastrous. During this time, or prior to this time, the original data to be supplied to the problem should be connected to an input medium that can be used by the machine and by the program that has been written.

Program Check-Out

Program check-out is a process of determining whether or not the program just written (or an old program just modified) will cause the computer system to do the things that the programmer has instructed it to do. Usually, program check-out consists of two steps, the first of which is the more important. This first step, known as *desk-checking* the program, consists of completely reviewing the program, starting with the problem definition and progressing through the block diagramming and coding stages. Almost always taking place before the program is punched into cards, desk-checking tries to find all the logical and clerical errors made by the programmer during the preparation of the program.

The second stage of program check-out involves testing the program on the computer system itself. When a program is written in a language other than machine language, which is almost always the case, the translator program that converts the programmer's coding into machine language will include automatic checks for commonly made clerical errors and omissions. Thus, on the programmer's first attempt to translate his program into machine language, he will more likely than not be presented with a list of errors of this nature that were made in preparing the program. This list is usually referred to as a *program diagnostic.* Once these initial clerical errors are diagnosed and, of course, corrected, the program can be successfully translated into machine language.

At this point, the logic of the program can be thoroughly tested using a set of test data that present to the program every conceivable circumstance that can be manifested by the data. If the program successfully treats all of these circumstances, then and only then is it ready to be put to work on real-life data. It has been the authors' experience that frequently programs otherwise fairly well prepared have not been afforded

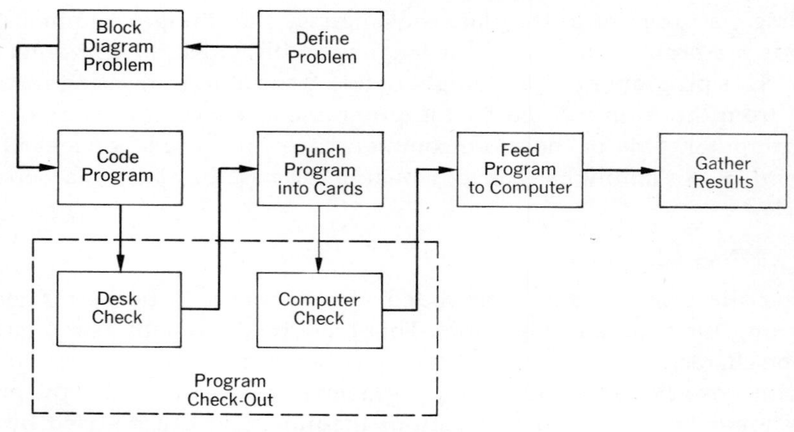

Figure 9–13. Steps in program development.

this important phase of program check-out. As a result, programs that are believed to be correctly prepared are set to work on data only to show, perhaps, after several hours of wasted work, that they include logical errors important enough to require substantial corrective efforts and result in often embarrassing results such as assigning boys to girls' gym classes, neglecting to record on transcripts courses successfully taken by college students, and writing payroll checks for negative amounts.

Execution

When finally checked out, the program is ready for application to the job for which it was intended. The program is loaded into the memory of the computer, and the data are made available to the computer system and the computer is set to work executing the program.

Of the steps outlined above, one of the most time-consuming is that of program check-out. Most programmers will agree that it takes almost as much time to check out (or, as they put it, "debug") a program as it does to write it in the first place. Figure 9–13 illustrates the steps discussed here necessary to prepare and execute a computer program.

Questions

1. Electronic digital computers operate so fast that their speeds are measured in terms of *microseconds, milliseconds,* and *nanoseconds.* What is the time period indicated by each of these three terms? You may want to consult a dictionary.
2. Make a list of analog devices found in common use today.
3. What is the most important difference between a digital computer and an adding machine or bookkeeping machine?

4. What are the basic parts of a computer instruction? What functions do they perform?
5. Some programming languages use instructions with one operand, some with two, and some with three. Try to discover how such instructions differ in operation from each other.
6. Show how the characters 76 TROMBONES would be represented in seven-bit code. Where would wordmark bits be turned on?
7. Determine how these numbers would be represented in binary form, that is, as numbers using only ones and zeros—(a) 1, (b) 4, (c) 15, (d) 16, (e) 31, (f) 32, (g) 2, (h) 7, (i) 8, (j) 100. You may wish to refer to Chapter 16 on number systems for help. However, try to figure these out without doing so.
8. Most activities can be block diagrammed. Prepare a block diagram showing the steps necessary to dial a telephone number. Prepare another showing how to cross a busy intersection (with traffic signals) as a pedestrian. Make sure you don't get run over.
9. Which of the two parts of program check-out do you think is most often neglected by programmers? Why?

10

Electronic Computer Components: Control, Arithmetic, and Memory

In the last chapter, the nature of computer operations and computer programming were discussed. This chapter examines in some detail how various parts of a computer system work, principally those involved with control of the system, arithmetic operations, and primary memory devices.

The five parts of a digital computer may be represented schematically as in Figure 10–1. Everyone concerned with or affected by data processing should understand the function of each computer component as well as the fundamentals of operation of some of the devices used for these components. Whole texts can be, and have been, written on any one of the five components of digital computers alone.

Control Unit

The heart of a digital computer is composed of a control unit and an arithmetic unit. These two units working hand in hand control and supervise electronically the operation of the entire computer system. The prime function of the control unit is to interpret instructions stored in memory and give signals to the rest of the computer, causing various functions to be performed. If the control unit accesses a multiply instruction, it must, through a complex series of switching and timing equipment, open and close many electronic paths or gates through which data may flow in order that the command be executed properly. It also must control all data paths to the input/output devices attached to the system.

The control unit functions in an orderly fashion through a series of switching and timing circuits. The switching circuitry consists primarily of *selecting, connecting,* and *hunting circuits.* For example, in an add command such as A 200,300—where we wish to add the contents of cell 300 to the contents of cell 200—the *selecting circuits* would select the addresses 200 and 300 from the whole set of memory addresses. It would select particular preidentified circuits from a group of related circuits. The *connect-*

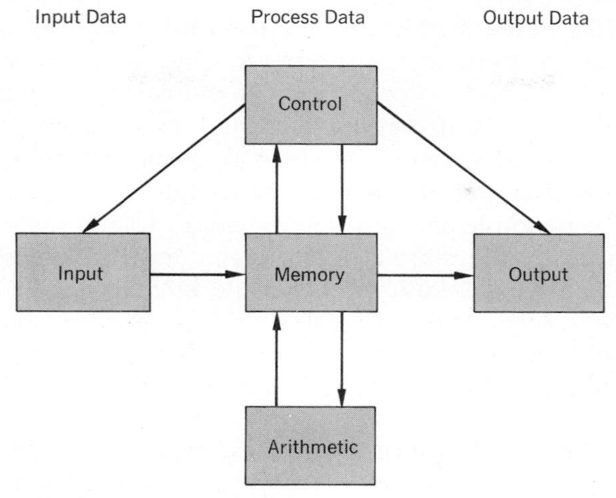

Figure 10–1. Computer system components.

ing circuits would then establish links or paths through which the required information would flow to various parts of the computer in order that the add operation be executed correctly. The *hunting circuits* would continue to monitor the state of other circuits in the computer to determine if error conditions existed, or if a higher priority job was to be executed prior to the one in progress, or if there were some kind of program interruption that should take place so that another high-priority program could be executed.

Figure 10–2. IBM System/360 Model 50. *(Courtesy, IBM)*

Timing circuits in the control unit are used to control the accessing and execution of instructions in the computer. They consist basically of two types, synchronous and asynchronous. If the computer consists of *synchronous timing circuits,* it may be classified as a *synchronous computer.* A synchronous computer is one in which electronic pulses spaced at equal intervals are used to step the computer through its access and execution cycles. This is accomplished through a "clock" inside the machine. The pulses produced by the master clock are counted and used to determine the stage of access or execution that should be taking place at that time. In *asynchronous computers,* no master clock is present; each switching operation itself controls the next switching operation to take place. Thus, every switching operation serves as a signal to the next one that is to take place.

In summary, the control unit through a series of switching and timing circuits can control when and how instructions in the computer memory will be executed.

Arithmetic-Logical Unit

This unit is composed of circuitry to carry out arithmetic and logical operations. Some of the arithmetic operations performed are to add, subtract, multiply, and divide and to shift information in a register to the right or left. The logical portion of this component, on the other hand, is used to compare numbers and make decisions, perform logical sums and products and look for "overflow" conditions in which the results of a computation require more memory space than provided. These operations are completed through a series of accumulators, adders, registers, and comparers. In each computer, the method used internally to carry out arithmetic-logical operations differs, although the result will be the same. For example, in the execution of a subtract command, some computers are provided with circuitry to take the data from one location in memory and subtract it from another location directly. Other computers may use a series of registers and accumulators to perform the same operation. In this latter type of computer, the data that is brought into the central processing unit from storage must be held temporarily somewhere. These temporary holding areas are usually referred to as registers and usually consist of no more than the equivalent of two words of information. Some computers tie two registers together and call this an accumulator. These types generally leave the results of their arithmetic operations stored here. In the IBM System/360, the results of arithmetic operations are left in registers. It is the programmer's responsibility to write program instructions that place the information in and extract the information from these general purpose registers.

The *adder* in the arithmetic-logical unit is the workhorse that performs the actual arithmetic operation desired. This is accomplished through a series of what are commonly known as *half-adders*. Using the terminology of the trade, two half-adders become one full adder, and a series of electronic circuits that utilize the principles of these half and full adders perform the various arithmetic functions. A more thorough discussion of the logical operation of these devices is included in the appendix following this chapter.

Comparers are used to indicate whether contents of the accumulator and storage registers are equal or unequal. They can be used to detect overflow conditions as well. For example, suppose we tried to add the decimal numbers 742 and 897 together but had only three positions in which to store the result. Our answer, 1639, could not be held in these three positions. It would appear in memory as 639. The comparer would detect this condition for us and turn on an indicator which we, in our program, could test in order to detect this situation. It is very important that the programmer know his data thoroughly for this reason. An undetected overflow makes a ream of paper run off as a result of hours of program execution just so much scratch paper.

Storage Unit

We are concerned here primarily with the main storage devices that exist or have existed in computers. The following chapter on input/output devices will discuss auxiliary storage devices and data organization concepts.

Earlier, we mentioned that one of the prime reasons a digital computer is such a valuable tool is because of its ability to store and recall information. The information stored can represent a set of instructions for the computer to execute sequentially as well as data to be operated upon by these instructions. These storage devices "remember" in much the same fashion that the box with the pigeonholes discussed earlier remembered. Where each pigeonhole had a number, so does each location in a computer's memory device. In each numbered pigeonhole was some kind of information (instructions or data); likewise, in each memory location some information will be stored. The number on the box in the pigeonhole example is analogous to the *address* of a location in memory and the contents of the box is analogous to the contents of a location in memory. Each memory device will vary with respect to the amount of information that can be held in one addressable location, but all use the same binary principle for the representation of data in any one addressable location. One computer may be able to store one of 64 different *characters* in an addressable memory location, and another may be designed to handle eight binary digits (a byte) in one memory location, while still another may contain a *word* (32 bits) in one memory location. For any particular computer, the programmer must know what he is referencing when he calls for the information in one memory location. He must know whether he is asking for a character, byte, or word in order that he may manipulate this data properly.

Although data and instructions are both stored internally and are always ready for immediate use by the computer, the control unit requires time to locate the instructions and data for processing. This is referred to as the *access time.* Access time is a very important consideration in storage devices. If very rapid access time is required, *core* memories will probably be used, but if access time is not the prime concern, then one may consider slower access devices, such as *drums* and *disks* for internal memories. In core memories, access times are measured in the millionths of seconds, whereas in drum and disk memories, access times are measured in the thousandths of seconds. These times may both seem very rapid (and they are) and one might wonder why we are worrying about split seconds, but obviously, the faster we can get to our data, the sooner we will be able to process it. In memories that possess millionths of seconds' access times, we can access one thousand or more pieces of data in the same amount of time that it takes the memory operating in thousandths of seconds to access one piece of data. Why not use core memories only, since they are faster? The answer to this is cost. In terms of the cost involved in storing one piece of information, core storage is much more expensive than drum or disk storage. Third-generation data processing systems are designed around reaching a happy medium between these various storage devices. They use core storage as their main storage device and drums and disks as auxiliary storage, primarily because of the cost factor.

We will discuss a few of the more common storage devices. While we are doing this, you must remember that no matter what kind of a device we are discussing, the data is always represented internally in one of two different states, one or zero. In some cases, this may be two different states of magnetism; in others, it may be the presence or absence of a spot on a cathode ray tube; and in still others use may be made of the presence or absence of a sound wave. This is why it is so important that you thoroughly understand methods of representing data other than the familiar alphabet and base ten numbering system.

As we mentioned earlier, magnetic cores, drums, and disks are the most frequently used memory devices. There are a few others that deserve mention prior to a more thorough investigation of the three listed above.

Electrostatic Tube Storage

This storage device consists of a tube that is very similar in operation to the picture tube on your television set. The picture on a television tube consists of a series of lines and each line is made up of a series of dots. These lines are projected on the tube so rapidly that the human eye cannot

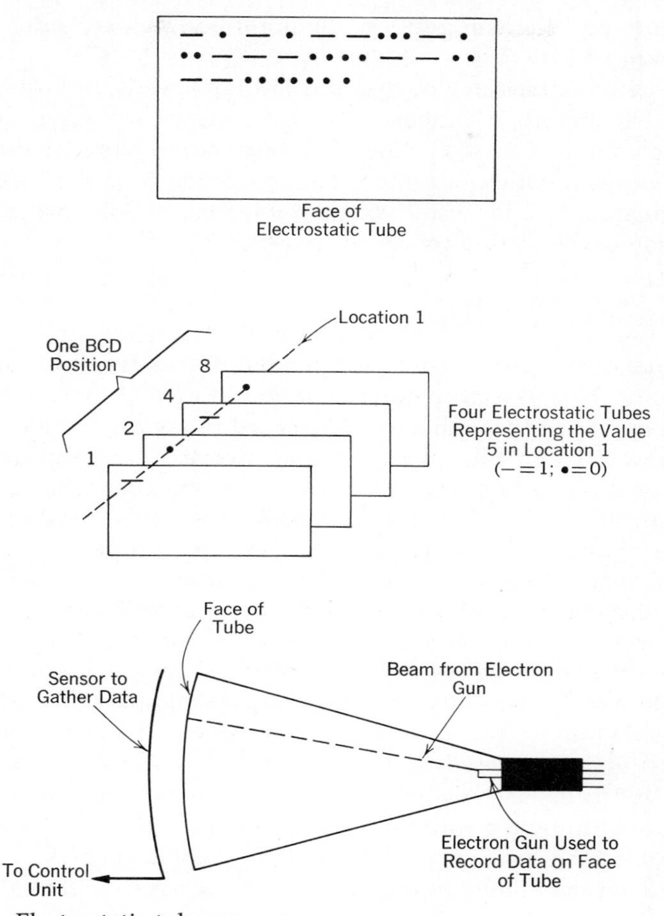

Figure 10–3. Electrostatic tube memory.

detect when one leaves and the other appears, giving the eye the sensation of a continuous flow. In electrostatic tube storage, the zero or one of the binary code is projected onto the face of the tube as a dot or a dash. If the face of the tube is visualized as a grid, it might appear as shown in Figure 10–3, where each dot or dash can be thought of as sitting in a box or location all its own. Thus, the dash in the upper lefthand corner might be considered to be sitting in location 0, the next dot in location 1, and so on. Here we have one bit stored in each location, which is not too useful by itself, but if we decide to "tie" four of these tubes together and use the contents of the upper lefthand corner of each as the contents of location 0, we can represent numbers in binary coded decimal.

To extract this information from memory (which, incidentally, does not destroy the information), a sensor is placed on the face of the tube which can pick up these dots and dashes, and to enter information into the memory an "electron gun" inside the tube "shoots" a dot or dash to the position specified.

This type of storage device operates at high speeds, but it is costly and very hard to maintain properly. In addition, as in your television set, when the computer is shut down, all information stored therein is lost. Memory devices which lose their contents when power is lost are called *volatile* memories and suffer considerable risk of losing the results of several hours' calculation in case of power failure.

Acoustic Delay Lines

This type of memory is now obsolete, but it does deserve some mention at this point. This device operated on a sound wave principle. If the speed of sound travelling through a particular medium is known, it can be determined how long it will take a sound wave to travel through a given amount of this medium. For example, since the speed of light is much faster than the speed of sound, this technique can be used to determine the range to a given gun emplacement. The lapsed time from the time the burst was sighted until the sound was heard was used to determine the range of the enemy emplacement. This could be calculated or looked up in tables very easily if one knew the speed of sound in air.

The medium used in acoustic delay lines, in most instances, was mercury. Data was entered into one end of a tube of known length, travelled through this tube in the form of a sound wave and was picked up at the other end and re-entered into the tube. While the data was travelling through the tube, it was being stored. To guarantee that it remained stored, it had to be fed into the other end of the tube again. If the control unit accessed this particular piece of data, it could be picked off as soon as it came out the other end of the tube. The access time for these acoustic delay times ranged from 75 to 175 microseconds, which places this storage device in between drum storage and core storage. It is faster than drum but slower than core. As with electrostatic storage, the information stored in an acoustic delay line was volatile, making this storage medium undesirable.

Drum Storage

This storage device consists of a steel cylinder coated with a ferric oxide material, which is easily magnetized and which will retain its magnetism

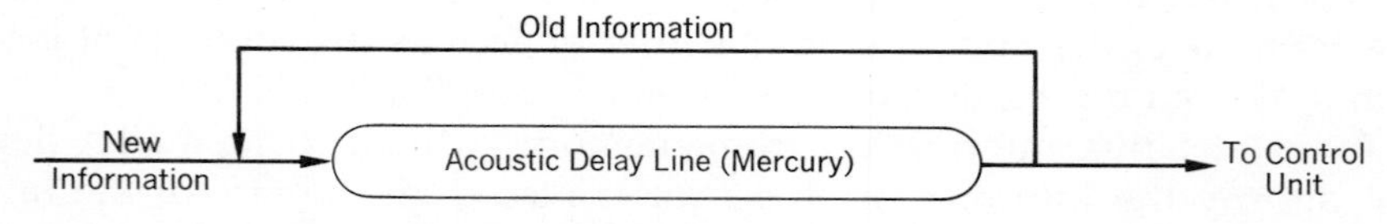

Figure 10–4. Acoustic delay line memory.

indefinitely. The speed of rotation of the drum is controlled by a precision motor that keeps it rotating at a constant rate. Magnetically, the drum is divided into *tracks* and *sectors*, each sector representing one addressable location. In one particular computer, the Royal-Precision LGP-30, the drum contains 64 tracks and each track contains 64 sectors as illustrated in Figure 10–5. Each sector can hold 32 bits of information. This scheme yields 4096 (64 × 64) addressable words of storage. To record and read information, a permanent head—a small electromagnet—is situated above each track. This particular computer has 64 permanent heads, one mounted above each track. To understand more clearly how information is recorded and read, we will need to examine the head in more detail.

The read-write head, shown in Figure 10–6, consists of an insulated piece of permeable material. It has the ability to change its state of magnetism very rapidly. This laminate is wound with wire which is connected to a source of electricity. As current is applied to this coil, the permeable material inside the coil becomes magnetized in one state or the other in much the same fashion as the electromagnet used in a scrap iron yard. One pole then becomes a north pole and the other a south pole. Just as the earth has a magnetic field about it, so does this tiny electromagnet. The direction of flow of these flux lines depends on the polarity of the head. Thus, if the polarity of the head is reversed (by reversing the current flow to the head), the flow of flux lines reverses. Now if the drum is rotating beneath these heads and the heads are very close to the drum, the material that was coated on the surface of the drum will record these magnetic fields and retain the information. Thus, either a polarity repre-

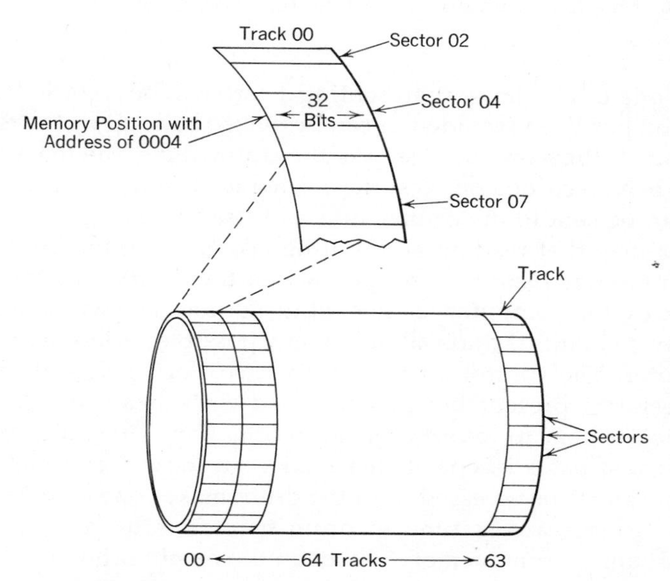

Figure 10–5. Drum memory components.

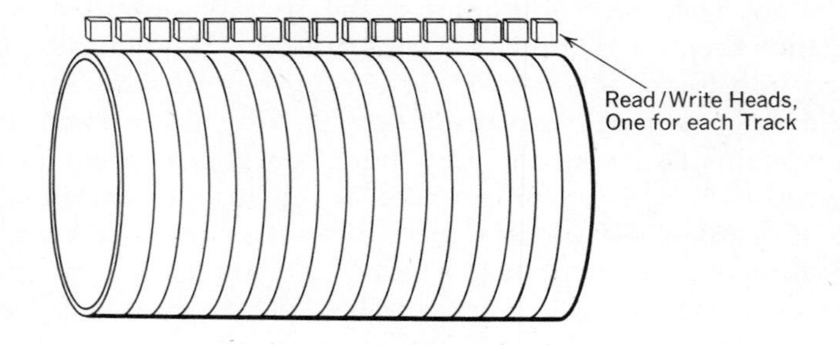

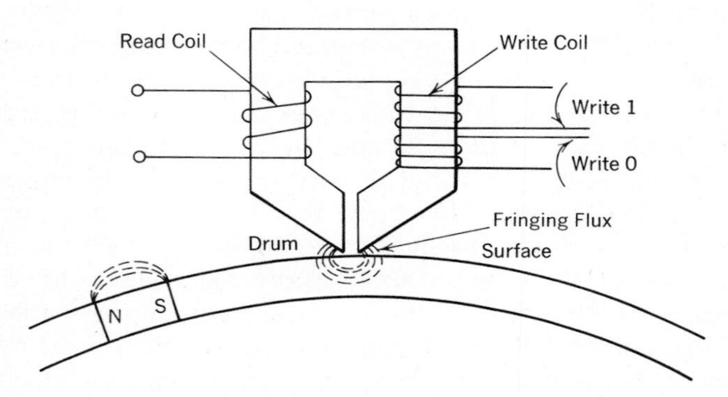

Figure 10–6. Magnetic drun data recording. *(Courtesy, IBM)*

senting a one or a polarity representing a zero will be recorded. Once the information has been recorded, it can be picked back up by the read-write head in much the same manner. As the drum spins, the magnetic spots that have been recorded on its surface generate a voltage in the head. This voltage can be sent to the control unit and used as data.

To guarantee that reading and writing take place at the proper time, a series of pulses is recorded on one track of the drum. This track is used as a clock by the computer to time all of its internal switching. Using a timing device in this fashion allows for any possible variation in the speed of the motor. The control unit monitors each clock pulse and when the proper sector is present beneath the read-write head, the control unit directs the memory to record or send information. Thus, if an addressed sector has just passed beneath the read-write head, the information in this sector cannot be accessed until the drum makes one complete revolution. This causes access time in drum memories to vary. An average access time for a drum memory will be in the neighborhood of five to ten milliseconds.

Magnetic Disk Storage

The magnetic disks used for internal or main memories in computers operate in much the same fashion as do magnetic drums. In the disk storage device, a circular disk of steel or beryllium is coated with a ferric oxide material. This surface is divided magnetically into tracks and sectors with a permanent read-write head mounted above each track.

As in the case of the drum memory, information is addressed by referencing its track and sector. The shaded portion in the diagram in Figure 10–7 represents the information stored in track 0, sector 0. In some computers, these disks are capable of handling the same amount of information as the drum discussed previously. The RECOMP computer uses a disk for an internal storage device and can store 4096 (64 tracks × 64 sectors) addressable words. Disks are also rotated by precision motors and controlled, like drum memory devices, by timed pulses to the control unit produced by a clock permanently recorded on one of its outermost tracks.

One significant problem that arises in the design of disk storage devices deserves mention at this point. Most children riding the merry-go-round at an amusement park like to ride horses on the outside of the wheel. There are many reasons for this, but probably the most significant is that

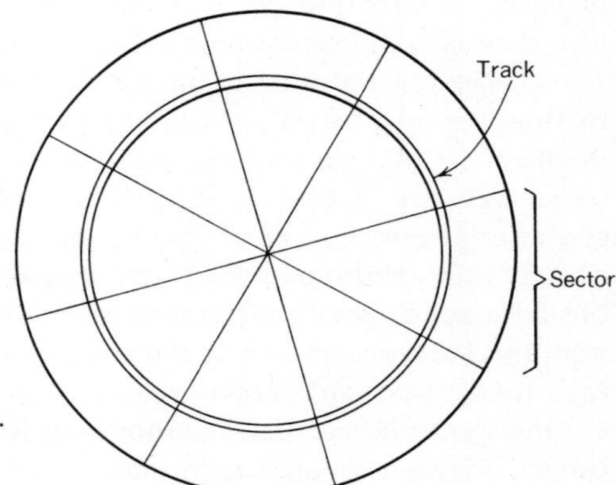

Figure 10–7. Magnetic disk memory.

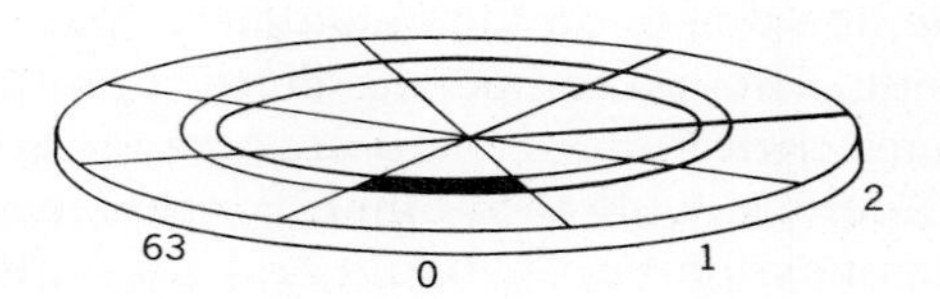

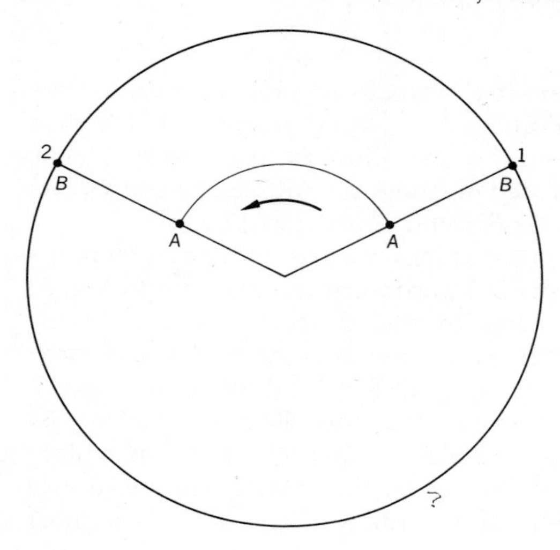

Figure 10–8. Disk rotation.

the horses on the outside of the merry-go-round travel much faster than those on the inside. This can be more completely understood by considering the time and distance required to go from point to point on the various parts of the wheel. The merry-go-round is rotating at a constant speed, possibly ten revolutions per minute, and each piece on the merry-go-round must hold its same relative position in the same amount of time. The pieces on the outside have farther to move than do the inside pieces in this period of time and hence must move faster to hold their relative position. Thus, although the angular velocity of the wheel is constant, the linear velocity of each piece differs, depending on its distance from the center of the wheel. See Figure 10–8. In moving from position 1 to position 2, each of the pieces A and B must arrive at the same time. Since B has a longer distance to travel than A, B must move faster in order to arrive at point 2 at the same time. For this reason, very few track men try to overtake their opponents on curves.

This example was used to illustrate what takes place in the disk storage device when it records information. We will suppose that each word on the disk consists of 32 bits. Since the inside words are much shorter, in physical size, than the words located on the outermost tracks, the information will be packed tighter on the inside than on the outside, for all the recording (whether on an inside track or an outside track) must take place in the same amount of time. Since the outside moves faster than the inside, the pulses on the outside are spaced further apart than those on the inside. This pulse-packing density on the innermost tracks of a disk becomes critical, for if the pulses are recorded too close together, they tend to interfere with each other. For this reason, in most disk memories, the innermost portion—about one-half—of the disk is never used.

Magnetic Core

In terms of cost per bit of storage, the magnetic core illustrated in Figure 10–9 is probably the most expensive type of storage device to date. This cost is offset, however, by the high reliability performance of the magnetic core. A magnetic core consists of a ring of ferromagnetic material much the same as that used in the read-write heads discussed previously. This enables the core, when exposed to a magnetic field, to accept and retain magnetism indefinitely. Cores can be magnetized in just a few millionths of a second. If a wire were placed in the center of one of these cores and current sent through the wire, a magnetic field would be set up around

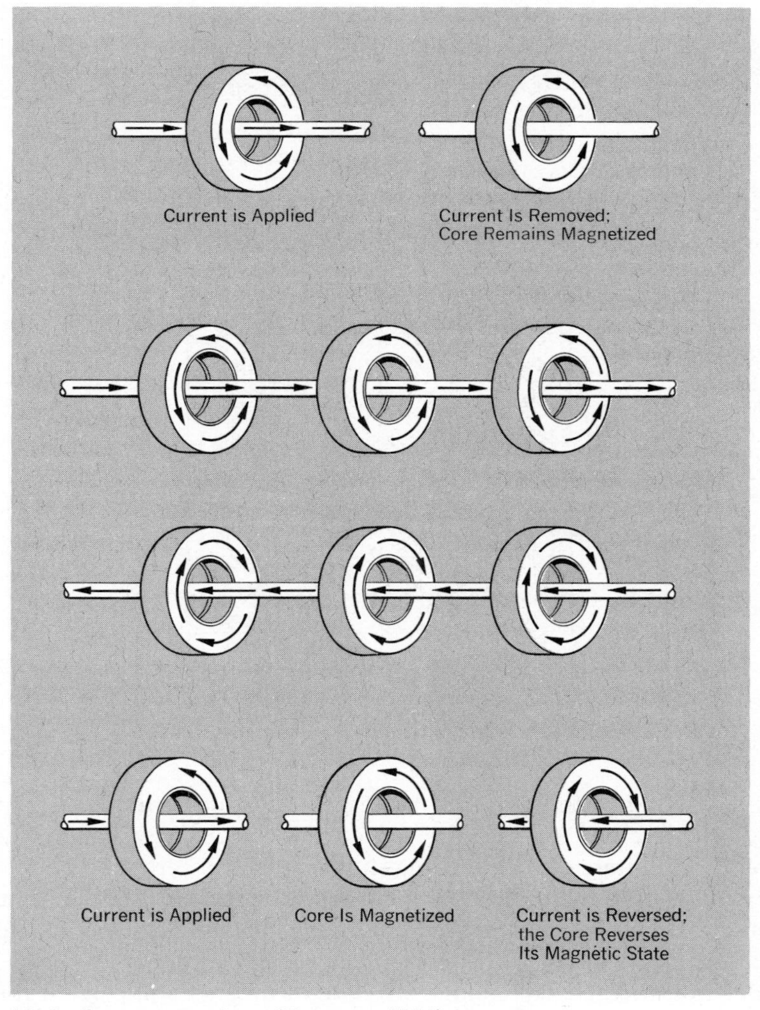

Figure 10–9. Core magnetism. *(Courtesy, IBM)*

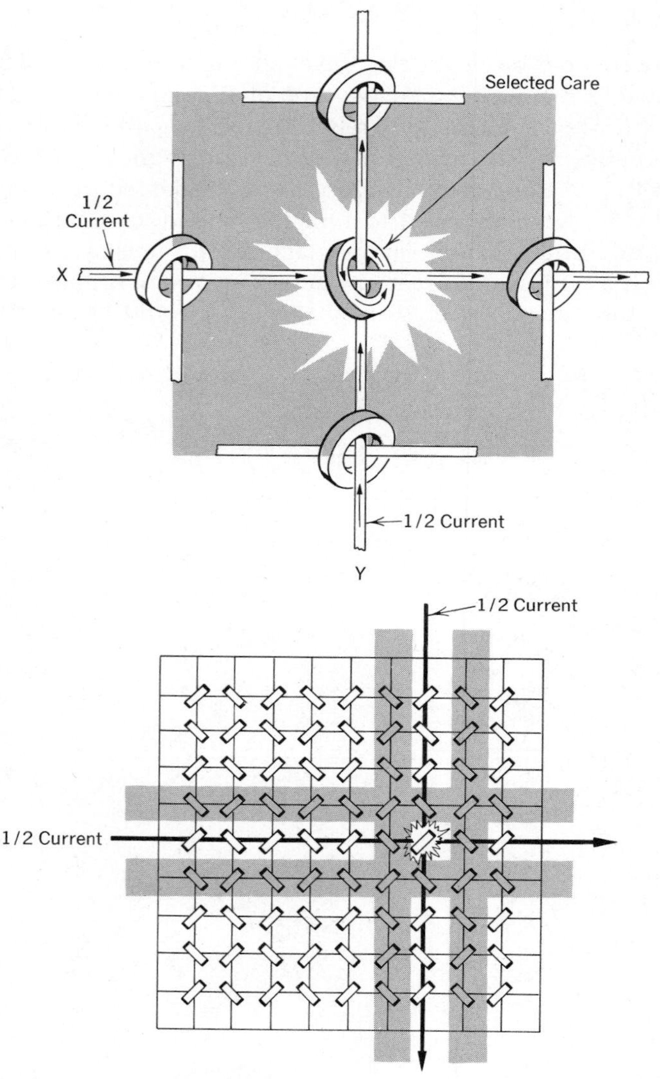

Figure 10–10. Core plane. *(Courtesy, IBM)*

the wire, owing to the current passing through the wire, and would be sensed and retained by the core. When the current is removed, the core will retain this state of magnetism. Thus, a one or a zero may be recorded merely by reversing the direction of the flow of current. In order that more information may be represented internally, these cores are set up in a matrix form on a plane with two wires used to magnetize the core. Thus, in order that a core may change its state of magnetism, current must be applied to both wires. In Figure 10–10, if one-half the current required to

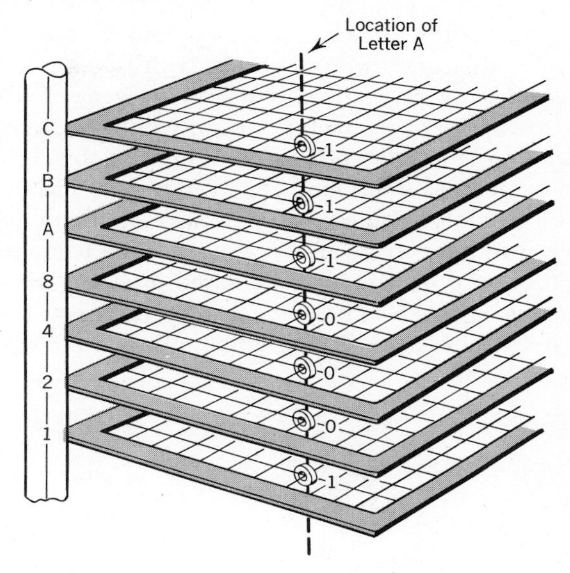

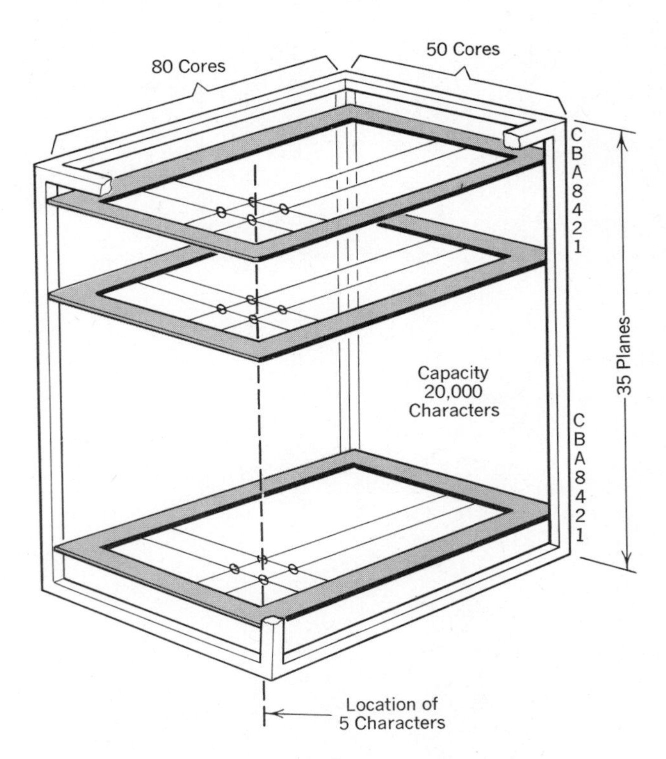

Figure 10–11. Core memory organization. *(Courtesy, IBM)*

change the state of any of the cores is applied to wires X and Y, the only core affected is that one through which both wires pass. Using a scheme like this allows us to pick one core out of an array of cores.

In order to represent characters in the computer, magnetic core *planes* are lined up one below the other and a complete BCD character or binary word may be represented. This constitutes one addressable location in this kind of memory. Some machines have as many as 256,000 of these addressable locations that can be used for main memory purposes. In order that this information, once recorded, may be sensed by the control unit, a sensing wire is also passed through the cores. The function of this wire is to detect the state of magnetism of a particular core. Thus, the X

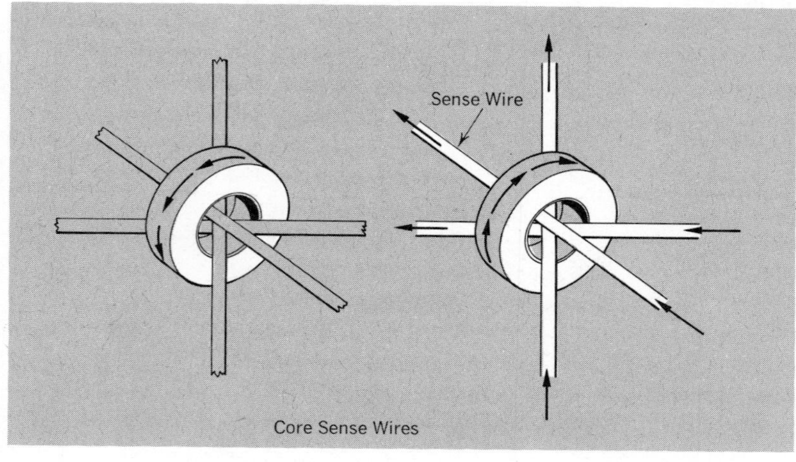

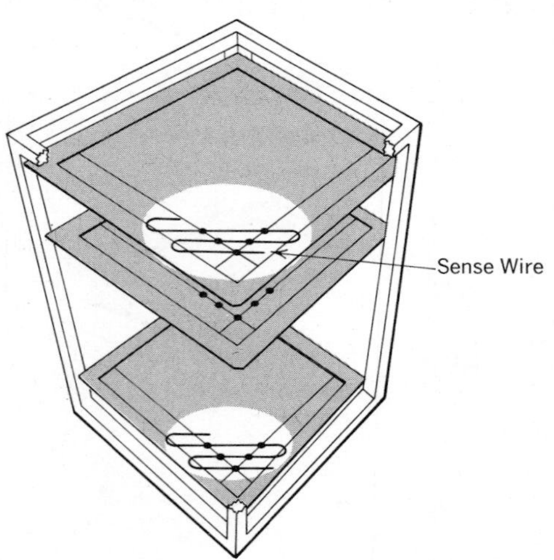

Sense Wire in Cord Plane

Figure 10–12. Magnetic core sense wire. *(Courtesy, IBM)*

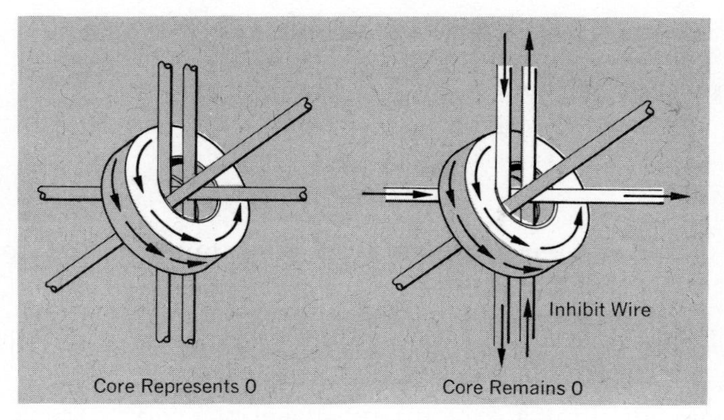

Figure 10–13. Magnetic core inhibit wire. *(Courtesy, IBM)*

and Y wires are used to record information, and the sense wire is used to determine what has been recorded. This description of magnetic core memories is not quite complete, however, for when information is read by the sense wire, all cores containing a 1 are reset to zero. This would make a core memory a *destructive* read-out device—highly undesirable. To overcome this deficiency, one more wire is strung through the core. After information from one location of core storage has been accessed, current is applied to the X and Y wires to try to produce 1's in all the cores. This third wire now performs its function, which is to inhibit the writing of ones in those cores that previously contained zeros. To do this, current is sent through the wire in a direction opposite to that required for writing a one. Thus the cores that were zero remain zero and those that lost their 1's get them replaced. Thus, although when reading information out of a core it is destroyed, its previous state is retained by regenerating the information that was previously present. Figures 10–11, 10–12 and 10–13 illustrate this organization of core memory.

Summary

Summarizing, we note that there are varied types of internal or primary storage devices, but the purpose of each is the same—to store information to be used by the computer during the execution of a program. This stored information may represent instructions, data, or both, but it is always represented in a language that can be used by that particular machine. All of these storage devices represent their information in one of two different states, regardless of the coding scheme used by the computer. Thus, in fixed word length machines, information is recorded as a series of ones and zeros in a word; in character machines, information is recorded as a series of ones and zeros to represent a character; and in decimal machines, the information is recorded as a series of ones and zeros to represent a decimal digit. All are characterized by the fact that reading information into memory is destructive while reading information out of storage is nondestructive.

Questions

1. Explain the difference between selecting, hunting, and connecting circuits.
2. Consider an electronic digital computer that has a memory device that stores three-digit decimal numbers in each memory location. Illustrate how an overflow condition could come about in one of these locations.
3. List what you think are the disadvantages of a volatile memory device as compared to a more permanent one.
4. Explain the difference in function between the magnetic core sense wire and inhibit wire.
5. One of the advantages of magnetic core memory devices over drum or disk devices is the absence of mechanical motion on the part of core. What do you imagine are the disadvantages involved with mechanical motion in a computer?

Appendix to Chapter 10

Operation of Adders

An adder is an electronic circuit that accomplishes mathematical operations by combining electrical impulses. A number of these adders make up an entire arithmetic unit of an electronic computer, which gives it the ability to add, divide, find square roots, and other such operations. Circuits inside adders can be broken down into four parts: (1) AND gates, (2) OR gates, (3) NOT gates, and (4) DELAY gates. A *gate* is an electronic device that combines electrical impulses or the lack of such pulses in circuits to produce other impulses. Whether or not a series of gates connected together and receiving a pattern of input pulses will produce a given output of pulses depends upon the kind of gates employed and the manner in which they are wired together. In general, the operation of gates or, as they are frequently called, *logical gates*, follows the rules of logical truth tables, as described below and in early chapters of introductory textbooks in logic. Through a series of gates, properly connected, addition of two binary numbers may take place. Gates operate on a pulse or no-pulse basis, making them amenable to binary operations. Thus, a pulse will be considered as the binary digit 1 and a no-pulse condition as a 0. Figure 10–14 illustrates the four types of gates used in arithmetic units of digital computers.

In the AND gate, we have a situation where in order to receive a pulse on the output side, *C*, all pulses, *A* and *B*, must be present on the input side. In the OR gate, a pulse will be present at *C* if there is a pulse present at *A* or *B* or both *A* and *B*. The NOT gate, or inverter gate, produces just the opposite pulse at the output terminal, *C*, that was present at the input terminal, *A*. The delay gate merely impedes the progress of a pulse for one clock cycle. The operation of the AND, OR, and NOT gates is summarized in Figure 10–15.

In adding two binary digits, four possible answers or cases may result (see Chapter 16):

+	0	1
0	0	1
1	1	0*c*

(where the *c* denotes carry)

AND

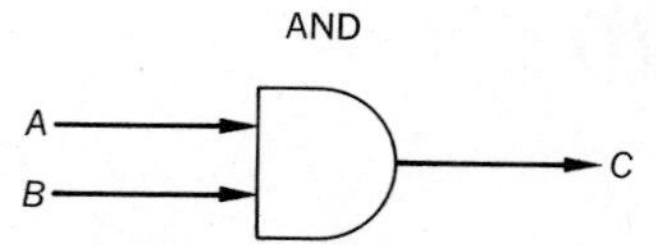

Pulses must be present at both A and B in order for a pulse to be present at C.

OR

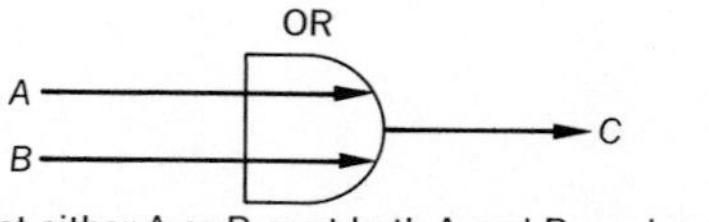

A pulse at either A or B or at both A and B produces a pulse at C.

NOT

A ——●—— C

If a pulse is present at A, there will be no pulse at C. If no pulse at A, then there will be a pulse at C.

DELAY

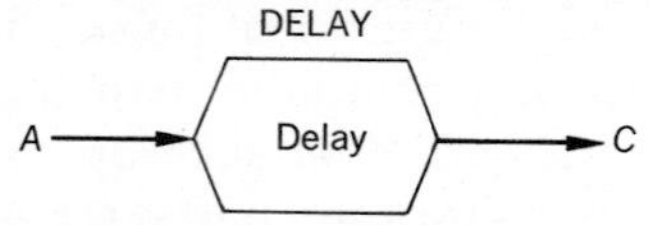

The pulse at A will be at C during the next clock cycle.

Figure 10–14. Logical gates.

In adding three-digit binary numbers, we must allow for a possible carry from the adjacent column to the right when adding the digits in a specified column. Thus:

$$\begin{array}{cccc} & c & c & c \\ 0 & 1 & 0 & 1 \\ \underline{0} & \underline{0} & \underline{1} & \underline{1} \\ 1 & 0 & 0 & 0 \end{array}$$

and

$$\begin{array}{cccc} & c & c & \\ 0 & 1 & 1 & 0 \\ \underline{0} & \underline{1} & \underline{1} & \underline{1} \\ 1 & 1 & 0 & 1 \end{array}$$

where the *c* denotes a carry from the adjacent column on the right.

Trying to control this operation in the computer by the use of adders becomes a relatively simple process. We will make a few observations first and then mechanize the process. In the addition of two binary digits, four results are possible. The half-adder handles this function. Schematically, a half-adder appears as shown in Figure 10–16.

We will examine the half-adder circuit considering four possible configurations for A and B. Notice that the A and B pulses enter both the AND and the OR gates to the left of the half-adder. If $A = 0$ and $B = 0$, then the output of the OR gate is 0; the output of the AND gate below it

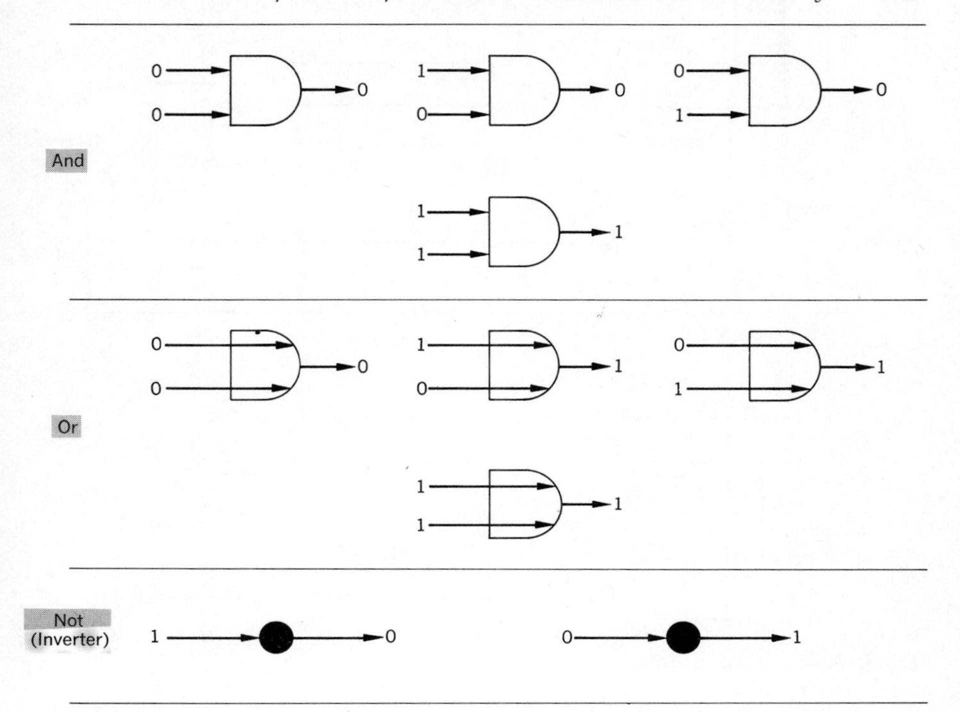

Figure 10–15. Summary of and, or and not gate operations.

is also 0. Thus, the carry becomes 0. Now, the other AND gate in the diagram has an input of 0 (from the top OR gate) and 1 (produced by the output of the lower AND gate (0) and the INVERTER). Thus, the output of this AND gate (1 and 0 input) produces 0, giving us: $A + B = 0$ and $c = 0$, which is what we expected. Assuming $A = 1$ and $B = 0$, we get a 1 out of the OR gate, a 0 out of the AND gate below it, and thus a zero carry. The input to the second AND gate becomes 1 (from the OR gate) and 1 (0 output from lower AND gate and inverted to 1). Thus, we get $A + B = 1$ and $C = 0$, as we expected. The case for $A = 0$ and $B = 1$ is identical to that described above. Finally, considering the case $A = 1$ and $B = 1$, we find that this produces a 1 out of the OR gate and a 1 out of the AND gate below it, giving us a 1 carry. The input to the second AND gate is 1 (produced by the first OR gate) and 0 (produced by the lower AND gate and the inverter), giving us 0 at the output of this AND gate. Our sum $A + B$ becomes 0 and we have a 1 carry, which we expected. See Figure 10–17.

A full adder has the added flexibility of being able to handle the carry digit that resulted as an output of the half-adder. A few more observations are in order before trying to diagram the full adder. The full adder is concerned with not only the addition of two binary digits, but also the con-

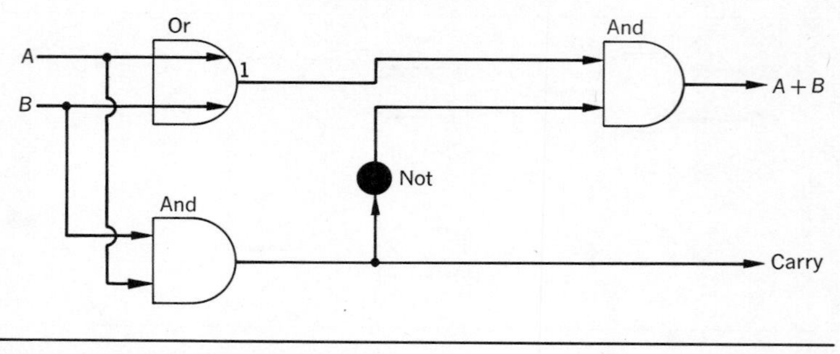

A = 1; B = 0: A + B = 1; Carry = 0

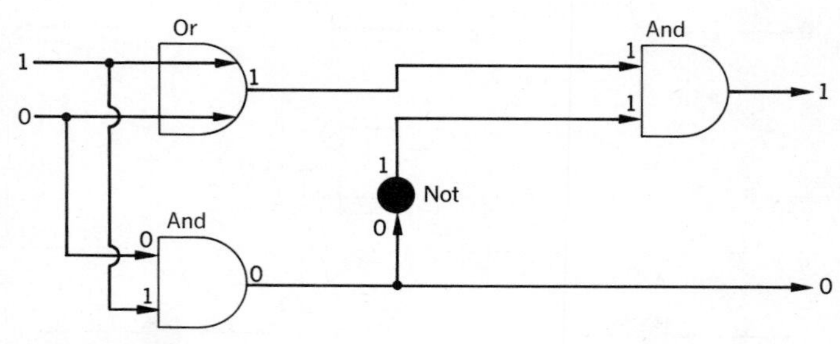

Figure 10–16. Half-adder.

sideration of the carry digit. Note that if A and B are both 1 and C is 1, we should get 1 for a total and 1 for a carry. These observations must be considered and implemented in the design of the full adder. Also, when a carry does occur, we want to be sure that we delay its pulse for one clock

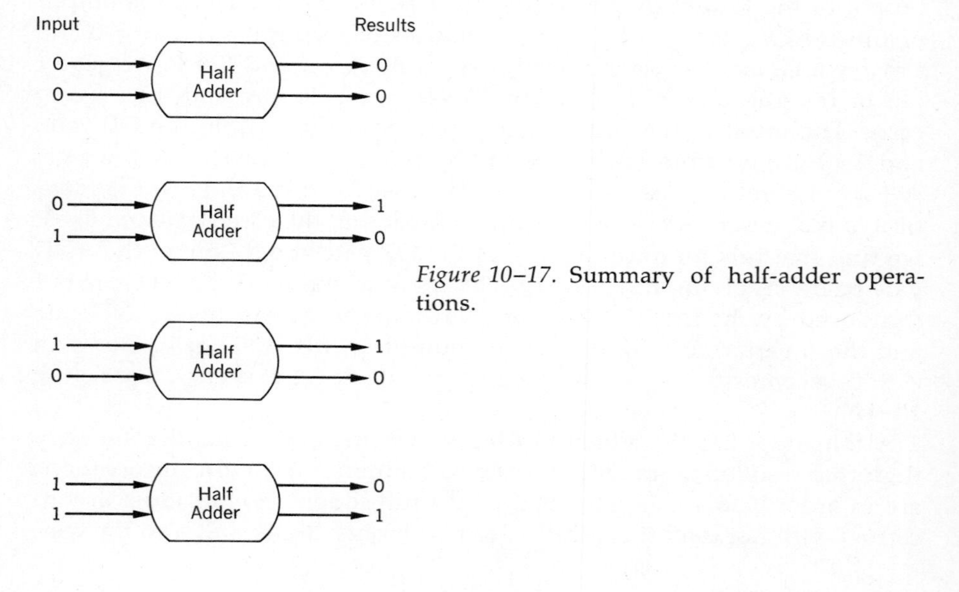

Figure 10–17. Summary of half-adder operations.

cycle until the digits in the next column are added by the circuitry. A schematic for a full adder is shown in Figure 10–18.

Consider adding the numbers 111_2 and 101_2 using the full adder in Figure 10–18. On the first cycle of operation, we are concerned with the addition of the least significant digits of each field:

```
1 1 1     A
1 0 1     B
-----
        1st cycle
```

For the generation of the sum of 1 + 1, the first half-adder will record a 0 at point 1, which will be received by the second half-adder, and since there is no carry on the first cycle, this will produce a 0 at point 2. The first half-adder generated a 1 at point 3, which is seen at point 4 and delayed for one cycle. Thus, the result of adding the first column of digits is 0 and 1 carry.

On the second cycle, this addition takes place:

```
  c
1 1 1   A
1 0 1   B
-----
    0   result
```

For the 1 + 0, the first half-adder will record a 1 at point 1. Now, this 1 at point 1 and the carry that was delayed on the last cycle are our inputs to the second half-adder. The output of this second half-adder (having 1 and 1 as inputs) will be 0 at point 2 and 1 at point 6. This carry at point 6 passes through the OR gate and is delayed at point 4 for one cycle. Our result has now been recorded as 00 and we are ready for the third cycle. On the third cycle, we observe this operation:

```
c
1 1 1   A
1 0 1   B
-----
  0 0   result
```

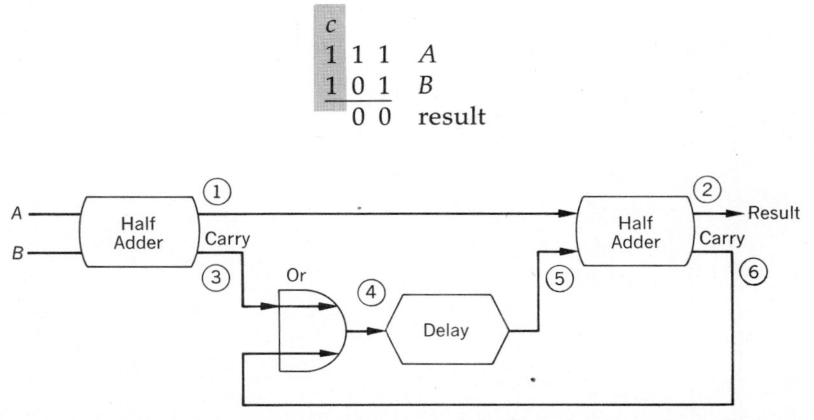

Figure 10–18. Full adder incorporates two half-adders, an "or" circuit and a delay.

The first half-adder records a 0 at point 1. This, along with the delayed carry from the last cycle, is seen by the second half-adder. This causes the second half-adder to record a 1 at point 2 as the result of addition of the third column. Now, the first half-adder also had a carry at point 3, which is delayed one cycle at point 4.

At this stage, the result appears as:

```
c
1 1 1   A
1 0 1   B
-----
1 0 0   result
```

At this time, the control unit recognizes the end of the field and the last carry that was delayed one cycle enters the second half-adder on the next cycle which records a 1 at point 2 and our result becomes, as it should be:

```
  1 1 1   A
  1 0 1   B
-------
1 1 0 0   result
```

11

Electronic Computer Components: Input/Output

The previous chapter considered those portions of digital computers that are directly involved in the accomplishment of the computer system's work. The memory devices examined there are often called *primary* memory devices because they make up the main memory of the system. This chapter considers input/output (I/O) devices that are connected to computer systems to facilitate making data available to programs being executed. These devices are known as *secondary* memory devices. The distinction between primary and secondary memory devices is this: Primary devices are those used by the computer system to store programs while those programs are being executed and for storing small amounts of data while those data are being operated upon by the system. Secondary memory devices are used to store large quantities of data and programs which, in order to be processed or executed, must first be loaded into the computer system's primary memory. Although not all input/output devices are secondary memory devices, it is true that secondary memory devices when *on-line* to the system, that is, when the data stored therein can be immediately accessed by the computer system without human intervention, are input/output devices. Therefore, the discussion here will be oriented towards input/output devices, with the understanding that many of these devices are used for *off-line* mass data storage.

Input/Output Devices

Input/output, or I/O, devices, as the name implies, are used to enter information into the primary memory device of the central processing unit of the computer or to extract and store information from the memory device of the central processing unit. These devices vary from computer system to computer system and we cannot, in this text, begin to cover all of them. We will discuss, however, some of the more commonly used devices in third-generation data processing systems. Figure 11–2 shows the various types of input/output devices used in third-generation data

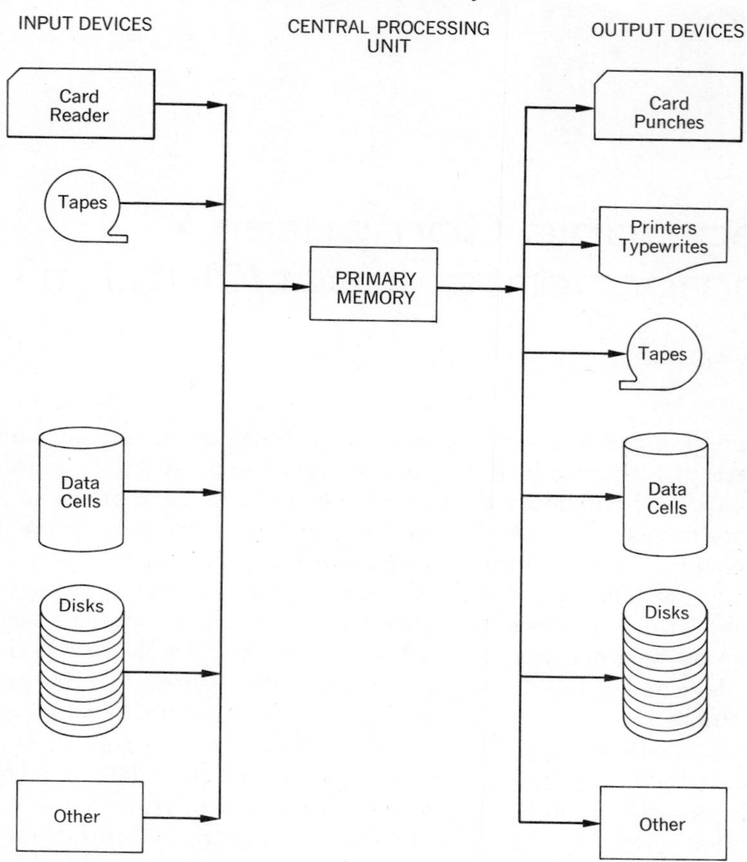

Figure 11–1. Input/output devices.

processing. In this section, we will examine card readers, line printers, data cells, magnetic tape, and disk packs. These are the most commonly used devices and every data processing student should be familiar with them. Information relating to the other devices mentioned in Figure 11–2 may be found in manufacturers' manuals. The operations of these devices follow, in general, the same principles as those discussed here.

Card Reader-Punches

Card reader-punches, such as that shown in Figure 11–3, are used to read and punch 80-column cards. Reading speeds may be as high as 1,000 cards per minute and punching may be accomplished at speeds up to 500 cards per minute. The information punched into cards comes from primary memory and would consist, typically, of 80 characters—blank

Punched Cards	Edge Punched Cards (Input Only)
Magnetic Tape	Punched Tickets (Input Only)
Punched Paper Tape	Transactor Terminal (Input Only)
Typewriter Console Monitor	Photographic Copy
Remote Typewriter Terminal	Graphic Plotters
Optical Scanner (Input Only)	Computer
Cathode Ray Tube Light Pen (Input Only)	Telemetry Devices
Telephone Dial (Input Only)	Data Cells
Disk Packs	Plastic Cards
Voice	Cathode Ray Tube Screen
Magnetic Drums	Magnetic Ink Character Reader (Input Only)

Figure 11–2. Third generation data processing input/output devices.

or otherwise—that are to be recorded into the 80 columns of the card. Similarly, information read from a card goes into primary memory where it is ready for processing in accordance with the program being executed.

Reader-punches have the ability to select cards being read or punched

Figure 11–3. IBM 2540 card read punch. *(Courtesy, IBM)*

into one of five different pockets—three from each side as pictured in Figure 11–4. Thus, if reading and punching is taking place at the same time, the common pocket may be used to merge cards from both the reader and the punch. Cards entering from the read hopper are checked for a hole count first, then read, and then, if selection is to take place, sent to pocket 1 or 2. If no selection is to take place, they are routed to the normal read (NR) pocket. Cards entering the reader-punch from the punch hopper are read (if they are not blank), punched, and then checked to guarantee the accuracy of the information just punched. Then, if selection takes place, they are directed to the 4 or 8 pocket. If no selection takes place, they are dropped into the normal punch (NP) pocket. Note that the middle pocket is labeled 8/2. The 2 is used if the card is being routed from the read side, and the 8 is used for cards entering from the punch side. The reason for the punch-read station is explained by the fact that some reader-punches have the ability to read and punch the same card where others do not.

These units are buffered in a variety of ways. Some have no buffering whatsoever, whereas others contain buffers on the punch side only (since it operates at one-half the speed of the reader); one model (IBM 2540) has both the read side and the punch side buffered. IBM 2540 readers operate in two different data modes and are used with some models of the System/360. In the first mode of operation, the 256 different bit combinations required for the extended binary coded decimal interchange code (EBCDIC) may be read and punched. In the second data mode of operation, the low order six bits of bytes read from the processing unit are punched alternately into the upper six and lower six rows of a card, allowing 160 truncated bytes to be placed in the card. This mode of operation has been referred to in the past as *column binary*. When this punched information is read, it is done so column by column and sent to the CPU byte by byte. The two high order bits of the eight-bit byte are always sent in as zeros.

Reading in most third-generation readers is accomplished by the use of photoelectric cells that convert the light passing through the holes in the card into electrical energy which may be sensed by the central proces-

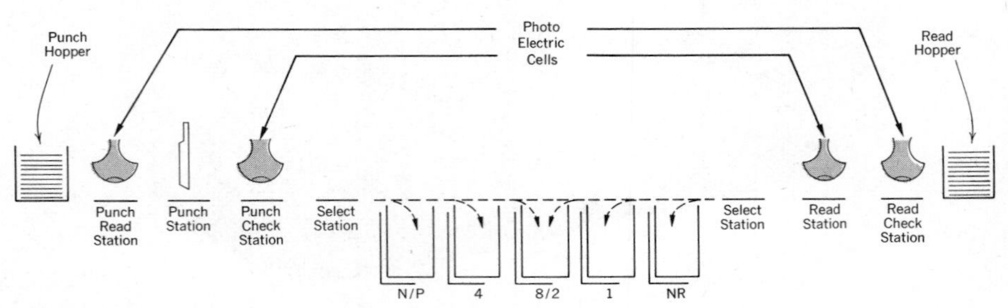

Figure 11–4. Schematic of card reader-punch.

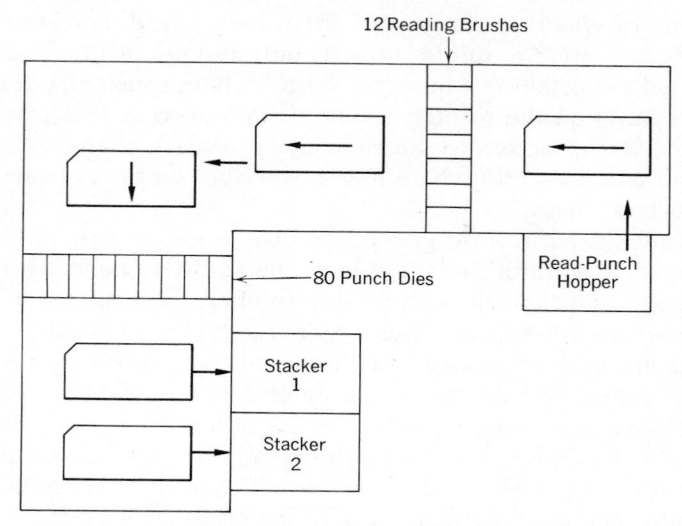

Figure 11–5. Schematic of operation of IBM 2520 card read-punch.

sor. The IBM 2520 card read punch, shown in Figure 11–5, both reads and punches cards at the rate of 500 cards per minute. In this device, every card passes through a reading station as well as a punching station. The punch station need not be activated, however, if reading only is desired.

The punched card is the basic unit of information used in most data processing applications, but entering the information contained in this card into the computer is a slow process. For this reason, the data on the cards is usually transferred to disk or tape prior to processing. This operation is accomplished off-line—that is, apart from the main computer system. Thus, when the main computer is available to process the data, it can do so without having to wait for a slow card reader.

Printers

In third-generation data processing, the most common type of printing device is the chain printer. Printing is accomplished in this device by placing a paper form between a moving chain containing the character set for the computer and a magnetically controlled hammer. (See Figure 11–7.) The characters of the data set are repeated on the chain until all of the space on the chain has been utilized. The chain moves at approximately eight miles per hour and as the desired character passes the position in which it is to be printed, a magnetically controlled hammer strikes the paper which is in turn pressed against the chain and the character becomes recorded on the paper form. Printing takes place at a rate up to 1,100 132-character lines per minute. Printing speeds are affected by many factors, one of which is the type of chain being used. For example, if a particular application required numeric output only, printing speed may be increased by installing a numeric chain (a chain consisting of the characters 0–9 only) on the printer. Using a chain such as this would allow the hammer faster access to the characters, for each character would be present more times on this chain than it would be on a universal character (240 characters) chain.

The printers used in third-generation data processing are all controlled and buffered by control units that have the ability to handle up to three printers each. The characters on these printers are printed ten to the inch and the lines may be spaced either six or eight to the inch. After each line is printed, the printer executes an automatic space in anticipation of the next printed line. Should the programmer desire other types of spacing to be performed, he may, through the use of a carriage tape identical to that explained in the unit record section, instruct the printer to execute an automatic skip to any desired channel. The printer will automatically skip to this channel at speeds up to 75 inches of paper per second. The ribbon used for conventional printing may be replaced by one containing magnetic ink in order that the American Banking Association approved type may be printed. Characters used with this type of ribbon are similar to those found at the bottom of your personal checks. These symbols, printed on checks with magnetic ink, may in turn be read by an input device called a magnetic ink character reader.

Figure 11–6. IBM 1404 chain printer. *(Courtesy, IBM)*

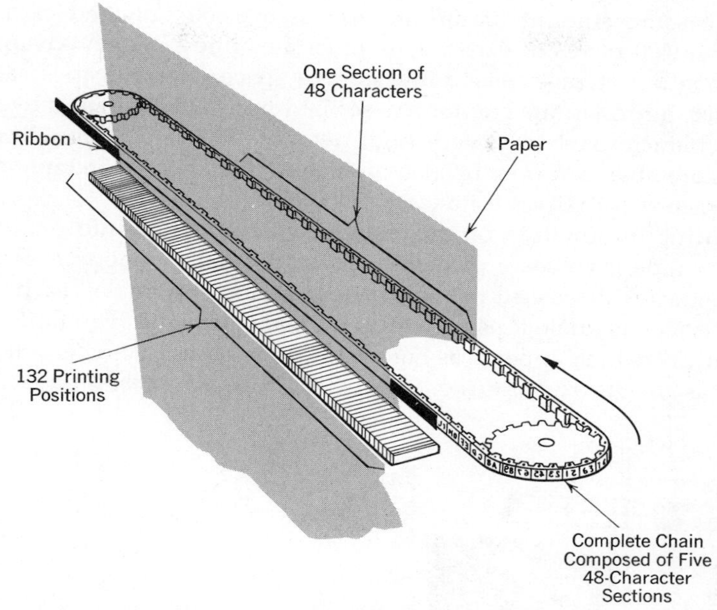

Figure 11–7. IBM 1403 print chain. *(Courtesy, IBM)*

Printing speeds are slow compared to processing speeds. For this reason, most of the output of a particular computer run is placed on disk or magnetic tape and is converted to the printer at a later time by a computer used primarily for this purpose. This allows the more expensive and elaborate main computer system to spend most of its precious time processing data instead of printing reports. Most programs will be written with the option of printing on-line or writing the output on tape to be printed off-line at a later time, if the system is flexible enough to allow off-line printing.

Magnetic Tape

Prior to the introduction of third-generation devices, magnetic tape was the most widely used input/output medium in most data processing installations. Magnetic tape used in data processing is similar in appearance to that used in tape recorders. It consists of a flexible plastic strip coated with a thin layer of iron oxide on one side. This is the side used to hold information. The opposite side of the tape has no coating and acts as an insulator between surfaces when the tape is wound on the reel. A full reel of tape consists of 2,400 feet of one-half inch tape. Each reel of tape is approximately 10.5 inches in diameter and when completely loaded can hold the same amount of information as 800,000 punched cards. This represents 400 boxes of cards. This illustrates one obvious advantage of using magnetic tape—conserving storage space. Not all tapes can store this much information. The tape described here is known as a hypertape and is characterized by a very high density of data storage. Other tape systems are able to store much less data than this, the most common being 800 characters (or ten card images) per inch.

Recording information on magnetic tape and reading information from magnetic tape involves a principle similar to that of magnetic drum and disk memories discussed in the previous chapter. Actually, each track of these devices is analogous to a strip of magnetic tape. The tape drive, a schematic of which appears as Figure 11–10, handles two reels of tape, one known as the *file reel* and the other as the *take-up*, or *machine, reel*. Tape

Figure 11–8. IBM model 729 IV magnetic tape unit. *(Courtesy, IBM)*

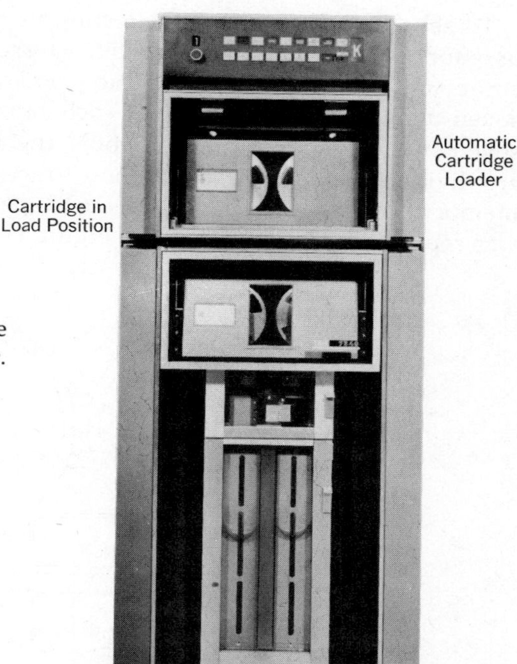

Figure 11–9. IBM hypertape drive with automatic cartridge loader. *(Courtesy, IBM)*

is passed from the file reel through a vacuum column to the read-write head assembly, through another vacuum column, and finally to the take-up reel. Operation of tape drives is similar to that of movie projectors. When information is to be recorded or read, the unit will start and when the information has been written on tape or read into memory, the unit will stop. This forces the tape drives to start and stop very rapidly. To keep the tape from breaking during these quick starts and stops, vacuum columns with photoelectric eyes are employed. When the tape in that column rises above or drops below a predetermined level, the cell actuates a drive mechanism that either allows more tape to spin off the file reel or causes the take-up reel to wind in slack.

The tape moves through the head assembly at speeds up to 112.5 inches per second in hypertape units. Although the tape is moving at such high speed, the read-write head is sensitive enough to be able to polarize itself so quickly as to record the data on tape in such a way that the data appear as though recorded with the tape motionless. Data are recorded on tape in *channels.* (See Figure 11–11.) The read-write head assembly consists of a reading and writing head for each channel of the tape. Thus, in nine-channel tape, the read-write head assembly consists of nine read-write heads. The most common number of channels in use in third-generation data processing is seven- or nine-channel tape.

To get a better picture of the technique used to record data on tape, let us suppose that the characters 15DOT are sitting in memory (BCD machine) and we wish to place these characters on magnetic tape. The seven channels of this one-half-inch tape may be associated with the seven bits in memory used to hold the information 15DOT. Channels are divided into C, B, A, 8, 4, 2, and 1 sections, as is each core position in memory. The data will be recorded on tape in much the same fashion as it was represented in memory. (See Figure 11–11.) Note first that even parity

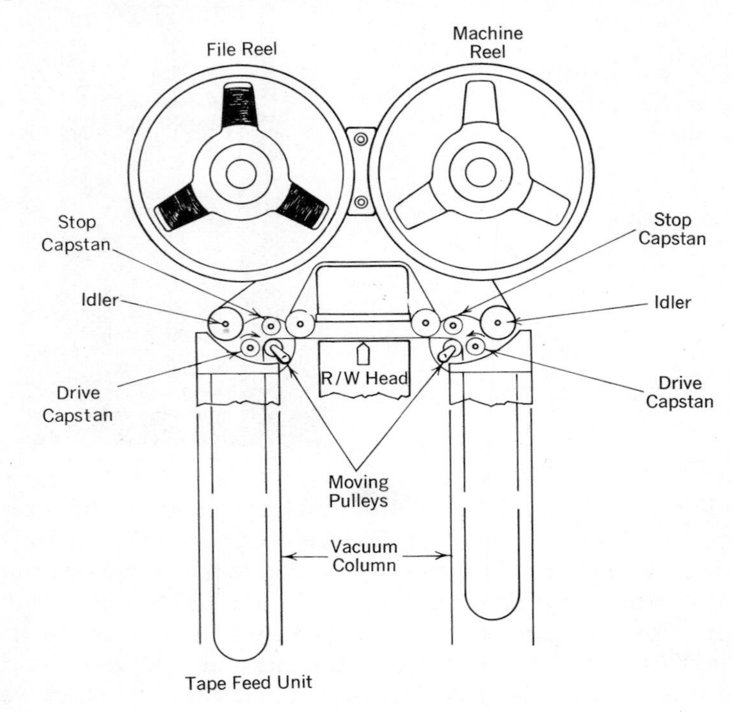

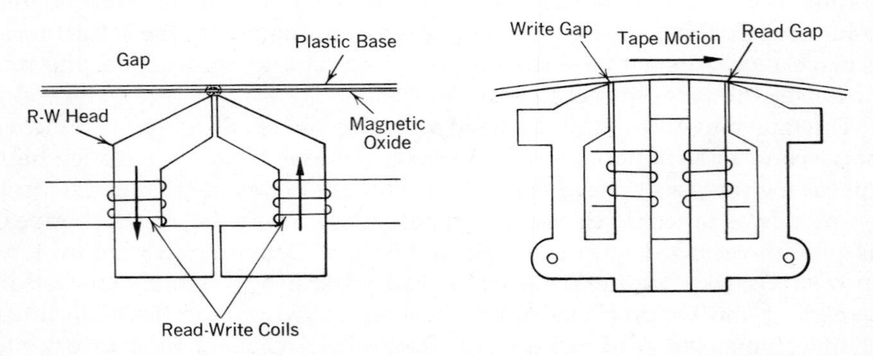

Figure 11–10. Magnetic tape drive. *(Courtesy, IBM)*

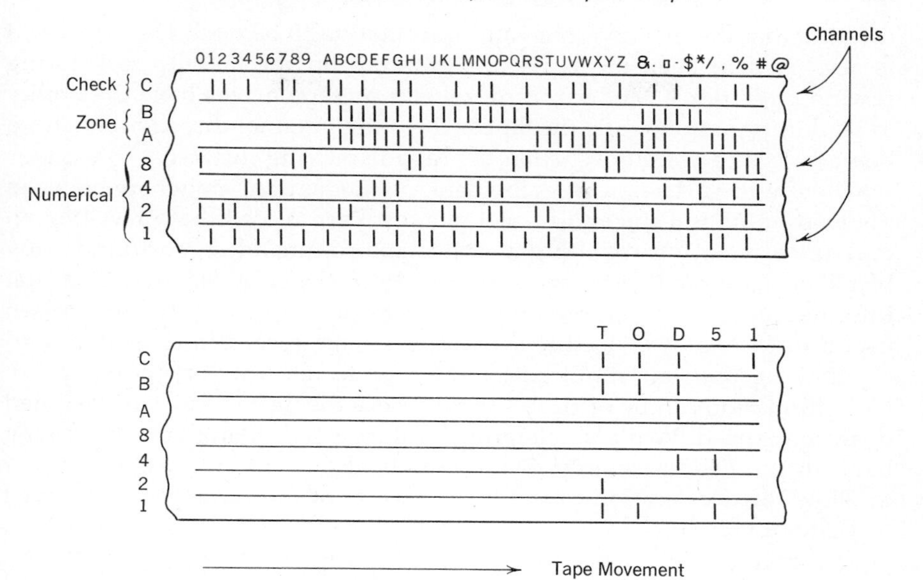

Figure 11–11. Seven-channel tape.

is used in recording data and secondly that the data appear to be written backwards. This is because the 1 was written first and the T last. This will cause the 1 to enter storage first when the tape is read so the data will appear in memory in exactly the same form as it was when it was written. The reader should note the analogy between the seven channels on the tape and the seven bits in each core position used to represent a BCD character. In using nine-channel tape, each position can be used to store a byte of core storage. As we have seen, a byte is a System/360 unit of data that consists of eight binary digits or bits. These eight bits plus the check bit are the reason for using nine-channel tape. For a BCD machine, one column of bits on the tape represents one character in storage and for byte machines, one column of the tape represents a byte as it appeared in core storage.

Since the information recorded on magnetic tape is invisible to the naked eye, some means must be used for detecting the beginning and the end of usable information on the tape. This is accomplished by the use of aluminized stickers which may be placed on the tape at any place. These "spots," shown in Figure 11–12, are used to indicate the beginning and end of usable data on the tape. The spot at the beginning of the tape is called the *load point;* the spot at the end of the tape is called the *end-of-reel marker.* Each of these is situated approximately eight to 12 feet from the end of the tape. The load point is used to position the tape in the tape unit in preparation for processing. The end-of-reel marker is detected by the program and prevents the tape from running off the file reel by indicating that there is no more valid information to be read. The load point is also used to keep the tape from running off the take-up reel during rewind operations. Modern third-generation tape drives have the ability to read information while the tape is traveling in either direction. Writing, however, takes place only when the tape is moving forward.

When writing data on tape, the data may be written anywhere between the load point and the end-of-reel marker. Each record that is written on tape (as a result of executing a write tape command) is surrounded by blank tape referred to as an *inter-record gap* (IRG). A *tape record* is that information contained between two interrecord gaps. The IRG serves two useful functions. It is used to separate one tape record from another and to allow for the time required for the tape to reach its operating speed. No information can be recorded on tape until the unit reaches its designed operating speed. While accelerating to this speed, blank tape is passing beneath the head assembly. Blank tape is also "written" in this manner to allow for deceleration of the tape drive after the completion of a read or write operation.

To provide a clearer perspective as to the organization of data on tape, let us examine a card-to-tape conversion. Suppose we wish to read a card and then transfer the information in memory that was read from this card onto magnetic tape. In this example, we will be creating an 80-character tape record. Keep in mind that the tape must be running at its designed operating speed before any writing may take place. For a hypertape, this requires that approximately 0.2 of an inch of tape be fed. Now, the contents of one punched card (80 characters) can be held in approximately 0.03 inch of tape. This would cause our tape to appear as shown in the upper portion of Figure 11–13. This implies that we are using only

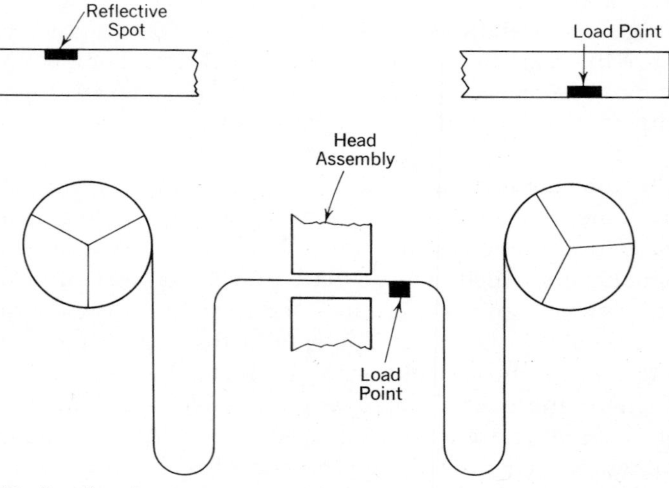

Figure 11–12. Load point.

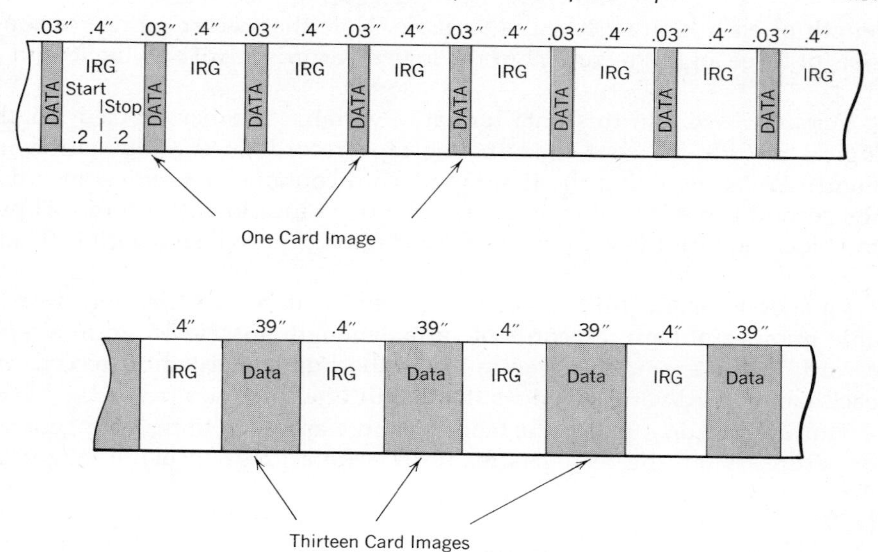

Figure 11–13. Magnetic tape record blocking.

one-thirteenth of our tape to store usable data, obviously a wasteful situation. The remainder of the tape is used by space required to stop and start the tape. In order that we may use the tape more effectively, we will *block* our records. In the example above, were we to read 13 cards into storage and write them all at once, we would produce a 1,240-character tape record and use effectively one-half of our tape as shown in the lower portion of Figure 11–13. This grouping of logical records to form a tape record is called *blocking,* and the number of *logical records* that appear within a tape record is called the *blocking factor.* In the example above, assuming one punched card is a logical record, our blocking factor is 13.

Magnetic Tape Data Organization

There are four basic techniques used to organize data on magnetic tape. These are the fixed-fixed format, the fixed-variable format, the variable-fixed format and the variable-variable format. Each of these is illustrated in Figure 11–14.

Fixed-Fixed. If a block of information is to consist of a fixed number of logical records, all having the same length, then the file is said to have a fixed-fixed format. Each logical record has the same length and each tape record has a blocking factor of 3. The length of the logical record is fixed as is the blocking factor.

Fixed-Variable. In this format, the blocking factor is fixed but the length of each logical record is variable. Note that each tape record consists of three logical records, but the logical records are of varying lengths.

Variable-Fixed. In this data format, a variable number of fixed-length logical records are contained in one tape record. In the illustration in Figure 11–14, note that the first tape record contains five logical records, the second three logical records, and the third four logical records. Thus, the blocking factor is variable, but the length of the logical record is fixed.

Variable-Variable. In this form of storing data records on tape, a variable number of logical records of variable length are used to form a tape record. In the example in Figure 11–14 the number of logical records in each tape record varies, as does the length of each logical record.

This discussion of magnetic tapes is, and was meant to be, very general in nature. When the reader is ready to write a program using magnetic

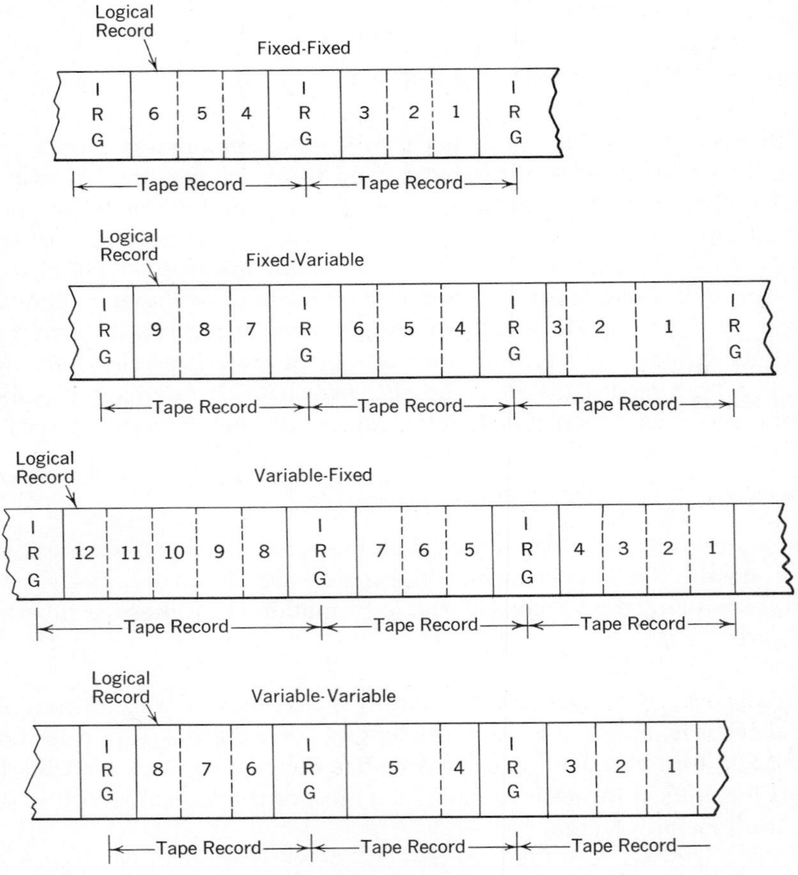

Figure 11–14. Magnetic tape data organization formats.

tape processing, he will undoubtedly want to refer to the manufacturers' manuals for specific details. It is important that the reader notice that magnetic tape is a *sequential* file storage device. That is, the first record on tape must be read before the second record and the second record read before the third and so on. The records on tape are stored in some kind of sequence according to a key in the logical record. To process record 7 shown in Figure 11–15, we must first read records 1 through 6. This has many advantages and many more disadvantages. Ideally, we would like to process any record we wanted at will without having to read all of the others, but because of the sequential nature of magnetic tape storage, this cannot be accomplished. The solution to this problem is achieved by manufacturers of direct access devices such as data cells and disks, a discussion of which follows later.

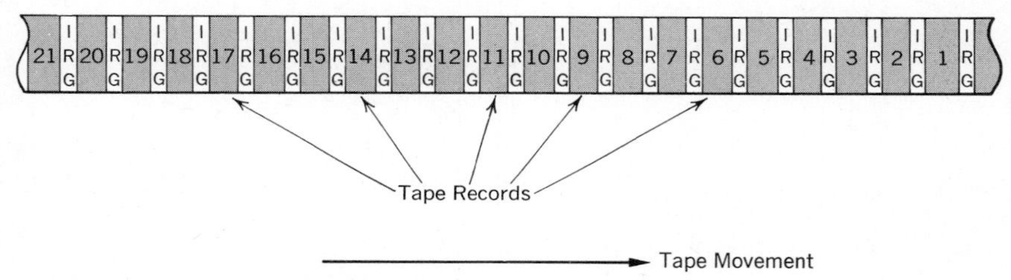

Figure 11–15. Record sequence on tape.

In making the transition from punched card processing systems to magnetic tape processing systems, many factors must be considered. First, each reel of tape is indistinguishable from the next. All reels of tape look alike and must have some means of external as well as internal identification labeling. Second, the records to be processed are not physically separated as is the case with cards. This means that a clerk may not reach in and physically remove a record, insert a record, or change the order of a file. Third, the operations of sorting and merging files no longer can be done on off-line equipment, but must be done through the computer system. Fourth, when an error on reading or writing occurs, the operator can no longer run out the file and restart. Checks must be provided in the program to handle situations such as this. Finally, some way of indicating when a job is complete must be provided. The operator no longer can tell when the job is done by placing the last handful of punched cards in the read hopper. These and other considerations must be provided for when processing data using magnetic tape.

Data Cells

Third-generation data processing requires the maintenance of very large files of information. This requirement has resulted in the development

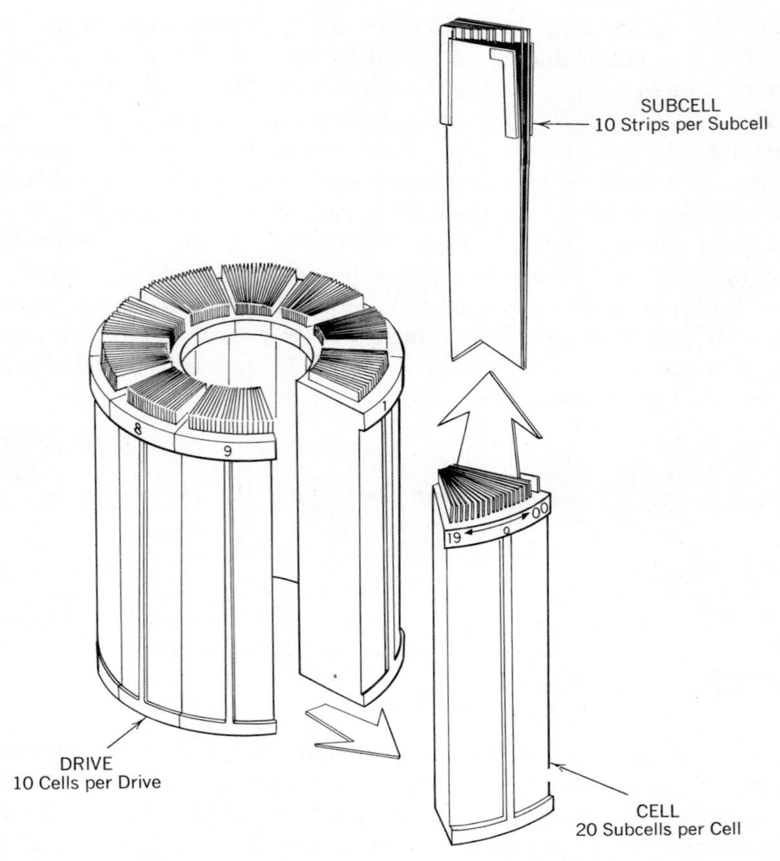

Figure 11–16. IBM 2321 data cell drive, data cell, and subcell. *(Courtesy, IBM)*

of hardware capable of handling large data files with relatively fast data transfer to the central processor. The data cell is one of these devices. It appears in Figure 11–16. Data cells feature large storage capacity (418 million bytes per cell), medium speed accessibility (600 milliseconds maximum to any record), data file removability (change time about one minute), fast data transfer to the CPU (55,000 bytes per second), and a large volume of data available at a single on-line computer access.

Data cells consist of a cylindrical array of ten cells, each having twenty subcells. Each subcell consists of ten strips of material similar to magnetic tape on which information is recorded. A drive motor positions any one of the ten cells beneath an access station. Then, a subcell is selected and from this subcell one of the ten strips is withdrawn and wrapped around a drum. The read-write head associated with this drum reads or writes on this strip and then the strip is returned to its original location in the subcell. (See Figure 11–18.) Each strip consists of 100 tracks of information,

Figure 11–17. IBM data cell drive. *(Courtesy, IBM)*

thereby giving us the same storage capacity as would be provided by 2,000 drum memories consisting of 100 tracks of information each. The read-write head associated with the drum that the strip is wrapped around has only twenty heads. To access each of these 100 tracks of information, the head has the ability to place itself in one of five different positions, giving us 100 (20 × 5) different positions from which to access data. This corresponds to the 100 tracks of information contained in each strip. Each data cell has the ability to handle 400 million bytes, or over 800 million decimal digits of user information. Each track can contain up to 2,000 bytes of information. Since there are 100 tracks per strip, we observe that each strip may contain as many as 200,000 bytes or characters of information. The storage capacity of a strip varies with the data format used in a particular track. Data on tracks is stored in a count-key-data format. That is to say, an indication is given by the count field as to the length of the record being accessed. The key is used in much the same fashion as a control field is used in punched card processing. The data that follows the key field is the actual data to be processed. This scheme must be used in order that the program may determine the length of data fields, since all data is assumed to be variable in length. In addition to the count-key-data format of storing data on a strip, each record is preceded by an address marker to indicate to the read-write head which position is being accessed. (See Figure 11–19.) Each track may consist of one or many records, depending on the data requirements of the job to be processed.

Use of direct access devices such as the data cell enables the central processing unit to answer inquiries about any record in the file without regard to its location. To do this on magnetic tape would be a tedious task, for if the record to be accessed were near the end of the tape, each record prior to this one would have to be read first. In the case of the data cell, the strip with the desired record may be accessed as quickly as any

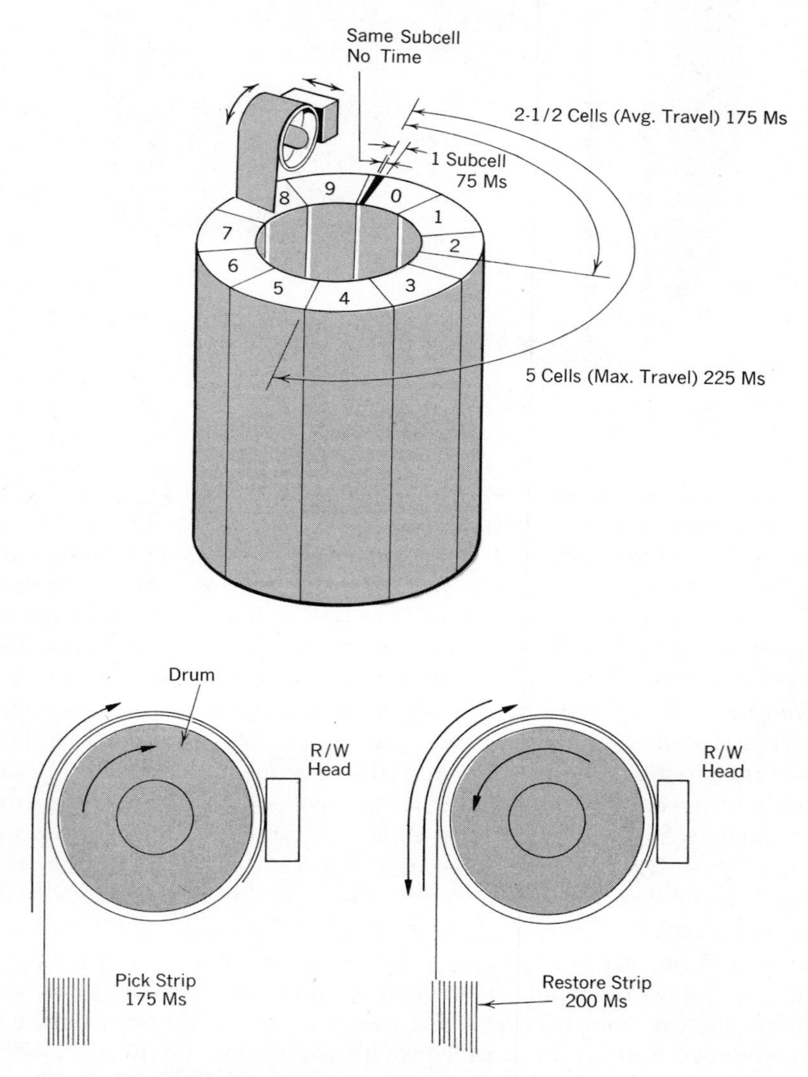

Figure 11–18. Data cell access procedure. *(Courtesy, IBM)*

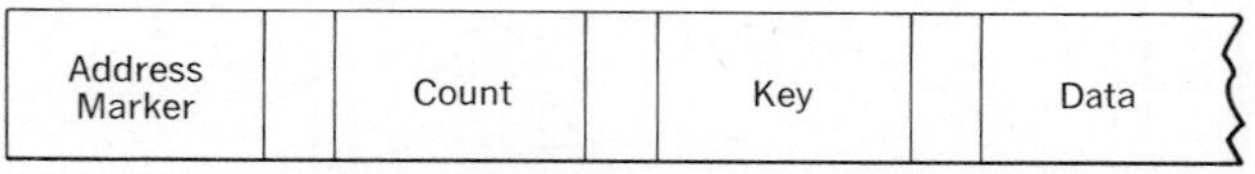

Address Marker		Count		Key		Data

Figure 11–19. Schematic of typical record found in any tract of the 2321 data cell.

other without regard for its relative location in the cell, hence the name *direct access* which has been appended to all nonsequential data storage devices.

Disk Storage

Another direct access device used in third-generation data processing applications is the 2311 disk storage drive shown in Figure 11–20. One of these storage devices has the ability to store 7.2 million characters of information with an average access time for any one record of 85 milliseconds. Once the data on the disk pack has been located, it can be transferred into core at a rate of 156,000 characters or bytes per second.

The 2311 disk storage device contains a removable 1316 disk pack. Each of these disk packs is composed of six 14-inch disks. Data is recorded on ten of the 12 surfaces available in the pack. The top surface and bottom surface are not used. (See Figure 11–21.) This is because the arm that accesses the data from the surface of the disk must ride on a cushion of

Figure 11–20. IBM 2311 disk storage drive. *(Courtesy, IBM)*

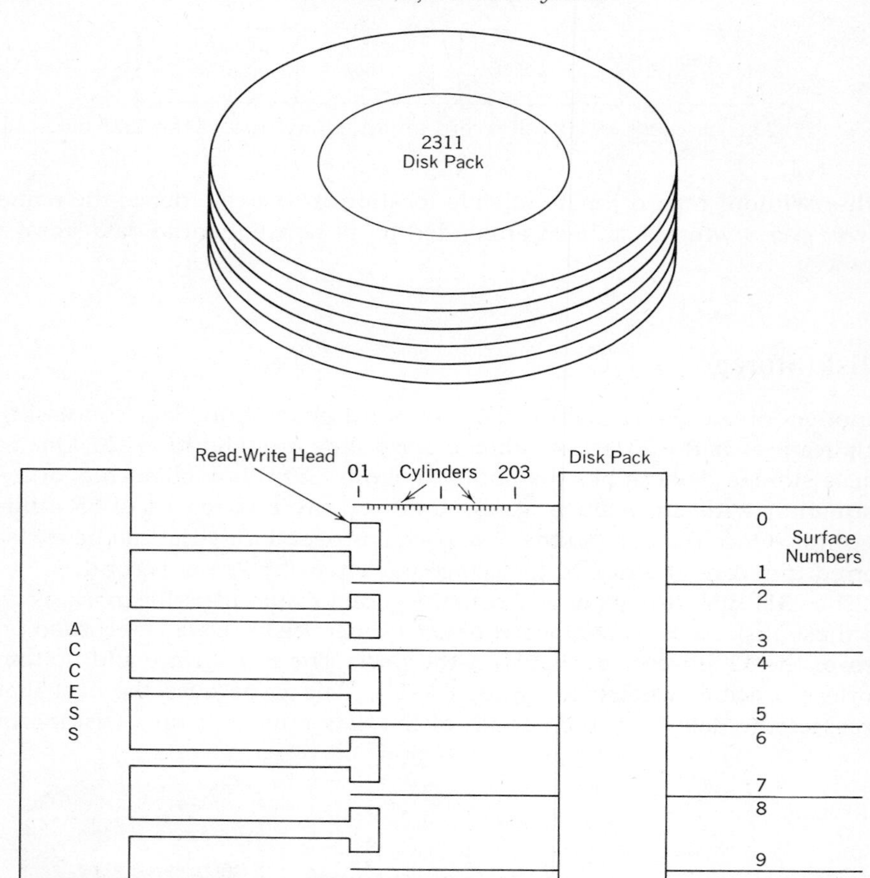

Figure 11–21. Disk pack and read-write heads. *(Courtesy, IBM)*

air, and this cushion cannot be provided by one surface alone. When the disk pack is mounted in the storage unit, information may be read or written using read-write heads similar to those used in the data cell. These read-write heads are mounted in pairs on a moveable arm as shown in Figure 11–22. The movable arm has the ability to position itself in

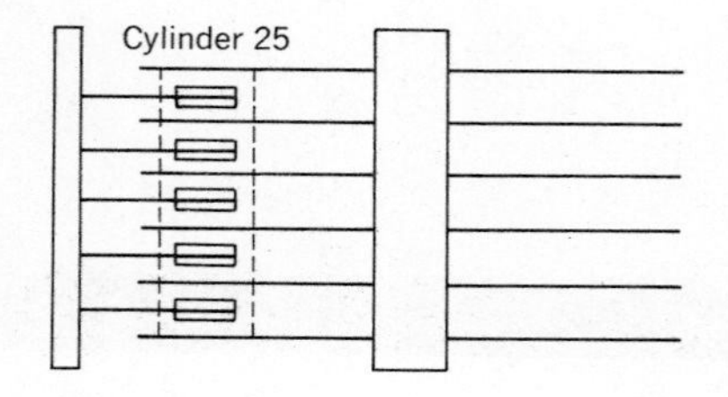

Figure 11–22. Access mechanism at cylinder 25.

one of 203 different positions. Each of these positions will be referred to as a cylinder. Thus, if the arm is in position 25, all heads are positioned to access information from cylinder 25. Thus a cylinder of information is all of that information contained on ten disk faces at a specified distance from the center of the disk pack. Each disk surface may be thought of as being divided into 203 tracks. (See Figure 11–23.) Note that we refer to a *track* on a particular disk surface, but the aggregate of all the tracks for a given position of the movable arm is referred to as a *cylinder.* Each disk surface may be thought of as being composed of 203 tracks, and the entire disk pack is composed of 203 cylinders. Each track has the ability of storing 3,600 bytes or characters of information. There are 200 usable tracks per disk surface giving us 720,000 bytes of information per disk face and with ten disk faces, we are provided with the ability to store 7.2 million bytes of information. The sector concept discussed previously for internal disk memory devices is not used in third-generation data processing disk storage devices. One might question the fact that the arm may be positioned in one of 203 different positions yet we can use only 200 cylinders to store data. The other three cylinders are used as auxiliary storage in case one of the 200 prime storage areas becomes damaged in some way. This could be a result of a scratch in the surface of the disk or the like. Actually, the programmer never realizes that one of the alternate tracks is being used by the system. Should the system detect a bad track, it will automatically shift its data to one of the auxiliary cylinders. Data is accessed on the disk storage device by referencing a particular cylinder and read-write head. Thus, the data at cylinder 57, head 4 would be found by positioning the access arm to cylinder 57 and then switching on the head associated with disk face 4.

Data stored on the disk pack uses the same format as that discussed for the data cell: count-key-data. Each record also has its own address marker.

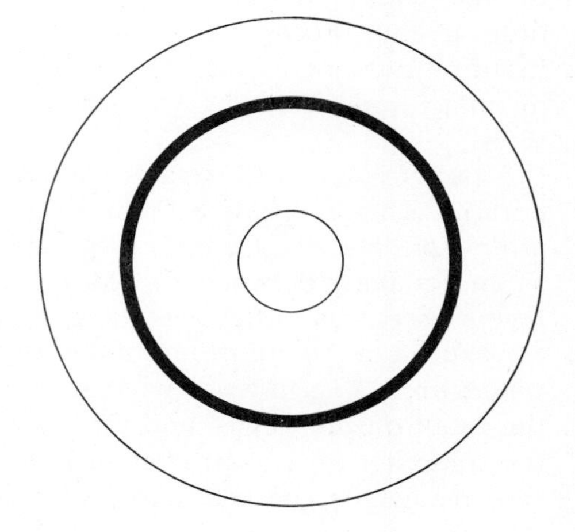

Figure 11–23. Typical disk surface showing one track.

Figure 11–24. IBM 2314 direct access storage facility consisting of a "cluster" of nine disk packs. *(Courtesy, IBM)*

Buffers

Prior to the introduction of third-generation data processing hardware and techniques, most commercial applications were limited in operating speed by the speed of operation of the input/output device. Programs limited in this fashion were classified as being *input/output bound.* Most manufacturers recognized this problem and poured sizable amounts of money into development of devices that could handle input/output operations at much greater speeds. The input/output problem was alleviated somewhat by the development of high-speed printers, faster tape drives, and special features on external disk storage devices, but along with the introduction of these faster devices came demands for processing a larger volume of data, and the input/output problem plagued manufacturers again. During most input/output operations on second-generation systems, the central processing unit was forced to sit idly by while data was brought into or removed from the memory of the computer. Thus, very little, if any, processing of data was accomplished by the CPU during input/output operations. As an attempt to make use of this idle time, manufacturers decided to incorporate *buffers* for their input/output devices.

A buffer is an auxiliary data storage device designed to hold data temporarily. This device is used to compensate for the difference in the rate of flow of data when transferring data from one device to another. It acts as an equalizer between two components operating at different speeds. In our case, this buffer was designed primarily to attempt to match the slow speed of the input/output device with the higher speeds of the computer, providing us with what seemed to be simultaneous operation of the input/output device and the central processing unit. For example, if the computer must wait after each read command for a card to enter the card reader, be checked, and sent to storage, many precious seconds of

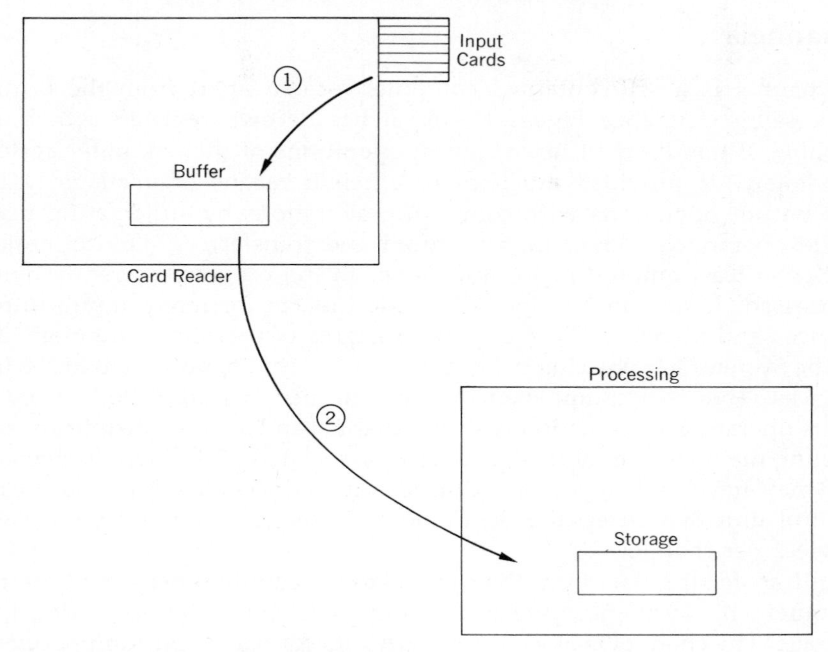

Figure 11–25. Operation of buffer device.

processing time are lost. It would be much more desirable to transfer the card image from the reader to storage at electronic speeds instead of electromechanical speeds. To do this, the card reader was provided with a buffer, which, while processing was being done, received the card image. Then, when the computer requested a card to be read, it could be transferred to core storage at electronic speeds from this temporary storage device. Then, while that data was being processed, another card was read mechanically and its contents stored in the buffer.

In Figure 11–25, the transfer of data from the read hopper to the buffer takes place while the program in memory is being executed. Then, when the program requests data to be read from the reader, it is merely transferred from the buffer to storage electronically and the next card image is automatically placed in the buffer in anticipation of the next read command. This technique works fine if the read commands in the program are spaced far enough apart to allow for reloading the buffer. But, if a read command is executed while the buffer is being loaded, the CPU is forced, once again, to wait for an electromechanical operation to be completed. As internal processing speeds have increased, it has become impossible for buffer devices to keep up with these processing speeds. Once again, computers have become input/output-bound. This situation has led to the development of *channels*, which are used on most third-generation data processing equipment.

Channels

A channel is a self-contained computer located apart from the central processing unit. (See Figure 11–26.) It has its own registers which are capable of handling all input/output operations of the computer system separately. It provides much more efficient means of *overlapping* input/output operations with computing operations by anticipating read-write operations sooner than required and transferring data to storage with the least amount of inconvenience to the program currently being processed. It has the ability to provide linkage for many input/output devices and therefore allow for a high degree of peripheral simultaneity. In the System/360, one channel has the capability of handling up to 256 I/O devices. This is accomplished through the use of *control units.* Control units operate in conjunction with the channel and are responsible for controlling the operation of the I/O devices associated with them. Each channel may have as many as 16 control units associated with it, and each control unit may direct the operation of 16 devices giving 256 (16 × 16) devices per channel.

In transferring data from the channel to the central processing unit, the channel will "steal" machine cycles from the CPU in order to get data into storage. The channel is always given priority for data input/output operations. Thus, a program will be interrupted for one or two machine cycles (a matter of microseconds) in order that the channel may supply the CPU

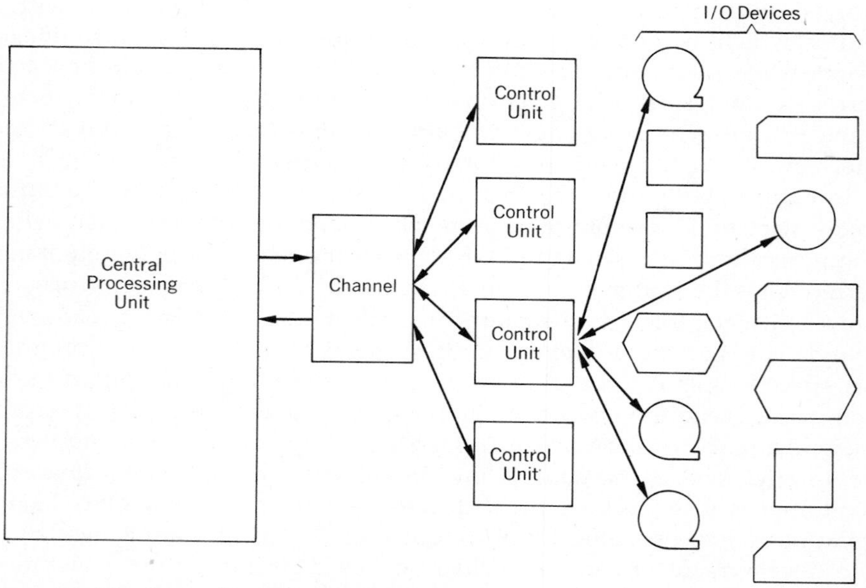

Figure 11–26. Channels and control units.

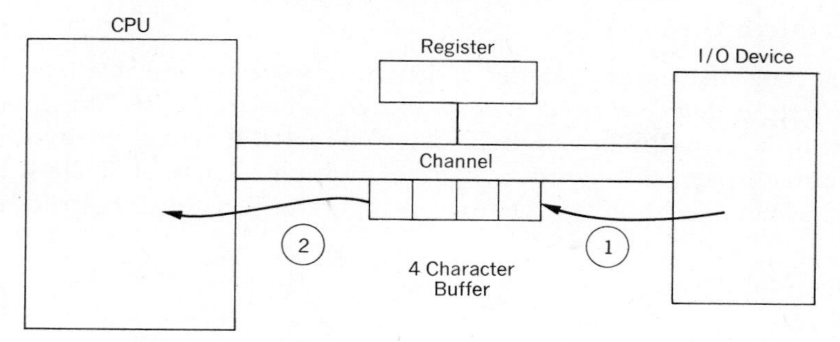

The channel gathers four bytes of information from the I/O device, looks at its register to see where this information is to go, steals a few machine cycles, places these four bytes into storage, and returns control to the CPU.

Figure 11–27. Operation of channel.

with data. The channel actually anticipates the data required by the CPU and places it into storage before the CPU must use this data. In moving data from the I/O device to the CPU, the channel can move four characters or bytes of data at a time, which requires only a few machine cycles.[1] Then the CPU goes back to work processing the program while the channel is gathering another four characters of information. (See Figure 11–27.) When this has been gathered, the channel will "steal" a few more machine cycles and transfer this data into storage. Thus, processing time is, relatively speaking, not affected by input/output operations. Note that the channel always has priority over the CPU as far as access to main storage is concerned. The buffer of the channel must be ready to accept more information from the input/output device and thus must unload what it has gathered immediately. Associated with these channels are buffers, and the I/O devices themselves also have buffers as does main storage. This gives all of the features of a buffered system as well as those of a channeled system. A computer may have more than one channel associated with it, giving us the added capability of using the alternate channel if the main channel is in current use.

Selector Channel

This channel can operate only one control unit at a time and may have up to eight of these control units attached. The maximum number of selector channels that may be attached to a computer system is six.

[1] A byte is a unit of data recorded in System/360 computer systems. More detail is afforded bytes in the final section of this book. At this point, it will suffice to consider it as a character of data.

MULTIPLEX CHANNEL

This type of channel has the ability to operate several relatively slow input/output devices at one time as shown in Figure 11–28. This mode of operation by a multiplex channel is referred to as the byte interleave mode. The other mode of operation by the multiplex channel is the "burst mode." When a multiplex channel is operating in the burst mode, its

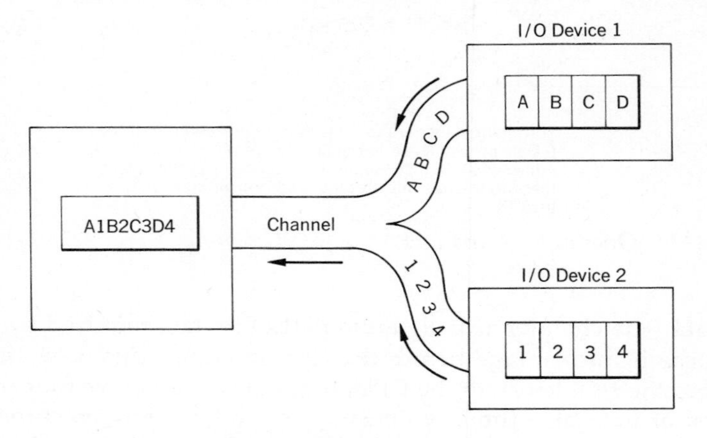

BYTE Interleaved Mode of Operation: Note that each byte from I/O devices 1 and 2 are interleaved and when data enters storage, it appears mixed. This allows for better utilization of time when using slow input/output devices, i.e., card readers, printers, etc.

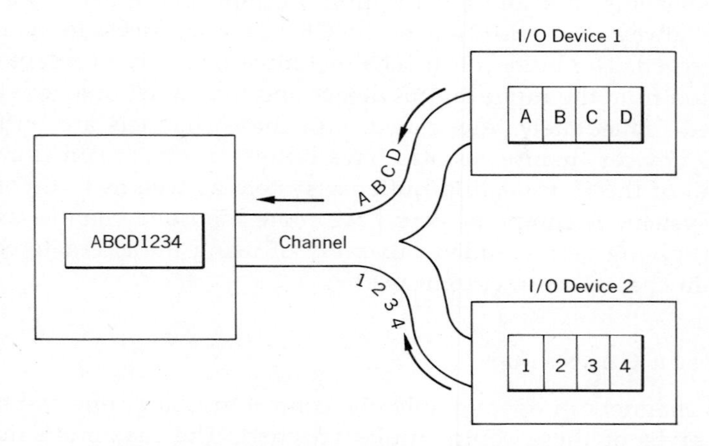

Burst Mode of Operation: Information is sent down the channel in bursts from the I/O devices. This type of operation is used for faster type I/O devices, i.e., tape, disk, etc.

Figure 11–28. Operating modes of multiplexor channels.

function is reduced essentially to that of a selector channel, that is, outputting large amounts of data through one control unit rather than small amounts each to several control units as in byte interleave mode.

The selector and multiplex channels have three common characteristics:

1. Each is a stored program computer in itself.
2. The program for these channels is stored in the CPU of the system.
3. The commands that start the channel programs are part of the main line program being executed.

It is beyond the scope of this book to discuss in detail the operation of channels or to examine the commands used to actuate a channel program. Our intention is to familiarize the reader with the necessity and function of channels in third-generation data processing systems. The efficiency of all computer systems—first, second, or third-generation—is measured in terms of the quantity of data that can be processed accurately in a given period of time. This ability is increased by the use of faster input/output media. The channel is nothing more than a better, faster, and more efficient means of connecting input/output devices to the central processing unit. They are a must for improving system efficiency in processing data in the third generation.

Data Organization

When direct access storage devices (DASD's) are used, data may be arranged in one of four different patterns: (1) sequential; (2) indexed sequential; (3) direct; and (4) partitioned.

Sequential Organization

Sequential arrangement of data on DASD's is tape-like in nature; that is, the physical records on the DASD are arranged in sequence in anticipation that they will be processed in this fashion. The records are generally placed on the file, using the key to sequence the data properly. The records are read and updated in the same sequence that they appear on the file. An insertion involves moving all of the records down one location on the file to make room for the new record being inserted. This type of organization has the disadvantage of not being able to locate individual records quickly nor being able to add or delete records without rewriting the entire file. In general, this type of data organization should be reserved for those applications in which most of the records are processed each time the file is used.

Indexed Sequential Organization

Indexed sequential arrangement of data on DASD's also allows for processing a file in a sequential nature, but it has the added flexibility of being able to locate an individual record very quickly. This is accomplished by referencing indexes associated with the file. For example, a file might have a cylinder index stored on cylinder zero, which contains the address of the highest numbered record on any cylinder. This index will point the movable arm to the correct cylinder immediately. Once the arm reaches the desired cylinder, it will search a track index to determine what track or surface in that cylinder the desired record is on. Once this has been determined, the proper read-write head can be actuated and the desired record read.

In the schematic shown in Figure 11–29, we wish to locate record number 12570. To do this, we search the cylinder index to find that this record is located somewhere in cylinder 3. Then the arm is positioned to cylinder 3; we search the track index and find that this record is on disk face 6 of cylinder 3. Now all of the information on track 6 is read into memory and searched for the desired record. By using overflow tracks in each cylinder, this system allows for very quick insertion and deletion of records. This is the most popular form of data organization on direct access storage devices.

Partitioned Organization

In partitioned data organization, the file is divided into several parts, or "members." Within each of these members, the data is arranged sequentially. In this type of organization, a directory containing the names and locations of these members within the file is searched to find the location of a particular member. This directory is arranged alphabetically.

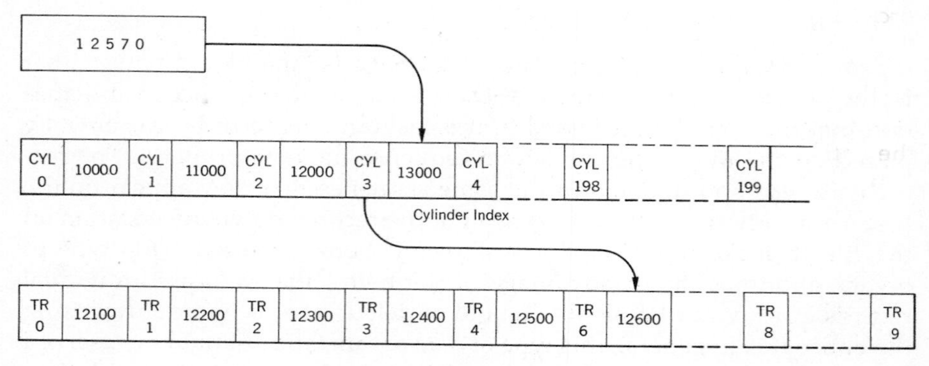

Figure 11–29. Indexed sequential record accessing.

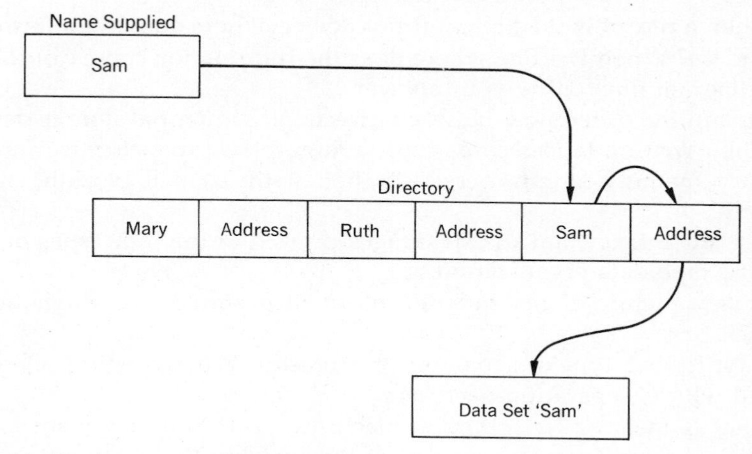

Figure 11–30. Accessing partitioned records.

The programmer merely supplies the name of the file he wishes to process and the directory is searched for a "hit" on the name. The address of the data set desired resides beside the name and the arm can be positioned directly to this location. This type of data organization is used primarily for the storage of sequential data, such as programs, subroutines, and libraries.

Direct Organization

Direct (or random) organization stores and retrieves records directly using a scheme of converting the key into an actual address to which the device may position itself and find the desired record. The programmer is responsible for establishing the relationship between the key of the record and the address of the record on the direct access storage device. Much research is currently being done in the area of generating random or direct addresses for data with given keys. The big problem here lies in the fact that different keys may produce the same address, and having the same address for two records is not a desirable situation. These problems are fairly easy to overcome, but it is beyond the scope of this book to get involved in a detailed discussion of key randomizing schemes.

Questions

1. Explain the difference between primary and secondary storage devices.
2. Make a list of devices that involve only input operations, only output operations, and both input and output operations.

3. When a record is read by an input device, where does the information read go? When written, where does the information come from? Draw a diagram illustrating your answer.
4. Explain the differences between direct and sequential storage devices.
5. When writing tape records with a large blocking factor, is more primary memory storage required than with a small blocking factor? Why?
6. List advantages and disadvantages of each of the four types of magnetic tape data organization.
7. Draw a picture of a cylinder of information stored on a magnetic disk pack.
8. A buffer is a type of separator or protector. What is being separated, and why is separation necessary?
9. What is meant by a computer machine cycle? You may want to refer back to the chapters on unit record processing to get started.
10. Explain in your own words the difference between a selector and a multiplexor channel.

12

Programming CYBERNAC, A Hypothetical Computer

It is the belief of the authors that in learning to program an electronic computer, the student does best by learning to program a computer in actual use. This more thoroughly prepares him in terms of appreciating the detail with which computer programs must be prepared and also provides him with a skill that he can use profitably if he should ever find himself in a position to program that computer in a real-life application. In deference to this opinion, we have devoted an entire section of this book to an introduction of System/360 Assembly Language programming, a section that will, we believe, prepare those who desire to become professional computer programmers in the most adequate fashion. The System/360 computer promises to be the most widely used computer in the future, and skill in programming in 360 Assembly Language is a prime requisite for the professional programmer.

However, those who have had little or no experience in computer programming and operation find learning to program in 360 Assembly Language somewhat arduous. It is the purpose of this chapter to present a hypothetical computer that embodies all of the operating and programming characteristics of real computers but which has minimal requirements with respect to detailed knowledge of computer operation. An understanding of CYBERNAC, our hypothetical computer, will form the basis of understanding for *any* digital electronic computer. What is more, programs written in the CYBERNAC programming language can be executed on a real electronic computer if one is available and if it seems desirable to do so.

Introduction

CYBERNAC (Clark's Youthful, Benevolent and Easily Routined Numeric and Alphabetic Computer) was designed by John Clark of Orange Coast College as an aid in learning computer programming.

Different people see the process of computer programming as consisting of different steps, ranging from two or three to over a dozen. In any case, the basic ideas in all of these steps include the idea of problem definition and the development of a logical, systematic procedure to be followed by the computer to arrive at the solution to the problem. These are the most intellectually challenging ideas that the computer programmer faces. CYBERNAC was designed to help students of programming learn skills in developing systematic and logical procedures to be followed by a computing device when solving a problem. Since no problem can be solved—by man or machine—until a man first understands how the solution is to be reached, and since this understanding is predicated upon a thorough understanding of the problem itself, it follows that developing the skills necessary in designing procedures to solve problems will also develop skills needed to analyze them.

The problem is analyzed and a systematic way developed for a computing device to arrive at a solution through the development of a *block diagram* depicting the logical steps to be taken by the computer in the problem's solution. The programmer is then ready to convert his method of solution—that is, his block diagram—into instructions to be executed by a computer. This process, usually called *coding*, consists of converting the logic expressed in the block diagram into a set of instructions to be performed by the computer. These instructions may be written in one of a number of different computer languages, depending upon the particular computer system and other features available to the programmer in his computer installation. The coded program is usually called a *source program*, which is actually a sequential list of instructions to be executed by a computer. The source program is then punched into cards or recorded in other input media and presented to the computer system where, perhaps after considerable manipulation, the instructions are executed.

For the programming student, CYBERNAC provides an easily coded computer the language of which can be used to translate block diagrams into computer instructions which can then be executed by an actual computer if desired to determine if the block diagram, that is, the programmer's logic of problem solving, is correct. Essentially, CYBERNAC is a highly simplified computer which allows the programmer to concentrate upon the logic of solving his problem without being excessively bothered by intricate details of computer operation and coding.

Experienced programmers would call CYBERNAC a *simulator*. By the term simulator they mean a program that makes one electronic computer behave as if it were a different electronic computer. Specifically, CYBERNAC is a computer program written in a programming language known as FORTRAN, which causes real computers capable of executing FORTRAN programs to behave as if they were computers with the characteristic features of CYBERNAC. To operate and program CYBERNAC, it is not necessary for the programming student to understand either the FORTRAN programming language or the details of the computer that is performing the simulation. It is enough to understand the simple characteristics of CYBERNAC and to use this understanding to code the flow charts he has prepared into CYBERNAC language to see if CYBERNAC will do what he thinks he is telling it to do.

CYBERNAC Machine Characteristics

The CYBERNAC, like all other electronic computers, consists of five basic components as shown in Figure 12–1. These are the memory unit, the input devices, the output devices, the arithmetic unit and the control unit. These five basic units are related to each other from a conceptual standpoint as shown in Figure 12–2.

Control Unit

The *control unit* shown at the top of the diagram controls the activities of the other four components by interpreting instructions stored in the memory of the computer. The CYBERNAC is a *stored program* computer; that is, the set of instructions the computer is to execute is stored in the memory of the computer and processed sequentially by the control unit, which, in response to the instruction being executed at the time, causes the other components of the system to perform such functions as adding, printing the contents of memory locations, and so on. The processes that take place during the execution of a CYBERNAC instruction will be discussed in detail later.

Memory Unit

The *memory unit* of CYBERNAC is a device that contains data and instructions. Both data and instructions are placed into memory by the programmer using input devices, which will be discussed below. Units of data, called data words, and CYBERNAC instructions occupy portions of memory known as *memory cells.* The CYBERNAC memory device has 99 memory cells numbered from 01 to 99. These numbers are known as the *addresses* of the memory cells and, of course, each memory cell has its own address that identifies it from the other cells in the memory device. The student should make sure that he understands that a memory cell can contain one of two things: either a data word or an instruction. Data words consist of either numeric or alphabetic data. A memory cell can contain numeric data in the form of a decimal number with the following format:

±XXXXXX.XXXX

From this, it can be seen that the largest positive number that can be

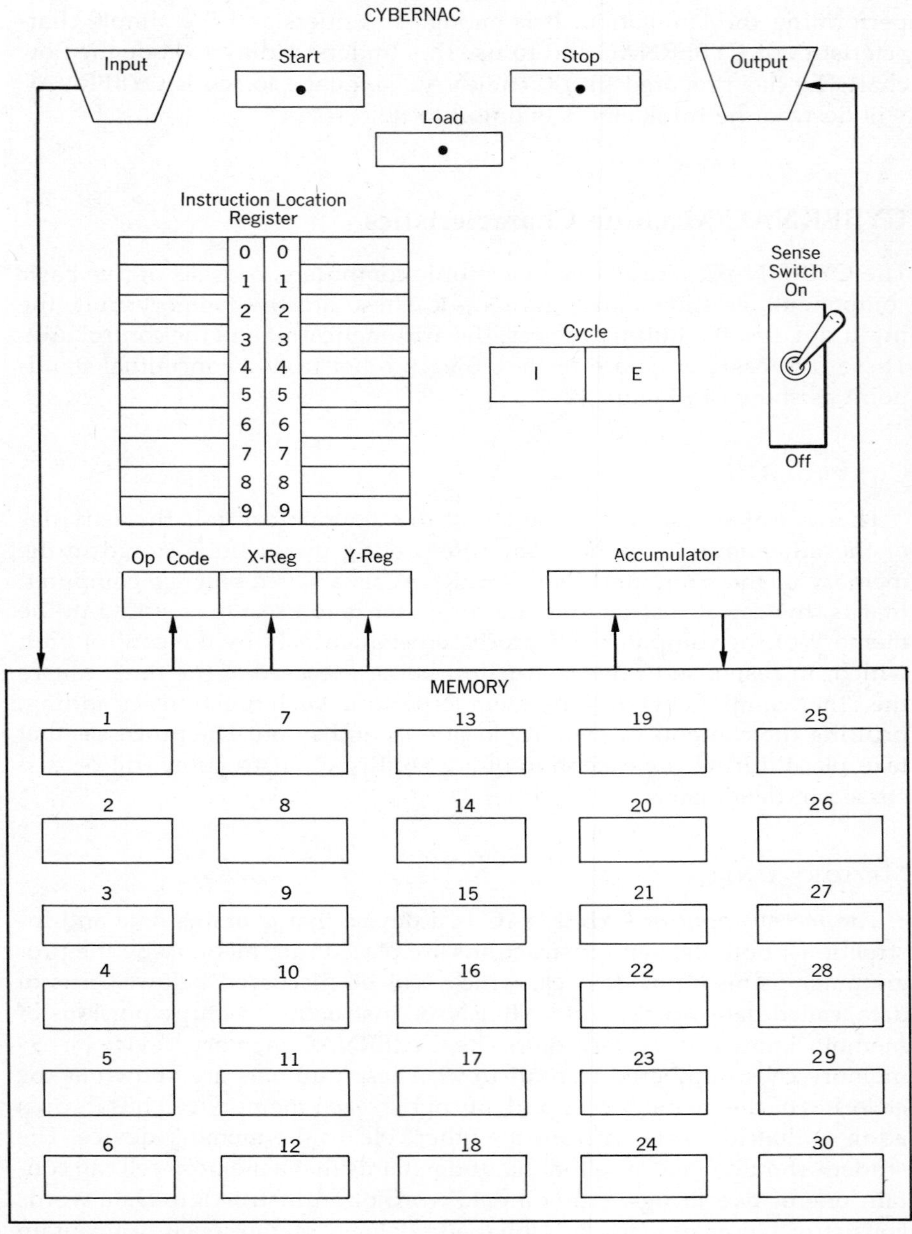

Figure 12–1. Cybernac.

stored in a memory cell (and consequently the largest number that can be handled by CYBERNAC) is

$$+999999.9999$$

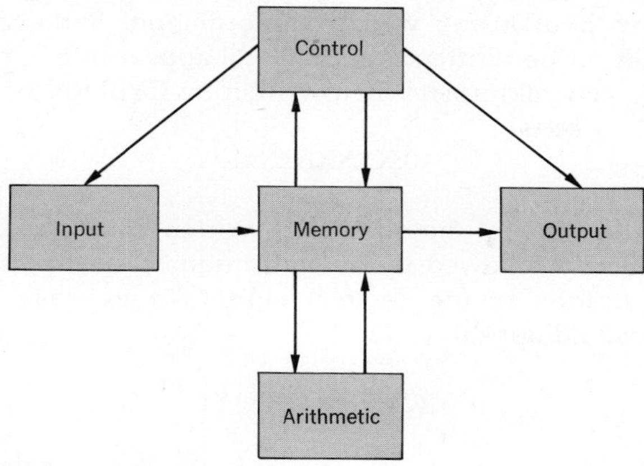

Figure 12–2. Cybernac components.

and the smallest positive number greater than zero is

+000000.0001

As you would expect, the smallest negative number is

−000000.0001

and the largest negative number is

−999999.9999

Each memory cell in CYBERNAC always consists of twelve positions—that is, ten positions containing decimal digits and two more for the decimal point and sign; thus the CYBERNAC is a *fixed word length* computer. Each data word occupies one memory cell, no matter how long the data word is. Thus, the number 5.7 occupies as much space in memory as 5678.348 because the first number is stored in memory cell as

+000005.7000

and the second as

+005678.3480

Occasionally, calculations performed by CYBERNAC may yield numbers that exceed the capacity of CYBERNAC memory cells. In this case, the resulting data is said to have *overflowed* the memory cell. In most computers, the high order positions of the data overflow out of the memory cell and are lost. CYBERNAC, however, is able to overflow out of the memory cell without losing valuable information. If the contents of a memory cell are to be written out, they will appear in a *normalized form*, which has this general format when written by CYBERNAC:

0.XXXXE±XX

The significant portion of the number is written, in this case, as 0.XXXX, and is immediately followed by an indication of an exponent of ten to indicate the location of the decimal point. For example, the number 312467581628 would appear as

3.12467581628E+11

The E+11 tells us to multiply the significant portion of the number by 10^{+11}. Most of the problems solved by CYBERNAC, however, consider data that do not exceed the normal limits of the memory cells. Data appearing in normalized form as written from memory cells may indicate some error in calculation procedure or in preparing the data to be processed.

Data words consisting of alphameric information can be stored in memory cells, too, in the following form:

YYYYY

where each Y represents one of the 26 letters of the alphabet, the numbers 0 through 9, plus blanks and the various special characters available in Hollerith code. Again, as in numeric data words, each alphameric word of five characters occupies one memory cell and each memory cell used to contain alphameric data words will consist of exactly five characters. Thus, the characters

EOJ

and

A2J9

occupy as much space as

IT IS

An important characteristic of all computer memories, including CYBERNAC, is known as *destructive read-in* and *nondestructive read-out*. Destructive read-in means that a data word read into a memory cell replaces the data word that was there previously; that is, the old data is destroyed. Nondestructive read-out means that information can be read from a memory cell, as in an output operation, for example, without destroying that data; it is still in the memory cell and can be used for further purposes.

INPUT/OUTPUT

The *input device* of CYBERNAC is an IBM card reader. Information to be stored in CYBERNAC memory is first punched into IBM-type punched cards using an IBM card punch. These cards are then made available to CYBERNAC by placing them in the feed hopper of the card reader. When CYBERNAC executes instructions causing it to read instructions or data, cards are fed through the card reader and the contents of the cards are stored in the memory location indicated in the read instruction. Information punched into cards to be presented to CYBERNAC *must* adhere to the following rules:

1. CYBERNAC instructions punched into cards must begin in card column one.
2. Numerical data words punched into cards must be located in card columns 10 through 21 inclusively. A number punched into these columns may have no more than ten digits and the decimal point should be punched. Leading zeros and the sign of positive numbers may be punched but are not necessary.

For example, the number 468 would be punched into a card as follows:

468

These four characters will be recorded in the indicated memory location as

+000468.0000

Observe that it does not matter where in the twelve data columns the digits of the numerical data word appear. As long as the programmer includes the decimal point when punching the card, the value will be stored in a memory location in the general format above. Should the programmer neglect the decimal point, CYBERNAC will load his data word into a memory location as a ten-digit number the decimal point of which is between the sixth and the seventh digits. Thus, in the example above, if the data word had been punched as

468

with the four in card column ten, it would appear in the memory cell as

468000.0000

The *output device* for CYBERNAC is a typewriter. The contents of memory location will be typed out by the typewriter when CYBERNAC is executing a write instruction. Numerical data will have leading zeros and positive sign identification suppressed automatically.

ARITHMETIC UNIT

The *arithmetic unit* of CYBERNAC is a register called the *accumulator*. The accumulator can be considered to be the workbench of the computer. The results of all arithmetic operations are performed on data words that were first located in the accumulator. For example, in adding the contents of memory location 40 to the contents of memory location 56, the contents of one of the memory locations must first be placed in the accumulator and the contents of the other memory location should then be added to the accumulator. After this addition operation, the accumulator will contain the sum of the contents of both of the memory locations. If this sum is to be divided, say, by the contents of another memory location, this can be accomplished by an instruction which divides the accumulator by the contents of that memory location. The quotient would then be found in the accumulator. The contents of the accumulator can never be typed out by the typewriter; they must first be moved to a memory location and the contents of that memory location are then typed out, using an output instruction.

INSTRUCTION LOCATION REGISTER

The instruction location register is a memory-like device that contains the *address* of the next instruction to be executed. It can be considered the bookmark of the computer because it keeps track of where in memory the control unit is to look for the next instruction. The instruction location register is incremented by one during the execution of each CYBERNAC instruction. The contents of this register may be changed by a program instruction designed for this purpose and generally called a "branch" instruction because it causes control to branch or transfer to a memory location that is not in sequence with the program instructions as they are stored in memory.

SAVE REGISTER

The save register is a special purpose register that, after the execution of an unconditional branch instruction, contains the address of the instruction which immediately follows (sequentially) the branch instruction. It is useful for providing a means to return to the main program after branching to and executing a subroutine.

CYBERNAC Instructions: Basic Format

A CYBERNAC instruction consists of three basic parts: an operation code and two operands, the *X*-address and the *Y*-address. The operation code is a two-digit number that indicates to the control unit which of the several operations available on the CYBERNAC is to be performed. The operands indicate which of the memory locations are to be involved in the operation. For example, an instruction to read 15 cards and store their contents into memory locations 3 through 17 would look like this:

Op Code		X-Add		Y-Add
36	–	03	–	15

The operation code 36 is interpreted by the control unit, which causes the card reader to begin reading cards and to continue reading until 15 cards have been read. The contents of these cards, which in this case must be numeric, are stored in sequential memory locations beginning with location 3. This instruction, when prepared by the programmer, would have been punched as follows:

Card columns	123456789 . . .
Instruction	36–03–15

Observe that the instruction begins with card column one and continues without skipping any columns until the entire instruction is punched in the card. The operation code and the two operands are separated by dashes (–).

More often than not, CYBERNAC instructions do not include a Y-address. Consider an instruction to add the contents of memory location 38 to the contents of the accumulator:

Op Code		X-Add	Y-Add
21	–	38	

The operation code 21 causes the addition operation to take place with the contents of memory location 38 being added to the contents of the accumulator. The student should understand that the contents of the accumulator before the add operation have been replaced by the sum resulting from the add operation and that the contents of memory location 38 have remained unaltered by the add operation.

CYBERNAC has a number of instructions and a description of each is included as an appendix to this chapter. In the sample programs that follow later in this chapter, many of these instructions are used and will be discussed in terms of their functions in that particular application. The reader may wish to refer to the appendix for more detailed discussion of the instructions as he examines the sample programs.

Branching

Branch instructions differ from other instructions. No data is transferred with the execution of a branch instruction. When the conditions are met for the branch instruction the instruction location register (ILR) is set equal to the contents of the X-register. The purpose of the X-register will be explained later. There are two types of branch instructions in CYBERNAC: unconditional and conditional.

Unconditional Branch

A break in the sequential processing of the program is an unconditional branch. The contents of the ILR is stored in the save register and the content of the X-register is placed in the ILR during the execution of the unconditional branch. During the instruction cycle the ILR is advanced to the address of the next sequential instruction. It is this value that is placed in the save register.

Conditional Branches

Branch If Accumulator = 0. If the accumulator has a zero value at the time this instruction is executed the contents of the ILR are replaced by the contents of the X-register.

Branch If Accumulator Negative. If the accumulator has a negative value at the time this instruction is executed, the contents of the ILR are replaced by the contents of the X-register. With conditional branches, if the conditions are not met (that is, accumulator = 0 or accumulator positive), the next sequential instruction is executed.

Branch Back

When a branch back instruction is executed, the contents of the save register are placed in the ILR. This instruction is used in subroutine linkage.

Index Registers

CYBERNAC is equipped with five index registers numbered from 01 to 05. An index register is a special area of memory which can contain a two-digit number that can be used to modify the X-address of an instruction. Index registers are primarily useful in looping operations which process data contained in several memory cells. For example, if one were to write the instruction, 21–41–02, one is said to have "tagged" the

X-address of the instruction with the contents of index register two. In this case, we are adding to the accumulator the contents of the memory location the address of which is equal to the sum of 41 and the contents of index register two. If index register two contained 13, then the effective instruction executed would be 21–54.

Sense Switches

CYBERNAC has three sense switches, which give the programmer the ability to slightly modify his program from time to time to meet special conditions and to cause CYBERNAC to perform special functions. CYBERNAC sense switches are set by setting the equivalent computer sense switches.

Sense switch 2. Trace. Types instruction number and accumulator contents after the instruction has been executed.

Sense switch 3. Lists input information and location into which it is stored.

Sense switch 4. Branch if sense switch 4 is on. Instruction format: 46–XX. If sense switch 4 is on and the above instruction is executed, the instruction location register is set to the value XX. The next instruction CYBERNAC executes will be found in location XX.

Load Button

The CYBERNAC load button is used to load programs and other information into CYBERNAC memory cells. The load button is pressed after one or more cards are placed in the feeding unit of the card reader. Pressing the load button causes these things to happen:

1. The first card is read and its contents are placed into memory location one. This card must contain a read instruction or CYBERNAC will execute an error halt.
2. The instruction location register is set to one.
3. A CYBERNAC operation is begun. This CYBERNAC operation, because it is initiated by a signal from the load button, is slightly different from the ordinary CYBERNAC operation. In this case, the instruction location register, after the execution of the instruction in memory position one is set to a value that is equal to the contents of the X-register, which is equal to the X-address of the instruction on the first card.

The load button, in performing its function of storing programs and other information into memory, works in conjunction with a *load card.* The function of a load card is to instruct the computer to load a program into memory. Recall that pushing the load button on CYBERNAC causes one card to be read, its contents to be stored in memory position one, and control of the computer to be directed to memory position one for the first instruction to be executed. The first card of any program to be loaded and executed by CYBERNAC must be a load card. This card contains an instruction of the format: 36–XX–YY. The operation code 36 tells the computer to read numerical data from cards; YY indicates the number of such cards to be read; and XX indicates the memory position into which the first piece of data is to be loaded. The remaining data will be loaded sequentially into memory following that location. The data, in this case, are the program instruction cards. Thus, the load card instructs the computer to read a number of program instruction cards, store these instructions, one per memory cell, sequentially in memory, starting with the memory cell whose address is indicated by XX, and, finally, indicates to the computer that the next instruction to be executed is at the address indicated by XX. The instruction at XX is, of course, the first instruction of the program to be executed.

CYBERNAC Operation

A CYBERNAC operation is an activity during which one CYBERNAC instruction is executed. This activity consists of two cycles—the instruction cycle, and the execution cycle.

Instruction Cycle

During the instruction cycle, the operation code of the instruction, the address of which is in the instruction location register, is moved into the *op-code register*. It is the purpose of the op-code register to contain the operation code of the instruction being executed. This register is consulted by the control unit to determine what functions CYBERNAC must perform in order to execute the instruction. The X-address and the Y-address of the instruction being executed are, during the instruction cycle, moved to the X- and Y-registers where the control unit will find information it needs for execution of the instruction. Finally, the instruction location register is incremented by one.

Execution Cycle

During this cycle, the instruction in the op-code, X-, and Y-registers is executed. The necessary switching circuits are set up to carry out the operation found in the op-code register. The memory cell referenced by the X-register is located and the information in this memory cell is used in execution of the instruction. The information in the Y-register, when other than blank, is used to control input and output operations by counting the number of memory cells read (and written out) or the number of memory cells into which data have been stored. This is done by decrementing the Y-register by one for each memory cell processed until the Y-register reaches zero, which halts the execution of the input/output operation. Following the completion of the execution cycle, an instruction cycle is immediately initiated.

Sample Program: Averaging Pairs of Numbers

To illustrate the operation of CYBERNAC, and consequently the basic operation of all digital electronic computers, we will examine some simple applications. The first of these finds the average of a series of pairs of numbers.

Problem Input

The input data for this application consists of a deck of cards organized as shown in Figure 12–3. Each unit of data consists of two values, A and B, which are punched into separate cards. The computer is to read each unit of data (two cards) and find their average.

Program Output

The computer typewriter is to type out both numbers, A and B, and their average for each unit of data processed in this format:

A B Average

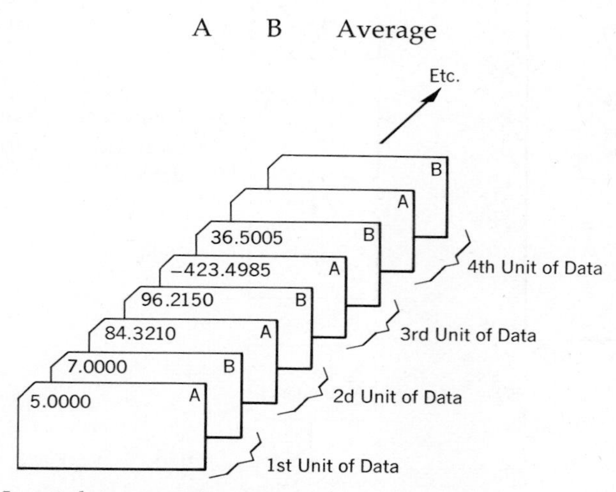

Figure 12–3. Input data averaging program.

Block Diagrams

Block diagrams to accomplish this task are shown in Figure 12–4. As you can see, there is a general block diagram that shows, in boxes 1, 2, and 3, that the data are read, their average calculated, and the results, with the original data, are written. Following this, the program branches back to the read operation and repeats the process on the next pair of data cards.

The reader will observe that this program continues indefinitely in this *program loop*. There is no provision made to cause the computer to cease executing the program once all of the data cards have been processed. Actually, this is a pretty sloppy way of going about things and no programmer would consider writing a program in this fashion. What will happen is this: The card reader will try to read a card that is not there (because all the data cards have been read and processed) and the computer will stop because this input device is unable to perform its function. The computer will stop to be sure, but in a manner that most consider to be very poor programming form. However, for the purposes of this very simple example, we will forget about such matters and will consider them in the next sample program.

Figure 12–4 also shows a detailed block diagram of the calculations to be performed in box number 2. Box 2–1 indicates that the first piece of

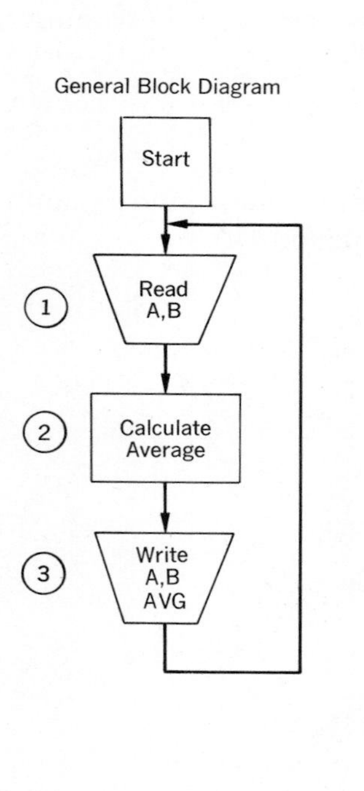

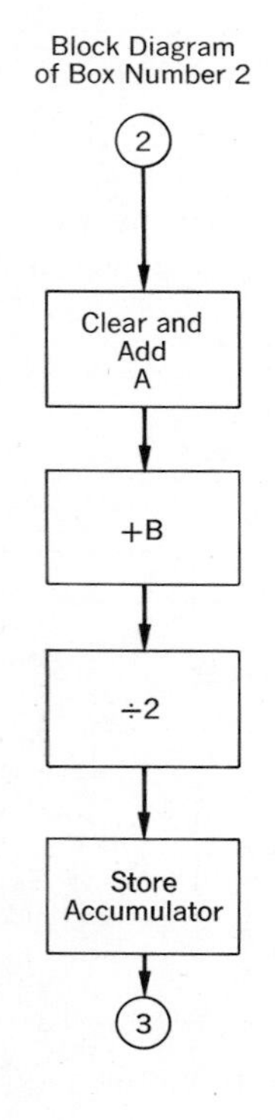

Figure 12–4. Averaging pairs of numbers with block diagrams.

data, A, will be moved from the memory position into which it was read and stored to the accumulator. This operation is known as clearing and adding the contents of a memory position to the accumulator. Now (box 2–2), the memory position containing the other piece of data, B, is added to the contents of the accumulator. The accumulator now contains the sum of A and B. The contents of the accumulator is now divided by the contents of a memory cell that contains the constant data word 2 (box 2–3). The accumulator now contains the average of A and B and (box 2–4) these contents are stored into a memory position in preparation for writing since data cannot be written directly from the accumulator, only from a memory cell.

PROGRAM CODING

The body of the CYBERNAC coding sheet is used to code the instructions that are to perform the work and to indicate what constants are to be loaded into memory to be used by the program. At this point, it would be well to discuss the difference between *constant* data and *variable* data as the terms are used in computer programming. Constant data are those that the programmer makes available to the computer for use in a program and that never change throughout the execution of the program. In our example here, we use the value two in calculating the average of the input data. This value never changes during the execution of the program (hence, it is a data constant) and must be stored in a memory cell so that the computer has access to it during the process of executing the program. Variable data are data upon which the program works and which change with each repetition or iteration of the program. In our example here, A and B are variable data words which take new values every time a new set of data cards are read. After processing one set of data, the program loops back, reads a *new* set of data, and repeats the same operations on these new data as it did before. This illustrates one of the most advantageous features of the stored program computer—its ability to loop back and execute the same program segment over and over again without the necessity of reloading the program into memory. Obviously, it is no trick to add two numbers together and then find their average by dividing by two. However, there is a trick to performing these calculations again and again at the rate of several per second. This trick is made possible through the use of the stored program concept and the notion of looping. Thus, electronic computers perform thousands of simple (or complex) calculations in a very short time on large numbers of data.

The CYBERNAC coding sheet provides space in the lefthand portion of the form for the programmer to make notations as to the organization of his program. This information is not punched into program cards, but remains on the coding sheet as a record of what his program is accomplishing. Near the center of the form is a column that the programmer uses to indicate which memory cells are to be used to contain his instructions. Since instructions are to be executed sequentially, the programmer will number his instructions sequentially, using this column and beginning with the memory cell that is to contain the first program instruction. These numbers are not punched into the program cards. Just to the right of the memory cell number is space for the programmer to write his instructions using the instruction format discussed above. He writes a two-position operation code, a two-position X-address and a two-position Y-address, each separated from the others by dashes. These instructions are punched into cards beginning with card column 1 and extending through column 8 for instructions having both an X- and a Y-address. Instructions using only an X-address will extend only through card column 5. Finally, at the far right of the coding sheet is space for the programmer to note to himself the nature of the constants and/or data to which the instruction addresses refer.

Figure 12–5 shows the coding of the program that averages pairs of numbers. The load card indicates that the first instruction is to be stored at memory cell 01. The remaining instructions will be stored in sequential locations following memory cell 01. The load card shows that eight cards are to be read and loaded. Seven of these will be program instructions and will be stored in memory cells 01 through 07. The eighth card read contains a constant data word, 2, which will be stored sequentially following the program instructions into memory cell 8. Let us examine each of the seven instructions of this program. Each instruction will be identified by the address of the memory cell into which it is stored.

Instruction 01: 36–25–02. This is a read instruction. The operation code 36 causes the card reader to read cards containing numerical information. The Y-address (02) indicates that two cards are to be read; the X-address (25) indicates the first memory cell into which these data read are to be sequentially stored. In this case, the two cards read are data cards containing A and B. A is stored in cell 25 and B in cell 26.

Instruction 02: 20–25. The operation code 20 is an instruction to clear the accumulator to zero and then add to it the contents of the memory cell indicated by the X-address, in this case 25. The effect of this instruction is to take data A, stored in memory cell 25, and place it in the accumulator.

Instruction 03: 21–26. The 21 operation code causes the contents of the memory cell specified in the X-address to be added to the current contents of the accumulator. In this case, the contents of cell 26, B, is added to the contents of the accumulator, A. The result of this operation, A + B, is in the accumulator.

CYBERNAC coding sheet

Programmer	Program	Load Card		Page 1 of 1	Date
J. CLARK	AVG. PAIRS OF NOS.	36-01-08			4-30-67

Program Organization	Cell	OP	X	Y	Const./Data
Read A and B	01	36	25	02	
A to Accumulator	02	20	25		A
Add B to Accumulator	03	21	26		B
Divide Accumulator by TWO	04	24	08		TWO
Store results	05	25	27		AVG
Write A, B, results	06	38	25	03	A, B, AVG
Loop Back to "Read A and B"	07	49	01		
CONSTANT 2	08	2	00	00	TWO
	09				
	10				
	11				
	12				
	13				
	14				
	15				
	16				
	17				
	18				
	19				
	20				
	21				
	22				
	23				
	24				
INPUT DATA {	25				A
	26				B
RESULTS	27				AVG
	28				
	29				
	30				

Figure 12–5.

Instruction 04: 24–08. This instruction divides (operation code 24) the contents of memory cell 08 into the contents of the accumulator. Memory cell 08 contains a constant data word of 2 that was stored there by the load card, which was the first card read by the computer, and which contained an instruction (36–01–08) that caused the computer to read eight more cards. After this divide operation, the accumulator contains the quotient (A + B)/2.

Instruction 05: 25–27. The operation code 25 causes the contents of the accumulator to be stored in the memory cell specified in the X-address—in this case, cell 27. The previous contents of the memory cell are replaced by the data coming from the accumulator. After the execution of this instruction, the quotient (A + B)/2 is found both in the accumulator and in memory cell 27.

Instruction 06: 38–25–03. The operation code 38 causes numerical information from the memory location specified in the X-address to be typed out. The Y-address of the instruction (03 in this case) indicates how many memory cells are to be written. This instruction will cause the contents of three memory cells to be written out: 25, 26, and 27. These memory cells contain, respectively, A, B, and (A + B)/2—the average of A and B. If the first two data numbers were 5.0 and 7.0, then the output would be as follows:

5.0000   7.0000   6.0000

The output has spaces between the numbers by virtue of the fact that leading zeros and the + sign are suppressed automatically. Actually, 12 characters are typed out for each memory location, but the sign (positive) and the leading zeros are typed out as blanks or spaces that are, of course, invisible. Thus, there are seven blanks between the left margin and the character 5, seven more between the last zero of 5.0000 and 7, and seven again between 7.0000 and 6.

Instruction 07: 49–01. The 49 operation code indicates an unconditional branch to the memory cell indicated by the X-address (01) for the next instruction. In operation, this instruction replaces the contents of the instruction location register with the X-address of the branch instruction so that on the following instruction cycle, the next instruction is accessed from the memory cell indicated by the X-address.

Memory cell 08 contains the constant 2 we have already discussed. Figure 12–6 shows in step-by-step fashion the contents of various memory locations during the execution of these seven instructions. The seventh instruction (49–01) is the looping instruction that causes the entire process to continue, in this case, indefinitely.

Figure 12–7 shows an output from executing this program with the trace feature employed and using three units of sample data (see sense switch 2). The contents of the accumulator are typed out after the execution of each instruction. The output is typed out between instructions 5 and 6 because the contents of the accumulator is listed after the execution of the sixth instruction is completed.

Review of Program Loading and Execution

Looking over the program execution above, one can observe that several steps were necessary for the program to be executed successfully. First,

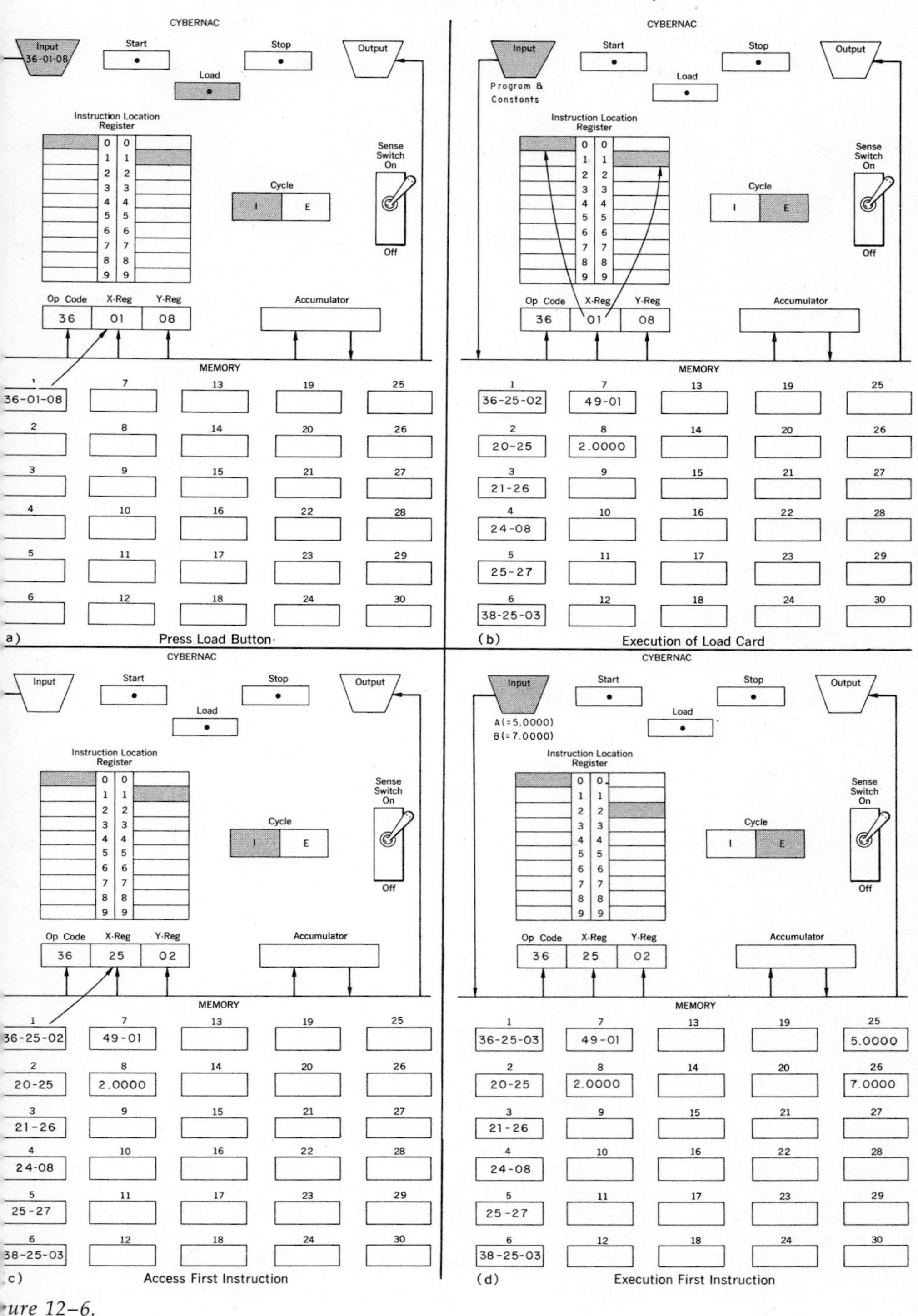
CYBERNAC
Input
36-01-08
Start
Stop
Output
Load
Instruction Location Register
Sense Switch On
Off
Cycle
I
E
Op Code
X-Reg
Y-Reg
36
01
08
Accumulator
MEMORY
36-01-08
a)
Press Load Button
CYBERNAC
Input
Program & Constants
Start
Stop
Output
Load
Instruction Location Register
Sense Switch On
Off
Cycle
I
E
Op Code
X-Reg
Y-Reg
36
01
08
Accumulator
MEMORY
36-25-02
20-25
21-26
24-08
25-27
38-25-03
49-01
2.0000
(b)
Execution of Load Card
CYBERNAC
Input
Start
Stop
Output
Load
Instruction Location Register
Sense Switch On
Off
Cycle
I
E
Op Code
X-Reg
Y-Reg
36
25
02
Accumulator
MEMORY
36-25-02
20-25
21-26
24-08
25-27
38-25-03
49-01
2.0000
c)
Access First Instruction
CYBERNAC
Input
A(=5.0000)
B(=7.0000)
Start
Stop
Output
Load
Instruction Location Register
Sense Switch On
Off
Cycle
I
E
Op Code
X-Reg
Y-Reg
36
25
02
Accumulator
MEMORY
36-25-03
20-25
21-26
24-08
25-27
38-25-03
49-01
2.0000
5.0000
7.0000
(d)
Execution First Instruction

ure 12–6.

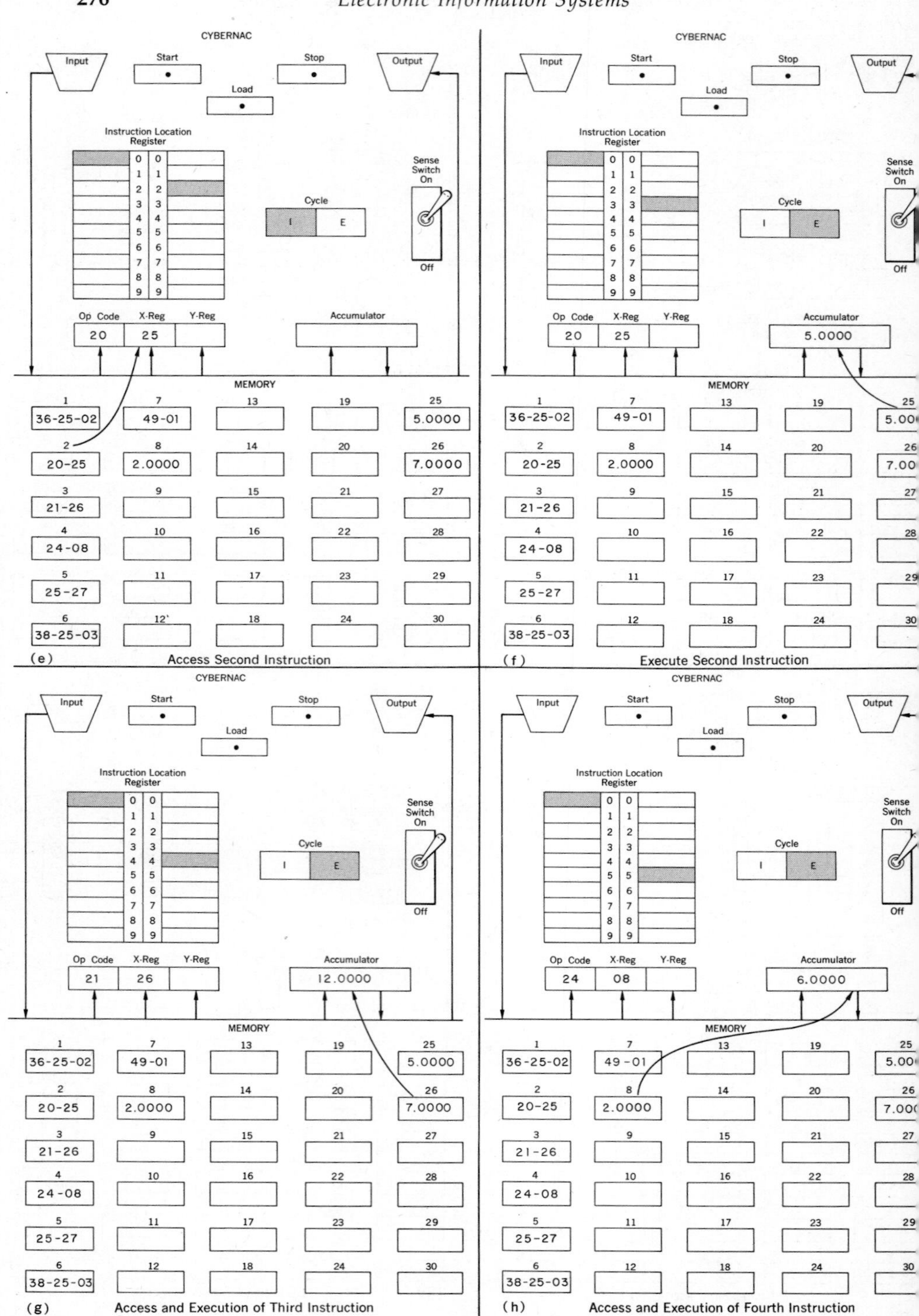

Figure 12–6. Continued.

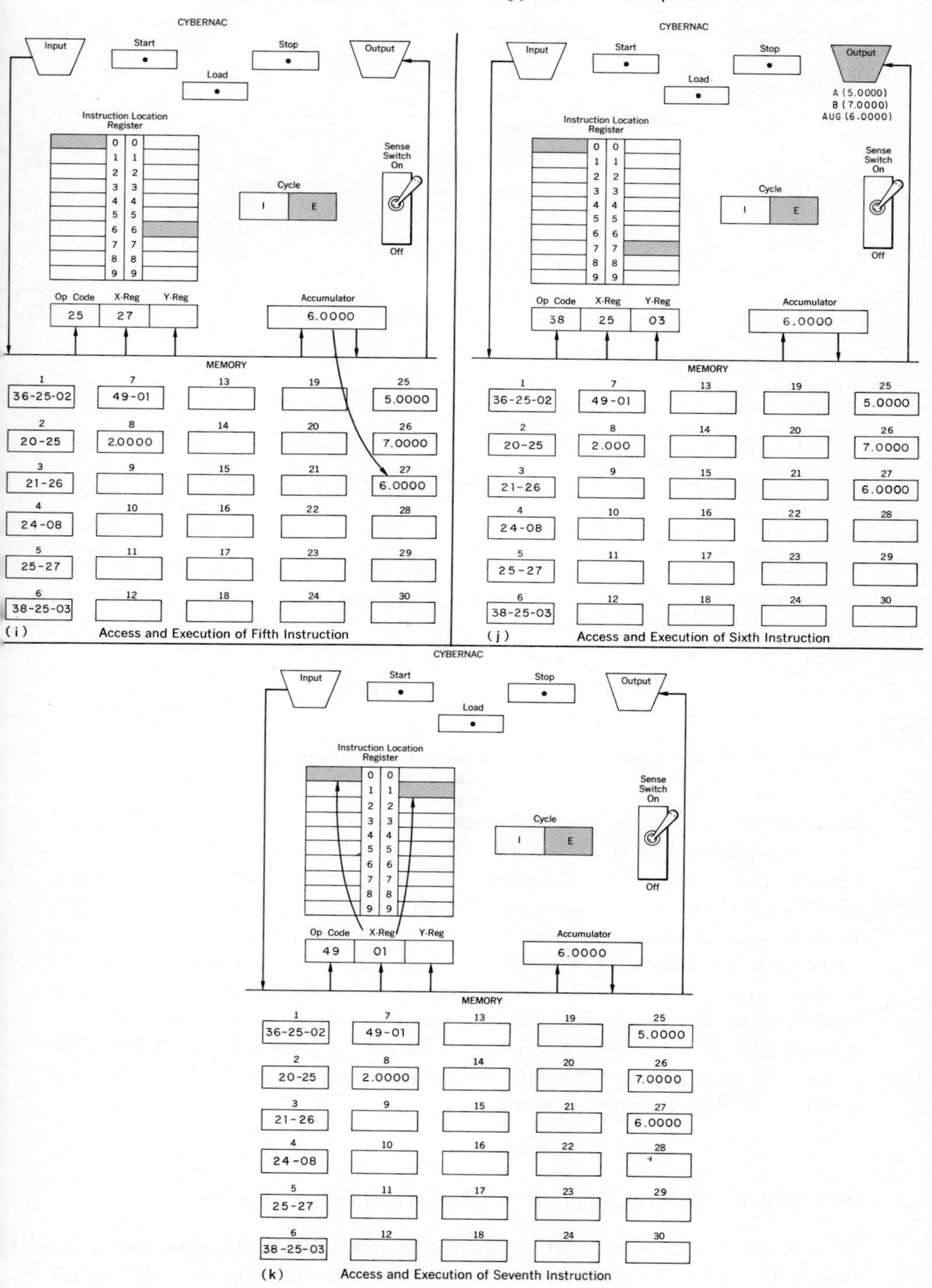

gure 12–6. Continued.

Instruction		Accumulator		
1		0.0000		
2		5.0000		
3		12.0000		
4		6.0000		
5		6.0000		
	5.0000		7.0000	6.0000 (1st pair and average)
6		6.0000		
1		6.0000		
2		84.3210		
3		180.5360		
4		90.2680		
5		90.2680		
	84.3210		96.2150	90.2680 (2nd pair and average
6		90.2680		
1		90.2680		
2		−423.4985		
3		−386.9980		
4		−193.4990		
5		−193.4990		
	−423.4985		36.5005	−193.4990 (3rd pair and average)
6		−193.4990		

Figure 12–7. Trace of program average pairs of numbers.

the program had to be loaded into memory. Second, constants to be used by the program had to be stored in memory. Then, the computer had to be directed to the memory location containing the first instruction to be executed. Finally, the program itself had to cause successive units of data to be read and stored into memory as required. Loading the program and constants and indicating the address of the first instruction to be executed is the purpose of the load card, which is read upon the pushing of the load button. Programs invariably contain instructions to access the required data from whatever storage medium is used to store them. One never writes a program to deal with data already stored in the primary memory of the computer system.

Sample Program: Payroll Calculations

This short program is another example of CYBERNAC operation. The reader is urged to examine each instruction and to make sure he understands the operation of each. Note especially the use of the *conditional branch* instruction, 44–XX, which causes branching to the memory cell the address of which is indicated by the X-address (XX) of the instruction only if the contents of the accumulator are zero.

Program Input

Each employee's pay record for this application consists of four figures: the number of hours he has worked this pay period, the amount of money he is paid per hour, the amount of deductions to be deducted from his pay every pay period, and the amount of net pay he has earned so far this year, that is, his year-to-date (YTD) net earnings. These data will be on data cards arranged for each employee as shown in Figure 12–8.

Program Output

For each employee, a line of information is to be written by the typewriter showing his net pay for this period and the amount of year-to-date earnings at the end of this pay period. To calculate his net pay for the current pay period, multiply hours times rate and subtract deductions.

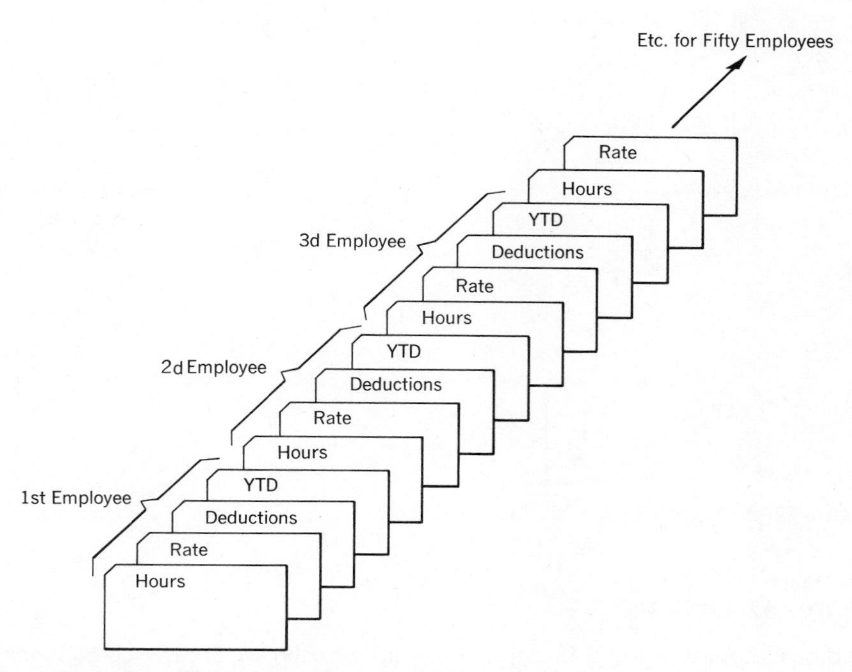

Figure 12–8. Payroll program input data deck.

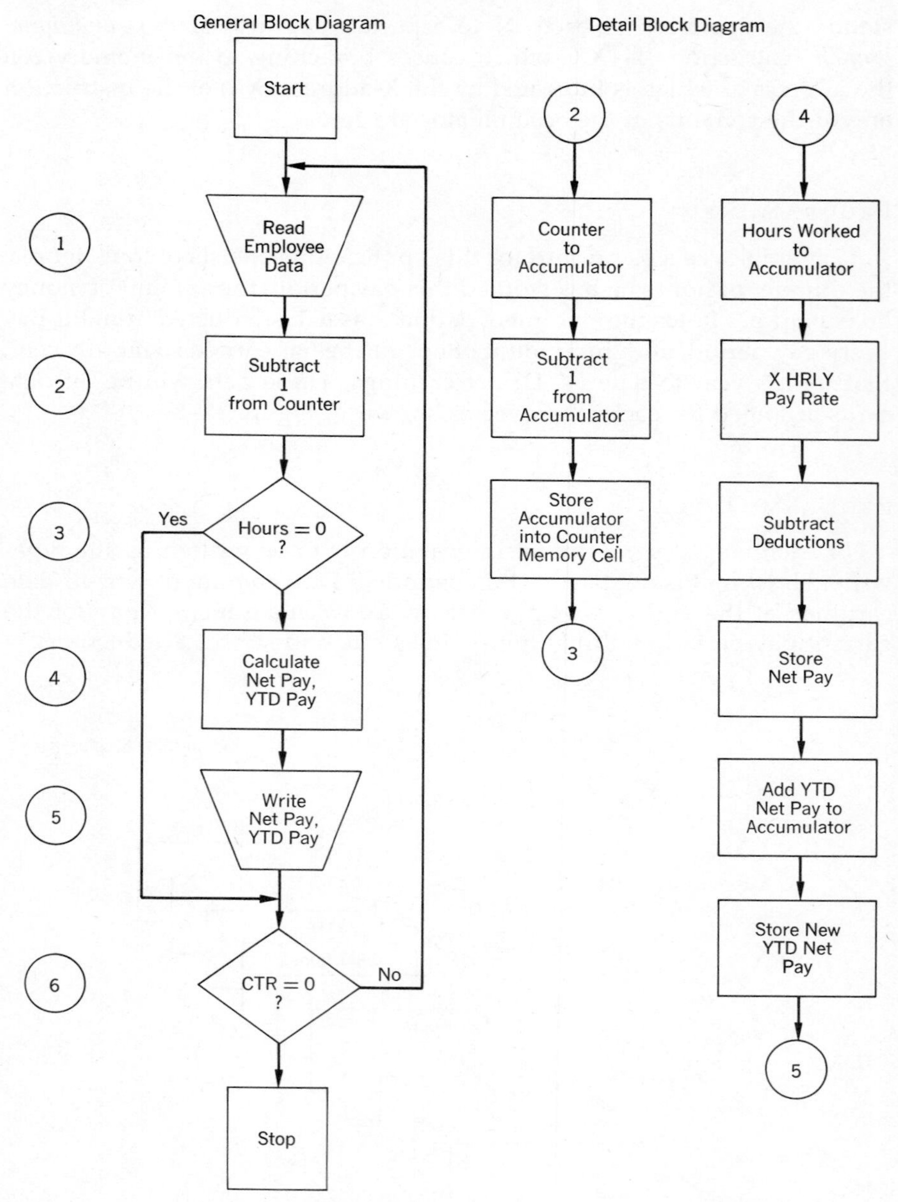

Figure 12–9. Payroll program block diagrams.

Block Diagrams

Block diagrams for this application are shown in Figure 12–9. Block 1 shows that employee data cards for one employee are to be read and stored in memory. Block 2 subtracts one from a counter. A counter in this application starts out at the beginning of the program as a constant 50 stored in memory to indicate that there are exactly 50 employees for whom net pay and current YTD pay are to be calculated. Every time an employee pay record (consisting of four data cards) is read, the value one is subtracted from the memory position that started with a value of 50. Clearly, when the contents of this memory location are zero, all 50 employee pay records have been processed. The value remaining in the counter is examined in box 6. The computer is programmed to halt when its value reaches zero.

Box 3 determines whether or not the employee has worked at all this pay period. If he has not, then the calculations of a new net pay figure are not performed and there is no output for that employee at all. Box 4 repre-

CYBERNAC coding sheet

Programmer	Program	Load Card		Page	Date
Brightman	Payroll	36 - 01 - 19		1 of 1	4-30-67

Program Organization		Cell	OP - X - Y	Const./Data
Read Data		0 1	36 - 20 - 04	Data
Counter to Accumulator		0 2	20 - 19 -	CTR
Subtract 1		0 3	22 - 18 -	1
Store Counter Back		0 4	25 - 19 -	CTR
HRS to Accumulator		0 5	20 - 20 -	HRS
If zero, Branch to "Test Counter"		0 6	44 - 14 -	"TEST CTR"
Multiply RATE X HRS		0 7	23 - 21 -	RATE
Subtract DEDUCTIONS		0 8	22 - 22 -	DEDUCTIONS
Store NET PAY		0 9	25 - 24 -	NET PAY
Add YTD to Accumulator		1 0	21 - 23 -	YTD
Store NEW YTD		1 1	25 - 25 -	NEW YTD
Write NET PAY; YTD		1 2	38 - 24 - 02	NET PAY; NEW YTD
Counter to Accumulator		1 3	20 - 19 -	CTR
Test Counter, if zero, go to "stop"		1 4	44 - 17 -	STOP
Store Counter back to memory		1 5	25 - 19 -	CTR
Branch to "Read Data"		1 6	49 - 01 -	
STOP		1 7	48 - -	
	Constant 1	1 8	1 . 0000	1
	Constant 50	1 9	50 - 0000	CTR
INPUT DATA	Hours Worked	2 0	- -	HRS
	Hourly Pay Rate	2 1	- -	RATE
	Deductions	2 2	- -	DEDUCTIONS
	YTD Net Pay	2 3	- -	YTD
RESULTS	Net Pay this Period	2 4	- -	NET PAY
	New YTD Net Pay	2 5	- -	NEW YTD
		6	- -	
		7	- -	
		8	- -	
		9	- -	
		0	- -	

Figure 12–10.

sents the calculations necessary to arrive at the appropriate output data and is explained in detail in the block diagram of box 4.

Box 5 shows the outputting of the data, and box 6 tests the counter to determine if 50 employees have been processed. If the counter is not equal to zero, then 50 employees have not been processed. If it has, then the computer is to execute a halt instruction, which will stop the execution of this program.

PROGRAM CODING

Figure 12–10 shows the coding of the program. The reader should examine each instruction and make sure that he understands the operation of the entire program. The best way to do this is to sketch out the contents of various memory positions and the accumulator. The reader is urged to do this.

Questions

1. Design a way to modify the payroll program in this chapter to treat any number of employees. Modify the program so that the computer operator can supply any number of complete pay records and the computer will execute a halt instruction after the last record has been processed.
2. Write a program to calculate and write out 25 values of F where:

$$F = D\left[\frac{A^2 + B}{C} - 5\right]$$

Data input consists of 100 data cards consisting of 25 sets of data organized sequentially as A, B, C, and D for each set.

Appendix to Chapter 12

Basic CYBERNAC—Instruction Set

Input/Output Instructions

READ NUMERIC 36–XX–YY

The contents of the next YY cards are read and stored in locations XX through XX + YY − 1.

The previous contents of these locations are destroyed. (Instructions must start in card column 1. Data in card columns 10 to 20.)

WRITE NUMERIC 38–XX–YY

The contents of YY locations starting with location XX through XX + YY − 1 are written on the output device. (Output correct to four decimal places truncated.)

READ ALPHAMERIC 37–XX–YY

Reads alphameric characters punched in card columns 1–5 of the next YY cards into location XX through XX + YY − 1.

WRITE ALPHAMERIC 39–XX–YY

Write the alphameric characters stored five to a cell from cell XX to cell XX + YY − 1. Output six cells to a line.

SPACE 34–XX–01

Space XX times before write with no carriage return.

RETURN CARRIAGE 34–XX–02

Return carriage XX times before write.

SUPPRESS RETURN CARRIAGE 00–XX

This instruction suppresses the carriage return operation, which occurs *automatically* after every write operation. There will be no automatic carriage returns after write operations following this entry. All carriage returns desired must be programmed using the return carriage instruction.

REINSTATE RETURN CARRIAGE 01–XX

This instruction reinstates the automatic carriage return feature which will cause a carriage return to take place after every write operation following the reinstate return carriage entry.

Arithmetic Instructions

CLEAR AND ADD 20–XX

The contents of location XX are placed in the accumulator. Previous contents of the accumulator are destroyed. The contents of location XX remain the same.

ADD 21–XX

The contents of location XX are added to the contents of the accumulator. The sum is placed in the accumulator. Previous contents of the accumulator are destroyed. The contents of location XX remain the same.

SUBTRACT 22–XX

The contents of location XX are subtracted from the contents of the accumulator. The difference is placed in the accumulator. Previous contents of the accumulator are destroyed. The contents of location XX remain the same.

MULTIPLY 23–XX

The contents of location XX are multiplied by the contents of the accumulator. The product is placed in the accumulator. Previous contents of the accumulator are destroyed. The contents of location XX remain the same.

DIVIDE 24–XX

The contents of the accumulator are divided by the contents of location XX. The quotient is placed in the accumulator. Previous contents of the accumulator are destroyed. The contents of location XX remain the same.

STORE 25–XX

The contents of the accumulator are moved to location XX. Previous contents of location XX are destroyed. The contents of the accumulator remain the same.

Logic Instructions

BRANCH 49–XX

The instruction location register is set to the value XX. The next instruction CYBERNAC executes will be found in location XX.

BRANCH NEGATIVE 43–XX

If the value in the accumulator is negative, the instruction location register is set to the value XX. The next instruction CYBERNAC executes will be found in location XX. If the value in the accumulator is zero or positive, the instruction is treated as a no-operation.

BRANCH ZERO 44–XX

If the value in the accumulator is zero, the instruction location register is set to the value XX. The next instruction CYBERNAC executes will be found in location XX. If the value in the accumulator is negative or positive, the instruction is treated as a no-operation and the next sequential instruction is executed.

NO-OPERATION 41–XX

This instruction performs no operation. Execution passes to the next instruction in sequence.

HALT 48

This instruction causes the execution of instructions to terminate. The program may be restarted by pushing the start button.

13

Computer Programming Systems

Machine Language versus the King's English

In previous chapters, the two basic functions of computer programming were discussed: block diagramming and coding. There it was noted that block diagramming, that is, problem definition and solution development, is the most challenging intellectual activity performed by computer programmers. Once the block diagram is developed, the logic of the solution to the problem as expressed by it is translated into computer instructions. This process of translation, coding, could be a fairly simple clerical operation if it were not for the exacting manner in which computer instructions, constants, data, and results must be arranged in the memory of the computer. Coding his block diagram in machine language, the programmer finds himself overwhelmed with the minutia of memory allocation, numerical operation codes, numerical data addresses, instruction addresses, and other matters which make the job of machine language coding prone to error. What is more, if, when testing his program, the programmer discovers that some instructions have been left out, it may be next to impossible to insert them into the program without rewriting most of the program or developing complex patching networks, since the sequence of memory allocation will be disrupted by the inclusion of the missing instructions.

Most programmers and certainly nonprofessional users of electronic data processing equipment well might wish that one could simply write a few sentences in English to which the computer could respond. Why not design a computer that responds to plain English? Why burden the computer user with strange and exotic numbers representing operation codes and with the necessity to understand in detail how the computer executes instructions, transfers data, and other technical matters? Probably, the most important reason why computers cannot make use of "plain" English is that English is a very complex language and computers are remarkably limited. English is ambiguous. Computers must be instructed in quite nonequivocal terms. English as normally spoken by the computer programmer is generally beyond the cognition of even the most advanced computers. Programming systems are an effort to make the task of preparing computer instructions easier in two ways: first, by making the instructions a programmer writes for a computer more like the English language and less like machine language, and second, by performing the clerical detail involved in allocation of memory positions for instructions, data, constants, and results. The programmer codes his program using a programming language that is essentially unintelligible to the computer that will execute his program. This language consists of *mnemonic* op codes that are easy for the programmer to understand but are unlike the alphameric op codes the computer system's control unit must analyze in order to cause the appropriate functioning of the system. Moreover, instead of using actual computer memory addresses when referring to instructions, data, and constants stored in memory, the programmer will use *symbolic* addresses. A symbolic address is a word or a set of characters that the programmer designs to help recall the function of the instruction stored at the memory positions to which the symbolic address is made equivalent and to recall the nature of information stored at the address in the case of constants and data. For example, the first instruction of a program may read some data cards. This instruction may be stored, say, at memory location 750. After reading the data cards, various processing functions are performed on the data, and results are then printed out in the form of one line of a report. Following this output, the computer must branch back to the first instruction in the program again. The programmer can write an instruction that would cause transfer of control back to memory position 750 for continued reiteration of this program. Or, using a programming system, he can forget about where in memory the first instruction is located, and let the computer system itself store the program instructions in memory. In doing this, he would assign some *symbolic label* to the memory location containing the read instruction. Let us say that he assigns the label START to this instruction. Now, instead of writing an instruction to "Branch to 750," the programmer writes an instruction to "Branch to START." The programmer does not know where the read instruction is stored in the computer memory, nor does he care. He lets the computer system itself load his instructions in memory and the system, while doing this, will automatically associate the label START with memory position 750.

The purpose of this kind of programming system, then, is twofold. First, it translates mnemonic op codes into machine language op codes that the computer system can execute and it provides for automatic memory allocation and addressing through the use of symbolic addresses by the programmer. A programming system that causes the computer system to perform these functions is itself a program. It may be thought of as a translator program that translates the program written by the programmer, called the *source* program, into the *object* program that is executable by the computer system. Programming systems are programs that are usually provided by the computer manufacturer as part of a software package which the manufacturer makes available to users of his equipment. *Software* is a term used in electronic data processing to mean any program which causes computer systems to perform general functions. Programming systems, together with operating systems to be discussed in the chapter to follow, are the two most important elements of a manufacturer's software package. As far as the programmer is concerned, making use of a programming system is a process consisting of preparing the source program; loading the programming system, called the *processor,* into the memory of the computer system used to translate the source program into an object program; executing the processor program—that is, causing the computer system to perform the translation; loading the resulting object program into the computer system that is to execute it; and starting execution. This sequence of events is shown in Figure 13–1. It is important to understand that two object programs are processed by the computer systems used. One object program is the processor program, which translates the source program into machine language. The other is the machine language object program itself, which does the work.

Figure 13–1 also shows another convenience that most programming systems offer the programmer. After processing the source program, a listing of the source program, the object program, and some indications of clerical errors made by the programmer may be provided by the computer system performing the processing. This sort of information is very useful to the programmer in determining whether or not he has correctly coded the program and in correcting errors. It is not always necessary that the processor provide a listing of the object program resulting from the translation of the source program. In fact, in the case of some programming languages used by scientists and engineers who are not familiar with computers, it is better to provide only minimum indications of the nature of the object program itself and to provide maximum help in diagnosing errors occurring in the source program. In modern computer systems, various kinds of processor programs, and the object programs which result from their execution, are stored on magnetic tape or magnetic disks as partitioned data sets. The object program can then be automatically loaded back into the same computer that produced it and execution can commence immediately giving the illusion that the computer system is in fact executing the source program.

The above discussion points up the two basic parts of any programming system: the *source language,* and the *processor.* The source language, of course, is the set of instructions and grammar rules used by the programmer to code the logic of his block diagram. The processor is the program that translates the source program into machine language. Using programming systems, programmers need only learn the relatively simple rules of the source language and are relieved of the necessity of detailed

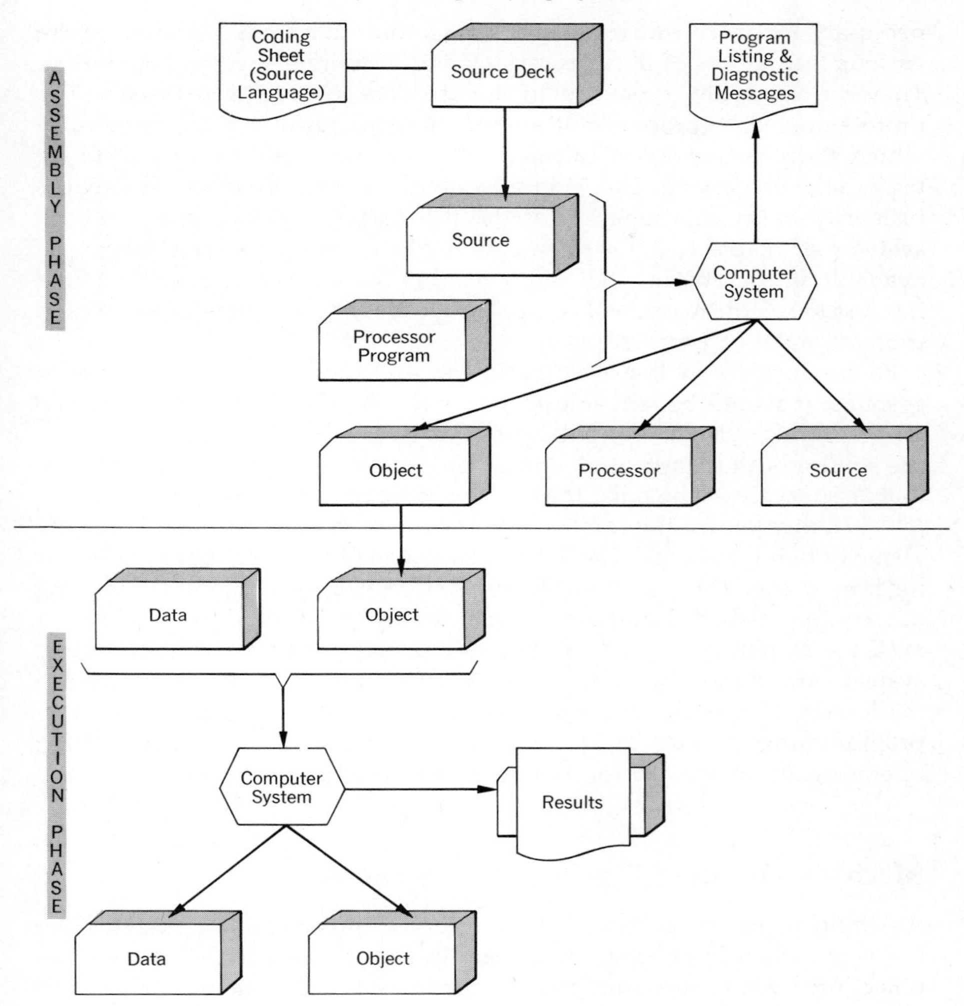

Figure 13–1. Programming system.

understanding of the equipment that is going to perform the work. Indeed, some fairly advanced programming systems can be learned in a few hours of classroom instruction. Scientists and engineers can code their program and send the coding sheets to a data processing center, where their programs are punched into cards and submitted to a computer system for execution. The programmers in these situations may not even know what kind of computer is doing the work and could not care less. However, these people cannot be considered to be data processors in the sense that they are professionally engaged in data processing. Instead, they are users of a calculating device who are professionally occupied in other fields, say, mathematics, physics, psychology, and so forth. It is not necessary for these individuals to have a thorough understanding of the various techniques of data processing and of computer system operation. They are primarily interested in the answers to specific problems. The professional data processor is more concerned with the techniques by which those answers are calculated and in the hardware and software used in the processing. The remainder of this chapter, therefore, is devoted primarily to an investigation of the three basic types of programming systems available today with mention of the various source languages available in each basic type. Although this information is usually of little interest to scientific users of computer systems, it is of vital importance to professional data processors.

Before turning to the examination of specific types of programming systems, it would be valuable to point out the basic difference between programming systems, the subject of this chapter, and operating systems, the subject of the chapter to follow. A programming system is a program—that is, software—which has the basic purpose of making the programmer's job easier by permitting him to code his program in a language which, by virtue of being more like the English language (however slightly), is easier for him to use. Thus, a programming system is useful in terms of making the coding task of computer programming more efficient. Operating systems, as will be seen, have the basic purpose of making the computer system—the hardware—operate more efficiently by providing for automatic execution of generalized operating necessities. In a nutshell, then, programming systems make for more efficient computer programming; operating systems make for more efficient computer operation.

Machine-Oriented Programming Systems

As their name suggests, machine-oriented programming systems are those in which knowledge of the equipment to be used to execute the object program is very important to the programmer. There are two basic types of machine-oriented programming systems: *assembly* systems, and *macro* systems. Writing a program in an assembly system, sometimes called a *symbolic* system, is a good deal like writing the program in machine language, the most important difference being that basic mnemonics are used instead of actual machine operation codes and symbolic addresses are used instead of actual numeric memory addresses of the computer being used. In addition, most assembly systems offer some provision for diagnosis of clerical error.

Assembly Systems

Assembly systems are usually thought of as one-for-one systems in that one source language instruction, called a *statement*, is translated by the processor into one machine language instruction. For example, the instruction

A SUM, INPUT

written in IBM 1620 Symbolic Programming System—which causes the adding (the operation code A) of the contents of the memory location referred to symbolically by INPUT to the contents of the memory location identified as SUM—would be translated, or *assembled*, by the processor as

21 14089 13457

In this case, the mnemonic operation code A has been translated into the numeric operation code—21—required for execution by the 1620. The memory addresses containing the data to be added together referenced by INPUT and SUM have been assembled into the numeric memory addresses 14089 and 13457.

As in the case with other programming systems, instructions written in an assembly, or symbolic, language are called *statements*. There are three basic types of assembly statements: imperative, declarative, and control. *Imperative statements* cause the computer to perform some arithmetical or logical function. The statement,

A SUM, INPUT

is such an imperative statement. *Declarative statements* define the symbols to be used to refer to the memory locations used to store data, constants, and program instructions. The 1620 SPS statement,

INPUT DSS 80

will cause the assembler to set aside 80 positions of memory (the programmer need not know where) and will make the label INPUT synonymous with the numerical memory address of the 80-position area so reserved. Unlike imperative statements, declarative statements do not cause the processor to generate machine language instructions, but only indicate to the processor that when a symbol is used in the source program, in our case INPUT, the processor should replace that symbol in the machine language object program it is assembling with the actual numerical address of the 80-position area it has reserved as referenced by that symbol. *Control statements* are used to indicate to the processor program matters of importance with respect to the assembly process and the equipment to be used in assembly and execution. As with declarative statements, control statements do not cause machine language instructions to be generated. Control and declarative statements, being instructions to the processor, are executed while the source program is being assembled into machine language—that is, at *assembly time.* Imperative statements, on the other hand, are executed as part of the object program execution—that is, at *object time.*

Inasmuch as assembly languages are closely tied to the computer system for which they are designed, most computers today have such a programming system available. The IBM 1620 Symbolic Programming System (or 1620 SPS) and the IBM 1401 SPS are examples of this type of one-for-one programming system. To give the reader a better appreciation of the relationships between the source language, the function of the processor, and the resulting machine language program, an analysis of a very simple 1401 SPS program is presented in the appendix to this chapter. The reader will find it helpful to trace through this program as a means of understanding the relationships between the block diagram, the source language coding, and the action of the processor in translating the source program into machine language.

MACRO SYSTEMS

The machine-oriented programming system described above is known as an assembly system, or a one-for-one system, which generates one machine language instruction for each source language statement processed. Another, more sophisticated type of machine-oriented system is one that has the capability of generating more than one machine language instruction for each source statement. Such a programming system is known as a *macro* system, and statements given in the source program which cause more than one machine language instruction to be produced by the processor are known as *macro statements.* For example, a programmer may know that there is a macro available to the processor, which causes standard heading information to be printed on forms when called for by the source program. In this case, the programmer would enter the macro operation code (say, HEAD) on his coding sheet, and the processor will insert into his source program the SPS instructions and constants that will cause the standard heading to be printed out. These instructions might be many in number, but the programmer need only provide the processor with the operation code HEAD in order to indicate that these headings are to be printed out. Manufacturers of computing equipment usually provide a number of macros with the assembly system software. The IBM Autocoder assembly language, used with the 1400 computer systems and a close relative of 1400 SPS, is an example of one such system. Available as standard macros for use with the Autocoder source language are macros that add numbers, subtract, multiply, divide, compare fields of data, and provide branches to different locations, depending upon the basis of the comparison (high, low, or equal comparison). Of course, the user of the system is provided a means to prepare his own set of macros, in addition to the standard macros provided by the manufacturer, for his own special needs.

Machine-oriented programming systems are widely used today and promise to continue their popularity even with the advent of third-generation computer systems such as the IBM System/360, which make more sophisticated programming systems more valuable for general use. Because machine-oriented systems do require considerable sophistication on the part of the programmer, with respect to the way the computer being used operates, it is possible to prepare programs that operate much more efficiently than is generally possible with a higher level programming system such as those to be discussed below. Knowledge of machine language execution and assembly language coding is a prime necessity for the professional programmer because it develops an understanding of the equipment being used and how it works. It is possible today to program computers without this understanding, but it has become apparent at manufacturers' education centers that programmers who program exclusively with high-level languages and who do not understand the details of machine language program execution have more difficulty in learning to program third-generation computers in assembly language than those who have been working with some other machine-oriented programming system. This in itself would not be important if it were not for the general recognition in the computer industry that programming the third-generation computer system and particularly the IBM System/360 series is most effectively done in System/360 Basic Assembler Language. The sections that follow discuss briefly higher level programming systems and the source languages used by programmers employing that particular system. It should be kept in mind that the two basic parts of programming systems—the source language and the processor—exist in each system. The primary difference between the systems is the viewpoint taken by the programmer toward his problem and toward the computer system used to execute his program.

Procedure-Oriented Programming Systems

Machine-oriented programming systems require thorough understanding of the computer system, or hardware, to be used in the execution of the program by the programmer. Procedure-oriented programming systems are those which remove as much as possible any necessity on the part of the programmer for understanding how the computer system will go about executing his program. Procedure-oriented programming systems let the programmer concentrate on expressing the procedure or logic of solving his problem. He need not even know what kind of computer system will be used for its execution.

Machine-oriented programming systems are often called assemblers, whereas procedure-oriented systems are called compilers. This is because the procedure-oriented systems usually compile many machine language instructions from one source language statement. The result is an elaborate machine language program that the source language programmer is unlikely to understand at all. Procedure-oriented programming systems represent the most nearly successful effort so far to enable computers to program themselves. The processor for these kinds of systems is, then, a program the purpose of which is to write another program. The input to the processor program is the procedure needed to solve the problem being considered by the programmer. There are four fairly widely used procedure-oriented programming systems: FORTRAN, ALGOL, COBOL, and PL/1. Each of these is discussed briefly below.

FORTRAN

The FORTRAN programming language is probably the most widely used programming language today. There are more than 100,000 FORTRAN programmers now making use of this programming system, and as the numbers of computers in operation increases, this number will grow apace. FORTRAN processors have to be prepared for almost every computer system of any consequence. As a result almost anyone, with a minimum of effort, can learn to program almost every computer system. The programs he writes will probably not be efficient in terms of execution time and memory utilization, but his problem can be solved. What is more, the FORTRAN program he wrote for one computer system will probably also be executable on other computer systems. However, it is important to understand that there are many different types of FORTRAN processors for different types of computers. In general, it may be said that FORTRAN is a machine-independent programming language; however, a FORTRAN source program written for execution on a large, sophisticated computer system will use features that are not available on smaller systems. There are four basic FORTRAN programming languages around which minor modifications are made to fit the language and the processor to a specific computer system. These are FORTRAN (with Format), FORTRAN II, FORTRAN IV, and FORTRAN VI. FORTRAN VI is the most involved of the four, usually requiring quite a large computer system for compilation and execution. The other variations range downward in complexity from FORTRAN VI. Usually, FORTRAN (with Format) and FORTRAN II may be processed by any FORTRAN processor. Similarly, FORTRAN (with Format) can be compiled by any of the other processors.

Figure 13–2 shows a sample FORTRAN program. It reads a punched card, adds together two data fields, multiplies this sum by three, and types the result on the console typewriter. It then reads another card and re-

IBM

FORTRAN CODING FORM

Program SAMPLE | Programmer BRIGHTMAN | Date | Punching Instructions: Graphic, Punch | Card Form # | Page 01 of 01 | Identification 73–80

C FOR COMMENT — STATEMENT NUMBER (1–5) | Cont. (6) | FORTRAN STATEMENT (7–72)

```
C     SAMPLE FØRTRAN PRØGRAM
    1 READ 2,IØTA,JACK
    2 FØRMAT(30X,I3,I2)
      MAX=(IØTA+JACK)*3
      TYPE3,MAX
    3 FØRMAT(I5)
      GØTØ1
      END
```

Figure 13–2. Fortran program.

peats this process indefinitely. (The perceptive reader will note that no provision has been made to stop the program if there are no more data cards to be processed.) The first statement in this program causes a card to be read by the card reader of the computer system. The data to be read from the card will henceforth be referred to by the programmer as IOTA and JACK in the same manner that symbols were used to refer to memory positions in 1401 SPS discussed in the preceding section. The 2 following the word READ references the number of the FORTRAN statement which indicates where in the card the two data fields are located. Statement 2, the specification statement, indicates that the format of the data is according to the information within the parentheses. Thus, the 30X tells the system that the first 30 columns of the card are to be ignored. The I3 indicates that the data word called IOTA is in the next three card columns as a three-position integer. The I2 indicates that the data word called JACK immediately follows the last data field and is a two position integer.

The third statement in this program is an arithmetic statement that expresses algebraically the procedure to be followed in calculating. The result field will be referred to by the programmer as MAX and the information to be placed in this field (or memory position) is calculated by adding the two data fields IOTA and JACK together and multiplying this sum by the constant value 3. An asterisk in FORTRAN is an operation that causes multiplication. Algebraically, this arithmetic statement can be rewritten as:

$$\text{MAX} = (\text{IOTA} + \text{JACK})3$$

The calculations are performed as described above and the results are placed in a memory location that the programmer can henceforth refer to by the name MAX. It is important to observe that the names used in FORTRAN programs to identify data and results are essentially arbitrary. We could just as well have used such names as K45, NANCY, and LOVE in place of IOTA, JACK, and MAX.

The fourth statement causes the information in the memory field called MAX to be typed out in accordance with the specifications provided by statement number 3. Statement number 3, another format statement, indicates that these data are to be typed out as a five-position integer.

The GO TO statement is equivalent to an unconditional branch as used with CYBERNAC. It indicates that the next instruction to be executed is statement number 1. The END statement is a signal to the FORTRAN processor that the last source statement has been reached and that compilation can be terminated.

The beauty of FORTRAN programming is its close relationship to typical mathematical expressions of calculation. In the problem above, the formula to be solved was:

$$MAX = (IOTA + JACK)3$$

and the FORTRAN statement that caused the computer to perform the calculations necessary to solve this equation for MAX was:

$$MAX = (IOTA + JACK)*3$$

This similarity of means of expressing the calculations or procedures to be performed between mathematics and FORTRAN has given FORTRAN its name. The initials FORTRAN stand for FORmula TRANslator and clearly indicate that it is a programming system designed for ease of mathematical and scientific users.

There are probably as many nonprofessional FORTRAN programmers as there are professional data processors who use this system. Most college programs in the sciences, engineering, and even business (although FORTRAN is not the most advantageous language to use for business computer applications) require the ability to program in the FORTRAN language.

ALGOL

FORTRAN, as a programming language, was developed in the United States. While its development was taking place, in Europe another similar programming system was being developed which provided essentially the same features as FORTRAN. This language, now used extensively in Europe, is known as ALGOL (ALGebraic-Oriented Language), or sometimes as IAL (for International Algebraic Language). The language has many similarities to FORTRAN, particularly FORTRAN IV. ALGOL users maintain that it is easier to use and easier to learn. However, because of its wide acceptance, FORTRAN continues to be the favored procedure-oriented language for nonbusiness applications.

COBOL

In 1959, a number of computer manufacturers and large computer system users joined forces to develop a programming language that would be common to all computer systems and, because of its close similarity to the English language, would be quick to learn and easy to use. The result of this joint effort of over 30 organizations is the COBOL (COmmon Business-Oriented Language) programming language and processor. Its initial specifications were given in a document published in 1960 by the group responsible for its initial development—CODASYL (COnference on DAta SYstems Languages). This group, composed of businesses, computer manufacturers, military users of computing equipment, and government agencies, was formed out of the need for a common programming language to be used for commercial purposes, much as FORTRAN had become the common scientific programming language. Whether or not CODASYL was altogether successful, or even the degree to which it was successful, was a question giving rise to considerable debate until the introduction of third-generation computer systems in 1964 which, because of their exceptional speeds, could economically process COBOL source programs. Up until the announcement of the third-generation computers, compilation time of COBOL source programs on most equipment was such a lengthy procedure that the language was considered by many to be unfeasible. COBOL processors were developed, however, for a wide range of medium- and large-scale computer systems, and since its original development, COBOL has become more efficient. Now, with the advent of the new computer systems, we can expect to see more widespread use of this commercial programming language.

Many advantages have been claimed for the COBOL programming system. The language more closely resembles English than any other system yet developed. For this reason, programmers will be less likely to make clerical errors and can encode their programs more quickly. Documentation is improved because of the similarity to English and the consequent ease with which the logic of the source program can be followed from the coding. Too, it is easier for more than one programmer to work on the same program because communication between the programmers is easier as a result of standardized routines for input and output. Although the purpose of COBOL is to provide the programmer with a programming system that removes him from the responsibility of understanding in detail the computer being used to execute his program, it is considered by most professional data processors that learning COBOL (or any high-level programming language) as the sole tool in the programmer's bag of tricks is a bad practice. It seems apparent that a COBOL program is more or less efficient as the programmer is more or less familiar with the computer system to be used. To this extent and in view of the differences between COBOL processors from one computer system to another, it is clear that COBOL is not nearly as machine-independent as its designers would have liked it to be. The 1401 COBOL processor, for example, first translates the COBOL source program to 1401 Autocoder, then assembles the Autocoder program into 1401 machine language. A programmer using COBOL with this system would do well to be quite familiar with 1401 Autocoder in order to most effectively check out and debug this program. But familiarity with 1401 Autocoder requires familiarity with 1401 machine language program execution. This is a case in point, then, of the necessity for professional programmers to understand hardware, even when using high-level programming languages. However, as one of many skills available to the professional commercial programmer, COBOL is a valuable tool and will become more valuable to him as the language and the processors for it continue their development.

COBOL programs are divided into four divisions, the identification division, the environment division, the data division, and the procedure division. The identification division serves the purpose of identifying the program by listing the name of the program, the name of the programmer, the installation at which the program was written, the date it was compiled, security classification, and any remarks the programmer thinks appropriate. This identification appears with the listing of the source program as provided by the processor when compiling the program.

The environment division specifies for the processor the specific characteristics of the computer system on which the object program is to be executed and on which the source program is to be compiled.

Probably the most rigorous part of any COBOL program is the data division that specifies the input and output characteristics of the job to be executed. Because of the great variety of input/output devices available to every possible computer system and the different computer instructions needed to operate these devices properly as the job requires, it is necessary to specify the nature of the input data, the output required, and the formats of these data with great care. The fact that different computers use different means of representing data internally—binary, alphameric, BCD, and so on—only complicates the situation. It is this division of the COBOL system that illustrates most vividly the difficulty of developing a truly common programming language.

The procedure division is used to specify the calculations to be performed and the other work to be done in the execution of the program. This division of the program makes use of COBOL *verbs* such as READ, WRITE, MOVE, ADD, DIVIDE, COMPUTE, GO TO, and so on. A statement to calculate the sales commission to be paid a salesman might look like this:

COMPUTE COMMISSIONS = SALES * RATE + BONUS − DRAW.

In this case, the sales commission rate is multiplied by the amount of sales, a bonus is added to that, and whatever amount the salesman has taken out of his drawing account is deducted to find the amount owed to him.

PL/1

Within two years after the introduction of COBOL to the computer industry, consideration was given by IBM and a group of computer users known as SHARE to the development of a programming language that would combine the advantages of FORTRAN and COBOL in such a way that one language would serve all of the purposes of a typical computer installation, whether the applications being programmed at the installation were of a commercial or scientific nature or some mixture of the two. In addition, it was clear that FORTRAN and COBOL with their orientation toward card and tape systems were inadequate programming media for programs being written for modern computer installations using operating systems and real time program execution. To satisfy these needs work was begun on what then was known as NPL, or New Programming Language. In 1965, IBM announced the forthcoming availability of the new language to users of their System/360 line of computer systems. The name of the language is now PL/1 (Programming Language 1).

Compared with FORTRAN, PL/1 is more flexible and yet employs the same advantages of ease of specifying computational procedures. At the same time, much of the flexibility of input and output available to COBOL users is also available in PL/1. However, as of this writing, availability of PL/1 processors for existing installations does not exist and there seems to be some doubt in the industry as to its potential when used even with third-generation computers. PL/1, like COBOL, *cascades* down into lower level languages. That is to say, a PL/1 source program processed on an IBM System/360 computer will first be translated into System/360 Assembly Language, then into machine language. Once again, for program check-out purposes, this requires considerable knowledge on the part of the programmer as to how the System/360 works, even though the language is described by its developers as a "machine-independent" programming tool. Most operating installations have adopted a "wait and see" attitude toward this new programming system, which seems to promise so much.

Problem-Oriented Programming Systems

Problem-oriented programming systems attempt to relieve the programmer of not only an understanding of the computer system being used to execute his program, but also to excuse him from the requirement of specifying the procedure to be followed. Such a programming system is possible for jobs which involve very standardized procedures and therefore require that the program only specify a description of the input data. The processor does the rest.

Report Generators

A great number of applications of computer systems for commercial purposes consists of compiling and printing standardized reports. Usually the logic of the calculations and operations to be performed by the system is little changed from one report format to another. Report generators are generalized programs that programmers can call upon to produce these reports. In making use of them, the programmer must describe the data, specify the calculations to be performed, and indicate the format of the output. How the calculations are performed, how the output is produced, and how the data are treated to achieve the desired results are left to the report generator.

There are two basic types of report generators in use today. One of these types consists of a program that operates upon the data itself and produces the desired report directly, using the specifications provided by the programmer as additional data. The other type is often called a report *program* generator because it does not produce the report, but rather produces a source or an object program, using only the programmer specifications as data. This program is then assembled, if necessary, and applied to the data to produce the report.

Tabular Languages

Tabular languages represent an effort to reduce the difficulty of encoding the logic of a block diagram correctly into a source language (or object language) program. In this attempt, techniques familiar to statisticians and students of decision theory are used to develop a means of combining problem analysis, logic description, and program coding into a single documented activity. From the programmer's standpoint, his job involves stating the conditions under which certain actions by the computer system are to be taken. He is able to state the logic of his problem in such a way that the procedure for its implementation is implied. For example, if a customer orders more than 1,000 units, and if he has been a customer for more than one year, and if the amount of time it takes the customer to pay his account is less than 60 days, then the customer qualifies for a discount percentage on this purchase of 15 per cent. The "IF . . . THEN" type of logic described above is essential to tabular programming systems, and the systems make use of decision table techniques in developing the proper object program instruction sequence to get the job done. Users of these systems apparently regard them very highly as efficient tools for many commercial applications. As further work and research in the nature of programming systems proceeds, more widespread use of tabular languages may be seen.

Advantages of Programming Systems

Compared to programming in machine language, programming with the use of a programming system is by far more desirable. Certainly the programming, and, in particular, the coding of the computer program is more quickly accomplished. There is no doubt that a computer, in the execution of the programming system processor, can accomplish the clerical tasks needed to organize an object program more efficiently than can a human programmer. Also, it is easier to train programmers in programming systems because the coding is more easily understood, often by virtue of its similarity to English grammar. Diagnostic aids available with these systems often make program check-out much easier than if only machine language programming were used. Documentation, too, is improved with the use of programming systems. It is much easier for one who has not written the program, for example, to examine a COBOL program than a 1401 machine language program and determine what is being accomplished. This is true, also, of the lower level languages through the use of comments that appear on object and source program listings. Finally, although it is certainly desirable that professional programmers understand the operations of the computer systems for which they write programs, it is also desirable that they be relieved of the chores of programming in absolute or machine language. The machine independence that becomes available to the programmer through the use of programming systems is one of their greatest advantages.

Questions

1. What does the word mnemonic mean? Why is it used to describe source language instructions?
2. Explain the basic difference between macro systems and assembly systems. Give some examples.
3. What are the functions of the two basic parts of a programming system? Describe how these operate in the sample 1401 SPS program illustrated in the appendix to this chapter.
4. Try to write a FORTRAN program that would read three numbers from a card (card columns 1–5, 11–15, and 31–35), which we will call MAIZY, NANCY, and JILL; find their average (called JANE); write it out; then go back and read three more cards. Do not worry about running out of cards.
5. What has been the relationship of software development to the use of computers by business organizations?

Appendix to Chapter 13

Analysis of 1401 SPS Program

The purpose of this appendix is to illustrate the operations of an assembly type of programming system. Each of the steps involved in using a programming system is discussed: block diagramming, coding, assembly, and execution.

Program Input

Data cards with the following fields:

Card columns 1–20: Product name
Card columns 31–35: Product number
Card columns 41–45: unit cost

Program Output

A report listing each product number with its respective product name and unit cost and a total of the unit costs of each product card processed.

Block Diagram

A block diagram showing the sequence of steps in this program is shown in Figure 13–3. The numbers below refer to the annotated numbers on the flow chart.

1. Our report must have columnar headings in order to produce the following report format:

PRODUCT NUMBER	PRODUCT NAME	UNIT COST
.	.	.
.	.	.
.	.	.
.	.	.
.	.	.
	TOTALS	

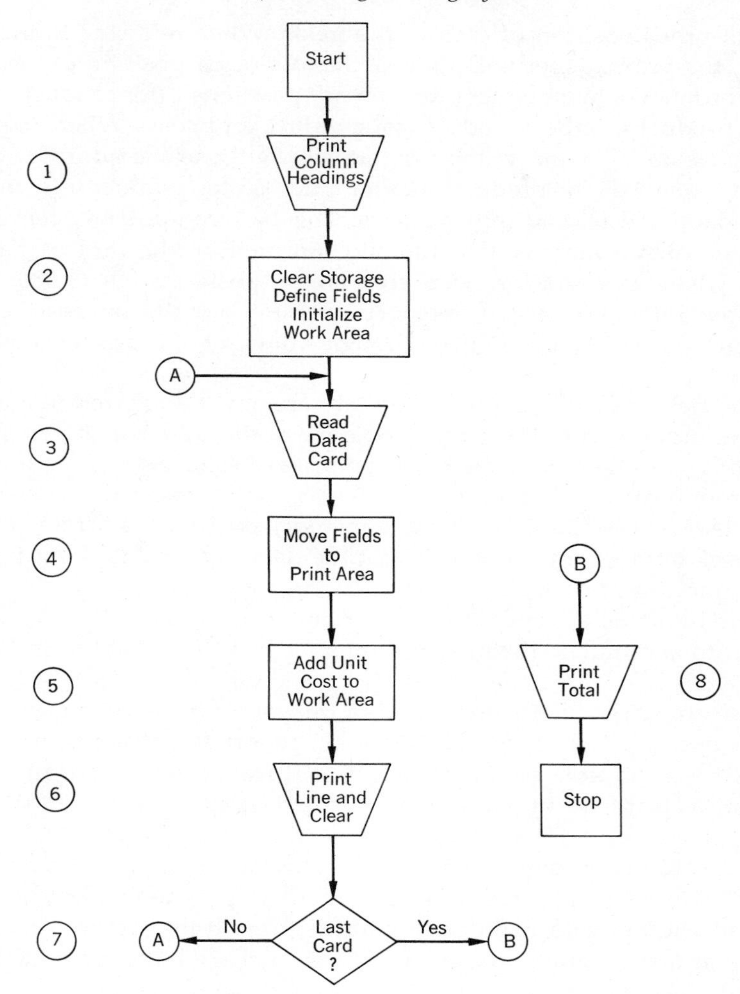

Figure 13–3. Block diagram of a sample program.

Block number one indicates that the constant information PRODUCT NUMBER, PRODUCT NAME, and UNIT COST are to be printed out as column headings.

2. Block number two indicates the necessity to establish a work area in memory for the purpose of accumulating the total of the unit cost figures read in from each card in the data file. It is also necessary to clear certain areas of memory, as will become clear later. The cards in our data file each have three fields and when this card is read by the 1401, all 80 characters on the card (remember that a blank is a valid character for electronic computers) are placed into the first 80 memory positions. In order that the three data fields read into these memory positions are defined properly, a field definition mark, called a word mark, must be placed in

the high-order position of each of the fields. When referring to the field of data, the programmer will address the low-order position of the field. Thus word marks must be set into memory positions 1 (for product name), 31 (for product number), and 41 (for product unit cost). When referring to these fields in memory, the programmer will use the address 020 for product name, 035 for product number, and 045 for product unit cost.

3. A data card is read into memory. The 1401 computer system is designed in such a manner that the 80 characters on the card being read replace whatever characters were in memory positions 001 to 080. Word marks put into these eighty memory positions for the purpose of field definition, as above, remain even though a new set of characters has been read.

4. The fields of data read in on the card are now transferred in memory from the input area to the area of memory in the 1401 which is reserved for setting up a line of characters to be printed. This area of memory extends from position 201 through 232. When a print instruction is executed by the 1401, every character in these memory positions is printed on one line. Block number four indicates that the data to be printed out is to be moved into the print area.

5. The input field, product unit cost, must be added to the work area in order to accumulate the total that must be printed out at the end of the listing.

6. The characters that were set up in the print area of memory by step four are now printed out on one line of the report. It will also be necessary to clear the print area so that data left in it from the last card processed will not be printed out together with the desired output from the next card.

7. The card reader device is tested to see whether the last card has been read. If there are more cards to be read, then our program will branch back and read another card and continue processing. If the last card has been read, then our program will print out the total we have accumulated in the work area and stop.

Coding

After preparing a block diagram as shown in Figure 13–3, the programmer next proceeds to write the program in the language of the programming system he is using. In our case, this is 1401 Symbolic Programming System. Figure 13–4*a* and *b* illustrate what the coding of this problem looks like. Each line of the coding sheet indicates the information to be punched into one IBM punched card. In the upper right corner of the coding sheet, it can be seen that columns 1 and 2 of each card will contain the page number of the coding sheet from which the card was punched. In the body of the coding sheet, near the left margin, it can be seen that card

IBM — INTERNATIONAL BUSINESS MACHINES CORPORATION — **IBM 1401 SYMBOLIC PROGRAMMING SYSTEM** — CODING SHEET — FORM X24-1152-2 PRINTED IN U.S.A.

Program: SAMPLE PRØGRAM — Page No. 01 of 2
Programmed by: BRIGHTMAN — Date: 4-28-67 — Identification: ____

LINE	COUNT	LABEL	OPERATION	(A) OPERAND ADDRESS	±	CHAR. ADJ.	IND.	(B) OPERAND ADDRESS	±	CHAR. ADJ.	IND.	d	COMMENTS
3–5	6–7	8–13	14–16	17	23		27	28	34		38	39	40–55
010			CTL	55									
020			ØRG	0401									
030		STEP1	CS	0332									
040			CS	0299									CLEAR PRINT AREA
050			MCW	UNTCST				0275					MØVE HEADINGS
060			MCW	PRDTNM				0255					TØ
070			MCW	PRDTNØ				0225					PRINT AREA
080			W										PRINT HEADINGS
090		STEP2	CS	0332									CLEAR PRINT AREA
100			CS	0299									
110			MCW	ZERØS				WØRK					INITIALIZE WØRK
120			SW	0001				0031					DEFINE FIELDS
130			SW	0041									
140		STEP3	R										READ DATA CARD
150		STEP4	MCW	0045				0273					CØST TO PRINT
160			MCW	0020				0263					
170			MCW	0035				0219					NUMBER TØ PRINT
180		STEP5	A	0045				WØRK					WØRK + CØST
190		STEP6	W										WRITE A LINE
200			CS	0273									CLEAR PRINT AREA

Figure 13–4a.

IBM — INTERNATIONAL BUSINESS MACHINES CORPORATION — **IBM 1401 SYMBOLIC PROGRAMMING SYSTEM** — CODING SHEET — FORM X24-1152-2 PRINTED IN U.S.A.

Program: SAMPLE PRØGRAM — Page No. 02 of 2
Programmed by: ____ — Date: ____ — Identification: ____

LINE	COUNT	LABEL	OPERATION	(A) OPERAND ADDRESS	±	CHAR. ADJ.	IND.	(B) OPERAND ADDRESS	±	CHAR. ADJ.	IND.	d	COMMENTS
3–5	6–7	8–13	14–16	17	23		27	28	34		38	39	40–55
010		STEP7	B	STEP8								A	LAST CARD TEST
020			B	STEP3									LØØP BACK
030		STEP8	MCW	WØRK				0273					WØRK TØ PRINT
040			MCW	TØTALS				0259					TØTALS TØ PRINT
050			W										PRINT A LINE
060			H										HALT
070	09	UNTCST	DCW	*		UNIT CØST							
080	12	PRDTNM	DCW	*		PRØDUCT NAME							
090	14	PRDTNØ	DCW	*		PRØDUCT NUMBER							
100	06	ZERØS	DCW	*		000000							
110	06	WØRK	DCW	*									
120	06	TØTALS	DCW	*		TØTALS							
130			END	STEP1									
140													
150													
160													
170													
180													
190													
200													

Figure 13–4b.

columns 3, 4, and 5 will contain a number representing which line on the page was used in preparing the card. Together, the page number and the line number serve to sequence the instructions in the order in which they were written. Since the 1401 is a two-address computer, the coding sheet provides space for the programmer to indicate an *A*-operand and a *B*-operand as well as an operation code for each instruction. The label field is used by the programmer to indicate to the processor which instructions, constants, and work areas are to be referenced by a symbolic label and what that label is. Card columns 40 through 55 are made available to the programmer for any comments he cares to punch into the source cards to aid in identifying sections of his program. The following is a line-by-line description of the program shown in Figure 13–4*a* and *b*. The labels used in the program (STEP 1, STEP 2, and so on) refer to the numbered symbols of the block diagram in Figure 13–3.

PAGE ONE (Figure 13–4a)

Lines 010 and 020. These cards are known as processor control cards. The first, CTL55, indicates to the SPS processor the size of the 1401 computer used to assemble the object program and the size of the 1401 that will be used in executing the object program. The ORG0401 statement tells the processor that the programmer wants the first character of this program to be located in memory position 401. The rest of the program will follow sequentially from 401.

Lines 030 and 040. The instruction, CS, is one which causes areas of memory to be cleared to blanks. As used here, these two instructions together clear the print area, 201 to 332. A comment is punched into this card, as with most of the cards to follow, to indicate the basic function of the statement.

Lines 050 to 070. These three instructions move constant information from where it is stored in memory to the print area in preparation for printing the columnar headings. The operation code, MCW, means move characters until a word mark is reached. Move operations in the 1401 memory proceed character by character from right to left. Word marks, placed in the high order position of the field being moved, will terminate the instruction and the system will then proceed to the next step of the program. In the case of these instructions, constant information must be stored in memory in order that the correct information be moved into the read area. To see how this was done, examine Figure 13–4*b*. Lines 070, 080, and 090 contain SPS statements that cause constants to be loaded into memory. The DCW operation code means "define a constant with a word mark." The labels, UNTCST, PRDTNM, and PRDTNO, are the symbolic labels that the programmer wishes to use when referring to these constants. The asterisk immediately following the DCW operation code is a signal to the processor to place this constant in memory wherever the processor finds most convenient. Because of this, the programmer will not know the actual machine address of the constants, but he will be able to use them nevertheless because of the labels that are synonymous with their memory addresses. The constants themselves are punched into the card containing the DCW entry, starting with card column 24. Finally, the count field contains a number that indicates to the processor the number of characters in the constant. The move operations in lines 050, 060, and 070 on page 1 cause the constants loaded into memory by the DCW statements on page 2 to be moved into the print area in preparation for printing of the columnar headings UNIT COST, PRODUCT NAME, and PRODUCT NUMBER.

Line 080. This instruction, W, causes the entire contents of the print area of the 1401 memory to be written as one line on the paper in the printing device. The print area contains the column headings moved into it by the previous three instructions and this information is printed out. Figure 13–5 shows the entire report produced by this program when applied to 47 data cards of the format specified above under *Program Input.* On the report can be seen the headings printed by this operation.

Lines 090 and 100. The print area is cleared of the heading information just printed so that this data will not interfere with future printing operations.

Line 110. This operation sets the memory area to be used to accumulate the sum of the unit cost figures from each data card to zero. This is accomplished by moving a field of zeros into the work area. This field of zeros was set into memory as a constant in the same manner as the heading constants were placed into memory. Lines 100 and 110 on Figure 13–4*b* show the DCW entries that establish a constant field in memory containing six zeros and setting aside six positions of memory labeled, WORK, to be used to accumulate the total.

Lines 120 and 130. SW (set word mark) is an operation that causes word marks to be associated with the memory positions specified in the *A*- and *B*-operands of the instruction. In the case of these two instructions, word marks are set in three memory positions that will be the high order positions of the three data fields read into the card input area when a data card is read. In this way, a word mark is established in the high order positions of the data fields so that these fields can be then moved to the print area for printing and the unit cost field can be added to the work area.

Line 140. This operation causes the card reader device attached to the 1401 to read a card and place all 80 characters (including blanks) into the

PRODUCT NUMBER	PRODUCT NAME	UNIT COST
00001	ACTUATE REPEAT KEY	00250
00002	PUNCHING GUIDE	00128
00003	INDEX KEYBOARD	24500
00005	DEPRESS MOTER BAR	05324
00006	INDEX CIPHER	00298
00007	PULL TOTAL KEY	00252
00010	PUSH NON-ADD KEY	00986
00011	LEFT HAND CARD HOLD	00530
00012	SENSING GUIDE	00423
00013	LEFT HAND CONTROLS	02150
00014	DOWNWARD STACKER	00135
00015	SEQUENCE STACKER	00250
00016	SHINGLED EDGE CARDS	00025
00017	EJECT CARD STACKER	00243
00018	REPEAT KEY	00098
00019	PLASTIC END STOP	00540
00021	STACKER SPRING	00015
00022	LOWER CARD SHELF	00520
00023	RIGHT FIELD FINDER	00257
00024	UNIVERSAL KNOB	00036
00025	ON PLUG	00052
00026	OFF PLUG	00546
00027	FINGER GLOVES	00125
00028	THUMB GLOVE	00098
00029	KEYSORT PUNCH	05863
00030	COLUMN INDICATOR	00042
00031	SUBTRACT BAR	00201
00032	PARALLEL KEYSORT NUT	00025
00033	BEVELED EDGE CARD	00350
00034	UPRIGHT PIN	00030
00035	BACK PLATE	00215
00036	KEYSORT GROOVER	00150
00037	FOOT LEVER	00530
00038	ROTATING FOOT LEVER	05689
00039	WHIP HANDLE	00254
00040	VARIABLE DATA RACK	98635
00041	FIXED DATA RACK	65832
00042	MARKING INK	00254
00043	TEMPLATE	00025
00044	LEFT GUIDE	00021
00045	RIGHT GUIDE	00024
00046	CHIP TRAY	02354
00047	OPERATING HANDLE	00369
	TOTALS	218644

Figure 13–5. Sample program output.

first 80 memory positions of the 1401 memory—that is, memory positions 001 to 080. The word marks that were set in the card input area at 001, 031, and 041 are left undisturbed by this reading operation; however, any characters that were in the card input area are replaced by the 80 characters in the card just read.

Lines 150, 160, and 170. These instructions move the three data fields from the card input area to the positions in the print area which will cause them to be printed out in the correct place on the report. The programmer here addresses the low order positions of the input data fields (positions 045, 020, and 035) and moves them to the low order positions of the fields in the print area. The word marks set in the high order positions of each of the three input data fields (001, 031, and 041) stop each of the three move operations.

Line 180. The instruction, A, causes the contents of the field addressed in the *A*-operand of the instruction to be added to the contents of the field addressed in the *B*-operand. In the case of this add instruction, the input field at 045—that is, the unit cost field of the input card—is added to the work area. Recall that earlier in the program the work area was started at a value of zero. Each time a data card is read and processed, the unit cost field is added to the work area. Refer back to Figure 13–3, which shows the block diagram for this program. Observe that the work area is initialized before the first data card is read. Thereafter, until the last card has been processed, the work area contains the amount left in it from the last card. In other words, the branch from Step Seven on the no last card test is to Step Three. In this way the programmer is sure that the work area is set to zero only at the beginning of his program.

Lines 190 and 200. Now the contents of the print area—that is, the data fields read in from the last card—are printed on the report under the appropriate column headings. After printing, the print area is again cleared to make way for the next data fields.

PAGE TWO (Figure 13–4b)

Line 010. This instruction tests the card reader device to determine if the last card has been read. Its meaning is this: "If the last card has been read, branch to Step Eight for the next instruction to be executed. If the last card has not been read, continue to the next sequential instruction." The character, A, in column 39 of this instruction indicates that the branch to Step Eight is to be taken only if the last card has been read. This character distinguishes this conditional branch from an unconditional branch instruction, which would cause transfer of control every time the instruction was encountered. Again referring to the block diagram in Figure 13–3, Step Eight is the first of those instructions that cause the final total to be printed out and the computer to halt. These are the things that must be done after the last card has been processed.

Line 020. If the last card has not been read, then this is the instruction that will be executed after Step Seven. This is an unconditional branch and will transfer control back to Step Three, which will cause another card to be read and processing will continue.

Lines 030 and 040. If the last card has been read, then the total of the units costs must be printed out along with the constant word, TOTALS. These two instructions move the area called WORK to the print area as well as the constant, TOTALS, which was put into memory by a DCW statement on line 120.

Line 050. The information put into the printing area in Step Eight is printed out by this instruction.

Line 060. This is a halt instruction. It causes the execution of this program to halt.

Lines 070 through 110. These statements, which have already been described above, cause the constants needed by the program to be stored in memory.

Line 130. This is a control statement that tells the SPS processor that the last source statement has been processed and that no more program instructions will have to be translated into machine language for this particular program.

Observe that in the coding of this program, the programmer was able to refer to the location in memory of certain instructions (Step Three and Step Eight) without knowing where in memory these instructions would be stored. Similarly, he was able to use constants without knowing where in memory they were located. In the translation process conducted by the SPS processor, the labels that the programmer has used as operands in his program will be replaced by the actual machine address of the constant or instruction that is being addressed symbolically. Figure 13–6 shows the results of the translation performed by the processor and the resulting machine language program. The characters to the left of the center line are the 1401 SPS statements as coded on the coding sheet and punched into the source deck. Across the top of the left portion of Figure 13–6 are column headings for page number, line number, the count field punched in the source cards, and so on. To the right of the center line, the column headings indicate the memory location containing the machine language instructions and constants, the instructions, the contents of the 1401 instruction registers just before the instructions are to be executed, and the comment field as punched into the source cards.

By comparing the source statements with the resulting machine language instructions, the reader can get a good appreciation of the advantages of programming in 1401 SPS rather than machine language. For example, on page 1, line 050, the SPS source statement written by the programmer (MCW UNTCST 0275) involved moving the constant, UNIT COST, to the print area of the 1401 memory in preparation for printing the column headings. This instruction was translated, or assembled,

```
                                                                                                   PAGE  1
PG LIN CT LABEL  OP  A OPERAND    B OPERAND    D  LOC   INSTRUCTION  A/REG B/REG   COMMENTS

 1 010           CTL 55
 1 020           ORG 0401
 1 030  4 STEP1  CS  0332                         0401  / 332        0332
 1 040  4        CS  0299                         0405  / 299        0299          CLEAR PRINT AREA
 1 050  7        MCW UNTCST       0275            0409  M 524 275    0524  0275    MOVE HEADINGS
 1 060  7        MCW PRDTNM       0255            0416  M 536 255    0536  0255         TO
 1 070  7        MCW PRDTNO       0225            0423  M 550 225    0550  0225      PRINT  AREA
 1 080  1        W                                0430  2                          PRINT HEADINGS
 1 090  4 STEP2  CS  0332                         0431  / 332        0332          CLEAR PRINT AREA
 2 000  4        CS  0299                         0435  / 299        0299
 2 010  7        MCW ZEROS        WORK            0439  M 556 562    0556  0562    INITIALIZE WORK
 2 020  7        SW  0001         0031            0446  , 001 031    0001  0031    DEFINE FIELDS
 2 030  4        SW  0041                         0453  , 041        0041
 2 040  1 STEP3  R                                0457  1                          READ DATA CARD
 2 050  7 STEP4  MCW 0045         0273            0458  M 045 273    0045  0273    COST TO PRINT
 2 060  7        MCW 0020         0263            0465  M 020 263    0020  0263
 2 070  7        MCW 0035         0219            0472  M 035 219    0035  0219    NUMBER TO PRINT
 2 080  7 STEP5  A   0045         WORK            0479  A 045 562    0045  0562    WORK & COST
 2 090  1 STEP6  W                                0486  2                          WRITE A LINE
 3 000  4        CS  0273                         0487  / 273        0273          CLEAR PRINT AREA
 3 010  5 STEP7  B   STEP8                     A  0491  B 500 A      0500          LAST CARD TEST
 3 020  4        B   STEP3                        0496  B 457        0457          LOOP BACK
 3 030  7 STEP8  MCW WORK         0273            0500  M 562 273    0562  0273    WORK TO PRINT
 3 040  7        MCW TOTALS       0259            0507  M 568 259    0568  0259    TOTALS TO PRINT
 3 050  1        W                                0514  2                          PRINT A LINE
 3 050  1        H                                0515  .                          HALT
 3 060  9 UNTCST DCW *                            0524            .UNIT COST
 3 070 12 PRDTNM DCW *                            0536            .PRODUCT NAME
 3 080 14 PRDTNO DCW *                            0550            .PRODUCT NUMBER
 3 090  6 ZEROS  DCW *                            0556            .00000
 4 000  6 WORK   DCW *                            0562            .
 4 010  6 TOTALS DCW *                            0568            .TOTALS
 4 020           END STEP1                              / 401 080

          33 CARDS
```

Figure 13–6. Assembly of a sample program.

by the processor as M524 to 275—that is, "move the contents of the field at 524 to the field at 275." Now, look down the column of the figure headed with LOC. This column contains the memory addresses of instructions and constants stored in memory. Seven lines up from the bottom we find the number 524, which indicates the memory location of the instruction or constant to the right of that address. In this case, we see the characters,

SPS Mnemonic Operation Code	Machine Language Operation Code	Function
CS	/	Clear Storage
MCW	M	Move field from A-field to B-field
W	2	Write a line
SW	,	Set word mark
R	1	Read a card
A	A	Add A-field to B-field
B	B	Branch
H	.	Halt

Note: CTL, ORG, DCW, and END are control statements to the processor as described in text description

Figure 13–7. SPS instruction codes and machine language equivalents as used in sample SPS program.

UNIT COST, preceded by a period, which indicates that in memory there will be a word mark in the high order position of that constant field In assembling the move instruction on page 1, line 050, the processor has put the address of the constant, UNIT COST, into the *A*-operand of the completed machine language instruction. In this way, the programmer need not know where in memory the constant was stored; the processor took care of that detail for him. Similarly, in the case of the branch instruction at Step Seven, which reads B STEP8, the instruction is assembled as B 500A (the A indicates that this branch is to take place only if the last card has been read). The machine address 500, it can be seen from the location column, is the address of the move instruction that the programmer wants executed if the last card has been read. Once again, the programmer did not need to know the memory address of the move instruction at Step Eight; the processor was able to provide it for him. To aid the reader in tracing through the other instructions as assembled and shown in Figure 13–6, Figure 13–7 is a chart of the various 1401 SPS instruction codes and their equivalent machine language instructions in the order in which they appear in the sample program.

14

Operating Systems

The Process of Program Execution

Consider what must be done to execute a program after the programmer has written it. If the program has been written in a high-level language such as COBOL, PL/1, or FORTRAN, it must first be complied. This involves loading into the computer memory the appropriate processor program and submitting the source program to the computer via some input device, often a card reader, in order that the processor program may either translate it first into an assembly language and then into machine language, or translate it directly into machine language. During processing, clerical errors made on the part of the programmer will be discovered and diagnosed by the processor, which causes a list of these to be printed by a printing device on line to the computer. The computer operator returns the source program to the programmer, loads another program into the computer's main memory, sets up the input data for this new program into the required input devices, and sets the computer to executing this job. Later, the programmer returns with his program after correcting the errors and another attempt is made to compile it. Again, the operator loads the compiler program into main memory and submits the source program to the computer. This time, if the compilation is successful, the programmer will want to check out the program to ascertain that the logic of his program will cause the computer to do the things to the data that should be done. To do this, he tries executing his program with sample data. Knowing in advance the results of the calculations that should be performed on these sample data, he is able to determine if the job is being done correctly. If it is not, then he must find his logic errors, correct them, recompile, correct any clerical errors that are indicated by the compiler, and try his sample data again. Finally, after perhaps several attempts at checking out his program, he is satisfied that it is correct and is ready for a production run.

The above process, called *program check-out*, or *program debugging*, is time-consuming from the programmer's standpoint—usually as much time is spent in checking out a program as is spent in initially writing it—as well as from the computer's standpoint. There is almost nothing that can be done to eliminate the need for program check-out. Programmers, being human, are not infallible and are bound to make mistakes. Naturally, these mistakes must all be found before the program is ready for a production run. Nevertheless, from a computer standpoint, the time spent in loading compilers, testing, and debugging programs and returning to a production run is wasteful. While data are being loaded into card readers or mounted on tape drives or disk drives, while programs are being loaded into memory, and other programs are being stored away, the computer is doing no work in a production sense. Having a computer stand idle during program change operations necessary to switch from one job to another can be a very expensive luxury, costing as much as $500 per hour for some elaborate computers.

Program check-out, of course, is only one kind of activity involving program changes in a typical computer installation. During the workday of a fairly large computer, it will be called upon to execute many different kinds of programs requiring many different kinds of set-ups. Tape reels must be changed, different paper loaded into printers, perhaps cards loaded into card readers, switch settings adjusted on the computer console, and other general computer operation activities. These activities require time—time during which the computer is standing idle, waiting for operators to make routine decisions, to perform routine clerical operations such as recording the processing time of the last run, for example, and making physical adjustments to the computer system.

In the past, little could be done to eliminate this wasted time. Computers were less expensive than at present, and wasted time did not mean necessarily a good deal of wasted money. In those good old days—days that are still enjoyed by many a smaller computer installation—computer operators loaded programs and the data upon which they were to execute manually, following a set of instructions prepared by the programmer who wrote the program. These instructions usually told the operator two things: what he was to do, and what he should expect the computer to do. Because the computer operators usually knew little about the programs they were executing, the instructions had to be written in very simple terms, using the same techniques as used to write a computer program. That is, instead of telling the operator to mount the accounts receivable tape on the input tape drive, the programmer, to assure that the operator would put the correct tape on the proper drive, would find it necessary to instruct him to mount tape 467 on tape drive 4. In addition, the operator was told to make certain switch settings, perhaps to enter some information manually to the system through the console, and perform other duties. As you might expect, the more elaborate these operator instructions, the greater the chance that mistakes in machine operation would occur. Also, the more elaborate the operator instructions, the less effective the object program was likely to be since the programmer was unable to rely upon his ingenuity to cause his stored program to do those things that he wanted done and had to count on the work of the computer operator instead.

At this point, the chief problem of electronic computer operation should be clear: modern computers, as expensive as they are, can be economically justified only because of the great processing speed, or more accurately, great *throughput* speed of the system. Requiring an expensive machine to spend any appreciable time standing idle while human operators who are relatively slow and inaccurate perform routine operations is wasteful. In fact, where large complex electronic systems are needed, it is more economical to make the system even larger to eliminate as much as possible the need for human intervention during operation. If a way can be found to eliminate the need for human operators entirely, this might even be better. As an example, consider a computer system in which all the assemblers and compilers are permanently stored on some on-line secondary memory device, say a magnetic disk file, and that a library of subroutines and frequently used programs are similarly stored. Furthermore, data files frequently processed might also be stored permanently on an on-line basis.

Now our programmer with his source program to be compiled need only present his deck to the system and ask it to compile his program and to store the resulting object program away somewhere on magnetic disk or magnetic tape so that he may execute it when he might want to. This can be done now without the need of an operator removing the production job being executed and reloading the computer with the compiler program and then presenting the source program to be processed.

Here is what happens. First, remember that the computer system is executing a production program, using data that are coming into the system from some input device. When the source program our programmer has written is presented to the computer system, a program, the purpose of which is to determine what programs are to be executed by the system, senses that a new job is being presented at one of the input devices, in this case a card reader. Let us assume that in this installation the processing and check-out of source programs has priority over any production program being executed. Along with the source deck, the programmer has included a control card. This is the first card that the card reader reads. The controlling program examines this first card and from it learns that this is, say, a PL/1 program to be compiled and stored on magnetic disk and that a diagnostic message indicating clerical errors in the source program is to be displayed on an on-line printer. The controlling program causes the production program being executed by the computer to be interrupted and the contents of the computer's memory to be temporarily stored away on an on-line secondary memory device, magnetic tape, or disk. The PL/1 compiler is called into main memory from the on-line device on which it is normally stored; the cards of the source deck are read by the card reader; and the source instructions are compiled. The resulting object program then is also stored on a secondary memory device and the diagnostic message, if any, is printed along with an indication of where in the computer system the object program is stored and how many storage locations are needed to contain it. Following this, the controlling programs calls the production program that was interrupted back into main memory and sets the system back to its execution.

Thus, a program in the process of execution was interrupted and stored away; a new program to be executed was loaded (this was the PL/1 compiler); this program was executed; the first program reloaded; and the computer system returned to the execution of the initial program. All the operator had to do to cause all this to happen was to present the interrupting message to the system. This was done via the control card at the front of the source deck. Observe that *four* programs have been involved in this operation: the production program, the compiler program, the controlling program, and the source program to be compiled. The controlling program and the other programs and devices over which it has control are the subject of this chapter.

Monitors

The controlling program in the above example is known as a *monitor*, and the other programs and devices over which it has control comprise the *operating system.* A monitor program serves the purpose of increasing the operational efficiency of the computer system. It does this by performing tasks that otherwise would have to be accomplished by a computer operator in accordance with instructions written to them by the programmers. By standardizing these essentially routine tasks, it becomes possible to write instructions to cause the computer to perform them. This set of instructions is known as the *monitor program*, although it goes by many different names: supervisory control program; executive routine; executor; and supervisor.

Monitor programs vary in size and complexity, depending upon the system and the applications being executed on the system. Some monitors are very simple, amounting to 100 instructions or less and doing little more than searching a program library for object programs and subroutines called for by the job in question. At the other end of the scale are huge programs which sequence jobs, set up queues of programs to be executed in accordance with an established priority system, and control the affairs of a real-time or shared-time system. (See Chapter 15 on real-time systems.)

Programs Within Operating Systems

An *operating system* is a set of programs and related hardware devices placed under control of the monitor program to assure computer system operation with a minimum of time delays for operational functions. Because of the close relationship between the monitor and the operating system, many use the two terms synonymously. However, it is useful to consider the system separately from the program that controls it.

Often, operating systems and their individual programs are known as software, in contrast with the hardware, or computer devices, that the systems are used to control. In the face of increasing complexity of computer operational and programming techniques, users of electronic data processing equipment look to software packages offered by the manufacturer of the equipment as a crucial factor in deciding which system to buy or lease. The programs within the software package offered by the manufacturer are of two basic types. There are those routine programs that serve specific purposes in terms of the installation's data processing needs. A department store may have a customer billing program as part of the operating system which can be loaded into memory and executed when necessary; a bank might have a program that is used once a day to update depositors' accounts. Frequently, these programs are written by the user in order to tailor them to his unique requirements, but business applications common to many businesses are usually programmed by manufacturers and made available in the software package.

The other general category of programs within operating systems includes programs concerned with specific operational needs of the computer system itself, such as maintaining the library of object programs and subroutines, controlling input and output operations, compilation and assembly of source program, and other functions.

The remainder of this chapter deals with the specific functions of operating systems as they have been developed so far. The ultimate operating system is known as a *total information system,* an outgrowth of *real-time systems.* These advanced types of operating systems will be discussed in the next chapter.

The Library

The simplest type of operating system is one that consists of nothing more than a monitor program that searches for an object program among several stored on magnetic tape or disk, loads it into memory, and starts its execution. Such a program may use little more than a hundred memory locations. In many operating systems, the monitor is in permanent residence in main memory. All other programs are expected to occupy and to use other memory locations.

When a program in the library is to be executed, a card is presented to the system. This card is generally called a "call" card since it is used to call for the program in the library which is to be executed. The call card usually is punched with the characters CALL followed by the name of the object program to be brought from the library and loaded into memory. Assume that we have available to us a library of object programs stored on magnetic tape. We wish to execute a program entitled UPDAT, which has the purpose of reading a series of cards on which are recorded transactions involving the removal from and additions to a small parts inventory and updating the records of inventory items that are kept in a file recorded on magnetic tape. To accomplish this, we must mount the inventory file tape on the tape drive called for by the object program, prepare a card with the characters, CALL UPDAT, punched into it, and present this card together with the transactions cards to the system via a card reader.

Reading the call card causes the monitor program to rewind the tape on which is stored the library of object programs available. Then it causes reading of the names of each program sequentially through the tape until it comes to the one entitled UPDAT. It does this by comparing each program title it reads from the tape with the characters, UPDAT, read from the call card until it gets an equal comparison. Having thus found the desired object program, it then loads it from the tape into main memory and causes execution to begin. The object program then calls for the transaction cards that are available at the card reader and uses them to adjust the inventory records available from the file of inventory records on the inventory tape.

While the computer is in the process of executing the UPDAT program, the computer operator can be occupied by mounting tapes and preparing input cards and other activities in preparation for a program to be executed later. The most significant advantage of this simple library monitor is the ability to *stack* jobs. This means that a series of jobs to be executed by the computer system can be loaded into a card reader and the monitor will cause them each to be executed in accordance with the control card for each job. Some jobs will involve programs in the library and the control card will be a call card as in the above example. Others may involve executing a program that is not in the library. The control card for such a job would be a load card which would cause loading of the object program from some source other than the program library tape. In this way, the monitor, although only a simple search program, essentially, enables the computer to execute jobs one after the other with no wait while the operator loads the object program and prepares the input and output devices.

Other, more complex operating systems are basically similar to this library monitor in operation. Their complexity involves the use of other programs, rather than in the use of more difficult concepts. Other operating systems have some provision for library maintenance and in this respect can be considered to be outgrowths of this simplified system. This system illustrates the basic nature of the operating system—that is, a monitor program that has control over a set of other programs designed to perform some function, whether in a production sense, as with this library example, or a function related to maintaining the operational efficiencies of the computer system itself.

Input/Output

Even greater efficiencies could be enjoyed in the simple library system above if standardized input/output procedures were employed by every programmer using the system. In fact, requiring every programmer to conform to established procedures for input and output operations enables the development of standardized programs that relieve the programmer of the necessity of writing complicated input and output instructions at all. Approximately 40 per cent of a business-application computer program consists of instructions written for the purpose of reading input data or writing output results. The purpose of input/output routines in operating systems is to permit the programmer to concentrate on the logic of the processing task without becoming bogged down in detailed input/output programming. Programming the reading, writing, and manipulation of records is a tedious chore common to most programming jobs treating large files of records. It is a job that can be standardized in the sense that one set of instructions to read records from one file can probably be used for other files. If programmers can be made to conform to certain rules about such input and output operations, then a common program can be used by all. Input/Output Control System, or IOCS, is just such a program.

Functions of IOCS

IOCS performs such functions as blocking and deblocking of records, processing of tape labels, and writing checkpoint records.

Blocking and Deblocking. IOCS will relieve the programmer of the tedium of record manipulation when writing a program to process records stored in blocked form. Generally, a business programmer is interested in processing data in the form of records and transactions. You will recall that files of records are stored on magnetic tape or disk or in data cells in blocked form, that is, as physical records. A *file*, for example, is a collection of all the *logical records* available with respect to some function of the business; for example, a file of employee records, a file of customer records, of inventory records, and so on. A logical record is a set of facts about a specific item in the file; for example, a specific employee, a specific customer, a specific item of inventory. A *physical record* is a group of logical records grouped together to increase the efficiency of data storage on the device used to store the entire file. The process of *blocking* involves grouping the logical records into physical records, and the *blocking factor* represents the number of logical records in a physical record. Thus, a file of 1,000 logical records about employees might be stored on magnetic tape with a blocking factor of ten, that is, as 100 physical records each containing ten logical records about individual employees. A programmer wanting to write a program to calculate earned retirement benefits for each of the 1,000 employees really does not care much how the individual records are stored on the tape. He must examine the employee record for earnings and retirement status, perform the necessary calculations, then proceed on to the next employee record.

However, records stored in blocked form must be read from the tape in blocks; this is the nature of the magnetic tape device on which the records are stored. Thus, the programmer must read from the tape an entire physical record. Once this physical record is in main memory, he must then extract one logical record from the block of logical records he has available in memory. This is called *deblocking*—that is, separating logical records out of the physical record in which they are stored. Once the programmer has deblocked a logical record, it is then ready for processing. If, after processing, the record is updated or otherwise changed and requires rewriting back on the tape in its new form, the programmer must reblock the record before this can be done for the same reason as above: records can only be read from and written on tape (or magnetic disk) in blocked form, as part of a physical record.

Reading and Writing of Physical Records. Because the programmer relies upon IOCS to block and deblock records, he should not have to concern himself with knowing when a new physical record should be read into memory or when a physical record has been completely processed and requires writing back on the storage medium. IOCS will do these things for him when required by the nature of the records. The programmer need only concern himself with processing the individual logical records. All the reading and writing of physical records is done for him. IOCS performs all the blocking and deblocking required to make a logical record available to the programmer for individual treatment. In general, the programmer calls for a logical record using an instruction such as GET PAYREC, GET being an operation code and PAYREC being an operand. IOCS will cause an entire physical record to be read into memory and one logical record to be made available to the programmer in the memory location identified by the label PAYREC. After processing this record, IOCS, when sensing another GET instruction will bring the second record out of the block already in memory and make it available for processing. IOCS will continue to function in this manner until all the logical records in the physical record in memory have been processed. Then, it will read another physical record and make the first logical record in it available and so on.

If the records in the file are to be written back into the file after processing, as in an updating operation, IOCS will perform the writing of logical records just as it performed their reading. In this case, when the programmer has programmed all the instructions necessary to process a logical record, he then need only write the instruction, PUT PAYREC, and the logical record he was working with is stored in memory by IOCS. After a series of such PUT instructions, a physical record will be assembled with the appropriate blocking factor and then written back on the device that stores the file.

In the example above, the programmer need not know where on the magnetic tape or disk the file of records identified by the name PAYREC is stored or even how many logical records there are in the file to be processed. He can concentrate entirely upon the operations to be performed on the data—IOCS takes care of all of the tasks necessary to get the individual records from the file and put them back.

Error Checking. Input and output devices tend to be error-prone. This is not because they are poorly manufactured, but rather because they are called upon to perform truly miraculous feats. We have studied various input/output devices in Chapter 11, and have observed that in order for them even inadequately to keep up with the fast processing speeds of the central processing unit, they must perform physical tasks at speeds that insure errors. A spot of dust on magnetic tape or disk file, a fault or blister on the surface of a tape or disk, a faulty punch die in a card punch, and many other phenomena can cause correctly processed data to be written incorrectly or not written at all. One of the functions of IOCS is to detect such errors and correct them without the necessity of stopping the program and without requiring the programmer to program error checking routines for each program written.

In order to perform this function, IOCS relies upon rather elaborate error-detection devices built into the hardware. Input/output devices are now being built with a wide variety of error-checking features. Still, even if such features reduce the chance of making an error to one out of a million, a magnetic disk drive transmitting data at 55,000 characters per second might be expected to make an error once every 20 seconds or so. Clearly, the reliability of input/output devices requires a chance of making an undetected error that is very small, indeed. In general, an undetected error occurring during processing will probably continue to go unnoticed until some time later when the data are being analyzed or otherwise used. Almost everybody has heard of someone who received a check produced by a computer system that had misplaced the decimal point giving the payee of the check either many times more than he deserved or many times less. This is not the kind of error that can be treated by IOCS. IOCS has routines designed to handle *detected* errors. In the case of miswriting on magnetic tape, for example, the routine might try to write again several times and if still unable to write correctly, skip a portion of the tape and try to write again. Were it not for these routines which are a part of IOCS, the programmer would find it necessary to program these routines as part of every program written.

Label Checking and Writing. Files of records kept on magnetic tape or disk are identified by a label or name. IOCS contains routines designed to check the labels of data files to assure that the correct file is mounted on the tape or disk drive for processing and to write labels for files newly being written. Such label checking routines are safety devices used to assure that data files are not inadvertently destroyed because they were inaccurately identified by the computer operator and to prevent wasting valuable time processing data from the wrong file.

Checkpoint Procedure Implementation. When a program in operation is to be interrupted by the operating system to permit another program to be loaded into memory and executed, some procedure is necessary to permit reinstating the first program without having to start it all over again from the beginning. For example, a program which requires seven hours for completion may have to be interrupted after five hours of processing in order for a short but high-priority program to be run. A *checkpoint procedure* is one that writes the contents of the computer memory and registers on an on-line storage device, so that when the interrupting program is finished, the program that was interrupted can be loaded back into memory and its execution continued without losing the five hours of work that took place before the interruption. Before the development of this feature of IOCS, programmers, when preparing a program which would require considerable time to process, would write their own checkpoint routines. These routines would cause the contents of memory and registers along with intermediate data results to be stored on an on-line device from time to time, so that at any time during the execution of the program there would be a record of the condition of the system as it stood not too long ago—say, every ten minutes or so. Because of this record, the program could be stopped and then restarted at a later time with a loss of only a few minutes of processing time. Including these checkpoint procedures in IOCS relieves the programmer of this task. Again, he needs consider only the logic of processing the records in the file.

SPOOLing

A *buffer* is a data storage device used to receive output data from the central processing unit. The data are stored there until the output device on which the data are to be written becomes available for use. Similarly, input data coming from an input device will be stored in a buffer before entering the central processing unit. In this way, the central processing unit, which operates at speeds much greater than those possibly achieved by input/output devices, need not wait while these devices perform their operations. A buffer, then, as the term is used here, is a device that separates computer components (for example, central processing unit and input/output devices) that operate at different speeds so that the faster of the devices can continue operating while the slower devices perform their functions.

Large computer systems to which are attached many different kinds of input/output devices can effect more efficient operations if several of these devices can be operated at the same time. Because of the introduction of buffers into the system, the processing unit generally can continue executing while input/output operations are being performed; thus there is every reason to expect that the same process of buffering can permit the simultaneous operation of input/output devices and other kinds of peripheral equipment. Such operation is possible and is called *SPOOLing* (Simultaneous Peripheral Operation—On Line). SPOOLing is accomplished by IOCS through the programmed control of special hardware features that permit temporary storage of data in buffers and of instruction registers that permit IOCS to control the activities of the central processor in such a way as to provide minimum interference between it and the peripheral devices being operated. A computer system engaged in a SPOOLing operation has the appearance of performing many feats at once. Actually, the central processor is still only executing one instruction at a time, but the hardware features available to IOCS permit it to control the various peripheral devices quite independently of the processing unit when necessary.

As an example, consider a computer system to which are connected three on-line printers, each capable of printing 1,200 lines of information per minute. Together, these printers can print 60 lines of information every second. Let us assume, for the sake of simplicity, that the program being executed generates 60 lines of output data every second. A SPOOLing operation in this situation would require six buffers, two for each line printer. The first 60 lines of output would be stored in three buffers. After being thus stored, IOCS would cause the printing of the contents of these three buffers to commence. While this printing is going on, the processing unit would continue to execute the object program and would store the resulting data in the three buffers not being used by the printing operation. When the information contained in the first set of buffers is completely written, IOCS will cause the contents of the second set of buffers to be printed and the processing unit will now store the results of its continued processing in the first set again. In this way, both the processing unit and the printers are operating at top speed and there is no necessity

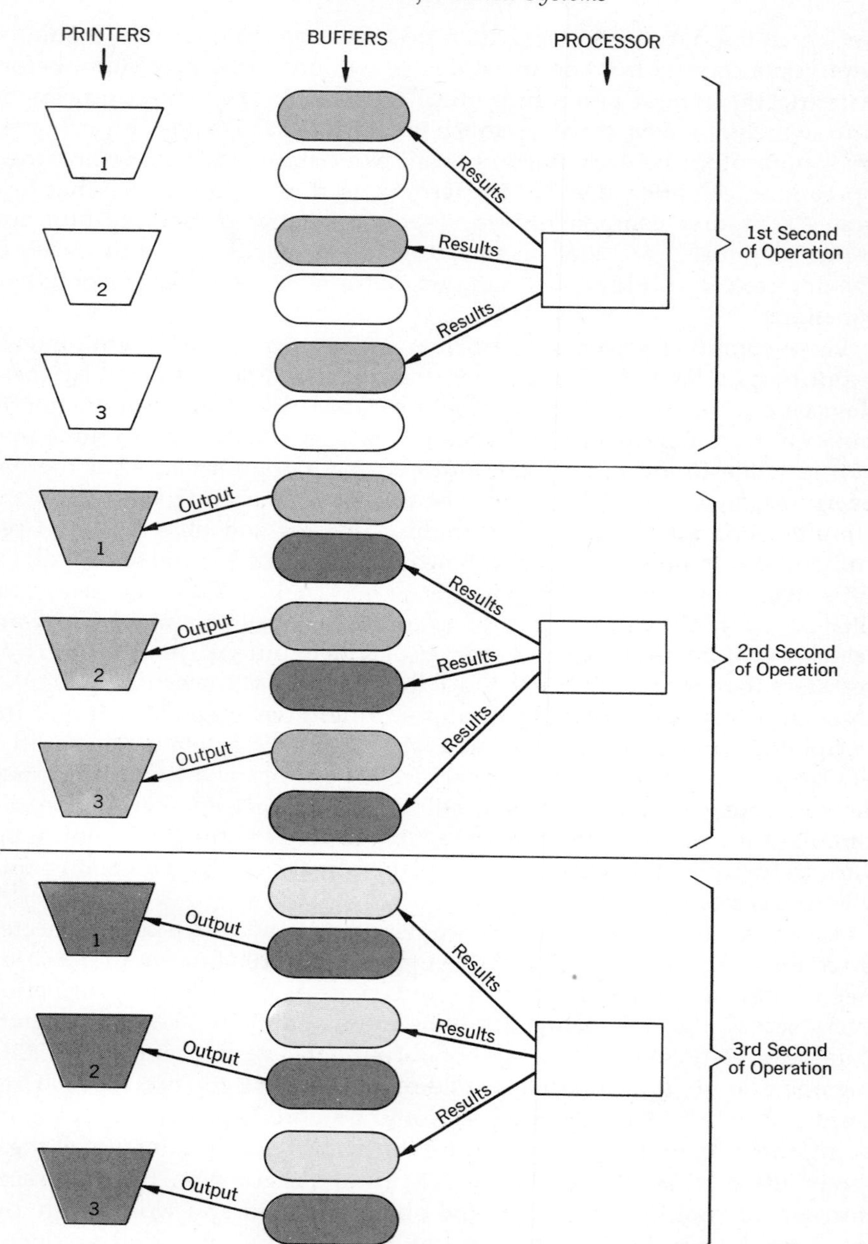

Figure 14–1. A SPOOLing operation.

for either to wait for the completion of the other's operation. Figure 14–1 illustrates this principle.

In actual situations, there is not perfect coordination between the activities of the processor and the peripheral equipment as in this example. However, even though both must frequently wait for each other, the operation described above is much more efficient in terms of throughput than if the SPOOLing of the printers and overlapping of the operation of the printers and processing unit were not possible.

IOCS Macro Statements

As we have observed, a programmer is interested in processing one logical record at a time, and his work is considerably simplified if IOCS can provide him with one such record when he calls for it and allow him to indicate through program coding when the processing of that record is complete so that it can be replaced into the file when necessary. IOCS includes provisions that permit programmers to do this without becoming concerned with details of input/output operations. These provisions are called macro statements and are of the type of macro instruction discussed in Chapter 13 on programming systems in that one such macro statement generates many machine language instructions. This concept is most easily understood pictorially. Consider Figure 14–2. Here, the monitor program, which controls the operating system, and IOCS are shown as being permanently in residence in main memory of the computer system. The object program, which is loaded into memory temporarily until its execution is completed, includes certain machine language IOCS link instructions which were generated during the compilation of the source program in response to IOCS macro statements written into the

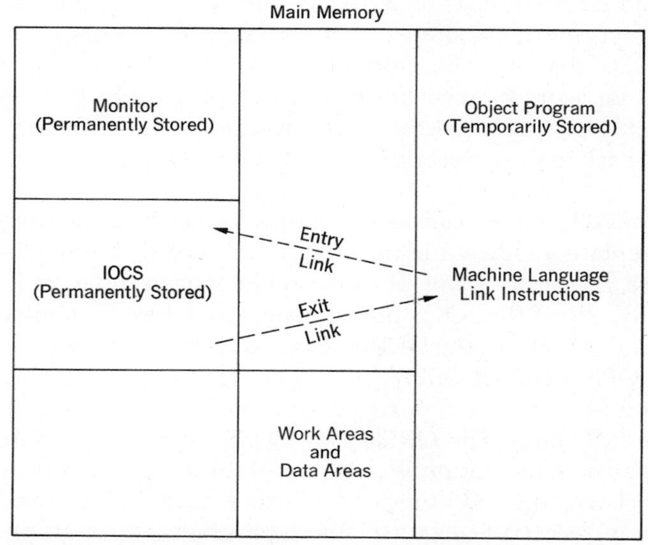

Figure 14–2. Memory utilization during processing of object program requiring IOCS.

source program by the programmer. There are four macro statements in common use with IOCS processors: GET, PUT, OPEN, and CLOSE.

GET. The GET macro, when processed by the IOCS processor during the compilation of the source program, generates instructions that cause a routine contained in the IOCS program to be executed; this program had been stored in memory during the loading of the object program. After the IOCS functions relating to reading a block of records into memory have been executed, control of the processing unit is returned to the object program. Look again at Figure 14–2; if the link instructions were the result of a GET macro in the source program, they would cause transfer of control, via the entry link, to a portion of the IOCS program that causes the performance of all the steps necessary to make one logical record available to the programmer for processing. Once this has been accomplished, the exit link established in the IOCS routine would return control to the object program.

For example, imagine that you are preparing a 1401 program to process records contained in a card file. Assuming that each card contains one logical record, your task as a programmer is to issue instructions to read a card, test to see if it is the last card, and perhaps program other manipulative routines. This might require several program instructions. However, using 1401 Autocoder with IOCS, your job as a programmer is simplified to issuing one instruction: GET CARD. When the source program you have written is processed, this macro instruction will cause a series of machine language instructions to be generated which will cause the computer to read a card and do all of the detailed checking and manipulation for you. Other, more elaborate computer systems and operating systems would require that the IOCS processor generate machine language instructions that would cause branching out of the object program into IOCS, which then preforms the necessary functions, and then control is transferred back to the object program. This is the situation in Figure 14–2.

PUT. The PUT macro causes generation of machine language instructions that replace a logical file into the file of records being processed. In cases where the records are blocked, reblocking is done automatically. Conceptually, all of the IOCS macro statements operate similarly. Thus, the remarks made about the GET macro above hold for the PUT macro, as well as for OPEN and CLOSE.

OPEN and CLOSE. The OPEN and CLOSE macros generate machine language instructions that provide for label checking and opening of a file and for label writing and other end-of-processing duties. Together, they provide some protection against object programs, through programmer error, inadvertently processing the wrong file since the GET and the PUT macros will not perform their function on a file unless the particular file called for has been first opened. Closing a file with the CLOSE macro prevents further processing of any record in the file until it has been opened again.

IOCS: A Hybrid System

The distinction between an operating system and a programming system lies in the purposes to which the systems are put. Operating systems are designed to control the computer system itself and consequently are more directly related to the hardware used in the system. Programming systems, on the other hand, are for the purpose of aiding the programmer by making the job of writing computer instructions more like that of writing English. IOCS, through its function of controlling input and output hardware devices, and because it frequently requires special hardware features built into the computer system itself, can be considered quite appropriately as a part of the operating system. On the other hand, since clearly the greatest value of IOCS lies in the ease with which it permits programmers to read and write records being processed, one might also consider it to be a programming system. In the final analysis, IOCS is a combination, or hybrid, system involving aspects of both kinds of systems. The categorizing of IOCS as an operating system, as we have done here, rather than as a programming system is purely academic.

Multiprogramming

Electronic computer systems consist of elements that operate at different speeds. As we have seen, a processing unit capable of executing several thousand program instructions per second may be coupled with output devices that can record the results of calculations at much slower speeds and with input devices able to provide data for calculations at speeds that do not begin to approach the ability of the processor to handle them. Because of the divergent speeds of the various computer system elements, buffering techniques have been developed to separate the operating devices from each other so as to allow each to operate at speed more closely approaching the optimum.

The efficiency with which a program is executed by a computer system is dependent not only upon the efficiency and coordination of the hardware, but also upon the nature of the program itself. Some programs require little calculation and great quantities of output, for example. Others might require considerable internal processing time, but a minimal amount of time to record the results of the processing. The first of these examples is a program typically called *I/O-bound*. By this, it is meant that the total throughput time required to process the program is limited by the speed of the input/output devices being used to record the output and to provide the input data to the processing unit. Other programs requiring considerable processing time are known as *process-bound* because their throughput time depends upon the internal speed of the processing unit. When an I/O-bound program is being executed, the processing unit spends a good deal of time waiting while the input/output devices perform their function. Similarly, when a process-bound program is being executed, input/output devices are standing idle much of the time. *Multiprogramming* is a feature of advanced operating systems which attempts to increase the general throughput of the computer system by executing more than one program at once. Ideally, the set of programs being executed together would contain a combination of process-bound and I/O-bound programs in such a way that both the processing unit and the input/output devices are operating at maximum speed. Thus, while the output device, say, is recording the results of the minimal calculations involved in the I/O-bound programs, the processor is executing a portion of the process-bound programs which does not require input or output functions. If two such programs are being executed together, it is clear that separate input/output devices are needed for each program. Computer systems so complex as to justify an operating system sophisticated enough to permit multiprogramming will be equipped with multiple input/output devices and the related hardware devices needed to control them.

Basically, multiprogramming operates as follows. An object program to be executed is loaded into memory. Let us assume that this is an I/O-bound program. Soon after execution starts, this program calls for some elaborate input/output operation. When this happens, the input/output devices involved are set to the required tasks, and another program is loaded into memory, say a process-bound program. The processing unit is then turned to the operations called for in this program; these will continue until the input/output devices have completed their functions for the I/O-bound program. When this happens, the I/O-bound program is reloaded into memory after the temporary results of the other program are stored away, and execution of the I/O-bound program continues until it again calls for input/output functions, at which time the transfer of programs in memory takes place again. The two programs in this example are not being executed simultaneously; rather, they each come to the attention of the processor in turn. The cycle described above may take place every two or three seconds or perhaps over longer intervals of time. The advantage gained is more effective use of the central processor because it can continue executing a program while waiting for the input/output devices to complete their operations. If the computer system's main memory is large enough or the programs to be executed small enough, or both, then both object programs can be stored in memory and control transferred from one to the other, thus precluding the necessity of loading and reloading each program in its turn. This, of course, would result in even more efficient throughput.

Multiprogramming works most ideally in a situation in which programs to be executed over a period of time, say, a few hours or a day, are indicated to the operating system and made available to it, together with their respective data, by on-line input/output devices. The operating system, provided with information as to the frequency and duration of input/output operations of each of the programs, is then in a position to schedule which programs are to be executed when and in combination with which other programs so as to maximize the system's throughput. Elaborate operating systems capable of coping with this type of operation are generally available for use with large computer systems.

Utility Systems

Usually under the control of the operating system or monitor there are a number of programs called utility programs or utility systems, the purpose of which is to perform basic data processing functions that are required in common by many different types of applications. These programs are briefly described below.

File Conversion Routines

Frequently, a file of data on a particular storage device requires storing or rewriting on another storage device. It may be desirable, for example, to rewrite a file that has in the past been stored in a card file on magnetic tape. Similarly, magnetic tape files may need to be written on magnetic disk, and so on. Programs are available from equipment manufacturers which perform these functions in standardized ways so that installations requiring such operations need not program them, but can, by adhering to standardized practices required by the programs, simply cause them to be executed upon the data requiring refiling.

Conversion programs have been prepared to provide conversion from any storage media to any other. The programmer need only indicate the format of the file to be converted and the format of the new file to be prepared. Such programs automatically provide record blocking when writing a tape or disk file; they can be instructed to generate card sequence numbering when preparing a card file; and in other ways they perform rather routine tasks needed to properly prepare a file for the storage medium.

Program Testing and Diagnosis

Even though prepared with meticulous care, programs usually contain errors that need to be corrected before the job of programming can be considered as completed. Program errors generally fall into three categories: programmer clerical errors, programmer logical errors, and, more rarely, equipment malfunction. Clerical errors are usually detected by the programming system used to translate the source program into machine language. Operating systems also include testing and diagnostic routines to help the programmer discover his logical errors and to provide for their correction, frequently without the necessity of recompilation. It is not within the scope of this book to dwell in detail as to how these work. However, two examples may illustrate their basic nature.

Some testing systems include a *trace program*, which causes the contents of the computer registers and other important information to be listed out after the execution of each machine language instruction in the object program. Such a listing is helpful to programmers in tracing through the logic of their programs to determine if the computer is really doing what they believe they instructed it to do. Many test systems include *storage print routines* and processor halts, which cause the contents of the computer memory to be listed out from time to time during the execution of the object program and to cause the execution of the object program to halt from time to time to permit console inquiry as to the contents of certain memory locations and registers. Again, these functions permit the programmer to check on the progress of the object program during various stages of its execution, thus permitting comparisons to be made between the programmer's understanding of the logic of his program and the logic that is actually performed by the computer.

Housekeeping Routines

Everything that a computer does is in response to instructions received, either from a stored program or from instructions entered from a console device such as a typewriter or a set of console switches. Before the execution of some programs, it is often necessary to prepare the computer by clearing its memory to blanks or zeros. Programs must be loaded into memory by the computer, which during the operation is executing a program that causes the loading. It is necessary from time to time to cause the contents of the computer's memory to be printed out for program checkout purposes. This printing is also accomplished by the computer through the execution of a set of instructions. Most manufacturers provide to computer users programs to perform mundane tasks such as these and make them available in the software package or operating system. Their purpose is to make the day-to-day operation of the computer easier without the necessity of excessive console manipulation or program writing.

Sort Systems

Sort systems are programs designed to sequentially order records in a file by some key. A file of employee records, for example, may require ordering by employee number for some applications, by employee name in another. Sort systems are provided as part of programming systems to aid in the arranging of data by sorting without requiring very much programming. A programmer need only identify the field by which the records are to be sorted and the rest of the sorting task is left almost entirely to the operating system.

Sorting is such an important data processing activity that there are few computer systems designed today that do not include a generalized sort system in the basic software package.

Emulation

The advent of third-generation computers brought with it the problem of program conversion from programs to be executed on the old system to programs to be executed on the new third-generation systems. Computer installations with thousands of operating programs written and debugged for one computer system face monumental expenses involved in rewriting their programs so as to be able to use the new computers. One way to solve this problem involves writing programs, much like source language compilers, to translate programs written for one machine into programs that could be executed by a different computer.

Another way involves designing hardware features of the new computers which can be used with special programs to cause the new computer to behave as if it were another computer and therefore be capable of executing programs written for the older computer. This technique is known as *emulation,* wherein one computer, through software and hardware combined, is made to behave as if it were another computer. *Emulation* should not be confused with *simulation,* which does essentially the same thing but is strictly a software feature and does not involve any special hardware configuration or features as is the case with emulation. Simulation, furthermore, is usually a slow process; that is, an IBM 1401 program executed on an IBM 1620 computer will take considerably longer than the same program executed on the 1401 for which it was originally written. Emulation, on the other hand, because of the high processing speeds of third-generation computers, permits more rapid execution of programs than is possible on the equipment for which the program was originally written. Many programs, for example, written for the IBM 1401 take two and one-half times as long to execute on the 1401 than on the IBM System/360 with a 1401 emulator.

Operating Systems and the Third-Generation Computers

The incredibly high speed of third-generation computers makes it essential that these machines be designed to operate with a minimum of necessary computer operator functions. Because of this, most manufacturers of third-generation equipment have gone to great lengths to develop and make available to users of this equipment elaborate operating systems that make the job of production little more than indicating which programs are to be executed and assuring that the data called for by these programs are available to the computer system.

The first third-generation computer to be announced and the most widely used of this variety of computer system is the IBM System/360, which really is not a computer but rather is a family of computers, each with different capabilities and uses. System/360 computers are the most widely used of the third-generation computers, and it may be of value at this point to describe the operating systems available with this equipment as an example of the range of duties and functions of modern operating systems.

There are two general types of operating systems available to System/360 users: Operating System/360(OS), and Basis Operating System (BOS). Also available are DOS (Disk Operating System) and TOS (Tape Operating System), which will be used extensively in hardware systems oriented around disk and tape input/output devices. BOS is primarily for use with System/360 computers with relatively small memory capacity, that is, between 8,000 and 32,000 bytes of memory (a byte is a group of eight binary digits). OS is available for larger machines (up to 1,024,000 bytes of main memory) and can, as one would expect, perform more elaborate functions.

Operating systems for the System/360, furthermore, are characterized by special modifications and versions for various models in the System/360 series; these are shown in Figure 14–3. In addition to the 8K and 16K Basic Operating System and the Operating System/360, there are special versions of operating systems for the Model 20, a card processing computer for smaller business applications, and the Model 44, a fast, low-cost model primarily for scientific use. Across the top of the figure, Basic Programming Support is an operating system, the primary purpose of which is to make the processors available for certain languages. This type of processor, like BOS, is useful mainly with smaller models of System/360. The full operating system, or OS, becomes available only to users of 64K machines or larger and provides the full range of features available on this family of computers. 16K computers have available 16K BOS, which also provides all of the features if disk storage devices are used. Model 20, 44, and 67 are more specialized members of the family and are able to provide limited operating system service. The Model 67 Time Sharing System will offer language processors in a *conversational mode*. By this it is meant that programmers or others who wish a program to be executed can present their program to the computer system via an on-line terminal device in a manner that gives the appearance of talking to the computer system and receiving answers back. This is described in more detail in Chapter 15, Real-Time Systems.

	Basic Programming Support	Basic Operating System (8K)	Basic Operating System (16K)	Operating System/360	Model 20 Support	Model 44 Support	Model 67 Time-Sharing System
Assembler	x	x	x	x	x	x	x*
Fortran IV	x		x	x		x	x*
Cobol			x	x			x
PL/1			x	x			x*
RPG	x	x	x	x	x		
Utilities	x	x	x	x	x	x	
Sort/Merge	x	x	x	x	x		x
Tele-Processing			x**	x			x
Control Program		x	x	x		x	x

*Conversational

**16K Disk Only

Figure 14–3. IBM System/360 operating systems.

The various features of the operating systems available to System/360 users range from Assembly language processors to Teleprocessing as shown in Figure 14–3. Processors are available for five different programming languages including a machine-oriented processor, 360 Assembler Language, procedure-oriented languages, Fortran IV, COBOL, and PL/1, and problem-oriented languages, RPG, and SORT/MERGE. In addition, teleprocessing is available in five out of the seven available systems. The control program shown on the bottom of Figure 14–3 is a program in the operating system which relocates programs being executed to different areas of main memory to better facilitate multiprogramming and allows for more flexible selection of monitor functions and library control.

Figure 14–4 illustrates the conceptual organization of the 16K Basic Operating System. At the top of the figure, the control program is shown controlling the activities of the supervisor, which otherwise is in control of the operating system. The supervisor and control program work together to schedule loading and relocation of programs to be executed into the main memory of the system. The supervisor also controls the flow of jobs into the system, SPOOLing, and teleprocessing. The supervisor makes available to the central processing unit the service facilities, language processors, sorting routines, program testing routine, and the various utilities. The housekeeping programs available in this system are shown as part of the utilities as initializing programs.

The foregoing discussion does not attempt to provide a full understanding of System/360 operating systems, but it does provide an illustration of how a modern operating system is organized and of the relationship between the supervisor and the various programs and routines under its control. Figure 14–5 represents how operating systems and resident programs are arranged in primary and secondary memory.

Man Still the Master

In recent years, the development of operating systems has taken a leading role in the continued development of electronic data processing. Because of the developmental efforts in this area, electronic data processing is acquiring an intensified aura of sorcery and mystification. From its outward appearance, a large computer system operating under control of an operating system looks a great deal like an electronic brain under its own control, choosing which jobs to perform, rejecting some because of errors it has discovered, instructing the human operator to mount tapes, set switches and change paper, writing error diagnostics to programmers, and in other ways behaving in a dictatorial manner. This has prompted some to envision humans as soon becoming the slaves of their computing machines, doing their bidding rather than the reverse. This fear can be quickly resolved by recognizing that the operating system is a product of man's

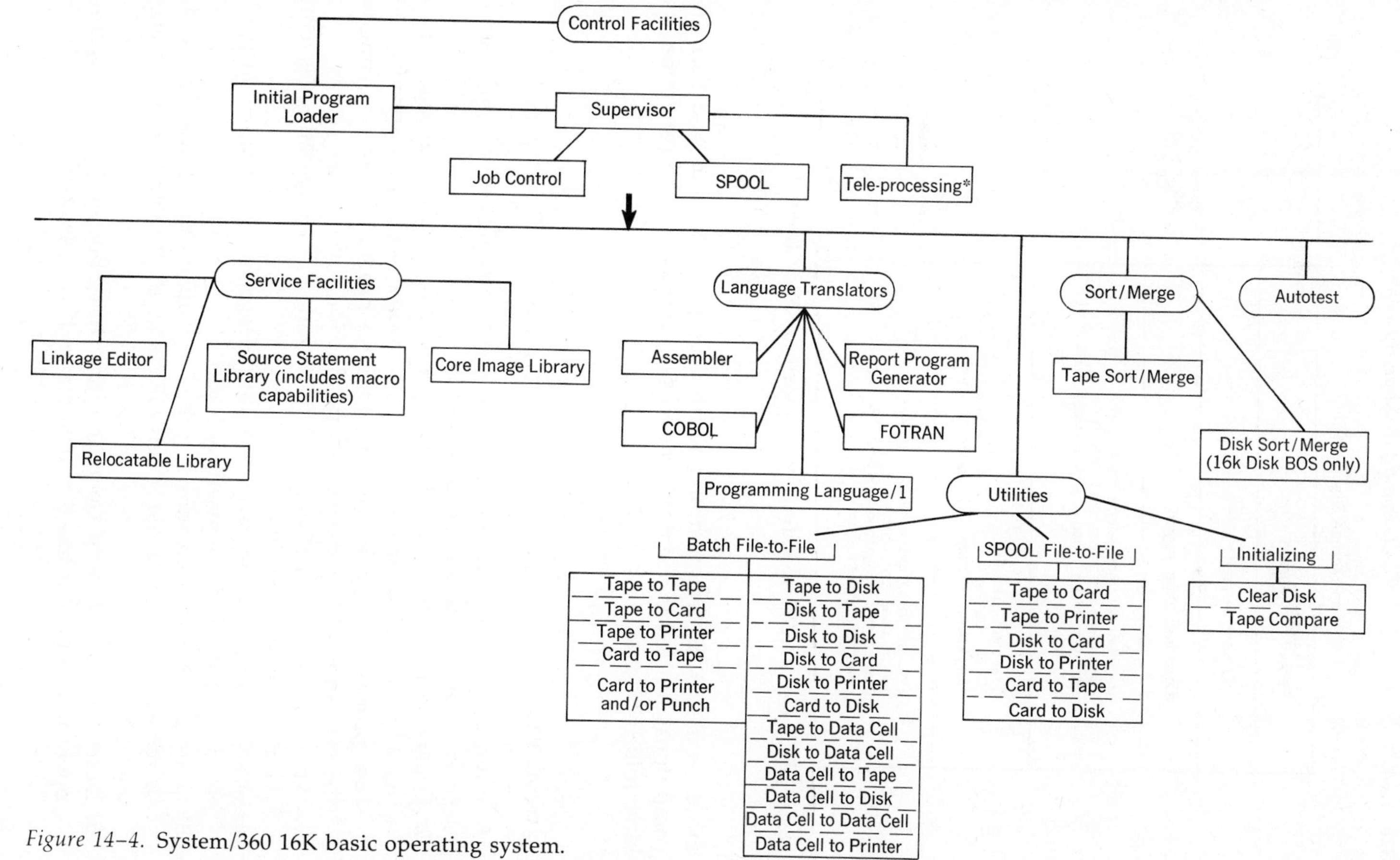

Figure 14–4. System/360 16K basic operating system.

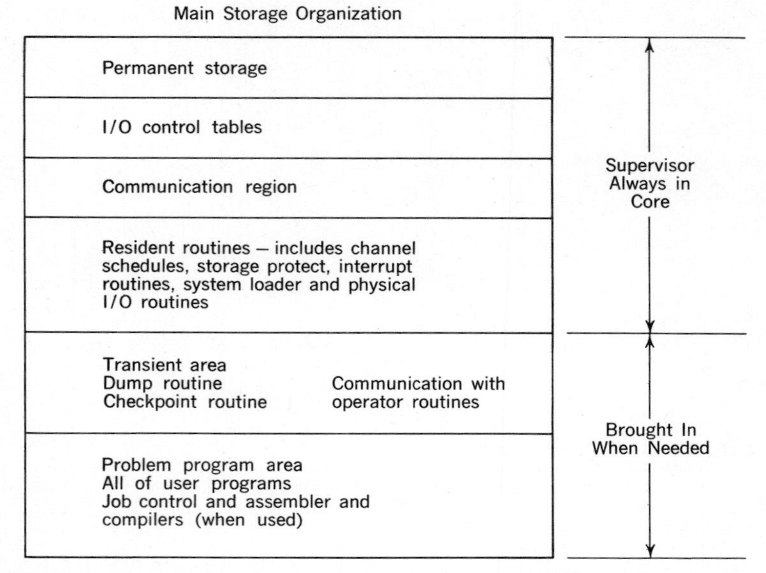

Figure 14–5. System/360 operating system memory allocation.

mind, is a system designed and written by programmers, and that the computer is limited in what it can do to what it is that the programmers have told it to do.

Questions

1. What can programmers do to reduce the amount of *computer* time spent in program check-out operations?
2. Draw a systems flow chart depicting the major steps and decisions that must be made in interrupting the execution of a computer production run, processing and testing a new source program, then returning to the execution of the interrupted production run.
3. What are the two types of programs included in an operating system? What are their functions?
4. Draw a picture of the various input, output, and work areas in main memory that would be used by IOCS.
5. Draw a block diagram showing the basic operations of IOCS on a file of records to be updated when GET and PUT instructions are executed.
6. Describe a SPOOLing operation that uses both input and output operations and that has five printers and five card readers.

7. Explain the difference between I/O-bound processing and processor-bound processing.
8. Explain the use and value of placing a control card in front of a source deck when loading a program for execution.
9. What is the function of a monitor program?
10. Give an example of a physical record and explain its relationship to logical records.

15

Real-Time Systems

Imagine that you are depositing your monthly pay check at a bank teller's window. Your wife, unknown to you, perhaps, is at another window presenting to that teller a check against your joint checking account for a large sum. The teller serving your wife checks the account to determine if there are sufficient funds to cover the withdrawal and, as there has not been time enough to record the deposit you have just made, returns to your wife with the news that she cannot have the money. Legally, your wife has every right to demand the money she knows is in the account because of your recent deposit. Yet, because of the time delay in processing the information that your deposit has been made to the account, the bank is unable to determine accurately how much is actually on deposit and therefore is unable to serve you as efficiently as it might want to. Most banks would be unable to account for the deposit until the following morning after all the deposits and all the withdrawals for the day had been processed in a *batch*.

One way for a bank to provide up-to-the-minute information about any one of perhaps thousands of accounts is to design a system in which the tellers record in the accounts each deposit or withdrawal—that is, each *transaction*—as it is made. Done manually, this would be a time-consuming procedure in which tellers would spend more time adjusting accounts than waiting on customers, and in which each customer would have to wait while his account was updated before his transaction was completed. This manual process could be accelerated by the introduction of a telephone at each teller's window and clerks to record transactions into the accounts as reported to them by the tellers over the telephones.

At this point the bank manager might wonder if the increased customer service of this *direct access processing* technique is worth the increased cost over the previous batch processing methods. More clerks are needed, customers still must wait longer for each transaction than when batch processing techniques were used and voice transmission of data over the telephone is significantly more error prone. Today's data processing technology permits further savings and efficiencies. The clerks and the accounts they keep can be replaced by direct access devices we have discussed in Chapter 11. The telephones might be replaced by keyboard devices which allow tellers to key in the information to be used to update a customer's account. Indeed, one can imagine optical scanning devices which can read the information presented to them by depositors and cause updating to take place without tellers. Other machines can dispense cash to customers after data files are consulted for status with respect to funds on deposit. These input/output and storage devices would be, of course, controlled by a central processing unit, or computer.

The elimination of tellers and clerks and the improved customer service provided by this system are more likely to justify the increased costs of the system over the old batch methods. Customers now wait even less time than previously and records are more accurately kept since the number of humans, with their propensities to err, who handle the data is reduced. Moreover, with customer accounts always kept up-to-the-minute, the bank is better able to handle its own financial affairs because it has a better grasp on its most important liability—depositors' accounts. The system described above—and it is not unlike those used in some progressive banks today—is known as a *real-time system.* A depositor writes a check or withdrawal slip, presents it to the system—either to a human or to a device able to read the withdrawal document he has prepared—his accounts are checked and updated, and the cash he wants to withdraw, assuming sufficient funds in his account and proper identification, is presented to him a few seconds after he initiates the transaction.

Real-Time Defined

Real-Time Systems

The term *real-time* is most closely associated with immediacy. In the example above, the depositors' accounts are updated immediately as transactions involving their accounts occur. Thus, a real-time system is one in which data presented to the system is processed immediately upon receipt and the results of the processing made immediately available for further use. Clearly, in order to appreciate the meaning of real-time, a definition of *immediate* is needed. Immediacy in real-time systems is measured in terms of *response time*—the amount of time that elapses between the presentation of a transaction to the system and the completion of the processing of that transaction, including the output of results. Response times range from 0.1 microseconds to over 15 minutes. As might be expected, the response time needed for some applications of real-time systems is not the same as for others. A bank depositor might be satisfied to wait ten or twenty seconds for his deposit receipt, while such a delay in firing a retrorocket on an orbiting space capsule could be disastrous. However, both of these applications are properly called real-time. Some authorities envision degrees of real-time: "Real-time is a matter of degree, with the system becoming less real-time the longer it takes for a response."[1] Probably, however, it is more useful to consider a real-time system as one in which the response to the presented transaction is soon enough to permit appropriate action based on the response and which treats each transaction individually or with a minimum of batching consistent with the desired response time per transaction.

Real-Time Operation

The Federal Bureau of the Budget defines a real-time operation as follows:

> The use of the computer as an element of a processing system in which the times of occurrence of data transmission are controlled by other portions of the system or by physical events outside the system, and cannot be modified for convenience in computer programming. Such an operation either proceeds at the same speed as the events being simulated or at a sufficient speed to analyze or control external events happening concurrently.[2]

This definition points up another feature of real-time systems. Because the system is controlled by a computer that in turn is controlled by a program, the controlling program must not be changed as a matter of routine once the system is implemented. It is easy to imagine writing a computer program to batch-process the day's transactions and perhaps to change the program as frequently as new situations arise in the processing application. In this manner, program changes may be thought of as routine and expected. In a real-time operation, however, the program is *not* to be changed in a routine fashion; users of the system must conform completely to the system, and the system must be able to cope with every conceivable situation arising from the transactions presented to it.

Thus, in our bank example, the program controlling the system must be able to respond appropriately whatever the nature of the transaction presented to it: a depositor attempting to overdraw his account, a nondepositor attempting to withdraw funds fraudulently, a depositor whose name and account number are inconsistent because he is erroneously depositing funds to the wrong account, and many other situations. This draws attention to current thinking about real-time systems and the future. Some observers of automation anticipate the day when machines may take over all or most of the commercial functions now performed by humans. Although this may in large part be true, the fact remains that it is impos-

[1] "Real-Time Overview," *Automatic Data Processing Newsletter*, The Diebold Group, Inc., X (August 16, 1965).

[2] Executive Office of the President, Bureau of the Budget, *Automatic Data Processing Glossary*, U.S. Government Printing Office, 1965, p. 67.

sible for a programmer who is preparing the controlling program for a real-time system such as the one in our bank example to foresee all the possible transactions and combination of transactions that will be presented to the system. There will always be a need for humans to handle exceptional transactions: the good customer who has the bank president's permission to overdraw his account for a few days as a short-term interest-free loan; the customers who do not remember their account numbers but who nevertheless have the legal right to withdraw funds they have on deposit; and countless other situations that cannot be adequately anticipated.

Real-Time Systems Versus Conventional Systems

The most significant difference between a real-time system and a conventional system is set forth in the definition of a real-time system: transactions presented to the system are processed immediately and the results are made available soon enough to have an immediate effect upon the situation that initiated them. Until the mid-1960's, most automated data processing systems employed batch-processing techniques in which transactions were collected over time—days or weeks—and were then processed all at once. Customer billing, payroll calculations and checks, production reports, and the like were scheduled time on the processing system, and during this time were processed all the transactions that had been gathered since the last scheduled "run." In our bank example, the day's transactions—deposits and withdrawals—were collected during the day and run at the end of the day, thus updating all customer accounts at once rather than treating them individually as transactions occurred. More often than not, the transactions were processed against a master file, say, of customer checking accounts or of employee payroll records, and the master file was kept on a sequential storage device such as magnetic tape. Transactions had to be sorted into the same sequence as the master file and as the master records were read sequentially from the file, any transactions affecting that record were processed and the updated record stored back in sequence.

With the increased use of direct-access devices such as magnetic disk it becomes more feasible to process each transaction as it occurs rather than to batch a number of transactions for processing all at once at a later time. However, there is no physical reason why individual treatment cannot be given to each transaction even though the master file is stored on a sequential device. The master file would have to be read sequentially until the desired record is found. Then the transaction can be processed and the master file can then be sequentially searched for the master record, for the next transaction. However, at computer speeds, this physical searching of a master file stored sequentially is relatively time-consuming. Better computer utilization is achieved with a sequentially accessed master file if the transactions are batched and processed in the same order as the master record.

Direct-access devices give the data processing system the ability to process transactions as they occur while at the same time minimizing the amount of time needed to search the master file for the appropriate record. Thus, since real-time systems involve immediate and individual treatment of transactions (although some amount of batching may be acceptable, depending upon the system's response time requirements), they operate on a direct processing basis, whereas conventional systems operate generally in a batch-processing manner.

There are other important differences between real-time systems and conventional systems. Real-time systems are typically larger than conventional systems both from a hardware and from a software standpoint. The program controlling a real-time system may include hundreds of thousands of program instructions, which may have taken hundreds of man-years to develop. The memory size needed to handle programs of this magnitude is considerably larger than those needed for more conventional applications. The largest computer systems ever conceived have been of the real-time variety and include such well-known computer configurations as the BMEWS (Ballistic Missile Early Warning System), the Project Mercury system used to control space shots, and SABRE, a system used for airline seat reservations.

Real-time systems are, furthermore, more complex than their conventional cousins. As will be discussed later, a real-time system frequently involves quite complex aggregations of data processing and communications hardware as well as complex programs to control the system.

Finally, real-time systems can be considered to be the next step in the evolution of electronic data processing techniques—the fourth generation. Some see the future of electronic data processing as involving computers with billions of characters of direct-access data operating on a real-time basis to handle problems which, because of their complexity, are out of reach of today's most capable system. Even now, real-time systems are handling data processing problems of a much more vital and dynamic nature than those with which conventional systems could hope to cope. Control of manned satellites, moon rockets, intercontinental ballistic missiles and of enemy aircraft warning systems are a few of the current applications.

Development of Real-Time Systems

Prior to the development of mechanical techniques of data processing, data processing was accomplished manually, using a system which today we might call direct-access processing. Human clerks, best characterized perhaps by Dickens' Bob Cratchett, sitting at high desks wearing eye shades and sleeve protectors processed each transaction as it was presented to the system. Some efficiencies might be enjoyed through specialization of labor and consequently the introduction on a limited scale of batch processing. Basically a direct access system, this could hardly qualify as a real-time system because of the lack of immediacy of results.

The introduction of hardware to speed the processing of data on a batch basis, while increasing data processing efficiency in terms of man-hours expended, actually removed it further from the ideal situation in which the results of a transaction are available as soon after the event as needed. During the first half of the twentieth century, batch processing was the rule in automated data processing. The development of direct access processing and the development of data communication techniques were both essential to the realization of real-time systems. In our bank example, the ability to reach a customer's account record individually without the necessity of searching through the entire file of accounts and the telephone link between the teller and the clerk processing the accounts were both important aspects of the improved system. Furthermore, when replacing the account clerk with a computer which also serves to control the entire system, we require that the computer be linked to the communication system as well as to the data. Thus, we see that three technological advances were needed to support the development of real-time systems: direct access data storage devices; direct linkage between the computer and the communications system; and communication terminal devices into which transactions are entered. In our example, the terminal devices were telephones. However, we noted that voice transmission is prone to human error. Other terminal devices have been perfected which allow for much greater accuracy. It should also be recognized that this rather complex system must be controlled by a program. Thus, the necessity for advanced programming techniques to produce the software needed by real-time systems is also an important feature of the development of real-time systems.

Technological advances are never made just for the sake of developing more complex methods of doing things. These developments would not have taken place had there not been the need to find a better way to solve industry's data processing problems. While batch processing techniques and its technological advances increased the ability to speed up the processing of data, the amount of data to be processed increased at a faster rate than the ability to process it. For example, the number of bank demand depositors rose from 27 million in 1939 to 47 million in 1957. Three and a half billion checks were written in 1939, 12 billion in 1957, and it is expected that by 1970 22 billion checks a year will have to be processed by the nation's banks.[3] Every business, large or small, has felt a similar

[3] R. S. Aldom, *et. al., Automation In Banking*, New Brunswick, New Jersey: Rutgers University Press, 1963, p. 13.

impact with respect to the amount of information that must be processed and the new techniques that must be used to do the job in order for the business to maintain a competitive footing in terms of efficient data processing and consequent lower operating costs. More and more businesses can be expected to turn to real-time systems—that is, data processing systems directly connected to a data communications network. In 1965, about 1 per cent of all computers in use were linked to a communications network in a real-time system. It is estimated that by 1975, when roughly four times as many dollars worth of computers will be installed as in 1965, 60 per cent of all computers will be so linked.

The first large-scale real-time system operational in the United States was a system, made operational in 1964, called AUTODIN (Automatic Digital Network). Developed by Western Union for the Department of Defense, it was at that time the world's largest digital communications network, linking more than 300 stations for transmission of data by magnetic tape, punched cards, and automatic sending and receiving devices. A more recent real-time system extending over a considerable geographic area is the American Stock Exchanges Am-Quote system, which makes information about security prices and transactions available in voice form to telephone inquiries. This system translates digital information into verbal information using an on-line limited-word vocabulary. It is able to handle 72,000 telephone inquiries per hour on any of the 1,100 securities traded on the American Exchange.

Types of Function

There are three fairly clearly defined functions that real-time systems can perform: problem-solving, record-keeping, and process-control.

Problem-Solving Systems

The objective of a problem-solving real-time system is to allow users of a computer to enjoy its use with about the same ease as with a desk calculator. Usually, this type of system is thought of as most useful to the scientist or engineer, who looks upon a computer as a computational device to be used as a tool to help him solve his problems. Using a variety terminal device, the individual user is able to present a program to the computer system and within seconds receive the results. The terminal device might be a typewriter into which the user types his information, and from which is typed the results of the calculations; it might be a cathode ray tube display unit, a card reader, or any one of many such terminal devices.

The key to this system is the *shared-time* basis under which all the users operate. Connected to the main computer may be many terminal devices.

Figure 15–1. On-line terminal devices used in real-time systems. *(Courtesy, IBM)*

A user approaching one of the devices expects to be able to enter his problem and with minimal time lapse have the results returned to him. However, while he is entering his problem, other users at other terminals are also entering problems or have entered them and are waiting for the results. They, of course, also expect quick service from the system; that is, they expect a short *turn-around* time. Turn-around time is the amount of time required to reverse the direction of data transmission in a communication channel—that is, the time lapse between entering a problem or transaction into the system and receiving the results. Each of these users is satisfied by the system through the use of a technique known as *multiplexing*, or *commutating*. A multiplexing operation is one in which a device termed a *multiplexor*, or *line control computer*, consults each on-line terminal device to determine whether a transaction is there and ready to be transmitted into the system. This process is known as *polling* the terminals. Each terminal is allocated a certain amount of time at regularly established intervals (measured in thousandths of a second) to process the problem entered from that terminal. The multiplexor, then, is a device that allocates a small amount of computer time to each terminal that is receiving a problem. Since the computer is able to perform calculations very quickly, in some cases millions of calculations per second, each user at a terminal may consider himself to be the only user of the computer even though there may be many other users simultaneously at different terminals who have the same impression. Thus each terminal has access to a high-powered computer on a time-shared basis. The *time slice* made available to each terminal is very small, but the computer operates at such speed that the wait between time slices is also very small, and a user at a terminal has effective exclusive use of the computer.

An example of a problem-solving real-time system is IBM's SHARE system in which as many as 40 users have access to a centrally located large-scale computer through on-line terminals. Each user has storage space made available to him in a magnetic disk file and when operating his terminal device is totally unaware whether or not the other 39 customers are using the computer. Each user has available to him the computing power of a very large, expensive system, yet pays only a small portion of the cost of maintaining the system since he shares its use with many others. Users of such a system may be wide-spread geographically. Figure 15–2 illustrates how one computer can serve many users in remote locations.

Educational institutions are developing time-sharing techniques to provide students and researchers computer time on an immediate basis. In this case, students use the computer to solve problems or perhaps as a study aid through the use of computerized lesson plans much like programmed textbooks. At the same time researchers solve problems and the school administration schedules classroom assignments and does other administrative tasks. None of these three sets of users are noticeably delayed in their work because they share the use of the computer.

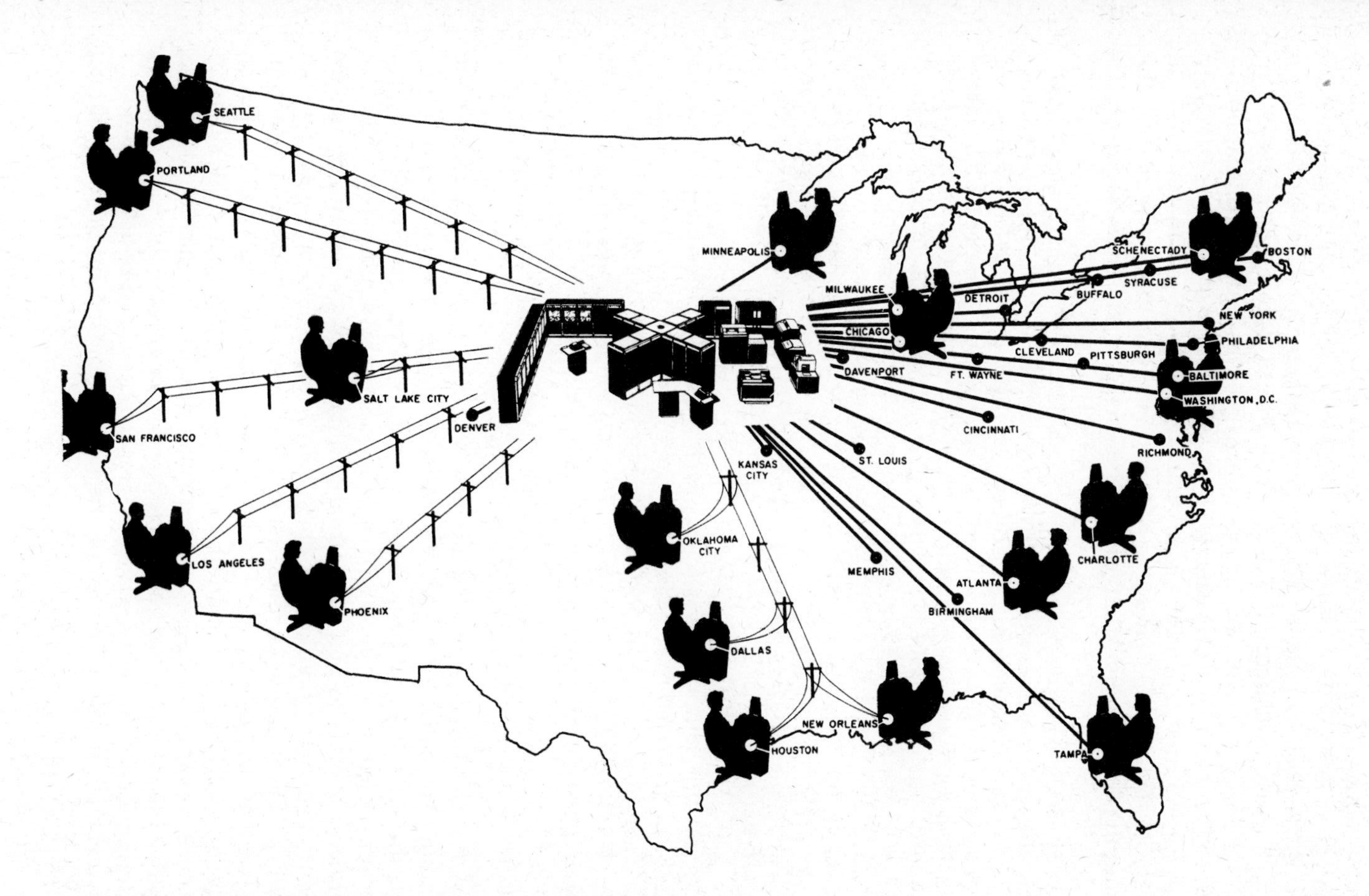

Figure 15–2. Shared-Time system. *(Courtesy, The Diebald Group, Inc.)*

One educational system using the shared-time approach to make a General Electric 235 computer available to students and researchers is the DATANET-30 system at Dartmouth University. This system makes use of a technique becoming common in shared-time applications known as *conversational mode.* As its name implies, this mode of operation involves the user in conversation with the computing system; the computer asks for information and the user provides it as required. In the following example, Figure 15–3 shows in italics the information provided by the computer and in bold-face type, the information replied by the user.

> Briefly, what occurs is this. The user dials a number which connects him to the computer installation. When the connection is established, he types, "HELLO." The computer then requests his user number which he types in reply. This is followed by the computer asking for the name of the language system which the user wishes. In this case, he answers "ALGOL." In [Figure 15–3], it should be noted that the underlining is for illustration only. The computer does not underline its portion of the conversation.
>
> The computer follows language determination by asking the user if he wishes to write a new program or recall a "saved" one. In this case the user desires an old program already on file. The computer asks its name. The user supplies it. The computer then retrieves this program from disk storage and states that it is "READY."[4]

This kind of computer system has exciting possibilities for the future. It has been predicted that in time, putting the computation power of a large-scale computer to use through remote terminals will be as common in the future as telephone usage is today. The development of real-time problem-solving systems is a major step in this direction.

Record-Keeping Systems

A record-keeping real-time system is one in which many records are maintained with a minimum of calculation for any one transaction affecting the records. Our bank example is a real-time system of this type. Another such system now in use is known as Telecredit. Telecredit is a service available to businesses that maintain a check-cashing service for their customers. Frequently, these businessmen are plagued by bad checks. Leasing the Telecredit system for between $75 and $300 per month, they have available to them records of fraudulent check-passers, stolen checks, and other information that helps them determine the safety of cashing a particular check for a particular individual. Basically, the system works like this. A cashier at a supermarket, drug store, or other business offering a check-cashing service is presented a check by a customer. The cashier dials a direct-line telephone to a centralized information bureau

[4] John W. Weil, "The Impact of Time Sharing on Data Processing Management," *DPMA Quarterly*, II (January 1966), p. 1.

```
HELLO
USER NUMBER--X86589
SYSTEM--ALGOL
NEW OR OLD?-OLD
OLD PROBLEM NAME--QUEUE
READY.

620 CONFIDENCE FACTOR := .26;
RUN


QUEUE     13:15     TUES.     8/17/65

DARTMOUTH ALGOL.

JOB SHOP SCHEDULE ANALYSIS

ENTER JOB IDENTIFICATION ? 35
ENTER PRESENT STATION NUMBER FOR JOB  35  ?  6
ENTER NUMBER OF HOURS JOB 35 HAS BEEN AT STATION  6?  1.25

JOB NUMBER 35  WILL BE COMPLETED IN  12.75 HOURS
WITH 80 PERCENT CONFIDENCE.


TIME = 2 SECS.


GOODBYE

*** OFF AT 13.18.
```

Figure 15–3. Conversational mode computer input/output. (Courtesy of DPMA Quarterly.)

maintained by Telecredit. Over the telephone, he relates information about the check and about the customer and his identification to a clerk at the Telecredit office. The clerk types this information into an on-line typewriter. A computer, receiving this information, searches its information files which are maintained on magnetic disk. If the check is stolen, or if the customer is a fugitive criminal or otherwise a high risk, the computer relates this information to the clerk who passes it on to the cashier. If there is no derogative or negative information about the check or customer, the cashier is thus informed and is then better able to decide to cash or not to cash the check.

Record-keeping real-time systems as small as that in our bank example or as large as that in the Telecredit system promise a wide variety of uses in industry: inventory records for manufacturers, customer records for retail stores, personnel records for all kinds of businesses, student records for school districts, and many other similar applications. These systems all have certain characteristics common to record-keeping systems: they involve storage of large numbers of records in a file and require a minimum amount of calculation for each inquiry about a record.

Process-Control Systems

The objective of a process-control system is to control or monitor an industrial process such as petroleum refining, papermaking, or other continuous-process manufacturing technique. There are two varieties of process-control systems: open loop and closed loop. The simplest type of open loop process-control system is shown in Figure 15–4. In this process, pieces of steel moving along a conveyor are being milled to a specific thickness. After the steel moves under the milling head, a feeler attached to a dial indicator—a simple analog computer—measures the thickness of the steel. The machine operator consults the dial indicator and compares the measurement he reads there with the measurements required by the job he is doing. If it is not satisfactory, he adjusts the controls until it is. This example illustrates the basic elements of an open loop system: a continuous process, a measuring device, and an operator to whom the measurement information is presented and who takes action based upon that information.

The chief difference between an open-loop system and a closed-loop system lies in the method of implementing needed corrections to the process. In the open-loop example above, corrections were made by an operator who adjusted controls in accordance with information provided him by the computer. A closed-loop system performing the same milling operation eliminates the need of an operator by the introduction of devices that compare the actual measurement with the desired measurement, calculate the required correction and adjust the controls as necessary to bring the cutting head into the appropriate height for the desired thickness. This type of process-control system is an example of automation (which, incidentally, is a word coined by John Diebold, the founder of a

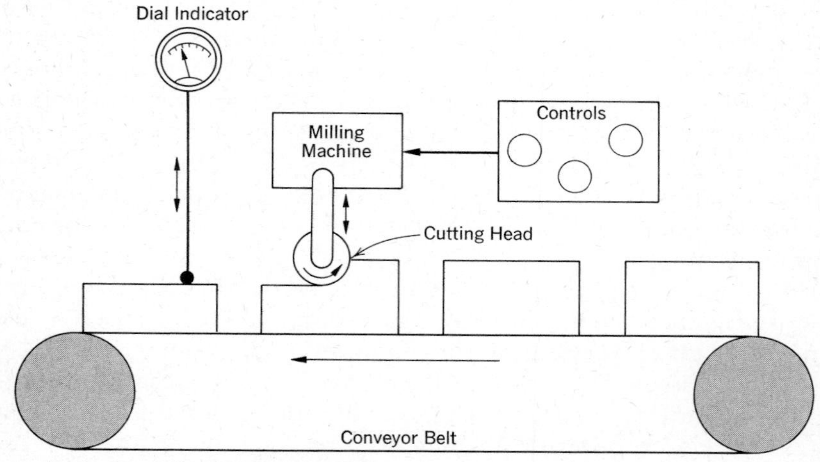

Figure 15–4. Open-loop control system.

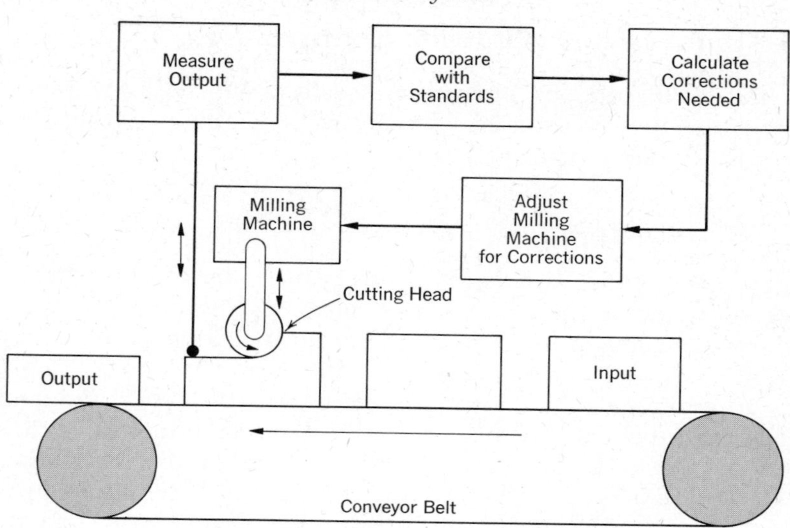

Figure 15–5. Closed-loop control system.

management consulting service devoted to automated business techniques). The essences of a closed-loop system and therefore of automation is the *feedback loop.* Figure 15–5 shows the feedback loop of our continuous milling operation as composed of the measuring device, a comparing unit, a correction calculator, and a correction maker. It can be seen that the nature of a feedback loop is such that the output of a process is measured and this measurement information is fed back into the process in such a way that the nature of the output is controlled automatically with minimal need for human adjustments.

Thus, the difference between an open-loop process-control system and a closed-loop process-control system, that is, the difference between a nonautomated process and an automated process, is one of feedback with human intervention (open-loop) or feedback without human intervention (closed-loop/automation). In an open-loop system, the computer indicates to an operator, by typewriter, indicator, or other display devices guides for more efficient operation. In a closed-loop process-control system, the computer itself effects the necessary corrections.

In general, process-control systems have been widely introduced in a variety of industries. The picture of a factory that is completely automated —a picture that frightens labor leaders as much as it delights factory managers—is one which depends entirely on the closed-loop process-control system. The realization of this dream (or nightmare) is still to be looked forward to and will require technological advances surpassing those now available.

Real-Time Systems Hardware Configurations

Hardware configurations in real-time systems can be categorized into four basic arrangements: basic systems, multicomputer systems, duplex systems, and multiprocessing systems.

Basic Hardware Configuration

Figure 15–6 shows two kinds of basic real-time configurations. The upper configuration includes all the elements necessary to qualify a computer system as real-time: communication lines linking a central processing unit with direct access files and with terminal devices. Two basic kinds of terminal devices are represented here—the typewriter, and the cathode ray tube (CRT) display unit. It is important to observe that this system in operation will allow only *one* terminal on the communication line to be used at once, and when it is used, the other terminals are effectively shut off and cannot enjoy access to the system until the terminal in operation has completely finished its operation.

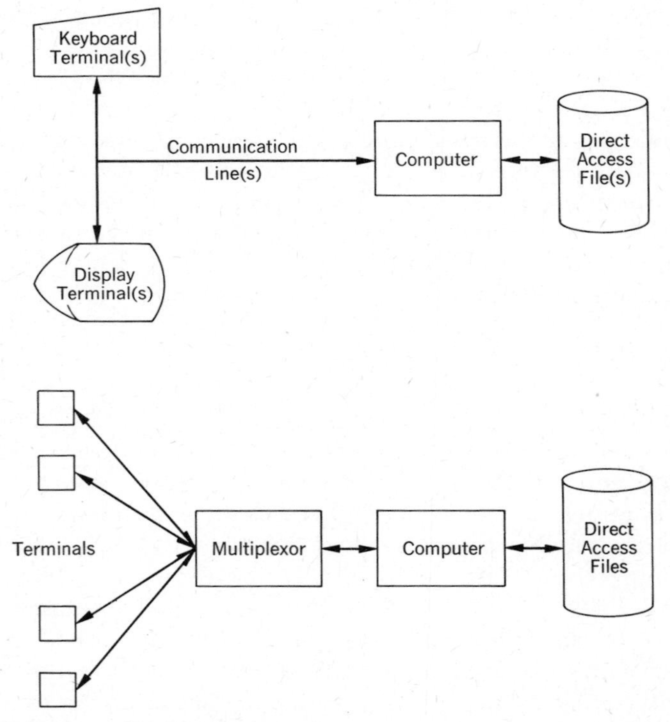

Figure 15–6. Basic real-time systems.

To provide for the likelihood that more than one terminal will require access to the system during the same time period, the basic configuration can be modified by the addition of a multiplexor or line control computer. This modification is shown in the lower part of Figure 15–6. As discussed earlier, the multiplexor is a device that provides each on-line terminal with a time-slice in such a way that users at each of several terminals are unaware that the computer is being used by anyone other than themselves. The multiplexor, then, is a stored-program computer with the special function of handling input/output operations of the system. Typically, this is accomplished in two ways: *queuing* and *commutating*. Queuing involves placing in a waiting line a terminal into which a user has entered a transaction. The terminal will have its transaction processed when its turn at the computer arrives. Some priority system may be programmed into the multiplexor or it may work on a first-come, first-served basis. Queuing is the technique used in the real-time systems developed for airline reservation bureaus.

Commutating causes a terminal that has an awaiting transaction to be allotted a small time slice every so often until the transaction is completed. In this way, it appears as if the computer is processing several transactions at once. Actually, this is not the case. The computer processes the transaction at terminal A for a short period, stores that transaction away and then proceeds to process the transaction at terminal B for a while, then stores it away and on to the transaction at terminal C, and so forth. The time lapse before the computer returns to terminal A is usually too short to inconvenience the user at that terminal even if he notices it.

The addition of the multiplexor to the basic system makes it much more flexible and increases the utilization of the central processing unit considerably since the relatively long time period needed by the user to key in his transaction—perhaps several seconds or even minutes—can be used by the processing unit to process transactions at other terminals.

Multicomputer Configurations

A multicomputer real-time system is one that makes use of more than one computer. Typically, these systems use one small or medium-sized computer to handle housekeeping so that a larger computer can devote all its time to computational tasks. The large computer is directed to its tasks by the smaller computer and for this reason, this type of configuration is frequently called a master-slave system. As shown in Figure 15–7, both computers have storage devices attached so that stored data can be available when needed. Direct-access data are usually on-line to the master computer, which thus qualifies this system as real-time; other storage devices can serve the slave computer.

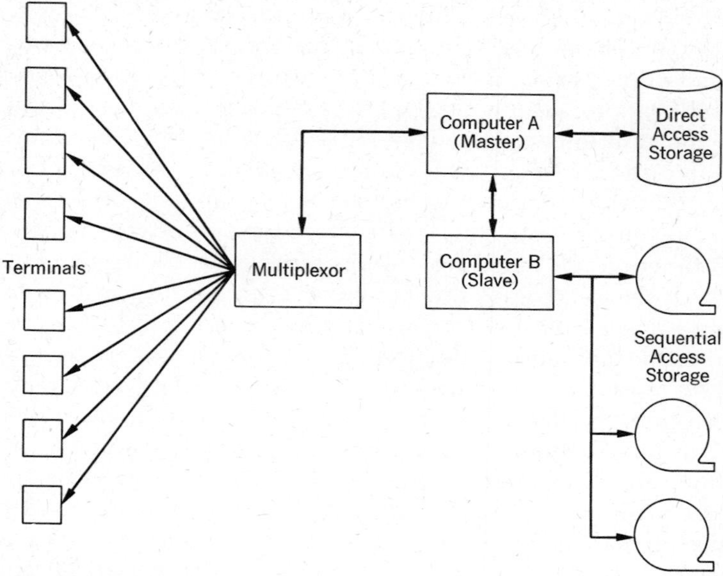

Figure 15–7. Multicomputer real-time system.

Duplexed Configurations

A duplexed real-time system is one in which two computers perform identical tasks at the same time or *in parallel.* In Figure 15–8 a transaction entering one of the terminals is processed by both computer system A and B at the same time. Which system is directly on-line to the terminal being used is determined by the switch. The purpose of such a system is to provide back-up in case one of the computer systems should malfunction; also, it is an important configuration for applications in which perfect computer system operation is vital, as with calculating the retro-rocket firing time for an orbiting space capsule. In the system illustrated, if system A should malfunction, the switch will detect this and connect the input/output devices to system B, which is performing the same task. In this way, the probability of failing to accomplish a task because of computer system failure is greatly reduced. For the American moon shots, the computer system is to be quadruplexed—four computers operating in parallel—to minimize the chance of system failure.

Multiprocessing Configurations

In some instances, real-time systems may involve the execution of a wide variety of programs and call for data from a wide variety of sources. To satisfy diverse requirements such as these, a system can be developed which involves more than one computer and in which a transaction presented to the system will be processed by the computer best suited to handle that particular operation. Other computers on-line to the system can be used to process other transactions or *background programs*—programs of a relatively low priority—which can be executed while the system is not called upon to satisfy real-time transactions and would therefore be standing idle. In this way, the system is in fact executing more than one program at once and is using more than one computer to do it.

Real-Time Systems Software

Any computer system ultimately looks to the programs it executes in the accomplishment of the system's objective. Although the hardware devices may be awe-inspiring, the programs that control the hardware are the more significant part of the total system's operation. The controlling programs, or software, of real time systems are of three basic types: object programs, supervisory programs, and support programs.

The object programs in a real-time computer system are very similar in purpose to the object programs on file in a more conventional system. They are also called operational programs and ordinary processors. Their purpose is to perform the calculations and manipulations to the data as required by the transactions entered through the terminals. Supervisory programs, frequently called monitors or executors, coordinate the work of the object programs and schedule the processing of transactions by maintaining queues when required and by allocating time slices. The supervisor program system can be considered to be the master of a set of object programs, which in effect is a group of subroutings called upon by the supervisor when needed. The supervisor and the object programs together comprise the complete *operating system.* The support system is used

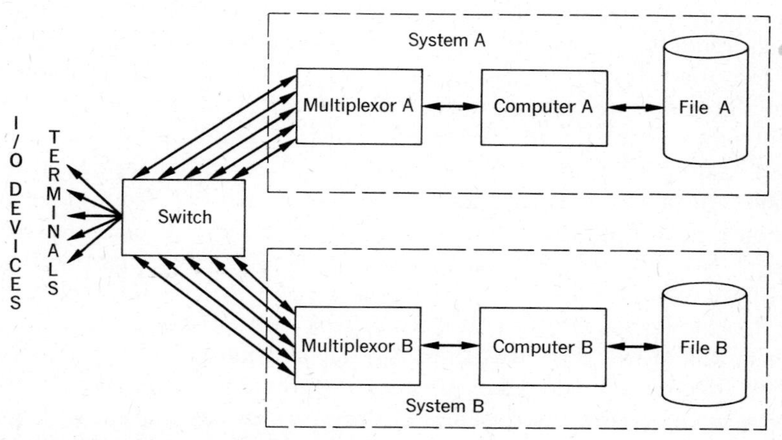

Figure 15–8. Duplexed real-time system.

in addition to the object programs and supervisor to serve additional operating and maintenance efficiency. They provide diagnostic aids in the case of system malfunction; they serve to install and revise the operating system; and they are used to maintain and reorganize data files.

The Total Information System

At the turn of the century, industrialists like John D. Rockefeller and Henry Ford could carry the essential records of their businesses in their heads. This was a total information system. All the pertinent information about the business was immediately available to the decision-maker. However, as businesses grew, and as the needed records and the amount of data to be stored and processed increased accordingly, it became impossible for one man to have at his immediate recall all the pertinent information needed to help him make an informed decision. Inevitably, time lags in information flow within the business enterprise grew and decision-making consequently became less well-informed. Businessmen recognize the need for fast handling of industry's most important single commodity: information. Therefore, they have turned to real-time systems recently as an answer to the problem of making decisions based upon the best quality information possible.

Many observers refer to this phenomenon as the second industrial revolution, the revolution of information flow. Because of today's technology which permits storing on-line to a computer millions of characters of data, business information systems are beginning to be able to return to the total information system which was characteristic of the industrial giant of several decades ago. This is a real-time system in which all the vital information about the business is available to management on an essentially no-time-lag basis. Any corporation, no matter how widely spread geographically, can have centrally located information files available completely to corporate decision-makers wherever in the corporation they may be. Moreover, management can be as close to this information as they choose through the use of display terminals in executive offices and at other points within easy access to decision-makers at all levels.

One example of this kind of real-time total information system is Westinghouse Electric Corporation's Tele-Computer Center. The Center is located near Pittsburgh and is the core of a large information system housing two Univac 490 real-time computer systems. Customer orders and other information is typed into teletype devices stationed in more than 300 offices, factories, and sales offices throughout the United States and Canada. The computers identify the data being received. If, for example, a customer order, they process it, reduce inventory levels accordingly, send shipping instructions to the proper warehouses, and prepare and send the customer invoice. When inventory levels reach pre-established reorder points, purchase orders are prepared and sent to manufacturing facilities or vendors.

In addition, the system maintains records of over 200,000 stockholders, keeps track of the financial results of manufacturing operations of all divisions of the company, produces payroll checks, and prepares statistical reports of the corporation's sales. According to Westinghouse Controller, F. E. Dalton, "Our officials are now in a better position to make decisions on how best to deploy the resources of money, manpower, and facilities available to them."

Some companies are developing information "war rooms" similar to the war rooms now employed in the United States national defense system. The most advanced of these is Sperry-Hutchinson's management information room at their New York headquarters. This theater-like room, now used for lecture-type presentations with elaborate audiovisual aids is wired to receive information from direct-access devices connected to closed circuit television and other terminals to make available a wide gamut of information to those who use the room for management conferences and decision-making activities.

The future of total information systems holds exciting promises. Many business systems involve low- and middle-level decision-makers (managers) who make rather routine decisions based upon rather routine information. A computerized information system may render such decision-makers obsolete and the entire system more efficient through removal of this human element. The impact of this phenomenon upon middle-manager personnel is surely to be as dramatic as the impact of automated production methods upon the rank-and-file production worker. The introduction of total information systems to business enterprises is indeed a second industrial revolution.

Questions

1. What is the difference between batch and sequential processing?
2. What implications can you see for the financial world when real-time data processing becomes widely used by financial institutions?
3. What role will third-generation computer systems play in the further development of real-time systems? Would this development be possible without some of the third-generation devices discussed in this book?
4. Give some examples of applications on each of the three types of real-time systems as categorized by function.

Part IV

System/360 Assembly Language Programming

16

Number Systems and Calculations

Examine the foundation of present day mathematics and mathematical thought and we may be surprised to learn that they are based upon several essentially undefined quantities and terms. For example, ask a mathematician to define something as apparently simple as a point and we will find him unable to do so. He can provide us with a physical model of a point, such as the period at the end of this sentence, but he would be unable to provide an unequivocal *definition* of one. An English teacher, knowing less about mathematics presumably than a mathematician, might define a point as "the intersection of two straight lines." Going further, perhaps, we look up the definition of a straight line to find it to be "the shortest distance between two points." Some would be satisfied with these definitions of point and line, but in reality, we have defined neither, for the definitions are circular, that is, one depends on the other. Rather than cope with this dilemma in a logical sense, mathematicians decide to regard *point* and *line* as undefined terms. Yet they derive whole systems of mathematics based on these undefined terms. Geometry, for example, is one such system. These observations about mathematics are not designed to weaken our confidence in it as a science, but rather to help us appreciate its relative nature. Should someone come along one day and remove one of the mathematician's basic axioms or postulates, this whole system would fall apart, since the system is meaningful only in relation to its initial assumptions.

One assumption concerning mathematics we all have come to accept has to do with the very number system upon which we base most of our mathematical thinking. Our number system, having ten symbols, 0 through 9, is a decimal, or base ten, system. The reason our number system is based upon the value ten and why, as a result, we learned to count to ten is predicated on the fact that we have ten fingers. If humans had four instead of ten digits on their hands, our number system most likely would be based on that number instead of ten.

Everything goes smoothly using this number ten as a base for a numbering system until we encounter someone or something that uses a different base. Suppose, for example, that we learned to count in the base ten system and Johnny across the street learned to count in the base four system. How would we tell Johnny that it is six o'clock and what would he be telling us if he said that he had just won 13 (read as "one-three," not "thirteen") marbles from Freddy? Johnny has his method of expressing quantities and we have ours. We need a means to convert quantities expressed in one number system to their equivalent in another system. If we had such a means, we could determine, for example, that Johnny's 13 marbles were seven marbles as expressed in our base ten or decimal system.

Why Different Number Systems?

This question can be answered in one word—communication. For many centuries man did not have a means of communicating a quantity to his fellow man. A shepherd might have kept track of his sheep when they went to pasture as follows: For each sheep that went out to pasture a stone was placed in a container. Each time a sheep returned from the pasture a stone was removed from the container. If the container were empty at the end of the day, the shepherd could feel relatively confident that all the sheep had returned. This shepherd would be unable, however, to express the quantity of sheep in his pen. We see here a need for a means of expressing quantities which could be understood by all with whom this shepherd might wish to communicate.

Means of communicating quantities using number systems were developed by the Egyptians around 3000 B.C. Systems were also developed by the Hindus, Chinese, Mayans, and other important civilizations or societies. In the development of techniques of expressing quantities, communication between different societies became a problem (and still is, for that matter). In order for the science of mathematics to have increased its influence on civilization, as it did, a means of standardization was necessary. The number system that became the standard in the world was base ten—a reflection, it is believed, of the number of fingers on our hands. Adoption of this system by the Arabic nations, one of the most mathematically oriented early civilizations, and the later invention of the printing press, which was initially used by countries that had adopted the base ten, or Arabic, system, gradually brought about the universal acceptance of the Arabic system of ten numerals and with it the decimal system of counting.

But why are there systems other than base ten? Once again, communication gives us the answer. Here the concern is not that of man to man communication, but rather man to machine communication. To communicate with machines, man must be able to express quantities in terms of the ability of the machine to deal with these quantities. Thus, we need other number systems such as binary, octal, and hexadecimal, which have, respectively, two, eight, and sixteen symbols as opposed to the ten symbols of the decimal system with which we are all so familiar. Since there are an infinite number of positive integers, there are an infinite number of possible number systems. In fact, the IBM System/360 has the capability of utilizing a number system with 256 symbols, that is, a base 256 number system. As data processors, concerned with man-machine communications, we will do well to understand the nature of number systems in general and be able to deal with systems other than base ten almost as readily as with decimal.

Base, or Radix, Ten

In discussing number systems, it is necessary to have some kind of reference point. Since we are fundamentally familiar with the base, or radix, ten numbering system we will use this as a frame of reference in the discussion that follows. To insure that each of us attaches the same meaning to quantities represented in bases other than ten, it is important that the reader be familiar with the concept of place value. Consider the case of an arbitrary three-digit number. The number represented by these three digits could vary from 000 to 999. If the three digits were initially zero, our number would appear as 000. Now suppose we are free to place the digit 1 in any one of these three positions. Our original 000 could be modified to 001, 010, or 100. Note in the first case the digit 1 has a place value of one (the new number represents one unit); in the second case, the digit 1 has a place value of ten (the new number represents ten units); in the third case the digit 1 has a place value of one hundred (the new number represents one hundred units). If we were free to place a 4 in any one of the three positions, we could represent 004, 040, or 400. Thus, in the first case we have four units; in the second case 40 units, or 4×10 units, and in the third case 400 units, or $4 \times 100 = 4 \times 10^2$ units. By this time, it should be clear that the position of the digit 4 in this three digit number is quite significant. Prior to the insertion of the digit four into any one position, the value of each of the positions has been predetermined. The reader will note that each position may be represented by a power of 10. In the base ten system, each position has a value of ten times that of the adjacent position on the right. For example, the number 6413 represents:

$$6000 + 400 + 10 + 3$$

or in our positional notation (using powers of ten) we have:

$$(6 \times 10^3) + (4 \times 10^2) + (1 \times 10^1) + (3 \times 10^0)$$

where $10^0 = 1$. Thus, an arbitrary four-digit number may be represented as:

$$(a \times 10^3) + (b \times 10^2) + (c \times 10^1) + (d \times 10^0)$$

where a, b, c, and d may be any one of the admissible digits in the base ten system (0, 1, 2, 3, 4, 5, 6, 7, 8, 9). The number of admissible digits in a number system is referred to as the base or radix of that system. If $a=5$, $b=2$, $c=7$, and $d=9$, we get:

$$(5 \times 10^3) + (2 \times 10^2) + (7 \times 10^1) + (9 \times 10^0) = 5279$$

It is important to observe that in the expression

$$(a \times 10^3) + (b \times 10^2) + (c \times 10^1) + (d \times 10^0)$$

the letters a, b, c, and d may vary over any of the admissible symbols in the base ten system, but the place value of each of these remains the same.

In order to generate a little food for thought, consider an expression such as:

$$ax^3 + bx^2 + cx + d$$

which you may recognize as a third degree polynomial. Suppose now that we are free to let the value of x vary. Note the x above is used as the base of the number system. For example, suppose x were to take on the value 5. Our expression then becomes:

$$(a \times 5^3) + (b \times 5^2) + (c \times 5^1) + (d \times 5^0)$$

In this case the base of this number is 5. What values may be assigned to the admissible marks a, b, c, and d?

Careful examination of the expression above should reveal that the letter d may be assigned the values 0, 1, 2, 3, 4. Why? Suppose d were permitted to take on the value 5. Then our expression becomes:

$$(a \times 5^3) + (b \times 5^2) + (c \times 5^1) + (5 \times 5^0)$$

and our rightmost position becomes a power of 5^1 indicating that this digit belongs in the next place to the left. Thus, in the base ten system, we have ten admissible marks and in the base five system there are five admissible marks, namely, 0, 1, 2, 3, and 4. Thus, the number 2143 in the base five system really means:

$$(2 \times 5^3) + (1 \times 5^2) + (4 \times 5^1) + (3 \times 5^0)$$

or:

$$(2 \times 125) + (1 \times 25) + (4 \times 5) + 3 = 250 + 25 + 20 + 3 = 298$$

in the base ten system.

Figure 16–1 illustrates the counting schemes of the two number systems we have examined so far. Note that in each system the counting scheme follows the same pattern: count in the rightmost position until the admissible marks of the system have been exhausted, then carry one to the position to the left of this and continue to count in the rightmost column. In terms of physical objects, then, the numbers 8 base ten and 13 base five represent the same quantity.

At this point, the reader should have a grasp on two major notions about number systems: the base of a number system and the admissible marks or symbols in the system.

Formation of Numbers

Numbers in the decimal system are formed by a summation of products. The individual product in this sum of products is made up of an integral power of the base ten multiplied by one of the admissible marks—0, 1, 2, 3, 4, 5, 6, 7, 8, 9. To form numbers using other base systems, the same idea used in forming numbers in the base ten system will be employed: a sum of products where each of the products is composed of an admissible mark times an integral power of the base being employed. Mathematically, the

Figure 16–1.

Base 10	Base 5
0	0
1	1
2	2
3	3
4	4
5	10
6	11
7	12
8	13
9	14
10	20
11	21
12	22

words above may be stated concisely as follows:

$$N = \sum_{i=-m}^{L} A_i r^i = A_L r^L + A_{L-1} r^{L-1} + \cdots + A_0 r^0 + A_{-1} r^{-1} + \cdots + A_{-m} r^{-m}$$

where N is the number; A_i is an admissible mark in the system; r^i is the radix or base of the system, and Σ, the Greek letter sigma, means "generate the sum."

Example: Express 14253.142 base five in the above notation.

$$\begin{aligned} 14253.142 = \sum_{i=-3}^{4} A_i 5^i &= A_4 5^4 + A_3 5^3 + A_2 5^2 + A_1 5^1 + A_0 5^0 + \\ &\quad A_{-1} 5^{-1} + A_{-2} 5^{-2} + A_{-3} 5^{-3} \\ &= (1 \times 5^4) + (4 \times 5^3) + (2 \times 5^2) + (5 \times 5^1) + \\ &\quad (3 \times 5^0) + (1 \times 5^{-1}) + (4 \times 5^{-2}) + (2 \times 5^{-3}) \end{aligned}$$

where $A_4 = 1$, $A_3 = 4$, $A_2 = 2$, $A_1 = 5$, $A_0 = 3$, $A_{-1} = 1$, $A_{-2} = 4$, $A_{-3} = 2$

Three systems are of primary importance in the study of digital computers: the binary system, the octal system, and the hexadecimal system. These systems use radix (or base) two, radix eight and radix sixteen, respectively. Thus, the binary system has two admissible marks (0, 1), the octal system has eight admissible marks (0, 1, 2, 3, 4, 5, 6, 7) and the hexadecimal system has sixteen admissible marks (0, 1, 2, 3, 4, 5, 6, 7, 8, 9, A, B, C, D, E, F). The point in each of the above that is used to separate the positive and negative powers of the radix is referred to as the binary point, octal point, and the hexadecimal point. This point in the base ten system is referred to as the decimal point.

Figure 16–2 shows the counting schemes of these four number systems. The counting schemes are analogous to those used in the previous section.

Consider the following examples:

$$\begin{aligned} 462.51_8 &= (4 \times 8^2) + (6 \times 8^1) + (2 \times 8^0) + (5 \times 8^{-1}) + (1 \times 8^{-2}) \\ 1011.01_2 &= (1 \times 2^3) + (0 \times 2^2) + (1 \times 2^1) + (1 \times 2^0) + (0 \times 2^{-1}) + (1 \times 2^{-2}) \\ \mathrm{A46.1C}_{16} &= (\mathrm{A} \times 16^2) + (4 \times 16^1) + (6 \times 16^0) + (1 \times 16^{-1}) + (\mathrm{C} \times 16^{-2}) \\ &= (10 \times 16^2) + (4 \times 16^1) + (6 \times 16^0) + (1 \times 16^{-1}) + (12 \times 16^{-2}) \end{aligned}$$

The subscript of the number (8, 2, or 16) indicates the number base employed. Thus, $\mathrm{A46.1C}_{16}$ is a hexadecimal number.

Addition

Once counting in a system has been mastered, the next logical step is learning how to add. Learning to add numbers in the base ten system involves memorizing an addition table which appears in Figure 16–3.

Decimal	Binary	Octal	Hexadecimal
0	0	0	0
1	1	1	1
2	10	2	2
3	11	3	3
4	100	4	4
5	101	5	5
6	110	6	6
7	111	7	7
8	1000	10	8
9	1001	11	9
10	1010	12	A
11	1011	13	B
12	1100	14	C
13	1101	15	D
14	1110	16	E
15	1111	17	F
16	10000	20	10
17	10001	21	11
18	10010	22	12
19	10011	23	13
20	10100	24	14

Figure 16–2. Counting schemes for decimal, binary, octal, and hexadecimal.

Using the table to find the sum of:

$$\begin{array}{r} 27 \\ +35 \\ \hline \end{array}$$

we find the entry corresponding to $7 + 5$ in Figure 16–3 and note that it is 12. Since the units position can hold only one digit, we place the 2 and carry the 1 as follows:

$$\begin{array}{r} 1 \\ 27 \\ +35 \\ \hline 2 \end{array}$$

Now, since we have a binary table (the operation of addition is used on *two* numbers), we cannot find $1 + 2 + 3$ directly from the table, so we look up the entry corresponding to $1 + 2$ and find 3. Then we look up the entry

+	0	1	2	3	4	5	6	7	8	9
0	0	1	2	3	4	5	6	7	8	9
1	1	2	3	4	5	6	7	8	9	10
2	2	3	4	5	6	7	8	9	10	11
3	3	4	5	6	7	8	9	10	11	12
4	4	5	6	7	8	9	10	11	12	13
5	5	6	7	8	9	10	11	12	13	14
6	6	7	8	9	10	11	12	13	14	15
7	7	8	9	10	11	12	13	14	15	16
8	8	9	10	11	12	13	14	15	16	17
9	9	10	11	12	13	14	15	16	17	18

Step 1	Step 2	Step 3
1 27 + 35 2	3{1 27 + 35 2	6←3{1 27 + 35 62

Figure 16–3. Decimal addition table and its use.

corresponding to 3 + 3 and find 6, giving us an answer of 62. Most of this is usually done so mechanically and automatically that we do not really become conscious of what is taking place. If we are to add in other systems, however, we must be totally aware of these processes.

Suppose we wish to add two numbers in the base six system. As with decimal addition, we will make use of an addition table. This base six addition table is shown in Figure 16–4. To add the numbers 43 + 24 in the base six system, we would proceed as follows. From the table find the

Base 6

+	0	1	2	3	4	5
0	0	1	2	3	4	5
1	1	2	3	4	5	10
2	2	3	4	5	10	11
3	3	4	5	10	11	12
4	4	5	10	11	12	13
5	5	10	11	12	13	14

Base 2

+	0	1
0	0	1
1	1	10

These tables are constructed by using the base 6 and base 2 counting schemes just as the base ten addition table was constructed.

Figure 16–4. Base six and two addition tables.

entry corresponding to 3 + 4. This number is 11. Write down the 1 and carry the other 1, thus:

$$\begin{array}{r} 1 \\ 43 \\ +24 \\ \hline 1 \end{array}$$

Now find the entry corresponding to 1 + 4 in the table. This number (5) is now added to 2 and the result, from the table, is 11. Thus our final answer is 111 base 6.

Step 1	*Step 2*	*Step 3*
$\begin{array}{r} 1 \\ 43 \\ +24 \\ \hline 1 \end{array}$	$\begin{array}{r} 5\left\{\begin{array}{l} 1 \\ 43 \end{array}\right. \\ +24 \\ \hline 1 \end{array}$	$\begin{array}{r} 5\left\{\begin{array}{l} 1 \\ 43 \end{array}\right. \\ +24 \\ \hline 111 \end{array}$

After using this table for several additions, we would find, hopefully, that we need not look up every entry, but could jot down the answer almost immediately.

As another example, let us examine the addition table for base two, or binary. (Keep in mind that the only admissible marks are 0 and 1.) Adding the number 101 to 011, following the same pattern as in the previous examples, we get the calculations shown in Figure 16–5. The previous examples were designed to make the reader aware of the process involved in addition and to emphasize the fact that addition is a binary operation and only two admissible marks can be handled at one time.

Step 1	Step 2	Step 3
$\begin{array}{rrrr} & & & 1 \\ & 1 & 0 & 1 \\ + & 0 & 1 & 1 \\ \hline & & & 0 \end{array}$	$\begin{array}{rrrr} & & 1\big\} & \\ & & & 1 \\ & 1 & 0\big\} & 1 \\ + & 0 & 1 & 1 \\ \hline & & & 0 \end{array}$	$\begin{array}{rrrr} & 1 & 1\big\} & \\ & & & 1 \\ & 1 & 0\big\} & 1 \\ + & 0 & 1 & 1 \\ \hline & & 0 & 0 \end{array}$

Step 4	Step 5	Step 6
$\begin{array}{rrrr} 10\left\{\begin{array}{l} 1 \\ 1 \end{array}\right. & 1\big\} & \\ & & 1 & \\ & 0\big\} & 1 \\ + \; 0 & 1 & 1 \\ \hline & 0 & 0 \end{array}$	$\begin{array}{rrrr} 10\left\{\begin{array}{l} 1 \\ 1 \end{array}\right. & 1\big\} & \\ & & 1 & \\ & 0\big\} & 1 \\ + \; 0 & 1 & 1 \\ \hline 0 & 0 & 0 \end{array}$	$\begin{array}{rrrr} 10\left\{\begin{array}{l} 1 \\ 1 \end{array}\right. & 1\big\} & \\ & & 1 & \\ & 0\big\} & 1 \\ + \; 0 & 1 & 1 \\ \hline 1 \; 0 & 0 & 0 \end{array}$

Figure 16–5. Binary addition.

+	0	1	2	3	4	5	6	7	8	9	A	B	C	D	E	F
0	0	1	2	3	4	5	6	7	8	9	A	B	C	D	E	F
1	1	2	3	4	5	6	7	8	9	A	B	C	D	E	F	10
2	2	3	4	5	6	7	8	9	A	B	C	D	E	F	10	11
3	3	4	5	6	7	8	9	A	B	C	D	E	F	10	11	12
4	4	5	6	7	8	9	A	B	C	D	E	F	10	11	12	13
5	5	6	7	8	9	A	B	C	D	E	F	10	11	12	13	14
6	6	7	8	9	A	B	C	D	E	F	10	11	12	13	14	15
7	7	8	9	A	B	C	D	E	F	10	11	12	13	14	15	16
8	8	9	A	B	C	D	E	F	10	11	12	13	14	15	16	17
9	9	A	B	C	D	E	F	10	11	12	13	14	15	16	17	18
A	A	B	C	D	E	F	10	11	12	13	14	15	16	17	18	19
B	B	C	D	E	F	10	11	12	13	14	15	16	17	18	19	1A
C	C	D	E	F	10	11	12	13	14	15	16	17	18	19	1A	1B
D	D	E	F	10	11	12	13	14	15	16	17	18	19	1A	1B	1C
E	E	F	10	11	12	13	14	15	16	17	18	19	1A	1B	1C	1D
F	F	10	11	12	13	14	15	16	17	18	19	1A	1B	1C	1D	1E

Figure 16–6. Hexadecimal addition table.

The addition table for hexadecimal would appear as in Figure 16–6. The addition of $6B_{16}$ and $A7_{16}$ is shown in Figure 16–7. The reader may have observed that since addition is commutative (that is, $x + y = y + x$), only one-half of any of the tables presented to this point need by used. For example, the base six addition table could be written as shown in Figure 16–8.

Multiplication

It is apparent now that if one can count in a specific number base, one can also construct an addition table, and having constructed this, he can add any two numbers in that base. Multiplication of whole numbers is really just repetitive addition, for example:

$$7 \times 3 = 7 + 7 + 7 = 21$$

One should, therefore, also be able to construct a multiplication table for any number system. Indeed, most of us have memorized one such table—

Step 1	Step 2	Step 3
1 6B + A7 2	7 {1 {6B + A7 2	→7 {1 {6B + A7 112

Figure 16–7. Hexadecimal addition.

+	0	1	2	3	4	5
0	0					
1	1	2				
2	2	3	4			
3	3	4	5	10		
4	4	5	10	11	12	
5	5	10	11	12	13	14

Figure 16–8. Condensed base six addition table.

base ten. An addition table can be used to construct a multiplication table. For example, if we wished to calculate the product 7×3 in the base ten system, all we need to do is add $7+7+7$. The sum $7+7$ can be found from the addition table to be 14. The sum $14+7$ would be found by adding $7+4$ getting 11 from the table and then adding $1+1$ and getting 2, thus giving our answer of 21. This technique would provide us with an entry for every space in any multiplication table for number bases. Once again, since multiplication is commutative, there is no need to construct the whole table. Suppose we examine the multiplication table for base six shown in Figure 16–9. To multiply 23×45 base six we would find the entry corresponding to 5×3, which is 23. Our partial product becomes:

$$\begin{array}{r} 2 \\ 23 \\ \times 45 \\ \hline 3 \end{array}$$

Now we find the entry corresponding to 5×2, which is 14; this added to 2 yields 20. Our partial product looks like this:

$$\begin{array}{r} 2 \\ 23 \\ \times 45 \\ \hline 203 \end{array}$$

x	0	1	2	3	4	5
0	0					
1	0	1				
2	0	2	4			
3	0	3	10	13		
4	0	4	12	20	24	
5	0	5	14	23	32	41

Figure 16–9. Base six multiplication table.

Now we find the entry corresponding to 4×3 to be 20. Our partial product is:

$$\begin{array}{r} 2 \\ 23 \\ \times 45 \\ \hline 203 \\ 0 \end{array}$$

$4 \times 2 = 12$. This added to 2 yields 14, giving us:

$$\begin{array}{r} 2 \\ 23 \\ \times 45 \\ \hline 203 \\ 140 \\ \hline \end{array}$$

Now adding as before (in base six, of course), we get:

$$\begin{array}{r} 23 \\ \times 45 \\ \hline 203 \\ 140 \\ \hline 2003 \end{array}$$

Figure 16–10 shows a multiplication table for hexadecimal, or base sixteen. Multiplying $6A_{16} \times B4_{16}$ we have:

$$\begin{array}{r} 2 \\ 6A \\ \times B4 \\ \hline 8 \end{array}$$

Now $(6 \times 4) + 2 = 18 + 2 = 1A$, using both multiply and add tables. Thus:

$$\begin{array}{r} 6A \\ \times B4 \\ \hline 1A8 \end{array}$$

Continuing, we calculate $A \times B = 6E$:

$$\begin{array}{r} 6 \\ 6A \\ \times B4 \\ \hline 1A8 \\ E \end{array}$$

$(6 \times B) + 6 = 42 + 6 = 48$

$$\begin{array}{r} 6A \\ \times B4 \\ \hline 1A8 \\ 48E \\ \hline 4A88 \end{array}$$

Given any number system, its base and its admissible marks, we can count, construct add tables, add, construct multiply tables, and multiply. These concepts and techniques may seem cumbersome at first, but only because we are so accustomed to performing arithmetic operations in base ten. If we were to practice doing arithmetic in hexadecimal, say, and were to memorize the addition and multiplication tables for that number system, as we have for decimal, we would find it no more difficult to use.

Complements

The operation of subtraction of positive numbers may be considered as the addition of a positive number to a negative number. In this way we can associate subtraction and addition. In many digital computers, subtraction is performed by the method of complements, and for that reason this technique deserves some mention here. Getting back to our old and

X	0	1	2	3	4	5	6	7	8	9	A	B	C	D	E	F
0	0															
1	0	1														
2	0	2	4													
3	0	3	6	9												
4	0	4	8	C	10											
5	0	5	A	F	14	19										
6	0	6	C	12	18	1E	24									
7	0	7	E	15	1C	23	2A	31								
8	0	8	10	18	20	28	30	38	40							
9	0	9	12	1B	24	2D	36	3F	48	51						
A	0	A	14	1E	28	32	3C	46	50	5A	64					
B	0	B	16	21	2C	37	42	4D	58	63	6E	79				
C	0	C	18	24	30	3C	48	54	60	6C	78	84	90			
D	0	D	1A	27	34	41	4E	5B	68	75	82	8F	9C	A9		
E	0	E	1C	2A	38	46	54	62	70	7E	8C	9A	A8	B6	C4	
F	0	F	1E	2D	3C	4B	5A	69	78	87	96	A5	B4	C3	D2	E1

Figure 16–10. Hexadecimal multiplication table.

familiar friend, the base ten number system, let us take a look at subtraction by the method of complements. Suppose we wish to subtract 4 from 7. This may be written as follows:

$$7 - 4 = 7 + (10 - 4) - 10 = 7 + 6 - 10 = 13 - 10 = 3$$

Using this technique we have subtracted and added 10 to our original problem and rearranged the terms. The portion in parentheses is called the tens complement of 4. Thus, instead of subtracting 4 from 7 directly, we have added six to seven and lopped off the tens digit, giving us the desired result, 3. Notice that the operation of subtraction has been reduced to one of addition. In subtracting 24 from 93, we would write the tens complement of 24 as $(100 - 24) = 76$ and add this to 93, giving 169, and then remove the high order 1, giving us 69, the desired result. Note that in finding the tens complement of 24 we subtracted it from the next higher power of 10 (100 in this case). In subtracting 34 from 754, we would take the tens complement of 34 $(1000 - 34)$, getting 966, add this to 754, giving 1720, and remove the high order 1 giving 720, the desired result. Why subtract 34 from 1000 in this case? Note that there are three digits in 754 and the number of digits in this number must be considered when complementing the 34, for if we had said that the tens complement of 34 were 66 and added 66 to 754, we would receive an erroneous result. In general, when complementing, the number of digits in the largest field must be used as a reference.

What happens when we try to subtract 55 from 37? If we complement 55, we get 45, and when we add this to 37, we receive 82. Observe that there is no 1 to remove in the high order position. The absence of this high order 1 indicates that our answer is negative and is in complement form. In order to obtain the correct result, we should complement 82 receiving 18 and attach a negative sign, giving us -18 as the correct result. Thus:

Step 1	*Step 2*
37	37
−55	+45
	82
	(no high order digit)

Complement of $82 = 18$, and since we had to recomplement, our answer is negative, so true result is -18.

Examples:

(1) $3142 - 27$

Complement 27 getting 9973.

Add 9973 to 3142 getting 13115.

Remove high order 1 to obtain 3115 as result.

(2) 872 − 954
Complement 954 getting 046.
Add 046 to 872 getting 918.
Note no high order 1. Recomplement 918 getting 082 and attach negative sign to 82 to obtain result of −82.

The observant reader has probably noticed that when complementing a number in the base ten system, all that is required is to subtract the units digit from 10 and the remainder of the digits from 9. Thus, in complementing 4,589,327, we subtract the 7 from 10 getting 3 and all other digits from 9. This gives us 5,410,673 as the complement of 4,589,327.

When considering complement arithmetic in other bases, the technique is exactly the same. If we complement a number in base six, for instance, we speak of it as the sixes complement and not the tens complement. For example, subtract 413 from 542 in base 6. Now we want to take the sixes complement of 413. To do this, subtract the 3 from 6 and the rest of the digits from 5. This yields 143 as the sixes complement of 413. Now add 143 to 542. This gives 1125 and removing the high order 1 results in $542 - 413 = 125$. To check this result, add $413 + 125$ and get 542. To subtract 25_6 from 431_6, we complement 25_6 as 531_6 and add this to 431_6 getting 1402_6. Removing the high order 1, we get 402_6 as the desired result. In trying to subtract 42_6 from 25_6, we complement 42_6 getting 14_6, then add this to 25_6 getting 43_6. Now, there is no high order 1, so we complement 43_6 and attach a negative sign leaving us with -13_6 as our result.

In digital computers which represent data in binary form, the same techniques used above are used. For example, to subtract 1001101_2 from 1100110_2, we complement 1001101_2, getting 0110011_2, and add this to 1100110_2, getting 10011001_2, and remove the high order 1, giving 11001_2 as our result. A convenient way to complement a binary number is as follows: scan the number from right to left leaving all rightmost zeros unchanged. Leave the first 1 encountered unchanged. From there on, from right to left, change 0's to 1's and 1's to 0's. For example, the twos complement of 10110100 is 01001100. Note the rightmost 0's and the rightmost 1 were not affected, but all other admissible marks were reversed. Figure 16–11 shows some examples of this technique.

In the System/360, all data is stored in binary and when operating in the binary mode, all negative numbers are represented in their twos complement form. For example, if we have a 32-bit (binary digit) word containing −13, it would appear as

11111111111111111111111111110011

where the 1's above could be represented by magnetic cores magnetized in one direction (say, north) and the 0's by magnetization in the opposite direction (south). Since the System/360 may be used as a fixed word-

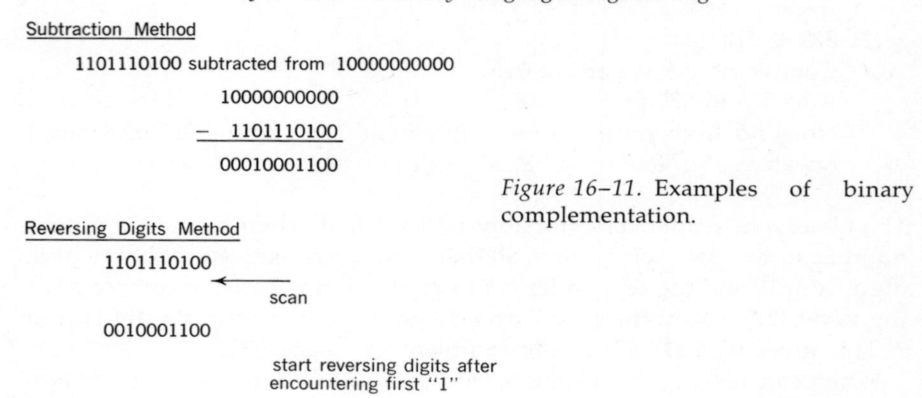

Figure 16–11. Examples of binary complementation.

length computer requiring, in this case, 32 binary positions for each data word, the high-order positions of negative numbers with small absolute values will consist of many ones.

This section has not been presented as an exhaustive study of subtraction using complements, but rather to make the reader aware of another technique of subtraction. Most computers have built-in circuitry which automatically complements data and the programmer need never know when or how this takes place. Should the programmer need to examine the machine's representation of data at some time, it will definitely be to his advantage to be aware of the techniques used in this section.

Integer Conversion Techniques

The man-to-machine communication problem is still with us at this point in our discussion. We have examined how the machine manipulates its data once it has received it internally and we are familiar with the techniques man uses to operate on his data. To complete the link between the man and the machine we must know how to convert data from man's representation to the form required by the machine and vice versa.

At the beginning of this chapter, we introduced the idea that a number in any base whatsoever can be represented as a polynomial. Thus, if representations in two different bases are to represent the same quantity we may set the polynomial representations of each equal to each other. For example, the number 473 base ten would appear as $(4 \times 10^2) + (7 \times 10^1) + (3 \times 10^0)$. If we are searching for the equivalent of this number in the base six system, we would set the above equal to $(a \times 6^3) + (b \times 6^2) + (c \times 6^1) + (d \times 6^0)$ and try to solve this equation for a, b, c, and d. At this point one might question the reason for using 6^3 as the leading term. On examination, it is found that $6^4 = 1296$, which is larger than 473, so obviously its coefficient would be zero, whereas $6^3 = 216$, which is less than 473 and it will have a nonzero coefficient. Returning to our solution of the equation $[(4 \times 10^2) + (7 \times 10^1) + (3 \times 10^0)] = [(a \times 6^3) + (b \times 6^2) + (c \times 6^1) + (d \times 6^0)]$, we note that we have only one equation and four unknowns, and to this point, our mathematical background has not provided us with a technique for solving for these unknowns. We do, however, know much about the above equation—in particular, that a, b, c, and d must be integers between 1 and 5. One of the theorems of number theory provides us with all the equipment we need to solve the equation above. This theorem says that if two numbers, in two different bases, are to be equal, their corresponding fractional and whole portions must be equal. Thus, all we need to do is devise a technique for getting a fraction and a whole portion on both sides of the above equation. Examining

$$473 = (a \times 6^3) + (b \times 6^2) + (c \times 6^1) + (d \times 6^0)$$

we see that dividing both sides by 6 will produce the desired result. Note that 6 is the radix of the number on the right. Dividing by 6 we obtain:

$$78\ 5/6 = (a \times 6^2) + (b \times 6^1) + (c \times 6^0) + d/6$$

Equating the fractions above we see that $5/6 = d/6$, which implies $d = 5$. Equating the whole portions above, we obtain $78 = (a \times 6^2) + (b \times 6^1) + (c \times 6^0)$. Dividing again by 6, we get:

$$13\ 0/6 = (a \times 6^1) + (b \times 6^0) + c/6$$

and $0/6 = c/6$, implying $c = 0$, and $13 = (a \times 6^1) + (b \times 6^0)$. Division by 6 gives:

$$2\ 1/6 = (a \times 6^0) + b/6$$

implying $1/6 = b/6$, or $b = 1$, and $2 = (a \times 6^0)$, or $a = 2$. Thus:

$$473_{10} = abcd_6, \text{ or } 473_{10} = 2105_6$$

As a further example, let's convert 3375_{10} to base sixteen:

$$3375 = (a \times 16^2) + (b \times 16^1) + (c \times 16^0)$$

Dividing by 16, we get:

$$210\ 15/16 = (a \times 16^1) + (b \times 16^0) + c/16$$

implying $c = 15 = F_{16}$ and $210 = (a \times 16^1) + (b \times 16^0)$. Dividing again by 16, we get:

$$13\ 2/16 = (a \times 16^0) + b/16$$

implying $b = 2$ and $a = 13 = D_{16}$. Thus:

$$3375_{10} = D2F_{16}$$

Close observation of the examples presented above will reveal that the technique is centered around the remainder on division by the base involved. Thus, the process involves repetitive division only. In our first example of converting 473 to base six, we could have proceeded as follows:

```
6 /473
    78 ———————————→ 5 remainder
6 /78
    13 ———————————→ 0 remainder
6 /13
     2 ———————————→ 1 remainder
6 /2
     0 ———————————→ 2 remainder
```

Reading the list of remainders from bottom to top we obtain 2105_6 as the desired result. Likewise in converting 3375 to base sixteen we proceed as follows:

```
                              Remainders
16 /3375
16 / 210 ———————————→ 15 = F
16 /  13 ———————————→  2
       0 ———————————→ 13 = D
```

Then reading upwards, we obtain $D2F_{16}$, the result obtained previously.

As one further example, let us examine the process of converting 375 to binary:

```
                         Remainders
2 /375
2 /187 ———————————→ 1
2 / 93 ———————————→ 1
2 / 46 ———————————→ 1
2 / 23 ———————————→ 0
2 / 11 ———————————→ 1
2 /  5 ———————————→ 1
2 /  2 ———————————→ 1
2 /  1 ———————————→ 0
     0 ———————————→ 1
```

Thus, $375_{10} = 101110111_2$.

These techniques provide us with quick methods for converting any whole number in base ten to any other base. Now consider the problem in reverse—that is, trying to convert a whole number from any nondecimal base back to base ten. Notice that in trying to convert 512_6 to base ten, the problem is reduced to one of evaluating the polynomial $5x^2 + 1x^1 + 2x^0$ when $x = 6$ or:

$$(5 \times 6^2) + 6 + 2 = 5 \times 36 + 6 + 2 = 180 + 6 + 2 = 188$$

Possibly an algebra course provides us with faster techniques for evaluating polynomials for particular values of the variable. One of these techniques involves synthetic division. For example, to evaluate $5x^2 + x + 2$ when $x = 6$, we can divide $5x^2 + x + 2$ by $x - 6$ as follows:

$$\begin{array}{r@{}l} & 5x + 31 \\ x - 6 \, \big) & \overline{5x^2 + x + 2} \\ & 5x^2 - 30x \\ \hline & 31x + 2 \\ & 31x - 186 \\ \hline & 188 \end{array}$$

Note the remainder 188 is the desired result. Doing the division synthetically, we would write the coefficients of the polynomial as follows:

$$5 \;\; 1 \;\; 2 \;\; \underline{/6}$$

The number in the bracket ($\underline{/\;\;}$) serves to indicate the base of the number we are converting to base ten. Then to perform the division, copy down the 5 as follows:

$$\begin{array}{lll} 5 & 1 & 2 \;\; \underline{/6} \\ & & \\ \hline 5 & & \end{array}$$

Then multiply the 5 by the 6 and write this under the 1:

$$\begin{array}{lll} 5 & 1 & 2 \;\; \underline{/6} \\ & 30 & \\ \hline 5 & 31 & \end{array}$$

Multiply the 31 by 6 and write under the 2:

$$\begin{array}{lll} 5 & 1 & 2 \;\; \underline{/6} \\ & 30 & 186 \\ \hline 5 & 31 & 188 \end{array} \quad \leftarrow \text{this is the result base ten}$$

Thus, $512_6 = 188_{10}$.

Converting 657_8 to base ten, we have:

```
6  5   7  /8
  48 424
---------
6 53 431
       ↖
        result
```

Thus, $657_8 = 431_{10}$.

Converting 1011011_2 to base ten, we have:

```
1 0 1  1  0  1  1 /2
  2 4 10 22 44 90
--------------------
1 2 5 11 22 45 91
                 ↖
                  result
```

Thus, $1011011_2 = 91_{10}$.

How about the conversion of $D2F_{16}$ to base ten? Since all of the arithmetic involved is in base ten, we must use the decimal equivalents of the D and F above when performing the synthetic division for the conversion of the bases. Thus:

```
D  2  F  /16
```

cannot be used directly, so we write it as:

```
13  2 15  /16
```

and then proceed as before, obtaining:

```
13   2   15  /16
    208 3360
------------
13 210 3375
          ↖
           result
```

Thus, $D2F_{16} = 3375_{10}$.

As a final consideration in converting whole numbers, we would like to consider the problem of trying to convert a number from one base (other than ten) to another base (other than ten) directly. To do this, the multiplication tables for the base to which we are converting must be at hand or have been memorized. The problem can be solved by using the techniques presented above and doing the operations in the base to which we are converting. For example, consider converting 342 base five to base six directly. Proceeding as before, we get:

```
3  4   2  /5
  23 235
---------
3 31 241
       ↖
        result
```

Thus, $342_5 = 241_6$. Notice that in this conversion, all of the arithmetic (addition and multiplication) was performed using the base six addition and multiplication tables presented earlier. In general, always perform the arithmetic in the base to which you are converting. This conversion could also have been accomplished by converting 342_5 to base ten, getting 97 and then converting 97 to base six getting 241_6, the desired result. The direct technique allows us to proceed from base to base without having to go through base ten first.

Now that we have covered the conversion of integers from one base to another, the next logical step to consider is operations on decimals. For example, we know that $43_{10} = 111_6$, but how does 43.27_{10} look in base six?

Decimal Conversion Techniques

The number .357 base ten can be represented algebraically as $(3 \times 10^{-1}) + (5 \times 10^{-2}) + (7 \times 10^{-3})$. To represent this number in base four, we will search for coefficients $a, b, c, d, \ldots$ as follows:

$$.357 = (a \times 4^{-1}) + (b \times 4^{-2}) + (c \times 4^{-3}) + (d \times 4^{-4}) + \cdots$$

Here we see that we have roughly the same problem we did when trying to convert integers from one base to another. In that case we tried to create fractions on both sides of the equality, whereas now we will attempt to create integers on both sides of the equality. Multiplying both sides of the equality above by 4 we obtain:

$$1.428 = (a \times 4^{0}) + (b \times 4^{-1}) + (c \times 4^{-2}) + (d \times 4^{-3}) + \cdots$$

Equating the integer portion of both sides, we obtain $1 = (a \times 4^{0})$, which implies $a = 1$. Equating the fractions we have $.428 = (b \times 4^{-1}) + (c \times 4^{-2}) + (d \times 4^{-3}) + \cdots$ Multiplying again by 4 we have:

$$1.712 = (b \times 4^{0}) + (c \times 4^{-1}) + (d \times 4^{-2}) + \cdots$$

Equating the integer portions, we have $1 = (b \times 4^{0})$, implying $b = 1$. Now,

$.712 = (c \times 4^{-1}) + (d \times 4^{-2}) + \cdots$ Multiplying by 4, we have:

$$2.848 = (c \times 4^0) + (d \times 4^{-1}) + \cdots$$

implying $c = 2$. Now $.848 = (d \times 4^{-1}) + (e \times 4^{-2}) + \cdots$ Again, multiplying both sides by 4 we get:

$$3.392 = (d \times 4^0) + (e \times 4^{-1})$$

implying $d = 3$. Stopping at this point and looking at the result, we have

$$.357_{10} = .abcde\ldots_4 = .1123\ldots_4$$

Notice that we could continue to generate digits for the base four representation of $.357_{10}$ and possibly never stop. This is one of the problems faced by the programmer trying to represent a fraction in base ten as a fraction in some other base. Obviously, it is not a happy situation, but one that must be either lived with or skirted through programming techniques. In a payroll application, it is important that every penny be accounted for and an inaccurate conversion should not occur. Thus, if a payroll calculation is done on a binary machine or a machine operating in the binary mode, the calculations are usually done in pennies and not in dollars and cents. Analyzing the process above, we see that converting decimals involves no more than repetitive multiplication by the base we are entering. A shorter method for the calculation above would appear as:

$$\begin{array}{rr} & .357 \\ & \times 4 \\ \hline \text{1st digit of answer} \rightarrow & 1.428 \end{array}$$

$$\begin{array}{rr} & .428 \\ & \times 4 \\ \hline \text{2nd digit of answer} \rightarrow & 1.712 \end{array}$$

$$\begin{array}{rr} & .712 \\ & \times 4 \\ \hline \text{3rd digit of answer} \rightarrow & 2.848 \end{array}$$

$$\begin{array}{rr} & .848 \\ & \times 4 \\ \hline \text{4th digit of answer} \rightarrow & 3.392 \end{array}$$

Keeping in mind that only the decimal portion is multiplied, the problem could be written as:

$$
\begin{array}{r}
.357 \\
4 \\
\hline
1.428 \\
4 \\
\hline
1.712 \\
4 \\
\hline
2.848 \\
4 \\
\hline
3.312
\end{array}
$$

and the answer may be written as $.1123_4$. Now we have the tools necessary to convert any decimal fraction to its equivalent in some other base.

The next logical step is the conversion of fractions represented in bases other than 10 to base ten. The synthetic division process described earlier works nicely for this type of conversion. One word of caution, however: in the results of the previous discussion of synthetic division, it should be understood that the answer was multiplied by $x^0 = 1$. This was so because the result of synthetic division is a coefficient of the lowest order of the number base in the original polynomial. Thus, when we converted $D2F_{16}$ to decimal, the result was:

$$3375 \times 16^0 = 3375 \times 1$$

because 16^0 was the lowest order place position in the original hexadecimal number. Since multiplication by 1 did not change the result, we did not make a point of multiplying by x^0. When converting decimal numbers, we must perform this operation. In these problems, the last power of the base used in the conversion must be used to find the correct result.

For example, in converting $.1123_4$ to base ten, we proceed as follows:

$$
\begin{array}{rrrrl}
1 & 1 & 2 & 3 & \underline{/4} \\
 & 4 & 20 & 88 & \\
\hline
1 & 5 & 22 & 91 &
\end{array}
$$

The 91 obtained above must be multiplied by 4^{-4} since the last power of 4 referenced in $.1123_4$ is -4. Thus, the correct result is

$$91 \times 4^{-4} = 91 \times 1/256 = 91/256 = .356$$

To convert $.11011_2$ to base ten.

$$
\begin{array}{rrrrrl}
1 & 1 & 0 & 1 & 1 & \underline{/2} \\
 & 2 & 6 & 12 & 26 & \\
\hline
1 & 3 & 6 & 13 & 27 & \times 2^{-5}
\end{array}
$$

Thus, our answer is $27/32 = .843$.

Once again, let us emphasize that these conversions are not exact. As a general rule of thumb, approximately 3.3 binary places should be used for each decimal place in order that the same accuracy be preserved. Thus, if the decimal number .507 is to be converted to binary, the binary representation should contain $3 \times 3.3 = 10$ binary places.

As a final note on conversion techniques, we would like to present a direct method of converting a number in any base back to base ten. This does not involve any new concepts, but does point out that the integer and decimal portions of a number do not necessarily have to be converted individually. Let us convert 523.14_6 to base ten. Using the synthetic division technique, we have:

```
5  2    3     1     4  /6
  30  192  1170  7026
5 32  195  1171  7030 × 6^-2
```

Thus, our answer becomes

$$7030 \times 6^{-2} = 7030/36 = 195.28$$

We could have converted the integer and fraction individually, obtaining:

```
5  2   3  /6
  30 192
5 32 195←integer

1  4  /6
   6
1 10 × 6^-2 = 10/36
            = .28←fraction
```

Combining these, we would obtain 195.28 as above.

The reader might question the use of this technique on the conversion of numbers in a base larger than ten to base ten. To demonstrate that the technique is no different, convert $A2.D5_{16}$ to base ten. Using synthetic division, we could write

```
A  2  D  5  /16
```

but since we are doing the arithmetic in the base ten system, we should use the base ten equivalents of the A and D above. Since $A_{16} = 10$ and $D_{16} = 13$, we will rewrite the above as:

```
10   2    13      5  /16
   160  2592  41680
10 162  2605  41685 × 16^-2
```

Our answer becomes:

$$41685 \times 16^{-2} = 41685/256 = 162.832$$

Thus, $A2.D5_{16} = 162.832_{10}$.

The Hindu-Arabic notation was accepted as a labor-saving device in performing arithmetic calculations with pencil and paper and with some calculations. To save time and labor in computers, it was found feasible to introduce other number bases. Internal calculations were made much more easily and the overall reliability of the answer was increased. Manipulation of data in bases other than ten serves to reinforce and understand more completely calculations in the base ten system. Although most programmers need only a general understanding of the binary and hexadecimal number systems, systems programmers will need to know how to perform these calculations in detail. Most binary machines have preprogrammed routines to convert numbers from decimal to binary and back again and this routine is taken for granted by most programmers. The man who wrote this routine, however, had to know precisely how to get the job done. The demand for systems programmers is ever increasing and most programmers are going to be forced to become familiar with these and other logic techniques used in the design of computer programming and operating systems if they plan to keep pace and advance in the profession. This chapter was presented with this idea in mind, and in the belief that understanding breeds confidence.

Questions

1. The hexadecimal value 76DB represents what binary number?
2. What is the decimal equivalent of the hexadecimal number $3FA_{16}$?
3. What is the hexadecimal equivalent of 857_{10}?
4. What is the binary equivalent of 93_{10}?
5. What is the decimal equivalent of the hexadecimal number $BD5_{16}$?
6. What is the decimal equivalent of the binary number 10110011_2?
7. Construct a base seven addition table.
8. Use this table to add the base seven numbers $1465_7 + 3524_7$.
9. Convert the following number to binary and hexadecimal: 34.675_{10}.
10. Devise a technique for dividing two numbers in the same base.

17

System/360 Assembly Language: I

The introduction of the third generation of computers in 1964 and the subsequent delivery of thousands of IBM System/360 computer systems has started a far-reaching revolution in the computer industry and, consequently, in the field of data processing in general. It seems clear that the computer of the future will be of the third-generation variety in general and the System/360 in particular. In fact, more than one-half of all the computers on order throughout the world as of this writing are some model of the 360.

The System/360 is really a family of computers ranging in size and complexity from the Model 20, a card-processing machine discussed in this book under unit record processing, upwards through Models 30, 40, 44, 65, and 90, with a large number of variations and configurations in each model. The third generation of computers tries to combine the requirements of both commercial and scientific computer installations. Because of this, the System/360 promises to become as close to a universal electronic digital computer as has been seen so far. It cannot be overemphasized that professional computer programmers will soon be looking to the System/360 as the basic computer tool of the industry. For these reasons, a knowledge of the programming techniques that will be most commonly used for this important computer tool is essential to the serious student of data processing. In Chapter 13 of this book dealing with programming systems, the reader became acquainted with a number of different *programming languages.* A programming language is a language consisting of words and symbols that programmers use to instruct computers what to do. Although the programming languages discussed in that chapter are important and can be used with the System/360, probably the most widely used language in terms of programming the most widely used computer—the System/360—will be the System/360 Assembly Language.

Several approaches in the teaching of computer programming have been tried by various authors and teachers and each seems to have its particular advantages and disadvantages. We feel that while learning how to code in general is important, it seems to be more meaningful and more purposeful if it is done on a modern computer with an up-to-date language. For this reason, we have chosen the System/360 Assembly Language as our introductory language to computer programming. In learning to code hypothetical computers, the student certainly has all of the tools at his disposal, but he must now be concerned with making the transition to a language that is actually in use. The reader who, as a working programmer, will not be coding on a 360, but rather some other machine, will also be at a disadvantage, but we feel he will not be as badly handicapped as the student who learned on a purely hypothetical machine. The System/360 Assembly Language is so versatile that the student should have no difficulty in making the transition to coding any other binary, octal, character, hexadecimal, or decimal machine.

Basic Characteristics of System/360 Data Representation

Before entering into a discussion of the various instructions available in the System/360 Assembly Language Coding (ALC), the reader must become familiar with some basic concepts peculiar to all instructions and data in the System/360.

Bits, Bytes, Nibbles, and Words

The basic addressable unit in the 360 is the byte, which consists of eight binary digits (bits). A 360 with 64K positions of storage has 64,000 bytes, each of which is addressable by the programmer. Careful analysis of the byte reveals that in eight bits, 256 different configurations may occur. This is determined by noting that each position (being binary) can be on or off (two states) and that a byte contains eight of these positions, so there are $2^8 = 256$ different ways to configure information contained in one byte of storage. The IBM 1400 series computers, in comparison, can hold only 64 different configurations in one addressable storage position. This is one of several reasons why the System/360 is a much more versatile family of computers than the 1400 series. Two bytes make up a *half-word,* 4 bytes make up a *full word* or *word,* and a *double word* consists of 8 bytes. Thus, a 64K machine may be thought of as composed of 16,000 words or 16,000 32-bit positions.

Data in the 360 may be stored in one of three different modes: character, packed decimal or binary.

Character Mode Data Representation

In storing characters in the 360, a byte is considered to be divided into two four-bit *half-bytes,* or *nibbles.* The leftmost four bits of each byte are used to store the zone portion and the rightmost four bits are used to store the digit portion. Thus, the letter "A" in storage would appear as 11000001, where the 1100 corresponds to the 12 zone in the Hollerith Code and the 0001 corresponds to the digit 1. A "J" would be represented as 11010001 and an "S" as 11100010. The number 5 would appear in character coding as 11110101.

Analyzing these examples, we can see that when characters are represented internally in the 360, the leftmost four bits will be 1100, 1101, 1110, and 1111, corresponding to a 12, 11, zero, and no-zone, respectively. Thus, whenever character-type commands are used in the 360, data will be assumed to be in character format, that is, a zone, decimal, zone, decimal, and so on. The name STUDENT would appear in memory in character coding as:

11100010	11100011	11100100	11000100	11000101	11010101	11100011
S	T	U	D	E	N	T
byte 0	byte 1	byte 2	byte 3	byte 4	byte 5	byte 6

We can see that each byte may be considered to be two hexadecimal characters. Knowing the counting scheme for hexadecimal, we can write each byte as two hexadecimal characters. Thus, if a byte contained 11100100, we could rewrite it as E4 since $1110_2 = 14_{10} = E_{16}$ and $0100 = 4_{10} = 4_{16}$. In hexadecimal, the word "student" would appear as shown in Figure 17–1.

11100010	11100011	11100100	11000100	11000101	11010101	11100011	←Internal
S	T	U	D	E	N	T	←Character
E2	E3	E4	C4	C5	D5	E3	←Hexadecimal
byte 0	byte 1	byte 2	byte 3	byte 4	byte 5	byte 6	←byte Number

Figure 17–1.

Zoned Decimal Data Representation

When storing signed numbers in character form in the 360, the zone portion of the units position of the number is considered to be the sign of that number. For example, the number −562 would appear in storage (using the character form) in three bytes as:

11110101	11110110	11010010 (zone portion of units position)
(5)	(6)	(2)
byte 0	byte 1	byte 2

Note that the no-zone code is used in bytes 0 and 1, but that the 11 zone code is used in byte 2. The machine would consider this to be a negative number upon examination of the zone portion of the units digit. The number +562 would be coded just as above except that the zone portion of the units digits could appear as 1010, 1100, or 1111. Thus, a positive number has any one of these three zone configurations in the units position of the number, whereas a negative number must always have the 1101 configuration. Character and zoned-decimal modes of data representation as discussed above are known as the EBCDIC code—Extended Binary Coded Decimal Interchange Code.

The observant reader will perceive that storing decimal information in this fashion is not very efficient. Should we wish to store decimal data in the machine and not use one byte for each decimal character, we can go to a packed decimal format.

Packed Decimal

In representing data in this format, we use one byte to store two decimal digits. At first glance, this might appear to present a problem, for where or how shall we indicate the sign of this number? We shall agree that data represented in the packed decimal format will use the last four bits of the rightmost byte as a sign indicator. Thus, the number −562 would appear as:

01010110	00101101 (sign: 1101)
5 6	2 −
byte 0	byte 1

Storing data in this format seems to have one advantage at least—twice as many numbers can be stored in the same number of bytes. The number +233 in packed decimal would appear as:

00100011	00111100
2 3	3 +
byte 0	byte 1

Analyzing the format for representation of packed decimal information, we notice that in any one byte the largest decimal number which may be stored is 99. Can we store a larger number in one byte?

Binary

The answer to the question just asked is yes. Suppose we decided that our data is to be represented in binary. The largest binary number that could be held in one byte would be 255. This is so because one byte contains eight binary digits. Thus, the largest binary number that can be contained in a byte is 11111111_2. $11111111_2 = 255_{10}$; that is, 11111111 in base two or binary is equal to 255 base ten or decimal. (See Chapter 16 for details.) Thus, in the packed decimal form, we noted above that the number +233 required *two* bytes to be stored properly, whereas in binary, the number +233 could be stored in one byte as: 11101001. The reader who has become familiar with the chapter on number systems (Chapter 16) might question the ability of the machine to represent negative numbers in the binary mode. This can be done. When representing data in the binary mode, more than one byte is usually used. Should the data represented be negative, it will appear in the machine in its *two's complement form.* Thus, the leftmost bit can be considered to be the sign bit, for if the number is negative, it will be in two's complement form and this bit will be on. For positive numbers, this bit is always off. Suppose we wished to represent −135 in two bytes (a half-word). It would appear as

11111111	01111001
byte 0	byte 1

half-word

whereas +135 would appear in a half-word as:

00000000	10000111
byte 0	byte 1

half-word

Note that the maximum positive number that can be represented in a full word (four bytes) is $2^{31} - 1$, not $2^{32} - 1$. The first bit must be reserved for sign control. In general, should the first bit be on (1), the number represented is negative and is represented in two's complement form, whereas if the first bit is off (0), the number represented is in pure binary.

Boundaries and Boundary Alignment

A *boundary* is an imaginary separator existing between half-words, full words, and double words in memory. Nine bytes of data in memory, for example, would be separated from each other by boundaries as shown in Figure 17–2 on page 392. The address of any byte in core storage is used in determining whether or not a specific half-word, word, or double word lies on a particular boundary. In the last section, we noted that:

8 bits = 1 byte
2 bytes = half-word
4 bytes = full word, or word
8 bytes = double word

If a particular piece of data is located on a half-word boundary, then its address will always be divisible by two. For example, the data located in core position 3154 is said to be on a half-word boundary, whereas the data located in 3153 is not. Should the address of a particular piece of data be divisible by four, then we say it is located on a full word boundary, as in location 3156. Note that since anything that is divisible by four is also divisible by two (the converse is not true), every piece of data located on a full word boundary is also on a half-word boundary. Should the address be divisible by eight, then we can refer to the data as being located on a double word boundary. Thus, the data located in 3160, for example, is on a half-word boundary, a full word boundary, and a double word boundary since 3160 is divisible by two, four, and eight. The data located in 3158 is on a half-word boundary only. In general, to determine the particular alignment of a particular piece of data, we must determine whether or not the address of the data is divisible by two, four, or eight for half-word, full word, or double word alignment. Obviously, any data located at (or referenced by) an odd address is not on half-word, full word, or double word alignment.

Boundary alignment plays a very important role in the understanding of the functions of various ALC operations. In general, data in the 360 is always referenced by the leftmost byte of the field. For example, if the number 31416 were stored in zoned decimal form in locations 4154, 4155, 4156, 4157, and 4158, we would reference it by calling location 4154. Note that this data is on a half-word boundary, but not a full or double word boundary, for its location is divisible by two but not four or eight.

System/360 Registers, Addresses, and Memory Organization

Registers

The System/360 has sixteen *general purpose registers* and four *floating point registers.* The general purpose registers are addressed 0 through 15. These registers are part of main storage and are used in conjunction with many of the instructions to be discussed later in these chapters. Each register has a 32-bit (one word) capacity. The four floating point registers are 64 bits (one double word) in length. The discussion and reference to registers in this section will concentrate entirely upon general purpose registers.

Memory Organization and Addressing

System/360 memories are organized into *blocks* of bytes, each block containing 4096 bytes. A 16,000-byte memory, for example, would appear as shown in Figure 17–3. As we can see, a 16,000-byte memory (called a

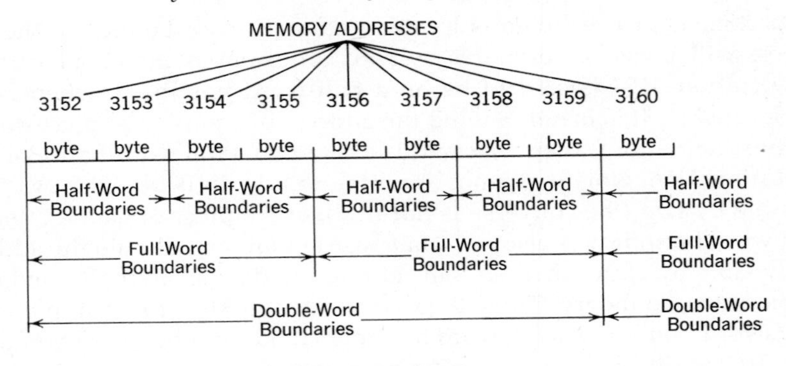

Figure 17–2. System/360 boundary alignment.

16K memory) has more than 16,000 bytes since it is constructed of multiples of 4096-byte blocks. An address referencing one of the bytes available in this memory device consists of two parts: a *base*, which identifies in which of the memory blocks the desired byte is located, and a *displacement*, which indicates which of the 4096 bytes in that block is being referenced. Typically, the programmer will store a base number in one of the 16 general purpose registers. An address, then, consists of the contents of this general purpose register (now called the *base register*) and the displacement. Thus, the effective address used by any instruction is equal to the *base address* (address in the base register) plus the *displacement*. The base register can be any one of the 16 general purpose registers. The rightmost 24 bits of this register are used as a base. The displacement is the relative address of a piece of information in a block of core storage consisting of 4096 bytes. At execution time, the effective address of an instruction is equal to the sum of the numbers in the base register plus the displacement referenced in the instruction being executed. For example, suppose we wished to reference location 8392. We would visualize core as being divided up into blocks containing 4096 bytes, as shown in Figure 17–3. Since $8392 = 8192 + 200$, this would indicate that we want to get to location 200 in the third block of core storage. Let us suppose we decide to use general purpose register nine as our base register. Then to get to location 8392, we would have 8192 stored in general purpose register nine and 200 as the displacement in our instruction. At execution time, the 8192 would be added to the 200, giving us an effective address of 8392. One might question the reason for using an addressing scheme as complicated as this. The reason should become clear as we continue this discussion. Note that those instructions calling for a displacement use only 12 bits rather than 24 bits, as would be required if we did not use the base-displacement technique, and in twelve bits we can get 4096 different configurations ($0 - 4095$). Note also that in using this concept, instruction lengths may be shortened. In general, all displacements must be posi-

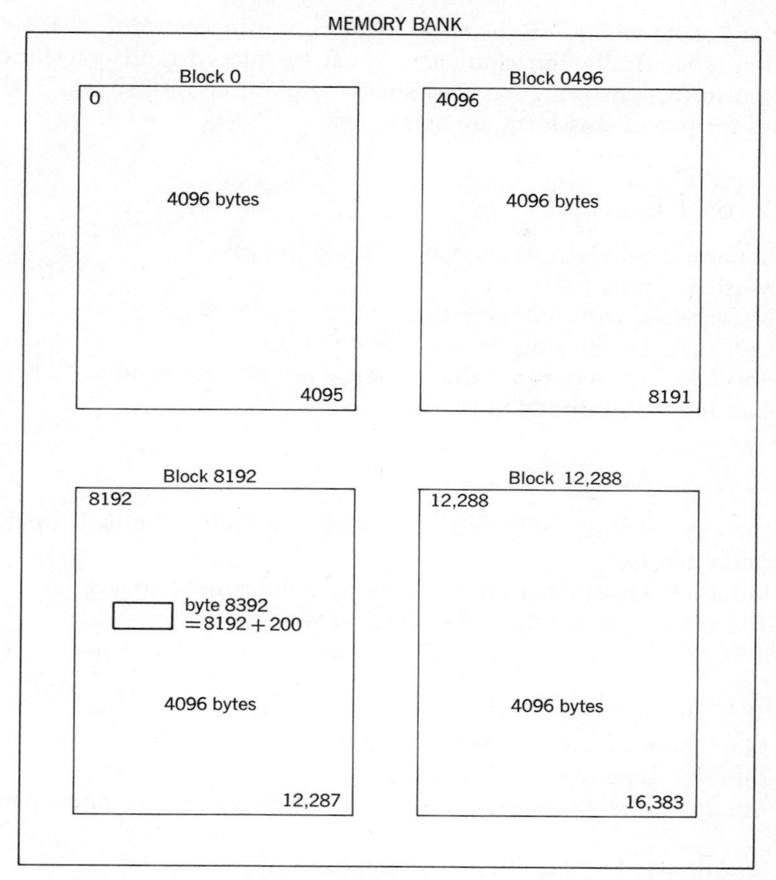

Figure 17–3. System/360 16K memory organization.

tive and less than 4096. Once the programmer has decided that he is going to use a particular register as a base register, he should use it exclusively for that purpose throughout his program.

Another question that arises frequently is how does one determine how many different base registers he will need to use in his program? System/360 programmers, to this date, have been following the general rule that approximately 40 pages of coding require 4,000 positions of storage. Thus, if 40 pages of coding is approached, or if the programmer is in doubt, he may assign another base register. At best, this is merely an educated guess.

System/360 ALC Coding Sheet

The coding sheets used in System/360 Assembly Language Coding are *free form* coding sheets; that is, the programmer is free to write his instructions as he wishes on the sheet with minimum restraint with respect to where specifically the characters must be placed (and consequently punched in the card). Figure 17–4 shows an ALC coding sheet.

Rules for use of this form are as follows:

Name (or Label)

1. Maximum of eight bytes may be used per label.
2. Must begin in column 1.
3. Must begin with letters A through Z or $, #, @.
4. Can include other digits in other positions.
5. Special characters other than $, #, @ are not permitted.
6. Can have no imbedded blanks.

Operation Code

1. Use mnemonics only; no numerical machine language operation codes may be used.
2. Must be separated from the label by one or more spaces.
3. The maximum length is five positions.

Operands

1. May use actual or symbolic address.
2. Must be separated by a comma.
3. Must be one or more spaces between first operand and operation code.
4. Nothing to be placed beyond column 71.

Comments

1. One or more blank spaces must be used to separate comments from operands.
2. Cannot extend beyond column 71.
3. An * in column 1 indicates that the entire card is a comment.

Continue

1. Any character in column 72 indicates that this statement is to be continued in column 16 of the next line.

Sequence

1. Use columns 73–80 for punching card sequence numbers.
2. This can be done automatically by the assembler.

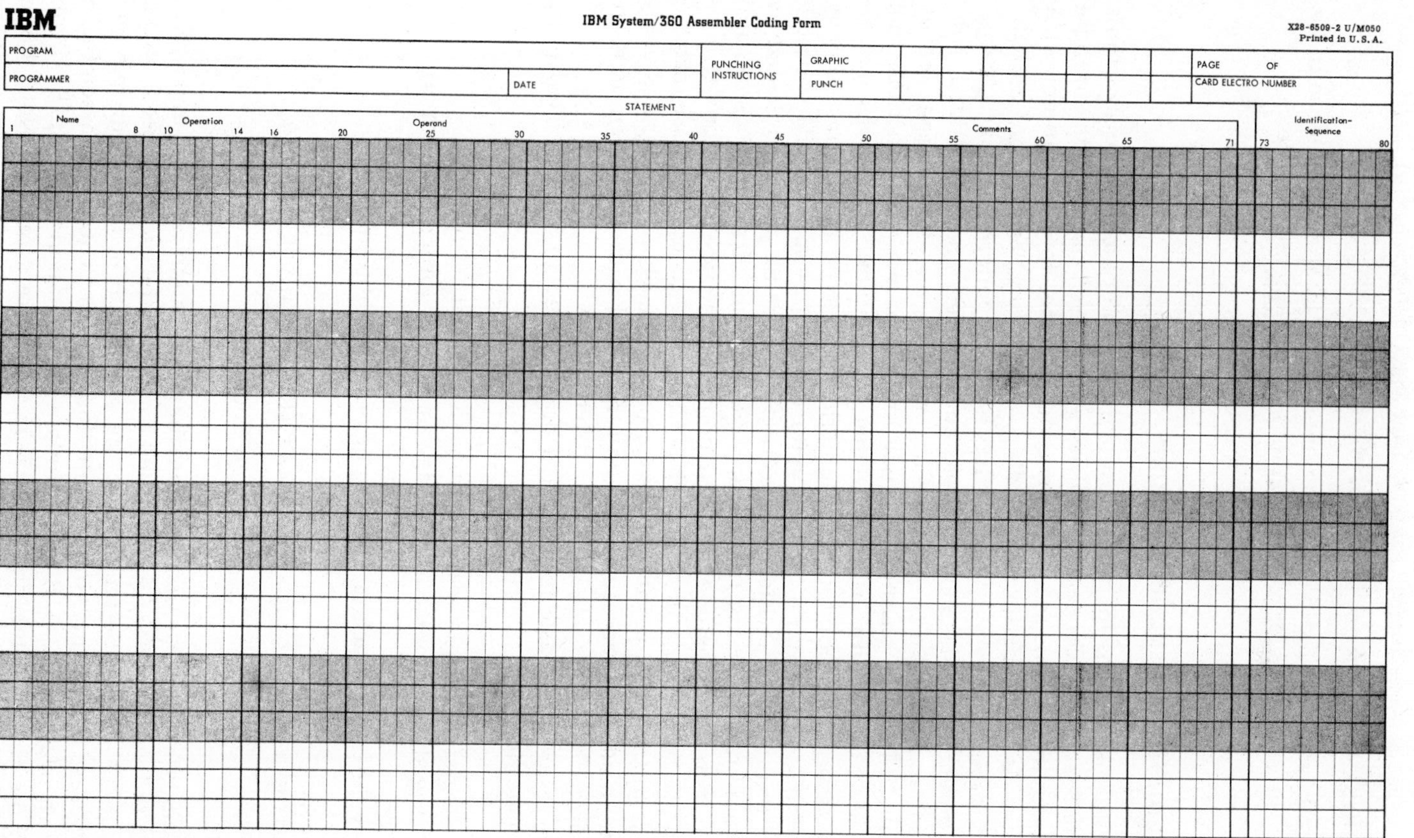
IBM

IBM System/360 Assembler Coding Form

X28-6509-2 U/M050
Printed in U.S.A.

PROGRAM		PUNCHING INSTRUCTIONS	GRAPHIC	PAGE OF
PROGRAMMER	DATE		PUNCH	CARD ELECTRO NUMBER

STATEMENT

Name 1 8 · Operation 10 14 · 16 20 · Operand 25 · 30 · 35 · 40 · 45 · 50 · 55 · Comments 60 · 65 · 71 · Identification-Sequence 73 80

Figure 17–4. (Courtesy, IBM)

ASTERISK OPERANDS

1. Indicates that the current contents of the location counter is to be used. The asterisk references the address of the operation code.

System/360 Instruction Formats

As with instructions for all electronic digital computers, the instructions for the System/360 consist basically of an *operation code* and one or more *operands.* In general, an operation code indicates to the computer what function is to be performed (adding, subtracting, and so on) and the operands indicate what the function is to be performed upon—that is, the contents of what memory areas and registers are to be added, subtracted, and so forth. In ALC coding, operands are always separated by a comma. In these chapters, we will limit ourselves to instructions that deal with fixed point arithmetic—that is, arithmetic operations that always assume the radix point of numerical data to be located immediately to the right of the rightmost digit in the data word—as opposed to floating point arithmetic, in which the location of the radix point is adjusted by the computer following the normal rules of multiplication, division, and other arithmetic operations. Fixed point arithmetic instructions will always use binary data in conjunction with some general purpose register; that is to say, fixed point arithmetic in the 360 is always performed using binary mode data representation, and the actual arithmetic operations are performed in a general purpose register.

There are two basic formats that are followed in writing fixed point instructions:

1. Register-to-register instructions (RR format).
2. Register-to-storage and storage-to-register format (RX format).

We will examine each of these types of instruction formats.

REGISTER-TO-REGISTER FORMAT (RR FORMAT).

Label Op Code R_1,R_2

This type of instruction will contain an operation code and make reference to two registers. A label, called a *name* on the coding sheet shown in Figure 17–4, may be attached to the instruction if desired for reference purposes. In the machine, the RR format instruction will assemble as shown in Figure 17–5. Bits 0–7 contain the operation code, bits 8–11 contain the first register, and bits 12–15, the second register. Note the instruction uses 16 bits of core storage or two bytes. Operand 1 is the re-

ALC Form

Label	Op Code	Operand 1		Operand 2
ADD	AR	4	,	5

Assembled Instruction Stored in Memory

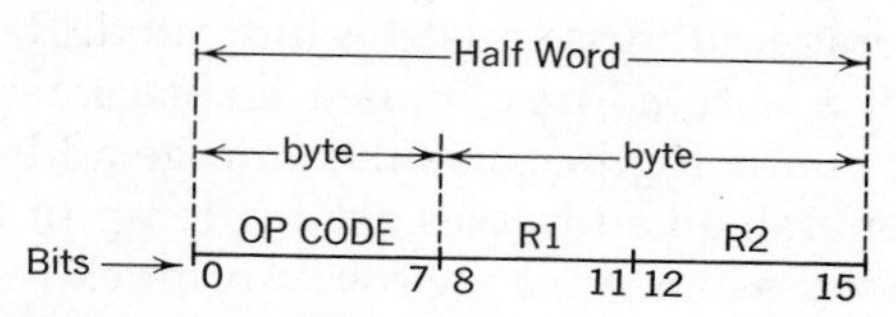

Figure 17–5. Register to register instruction.

ceiving register in these instructions. Those familiar with the IBM 1620 will recognize this kind of data transmission. The operands will be decimal numbers representing one of the registers 0–15. For example, the instruction

Op	*Operands*
AR	4,5

would add the contents of register 5 to register 4. Thus, register 4 would contain the sum of the amounts in registers 4 and 5 after execution. The contents of register 5 would be left unchanged.

As examples of this type of operation, consider these three instructions:

Op Code	*Operands*	
LR	7,6	Loads the information from register 6 to register 7.
AR	7,6	Adds register 6 to register 7 and holds the sum in register 7.
SR	7,6	Subtracts register 6 from register 7 and holds the difference in register 7.

Then consider the following routine:

Op Code	*Operands*
LR	5,6
AR	5,6
SR	5,6

What would be the contents of register 5 after the execution of these instructions?

REGISTER-TO-STORAGE OR STORAGE-TO-REGISTER FORMAT (RX FORMAT)

In this case, the assembled instruction will appear as in Figure 17–6. Note that the instruction is a full word in length. The reason for this, of course, is that a storage address must be indicated. Recall that each address is made up of a base address plus a displacement. At first glance, this format may be confusing because the storage address is made up of X_2, B_2 and D_2. In general, all addresses are made up in this fashion.

X_2 is a register used as an *index register.* An index register is a general purpose register used to store a number that is to be added to the displacement portion of the address. For example, earlier in this chapter, we discussed how memory position 8392 was addressed using a displacement of 200 and referencing a base register that contained the first memory location of the block we wanted to access (8192). If we wanted to access a memory location 30 bytes beyond 8392, we might do this by *indexing* the address of an instruction that would normally refer to 8392. This indexed instruction would reference a base register (containing 8192), an index register (containing 30), and a displacement (of 200). The effective address would then be:

```
  8192 (base register)
+   30 (index register)
+  200 (displacement)
  ----
  8422
```

B_2 of the RR instruction shown in Figure 17–6 is the base register to be used in conjunction with the instruction and D_2 is the actual displacement (0-4095). Thus, the storage address is actually made up of the displacement plus low order 24 bits of the general purpose register indicated by X_2 plus the low order 24 bits of the general purpose register indicated by B_2. Thus, the instruction:

Label	*Op Code*	*Operands*
	L	4,SAM(3,9)

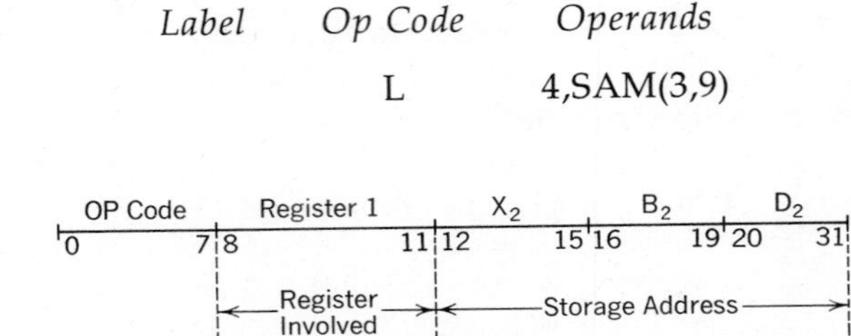

Figure 17–6. Storage to register and register to storage instruction.

would load the full word of data located at the address equivalent to the label SAM plus low order 24 bits of register 3 plus low order 24 bits of register 9 into register 4.

In general, for this discussion we will not be using an index register so the entry for X_2 will always be 0. Note that in this case, an entry of 0 does not refer to register 0, but to the fact that there is no indexing on this instruction. For example:

```
L   8,A(0,9)
```

would load the full word located at a memory address that is synonymous with the label "A" plus the contents of general purpose register 9 (the base register) into register 8. The 0 indicates that we do not wish to have the contents of any index register added to this address. We can now see that, in actuality, the effective address of every instruction is generated as follows:

X_1	B_1	D_1

Add D_1 to rightmost 24 bits of B_1, then add this to rightmost 24 bits of X_1. Thus, if X_1 contained 1962 in its rightmost 24 bits, B_1 contained 5013 in its rightmost 24 bits and D_1 contained 2025, the effective address to be used by this instruction would be:

$$\begin{array}{r} 1962 \\ +5013 \\ +2025 \\ \hline 9000 \end{array} = \text{effective address}$$

(This discussion has been included for completeness of the topic only; actually, we will be using no index registers in these chapters, so this entry will always be zero.)

Translation of Assembly Language to Machine Language

At this point, it would be well to observe that the System/360 really cannot execute Assembly Language instructions. The programmer codes his program in ALC to be sure, but the 360 really executes a *machine language translation* of the ALC program. Briefly, in preparing an ALC program for execution, the programmer first *assembles* his program. This means that he causes the 360 to translate his ALC program (usually called a source program) into a machine language program (an object program). The object program is then executed upon the data that require processing. It is important to understand that *two* programs are executed and at different times: the *processor program*, which translates the ALC program into machine language, and the *object program*, which actually does the work. The processor program, in ALC programming, is executed at *assembly time* and the object program at *object time*.

These things were more thoroughly discussed in Chapter 13, Computer Programming Systems. However, in the discussion of ALC instructions which follows, it is important to realize that some instructions are executed at assembly time and others at object time. *Declarative instructions* are executed at assembly time and *imperative instructions* at object time. Declarative instructions are signals to the processor program to perform some function, such as causing certain areas of memory to be reserved for special purposes during the execution of the object program. Imperative instructions cause such functions to be performed as addition, subtraction, and so on, during the execution of the object program—that is, at object time.

Fixed Point Instructions

The primary target of fixed point arithmetic instructions will be in addressing half-words or full words of information. In using these instructions, we will be dealing primarily with fields having values expressed in binary form. All negative numbers will be stored in their two's complement form, implying that the first bit will be used for sign control. For fixed point arithmetic operations, we will always use at least one of the 16 general purpose registers (numbered 0–15). These instructions will be concerned primarily with register-to-register operations or register-to-storage operations.

Data storage areas will be defined to the assembly language processor by the use of declarative instructions. Prior to entering into a detailed discussion of the operation of various fixed point instructions, we will discuss some of the declaratives available to the programmer. A thorough understanding of these is a prerequisite to understanding the operation of fixed point instructions.

Declaratives

In general, a declarative statement is one which causes the processor to reserve areas of memory for some special purpose or to associate symbols or labels with particular memory addresses.

Define Storage (DS). This declarative is used to reserve storage locations to be used at a later time by the programmer. If a label is associated with the DS, this label will be associated with the leftmost byte of the area being defined. It is important to note that the use of a DS does not guarantee that the particular area of core referenced will be cleared. The general format for a DS will be:

DS *d* *t* L*n*

where *d* refers to a duplication factor that indicates how many areas are to be reserved; *t* refers to the type code—H for half-word, F for full word, and D for double word; and *n* is the length attribute of the data, indicating the size of the field. If a length attribute is used, it will override the *t* entry. For example:

Label	*Op Code*	*Operand*
NAME	DS	3D

would set up three double-words (aligned on a double word boundary) and associate the label NAME to the leftmost byte of the first double word. Thus, we reserve 24 bytes of core with the label NAME associated with the first byte of this 24-byte area. The length attribute of NAME would be eight bytes, since we are associating it basically with a double word.

Label	*Op Code*	*Operand*
ONE	DS	F

would give us automatic alignment on a full word boundary, reserve one full word of core storage (four bytes), and associate the name ONE to the leftmost byte of this four-byte area. It is very significant to note that the F above forces alignment on a full word boundary. Suppose we tried to set up two storage areas in core using the following:

```
SAM  DS  H
JOE  DS  2F
```

The area referenced by SAM would consist of one half-word of core storage and JOE, two full words of core storage. The question now arises as to whether these areas will be adjacent to each other. The answer to this is, not necessarily. Suppose SAM were assigned to locations 0 and 1. Then could the processor assign JOE to bytes 2, 3, 4, 5, 6, 7, 8, and 9? Since JOE must be aligned on a full word boundary, we know that its address must be divisible by four. JOE cannot be assigned as above (bytes 2-9) since two is not divisible by four. Thus, core storage assignments for the declara-

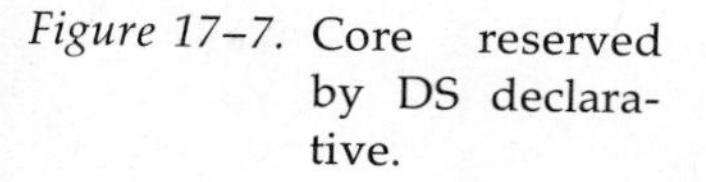
Figure 17–7. Core reserved by DS declarative.

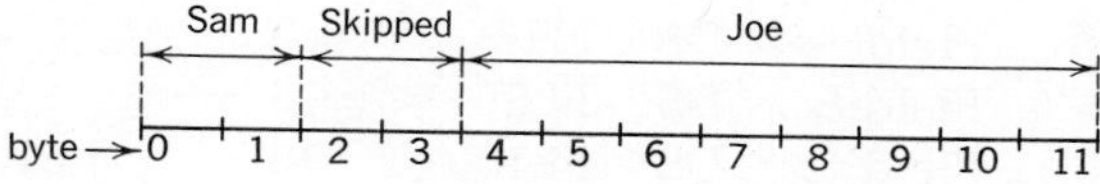

tives above would appear as in Figure 17–7. Note that bytes 2 and 3 have been skipped in order to force full word alignment for JOE. Actually, the name SAM refers to byte 0 and JOE to byte 4. The length attribute of a DS may be a maximum of eight. Should we use

```
DS   FL4
```

we would reserve four bytes (a full word), but since the length attribute overrides the type code (F above) we would not necessarily receive the proper alignment. Likewise,

```
DS   FL2
```

would give us two bytes of storage (rather than a full word). The two bytes are not necessarily aligned on a full word boundary.

Using the declarative

```
DS   OF
```

will not reserve any core storage at all but will advance the location counter to the next full word boundary. Thus, using the following:

```
ONE     DS   OF
TWO     DS   H
THREE   DS   H
```

would force the location counter to be advanced to the next full word boundary. Then the half-word that follows would be aligned on both a half-word and a full word boundary, and the last half-word would be aligned on a half-word boundary. (See Figure 17–8.)

The following chart will give a feel for the use of the DS, the duplication factor, the length attribute, and the type code. Assume that all of the following appear in the order listed.

Label	*Instruction*	*Length Attribute*	*Bytes Reserved*	*No. in Area*	*Aligned*
Field	DS H	2	2	1	Yes
Area 1	DS 2F	4	8	2	Yes
Area 2	DS D	8	8	1	Yes
Area 3	DS HL3	3	3	1	Yes*
Area 4	DS OF	4	0	0	Yes
Field A	DS 2H	2	4	2	Yes
Field B	DS FL8	8	8	1	Yes*
Field C	DS FL10	10	10	1	Yes*

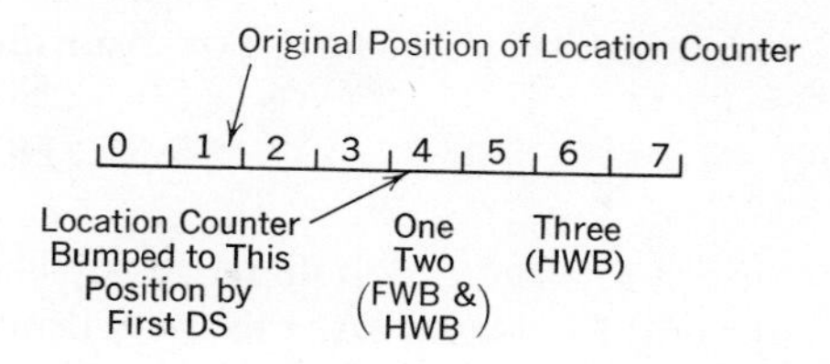

Figure 17–8. Boundary alignment using DS.

The asterisks in the chart indicate that alignment was not automatic but was a result of the previous DS forcing its alignment. Thus, if a full word has just been reserved on a full word boundary, then obviously the location counter is set up to receive a full word or half-word and give it proper alignment merely by taking the next available series of bytes.

Figure 17–9 pictorially represents the chart given above. We assume that the location counter is referencing a half-word boundary (HWB) just prior to encountering the first DS in the chart.

The reader might try to formulate the schematic appearing in Figure 17–9 and based on the chart, assuming that the location counter starts on a full word boundary. Note the difference in the amount of core used by the processor.

Define Constant (DC). This declarative is similar to the DS except that actual data are stored in the area that is reserved. As with the DS, the label associated with a DC references the leftmost byte of the reserved area. The general format for the DC is:

DC *d* *t* L*n* 'constant'

where the *d* refers to the duplication factor, *t* the type code, and *n* the length attribute. The constant itself will be in quotes. The same rules that were used for alignment with the DS apply to the DC. The constant that is stored will be converted to binary, right adjusted in the field, and com-

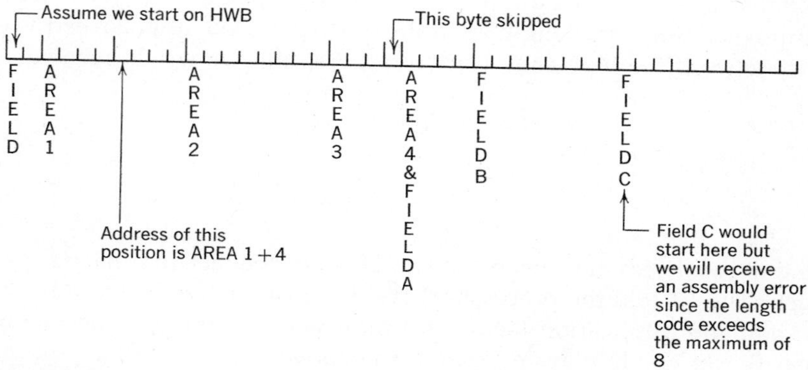

Figure 17–9.

plemented if necessary. For example:

SAM DC H '123'

would reserve one half-word of core, place 123 in binary in this area, and append the name SAM to the leftmost byte of this area. This would appear in storage as:

00000000	01111011

SAM
1/2 word (2 bytes)

If we had used

SAM DC H '+123'

we would have received the same result. Using

SAM DC H '−123'

we would obtain

11111111	10000101

SAM
half-word (2 bytes)

giving us −123 stored in its two's complement form.

The type code for a DC should never be D (double word), for in using binary numbers, we always deal with a 32-bit (one word) maximum.

If we were to use

TWO DC 2HL1 '200'

we would be specifying a duplication factor of 2, a half-word and a length attribute of 1. Since the length attribute has been used, it will override the type code (as if the type code were not there) and we would receive:

11001000	11001000

TWO
2 bytes

Note that two bytes have been used and the number 200 in binary appears in each. The L1 told the processor that this constant is to be stored in one byte, and the duplication factor of 2 indicates that this constant should appear twice. The H plays no role in the above.

The following chart summarizes the use of the DC.

Label	*Instruction*	*Length Attribute*	*Bytes Reserved*	*No. of Areas Reserved*	*Aligned*
FIELD	DC H'1379'	2	2	1	Yes
FIELD A	DC 3F'201'	4	12	3	Yes
AREA 1	DC H'33000'	2	2	1	Yes
AREA B	DC HL2'—1'	2	2	1	Yes

Note that if the L*n* does not appear then the length attribute is that required by the type code; however, if the L*n* is used, it will override the type code. In the definition of AREA 1 above, we have a slight problem, for in a half-word we cannot store a number as large as 33000. In this case, the processor will drop the high order bit and store an erroneous constant for us. In the definition of AREA B, we wind up with alignment only because the previous constant forced alignment. In general, when a length attribute is used, we cannot be assured of boundary alignment.

Address Constant (DC). The purpose of the address constant is to generate a four-byte field containing the address of a specified area. The format of an address constant declarative is:

DC A(C)

where C is the name of an area the synonymous address of which we wish to save. For example:

ADCON DC A(FIELD)

would reserve four bytes of information containing the address of FIELD; that is, if the address of FIELD were 3527, then ADCON would contain 3527 right justified.

To summarize the use of the DC, let us examine the following examples:

DC H'1379'	Places 1379 in binary in a half-word. Forces alignment on a HWB.
DC 3F'201'	Stores 201 in binary in each of three adjacent full words. Forces alignment on a FWB.
DC H'33000'	This number is too large to store in a half-word. A processor error would occur.
DC A(FIELD)	Generates the address synonymous with the label FIELD in one full word.

DC A(Q-94*60)	Generates the address of Q-94x60. Notice that arithmetic may be performed on addresses. The asterisk indicates multiplication.
DC HL2'—1'	Stores minus one in a half-word in its two's complement form. Boundary alignment is not forced.
DC A(B+40*10)	Stores the address of B+400.

Imperative Instructions

Declarative instructions are executed at assembly time and cause the object program to reserve memory for special purposes. Imperative instructions are executed at object time and cause machine functions to take place upon the data to be treated in the actual application. A few basic instructions are discussed here.

ADD (RX Format). This instruction adds one *full word* of data from core to the register specified. The data referenced in core must be stored on a full word boundary. The instruction

```
A 5,SAM(0,9)
```

will add one full word of information located at SAM to register 5 and retain the sum in register 5. SAM might have been defined as follows:

```
SAM DC F '100'
```

The above instruction would have added 100 (in binary) to register 5. Notice that in this add instruction SAM is the *displacement*; i.e., if the label SAM had been made synonymous with location 200, the displacement for the instruction above would have been 200 and the effective address 200 plus contents of rightmost 24 bits of register 9, the base register.

SUBTRACT (RX Format). This command functions in the same fashion as the add command except that the core storage location referenced is subtracted from the register indicated instead of added. Thus:

```
S 5,SAM(0,9)
```

would subtract the full word located at SAM from the full word contained in register 5.

LOAD (RX Format). This instruction takes a *full word* of information (on a full word boundary) and places it in the register indicated.

L 8,A(0,9)

will load register 8 with the full word located in location A.

Suppose we had used the following declaratives:

```
        DS   OF          (Sets location counter at
                          full word boundary)
CORE    DC   H  '300'    (Defines half-word constant of 300)
NEXT    DC   H  '-1'     (Defines half-word constant of -1)
```

These would have given us a full word of information on a full word boundary as shown in Figure 17–10.

The execution of

L 3,CORE(0,9)

would have placed the contents of these four bytes (one word) into register 3.

STORE (RX Format). The functions of the operands is reversed when using the STORE command. This command takes the contents of the register indicated and places it in core. The location in which the data is to be stored must be aligned on a full word boundary. For example:

ST 8,A(0,9)

would store the contents of register 8 into storage location A. Note the opposite use of the operands.

Half-Word Instructions (RX Format). The operation of the half-word instructions is similar to that of the full word instructions discussed above. As the name implies, only half-words of data are affected. The question is: which half? The only time this question becomes significant is when using the store half-word instruction. In this case, the rightmost 16 bits (last 2 bytes) of the register are stored in the half-word of core referenced. For the instructions that transfer data from core to registers, the half-word is picked up from core and extended to a full word prior to placing it into the register. In effect, all this does is to propagate the sign to the left. Thus, if the half-word picked up from core is positive, it will be extended to a full word by filling in 16 zeros. If the half-word picked up from core is negative, it will be extended to a full word by inserting 16 high-order 1's.

Figure 17–10.

The half-word variety of the instructions discussed above are:

LH	load half-word
STH	store half-word
AH	add half-word
SH	subtract half-word

All half-word instructions must be stored in memory on a half-word boundary and must, of course, operate upon half-words of data aligned on half-word boundaries.

In effect, half-word instructions operate on half-words of data by expanding them to a full word, performing the operation, and reducing the result to a half-word. The store half-word instruction stores the lower one-half of the referenced register in the memory location given in Operand 2.

Condition Code

At this stage in the development of our programming language and techniques, it will be well to mention that after some arithmetic instructions are executed, an indicator inside the 360 will be set indicating the algebraic sign of the outcome of the execution of that instruction. This indicator will remain in that state until another operation affecting the condition code is executed, at which time it is used to indicate the outcome of that particular operation. In between two arithmetic operations, this indicator may be interrogated and decisions made based on its setting. We will not attempt at this stage to discuss the interrogation of this condition code but will merely indicate its setting. The setting of the condition code is determined by the result of the previously executed arithmetic instruction according to the following chart:

Result	*Condition Code*
Zero	00
Negative	01
Positive	10
Overflow	11

We will have more to say about this later.

Example Programs

Prior to moving into more arithmetic operations in the following chapter, we should take the time to review a few examples of those presented here in order that we may reinforce the material to this point:

EXAMPLE 1

What is the result of executing the following program: assume register 9 in our base register.

Label	*Op Code*	*Operands*
CON 1	DC	F'5'
CON 2	DC	H'1'
CON 3	DC	H'3'
	L	3,CON1(0,9)
	AH	3,CON2(0,9)
	SH	3,CON3(0,9)

Solution. The declaratives would generate:

00	00	00	05	00	01	00	03

(8 bytes of information)

↖ ↖ ↑ *1 byte*

CON1FWB — CON2HWB — CON3HWB

Note that we are using hexadecimal representation and two hexadecimal characters equal one byte.

The load command would produce:

0	0	0	0	0	0	0	5

REG3 ↖ ↖ ↖ 1 byte

The add half-word command would produce:

0	0	0	0	0	0	0	6

REG3 Condition Code = 10

The subtract half-word command would produce our result:

0	0	0	0	0	0	0	3

R
E
G
3

Condition Code = 10

EXAMPLE 2

How is the condition code set following this series of instructions?

Label	*Op Code*	*Operands*
CON1	DC	H'2'
CON2	DC	F'3'
CON3	DC	F'−5'
ANS	DS	F
	LH	0,CON1(0,9)
	A	0,CON2(0,9)
	A	0,CON3(0,9)
	ST	0,ANS(0,9)

Solution. The declaratives would set up areas as follows:

00	02

(2 bytes on a HWB)

C
O
N
1

00	00	00	03

(4 bytes on a FWB.)
(This is not necessarily adjacent to above. Why?)

C
O
N
2

FF	FF	FF	FB

(4 bytes on FWB adjacent to CON2.)
(Note that hexadecimal representation is used.)

C
O
N
3

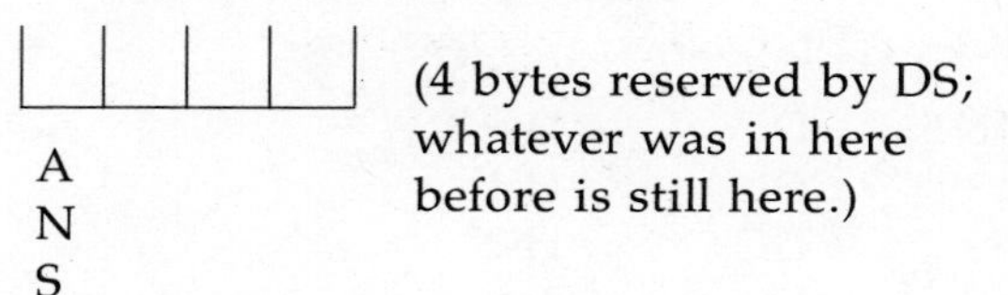

The load half-word instruction would result in:

00	00	00	02

Condition Code = ??

R
E
G
0

After the add, we have:

00	00	00	05

Condition Code = 10

R
E
G
0

and after the second add, we get:

00	00	00	00

Condition Code = 00

R
E
G
0

After the store answer instruction, the memory location called ANS contains:

00	00	00	00

Condition Code = 00

A
N
S

Thus, the condition code will be sitting at 00 after execution of this program. The store answer instruction does not affect the condition code.

EXAMPLE 3

What is the HEX representation of the information stored in ANS to ANS + 5?

	Label	*Op Code*	*Operands*
1.	CON	DC	H'−3'
2.		DC	H'1'
3.		DC	H'2'
4.	ANS	DS	3H
5.		LH	0,CON(0,9)
6.		LH	1,CON+2(0,9)
7.		LH	2,CON+4(0,9)
8.		AR	0,1
9.		AR	1,2
10.		AR	2,0
11.		STH	0,ANS(0,9)
12.		STH	1,ANS+2(0,9)
13.		STH	2,ANS+4(0,9)

Solution. The result of the execution of each step is shown. (Note that 2 hexadecimal characters equal one byte.)

1. FFFD
2. 0001
3. 0002
4. 3 half-words reserved
5. FFFFFFFD REG0
6. 00000001 REG1
7. 00000002 REG2
8. FFFFFFFE REG0
9. 00000003 REG1
10. 00000000 REG2
11. FFFE + 2 more half-words in ANS
12. FFFE0003 + 1 more half-word in ANS
13.

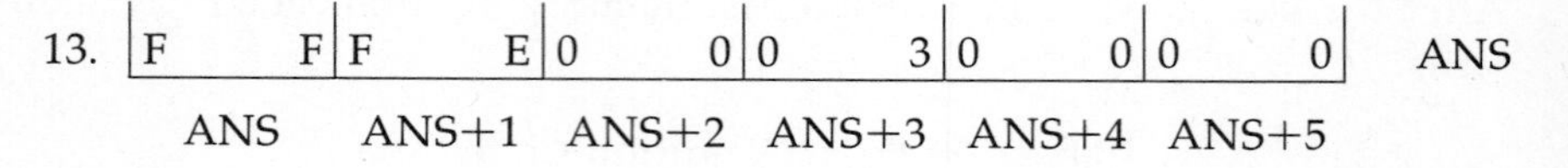

Summary

The purpose of this chapter was to introduce the basic notions of data storage and programming for the IBM System/360 Assembly Language. Naturally, one cannot expect to become an ALC programmer by reading one short chapter. However, the purpose here is not to teach 360 programming, but rather to illustrate the basic features of the 360 and the basic considerations of its programming. In the chapter to follow, more instructions and more programming considerations will be encountered.

Questions

1. The hexadecimal value 76D8 represents what binary number?
2. What is the hexadecimal equivalent of the following binary number? 10110111011011001
3. A byte in storage contains the binary value of the decimal number 100. If this number were negative, what would its bit pattern be?
4. From the following series of declaratives, which instruction does not begin on a half-word boundary?

```
FLD1    DS    F
FLD2    DS    H
FLD3    DS    D
CON2    DC    C'-3100'
CON4    DC    H'6400'
```

5. Which of the following symbols (names) has the greatest length attribute?
   a. ONE DC F'123456'
   b. TWO DC H'-123456'
   c. FOUR DC CL4'123456'
   d. FIVE DC 4C'123456'
6. In the execution of the instruction: L 3,FIELDA(0,9)
   a. What is the function of operand 2?
   b. What are the restrictions on boundary alignment?
   c. What restrictions are placed on operand 1?
   d. Is it necessary to clear operand 1 prior to executing this command?
   e. What is the displacement?
   f. What base register is being used?
   g. What index register is in use?
7. What byte of an area is the name of a declarative associated with?
8. What is the difference between the DC and DS assembler instructions?
9. Given the declaratives listed below and the fact that the first declarative has been assigned to location 984:

Assigned Location			
984	FIELD1	DS	F
988	FIELD2	DS	D
—	FIELD3	DS	F
—	FIELD4	DS	D
—	FIELD5	DS	F
—	FIELD6	DS	D

Can these declaratives be rearranged so as to use less storage?

18

System/360 Assembly Language: II

The instructions and examples in the last chapter were introduced to generate a feel for the System/360 Assembly Language. We cannot solve any earth-shaking problems with only those instructions. In this chapter, we will introduce some commands and concepts that should enable us to execute an elementary 360 ALC program.

Multiplication

When multiplying, we can use either full words or half words. If we are multiplying a full word by a full word, we are in actuality multiplying 31 bits and a sign bit by 31 bits and a sign bit. This will yield 62 bits + sign + one more bit. This extra bit is a high order zero if the result is positive and a one if the result is negative. The condition code is not affected by multiplication. Thus, our product contains two high order ones or two high order zeros, depending on the algebraic sign of the answer; that is, the answer will be:

00 + 62 bits of product	if positive
11 + 62 bits of product	if negative

Multiply RX Format

This is a full word multiply command. This command will multiply four bytes by four bytes. Its format is:

$$\text{M} \quad R_1,D_2(X_2B_2).$$

The register referenced must be an even-numbered one of an *even-odd* pair. The reason for this follows from the fact that the answer is to be held in registers and one register has but 32 bits, so we will "tie" two registers together in order that we may obtain our 64-bit product. Actually, we do not "tie" the registers together; the machine assumes this when it executes the multiply command. The storage address referenced $[D_2(X_2B_2)]$ should contain the multiplier and should be situated on a full word boundary. Prior to executing the multiply command, we must guarantee that the multiplicand is sitting in the *odd* register of the even-odd pair. The product will be contained in the even-odd pair of registers, with the sign in the *even* register. (By an *even-odd* pair, we mean 2 and 3 or 6 and 7, and so on, but *not* 3 and 4 or 7 and 8, and so on. The even register *must* come first.) The product will be right justified in the even-odd pair with algebraic sign control and the condition code is not set.

Example.

Label	*Op Code*	*Operands*
MCAND	DS	F
MPIER	DS	F
PRODUCT	DS	D
	L	5,MCAND(0,9)
	M	4,MPIER(0,9)
	ST	4,PRODUCT(0,9)
	ST	5,PRODUCT+4(0,9)

Explanation. We have chosen to use registers 4 and 5 for our even-odd pair. Then the multiplicand is placed into register 5. Recall that the load command operates on one full word. Then the multiply command is executed and the product, shown as a string of P's, winds up in registers

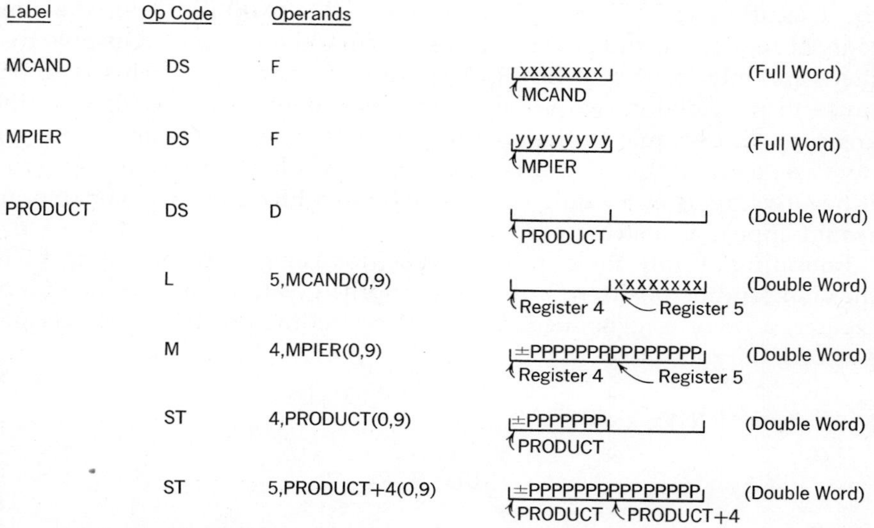

Label	Op Code	Operands		
MCAND	DS	F	xxxxxxxx (MCAND)	(Full Word)
MPIER	DS	F	yyyyyyyy (MPIER)	(Full Word)
PRODUCT	DS	D	(PRODUCT)	(Double Word)
	L	5,MCAND(0,9)	xxxxxxxx (Register 4, Register 5)	(Double Word)
	M	4,MPIER(0,9)	±PPPPPPPPPPPPPPP (Register 4, Register 5)	(Double Word)
	ST	4,PRODUCT(0,9)	±PPPPPPP (PRODUCT)	(Double Word)
	ST	5,PRODUCT+4(0,9)	±PPPPPPPPPPPPPPP (PRODUCT, PRODUCT+4)	(Double Word)

Figure 18–1. Multiplication procedure.

4 and 5 with the sign in register 4. Now we store each register (recall that the store command operates on one full word also) into the eight bytes reserved by the DS for the product. (See Figure 18–1.)

Suppose we wished to multiply two numbers together with two decimal places in each number assumed and that after multiplication we wished to half-adjust the product to two decimal places. If we were doing this by hand, we would multiply the numbers together:

```
      xx.xx     (This decimal not in core. It is
      xx.xx        assumed here.)
  ---------
  xxxx.xxxx
      .0050
  ---------
  xxxx.xx        (This is rounded result.)
```

To accomplish this task in 360 ALC, we would use the following pattern:

```
MCAND     DC    F'xx.xx'              (Assumed decimal place.)
MPLIER    DC    F'xx.xx'
PROD      DS    2F
ROUND     DC    H'50'
          L     7,MCAND(0,9)
          M     6,MPLIER(0,9)
          AH    7,ROUND(0,9)
          ST    6,PROD(0,9)
          ST    7,PROD+4(0,9)
```

This program works much the same way as the previous example. After the execution of the multiply instruction (M 6,MPLIER(0,9)), the contents of registers 6 and 7 would be as shown in Figure 18–2. Observe that there are only eight significant digits in our answer (P's). This is so because in multiplying two numbers together, the number of digits in the answer will be equal to the sum of the digits in each of the factors—in our case, eight. If the answer is positive, we will have eight leading zeros. If negative, register 6 would contain all ones, which in hexadecimal terms would appear as a string of F's.

Rounding off into the hundredths position is a process of adding a 5 to the thousandths position. If the thousandths position has a value of 5 or greater, a carry is generated into the hundredths position, thus accomplishing the rounding.

Multiply RR Format

MR R_1,R_2

R_1 must be an even register of an even-odd pair. The multiplicand should

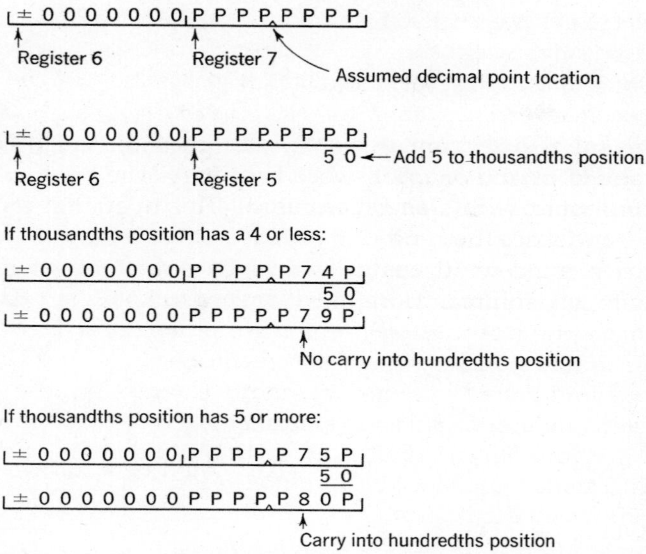

```
|± 0 0 0 0 0 0 0|P P P P^P P P P|
↑                ↑    ↖
Register 6       Register 7   Assumed decimal point location

|± 0 0 0 0 0 0 0|P P P P^P P P P|
                             5 0 ←— Add 5 to thousandths position
↑                ↑
Register 6       Register 5
```

If thousandths position has a 4 or less:

```
|± 0 0 0 0 0 0 0|P P P P^P 7 4 P|
                           5 0
|± 0 0 0 0 0 0 0 P P P P^P 7 9 P|
                         ↑
                         No carry into hundredths position
```

If thousandths position has 5 or more:

```
|± 0 0 0 0 0 0 0|P P P P^P 7 5 P|
                           5 0
|± 0 0 0 0 0 0 0 P P P P^P 8 0 P|
                         ↑
                         Carry into hundredths position
```

Figure 18–2. Rounding by the method of half-adjusting.

be in the odd register of the even-odd pair. R_2 may be any register. R_2 is assumed to be the multiplier.

Example.

Label	*Op Code*	*Operands*
MCAND	DS	F
MPLIER	DS	F
PROD	DS	2F
	L	10,MPLIER(0,9)
	L	7,MCAND(0,9)
	MR	6,10
	ST	6,PROD(0,9)
	ST	7,PROD+4(0,9)

Or, suppose we wished to square a number.

Label	*Op Code*	*Operands*
NUMBER	DC	F'*xx*'
	L	7,NUMBER(0,9)
	MR	6,7

This would leave the square of the number in registers 6 and 7 as a double word.

MULTIPLY HALF-WORD RX FORMAT

$$\text{MH} \quad R_1,D_2(X_2,B_2)$$

R_1 may be any register containing the multiplicand and $D_2(X_2,B_2)$ is the multiplier stored in core on a half-word boundary. The product winds up in R_1 as a full word with sign bits as usual. This operation can result in an overflow, and since the condition code is not set on any of the multiply operations, we could wind up in trouble. Thus, before using this command, as with any command, we must be sure to know our data.

Example.

Label	*Op Code*	*Operands*
MCAND	DS	H (This could be a full word)
MPLIER	DS	H
PROD	DS	F
	LH	14,MCAND(0,9)
	MH	14,MPLIER(0,9)
	ST	14,PROD(0,9)

Note that we did not use the STH command. Why? Had the multiplicand been a full word, we could have experienced the overflow mentioned above.

Problem. Write the instructions necessary to solve for Z where

$$Z = (A + B - C)\ W$$

Solution.

Label	*Op Code*	*Operands*
A	DS	F
B	DS	F
C	DS	F
W	DS	F
Z	DS	2F
	L	5,A(0,9)
	A	5,B(0,9)
	S	5,C(0,9)
	M	4,W(0,9)
	ST	4,Z(0,9)
	ST	5,Z+4(0,9)

Note especially the use of the *even-odd* registers. See Figure 18–3. Observe that the multiplicand (A + B − C) was formed in the odd-numbered register (5) so that the multiplier, W, can be multiplied against register 4 with no further manipulation of the multiplicand, A + B − C.

Division

As with multiplication, the condition code is not set after the division operation. The dividend used in the divide operation should contain 63 bits plus a sign. The divisor should contain 31 bits plus a sign. This will yield a quotient of 31 bits plus a sign and a remainder of 31 bits plus a sign.

RX FORMAT

The RX format for the divide command is:

$$OP \quad R_1,D_2(X_2,B_2)$$

where R_1 is the even of an even-odd pair of registers and this register and its odd counterpart contain the dividend. The dividend should be right justified in these registers with the sign in the left end of the even register. $D_2(X_2,B_2)$ refers to the core location of the divisor. The divisor should be a full word on a full word boundary. The quotient will be in the odd register with algebraic sign control and the remainder in the even register and will have the sign of the dividend attached. If the quotient cannot be held in one register (one word) an overflow will result.

Example.

Label	*Op Code*	*Operands*
DSOR	DS	F
DEND	DS	D
QUOT	DS	F
REM	DS	F
	L	2,DEND(0,9)
	L	3,DEND+4(0,9)
	D	2,DSOR(0,9)
	ST	3,QUOT(0,9)
	ST	2,REM(0,9)

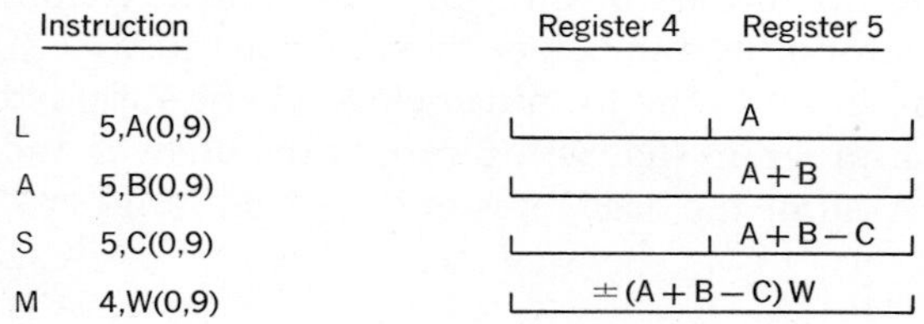

Instruction		Register 4	Register 5
L	5,A(0,9)		A
A	5,B(0,9)		A+B
S	5,C(0,9)		A+B−C
M	4,W(0,9)	±(A+B−C) W	

Figure 18–3. Register use in a sample problem.

Once again, note the function and operation of the even-odd pair of registers. At this point one might question the necessity of having the dividend stored in a double word. (See Figure 18–4.) Suppose the dividend were stored in a full word, rather than a double word. Would it be possible to get the sign in the even register? This question will be answered later.

DIVIDE—RR FORMAT

DR R_1,R_2

R_1 is the even of an even-odd pair of registers and contains the dividend right justified in the even-odd pair. R_2 contains the divisor and may be any register. The rest of the operation is similar to the divide RX format previously discussed.

Example. Calculate (D + A) C/D.

Label	*Op Code*	*Operands*
DSOR	DS	F (contains A)
QUOT	DS	F (contains B)
SAVE	DS	2F (contains C)
CON1	DS	F (contains D)
	L	3,CON1(0,9)
	LR	10,3
	A	3,DSOR(0,9)
	M	2,SAVE(0,9)
	DR	2,10
	ST	3,SAVE(0,9)
	ST	2,CON1(0,9)

Figure 18–5 illustrates these operations. The condition code was set by the add instruction given above only.

It is most significant to note that the difference between the operation of multiplication and division is that the divide command demands that the sign be set in the even register and that the multiply command does not.

In order to summarize the operations of multiplication and division, we present a final example combining the use of these commands.

Assume the values of W, Y, and Z in the formula below will be supplied by another program. Write a program that will compute the answer and place it in location RESULT. Assume the base register is register number 1.

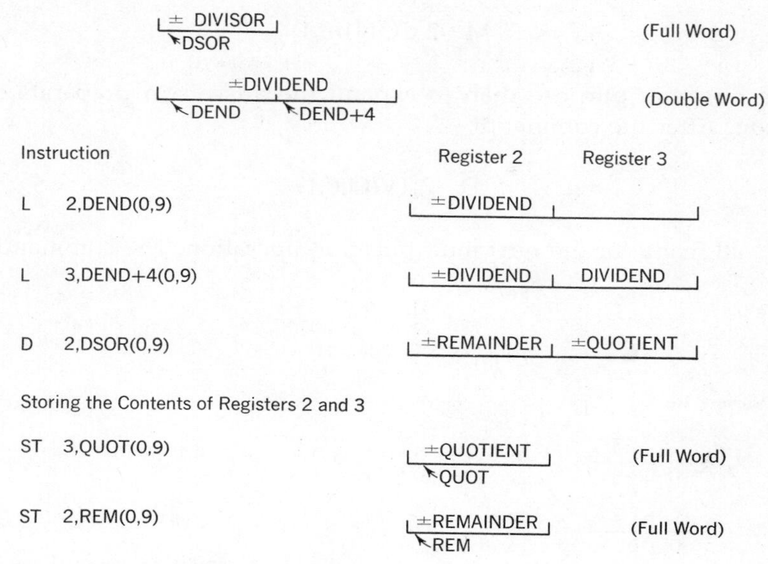

Figure 18–4. Division operation.

$$\text{RESULT} = \frac{W + Y - Z}{2} \times 3$$

Label	*Op Code*	*Operands*
CON1	DC	F'1'
RESULT	DS	D
W	DS	F
Y	DS	F
Z	DS	F
THREE	DC	F'3'
TWO	DC	F'2'
	L	3,W(0,1)
	A	3,Y(0,1)
	S	3,Z(0,1)
	M	2,CON1(0,1)
	D	2,TWO(0,1)
	SR	2,2
	M	2,THREE(0,1)
	ST	3,RESULT(0,1)
	ST	4,RESULT+4(0,1)

In the above solution, the command

M 2,CON1(0,1)

serves no other purpose than to expand the answer in preparation for division. After the command

D 2,TWO(0,1)

we are all ready for the next multiplication operation. The command

SR 2,2

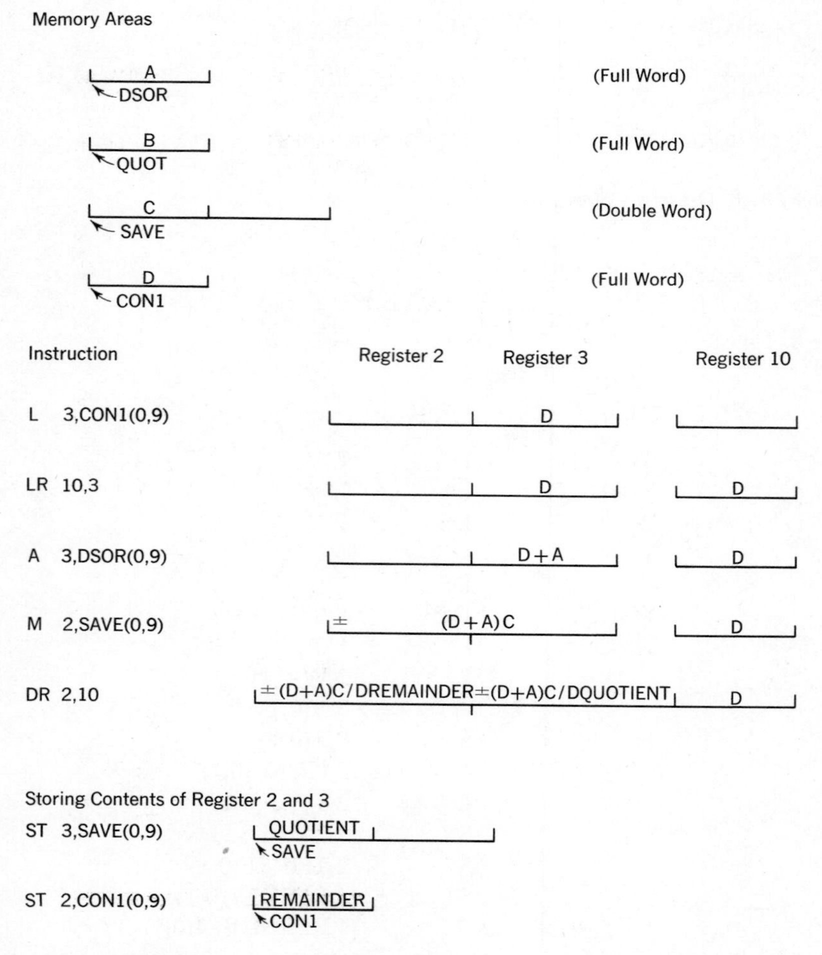

Figure 18–5. Calculation of (D + A)C/D.

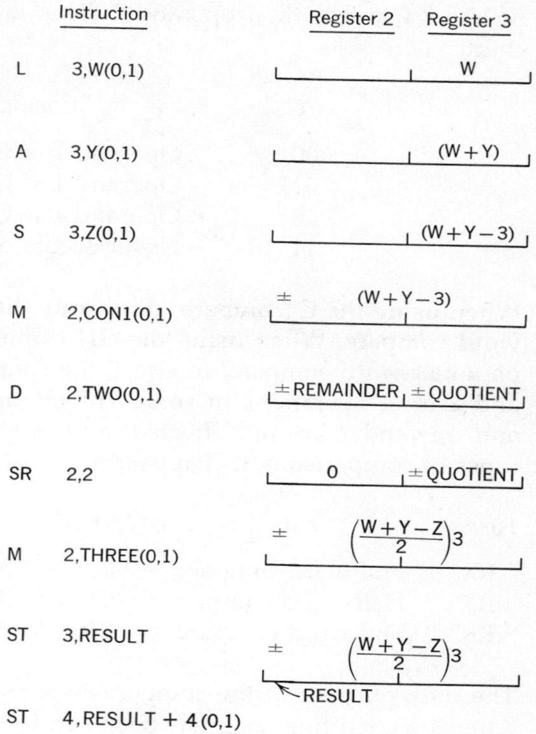

Instruction		Register 2	Register 3
L	3,W(0,1)		W
A	3,Y(0,1)		(W+Y)
S	3,Z(0,1)		(W+Y−3)
M	2,CON1(0,1)	± (W+Y−3)	
D	2,TWO(0,1)	±REMAINDER	±QUOTIENT
SR	2,2	0	±QUOTIENT
M	2,THREE(0,1)	± $\left(\frac{W+Y-Z}{2}\right)3$	
ST	3,RESULT	± $\left(\frac{W+Y-Z}{2}\right)3$ ← RESULT	
ST	4,RESULT + 4 (0,1)		

Figure 18–6. Calculation of $\left(\frac{W+Y-Z}{2}\right)3$

is not really necessary for the multiplication command automatically clears this register to zero prior to executing the command:

M 2,THREE(0,1)

Subtracting a register from itself, of course, leaves its contents zero. (See Figure 18–6.)

Comparing

During the course of executing a program, it will frequently become apparent that some way must be provided to analyze two fields and determine which is the larger. In System/360 ALC, we are provided with this capability via the algebraic compare commands. The compare command has two forms, RX and RR. The comparison is algebraic because the signs of the quantities being compared are taken into consideration. After every comparison, a condition code indicating the results of the comparison is set accordingly. The condition code is always set with reference to the first operand. If the condition code is 00, this implies that operand 1 is equal to operand 2. If the condition code is set to 01, this implies that operand 1 is less than operand 2. This is summarized in the following chart.

CC	*Comparison*
00	Operand 1 = Operand 2
01	Operand 1 < Operand 2
10	Operand 1 > Operand 2
11	Never occurs on comparing.

When using the C (compare command), the comparison is based on a full word compare. When using the CH command, the comparison is based on a half-word compare. In effect, the compare command subtracts operand 2 from operand 1 in some "phantom" registers (that is, operand 1 and operand 2 are not affected) and sets the condition code. The three types of comparisons will appear as:

Format	*Type*	*Op Code*	*Operand 1*	*Operand 2*
RX	Full word compare	C	Any register	Storage on FWB
RX	Half-word compare	CH	Any register	Storage on HWB
RR	Full word compare	CR	Any register	Any register

The only purpose of the compare command is to set the condition code. After the condition code has been set, we may test it and, based upon its setting, branch to various portions of our program.

Branching

BRANCH ON CONDITION (BC)

$$\text{OP} \quad M_1X_2B_2D_2$$

M_1 is the *mask* representing the condition to be tested and $X_2B_2D_2$ is the storage location to which we wish to branch should the condition exist. A mask, as we shall see, is a code word that the programmer develops to indicate the status of the condition code in which he is interested. Recall that the condition code may be set to 00, 01, 10, or 11. With each of these, let us associate the numbers 8, 4, 2, and 1, respectively, i.e.,

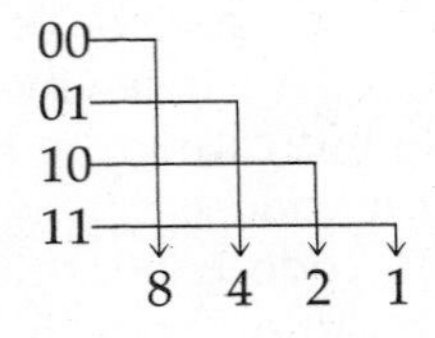

Using this BCD scheme, we can perform any one of 16 different tests; that is, should we use the number 3 in our mask, we are asking the machine if the 11 or the 10 condition exists. If we use the number 15 in our mask, we are asking the machine if the 00, 01, 10, or 11 conditions exist (this, in effect, gives us an unconditional branch, for one of these conditions will always exist). If we use the number 4 in our mask, we are asking only if the 01 condition exists. Testing the status of the condition code in this manner does not affect it. The only thing affecting the condition code is the execution of some arithmetic operations or the execution of a compare instruction.

Thus, the command:

BC 8,CORE(0,9) (Branch Equal)

will provide us with a branch to CORE if the 00 condition code exists. Otherwise, we will go to the next sequential instruction. The command

BC 12,CORE(0,9)

will give us a branch to CORE if the 00 or 01 conditions exist, and

BC 15,CORE(0,9)

results in an unconditional branch to CORE. In the illustrations above, it is assumed that CORE contains a valid instruction; otherwise, in taking the branch, an error condition would result.

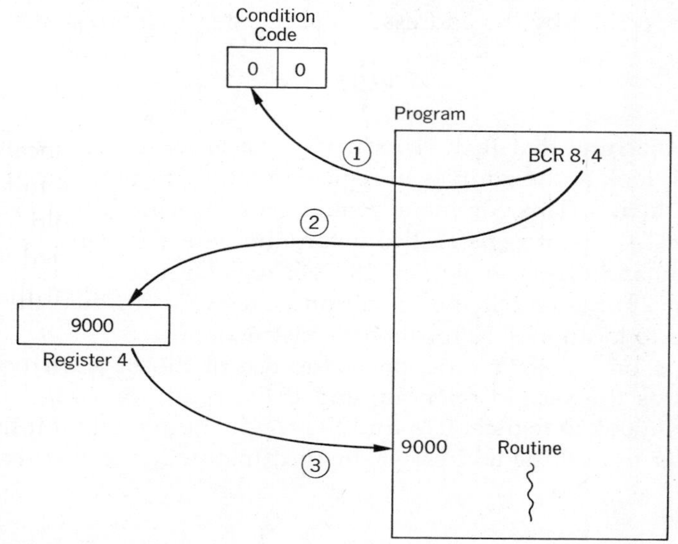

Figure 18–7. BCR execution.

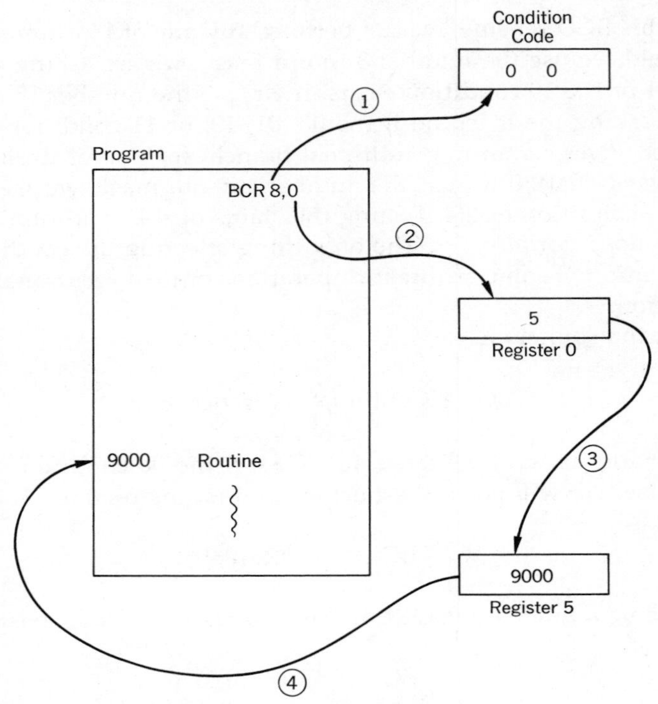

Figure 18–8. Branching on condition (RR format) operand 2 = 0.

The RR format for the conditional branch command is similar to the RX above except that if the condition is *true*, that is, if the condition code is in the status described by the mask, the computer will branch to the location specified by the address in the register referenced. For example:

BCR 8,4

tells the machine that if the condition code is set to 00, it should go to register 4, look at the address in register 4, and go to that location for its next instruction. This command would cause the machine to look at the rightmost 24 bits of register 4 to determine where it should look for its next command. Thus, in Figure 18–7, if register 4 contained 9000 in its rightmost 24 bits and if the condition code were 00, then the machine would go to location 9000 for its next instruction.

There is one major restriction to the use of the BCR. If register 0 is specified as the second operand, and if the condition code is satisfied, then it will look to register 0 to find the *register* number that it should look to in order to find the address of the next instruction to be executed. For example:

BCR 8,0

would look at the condition code, and if CC=00, then it would interrogate bits 12–15 of register 0 (and hopefully find something other than zero). It would then go to this register to find the address of the instruction to be executed next (See Figure 18–8).

Mnemonics for Branch Instructions

The reader might wonder why, since we are using an assembly language, there were not some mnemonics developed for all of these conditional branches. As a matter of fact, System/360 ALC does provide us with mnemonics for conditional branching. Figure 18–9 summarizes these mnemonics. Thus, the command

BL SAM(0,9)

would cause a branch to SAM if the condition code were set to 01 as would the command

BC 4,SAM(0,9)

Extended Mnemonic	Machine Code	Type of Branch
	General	
B	BC 15	Unconditional Branch
BR	BCR 15	Unconditional branch
NOP	BC 0	No operation
NOPR	BCR 0	No operation (R-R format)
	After Compare Instructions (A:B)	
BH	BC 2	Branch on A high
BL	BC 4	Branch on A low
BE	BC 8	Branch on A = B
BNH	BC 13	Branch on A not high
BNL	BC 11	Branch on A not low
BNE	BC 7	Branch on A ≠ B
	After Arithmetic Instructions	
BO	BC 1	Branch on overflow
BP	BC 2	Branch on plus
BM	BC 4	Branch on minus
BZ	BC 8	Branch on Zero

Figure 18–9. Branch mnemonics.

Additional Imperative and Declarative Instructions

Prior to moving into the storage to storage (SS format) type of instructions, we should investigate a few more register-type instructions and a technique for storing characters into core to be used for headings and other alphabetic outputs.

Load Positive Register (LPR)

LPR R_1,R_2

This command forces the absolute value of the data stored in R_2 to be loaded into R_1. Thus, if register 5 contains −8 and register 3 contains 27, the execution of

LPR 3,5

will cause register 3 to contain +8 and leave −8 in register 5.

Load Negative Register (LNR)

LNR R_1,R_2

This command causes the negative of the absolute value of R_2 to be placed in R_1. If register 3 contains 2 and register 5 contains 15, then execution of

LNR 5,3

will cause register 5 to be changed to −2. If register 3 had −2 in it originally, register 5 would still wind up with −2.

Load Complement Register (LCR)

LCR R_1,R_2

This command forces the negative of the contents of $R2$ to be loaded into R_1. Thus, if register 3 contains 2 and register 5 contains 15, then after execution of

LCR 5,3

register 5 would contain −2 stored in complement form, as is the case with all negative numbers. If register 3 contained −2 initially, then register 5 would contain 2 after execution of the above command.

LOAD AND TEST REGISTER (LTR)

LTR R_1,R_2

This command functions just like the load register command except that it forces a setting of the condition code. Thus, if register 5 contains −3 and register 7 contains 12, the execution of

LTR 7,5

would cause −3 to be loaded into register 7 and the condition code to be set to 01.

CHARACTER DECLARATIVE STATEMENTS

To this point, we have shown how to store fixed point data in memory and how it is manipulated arithmetically, but we have said nothing about storing characters in memory. The format for a declarative to set alphabetic and numeric constants in memory in character mode is shown below:

Label DC *d*C L*n* 'CONST'

Any name may be assigned according to the rules outlined previously. The DC tells the processor that we want to define a constant. The *d* is the duplication factor for this constant. The "C" is a requirement telling the machine that *characters* are to be stored; *n* tells the processor how many characters. The constant itself is placed between apostrophes. This entry may be used to place any EBCDIC character into core up to a maximum of 256 characters in one entry. One character will be entered into each byte according to the format discussed in the preceding chapter. For example:

Label	*Op Code*	*Operands*
CHARTER	DC	CL3'2AC'

would cause three bytes of information to be stored as follows:

11110010	11000001	11000011
2	A	C

If a duplication factor is used such as

NAME DC 2CL3'2AC'

then 2AC2AC will be stored in core with the name associated with the byte containing the first 2. Should we use

DC CL2'ABC'

then the C will be truncated when the data are stored with the result that AB is in storage. If we use

DC CL4'ABC'

we will receive ABC blank in the four bytes of storage declared. Anytime *n* is larger than the number of characters we wish to store, the right side of the constant will be *padded* with blanks.

Hexadecimal Declarative Statements

Should we wish to store hexadecimal data in the machine, we will use the same format as that used for declaring characters, except that the C becomes an X.

NAME DC *d*XL*n* 'CONST'

The maximum number of bytes used in one statement is 256 with two hexadecimal characters per byte, and the pad, if any, will be zeros instead of blanks. Also, the constant will be right justified in the area instead of left justified as with the character declarative. Each hexadecimal character we place between the apostrophes occupies one-half byte of core storage. Only hexadecimal characters are permitted—that is, 1 through 9, A, B, C, D, E, F. However, if only one hexadecimal character is specified, it will occupy one byte since the smallest addressable unit in the 360 is the byte. Thus:

Label	*Op Code*	*Operands*
X1	DC	X'1'

will be stored as

00000001
one byte

CONST DC X2'3AF2'

will be stored in two bytes as

$$\underbrace{00111010}_{\text{one byte}}\underbrace{11110010}_{\text{2nd byte}}$$

If n above had been 3 instead of 2, we would have stored this information in 3 bytes, but the first of these three would have contained zeros. The length code need not be specified. If it is not specified, the machine will examine the hexadecimal constant and store it using the appropriate number of bytes.

Sample Program 1

At this stage in the development of the Assembly Language Coding for the System/360, we should pause to examine more examples of ALC Coding in an attempt to solidify some of the ideas and instructions discussed.

PROBLEM

Calculate Z where all quantities are full word integers.

$$Z = |X| - 2\,(|X - |Y||)$$

where | | indicates *absolute value.* Assume $-2\,(|X - |Y||)$ will not occupy more than one word.

SOLUTION

Label	*Op Code*	*Operands*
X	DS	F
Y	DS	F
TWO	DC	F'2'
Z	DS	F
	L	1,X
	L	2,Y
	LPR	2,2
	S	1,2
	LPR	1,1
	M	0,TWO(0,9)
	LNR	1,1
	L	0,X
	LPR	0,0
	AR	0,1
	ST	0,Z

Instruction	Register 0	Register 1	Register 2
L 1,X		X	
L 2,Y		X	Y
LPR 2,2		X	|Y|
S 1,2		X − |Y|	|Y|
LPR 1,1		|X − |Y||	|Y|
M 0,TWO(0,1)	±00000000	2|X − |Y||	|Y|
LNR 1,1	±00000000	−2|X − |Y||	|Y|
L 0,X	X	−2|X − |Y||	|Y|
LPR 0,0	X	−2|X − |Y||	|Y|
AR 0,1	|X|−2|X−|Y||	−2|X − |Y||	|Y|
ST 0,Z	|X|−2|X−|Y|| (→ Z)		

Figure 18–10.

Figure 18–10 shows the contents of registers 0, 1, and 2 during the execution of this program.

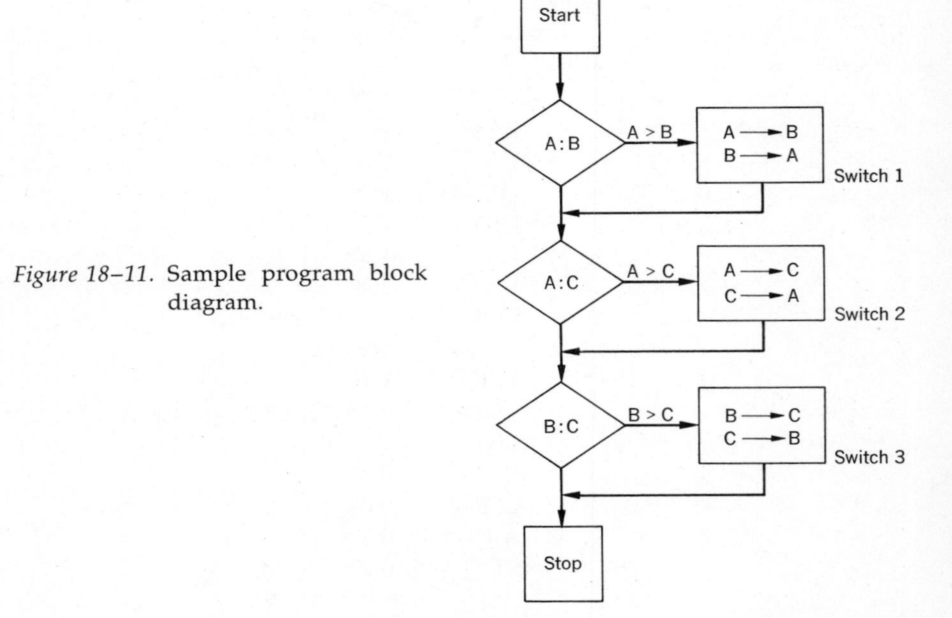

Figure 18–11. Sample program block diagram.

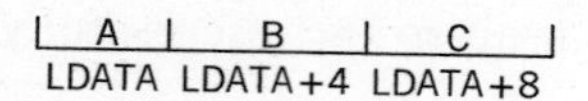


```
LDATA      DS     3F
           L      3,LDATA(0,9)
           C      3,LDATA+4(0,9)
           BH     SWITCH1
COMP2      C      3,LDATA+8(0,9)
           BH     SWITCH2
COMP3      L      3,LDATA+4(0,9)
           C      3,LDATA+4(0,9)
           BH     SWITCH3
STOP       STOP
SWITCH1    L      3,LDATA+4(0.9)
           L      4,LDATA(0,9)
           ST     3,LDATA(0,9)
           ST     4,LDATA+4(0,9)
           B      COMP2
SWITCH2    L      3,LDATA+8(0,9)
           L      4,LDATA(0,9)
           ST     3,LDATA(0,9)
           ST     4,LDATA+8(0,9)
           B      COMP3
SWITCH3    L      3,LDATA+8(0,9)
           L      4,LDATA+4(0,9)
           ST     3,LDATA+4(0,9)
           ST     4,LDATA+8(0,9)
           B      STOP
```

Figure 18–12. Sample program coding.

Sample Problem 2

Arrange three adjacent algebraic words, A, B, and C, with A stored at LDATA into ascending sequence. The block diagram and coding of this program are shown in Figures 18–11 and 18–12.

The reader should sketch the contents of the registers and memory locations (particularly the SWITCH routines) after the execution of each instruction in order to test his understanding of this program.

Up to this point, none of the sample problems and programs have presented very realistic or businesslike applications. This is because we have not yet examined all the instructions we need to write a realistic business problem. The purpose of the next chapter is to introduce some additional System/360 ALC operations and, finally, to write a short program more like those actually found in business applications.

Questions

1. What will be the content of general register 5 after executing the following instructions?

```
CONA    DC    F'1'
CONB    DC    H'-2'
        L     5,CONA(0,9)
        AH    5,CONB(0,9)
```

2. List the instructions required to successfully divide DVND by DVSR.

```
DVND    DC    F'12345'
DVSR    DC    F'+26'
```

3. What settings of the condition code are being tested in the following instruction?

```
        BC    11,OUT(0,9)
```

4. What will register 7 contain after the following instructions are executed?

```
        L     7,DELTA(0,9)
        C     7,GAMMA(0,9)
        BE    E
        BL    L
        S     7,GAMMA(0,9)
        B     OUT(0,9)
E       SR    7,7
        B     OUT(0,9)
L       AR    7,7
OUT     B     OUT(0,9)
DELTA   DC    F'444'
GAMMA   DC    F'111'
```

5. What instructions would be required to successfully multiply MCAND by MPLIER?

```
MCAND   DS    F
MPLIER  DS    F
```

6. List the fixed point instructions that affect the setting of the condition code.
7. What would the contents of AREA be as a result of executing the following instructions?

```
CON1    DC    F'—1'
CON2    DC    F'1'
AREA    DS    F
        L     1,CON2(0,9)
        LCR   2,1
        A     2,CON1(0,9)
        ST    2,AREA(0,9)
```

8. Assume there are three full word fixed point quantities in consecutive

storage words beginning at location AREA. Subtract three from each of these and then compute the sum of the first two minus the third. Do not change the original quantities in memory. Assume registers 2–8 are available for use and that your base register is register 9.

9. Code a routine which will test a location called KEY for the character 6. If a character 6 is present, branch to SIX; otherwise, continue on.

10. Write the instructions necessary to compute TOTAL PAY where

TOTALPAY = REGULARPAY+OVERTIMEPAY

and

REGULARPAY = 40*HOURLYRATE
OVERTIMEPAY = (HOURSWORKEDOVER 40)*
OVERTIMEHOURLYRATE

If a person worked less than 40 hours, calculate regular pay equals (number hours worked) * (hourly rate), and then branch to a location called LESS. Assume the following constants:

```
REGRTE    DS    F    (to nearest penny)
OVTRTE    DS    F    (to nearest penny)
HOURS     DS    H    (to nearest hour)
```

19

System/360 Assembly Language: III

Storage-to-Storage Instructions: SS Format

These instructions are designed to handle storage-to-storage operations. Using registers as intermediaries is not required for the storage-to-storage type of instructions. These instructions are designed to operate on *variable length data* as opposed to fixed data words which were discussed in the last chapters. Such data organization presents a problem: how does the computer know the length of the data fields involved? This information is provided by specifying the length of the data fields in the instruction itself. Should the length of the data fields to be operated upon not be specified, the machine will use the length attribute of the data as specified in the declaratives that establish the data fields. The SS format instructions are stored in six bytes or three half-words of storage each. When using these instructions, we may wish to specify two length codes (one for each operand) or one length code. These two types of SS format instructions are shown below.

Op Code	L_1,L_2	B_1	D_1	B_2	D_2	← Two Length Codes
Op Code	L_1	B_1	D_1	B_2	D_2	← One Length Code
|← 8 →|	← 8 →|	← 4 →|	←12→|	← 4 →|	←12→|	← Bits Used

The formats given above illustrate how SS format instructions are stored in memory. The programmer, using the assembly language, writes these

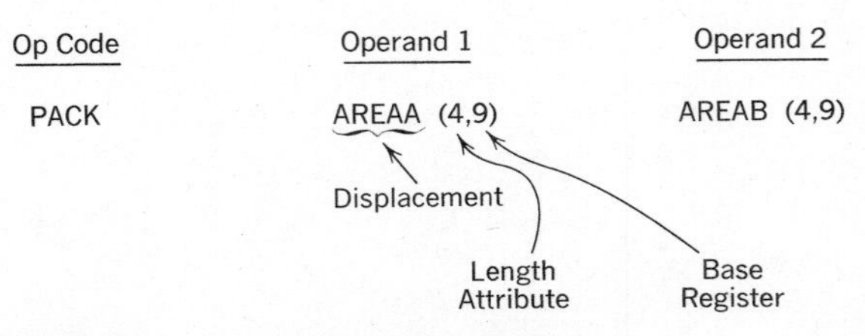

Figure 19–1. Format of storage to storage instructions.

instructions using a format as shown in Figure 19–1. Specific characteristics concerning the use of these instructions are discussed below.

PACK INSTRUCTION: SS FORMAT

Recall that in Chapter 17 we discussed various types of internal data representation. One of these was packed decimal. Should an area contain numerical character information, that is zoned decimal, and should we wish to convert these data to packed decimal, we would use the PACK instruction. The function of this command is to convert zoned decimal information (a numeric quantity stored in character form) into a packed decimal form. This instruction requires two length codes, which may be implied by the length attribute of the areas involved or may be included as part of the instruction. The instruction is executed from right to left. Suppose, for example, that AREAB contained

```
|F1|F2|F3|F4|    4 bytes of information
 ↖
 AREAB
```

and that we wished to pack this information into an area, say, AREAA, also four bytes in length.

```
AREAB  DC  CL4'1234'
AREAA  DC  CL4'    '
```

Now, if we issue the instruction:

```
PACK  AREAA,AREAB
```

we are indicating that the zoned decimal information in AREAB is to be converted to packed decimal form and placed in AREAA. The sign of the data in AREAB is taken to be the low order zone of this field. After issuing the PACK instruction above, AREAB will be unchanged and AREAA will contain:

```
|00|01|23|4F|
 ↖
 AREAA
```

The leading zeros in the field above are padded in automatically. Padding takes place until the length of the receiving field has been exhausted. Figure 19–2 illustrates the action of the PACK instruction. Note that all zones except the one in the low order position of AREA B are ignored.

Had we wished to specify the length code used in the declaratives for

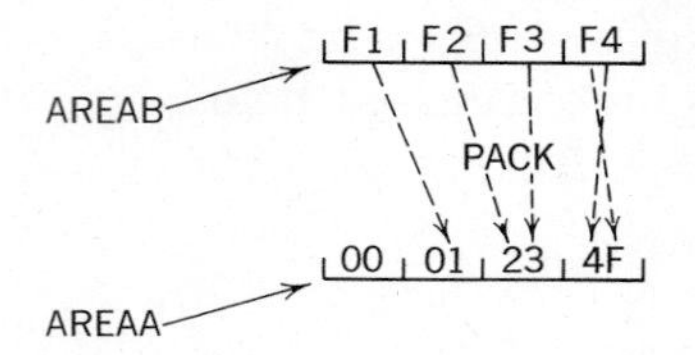

Figure 19–2. Action of the pack instruction.

the fields, assuming base register 9 is in use, our instruction would have appeared as:

PACK AREAA(4,9),AREAB(4,9)

Usually, when the length attribute of the affected areas is the same as the length desired in the instruction, the length codes will be omitted. A field may be packed into itself if the programmer desires. Thus, we could have used:

PACK AREAB,AREAB

Then, AREA B would be altered to a packed form.

As another illustration of the PACK instruction, examine the following:

Label	*Op Code*	*Operand*
PACKED	DC	X'1289C' (hexadecimal constant)
ZONED	DC	C'837' (character-mode constant)
	PACK	PACKED(,9),ZONED(,9)

Prior to execution of the PACK instruction, PACKED and ZONED appear as follows:

Byte 0	Byte 1	Byte 2
00000001	00101000	10011100
11111000	11110011	11110111

PACKED (top row); ZONED (bottom row)

After execution of the PACK instruction, ZONED is unchanged and PACKED will be changed to:

Byte 0	Byte 1	Byte 2
	(8) (3)	(7) (+)
00000000	10000011	01111111

PACKED

Since the length attributes were not specified in the PACK command, the machine assumes the attributes used by the declaratives.

Of course, if one has the ability to pack zoned decimal information, then the reverse operation should also be available.

Unpack Instruction: SS Format

This instruction performs the reverse of the PACK instruction. If the receiving field is not large enough to hold the packed information in a zoned decimal format, truncation of high order digits will result. If the receiving field is too long, zoned zeroes will be inserted in the high order positions of the field. For example:

```
UNPK   ZONED(,9),PACKED(,9)
```

executed on the following fields:

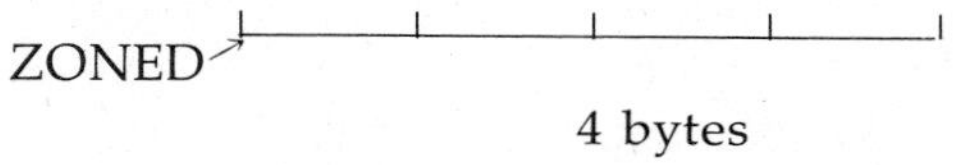

ZONED → | | | | | (4 bytes)

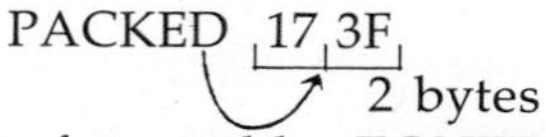

PACKED → |17|3F| (2 bytes)

would result in the field referenced by ZONED to be changed to:

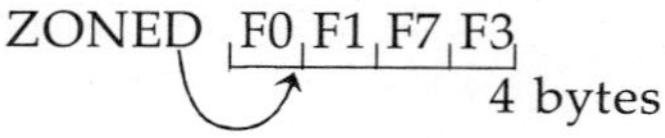

ZONED → |F0|F1|F7|F3| (4 bytes)

Notice that since four bytes were not required to hold the zoned information, the remaining byte was padded with a zoned zero.

Binary-Packed Decimal Conversion

Since all of the instructions we have discussed to this point operate on binary data, we must have a means of converting packed decimal information to binary in order that we may perform the desired arithmetic operations. This is accomplished by the use of the convert-to-binary instruction.

Convert to Binary

This instruction will get the packed information stored at the location specified by operand 2, convert it to binary information, and place it in the register specified by operand 1. Operand 2 must refer to a double word on a double word boundary. It is very important to note that this command operates on *packed information.* Keep in mind that we are trying to convert packed decimal digits when using this command. For this reason, if a valid digit is not present, our program will have a program error condition. The same will be true if the data in the sending field is too large. The following example should clarify the details of this instruction.

Assume PACKED contains

|00|00|00|00|00|00|25|5F|
↖PACKED

in a double word on a double word boundary, and that we issue the command

CVB 3,PACKED.

After execution of this command, register 3 will contain

00000000000000000000000011111111

in binary. Thus, +255 has been converted to its binary equivalent 11111111. After all arithmetic operations have been performed on this binary data, we will want to convert this binary information back to its packed decimal equivalent.

CONVERT TO PACKED DECIMAL

This command along with the store commands are two exceptions to the general role played by the operands. In this command, operand 1 will be a register containing binary information and operand 2 will be a double word sitting on a double word boundary. The machine will convert the decimal information in the referenced register and place it in the double word indicated by the second operand. When the machine converts this binary information to decimal, it will insert a C in the rightmost position of the packing area if the data are positive and a D if the data are negative. The packed information will appear in core as:

|D|D|D|D|D|D|D|S| where D = digit
S = sign.

In the previous example, if we were to execute the command,

CVD 3,PACKED

we would receive

00	00	00	00	00	00	25	5C

↖PACKED ↑ positive sign

in our double word.

When performing fixed point arithmetic operations, the processing sequence for the data will be similar to that shown in the block diagram in Figure 19–3.

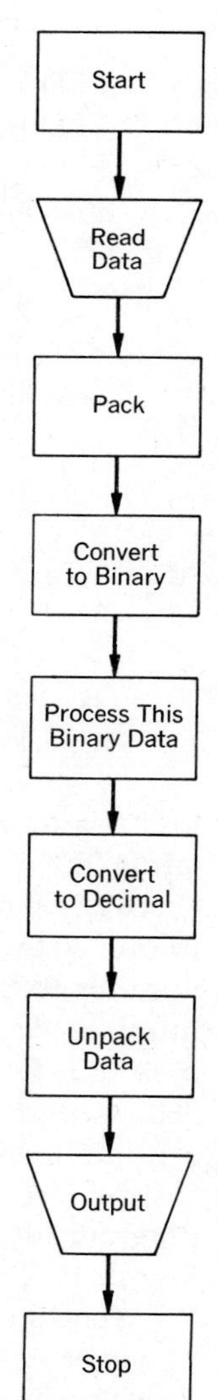

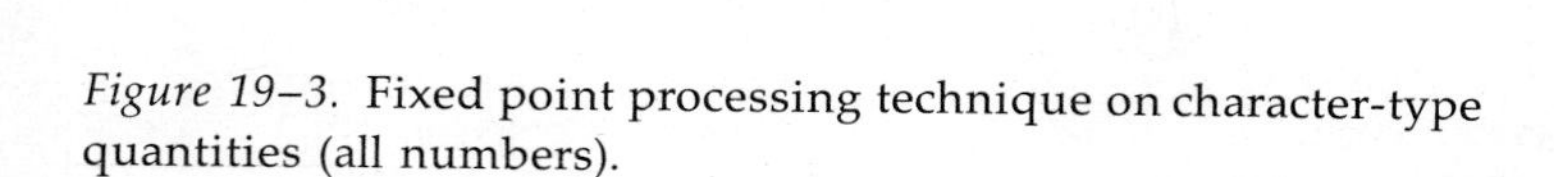

Figure 19–3. Fixed point processing technique on character-type quantities (all numbers).

Sample Program 1

The following example is designed to summarize the details of pack, unpack, convert to binary, convert to decimal commands. (See Figure 19–4.)

PROBLEM

Add FLDA to FLDB and retain the sum in FLDC in zoned decimal form.

Label	*Op Code*	*Operands*
FLDA	DC	C'123'
FLDB	DC	C'100'
FLDC	DS	CL3
PACKAREA	DS	D
	PACK	PACKAREA(,9),FLDA(,9)
	CVB	3,PACKAREA(0,9)
	PACK	PACKAREA(,9),FLDB(,9)
	CVB	4,PACKAREA(0,9)
	AR	3,4
	CVD	3,PACKAREA(0,9)
	UNPK	FLDC(,9),PACKAREA+6(,9)

After execution of the above program, PACKAREA will contain

|00|00|00|00|00|00|22|3C|

PACKAREA ↗ ↖ PACKAREA+6

Perhaps one might question the reason for all of this conversion. It certainly does not make programming any easier. It does, however, save execution time as well as storage space. This can be seen by recalling that in one byte a number as large as 255 can be stored. In the same byte the number 99 in packed decimal can be stored and in zoned decimal the number 9 can be stored. Thus, depending on the format of the data, one byte of information can contain as a maximum number 9, 99, or 255. The 360, as part of its instruction set, does have the capability of performing arithmetic operations on packed data. To be able to do this, the decimal instruction set must be included as a feature of your machine. The block diagram for processing data with this feature would appear as shown in Figure 19–5.

Execution of decimal instructions is costly in terms of time and space; however, they are more convenient to use for the novice programmer. This chapter will not present the detail of these instructions—not because we feel they are unimportant, but because we are attempting to introduce

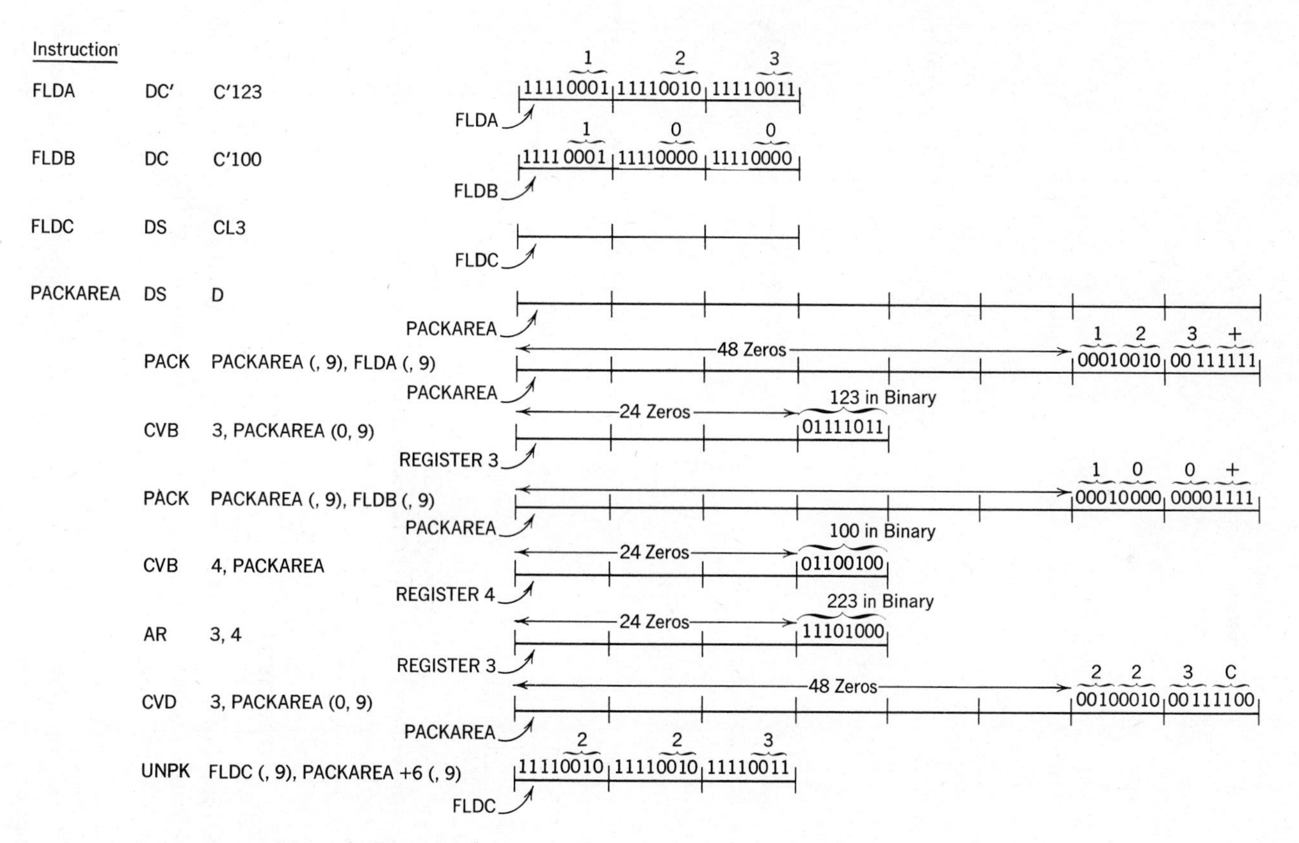

Figure 19–4. Execution of Sample Program 1.

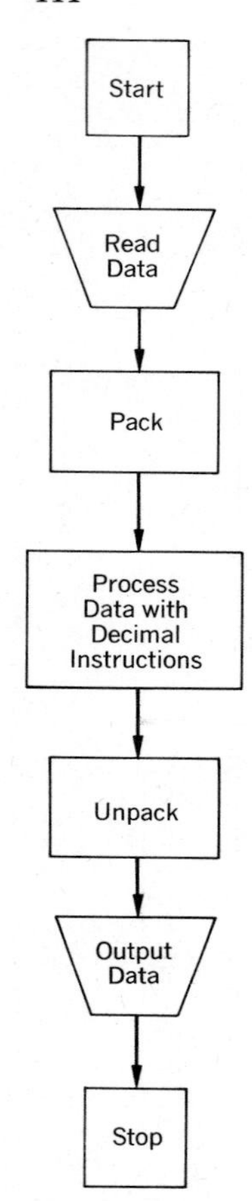

Figure 19–5. Arithmetic operations with decimal arithmetic instructions.

the student to basic programming concepts and instructions which will be applicable to any type of programming environment.

Data Movement

To this point in our discussion, we have not discussed any techniques or commands related to moving data around in memory. We shall do so now.

Move Characters

This command moves a maximum of 256 characters from one location in storage to another. The move takes place from left to right. The reason for the left to right move is that this command requires only one length code and in order to provide a right to left move, the length of both operands must be supplied. The format for this command is:

$$\text{OP} \quad L_1B_1D_1B_2D_2$$

or

$$\text{OP} \quad D_1(L_1B_1)D_2(B_2).$$

For example:

```
MVC   AREA(17,9),OUT(9)
```

will move seventeen bytes of information from OUT to AREA *regardless* of the size of OUT. Thus, if OUT is less then seventeen bytes in length, the data following OUT will be moved until the length code of the first operand has been exhausted. If the command,

```
MVC   AREA(,9),OUT(9)
```

were executed, the length attribute assigned to AREA would be used as the length attribute of the number of characters to be moved by the MVC. Suppose we were given IN and OUT as follows:

```
|____|____|____|____|____|        | A | B | C | D | E | F |
                                    O
  I                                 U
  N                                 T
```

and we executed the command,

```
MVC   IN(,9),OUT(9)
```

IN would then appear as:

```
| A | B | C | D | E |
  I
  N
```

The condition code is not set as a result of executing a MVC. In any storage-to-storage operation, the condition code is left unchanged.

On occasion, we may want to move only zones or only the numeric portions of a field. The System/360 ALC provides us with instructions to do this job also.

Move Zone

This instruction has the same format as the MVC instruction. This command will pick up the high order four bits of operand 2 and place them in the high order four bits of operand 1, one byte at a time. This instruction will be used on packed decimal data.

For example: Suppose CON and K1 were as follows:

```
 F1 F2 F3 F4 C5        F1
 CON                   K1
```

and we wished to move the zone from K1 to CON+4. Execution of the command,

```
MVZ   CON+4(1,9),K1
```

would produce:

```
 F1 F2 F3 F4 F5
 CON
```

Thus, if CON were printed out, we would see 12345 instead of 1234G, G being the alphabetic character equivalent of C5 or −5. This demonstrates a technique for clearing a zone from a signed zoned decimal field. In the example above, if the length code had not been 1, then the zone portion of anything following K1 would have been inserted over the zones in CON until the length code was exhausted.

Example Program Segments

Prior to entering into a discussion of shifting operations, we will examine a few examples to reinforce the ideas and concepts developed to this point.

Example 1

What is the equivalent core address of SAM assuming that the location counter starts at zero?

```
1.              DS   CL3
2.              DS   H
3.              DS   XL2
4.              DC   C'A'
5.              DS   F
6.        SAM   DS   D
```

Solution. (The asterisk indicates the high order byte of the area established by the declarative.)

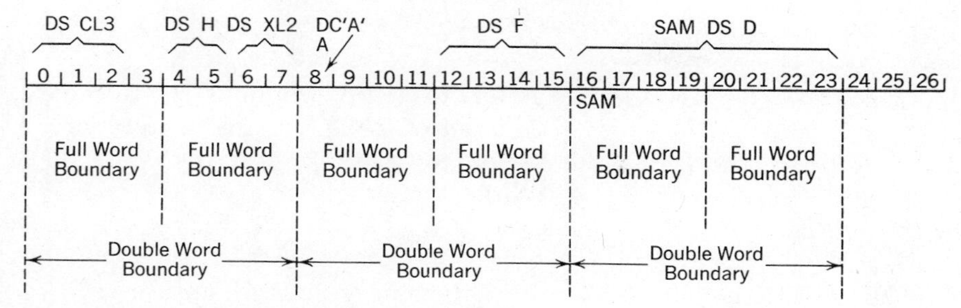

Figure 19–6. Example 1 memory assignment.

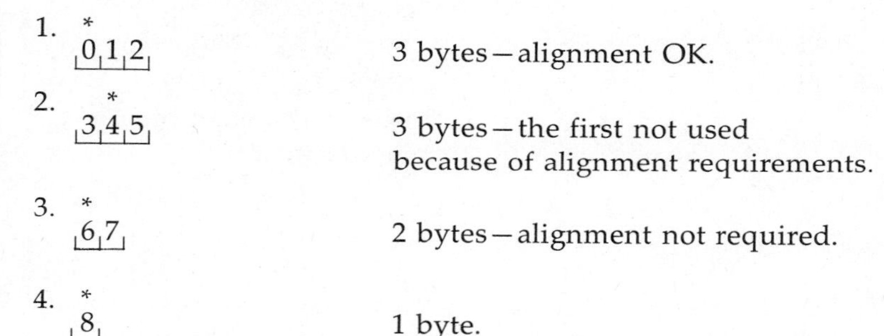

Thus, the equivalent core address of SAM is 16. Figure 19–6 illustrates the usage of the first 24 bytes of memory as indicated by these six declarative instructions.

EXAMPLE 2

What is the result stored in AREA after executing the following instructions?

1.	AREA	DS	CL4
2.	CON	DC	F'260'
3.	CON1	DC	F'59'
4.	WORK	DS	D
5.		L	0,CON(0,9)
6.		L	1,CON1(0,9)
7.		SR	1,0
8.		CVD	1,WORK(0,9)
9.		UNPK	AREA(,9),WORK(,9)

Solution.

1. └*┴─┴─┴─┘ — * refers to AREA. Contains 260 in binary;
2. └*┴─┴─┴─┘ — * refers to CON. Contains 59 in binary;
3. └*┴─┴─┴─┘ — * refers to CON1.
4. └─┴─┴─┴─┴─┴─┴─┴─┘ — Work.
5. 260 → Reg. 0
6. 59 → Reg. 1
7. −201 → Reg. 1 — In binary this will appear as: 11111111111111111111111100110111 4 bytes
8. 00 | 00 | 00 | 00 | 00 | 00 | 20 | 1− — WORK (hexadecimal).
9. F0 | F2 | F0 | D1 — AREA (hexadecimal) or 020J in extended binary coded decimal.

EXAMPLE 3

What is in AREA after executing the following instruction?

```
1.    AREA     DS      CL4
2.    ALPHA    DC      C'STUVWXYZ'
                       PACK    AREA(,9),ALPHA(,9)
```

Solution.

1. └─┴─┴─┴─┘ — 4 bytes reserved.
2. S | T | U | V | W | X | Y | Z — 8 bytes in EBCD.
or E2 | E3 | E4 | E5 | E6 | E7 | E8 | E9 — 8 bytes in hexadecimal.
3. 34 | 56 | 78 | 9E — AREA in hexadecimal.

Observe that since AREA was defined with only four bytes, the high order position of ALPHA (E2) was lost since the sign (E) required four bits.

EXAMPLE 4

What is in AREA after executing the following instruction?

```
1.    AREA     DC      CL5'ASJBTR'
2.    OUT      DC      X'93725'
3.    CON      DC      C'.,?'
4.             MVC     AREA(,9),OUT(9)
```

Solution.

1. | C1 | E2 | D1 | C2 | E3 | — 5 bytes (hexadecimal).
2. | 09 | 37 | 25 | — 3 bytes (hexadecimal).
3. | 4B | 6B | 6F | — 3 bytes (hexadecimal representation of the special characters).
4. | 09 | 37 | 25 | 4B | 6B | — 5 bytes (hexadecimal).

Note that the length of AREA determined the number of characters to be moved. Bytes reserved by declaratives are allocated sequentially in memory as shown in Figure 19–7. Note that five bytes were moved because AREA was defined as five bytes in length. The length of the receiving field (AREA) determines the number of bytes to be moved, so the first two bytes of CON were also moved.

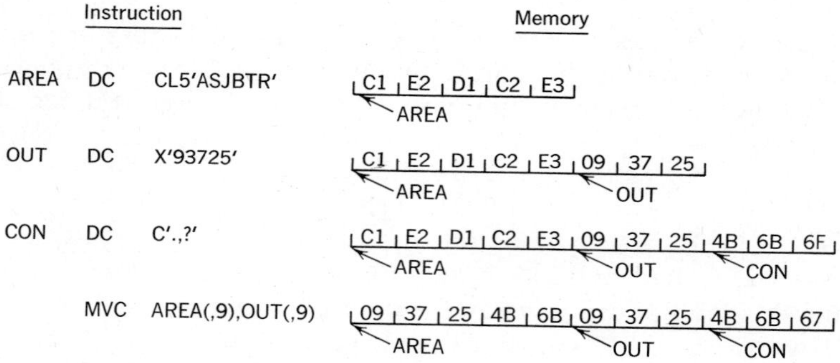

	Instruction		Memory
AREA	DC	CL5'ASJBTR'	C1 | E2 | D1 | C2 | E3 (AREA)
OUT	DC	X'93725'	C1 | E2 | D1 | C2 | E3 | 09 | 37 | 25 (AREA, OUT)
CON	DC	C'.,?'	C1 | E2 | D1 | C2 | E3 | 09 | 37 | 25 | 4B | 6B | 6F (AREA, OUT, CON)
	MVC	AREA(,9),OUT(,9)	09 | 37 | 25 | 4B | 6B | 09 | 37 | 25 | 4B | 6B | 67 (AREA, OUT, CON)

Figure 19–7. Example 4 memory assignments.

EXAMPLE 5

How can the following bit configuration be entered into core storage: 00011111?

Solution

Four different ways.

1. DC X'1F'
2. DC C'11' (An 11, 9, 8, 7 punch in one column of a card is a character that produces the desired bit configuration.)
   9
   8
   7
3. DC HL1'31'
4. DC FL1'31'

Figure 19–8 illustrates the constants set in memory by these declaratives.

Instruction	Memory	
DC X' 1F'	0001 1111 (byte)	
DC C' 11' 9 8 7	0001 1111	
DC HL1' 31'	0001 1111 (half-word boundary)	$(31_{10} = 11111_2)$
DC FL1' 31'	0001 1111 (full word boundary)	

Figure 19–8. Example 5 memory assignments.

Shift Commands

On occasion, various operations may be performed more efficiently if the programmer were able to shift data in a register to the right or to the left. Consider the decimal number 13 held in an eight-bit register. It would appear as:

0 0 0 0 1 1 0 1

Suppose we wished to multiply this number by eight. Rather than performing this multiplication using the multiply command, we could reason as follows: Since $8 = 2^3$ and since every position in the eight-bit register above represents an integral power of two, why not shift the number in the register to the left three positions, representing multiplication by 2^3, or 8? After shifting our register to the left three positions, its contents would be altered to

0 1 1 0 1 0 0 0

which is $104 = 8 \times 13$. This is merely one of the benefits derived from computers that have the ability to shift data to the right or left. As the reader becomes more sophisticated in his programming technique, he will encounter a myriad of uses for shifting operations.

Shift instructions in the System/360 Assembly Language operate on data in any one of the sixteen general purpose registers. There are two types of shifting operations, algebraic and logical. This chapter will not be concerned with logical shifts or logical instructions of any type, for that matter.

On a single algebraic shift, the 31 bits (disregarding sign) in the specified register are shifted to the left or right a specified number of positions. The sign of the data is not disturbed on an algebraic shift (hence, the term algebraic). On a right shift (algebraic) the low order bits in the register are lost and the sign is propagated in the high end. On a left algebraic shift, the high order bits are lost and zeros are filled in in the low order. Note that the effect of a right shift is to divide the number in the specified register by 2 (providing that number is even), whereas on an algebraic left shift, we are multiplying the number in the register by 2. As a result of every algebraic shift, the condition code will be set as follows:

CC = 00 if the result is 0.
CC = 01 if the result is negative.
CC = 10 if the result is positive.
CC = 11 if overflow resulted.

The first three condition code settings should be obvious to the reader by this time; the last one requires some clarification.

Executing a left shift carries with it the possibility of losing a significant bit. For example, suppose an eight-bit register contained:

S
0 0 1 0 1 1 0 1 (S indicates the sign bit.)

and we shifted this number to the left two places (keep in mind that the sign bit is not disturbed). The result of this shift is:

S
0 0 1 1 0 1 0 0

Note that the most significant bit of data has been lost. In this case, the condition code would be set to 11. As a general rule, we can say that if the bit lost on a left shift disagrees with the sign bit, an overflow will result. An overflow condition would also exist were we to try to shift the negative data,

S
1 1 1 0 1 1 0 1

left three places. This would force the zero out of the left end of the register giving us:

S
1 1 1 0 1 0 0 0

The bit lost (0) was different from the sign bit (1).

Shift commands are of the register to storage format:

OP $R_1D_2(B_2)$

The number of characters shifted is determined by the number indicated in D_2 plus the number indicated by the low order six bits of the base register (B_2). The SLA (shift left algebraic) and SRA (shift right algebraic) will be the only commands discussed. This is done primarily to make the student aware of shifting operations and not a master of them at this time. Suppose, for example, that register 4 contained

0 0 1 1 0 0

in its lower six bits. Then, execution of the command,

```
SLA   6,3(4)
```

would shift the contents of register 6 left $3+12=15$ places (note $001100_2=12$). If B_2 is not specified in the instruction, then the net effect of the number of places shifted is just D_2. For example, execution of

```
SLA   6,3
```

will shift the contents of register 6 left three places. To summarize shifting operations, we will solve a problem that we previously solved without the use of shift commands.

EXAMPLE

Solve for Z:

$$Z = |X| - 2(|X - |Y||)$$

Label	*Op Code*	*Operands*
X	DC	F
Y	DC	F
Z	DC	F
	L	5,X
	L	7,Y
	LPR	7,7
	S	5,7
	LPR	5,5
	SLA	5,1
	LCR	5,5
	L	8,X
	LPR	8,8
	A	8,5
	ST	8,Z

BALR-USING

At this point, the reader may be bewildered about the use of the base registers in Assembly Language instructions. In the example above, no base registers were indicated, whereas in most of the previous examples, the register used as a base *was* indicated. System/360 Assembly Language provides us with instructions that attach the base register being used to all subsequent instructions in that section of the program automatically. When using these instructions, we must indicate to the processor what register is to be used and what this register is to contain initially. Recall that the effective address of an instruction is equal to the displacement plus the contents of the base register in use.

The combination of instructions used to load a register with a base value properly and to associate that base register with each instruction will be the BALR-USING combination.

BALR is a mnemonic operation code for branch and load register. The format for the BALR is:

OP R_1,R_2.

This instruction places the address of the instruction following the BALR into R_1, and then branches to the address contained in the register specified by the second operand unless that operand specifies register 0. If R_2 is zero, no branch takes place. For example,

BALR 9,0

will place the address of the next instruction in register 9 and will not branch, but will continue executing the program in sequence.

BALR 9,6

will place the address of the next instruction in register 9 and branch to the address contained in register 6 for its next instruction.

The USING statement is a signal to the assembler that a particular register should be used as a base register for the section of the program that follows. The USING statement has the additional function of indicating to the processor what the contents of a particular register (usually the base register) will be.

In summary, the BALR-USING combination is used to identify a particular base register and to load it with its initial contents. It is most significant to note that the BALR is an executable machine instruction executed at object time, whereas the USING statement is an assembler instruction only, executed at assembly time. After assembly, the USING statement plays no significant role. If the statement,

```
USING * ,9
```

is used, the assembler will interpret this to mean that register 9 is to be used as a base register and the asterisk tells the assembler to place the address of the next instruction in register 9. In an assembly language program, the BALR-USING combination could appear as

```
BALR    9,0
USING * ,9
```

During assembly of the program, the assembler will execute the USING statement and attach base register 9 to appropriate instructions. After these instructions have been assembled, execution of the program takes place. At this time, the BALR is executed which loads register 9 with the address of the instruction following and then starts executing instructions in sequence. These instructions have been assembled with 9 as a base register, so when they are executed, they will use the contents of register 9 as their base. This number has been placed in register 9, by the BALR.

We will conclude this chapter with a sample problem and the System/360 Assembly Language program used to solve this program. Prior to doing this, we will indicate two more processor control cards and four macros we may use for input/output operations.

Control Cards

START Card

This card will always be the first instruction in our program. It occupies no memory. Two parameters will be associated with the START card. The first will be the name of this particular program. The second operand will be a self-defining value (SDV). If no SDV is present, the program will start assembling at location 0. For our program, we will use an SDV of 1B90 (hexadecimal), indicating that we want our program loaded starting with this location.

END Card

This card is used as a signal to the processor that the end of the source program has been reached. It will be the last card in the source program. One operand will be associated with this instruction. This operand will be the label of the first instruction to be executed at object time. This will usually refer to the BALR instruction.

Input/Output Operations

Since input/output programming is beyond the scope of this book, we will use special macros (precoded routines) for our input/output operations. We will assume that we have the following macros at our disposal.

RCARD—Read a Card

Eighty characters are read each time this macro is executed. The format of this instruction is:

```
RCARD   IOAREA,EOFADDR
```

where IOAREA is the name of the programmer's input area (probably defined as DS CL80) and EOFADDR is the address to which the programmer would like to branch after the last card has been read.

WLINE—Print a Line

This instruction causes the printer to write a line and to take a single space. The format of this instruction is:

```
WLINE   IOAREA,NOCHAR
```

where IOAREA is the name of the programmer's output area and NOCHAR is a decimal number between 1 and 132, indicating the number of characters he wishes printed. The printer attached to the 360 for the execution of our program can print up to 132 characters per line.

SK—Skip

The function of this macro is to cause the printer to skip to the next page. The format for this instruction is:

```
SK   1.
```

STOP—End Processing

This should be the last instruction executed at object time. This causes the machine to stop executing the program in progress and prepare to read the next program into storage.

Sample Exercise

Amortizing a Loan

The Friendly Lending Agency calculates the monthly interest on long- and short-term loans by multiplying the unpaid balance by the interest rate and dividing the result by twelve. For each payment received by the agency, the monthly interest is subtracted from the payment and the remainder is subtracted from the unpaid balance. They half-adjust all of their calculations to two decimal places (the nearest penny). Our job is to determine how many months must elapse on a given loan before the interest payment is less than the amount applied toward the unpaid balance. The Friendly Lending Agency punches the following information in cards. No decimal points appear in the cards.

Card Columns 1–7—Principal—2 decimal places.
Card Columns 8–11—Interest—4 decimal places.
Card Columns 12–15—Payments—2 decimal places.

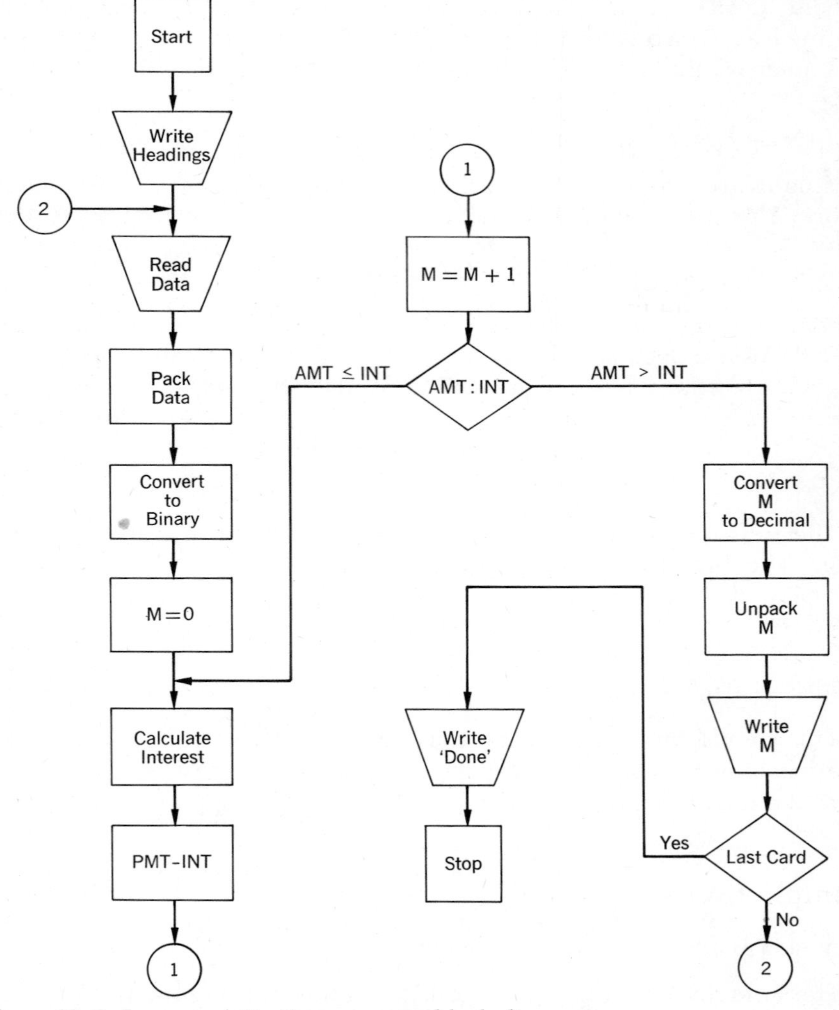

Figure 19–9. Loan amortization program block diagram.

The required output consists of XXX MONTHS for each card read. After the last card has been processed, print the message: DONE. A block diagram for this program appears in Figure 19–9.

CODING OF SAMPLE EXERCISE

```
Label       Op Code                 Operands      Comments
LOANPROB    START    X'1B90'
            BALR     9,0
            USING    *,9
            B        BEGIN
ZONE        DC       X'F0'
INPUT       DS       0CL80
PRIN        DS       CL7
INT         DS       CL4
PAY         DS       CL4
            DS       CL65
OUTPUT      DS       0CL11
ANSWER      DS       CL3
            DC       C'  '
            DC       C'MONTHS'
WORK        DS       D
ONE         DC       F'1'
HALFAD      DC       F'5000'
TENTH       DC       F'10000'
TWELVE      DC       F'12'
HEAD        DC       C'AMORTIZATION PROBLEM'
MESS        DC       C'DONE'
BEGIN       SK       1
            WLINE    HEAD,20
READ        RCARD    INPUT,EOJ
            PACK     WORK,PRIN
            CVB      2,WORK
            PACK     WORK,INT         CONVERT CONSTANTS
            CVB      3,WORK
            PACK     WORK,PAY
            CVB      4,WORK
            SR       5,5              CLEAR M
            L        6,ONE
            L        8,ONE
AGAIN       LR       11,2
            MR       10,3             INTEREST × PRINCIPAL
            D        10,TWELVE            Monthly Interest
            AR       11,7                 Add 5000
            SR       10,10
```

```
Label     Op Code    Operands                   Comments

          DR         10,8                       Drop 4 digits
          LR         10,4                       Payment   Reg. 10
          SR         10,11                      Payment—Interest
          SR         2,10                       Prin.—Amt.
          AR         5,6                        M=M+1
          CR         10,11                      Amt:Int
          BH         DONE
          B          AGAIN
DONE      CVD        5,WORK
          UNPK       ANSWER,WORK
          MVZ        ANSWER+2(1),ZONE
          WLINE      OUTPUT,11                  Write M
          B          READ
EOJ       MVI        OUTPUT,C'
          MVC        OUTPUT+1(10),OUTPUT
          MVC        OUTPUT(4),MESS
          WLINE      OUTPUT,11
          STOP
          END        LOANPROB
```

Concluding Remarks

With this introduction to System/360 Assembly Language coding, the reader should be ready to pursue and understand more sophisticated commands and topics of this language as well as prepare for some advanced operating system topics. This introduction to assembly language coding was not meant to be exhaustive or thorough in its treatment of the commands or topics, but rather to make the reader feel more at ease with languages of this caliber. The reader will find that after a basic understanding of the material in this chapter has been achieved, more advanced topics will come much more easily.

Questions

1. From the following series of sequential assembler definition instructions, which instruction does not begin on a half-word boundary?

```
FLD1    DS    F
FLD2    DS    H
CON1    DC    X'3100'
FLD3    DS    D
CON2    DC    C'—3100'
CON3    DC    X'6400'
CON4    DC    H'6400'
```

2. What would be in location PACKED as a result of the following operation?

```
ALPHA     DC      2CL5'ABCDE'
PACKED    DS      CL6
          PACK    PACKED(,9),ALPHA(,9)
```

3. What would be in location CONST1 as a result of the following set of instructions?

```
CONST1    DC      CL10'ABCDEFGHIJ'
CONST2    DC      CL4'JKLM'
CONST3    DC      CL3'123'
CONST4    DC      CL3'ABC'
          MVC     CONST1(,9),CONST2(9)
          MVC     CONST4(,9),CONST3(9)
          MVC     CONST1(,9),CONST2(9)
```

4. What would the location OUTPUT contain after execution of the following?

```
CONST1    DC      F'+1234'
PACKED    DS      D
OUTPUT    DC      C'ABCD'
          L       1,CONST1(0,9)
          CVD     1,PACKED(0,9)
          UNPK    OUTPUT(,9),PACKED(,9)
```

5. What fixed point instructions affect the condition code?
6. What is the content of AREA at the completion of the following:

```
AREA      DC      X'12342'
CON       DC      C'AJS'
CON2      DC      C'BK'
          MVZ     AREA(,9),CON(9)
```

7. Assume that the register being used as a base register contains 39300 and that indexing is not being used. What displacement is required to address location 40000?
8. The USING instruction tells the assembler that at object time general purpose register 11 will be loaded with what value?

```
          START   1000
BEGIN     BALR    11,0
          USING   *,11
```

9. Solve problem 10 of the previous chapter assuming the following constants.

```
REGRTE    DS    CL3       (2 decimal places assumed)
OVTRTE    DS    CL3       (2 decimal places assumed)
HOURS     DS    CL2       (1 decimal place assumed)
FOUR      DC    X'400C'   (1 decimal place assumed)
TOTPAY    DS    CL4       (2 decimal places assumed)
```

10. Write a program to rearrange the following record:

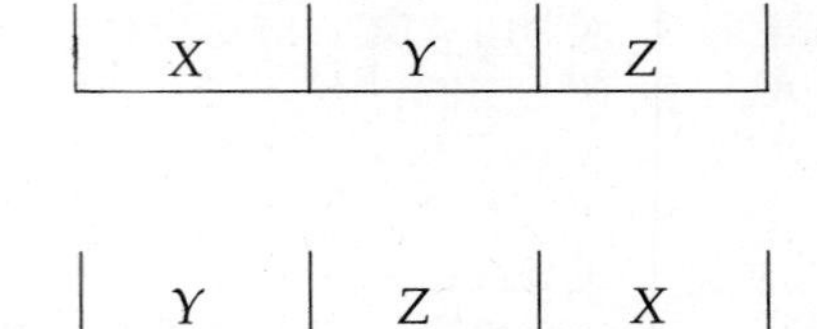

to

Assume X contains 16 *characters,* Y, 12 *characters* and Z, 12 *characters.*

Index